Handbook of Research on Social and Organizational Liabilities in Information Security

Manish Gupta
State University of New York at Buffalo, USA

Raj Sharman
State University of New York at Buffalo, USA

Information Science REFERENCE

INFORMATION SCIENCE REFERENCE
Hershey · New York

Director of Editorial Content:	Kristin Klinger
Director of Production:	Jennifer Neidig
Managing Editor:	Jamie Snavely
Assistant Managing Editor:	Carole Coulson
Typesetter:	Jeff Ash
Cover Design:	Lisa Tosheff
Printed at:	Yurchak Printing Inc.

Published in the United States of America by
Information Science Reference (an imprint of IGI Global)
701 E. Chocolate Avenue, Suite 200
Hershey PA 17033
Tel: 717-533-8845
Fax: 717-533-8661
E-mail: cust@igi-global.com
Web site: http://www.igi-global.com

and in the United Kingdom by
Information Science Reference (an imprint of IGI Global)
3 Henrietta Street
Covent Garden
London WC2E 8LU
Tel: 44 20 7240 0856
Fax: 44 20 7379 0609
Web site: http://www.eurospanbookstore.com

Library of Congress Cataloging-in-Publication Data

Handbook of research on social and organizational liabilities in information security / Manish Gupta and Raj Sharman, editors.

p. cm.

Includes bibliographical references and index.

Summary: "This book offers insightful articles on the most salient contemporary issues of managing social and human aspects of information security"--Provided by publisher.

ISBN 978-1-60566-132-2 (hardcover) -- ISBN 978-1-60566-133-9 (ebook)

1. Computer security--Management--Handbooks, manuals, etc. 2. Data protection--Management--Handbooks, manuals, etc. 3. Computer crimes--Prevention--Handbooks, manuals, etc. 4. Human computer interaction--Handbooks, manuals, etc. I. Gupta, Manish, 1978- II. Sharman, Raj.

QA76.9.A25.H365 2008

658.4'78--dc22

2008035140

British Cataloguing in Publication Data
A Cataloguing in Publication record for this book is available from the British Library.

Editorial Advisory Board

List of Contributors

Table of Contents

Detailed Table of Contents

Section I
Organizational Security

The first section of the book, titled "Organizational Security", hosts eight chapters on different aspects of organizational issues in information security. The section focuses on issues such as roles and responsibilities in organizational catastrophe contingency planning, soft techniques in understanding and thwarting organizational threats to information security, employee surveillance and monitoring, electronic insurance for security risks, social and cultural development in honesty credit system in organizational settings, role and organization-based access management, enterprise information system security life cycle management, and information security economics. Brief discussions on objectives and contributions of the chapters in the book are presented next.

This chapter examines the impact of catastrophes on information security and suggests who might have responsibility for maintaining an appropriate level of data protection when a catastrophe occurs. The author asserts that catastrophe contingency planning is very different from regular forms of business continuity and disaster recovery planning in terms of size, focus, scope, and content. Catastrophe contingency plans (CCPs) must comprehend a broad range of potential events affecting large numbers of humans and other living creatures, information processing capabilities, information and media, buildings, and infrastructure, and the like, each with its security considerations, and each characterized by its own roles, responsibilities and liabilities. The intent of the chapter is to encourage the development of more comprehensive and realistic CCPs, that is, plans that delineate roles and responsibilities clearly and liabilities should CCPs go awry.

An online business organization spends millions of dollars on firewalls, anti-virus, intrusion detection systems, digital signature, and encryption, to ensure minimal security breach. Nonetheless, a new virus or a clever hacker can easily compromise these deterrents, resulting in losses to the tune of millions of dollars annually. To minimize the financial loss, authors propose that online businesses should invest in e-risk insurance products as a complementary alternative, above the network security appliances. In this work, authors develop a Copula aided Bayesian Belief Network (CBBN) model, to assist insurance companies to design e-insurance products. The CBBN model does an e-vulnerability assessment (e-VA) and e-risk quantification (e-RQ). Authors first draw a casual diagram (BBN) stating the probable reason for security failure in an organization. Authors assume the marginal distributions for each of the nodes of the diagram. Using the CBBN model, authors compute the joint probability of the constituent nodes of the BBN. Next the conditional probability of each of the occurrences of the malicious event is arrived at. Authors then assume a loss distribution, and using the principles of collective risk modeling, authors arrive at the expected severity of the attack. The e-risk insurance companies compute the premium, by charging an extra (i.e., overloading and contingency loading), over the expected severity of attack.

Guoling Lao, Shanghai University of Finance & Economics, China
Liping Wang, Shanghai University of Finance & Economics, China

E-commerce mode aggravates information asymmetry so that honesty-credit problems become more serious. This chapter discusses the honesty-credit issue and honesty-credit system construction in e-commerce. It argues that the honesty-credit issue belongs to e-commerce security problems to some extent since it also destroys information integrity, confidentiality, and availability. The study of honesty-credit issue in e-commerce will help to promote social culture development as well as improve e-commerce security. Based on analysis of three game models, the chapter suggests the construction of social honesty-credit system mainly include four aspects: cultivate citizens' sense of honesty-credit, strengthen legislation, build mechanism of third-party authentication and regulate third-party service industry. At the end of the chapter, the case of Shanghai honesty-credit system construction of is introduced to describe China honesty-credit status.

Zhixiong Zhang, The College Board, USA
Xinwen Zhang, Samsung Information System America, USA
Ravi Sandhu, University of Texas at San Antonio and TriCipher Inc., USA

This chapter addresses the problem that traditional role-base access control (RBAC) models do not scale up well for modeling security policies spanning multiple organizations. After reviewing recently proposed Role and Organization Based Access Control (ROBAC) models, an administrative ROBAC model called AROBAC07 is presented and formalized in this chapter. Two examples are used to motivate and demonstrate the usefulness of ROBAC. Comparison between AROBAC07 and other administrative RBAC models are given. Authors show that ROBAC/AROBAC07 can significantly reduce administra-

Section II
Privacy and Social Engineering

The second section, Privacy and Social Engineering, contains seven chapters on privacy issues and social engineering threats and countermeasures. The chapters in this section cover policy-based privacy management, a country-specific privacy issues in banking sector, framework for defending against phishing attacks, context-dependent countermeasure against social engineering attacks, latest privacy enhancing technologies, social engineering taxonomy and countermeasures, and security challenges with social networking sites.

The growth of the Internet is increasing the deployment of e-services in such areas as e-commerce, e-learning, and e-health. In parallel, the providers and consumers of such services are realizing the need for privacy. The use of P3P privacy policies on Web sites is an example of this growing concern for privacy. Managing privacy using privacy policies is a promising approach. In this approach, an e-service provider and an e-service consumer each have separate privacy policies. Before an e-service is engaged, the provider's policy must be "compatible" with the consumer's policy. However, beyond compatibility, the policies may face pitfalls arising from improper specification, misapplication, and improper maintenance (e.g. failing to keep a personal privacy policy up-to-date). This can result in the loss of privacy and even lead to serious safety issues in certain cases. This chapter gives examples of how such pitfalls can arise and suggests ways to avoid these pitfalls.

Enabling customers to influence the way they are represented in the bank's databases, is one of the major personalization, responsiveness, and privacy issues of banking. In this chapter, authors reflect on the results from a qualitative study of the ways in which Australians think of privacy, security, and money. The authors find that changes in life stages, residence, and relationships motivate people to share additional personal information with their bank, in order to receive personalized services. The chapter's authors suggest ways in which privacy rights management can help customers better represent themselves in a flexible manner reflecting the changes in their lives.

Phishing scams pose a serious threat to end-users and commercial institutions alike. E-mail continues to be the favorite vehicle to perpetrate such scams mainly due to its widespread use combined with the ability to easily spoof them. Several approaches, both generic and specialized, have been proposed to address this growing problem. However, phishing techniques, growing in ingenuity as well as sophistication, render these solutions weak. To overcome these limitations, authors propose a multistage framework – the first stage aims at detecting phishing based on their semantic and structural properties, whereas in the second stage authors propose a proactive technique based on a challenge-response technique to establish the authenticity of a Web site. Using live e-mail data authors demonstrate that our approach with these two stages is able to detect a wider range of phishing attacks than existing schemes. Also, our performance analysis study shows that the implementation overhead introduced by our tool is negligibly small.

In recent years, the security research community has been very active in proposing different techniques and algorithms to face the proliferating security vulnerabilities. However, social engineering remains an alarming threat to most secured networks. Security administrators are certainly aware about the gravity of the human factor, whatever is the strength of the technological measures. The human factor is still a difficult-to-surround notion and a difficult concept to quantify. It is rarely considered in the early stages of the development life cycle of software, assuming traditional security considerations have been taken into account. In this chapter, authors discuss the added-value of context as a way to deal with social engineering. Based on a case study describing a typical attack, authors provide a first attempt to model this parameter.

Privacy-enhancing technologies (PETs), which constitute a wide array of technical means for protecting users' privacy, have gained considerable momentum in both academia and industry. However, existing surveys of PETs fail to delineate what sorts of privacy the described technologies enhance, which makes it difficult to differentiate between the various PETs. Moreover, those surveys could not consider very recent important developments with regard to PET solutions. The goal of this chapter is two-fold. First, authors provide an analytical framework to differentiate various PETs. This analytical framework consists of high-level privacy principles and concrete privacy concerns. Secondly, authors use this framework to evaluate representative up-to-date PETs, specifically with regard to the privacy concerns they address, and how they address them (i.e., what privacy principles they follow). Based on findings of the evaluation, authors outline several future research directions.

This chapter introduces and defines social engineering, a recognized threat to the security of information systems. It also introduces a taxonomy for classifying social engineering attacks along four dimensions: who or what the targets are, what media are used, how the attacks fit in an attack cycle, and the techniques used to execute the attacks. Additionally, the chapter discusses current social engineering countermeasures and how to map attack types to these countermeasures. Finally, the chapter ends with a discussion of future trends and technologies for defending against social engineering attacks. Use of the taxonomy should help security professionals and researchers understand social engineering attacks, and implementation of the discussed current and future countermeasures should help professionals reduce the risks associated with social engineering attacks.

Social networking has become one of the most popular applications on the Internet since the burst of the dot-com bubble. Apart from being a haven for teenagers and online marketers, social networking sites are increasingly adopted by the corporate community. The trend makes viable many new business models and applications. The popularity of these sites has altered the way society interacts, but it also greatly heightened the threats of cyber crime. Safety and crime issues aside, the massive amount of user-generated content in these Web 2.0 enabled social networking sites are becoming fertile grounds for viruses. Furthermore, these sites pose great challenges on how to protect copyrighted works as they are havens for digital content sharing. Society must learn to balance the benefits of social networking with its drawbacks as the phenomenon is an inescapable global trend, expanding at the speed of light.

Section III
Security Education and Awareness

The third section of the book, Security Education and Awareness, contains seven chapters on information security and assurance education and research issues. The section has chapters on design and implementation issues in information security curriculum and education and on research issues in emerging fields in information security.

Fraudulent e-mails, known as phishing attacks, have brought chaos across the digital world causing billions of dollars of damage. These attacks are known for their ability to exploit the human aspect of a computer system by pretending to originate from a source trusted by the victim. While technology defenses have been setup for protection, people are still succumbing to these attacks at alarming rates.

Therefore, educational techniques must implement to strengthen the human factor of security. Authors propose the use of a phishing IQ test that when used in classroom setting can help users build experience needed to identify phishing e-mail during their daily routine.

This chapter basically discusses the recent theories used in information security research studies. The chapter initially introduces the importance of the information security research and why it became so important recently. Following this introduction, "theory" is defined and the importance of the theories in information security research is mentioned. After this discussion, recently used theories (socio-technical systems theory, activity theory, distributed cognition theory, general deterrence theory, grounded theory, social cognitive theory) are listed and basic information about these theories as well as applications from the literature are given. Other recently used theories also summarized in a table in the next section. The chapter finally ends with concluding remarks on the theories and recommendations to the researchers in the information security area.

Information assurance education is an interdisciplinary endeavor that only when taken as a holistic and inclusive educational activity can be successful. When considering the design and implementation of a curriculum that is set to meet standards set by outside agencies, the educational institution must use a flexible and repeatable process. Building a curriculum on top of a strong foundation will empower and facilitate success. Meeting outside agencies' requirements, such as accrediting agencies, will close, if not eliminate any credibility gaps within an institution.

As with health and safety or legal compliance, management can hardly expect employees to comply with corporate information security policies, adopt security standards and follow security procedures if they don't even know of their existence. Information security awareness is therefore an essential component of effective information security management systems, supporting and enhancing the technical and procedural information security controls and contributing to the corporation's overall governance. In order to instill a genuine security culture throughout the organization, the awareness issue goes well beyond simply informing employees of their security obligations. To overcome the inevitable change resistance or inertia, employees have to be both informed and motivated to modify their behaviors, to "think secu-

information security researchers to be more aware of the research methodological options available to them. For each area, authors have provided background and existing research along side rationale on why this area is becoming important and vital in the field of information security research. The chapter introduces five key areas of information security research that are gaining recognition and credibility to significantly aid information security practice.

Section IV
Human and Interaction Issues

The last section of the book, Human and Interaction Issues, deals with human, behavioral, and psychological aspects of managing an information security program and practices. The section hosts chapters on different issues on the topics of linguistic steganography, password aspects, security issues with interactive systems, role of gender and social influence on security vulnerabilities, shill bidding detection, privacy, and security in large public displays and emotional trust factors.

This chapter develops a linguistically robust encryption system, LUNABEL, which converts a message into syntactically and semantically innocuous text. Drawing upon linguistic criteria, LUNABEL uses word replacement, with substitution classes based on traditional linguistic features (syntactic categories and subcategories), as well as features under-exploited in earlier works: semantic criteria, graphotactic structure, and inflectional class. The original message is further hidden through the use of cover texts—within these, LUNABEL retains all function words and targets specific classes of content words for replacement, creating text which preserves the syntactic structure and semantic context of the original cover text. LUNABEL takes advantage of cover text styles which are not expected to be necessarily comprehensible to the general public, making any semantic anomalies more opaque. This line of work has the promise of creating encrypted texts which are less detectable to human readers than earlier steganographic efforts.

The traditional approach to security has been the use of passwords. They provide the system with a barrier to access what was quite safe in the analogical world. The digital era provided the means to easily try

Shill bidding is where spurious bids are introduced into an auction to drive up the final price for the seller, thereby defrauding legitimate bidders. While shilling is recognized as a problem, presently there is little or no established means of defense against shills. This chapter presents an algorithm to detect the presence of shill bidding in online auctions. It observes bidding patterns over a series of auctions, providing each bidder a score indicating the likelihood of his/her potential involvement in shill behavior. The algorithm has been tested on data obtained from a series of realistic simulated auctions, and commercial online auctions. The algorithm is able to prune the search space required to detect which bidders are likely to be shills. This has significant practical and legal implications for commercial online auctions where shilling is considered a major threat. This chapter presents a framework for a feasible solution, which acts as a detection mechanism and a deterrent.

In this chapter, authors presented a novel concept for personalized privacy support on large public displays. In the first step, two formative evaluations were conducted in order to analyze the requirements of potential users regarding the protection of private information on large public displays. The insights gained in these evaluations were used to design a system that automatically adapts the information visible on public displays according to the current social situation and the individual privacy preferences of the user working on the display. In a third evaluation, the developed system was evaluated regarding its appropriateness for daily usage and its usefulness to protect privacy. The results of the evaluation showed that users are in general willing to trust system-based protection mechanisms, provided that they are well implemented. In this context, the proposed combination of pre-defined privacy profiles and context-adapted information visualization proved to be a good trade-off between usability and adequate privacy protection.

The sense of security, identified with the Japanese term, Anshin, is identified as an important contributor to emotional trust. This viewpoint suggests that designers should consider the subjective sense of security as well as objective security measures in designing systems and their user interfaces. A survey of users reveals both the personal and the environmental factors contributing to the users' sense of security when using the Internet. A more encompassing view of Anshin as including safety, reliability, and other non-functional properties of systems may provide additional insights for system design.

Foreword

I am pleased to write the foreword to this handbook of research in the area of information security, as its objectives and content provide valuable insights into various aspects of human, social, and organizational issues in information security. The topics covered in the book range from privacy to social engineering, to enterprise security management to security awareness, and address very timely and important issues in the area of information security. The book presents an excellent product of both the academic and the practical knowledge of the authors that will assist researchers and practitioners in gaining significant knowledge on various topics in the field of social and organizational issues in information security.

It is commonly acknowledged that that a large proportion of the breaches to information systems security are made by insiders such as employees, contractors, and partners. High incident rates of security breaches by employees of an organization can be, to a large extent, explained by the fact that internal threats and vulnerabilities to information security are not adequately managed. With more than 15 years of experience in information security related positions, I believe that the organizational efforts to manage information security are typically focused on vulnerabilities in technological assets such as hardware, software, and networking, while laying little emphasis on managing other organizational resources such as such as people, policies, processes, and culture. In addition to lack of focus on non-technological aspects of an organization, technology-focused security countermeasures and protection mechanisms are usually centered on external threats, such as hackers and viruses while leaving organizations open to breaches from the inside.

It is to be understood that that organizational security safeguards cannot be achieved by technology alone. There is a significant aspect of protection that ties with the attitudes, awareness, behavior, and culture of the people involved. Understanding and incorporating social and organizational aspects can potentially represent a vital component of any information security program towards achieving security. Proper attention and support for the human, social, and organizational factors should therefore be seen as a vital element of a successful security strategy. The overall information security program of any organization can be vastly strengthened if greater emphasis is placed on internal threats to information security as insiders handle information and systems in their daily activities. In particular, social and organizational aspects of information security are under represented in academic literature, organizational practices, and in security strategies. One important aspect of managing organizational information security is security awareness and training to all the stakeholders of organizational performance. People from all levels of an organization need to understand security concepts, how the issues may apply to them, and how to use the organizational resources to protect information. One important aspect of this handbook is that is has a few chapters on security awareness that provides excellent overview of challenges and solutions for threats arising from lack of security awareness in employees. In addition, the technology itself can make a contribution by reducing the demands upon users, simplifying protection measures, and automating a variety of safeguards.

When Manish approached me to write the foreword of this book, I was delighted at the prospect. I am pleased to be able to recommend this book to readers, be they those looking for substantive material on information security or looking to understand an important aspect of social and organizational liabilities in information security. The chapters in the book raise and discuss a number of pressing issues that organizations are facing today, and also offers an overview of potential solutions. The primary benefit of the book is in showing that successful security strategies rely on well-thought out and executed organizational processes, based not just upon information technology hardware and software products but also on social, cultural, and organizational aspects. The book provides both an initial step towards better understanding the process and peoples' aspects of managing information security and a detailed discourse on embarking on a continuous improvement of the security program.

John C. Walp Jr.
Corporate Information Security Officer
M&T Bank Corporation, Buffalo, NY

Preface

This handbook of research brings together chapters from renowned professionals and academicians from across the globe, on timely and critical topics on social and organizational issues of managing information security. The handbook aims to provide immense scholarly value and contribution to the fields of information technology, security, and management. Despite being a strongly emerging threat to organizational information security, there is evident dearth of research in the area. One of the key objectives of the handbook is to fill the gap in the existing literature on social and softer organizational dimensions of information security by providing the readers one comprehensive source of latest trends, issues, and research in the field. The book provides high-quality research chapters and industrial and practice articles on various topics ranging from employee surveillance to security education and awareness to security usability issues.

A NEW ORDER IN EVOLUTION OF SECURITY THREATS: EMERGENCE OF SOCIAL AND SOFTER ORGANIZATION ISSUES

As organizations are becoming increasingly dependent on technology and information systems for their operations and for sustaining strategic advantages, information security is playing an ever-important role in not only ensuring continuity of operations and protecting informational assets, but also in enabling business. In today's Internet age of interconnected electronic business environments, information security concerns are of paramount significance. At the same time, because of its openness and ubiquity, the Internet is being widely adopted as a cheaper and faster means of provisioning services and goods. Organizations are growing concerned with information security, as it is vital for their existence in protecting customer and corporate information, while managing its supply chain (Olivia, 2003). With the heightened concerns of security and rapid advancements in networking, communication, and mobility, as well as increases in risks and threats, management of information security has become one of the top business priorities within many organizations. It is becoming increasingly evident that the weaker links in an information-security chain are the people, because human nature and social interactions are much easier to manipulate than targeting the complex technological protections of information systems. Concerns and threats regarding human and social factors in organizational security are increasing at an exponential rate and shifting the information security paradigm.

While organizations are increasing spending on countermeasures to protect informational assets, there has been a disproportionate amount of allocation to non-technical countermeasures. Numerous surveys suggest that more than half of security breaches at companies occur due to actions taken by employees either indirectly or directly (Kaplan-Leiserson, 2003). However, organizations are not investing as much on non-technical measures such as security usability issues, compliance issues, motivational issues, security awareness, and so forth. Accidental or deliberate errors by individuals have adverse impacts through increasing an organization's vulnerability (Dutta & McCrohan, 2002). Practitioners and, increasingly, researchers in the field of information security, are realizing and admitting that information security depends more on peoples' aspects (human, social, and policy) than on technological. Improving organizational information security posture depends more on understanding and changing beliefs, attitudes, and behaviors of employees than on deploying latest technological systems. There are numerous studies that have documented actual and potential losses due to information security abuses by insiders (Burger, 1993; Loch, et. al., 1992; Panettieri, 1995). Beyond focusing on human and social elements, security practices and organizational factors such as policies, management philosophy, and organizational culture also play equally important role in improving information security program's effectiveness. Information security effectiveness is the ability of information security measures to protect against unauthorized or deliberate misuse of IS assets by people (Straub, 1990).

The relative lack of research on the topic of social and organizational aspects of information security in the existing literature on both broader areas of information security and human-computer interaction motivated work on this handbook of research to identify and fill gaps in the research. Despite a good amount of research on technical measures of information security, it is somewhat surprising that human and social factors have not been given sufficient attention, given that appropriate use of information systems involves human and social interactions and users' behavior, both end-users and system managers. This becomes even more important in light of the fact that the study of human-computer interaction has been the one of the most active areas of research within the field of information systems design and user. (Helander et. al., 1997). From a research standpoint, there are several areas that should be explored to better implement information security measures from a social and organizational perspective. Some of the considerations include users' resistance towards secure computing practices (Turnage, 1990), usability designs to lower user resistance (Al-Ghatani & King, 1999; Markus, 1983), ethical legitimacy of user behavior (Gordon, 1994; Gordon, 2000), motivational factors (Franklin et. al, 2007); and organizational policies and structure (Anderson, 1993). There are many key social and organizational issues to information security arising from human error problems such as a lack of adequate security training, lack of awareness about the importance of corporate and customer data, risks associated with insecure behavior, time and schedule pressures, absence of clear knowledge and communications regarding roles, responsibility and accountability, policies regarding use of organizational resources such as phones, e-mail, laptops, ans so forth. Instilling a security culture will entail different socio-cultural aspects that will support technical and other organizational security measures. This will help organizations to understand and increase trust between the different actors concerning information security within its organizational boundaries. Human and social factors in organizational security such as human error on information security are important issues that left unresolved can have adverse effects on industry (Carstens, 2008).

The book is aimed towards the primary audience of professionals, scholars, researchers, and academicians working in the fast evolving and growing field of information security. Practitioners and managers working in information technology or information security sectors across all industries would vastly improve their knowledge and understanding of critical human, social, and organizational aspects of information security. The book covers topics both on theoretical (research) aspects of securing information systems and infrastructure from social and organizational perspectives and real-world implications and implementations (practice) of the research.

There are 29 chapters in the handbook that are organized into four sections as follows:

I. Organizational Security
II. Privacy and Social Engineering

III. Security Education and Awareness
IV. Human and Interaction Issues

The first section of the book, titled ***Organizational Security***, hosts 8 chapters on different aspects of organizational issues in information security. The section focuses on issues such as roles and responsibilities in organizational catastrophe contingency planning, soft techniques in understanding and thwarting organizational threats to information security, employee surveillance and monitoring, electronic insurance for security risks, social and cultural development in honesty credit system in organizational settings, role and organization based access management, enterprise information system security life cycle management and information security economics. Brief discussions on objectives and contributions of the chapters in the book are presented next.

Chapter I of the book, "*Responsibilities and Liabilities with Respect to Catastrophes*" by Warren Axelrod, US Trust, USA, examines the impact of catastrophes on information security and suggests who might have responsibility for maintaining an appropriate level of data protection when a catastrophe occurs. The author asserts that catastrophe contingency planning is very different from regular forms of business continuity and disaster recovery planning in terms of size, focus, scope, and content. Catastrophe contingency plans (CCPs) must comprehend a broad range of potential events affecting large numbers of humans and other living creatures, information processing capabilities, information and media, buildings, and infrastructure, and the like, each with its security considerations, and each characterized by its own roles, responsibilities, and liabilities. The chapter encourages the development of more comprehensive and realistic CCPs, that is, plans that delineate roles and responsibilities clearly and liabilities should CCPs go awry.

Chapter II, "*The Complex New World of Information Security*" discusses the latest developments in the shifting threat landscape and their impact on the world of information security. It describes how we are now moving into a "third wave" of cybercrime where sophisticated criminals are applying relatively "soft" techniques that are more pervasive in their execution. The chapter argues that, as a consequence, information security countermeasures based on the latest information intelligence technologies will need to be complemented by softer, more pervasive techniques drawn from disciplines such as process engineering, policy development, behavioral science, psychology, and benefit management. The author, David Porter, Detica Corporation, UK, considers how these countermeasures can be fully realized in today's business environment and concludes by discussing future directions such as the growth in complexity and the rise of the surveillance society. The author hopes that by understanding these new imperatives, information security practitioners will be in a stronger position to protect their organizations from today's threats — and those of tomorrow.

In recent years, many studies have highlighted the unprecedented growth in security threats from multiple and varied sources faced by corporate as well as governmental organizations. People inside the organization with ready access to confidential or proprietary data can easily violate the organization security policy, maliciously or inadvertently, without being caught. In order to protect their reputation and valuable assets, many organizations take the dramatic but necessary step of deploying and operating employee surveillance and monitoring tools within their network perimeters. In **Chapter III**, "*Employee Surveillance Based on Free Text Detection of Keystroke Dynamics*", authors, Ahmed Awad E. Ahmed and Issa Traore of University of Victoria, Canada, discuss employee surveillance schemes from both technological and legal perspectives. They argue that keystroke dynamics could be used to fight effectively against insider threat, and as such it could play an important role in employee surveillance. They present a keystroke recognition scheme based on free text detection that goes beyond the traditional approach of using keystroke dynamics for authentication or employee performance evaluation, and consider using such information for dynamic user profiling. The generated profiles can be used to identify reliably perpetrators in the event of security breach. Such form of user profiling provides a very effective way of combating insider threat that is less intrusive to individual privacy.

An online business organization spends millions of dollars on firewalls, anti-virus, intrusion detection systems, digital signature, and encryption, to ensure minimal security breach. Nonetheless, a new virus or a clever hacker can easily compromise these deterrents, resulting in losses to the tune of millions of dollars annually. To minimize the financial loss, the authors of **Chapter IV**, "*E-Risk Insurance Product Design: A Copula Based Bayesian Belief Network*", propose that online businesses should invest in e-risk insurance products as a complementary alternative, above the network security appliances. In this work, the authors, Arunabha Mukhopadhyay, Indian Institute of Management Calcutta, India; Samir Chatterjee, Claremont Graduate University, USA; Debashis Saha, Indian Institute of Management Calcutta, India; Ambuj Mahanti, Indian Institute of Management Calcutta, India; and Samir K. Sadhukhan, Indian Institute of Management Calcutta, India, develop a Copula aided Bayesian Belief Network (CBBN) model, to assist insurance companies to design e-insurance products. The CBBN model presented in the book does an e-vulnerability assessment (e-VA) and e-risk quantification (e-RQ). Authors first draw a casual diagram (BBN) stating the probable reason for security failure in an organization, assuming the marginal distributions for each of the nodes of the diagram. Using the CBBN model, the joint probability of the constituent nodes of the BBN is computed and the conditional probability of each of the occurrences of the malicious event is arrived at. Authors then assume a loss distribution, and using the principles of collective risk modeling, arrive at the expected severity of the attack. The e-risk insurance companies compute the premium, by charging an extra (i.e., overloading and contingency loading), over the expected severity of attack.

E-commerce mode aggravates information asymmetry so that honesty-credit problems become more serious. **Chapter V**, "*E-Commerce Security and Honesty-Credit*" discusses the honesty-credit issue and honesty-credit system construction in e-commerce. It argues that the honesty-credit issue belongs to e-commerce security problems to some extent since it also destroys information integrity, confidentiality, and availability. The study of honesty-credit issue in e-commerce will help to promote social culture development as well as improve e-commerce security. Basing on analysis of three-game models, the authors, Lao Guoling and Liping Wang, of Shanghai University of Finance and Economics, China, suggest the construction of social honesty-credit system mainly include four aspects: cultivate citizens' sense of honesty-credit, strengthen legislation, build mechanism of third-party authentication, and regulate third-party service industry. At the end of the chapter, the case of Shanghai honesty-credit system construction of is introduced to describe China honesty-credit status.

Chapter VI, "*Towards a Scalable Role and Organization Based Access Control Model with Decentralized Security Administration*" addresses the problems that arise from the fact that traditional role-base access control (RBAC) models do not scale up well for modeling security policies spanning multiple organizations. After reviewing recently proposed Role and Organization Based Access Control (ROBAC) models, the authors, Xinwen Zhang of The College Board, USA; Zhixiong Zhang of Samsung Information System, USA; and Ravi Sandhu of University of Texas at San Antonio and TriCipher Inc., USA, present and formalize an administrative ROBAC model called AROBAC07. Authors used two examples to motivate and demonstrate the usefulness of ROBAC while providing a comparison between AROBAC07 and other administrative RBAC models. The authors show that ROBAC/AROBAC07 can significantly reduce administration complexity for applications involving a large number of organizational units. Finally, an application compartment-based delegation model is introduced in the chapter, which provides a method to construct administrative role hierarchy in AROBAC07. Authors show that the AROBAC07 model provides convenient ways to decentralize administrative tasks for ROBAC systems and scales up well for role-based systems involving a large number of organizational units.

There has been an unprecedented thrust in employing Computers and Communication technologies in all walks of life. The systems enabled by Information Technology are becoming more and more complex resulting in various threats and vulnerabilities. The security properties like confidentiality, integrity, and availability are becoming more and more difficult to protect. In **Chapter VII**, "*Enterprise Information System Security: A Life-Cycle Approach*", a life-cycle approach to achieve and maintain security of enterprises has been proposed. The chapter first examines enterprise information systems and then discusses the need for enterprise information system security and problems associated with security implementation. The authors, Chandan Mazumdar, Mridul S. Barik, and Anirban Sengupta from Jadavpur University, India, consider enterprise information system security as a management issue and detail the information security parameters. Finally, the chapter proposes security engineering life-cycle in detail including Security Requirement Analysis, Security Policy Formulation, Security Infrastructure Advisory Generation, Security Testing and Validation, and Review and Monitoring phases.

Most companies would agree that securing their information assets is worth some investment. It is thus plausible to assume that low levels of IT security investment indicate that only a small portion of the firm's business is IT asset value driven. It could also point to a misaligned corporate investment policy. Conversely, some firms may be investing more than is warranted, given the value of their information asset holdings, thereby wasting shareholder resources. The question then becomes: What level of IT security investment is enough? Several models exist to help companies set their IT spending in general and Information Security spending in particular. The leading model out there is the Information Technology Portfolio Management (ITPM) model, which is a financial portfolio management theory applied to the information technology realm to optimize IT spending based on a number of factors like business value, efficiency, and cost reduction among others. Despite current vigorous research at esteemed institutions like the Center for Information Systems Research (CISR) at MIT and at the Free University of Amsterdam, ITPM is still in its infancy and the field would benefit from alternative models. In **Chapter VIII**, "*An Alternative Model of Information Security Investment*", the author, Peter O. Orondo, president, Acclaim Consulting Group Inc., USA, proposes an alternative model of IT security spending that firms may readily apply when setting their Information Security budgets. The model is analytical and begins by developing a model for the business value of information. It then develops a model for the cost of an information security breach. Finally, the author presents a relationship between the value model and the cost model.

The second Section, ***Privacy and Social Engineering***, of the book contains 7 chapters on privacy issues and social engineering threats and countermeasures. The chapters in this section cover policy-based privacy management, a country-specific privacy issues in banking sector, framework for defending against phishing attacks, context-dependent countermeasure against social engineering attacks, latest privacy enhancing technologies, social engineering taxonomy and countermeasures; and security challenges with social networking sites.

The growth of the Internet is increasing the deployment of e-services in areas as e-commerce, e-learning, and e-health. In parallel, the providers and consumers of such services are realizing the need for privacy. The use of P3P privacy policies on Web sites is an example of this growing concern for privacy. Managing privacy using privacy policies is a promising approach. In this approach, an e-service provider and an e-service consumer each have separate privacy policies. Before an e-service is engaged, the provider's policy must be "compatible" with the consumer's policy. However, beyond compatibility, the policies may face pitfalls arising from improper specification, misapplication, and improper maintenance (e.g. failing to keep a personal privacy policy up-to-date). This can result in the loss of privacy and even lead to serious safety issues in certain cases. **Chapter IX**, "*Avoiding Pitfalls in Policy-Based Privacy Management,*" by George O. M. Yee and Larry Korba of National Research Council, Canada, gives examples of how such pitfalls can arise and suggests ways to avoid these pitfalls.

Enabling customers to influence the way they are represented in a bank's databases is one of the major personalization, responsiveness, and privacy issues in banking. **Chapter X**, "*Privacy and Banking in Australia*," draws on the results from a qualitative study of the ways in which Australians think of privacy, security, and money. The authors, Supriya Singh, RMIT University, Australia; Margaret Jackson, RMIT University, Australia; and Jenine Beekhuyzen, Griffith University, Australia, find that changes in life stages, residence, and relationships motivate people to share additional personal information with their bank, in order to receive personalized services. The authors suggest ways in which privacy rights management can help customers better represent themselves in a flexible manner reflecting the changes in their lives.

Phishing scams pose a serious threat to end-users and commercial institutions alike. E-mail continues to be the favorite vehicle to perpetrate such scams mainly due to its widespread use combined with the ability to easily spoof them. Several approaches, both generic and specialized, have been proposed to address this growing problem. However, phishing techniques, growing in ingenuity as well as sophistication, render these solutions weak. To overcome these limitations, authors, Madhusudhanan Chandrasekaran, State University of New York, Buffalo, USA, and Shambhu Upadhyaya, State University of New York, Buffalo, USA, propose a multistage framework – the first stage aims at detecting phishing based on their semantic and structural properties and the second stage proposes a proactive technique based on a challenge-response technique to establish the authenticity of a Web site. The authors in **Chapter XI**, "*A Multistage Framework to Defend Against Phishing Attacks*", use live e-mail data to demonstrate that their approach is able to detect a wider range of phishing attacks than existing schemes.

In recent years, the security research community has been very active in proposing different techniques and algorithms to face the proliferating security vulnerabilities. However, social engineering remains an alarming threat to most secured networks. Security administrators are certainly aware of the significance of the human factor irrespective of the strength of the applied technological measures. The human factor is still a difficult-to-surround notion and a difficult to quantify concept. It is rarely considered in the early stages of the development life cycle of software, assuming traditional security considerations have been taken into account. In **Chapter XII**, "*A New Approach to Reducing Social Engineering Impact*", the authors, Ghita Kouadri Mostéfaoui, Oxford University Computing Laboratory, UK, and Patrick Brézillon, LIP6, University Paris 6, France, discuss the added-value of *context* as a way to deal with social engineering. Based on a case study describing a typical attack, the authors provide a first attempt to model this parameter.

Privacy-enhancing technologies (PETs), which constitute a wide array of technical means for protecting users' privacy, have gained considerable momentum in both academia and industry. However, existing surveys of PETs fail to delineate what sorts of privacy the described technologies enhance, which makes it difficult to differentiate between the various PETs. Moreover, those surveys could not consider very recent important developments with regard to PET solutions. In **Chapter XIII**, "*Privacy-Enhancing Technologies*," authors, Yang Wang, University of California, Irvine, USA and Alfred Kobsa, University of California, Irvine, USA, provide an analytical framework to differentiate various PETs. This analytical framework consists of high-level privacy principles and concrete privacy concerns. The authors use this framework to evaluate representative up-to-date PETs, specifically with regard to the privacy concerns they address, and how they address them (i.e., what privacy principles they follow). Based on findings of the evaluation, authors also outline several future research directions.

Chapter XIV, "*Social Engineering and its Countermeasures*," introduces and defines social engineering, a recognized threat to the security of information systems. The chapter introduces a taxonomy for classifying social engineering attacks along four dimensions: (1) who or what the targets are, (2) what media are used, (3) how the attacks fit in an attack cycle and (4) what are the techniques used to execute the attacks. Additionally, the author, Douglas P. Twitchell, Illinois State University, USA, discusses current social engineering countermeasures and how to map attack types to these countermeasures. Use of the taxonomy should help security professionals and researchers understand social engineering attacks, and implementation of the discussed current and future countermeasures should help professionals reduce the risks associated with social engineering attacks. Finally, the chapter ends with a discussion of future trends and technologies for defending against social engineering attacks.

Social networking has become one of the most popular applications on the Internet since the burst of the dot-com bubble. Apart from being a haven for teenagers and online marketers, social networking sites are increasingly adopted by the corporate community. The trend makes viable many new business models and applications. The popularity of these sites has altered the way society interacts, but it has also greatly heightened the threats of cyber crime. Safety and crime issues aside, the massive amount of user-generated content in the Web 2.0-enabled social networking sites are becoming fertile grounds for all kinds of malware such as viruses and Trojan horses. Furthermore, these sites pose great challenges on how to protect copyrighted works as they are havens for digital content sharing. Society must learn to balance the benefits of social networking with its drawbacks as the phenomenon is an inescapable global trend. Author, Tom S. Chan, Southern New Hampshire University, USA, presents opportunities and security challenges that social networking sites pose in **Chapter XV**, "*Social Networking Site: Opportunities and Security Challenges*".

The third section of the book, ***Security Education and Awareness***, contains 7 chapters on information security and assurance education and research issues. The section has chapters on design and implementation issues in information security curriculum and education and on research issues in emerging fields in information security.

Fraudulent e-mails, known as phishing attacks, have brought chaos across the digital world causing billions of dollars of damage. These attacks are known for their ability to exploit the human aspect of a computer system by pretending to originate from a source trusted by the victim. While technology defenses have been setup for protection, people are still succumbing to these attacks at alarming rates. Therefore, educational techniques must be implemented to strengthen the human factor of security. Authors, James W. Ragucci, Syracuse University, USA, and Stefan A. Robila, Montclair State University, USA, in **Chapter XVI**, "*Designing Antiphising Education*", propose the use of a phishing IQ test that when used in classroom setting can help users build experience needed to identify phishing e-mail during their daily routine.

Chapter XVII, "*Theories Used in Information Security Research: Survey and Agenda,*" discusses the recent theories used in information security research studies. The authors Serkan Ada, Raj Sharman, and Manish Gupta, of State University of New York, Buffalo, USA, introduce the importance of the information security research and why it has become so important recently. Following the introduction, "theory" is defined and the importance of the theories in information security research is mentioned. The chapter then goes on to discuss recently used theories (socio-technical systems theory, activity theory, distributed cognition theory, general deterrence theory, grounded theory, social cognitive theory), while presenting basic information about these theories as well as applications from the literature. Other recently used theories are also summarized. The chapter finally ends with concluding remarks on the theories and recommendations to the researchers in the information security area.

Information assurance education is an interdisciplinary endeavor that when taken only as a holistic and inclusive educational activity it can be successful. Authors, Samuel P. Liles and Reza Kamali, of Purdue University Calumet, USA, suggest in **Chapter XVIII**, "*Information Assurance and Security Curriculum Meeting the SIGITE Guidelines,*" that during the design and implementation of a curriculum that is set to meet standards set by outside agencies, the educational institution must use a flexible and repeatable process. Building a curriculum on top of a strong foundation will empower and facilitate success. Authors suggest that meeting outside agencies' requirements, such as accrediting agencies, will close, if not eliminate any credibility gaps within an institution.

As with health and safety or legal compliance, management can hardly expect employees to comply with corporate information security policies, adopt security standards, and follow security procedures if they don't even know of their existence. Information security awareness is therefore an essential component of effective information security management systems, supporting and enhancing the technical and procedural information security controls and contributing to the corporation's overall governance. Author, Gary Hinson, IsecT Ltd, New Zealand, suggests in **Chapter XIX**, "*Information Security Awareness*," that in order to instill a genuine security culture throughout the organization, the awareness issue goes well beyond simply informing employees of their security obligations. To overcome the inevitable change in resistance or inertia, employees have to be both informed and motivated to modify their behaviors; "think security and act securely". The chapter explains the challenges and details information security awareness approaches that work, using quotations from others in the field to illustrate the points made.

Security training and awareness is often overlooked or not given sufficient focus in many organizations despite being a critical component of a layered defense. Organizations often purchase expensive hardware and software to help secure their organization, but fail to allocate resources to train employees who will install and configure the product. Similarly, organizations will devote many hours developing polices and procedures to protect sensitive information, but fail to allocate the appropriate resources to ensure awareness of those policies and procedures. Authors, Nick Pullman, Citigroup, USA, and Kevin Streff, Dakota State University, USA, in **Chapter XX**, "*Creating a Security Education, Training, and Awareness Program*," discusses how to design, create, and implement a formal security education, training, and awareness (SETA) program as a component of a layered defense strategy.

Chapter XXI, "*Information Security Within an E-Learning Environment*," introduces information security within the educational environments that utilize electronic resources. The education environment experienced a paradigm shift over the past number of years, due to the rapid growth in technology. This growth has made it possible for the education environment to utilize electronic services to enhance education methods. However, it is vital that all education environments (traditional or new ones) ensure that all resources (lecturers, students, and data) are properly protected against any possible security threats. Authors of **Chapter XXI**, E. Kritzinger, University of South Africa, Pretoria, South Africa, and S. H von Solms, Rand Afrikaans University, Johannesburg, South Africa, highlight the importance of securing information within the electronic environment. The authors present key aspects that must be addressed and implemented to ensure information security. The chapter also identifies four information security pillars that could assist top management to enhance overall information security management.

Authors, Donald Murphy from a northeast U.S. financial services firm and Manish Gupta, State University of New York, Buffalo, USA, and H. R. Rao, State University of New York, Buffalo, USA, present five emerging areas in information security that are poised to bring the radical benefits to the information security practice and research in **Chapter XXII**, "*Research Notes on Emerging Areas of Conflict in Security*". Authors have selected these five areas based on extensive literature review and emerging trends in information technology and security. This is a theoretical discourse, which considers a number of research issues and paradigms and explores the relevance of some interesting research areas that have far-reaching implications for IS research. The chapter stimulates discussions about the five covered research areas and in doing so provides a call for information security researchers to be more aware of the research methodological options available to them. For each area, the chapter provides background and existing research along side rationale on why the area is becoming important and vital in the field of information security research. The chapter introduces five key areas of information security research that are gaining recognition and credibility to significantly aid information security practice.

The last section of the book, ***Human and Interaction Issues***, deals with human, behavioral and psychological aspects of managing an information security program and practices. The section hosts chapters on different issues on the topics of linguistic steganography, password aspects, security issues with interactive systems, role of gender and social influence on security vulnerabilities, shill bidding detection, privacy, and security in large public displays and emotional trust factors.

Chapter XXIII, "*The Human Attack in Linguistic Steganography*" develops a linguistically robust encryption system, LUNABEL, which converts a message into syntactically and semantically innocuous text. Drawing upon linguistic criteria, LUNABEL uses word replacement, with substitution classes based on traditional linguistic features (syntactic categories and subcategories), as well as features under-exploited in earlier works: semantic criteria, graphotactic structure, and inflectional class. The original message is further hidden through the use of cover texts—within these, LUNABEL retains all function words and targets specific classes of content words for replacement, creating text which preserves the syntactic structure and semantic context of the original cover text. LUNABEL takes advantage of cover text styles which are not expected to be necessarily comprehensible to the general public, making any semantic anomalies more opaque. Authors, C. Orhan Orgun, University of California, Davis, and Vineeta Chand, University of California, Davis, suggest that this line of work has the promise of creating encrypted texts that are less detectable to human readers than earlier steganographic efforts.

The traditional approach to security has been the use of passwords. They provide the system with a barrier to access that was quite safe in the analogical world. The digital era provided the means to easily try thousands of passwords in a short period of time and now the password schema is no longer safe. Now it suffers of the password's contradiction: the fact that it requires both simplicity and complexity to be usable and safe. Being so, new technologies are required that can preserve the ease of use, but can provide stronger authentication processes. Authors, Sérgio Tenreiro de Magalhães, Faculdade de Ciências Sociais da Universidade Católica Portuguesa, University of Westminster, UK; Kenneth Revett, Departamento de Sistemas de Informação da Universidade do Minho, Portugal; Henrique M. D. Santos, Departamento de Sistemas de Informação da Universidade do Minho, Portugal; Leonel Duarte dos Santos, Departamento de Sistemas de Informação da Universidade do Minho, Portugal; André Oliveira, Departamento de Sistemas de Informação da Universidade do Minho, Portugal; and César Ariza, Bogomovil Ltda, Columbia, in **Chapter XXIV**, "*Using Technology to Overcome the Password's Contradiction*," present the latest advances in three technologies that can be used, unaided or together, to improve the safety of user/password schemas without significant changes in the protected information system architecture, despite the human factors that traditionally reduce the security of those systems. The chapter presents technologies such as Keystroke Dynamics, Graphical Authentication, and Pointer Dynamic.

Reducing the likelihood of human error in the use of interactive systems is increasingly important. Human errors could not only hinder the correct use and operation, they can also compromise the safety and security of such systems. Hence the need for formal methods to analyze and verify the correctness of interactive systems, particularly with regards to human interaction. **Chapter XXV**, "*Formal Analysis of Security in Interactive Systems*," examines the use of formal modeling and analysis of security properties of interactive systems. The chapter introduces some basic concepts in security and human-computer interaction, followed by formal modeling of human cognitive behavior and analysis of such systems. Authors, Antonio Cerone, United Nations University, China, and Siraj A. Shaikh, United Nations University, China, highlight the use of model checking to drive the system development to design secure user actions and sequences of actions. Authors also analyze the patterns of user behavior that may lead to security violation. Finally, particular areas of security protocol design where human interaction plays a key role are discussed.

It is estimated that over 1 billion people now have access to the Internet. This unprecedented access and use of Internet by individuals around the world, however, is accompanied by malicious and mischievous activities online. With the traditional crimes such as fraud, identity theft, and harassment now being committed with the use of the Internet, and networked home computers being exploited to carry out attacks such as denial of service, spamming, phishing, and virus/worm propagation, it has become important to investigate security and privacy issues as they pertain to individual Internet users. To date very little is known about what characteristics of Internet users affect their computing and online behaviors as they relate to security online. While some attention has been paid to understand the security issues affecting corporations, research investigating security issues as they relate to home users is still in infancy. Drawing from disciplines such as criminology, sociology, consumer fraud, and information security, **Chapter XXVI**, "*Internet Crime: How Vulnerable Are You? Do Gender, Social Influence and Education Play a Role in Vulnerability?*" seeks to find the role of computing skills and computer training, social influence, and gender on person's vulnerability to Internet crimes. Authors of the chapter 26, Tejaswini Herath, State University of New York, Buffalo, USA; H. R. Rao, State University of New York, Buffalo, USA, and Shambhu Upadhyaya, State University of New York, Buffalo, USA, assert that the findings of the study presented in the chapter are significant and shed light in this important area of Internet crime contributing to the information security literature.

Shill bidding is where spurious bids are introduced into an auction to drive up the final price for the seller, thereby defrauding legitimate bidders. While shilling is recognized as a problem, presently there is little or no established means of defense against shills. **Chapter XXVII**, "*Detecting Shill Bidding in Online English Auctions*," presents an algorithm to detect the presence of shill bidding in online auctions. The authors, Jarrod Trevathan, James Cook University, Australia, and Wayne Read, James Cook University, Australia, show that the algorithm observes bidding patterns over a series of auctions, providing each bidder a score indicating the likelihood of his/her potential involvement in shill behavior. The algorithm has been tested on data obtained from a series of realistic simulated auctions, and commercial online auctions. The algorithm is able to prune the search space required to detect which bidders are likely to be shills. This has significant practical and legal implications for commercial online auctions where shilling is considered a major threat. This chapter presents a framework for a feasible solution, which acts as a detection mechanism and a deterrent.

In **Chapter XXVIII**, "*Information Security at Large Public Displays*," authors Carsten Röcker, University of California, San Diego, USA; Carsten Magerkurth, SAP Research, Switzerland and Steve Hinske, Institute for Pervasive Computing, Switzerland, present a novel concepts for personalized privacy support on large public displays. In a first step, two formative evaluations are conducted in order to analyze the requirements of potential users regarding the protection of private information on large public displays. The insights gained in these evaluations are used to design a system that automatically adapts the information visible on public displays according to the current social situation and the individual privacy preferences of the user working on the display. In a third evaluation, the developed system is evaluated regarding its appropriateness for daily usage and its usefulness to protect privacy. The results of the evaluation showed that users are in general willing to trust system-based protection mechanisms, provided that they are well implemented. In this context, the proposed combination of pre-defined privacy profiles and context-adapted information visualization proved to be a good trade-off between usability and adequate privacy protection.

In **Chapter XXIX**, "*The Sense of Security and Trust*," the sense of security, identified with the Japanese term, Anshin, is identified as an important contributor to emotional trust. This viewpoint, put forth by the authors of the chapter, Yuko Murayama, Iwate Prefectural University, Japan; Carl Hauser, Washington State University, USA; Natsuko Hikage, Iwate Prefectural University, Japan and Basabi Chakraborty, Iwate Prefectural University, Japan, suggests that designers should consider the subjective sense of security as well as objective security measures in designing systems and their user interfaces. A survey of users reveals both the personal and the environmental factors contributing to the users' sense of security when using the Internet. A more encompassing view of Anshin as including safety, reliability, and other non-functional properties of systems may provide additional insights for system design.

Manish Gupta & Raj Sharman
State University of New York at Buffalo, USA

REFERENCES

Al-Ghatani, S. S., & King, M. (1999). Attitudes, satisfaction and usage: Factors contributing to each in the acceptance of information technology. *Behaviour & Information Technology, 18*, 277-297.

Anderson, R. (1993). Why cryptosystems fail. In *Proc. ACM CCS'93*, pages 215–227, Fairfax, VA, Nov. 1993.

Burger, K. (1993). The new age of anxiety. *Insurance and Technology, 18*(10), 48–54.

Carstens, D. S. (2008). Human and Social Aspects of Password Authentication. *Social and Human Elements of Information Security: Emerging Trends and Countermeasures.* Eds: Manish Gupta and Raj Sharman. IGI Global, Hershey, PA. 2008

Dutta, A., & McCrohan, K. (2002). Management's role in information security in a cyber economy. *California Management Review, 45*(1), 67-88.

Franklin, J., Paxson, V., Perrig, A., & Savage, S. (2007). An inquiry into the nature and causes of the wealth of Internet miscreants. In *Proc. ACM CCS'07*, Alexandria, VA, Oct./Nov. 2007.

Gordon, S. (1994). The generic virus writer. In Proc. Intl. Virus Bulletin Conf., pages 121-138, Jersey, Channel Islands, 1994.

Gordon, S. (2000). Virus writers - The end of the innocence? In *10th Annual Virus Bulletin Conference (VB2000)*, Orlando, FL, Sept. 2000.

Helander, M. G., Landauer, T. K., & Prabhu, P. V. (Eds.). (1997). *Handbook of human-computer interaction.* Amsterdam: Elsevier.

Kaplan-Leiserson, E. (2003). People and plans: Training's role in homeland and workplace security. *T+D, 57* (9).

Loch, K. D., Carr, H. H., & Warkentin, M. E. (1992). Threats to information systems: Today's reality, yesterday's understanding. *MIS Quarterly, 17*(2), 173–186.

Markus, M. L. (1983). Power, politics, and MIS implementation. *Communications of the ACM, 26*, 430–444.

Olivia, R. (2003). Will your information survive? *Marketing Management, 12*(1). Business Source Elite Database 10613846.

Panettieri, J. C. (1995). Information Week/Ernst and Young security survey. *Information Week, 555*, 32–37.

Straub, D. W. (1990). Effective IS security: An empirical study. *Information Systems Research, 1*(3), 255–276.

Turnage, J. J. (1990). The challenge of new workplace technology for psychology. *American Psychologist*, *45*, 171–178.

Section I
Organizational Security

Chapter I
Responsibilities and Liabilities with Respect to Catastrophes

C. Warren Axelrod
U.S. Trust, USA

ABSTRACT

This chapter examines the impact of catastrophes on information security and suggests who might have responsibility for maintaining an appropriate level of data protection when a catastrophe occurs. The author asserts that catastrophe contingency planning is very different from regular forms of business continuity and disaster recovery planning in terms of size, focus, scope, and content. Catastrophe contingency plans (CCPs) must comprehend a broad range of potential events affecting large numbers of humans and other living creatures, information processing capabilities, information and media, buildings, and infrastructure, and the like, each with its security considerations, and each characterized by its own roles, responsibilities and liabilities. The intent of the chapter is encourage the development of more comprehensive and realistic CCPs, that is, plans that delineate roles and responsibilities clearly and liabilities should CCPs go awry.

"... Brownie, you're doing a heck of a job."

– President George W. Bush to Federal Emergency Management Agency (FEMA) director Michael D. Brown in Mobile, Alabama, White House Press Release, September 2, 2005

"On September 12 [2005] Brown resigned ..."

See letter at http://www.cnn.com/2005/US/11/03/brown.fema.emails

BACKGROUND

In the wake of Katrina, a Category 5 hurricane that passed east of New Orleans on August 29, 2005, the levees were breached and New Orleans was flooded. There was plenty of blame to go around for the lack of preparation to prevent the breach and for the inadequacy of the rescue and recovery efforts. Local, state and national politicians and other government representatives were roundly criticized for their lack of planning and foresight and their failure to act appropriately and timely in the face of a mounting disaster and evolving catastrophe. On the one hand, the designers and builders of the levees were attacked for their having under-designed these protective structures. On the other hand, those responsible for responding to the event were first praised and subsequently pilloried for the inadequacy of their performance and the great suffering and destruction of property and lives that ensued.

Could this catastrophe have been averted? Or, if the risk of occurrence was considered too low to spend the extra funds on stronger and better designed levees, could the response and recovery process have been better organized and better planned?

Complete protection against such disasters is prohibitively expensive and usually cannot be justified based on the risks. But some level of planning and preparation is expected from our officials and emergency services. Someone has to take on the responsibility for developing and implementing such contingency plans. And, yes, some should be take the blame if the plans go awry and if it is apparent that the damage could have been averted.

Often it takes a tragedy to have better preventive and responsive measures put in place. The magnitude of the Indonesian tsunami of December 2004, with deaths estimated more than 200,000[1], was unprecedented in modern times and unforeseen. Before the event, monitoring devices were not considered necessary. After it happened, as is generally the case, perception of the likelihood of such a devastating event changed quickly, with pressure to build early warning systems in the Indian Ocean as exists in other oceans susceptible to earthquakes. Also, we are now seeing much greater responsiveness, in terms of warning coastal dwellers of a possible tsunami.

It is virtually impossible to predict major devastating events, natural or human-induced, in regard to scope, timing or both, as is very well argued in the book **The Black Swan** (Taleb, 2007). Therefore, it behooves those in power to plan for catastrophes as a whole. They must take responsibility for those plans, and step up to being strongly criticized and severely disciplined if their planning and responses are clearly inadequate and should have been more effective given the state of knowledge and capability prior to the event.

When the avian influenza (or bird flu) pandemic was originally confirmed to have infected human beings in 1997 (CDC, 2007), there were grave concerns that the outbreak would evolve into a human pandemic. Subsequently, there have been some efforts to plan for such a rampant spread of disease in humans, but there remain many who cannot or will not fathom the scope of the required Catastrophe Contingency Plan (CCP). A catastrophe, of the likes of a flu pandemic, would be unprecedented in modern times. The anticipated birdflu outbreak has been compared to the global flu pandemic of 1918. However, the world was not nearly as complex, intertwined and global 90 years ago, nor did it have today's multitude of interacting processes.

Today, with such reliance on nations' critical infrastructures and interdependencies within, between and across sectors, both domestically and internationally, the potential impact of a catastrophe, such as a pandemic, is huge.

There are many who view CCPs as merely simple extensions of regular business continuity and disaster recovery plans. However, as you will see from reading this chapter, CCPs not only include considerations that are very different from regular disaster plans, but they also involve more sophisticated and complex tools and methods. These methods go well beyond those prescribed for regular emergency preparedness and continuity planning.

There are others who think that the likelihood of a flu pandemic or other type of catastrophe is so small that it does not pay to invest in contingency planning. A particularly clear exposition of individuals' views on risk is contained in Michael Lewis's article in **The New York Times Magazine** (Lewis, 2007). Lewis discusses calculating the probabilities of occurrence of catastrophes, particularly natural disasters, and determining whether insurance can cover the losses. Lewis also examines the markets that have sprung up recently and which are geared to spreading the risk.

While the inevitability of a human avian flu pandemic is questionable (Grady, 2006), there is a strong sense that some form of pandemic will definitely occur in the foreseeable future, based on history and the ability of viruses to mutate into new forms and spread rapidly among humans. Some consider the potential impact of such catastrophes as being overstated, particularly since the Y2K meltdown was not nearly as calamitous as was predicted by pundits in the late 1990s. Of course, one might argue, that the potential impact of Y2K was largely mitigated through effective computer program changes. Furthermore, Y2K and the change in Daylight Savings Time, mentioned later, had predictable times and dates of impact, which is not the case for many natural disasters and for intentional and unintentional human activities leading to catastrophe.

This chapter is an attempt to lay out the factors and actions necessary to make up and implement a CCP and point to where the responsibilities lie for developing, maintaining, activating and supporting these plans.

INTRODUCTION

As mentioned above, there are many in business and government who have begun to recognize the urgent need for pandemic contingency planning. This has been in response to the prospect of human-to-human transmittal of a mutated avian influenza virus. They saw that existing planning efforts would not be sufficient in the event of such a pandemic. In support of this, the U.S. Government Accountability Office (GAO) issued a report on **Financial Market Preparedness** and concluded that further work must be done to improve the readiness of the securities markets against the potential onslaught of pandemics (GAO, 2007).

However, a pandemic is only one of many possible catastrophic events, although admittedly a very serious one. In the past decade or so, we have experienced a number of catastrophes, some caused intentionally, others through accidental human activities and still others through natural disasters. Such events include the terrorist attacks of 9-11, the Indonesian tsunami, hurricanes Andrew and Katrina, the Mount St. Helens volcanic eruption, the Kobe earthquake, and the Chernobyl nuclear electricity-generation plant meltdown.

Other catastrophic events are feared but thankfully have not (yet) been realized, except in books and on film. They include:

- an Ebola pandemic (as in the book and movie "The Hot Zone")
- a nuclear bomb exploding in a major U.S. city (as in the movie "The Sum of all Fears")
- the Three Mile Island near miss (similar to that contemporaneously depicted in the movie "The China Syndrome")
- a "dirty bomb" exploding in a metropolitan area (as in the made-for-TV movie "Dirty War" in a London, England context), and
- a sudden devastating climate change (as in the movie "The Day After Tomorrow")

While these latter events are fictional, each contains a seed of plausibility, so that they should serve as warnings.

Putting together continuity plans for such catastrophes is by no means simple. Catastrophe contingency planning is very different from traditional approaches to business continuity and disaster recovery planning in magnitude, focus, scope, context and content. You need to think about whether:

- your CCPs will work for a very large range of possible scenarios
- your computers, communications networks and their human support teams will be resilient enough to withstand catastrophic events and potential resulting infrastructure outages, and
- your computer, network and human systems are readily recoverable and can be brought back to "normal" operation in some form or other following a catastrophic event

It is usually a large effort (relative to regular continuity and recovery plan development, which itself is no small endeavor) to develop CCPs and to try to ensure that they will work under many unthinkable disastrous conditions. Not the least of these considerations is about who takes on the various roles, that is, who is responsible for developing and testing various components of the plan, and (unfortunately but realistically) who is to blame if there are negative repercussions from the plan's deficiencies when it has to be invoked.

In this chapter, we will examine the information security roles, responsibilities and liabilities related to catastrophes, with particular emphasis on those roles and responsibilities that relate to securing information assets prior to, during and subsequent to a catastrophe.

SOME DEFINITIONS

First, we will discuss some definitions. There are many definitions and interpretations of information security and contingency planning and these differences often lead to confusion. What follows is an attempt to reduce the confusion.

Information Security

Simply put, **information security** has to do with the protection of information assets. Such protection can take many forms and, as such, covers a broad array of disciplines.

It is commonly held that the purpose of information security is to ensure the **c**onfidentiality, **i**ntegrity and **a**vailability (the so-called ***CIA***) of information assets. Donn Parker argues that such a definition is inadequate and does not account for the risk aspects of security, particularly as they relate to going after the perpetrators (Parker, 2006).

However, even if we grant that the CIA definition of information security may be incomplete, it can still be helpful to compare confidentiality, integrity and availability to specific topics within the Common Body of Knowledge (CBK). The ten domains of the CBK are the foundation of the more respected certifications in the field, such as the CISSP or Certified Information System Security Professional (Krutz & Vines, 2001). In Table 1, we map each domain in the CBK against the three pillars of information security.

Many of the CBK domains cover all three areas of information security. Notably absent are the attributions of confidentiality and integrity to disaster recovery and business continuity. In general, inadequate attention is paid to confidentiality and integrity in contingency planning – a deficiency that we will address in this chapter.

It is noteworthy that the CBK includes physical security, which is often separate from information security within corporate structures. Despite this,

Table 1. CBK categories mapped to information security objectives

Common Body of Knowledge Domain	Confidentiality	Integrity	Availability
Security management practices	X	X	X
Access control	X		
Security models and architectures	X	X	X
Physical security	X		X
Telecommunications and network security	X	X	X
Cryptography	X	X	
Business continuity planning and disaster recovery planning			X
Law, investigation and ethics	X	X	
Applications and system development	X	X	
Operations security	X		X

there is a current trend for physical and logical (information) security to converge under one head, such as the senior risk officer. Also of note is that legal and ethical aspects are included in the CBK. Increasingly, legal interpretations and regulatory compliance are dominating the privacy space. In some companies, privacy and security are also subject to convergence within the risk organization. However, in other cases, they are separate groups with privacy being in the purview of legal and compliance departments and security residing in the technology and operations world. Bayuk (2008) provides a more detailed description of the various organizational structures.

For this chapter, we shall consider all of the CBK domains to be in scope and will move freely among them.

Privacy

While privacy is frequently achieved through security measures, it has a somewhat different slant than confidentiality or other aspects of sensitive information. Privacy has to do with a person's right to control which information about him or her should be collected, how it might be used, shared and disposed of. Table 2 shows how the CBK and ISO 17799 are related and what the predominant area(s) of applicability, i.e., security or privacy, might be.

Contingency Planning

Just as there are different thoughts as to the makeup of information security, so there are different views of contingency planning, which in general contains both business continuity and disaster recovery planning. It is usually held that business continuity has to do with the recovery of business operations following a damaging event, enabling business functions to be restored to some level that will allow the business to continue to operate. Disaster recovery, on the other hand, generally applies to the recovery of computer and network systems and support functions in the event that they become inoperable in their primary locations. However, the business functions and the computer-related functions are so intertwined that such distinctions are becoming less valid. Also, as the 9-11 terrorist attack demonstrated, events of large magnitude can affect virtually all functions and facilities of an organization.

For the sake of simplicity, I will refer to all planning related to the recovery and restoration of business and technology functions as contingency planning.

Table 2. CBK domains and ISO 17799 categories mapped to security and privacy

CBK Domains	ISO 17799 Categories	Security	Privacy
Security management practices	Security organization Security policy Personnel security	X	
Access control	System access control	X	X
Security models and architectures	Asset classification and control	X	X
Physical security	Physical and environmental security	X	
Telecommunications and network security	Communications and operations management	X	X
Cryptography	Asset classification and control	X	X
Disaster recovery and business continuity	Business continuity management Information security incident management	X	X
Law, investigation and ethics	Compliance		X
Applications and system development	System development and maintenance	X	
Operations security	Communications and operations management	X	X
	Information systems acquisition, development and maintenance	X	

Catastrophe

An area that appears to have received relatively little attention, from a definitional point of view, is that of a catastrophe. We are very familiar with localized, and even regional, events that disturb normal operations, yet are not considered catastrophes. Such events include the usual suspects of fires, floods, storms, and the like. They might result in a specific area, such as a city or state, being considered a "disaster area," and may indeed be catastrophic for the individuals directly involved. Yet it appears that true catastrophes are more far-reaching and devastating. The Indonesian tsunami and 9-11 terrorist attacks are certainly viewed as catastrophes, as are most wars, in that they adversely affect large numbers of people and take enormous efforts for recovery. But was the Mount St. Helens volcanic eruption a catastrophe? It was certainly a disaster, but probably would not be considered catastrophic since the lives of relatively few individuals were affected directly. On the other hand, Hurricane Katrina was disastrous in general, but catastrophic for New Orleans as it led to consequential events that destroyed a major city. The meltdown of the nuclear power plant in Chernobyl was catastrophic in that many became ill and died or suffered diseases from the radioactivity spewed into the atmosphere, but the threat of a meltdown was averted for the Three Mile Island nuclear plant near Middletown, Pennsylvania, so that a sure-fire catastrophe was avoided.

Sometimes the term is used for lesser events to indicate an escalation in the seriousness of the accident as in the case of the Utah mine collapse. When three of those attempting to rescue the trapped miners were themselves killed, the governor of Utah, Jon Huntsman, declared on August 17, 2007 that "… yesterday we went from a tragedy to a catastrophe."[2] This was certainly a very distressing, high profile disaster, but calling it a catastrophe might be viewed as political hyperbole.

Clearly the use of the term catastrophe is quite subjective. In this chapter, we will be addressing events that are likely to become catastrophic to the extent that are orders of magnitude more damaging than disasters that occur day-in and day-out throughout the world and cut across many sectors and parts of the infrastructure making recovery and reconstitution a long, painful endeavor. The experience of the destruction of the World Trade Center on 9-11 and the time it has taken (almost seven years) to decide what should be built at the "ground zero" site is illustrative of what can follow a major catastrophe.

IMPACT ON SECURITY AND PRIVACY

While the most publicized aspects of recent catastrophes have rightly focused on the human loss, pain and suffering caused by such events, there were also security issues that, while not as broadly communicated, severely impacted the confidentiality, integrity and availability of personal, confidential and other sensitive records. Here are some examples.

Following the destruction of New Orleans from the consequences of Hurricane Katrina, huge volumes of paper and electronic records, containing valuable, often irreplaceable, personal information, were exposed to the floodwaters and destroyed by them. Due to the extent of the flooding, both primary and any secondary repositories of data, such as health records and financial records, were often no longer usable and many of them would likely not be restorable from out-of-region sources. This no doubt contributed to the unbearable hardships endured and rampant fraud perpetrated in the wake of Katrina, particularly in regard to claiming eligibility for financial aid without having the proper credentials.[3]

Similarly, with the destruction of New York City's World Trade Center on September 11, 2001, many smaller companies lost their only place of business and even large firms had both primary **and** backup facilities destroyed in the collapsed buildings. Even when facilities were not destroyed, access to the area was denied for extended periods of time. Companies had not generally anticipated such extensive and total destruction from a single series of events and some thought that having redundant power supplies and alternative telecommunications providers was sufficient backup.

This loss of primary and backup facilities from a single event was also true of the blackout, due to a fire in a switching station, which occurred in the Downtown Manhattan area in August 1990, which selectively robbed buildings of power for up to several weeks. The Canadian ice storm of 1998, affecting the provinces of Ontario, Quebec and New Brunswick knocked out electric power to some areas for as long as a month. Also, the blackout of August 2003 in the northeastern states of America and eastern Canada knocked out a whole region and disabled many businesses' primary and backup facilities for an estimated total cost of $4 - 6 billion.[4] A number of businesses also found out that their disaster recovery plans were woefully inadequate for managing incidents with such broad areas of impact.

There are two main aspects of security and privacy as they relate to contingency planning. One is the need for inclusion of security and privacy in the contingency planning process (Axelrod, 1996); the other is the need to deal with the aftermath and avoid as many of the potential consequences in the planning stage. With regard to the latter, Rebecca Herold (2006) provides an excellent overview of the privacy issues that arise. The issues raised by Herold include the following:

- Personally identifiable information (PII) is lost and cannot be accounted for
- PII, particularly on paper, may have been viewed and misused by unauthorized persons
- Systems, which stored the PII, cannot be accounted for
- Systems documentation and persons able to operate the systems may not be available
- Inability of a company to contain and maintain PII may lead to loss of reputation
- Alternative means of transmitting or transferring PII may have been destroyed, leaving less secure alternative methods

- Stolen and looted items may contain PII, with the possibility of the information being used for fraud, identity theft, and other criminal activities
- Hurriedly assembled backup facilities may not have adequate physical security leading to potential compromise of PII
- Hurriedly restored systems may not provide the required access controls

Both Axelrod (1996) and Herold (2006) suggest measures that should be taken to achieve a higher level of confidence that control over sensitive and confidential information is maintained and that data and documentation required for reestablishing operations are appropriately stored.

RESPONSIBILITIES AND LIABILITIES

When it comes to CCP, initial concern about a particular impending catastrophe comes from many different sources. A senior manager may notice a newspaper article or read an article in an airline magazine on a long flight, as a result of which he or she may ask the question as to what his or her staff are doing about a particular threat or vulnerability. Another source may be industry or professional associations, which are generally on the lookout for upcoming risks as such notification represents an added service to the membership.

Whatever the means of introduction into the organization, and whoever the gatekeeper might be, the important question is who will take ownership of the process. Often it falls to the existing business continuity and disaster recovery planners. For example, the business continuity committee of SIFMA (Securities Industry and Financial Markets Association) has a membership of several hundred representatives from securities firms. When meetings were called to ensure a smooth transition of Daylight Savings Time (DST), after Congress had changed the dates on which it was to take effect, some 400 to 500 member firm representatives called into the planning and informational sessions. Similarly on the banking side, BITS (Banking Industry Technology Secretariat), the technology arm of the Financial Services roundtable, organized DST meetings for its members and directed them to important information sources, including software vendors' Web sites and the SIFMA Web site. In most of the member institutions, those already with continuity and recovery responsibilities took on these additional DST duties.

In general, the responsibility for developing contingency plans falls to a dedicated area or, in a smaller organization to an individual, usually in the risk or IT departments, depending upon the structure of the organization. In some cases, with a dedicated business continuity and disaster recovery group, the planning group may also be responsible for testing the plans directly or in an oversight role answerable to senior management. In other cases, the plans may be turned over to an operational area for maintenance and testing. Regardless of the specific structures in place in any particular entity, it is senior-level management and Boards of Directors who are ultimately responsible for ensuring the resiliency of their organizations.

It is really up to the planners themselves to ensure that adequate attention has been paid to security in developing and testing the various contingency plans. However, security is easily omitted from such plans. Consequently, practicing security professionals need to be assertive in ensuring that their views are heard and that there is top-level support for incorporating security into contingency plans. If not, then an actual disaster or catastrophe will very likely compound any underlying security issues or, if one does not experience a real disaster, auditors may well point out the omission of security, with resulting negative findings..

While the group that develops and validates the plans is often responsible for invoking the plans, it is ultimately senior management that is held liable if things go badly wrong.

DEVELOPING CONTINGENCY PLANS

The contingency planning process should follow a series of steps, some of which are completed during the preparation stages and others of which are activated when an incident actually occurs. In general, the **goals** of contingency plans are to:

- avoid, prevent and deter threats and vulnerabilities to whatever degree possible
- reduce the impact of an event should it occur
- provide alerts and warning, in anticipation of predictable events such as hurricanes, earthquakes and tsunamis
- send out alerts and notifications to those likely to be affected by an incident and to responders who are responsible for providing emergency assistance
- monitor events and collect information for potential forensics analysis, insurance claims, and charges against lawbreakers, and to assist in the recovery process
- respond to incidents in such a way as to minimize damage and losses, and
- restore facilities and operations to an effective level, up to and including the complete restoration of the pre-incident environment.

These steps must be documented and should be exercised as drills for the more likely disasters, such as fires and floods, for less common natural disasters, such as earthquakes, volcanic eruptions and tsunamis, and for man-made catastrophes, such as events involving biological or radioactive materials. However, it should be noted that the greater and more extensive the catastrophe, the larger the gap is likely to be between what may have been planned, developed and tested and what will need to be done should an actual catastrophe occur. The cost of preparing fully for every anticipated contingency situation is so prohibitive that one can only prepare for a small subset of all possible events. The extent of the preparation is also very much constrained by the availability of funds. However, in recognizing that actual events may vary considerably from those anticipated, it behooves the planner to provide a degree of flexibility and allow for decisions to be made as an event unfolds.

Catastrophe contingency planning is much more complex than was, for example, Y2K contingency planning, since activating and running catastrophe plans are so much more dependent on human beings, who may well be gravely affected personally by the catastrophic event and unable to function normally, if at all. Regular contingency plans invariably presume that some sufficient level of emergency personnel and equipment would be available in the event of a disaster. Such an assumption is likely not to be valid, particularly in the short term, for many potential catastrophes.

Not only is the scope of a CCP much more extensive than traditional business continuity and disaster recovery planning, but also creators of such plans must have high skill levels in an even broader range of business and technical disciplines.

An additional requirement for any contingency plan is "information security assurance," which means making sure that the confidentiality, integrity and availability of sensitive and business-critical information are preserved during and following a catastrophe. Such assurance is needed to verify, as best as one can, that systems will be able to sustain the upheavals and irregular processes that will surely occur when segments of the supporting infrastructure and the various interconnections are destroyed or unusable as a consequence of a catastrophe.

It is increasingly recognized that many catastrophe plans and tests may not be completed in time. The General Accountability Office made such a claim in regard to financial firms (GAO, 2007), either because of the lack of resources or because items have not been addressed at all. Attention must be turned to what to do when things do go wrong, as they surely will during and after a catastrophe. Whether the resulting environment is apocalyptic or disastrous depends largely upon how well everyone is prepared and how good the contingency plans prove to be.

Catastrophe contingency planners and managers need to bring at least the following experience, knowledge and skills to the table:

- knowledge of the industry sector(s) in which their organization(s) operate
- understanding of the business processes on which their organizations depend
- experience with business process modeling
- knowledge of system and network simulation technologies
- familiarity with risk assessment and business impact analysis tools
- experience with business continuity and disaster recovery plan development, implementation and testing
- experience with emergency preparedness planning and incident management, and
- experience with computer forensics methods

Many government agencies and industry groups have recently formed committees with pandemic contingency planning as their main focus. Government agencies are publishing requirements and reviewing readiness and disaster preparedness both for government agencies and for businesses over which they have oversight and regulatory responsibilities. An excellent resource for publications relating to a prospective influenza pandemic can be found on the BITS Web site (BITS, 2007).

In Table 3 we show some general and specific responses that will be required for expected and unanticipated events occurring at predictable and unknown times. Certain weather-related events, such as hurricanes, are predictable days and, with less precision, even weeks in advance. Earthquakes are less predictable, although expectations that they will occur at certain locations within a rough period of time are reasonably accurate and there are those who maintain that some animals are especially sensitive to pending earthquakes and tsunamis, and could provide some small window if their signs can be interpreted accurately. Similarly, pandemics can sometimes be projected from initial outbreaks, although actions can be taken to reduce the probability of their initial occurrence. And still other events, such as major electrical blackouts, are a surprise whenever they occur, although local brownouts and blackouts can be anticipated under heavy-load conditions, such as a blistering heat wave.

The greatest contributions to CCPs to date have come from traditional disaster recovery and business continuity experts. There is little question that the planning and recovery methodologies that these specialists have assembled over the years, which include risk assessment, business impact analysis, staff interviews, business continuity plan preparation, walkthroughs and incident management planning should form the foundation of any catastrophe contingency planning effort. However there are some very important differences between planning for catastrophes compared to a typical disaster such as a fire. Catastrophe contingency planning requires sophisticated approaches beyond those applied to traditional programs to deal with the added complexity. We now compare and contrast the two.

Regular Contingency Planning

Most contingency plans today are based on the assumption that disasters will likely be localized, well-defined events, such as fires, floods, tornadoes, and similar misfortunes. The goal of the plan is to secure backup resources, such as space, desks, computers, telephones, fax machines, supplies, and access to computer applications and data, at a site unlikely to be affected by any specific incident, so that business activities can be resumed at the backup location.

Usually an organization must balance distance, cost and convenience in selecting a disaster recovery site or a third party contingency service. The closer the backup facility, usually the easier it is to transport staff and materials—but the greater is the risk that an incident will affect both sites. On the other hand, distant sites tend to be more costly to maintain and test and, in the event of a disaster, could present transportation difficulties.

In this approach, preparations are made to survive broad-based events affecting buildings, transportation, utilities, and the like. Certain underlying assumptions are needed to make this approach viable, not least of which is that primary and backup facilities and resources will not both be destroyed or severely adversely affected by the same event.

The suitability of a backup site depends on such features as the distance from the primary site, separation of power and telephone grids, and independence of transportation systems. In Table 4 below, we show a number of factors, which exhibit differences between traditional contingency planning and catastrophe contingency planning.

Table 3. Catastrophe preparation and contingency planning activities

Event	Timing	Examples	General Responses	Specific Responses	Initiators, Implementers
Known	Known	Systems and facilities known not to be backed up.	Specific preventive measures.	Business impact analysis and prioritization. Replacement, elimination. Remediation contingency planning.	Internal Contingency Planning Team. Industry initiatives.
Expected	Unknown	Expected events (e.g., third-party system failures) which may or may not occur or may or may not have a significant impact.	Specific preparatory and emergency measures.	Business recovery/continuity planning. Disaster recovery planning. System and process integrity assurance program. Business interruption insurance.	Internal Contingency Planning Team.
Unexpected	Known	Unanticipated events likely to occur when a catastrophe happens. That is to say, while the timing of the catastrophe may not be known, there are events that are not anticipated prior to a catastrophic event, but could have been.	Risk analysis to determine the potential for failure. General preparatory and emergency measures.	Simulation of business processes and systems to bring out potential weak points. Risk assessment. Business impact analysis. Business recovery/continuity planning. Disaster recovery planning. System and process integrity assurance program. Business interruption insurance.	Internal Contingency Planning Team. Industry and national initiatives.
Unknown	Unknown	Unanticipated events that may or may not occur or may or may not have a significant impact.	General emergency measures.	Establish Incident Management Team with specific responsibilities and emergency response procedures. Coordinate with international, national and local Emergency Response Teams.	Internal Incident Management Team (IMT). Industry or Sector Incident Management Teams. International, national and local Emergency Response Teams.

Table 4. Comparisons between standard and year 2000 contingency planning

Factor	Traditional Contingency Planning	Catastrophe Contingency Planning
Distances between primary and backup business, operations and data center facilities.	Greater distance increases chance of independence of power and telephone grids, transportation systems, weather patterns, etc.	Distance not necessarily as significant a factor within continental U.S. for power and communications since a catastrophe, such as a pandemic, could have broad geographical impact. On the other hand, a regional event, such as might result from the detonation of a nuclear device, suggests establishing out-of-region backup facilities. Such out-of-region backup facilities have been mandated by finance sector regulators for so-called "core" institutions.
Off-site storage of documents, computer programs, data, supplies, etc.	Generally effective means of providing resources for restoration.	Restoration of programs and data may not be feasible since backup copies may also have been destroyed or otherwise unattainable.
Alternative power sources, telephone providers, etc. at both primary and backup facilities.	Generally provides good protection against incidents that affect a single provider, although many providers may be linked to one another or use each other's facilities.	Catastrophe, such as an earthquake, might affect all providers in the same region. Some concern that smaller providers will not be as resilient as larger providers.
Use of disaster recovery services for data center and network backup and third-party work-area facilities for backup of business units.	This is a means of protecting against a localized incident, assuming that an off-site data storage program is also in place, since third parties are less likely to be impacted by a local disaster.	Possibility of third party also being affected by catastrophes and communications to and from backup facility being affected. Also, huge demand might exceed capacity.
Notification of business and operations workers about off-hours incidents.	Assumes that telephone systems and notification systems are generally operational.	Telephone systems and notification systems and/or services may not be fully operational or even available. This suggests implementing "negative notification," whereby participants are given to understand that the CCP is invoked if they do NOT receive notification when an obviously catastrophic event has occurred.
Workers able to get to backup facility.	Assumes that transportation modes, including roads, are operational and that incident affects only workers' places of business and not their homes.	Variety of transportation modes might not be operational. Incidents may impact wide areas including businesses and homes, affecting workers ability to leave and/or travel between home and work. Pandemics or other types of catastrophe, such as earthquakes, will likely cause workers to stay with their families or to search for victims. This raises the issue as to whether there is sufficient network capacity to support a huge number of workers communicating from home.
Workers have access to backup facility.	Assumes that security systems, elevators, guard services, etc. are available and operational at backup facilities.	Power systems, transportation, guards, etc., may not be available during a catastrophe or in its aftermath.

Regular contingency plans are characterized by relatively few disaster scenarios—often the "worst case" is when a building is completely destroyed or is rendered inaccessible—and by the requirement to provide alternative resources and processing capability to keep the enterprise operating at an acceptable level. There is also an implicit expectation for localized incidents, such as fires and power outages, that suppliers, customers and business partners will not have been unduly affected by the same disaster. Therefore can be relied upon to be in operation and lend assistance particularly during the difficult early stages of recovery.

There are clearly regional disasters, such as hurricanes, earthquakes and regional power or telephone outages, which can also impact a firm's business partners. Such incidents might require a backup-to-backup solution in which a firm's backup facility needs to communicate with a business partner's backup facility, for example, assuming that the backup facilities reside outside the affected area. In general, most disaster recovery plans do not detail such scenarios. However catastrophe contingency planning brings this into the realm of higher probability.

However, we seldom see backup-to-backup CCPs and tests because of the low probabilities assumed for simultaneous catastrophes affecting an organization and its business partners. Increasingly regulators and auditors are looking to have financial firms, in particular, conduct backup-to-backup tests with their critical business partners and service providers.

Catastrophe Contingency Planning

While many of the components of regular contingency planning should be incorporated into CCPs, there are some major differences between the two—specifically there are add-ons for CCPs. CCPs should include both the narrower specifics of regular contingency planning as well as the broader more comprehensive approach to potential catastrophic disruptions.

Where utilities, such as telephone and electricity services, are impacted, then traditional disaster recovery might be applied, as long as backup facilities are not also affected by these or other incidents.

Where the problem is spread-out geographically, such as with a pandemic, transferring to another site may not resolve the problem since the backup environment might be impacted also.

Also, the nature of CCP problems might be difficult to identify and resolve because they may involve a large number of complex interactions. One can imagine that, even if primary physical facilities remain intact with power, telecommunications, computers, water, and transportation, standard recovery procedures may not work due to the nature of the catastrophe.

Thus, catastrophe contingency planning is characterized by the potential for a huge number of disaster scenarios versus relatively few scenarios under regular contingency planning. In addition, CCP scenarios may be such that standard restoration and recovery procedures simply will not work.

In some cases, such as a flu pandemic, health agencies have already determined how such a virus might spread throughout the world. A pandemic might originate in Asia and spread via Europe to North America. This may give the latter regions additional time to prepare for an onslaught.

Remediation Contingency Planning

Another type of contingency planning that is particularly important to a CCP arises from the possibility that remediation efforts will not be completed in time. Remediation contingency planning is targeted at coming up with alternatives which, it is hoped, can be effected within the available time.

MODELING BUSINESS PROCESSES

Why Models are Needed

The complexity of worldwide business processes, with trillions of interactions, makes it impossible for an individual, or even a group of individuals, to grasp the entire breadth and depth of all of the interdependent processes. This is clearly an area where computer-based models can not only assist in representing the processes and interactions, but may be the only means of doing so.

In order to understand the potential impact of failures caused by a catastrophe, the use of computerized models may be the only viable approach given the complexity and enormity of the situation. Such models facilitate the discovery of failure scenarios as well as provide the basis for preparing viable workarounds. They provide an understanding as to which systems need to have their integrity reviewed under recovery situations, and facilitate setting up effective emergency response procedures.

Various Approaches

However, building such models is neither simple nor quick. For them to be useful, models need to represent accurately all significant processes and their interdependencies. Added to this is the need to determine the probabilities of failure, due to various catastrophic events, of all nodes and links between nodes and then incorporate those probabilities into the computer model. The model should enable assessment of the likelihood of individual components failing on their own or due to the failure of one or more other components with which they interact.

The costs of interruptions of varying length are needed to calculate the business impact of failures. This analysis will suggest appropriate limits for the effort and money that should be expended on workarounds and recovery processes. Using risk assessment, analysts can estimate the expected loss using the probabilities and costs of failures.

Tools Available

A number of tools have been developed for process modeling, risk assessments, failure monitoring and reporting, business impact analysis and business continuity planning. Process modeling is traditionally based on simulation programming languages. These general business-process modeling tools can be used in the development of CCPs.

Some modeling and business impact analysis tools are static. These are more suited to measuring the losses relating to somewhat independent events and processes, not losses from the complex dynamic interactions that might be expected with catastrophic events. Dynamic modeling tools that account for feedback between processes and process delays are more appropriate for catastrophe analysis.

Business continuity planning tools are generally simple in construction, comprising databases of resources, word processing documents and graphical user screens. Their added value comes from their ability to load down data from human resources databases, to make key information immediately available and to facilitate the management and recording of an incident. The data contained in these systems can also be fed into automated notification systems.

Perhaps the least mature of the tools categories is that relating to the monitoring, reporting and fixing of real-time incidents. Such tools have the ability to monitor the health of the systems, including hardware, software and applications, and to participate in the restoration of service in the event of a failure. However we are seeing some progress being made in this area.

Skills and Responsibilities

The range of skills and knowledge required for modeling business processes is much broader than is needed on the technical side. The modelers must have strong working knowledge of the business so as to understand and correctly represent the processes that are described to them. The ownership of the models should fall to the business units whose processes are the subjects of the models. The business owners must validate that the models are truly representative.

SCENARIO DISCOVERY

As mentioned above, computerized tools can assist in the process of determining the broad range of potential catastrophe scenarios and their relative importance. Because of the enormous number of possible scenarios (literally the potential for millions of "coincident incidents"), it is necessary to limit severely the range of scenarios under consideration.

One approach is to use a probabilistic risk-assessment model along with an expected-loss threshold below which a specific response would not be developed. This would help ensure that high-impact low-probability events are included along with lower-impact high-probability events. Thus, even if you are 99.999 percent sure that the telephone system will be operating, the potential impact is so large that you would be advised to have some predetermined contingency plan to handle a mass telephone failure. While not suggesting returning to the days of carrier pigeons, other means of communication, such as a ham radio or radio telephone operating on batteries or a generator, might be considered.

Database of Past Problems

You should consider building an historical database of incidents that are occurring in the normal course of business, which impact your operation and from which you have previously recovered. The database should contain descriptions of events, their impact, workarounds (if any), and methods used to recover and/or restore the system back to normal operations.

The contents of the database can be expanded and enhanced by simulating outages or creating faults in test versions of systems, networks, etc. and capturing the events and the methods used to fix them in the same historical database. Additionally, one can look to external sources to provide data based on their own experience and research.

This database provides a good springboard for scenario development and for compiling lists of workarounds to be invoked in the event of future failure. The database should be in a form that can be readily searched using context-sensitive queries so that an event described in a natural language (e.g., English) can be translated into search criteria that come up with suggestions as to the cause and resolution of the event.

Responsibilities and Liabilities

An organization's risk management function should certainly be involved in the development of the risk aspects of the models. Risk professionals need to interface with the legal, compliance, audit and various business departments, as well as with senior management, in order to ensure that the scenarios posited are understood and accepted by the different constituencies.

It should also be recognized that catastrophes might subject organizations to unprecedented situations. A more complete portfolio of such events will require, in addition to internal data collection, tapping into professional societies and industry associations. Other sources include commercial publications, government agency publications, the general computer press, think tanks, consulting firms and advisory services.

The Internet is a very good source of catastrophe remediation and contingency planning information, particularly in regard to pandemics. There are many private and government Web sites that specifically cover catastrophic events and some of those address contingency planning. Web sites specializing in security and contingency matters are extending their interests to catastrophe scenarios.

Viable Workarounds

Once potentially significant scenarios have been identified, the question is—what next? The key is to come up with "what ifs," think them through and then develop workarounds that will function in the very unusual circumstances that will undoubtedly prevail in the aftermath of a catastrophe.

Traditionally, fixes and workarounds are based on assumptions about the environment, such as the availability and cooperation of service technicians, emergency services, vendor support, business partners, basic services (such as electricity, telephones) and so on. Under catastrophic conditions, it should be assumed that many of these support services might also be affected and therefore not be available, so that the proposed workarounds will have to allow for such extreme situations. It may be helpful to consider a few calamitous, but possible, situations and the type of measures that may have to be invoked, as follows:

- Typical emergency response procedures involve the notification of staff, vendors, emergency services, and so on. However, what if the telephone system is inoperative, along with radio, television and other means of broadcast or if some of these means of communication are saturated because of broad infrastructure and systems problems? One approach might be to introduce a "negative notification" procedure whereby those to be notified are given to understand that if they do not receive an "all clear," they must assume that there is a problem and take some appropriate predetermined action.
- If process modeling indicates the potential for a problem in one area rippling through to other areas, then the response might be to isolate or "quarantine" particular components. This might be particularly applicable to power and telecommunications utilities where a fault can quickly propagate throughout their systems. Cutting off failing components of the system increases the chance of survival of remaining components. Critical to this approach is assuring that the remaining healthy systems can in fact operate when other components are disconnected. Systems are not necessarily built to withstand this type of situation so that they may have to be modified and tested to ensure integrity under adversity.
- Outages in one segment of the infrastructure can lead to much higher use of other segments. For example, if computer-to-computer links are not operational, circumvention might involve increased telephone calls, faxes, and mailing of paper copy. This could overload the surviving telecommunications and mail delivery services. And physical deliveries may be hampered by excessive traffic if public transit is having problems and people take to the road. Consequently, the mass movement from one way of doing business to another could result in making the surviving systems practically unusable. This is the reason for efforts to obtain priority telecommunications and Internet services.

For CCP development, it is necessary to go beyond the regular assumptions of traditional contingency planning and to recognize that many long-held assumptions may not be valid in the face of a catastrophe. As a result, the impact of secondary and tertiary effects must be considered. This is not usually done in regular contingency planning.

In order to ferret out a broad range of possibilities, the business units and technical departments must meet with product vendors and other service providers to brainstorm the range of possibilities and walk through contingency modes. Also, organizations should be working with think tanks, government agencies and industry associations to learn to what extent vendors and supporters are developing their own contingency plans. For example, it is important to know whether your power and telecommunications providers have plans to isolate your region from the effect of outside regions and whether they can operate in a self-sufficient manner.

HISTORY OF PROBLEMS AND FIXES

In some cases, the "fix" documented in the historical database of past problems and their resolutions will likely prevent the incident from recurring, or greatly reduce the probability of recurrence. In other situations, the workaround used will become a recommended recovery procedure for catastrophic events.

Information Security Considerations

Assurance of System, Application and Data Integrity

Data and system integrity needs to be assured in three areas:

- **Continued operation of computer applications, data, underlying processes and processors**—Need to be assured that the changes performed to handle catastrophes have not compromised the normal operation of affected systems
- **Integrity of recovery processes needed to bring back failed systems**—Recovery routines and systems are easily ignored in the contingency planning process but they will likely be absolutely crucial to effective recovery during a catastrophe
- **Ensuring resilience in the face of workarounds**—Workarounds, such as manual processing, may have systems implications that could, in certain situations, create major processing problems for systems that are still active and for the recovery and restart processes.

Inventory of Systems and Interfaces

The system integrity project begins with inventorying all the systems, interfaces and infrastructure components that might possibly impact the business if they are rendered unavailable due to a catastrophe. The inventory should include what might be termed the applications' "dependency stack" which comprises various components on which the applications depend, such as servers, routers, "middleware" processes, processors, disk units, network devices, and so on. Interdependencies among applications should also be included.

While the applications development and the operations areas should play major roles in this process, the information security group must also take on responsibility for ensuring that appropriate levels of security are maintained throughout the project.

Integrity Reviews and Remediation

This phase consists of reviewing application program code, databases, etc., to see which components might fail and how they might affect other components. This type of review is not straightforward. In the integrity assurance case, a good understanding of the business process being supported is needed so as to be able to judge whether or not a problem exists and, if so, what a reasonable remedy might be. This type of contingency review is much more extensive than regular reviews and requires a great deal more thought, and consequently much more money and time per item than regular contingency planning. A couple of examples might be in order to indicate the nature of the problems to be encountered and how they might be remedied:

- A financial institution stated that it would not permit "open orders" to be carried in the event of a catastrophe. Assuming that this could be achieved (and some have expressed doubts that it is feasible), the question then arises as to whether the order-handling computer applications have been programmed in such a way that they can handle empty or static open-order files. Experience dictates that it might go either way. Specifically, if the program looks for an "end of file" prior to continuing, there could be a problem. If it is the reverse, the program should function, unless some other parts of the code fails when the number of open orders is zero.

- On one occasion a major central system in the securities industry failed for several hours. Programs feeding into that system did not detect that the system was down and continued broadcasting messages—which never arrived at their destination. While the central system in question is on an industry list of "must operate" systems, there are clearly instances, even today, in which even a critical system is not available. Corrective action needs to be taken to ensure the integrity of systems interfacing with other critical systems. It is often worse to have an event happen and not respond to it properly than having the event occur without seeing any response.

TESTING CONTINGENCY FAILURES

Testing for potential contingency failures falls into the following three categories:

- Assurance that recovery software and procedures are viable.
- Ensuring that computer applications are sustainable in the face of unprecedented combinations of failures.
- Determination that systems, other than those being specifically circumvented, will work in the event that workarounds are invoked, such as the suspension of affected business activities or reversion to manual procedures.

Recovery Software

Contingency projects primarily focus on day-to-day production applications. After all, these are the ones that are most visible and need to be up and running at all times. Jobs run infrequently—such as weekly, monthly, quarterly, and "on request" jobs—are, in the author's experience, often neglected in conversions and maintenance programs, since they are frequently omitted from inventories of systems. A particular category of occasional job, which is of major concern, is one that supports recovery activities. Since they are not considered part of regular production and since they may be activated only occasionally, they tend to be forgotten.

Compound Failures

In a typical production environment, some component or another fails practically every day. Data may be missing or garbled, calculations might go awry, hardware components break, and networks go down. Most failures are relatively minor and may not even be apparent to users. Some do have significant operational and financial impact but are often repaired in a fairly short time as technicians and support personnel plunge in and concentrate totally on the emergency until it is resolved. It is fortunately quite rare for many faults and incidents to occur at the same time but, when that does happen, recovery is not always guaranteed and consequences can be dire.

A number of compound failure scenarios can be envisaged. Here are some examples:

- A fault might "cascade" or ripple from one system to another and then to subsequent systems due to serial dependencies. As straight-through processing (STP) gains in popularity there will likely be increases in this pattern of failure.
- Another type of fault is one that "fans out" in parallel from a single source system to numerous dependent satellite systems. The push towards distributed systems, customer workstations and remote access via the Internet and other networks makes systems more vulnerable to fan-out failures.

- In a third situation, systems that depend on many supporting systems, data sources, etc., might be subject to the failure of several or many of the supporting systems and/or infrastructure services. Rapid growth in business-to-business, business-to-customer, as well as business-to-government interconnections increases the number and magnitude of dependencies on others for successful operation of an organization's systems.

It is difficult to prepare for, and respond to, complex and compound failures. As mentioned previously, it is unreasonable to expect that an individual or even a group of individuals can retain in their heads an overall detailed knowledge of all systems and processes within an organization. Consequently they are not able to analyze the myriad of events that might occur separately or in combination, and formulate strategies to fix abnormal situations. This points to the need for some form of automated assistance.

Failures Due to Workarounds

A third consideration is the potential failure brought about by workarounds or recovery procedures themselves. This is different from the situations above in that, in this case, the contingency operating environment will likely be different from regular operational modes. Consequently, fixes that worked previously might not work here. The key is to test systems running under conditions that they would see if particular fallback procedures were invoked.

For example, it might be decided that, if a particular data feed is not available, the data should be manually entered directly into the processing system. However, several preparatory checks need to be made. First and foremost, the capability to enter data manually obviously has to be available. It would be particularly troublesome to find out during an emergency that planned options cannot be invoked due to systems and procedures that have not been maintained and the loss of personnel knowledgeable in the emergency procedures.. However, it is increasingly unlikely that newer systems are built with manual entry capability since, for many such systems, the size of the potential manual effort precludes this option. Even if the manual-entry capability is built in, it may not have been tested since inception—and needs to be tested regularly. Furthermore, for the option to be usable, changes may have to be made, such as the addition of terminals, computer ports, and switches. And finally, trained staff needs to be available on call.

Some Unique Testing Situations

Testing of CCPs is different from regular testing in certain very important ways. In the first place, the impact may be so ubiquitous that it is not clear that, in any given test environment, all of the relevant components have been included. We must ensure that the systems operate over a period of time and also that they can handle unusually heavy volumes.

Multi-Day Tests

A catastrophe might appear to be a single event—but it is not. For example, the expectation is for a pandemic to hit in three successive waves. Many business processes have long cycles, lasting weeks and months, which might involve extended time delays and data retention or looking up historical data. As a result, tests should span the appropriate period of time.

Large-Volume Tests

Many test environments use subsets of sample data to expedite the testing process. This approach does test functionality but it certainly does not account for the potentially high volumes of data that may have to be processed and stored at the time of and following a catastrophe. The expectation of unusually high volumes is reasonable considering what we see from day-to-day failures. When a real-time application, such as an airline reservations system, is down then the telephone lines are swamped with customers seeking information. Some indication of the potential for diversion of traffic and increases in volume can be determined from process models for the major utilities and services and from business process models for organizations.

Responsibilities and Liabilities

While contingency planners should be involved and even manage the testing, this is an area where the operational areas and business units need to take ownership, and the various support areas should have specific assigned roles. With this structure, it is up to the business and operations owners to ensure that the tests are well attended by those invited to participate. If the planners or support areas are given the responsibility, it might be more difficult to ensure appropriate participation from other areas. Ultimately, the business and operational areas are the one who should be funding the effort and should be looked to if an actual event occurs and if the response is inadequate in any respect.

MONITORING AND EMERGENCY RESPONSE

Monitoring Tools

It is one thing for components to break and applications to fail. It is quite another not to know about it until it has wreaked havoc with all manner of business processes. How can those in command know what is happening quickly enough to make the right business decisions before too much damage has been done? The answer lies in the use of monitoring tools which continuously sense what is going on in applications, raise a flag if there is a problem and, optionally, go about fixing it. As mentioned previously, such a system would automatically build a database of its experience that can be drawn upon to help resolve a situation that may have shown up previously in a similar guise.

Emergency Response

A crucial component of the whole effort is the establishment of an incident management or emergency response team. Such a group is typically made up of representatives of senior management. In order to operate they need to be selected based on their knowledge of the business and their ability to respond effectively in disaster situations. They also require to have predetermined responsibilities and the tools and facilities to effect the response.

Many procedures for this group need to be tailored to specific catastrophes. For example, one has to allow for the possibility that the normal means of communication may not be available.

CONCLUSION

No one wants to think about the ramifications of a major catastrophe, but it is very necessary to do so in order to plan mitigation strategies to reduce the impact of horrendous events. How many lives would have been saved in Indonesia, for example, had there been a local early-warning system and concomitant procedures for tsunamis?

In this chapter, we looked at how catastrophe contingency planning differs from your regular run-of-the-mill approaches and pointed out how to account for the differences in developing, testing and maintaining those plans. While it is well nigh impossible to protect against all catastrophes, as Lucca point out (Lucca, 2006), planning for various catastrophic events is quite similar across events, even though they may vary widely.

Because the effect of a catastrophe can be devastating, even small improvements in the process will yield significant returns, which is a good reason to go through the catastrophe planning exercise. The hope is that planning for catastrophes will find its place in an organization's security and recovery repertoire. Just a minor improvement can make a big difference and make the effort worthwhile, and if damage can be contained and recovery expedited, even greater returns will be accomplished.

REFERENCES

Axelrod, C. W. (1999). Data Processing and Communications Security During Recovery and Repair. In S.F. Blanding (ed.), *Enterprise Operations Management Handbook, Second Edition* (pp. 631-640). Boca Raton, FL: CRC Press.

Bayuk, J. L. (2008). *Stepping through the Infosec Program*, Rolling Hills, IL: ISACA.

BITS (2008). *Pandemic Influenza Resources on File*. Retrieved May 1, 2008 from www.bitsinfo.org

GAO (United States Government Accountability Office) (2007). *Financial Market Preparedness: Significant Progress Has Been Made, but Pandemic Planning and Other Challenges Remain. Report to Congressional Requesters*. Washington, D.C.: GAO. Retrieved April 20, 2008 from www.gao.gov/new.items/d07399.pdf

Grady, D., & Kolata, G. (2008) How Serious is the Risk of Avian Flu? *The New York Times*. March 27, 2006. Retrieved April 20, 2008 from www.nytimes.com/2006/03/27/health/28qna.html?_r=1&ref=clogin

Herold, R. (2006). Addressing Privacy Issues during Disaster Recovery. *Information Systems Security*, January-February 2006,16-22.

Krutz, R. L, & Vines, R. D. (2001). *The CISSP Prep Guide: Mastering the Ten Domains of Computer Security*. New York, NY: John Wiley & Sons, Inc.

Lewis, M. (2007). In Nature's Casino. *The New York Times Magazine*. August 26, 2007, pages 26-33 and 49-53. Retrieved April 20, 2008 from http://query.nytimes.com/gst/fullpage.html?res=9C05E1DE103FF935A1575BC0A9619C8B63&scp=2&sq=nature%27s+casino&st=nyt

Lucca, C. (2006). Pandemic of Fear: Thinking about Disaster Recovery Planning. *The ISSA Journal*. November 2006, 20–22.

Parker, D. (2006). Making the Case for Replacing Risk-Based Security. *The ISSA Journal*. May 2006, 6-10.

Taleb, N.N. (2007). *The Black Swan*. New York, NY: Random House, Inc.

KEY TERMS

Business Continuity Plan: A plan for ensuring that businesses will be able to recover from the effects of a destructive incident and continue to operate at an acceptable level.

Catastrophe: A more far-reaching and devastating incident than a regular disaster. Cuts across many public and private sectors and infrastructures.

Contingency Catastrophe Plan (CCP): A specialized plan to minimize loss of human life and damage to resources and infrastructures and to facilitate recovery in the event of a catastrophic event.

Contingency Planning: A combination of business continuity and disaster recovery planning.

Disaster Recovery Plan: Generally a plan for enabling an organization to move to alternate system, network, and operational facilities in the event of an incident making the primary facilities unusable.

Incident Management: Policy and procedures relating to the response to and recovery from an incident.

Information Security: Protection of information assets by ensuring their confidentiality, integrity and availability.

Liability: Personal risk of being blamed for an incident and potentially being subject to adverse consequences.

Privacy: A person's right to control his or her personal information.

Risk: A measure of the expected loss of an event. The product of the magnitude of a loss and the probability of its occurrence.

Chapter II
The Complex New World of Information Security

David Porter
Detica UK Ltd., UK

ABSTRACT

This chapter discusses the latest developments in the shifting threat landscape and their impact on the world of information security. It describes how we are now moving into a "third wave" of cybercrime, where sophisticated criminals are applying relatively "soft" techniques that are more pervasive in their execution. It argues that, as a consequence, information security countermeasures based on the latest information intelligence technologies will need to be complemented by softer, more pervasive techniques drawn from disciplines such as process engineering, policy development, behavioral science, psychology and benefit management. The chapter also considers how these countermeasures can be fully realized in today's business environment and concludes by discussing future directions such as the growth in complexity and the rise of the surveillance society. The author hopes that by understanding these new imperatives, information security practitioners will be in a stronger position to protect their organizations from today's threats — and those of tomorrow.

INTRODUCTION

The Rise of the Cybercriminal

With the industrial and mobility revolutions of the 19th and 20th centuries behind us, we now find ourselves in the grip of the 21st century digital revolution. The widespread diffusion of telecommunications and computer technology is now having a profound effect on the way we live. From online banking and shopping through to social networking, the digital revolution is creating entirely new ways of working and socializing as well as challenging, and even destroying, many others.

The world of the financial criminal is evolving in a similar way. To put today's and tomorrow's threats in context, let us begin with the recent past. A couple of decades ago the techniques used were relatively "hard" — high on violence and low on intellect — and focused in execution, such as armed robbery and mugging. Traditional security countermeasures comprised of guards, dogs, fences and locks. As the digital revolution gathered pace in the late 1980s, criminals (both existing and newcomers) graduated into cybercrime, where the techniques used were "softer", requiring more intellect, less muscle and involved a broader range of execution. The new threats included hacking, virus attacks and various forms of electronic fraud involving credit cards, ATMs, checks, mortgages and insurance.

A range of preventative countermeasures similarly involved, such as access control systems comprising firewalls, website/e-mail content scanners and the like. Detection systems based on a body of rules (often wrapped up inside behavioral scorecards) that define the way that fraudsters and money launderers typically carry out their activities were also deployed. These rule-based systems are often founded on the "three Vs" of profiling — the volume, value and velocity (timing) of transactions. Countermeasures also included process controls such as recruitment screening, segregation, supervision and training. In the case of money laundering, much of this centered on the principle of "know your customer": training front office staff to verify the identity of customers opening new accounts and spot suspicious deposits or withdrawals. Last, but not least, information security standards have been deployed such as ISO17799.

Over the past few years, and into the present, we have seen a "second wave" of cybercrime, where criminals have moved further into "softer" and more sophisticated techniques that are more pervasive in their execution. This has been clearly demonstrated by the significant growth in:

- the Internet as a general vehicle for committing all kinds of frauds;
- Card Not Present (CNP) fraud as a result of the move from magnetic stripe to Chip-and-PIN credit cards;
- identity fraud (application fraud and account takeover) as a result of the significant increase in remote online banking and shopping as well as the indiscriminate publication and sharing of personal information on blogs, instant messaging, wiki pages, file sharing and social networking websites;
- sleeper fraud in which organized criminals imitate the behavior of genuine customers over an extended period of time, gain as much unsecured credit as possible and then default. This type of fraud is specifically designed to exploit the limitations of traditional record-matching technologies. The perpetrators are experts at distorting information to remain undiscovered until it is too late;
- insider fraud, where the perpetrators range from temporary contractors to permanent staff and all the way up to the most senior executives. All are in positions of trust and exploit inadequate processes, systems and internal controls. The original "opportunity takers", or people who exploit gaps in the system through temptation, incentive or pressure, have been joined by "opportunity makers" or professional criminals who have infiltrated a company and are immune to, and will indeed exploit, an organizational culture of trust and caring. Businesses where there are high levels of organizational or process change have been particularly vulnerable as well as those where there is unchecked staff authority, high staff turnover or low staff morale.

A "second wave" of cybercrime countermeasures have been, and are being, developed as a result:

- multi-factor authentication technologies such as one-shot password generators and biometrics based on voiceprints and fingerprints;
- insider fraud detection systems that use advanced clustering techniques and supermarket-style loyalty scoring to identify lone individuals that stand out from larger employee clusters because of anomalous behavior that is consistent with classic insider fraud psychology. They are fed by audit trails from key systems such as financial transaction logs, call centre logs, telephone logs, building entry logs, web server logs and print server logs. These are supplemented with records from Human Resources and Finance systems;
- detection systems based on "unsupervised" data mining methods that analyze large amounts of data in order to work out for themselves what is suspicious without having to refer to a checklist of rules. The output from these systems can then be turned into rule-based form in order to catch the criminals. These have helped banks begin to move closer towards "what we don't know we don't know";
- cross-industry data sharing to identify criminals before they have a chance to strike, the most significant example being the UK's Insurance Fraud Bureau;
- case management systems that are more closely integrated with detection systems and can handle a greater variety of multimedia such as scanned-in images, audio recordings, still images and moving images;
- e-Discovery, or the process of collecting and searching electronic documents for information relevant to civil litigation;
- revised information security standards such as ISO27001.

The Next Stage of Evolution

Financial crime showing no signs of slowing down. The third annual identity fraud study by Javelin Strategy & Research estimated US identity fraud losses to be $49.3 billion, with 8.4m US adult citizens (about 4% of the population) being the victims (Monahan, 2007). In the UK, the 2007 fraud report commissioned by the Association of Chief Police Officers revealed that fraud is costing the UK at least £13.9 billion per annum. This figure is a "conservative" estimate: the true cost rises to £20 billion when estimated losses from income tax fraud, under-reporting and fraudulent applications for European Union grants are added (Levi, 2007).

In light of these figures, information security is receiving an increasing level of attention and financial investment as organizations seek to contain the threat of theft, disruption, extortion and terrorism. Many organizations are in the process of selecting and deploying new technological solutions to supplement their existing ones. However, security is a chain that is only as strong as the weakest link and not all links are technical. Most security incidents have been, and always will be, a consequence of "softer" human failings such as a lack of awareness of threats and vulnerabilities, inadequately trained staff and competing business pressures resulting in the "tactical shortcut".

This is particularly relevant given that we are now at a transition point between the second and third waves of cybercrime. Criminals are demonstrating increasing levels of sophistication by moving even further into the "softer" end of the technique spectrum and applying their trade in a highly pervasive manner. Many of today's — and increasingly tomorrow's — threats rely heavily on social engineering: manipulating people (customers or employees) into performing actions or divulging confidential information about counter-fraud systems and processes. This is a modern take on a classic con trick but because it takes place over the Internet the attacker never comes face-to-face with the victim. Phishing and pharming are two well-known examples, while "Web 2.0" technologies such as blogs, instant messaging, wiki pages, file sharing and social networking websites are certain to create further opportunities for fraud and other forms of "Crime 2.0".

Given this shift in the threat landscape, a new range of information security countermeasures are now appearing. These are based on the latest information intelligence technologies that enable large volumes of complex data to be turned into relevant and actionable intelligence. These in turn are being complemented by softer, more pervasive techniques drawn from disciplines such as process engineering, policy development, behavioral science, psychology and benefit management. Figure 1 summarizes the discussion so far.

The relentless pace of the digital revolution is therefore driving us into a new world of information security and in the remainder of this chapter we will expand on the above themes and issues, with a particular focus on financial crime since this is often the end-goal of a security breach. We will begin by discussing the new world of information security and the "softer" countermeasures needed to keep pace with criminal evolution. We will then consider how these can be realized to their maximum potential in today's business environment and conclude by discussing future directions in this area, in particular the growth in complexity and the rise of the surveillance society.

THE NEW WORLD OF INFORMATION SECURITY

The Information Security Objective

Before discussing new developments in information security, let us first remind ourselves of the basic principles. Information is an asset which, like other important business assets, has value to an organization (and indeed fraudsters) and consequently needs to be protected. The first step is to define and implement a robust information security policy that addresses:

- **confidentiality:** ensuring that information is accessible only to those authorized to have access;
- **integrity:** safeguarding the accuracy and completeness of information and processing methods;

Figure 1. The evolution of threats and countermeasures

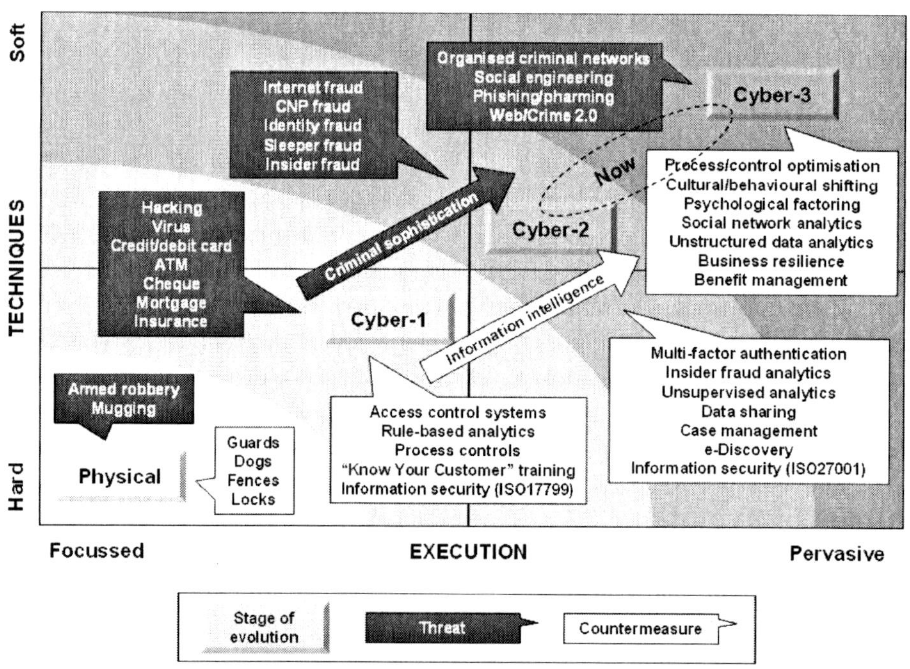

- **availability:** ensuring that authorized users have access to information and associated assets when required.

Information security is achieved by implementing a suitable set of controls in the form of policies, practices, procedures, organizational structures and software functions. These combine to form an Information Security Management System. This provides a framework for defining, implementing and continuously improving information security in order to provide cost effective protection of an organization's information assets commensurate with their perceived value and threat exposures (Porter, 2006). Security is however a very careful balancing act: too much slows down day-to-day business operations and degrades customer service, whereas too little makes the organization vulnerable to attack.

One of the biggest threats facing organizations is that posed by financial criminals such as fraudsters. In practical terms, there are two methods of securing against the fraud threat, namely prevention and detection. Prevention focuses on controls designed to reduce the opportunity for unauthorized use of corporate resources. They include perimeter defense technology such as firewalls, online content scanners and biometric access controls. They also include "softer" processes such as recruitment screening, segregation, supervision and training.

Many organizations rely heavily on such mechanisms. However, a prevention-centric strategy will only succeed if the prevention mechanism has been proved to be flawless. Otherwise its weaknesses will be exploited and it will be bypassed, especially by people who know the system. It is therefore essential that organizations have a means of detecting these individuals as quickly as possible. Detection focuses on the controls designed to alert the appropriate personnel that a fraud has been perpetrated. Such controls include authorization, internal auditing, whistleblower hotlines and automated detection systems (Porter, 2007).

Those responsible for information security and fraud containment cannot focus solely on external threats: the hackers, fraudsters and money launderers who exploit weak spots in an organization's defenses. A significant threat comes from inside, and not just outside, the organization; people in positions of trust habitually, and often all too easily, bypass internal control mechanisms. In its most recent report on occupational fraud, the Association of Certified Fraud Examiners revealed that insider fraud and abuse imposes enormous costs on US organizations. The median loss caused by the insider frauds in this study was $159,000, nearly one-quarter of the cases caused at least $1 million in losses and nine cases caused losses of $1 billion or more. Organizations participating in the study estimated that they lose 5% of their annual revenues to fraud. Applied to the estimated 2006 United States Gross Domestic Product, this 5% figure translates to approximately $652 billion in fraud losses (ACFE, 2006).

Organizations are therefore faced with not with the task of not only securing their organizational perimeter defenses against a range of external threats, but those coming from inside too — namely employees and customers.

Optimizing Processes and Controls

When it comes to information security, best practice recommends a "defense in depth" approach whereby an organization relies on multiple defenses — none of them perfect — to provide the strongest possible solution. Multiple layers of different types of control make fraud and abuse more much more difficult and significantly increase the chances of detection since single points of failure are eliminated.

However, even with multiple defenses, it is still possible for a fraudster to bypass a series of controls and checks. In reality layers of defense are like layers of Swiss cheese, each hole representing a vulnerability (Reason, 2000). When holes in different layers come into alignment, either by accident or design, then abuse and fraud can occur. For infrequent events, organizations may have little advance warning as they are difficult to predict. If these infrequent events have a high impact, the results can be devastating — examples such as the Barings and Enron frauds demonstrate this. Holes in defenses will change in shape, size and location over time. However, not all holes are alike — they can be caused by two very different types of weakness:

- "active failures" due to accident, negligence or malicious intent;
- "latent conditions" due to weaknesses in the environment such as inadequate supervision, poor training, unclear organizational structures or poorly designed computer systems.

It is often tempting for organizations to focus on fixing the active failures, i.e. patching and plugging holes as they are uncovered. However, it is often latent conditions that allow active failures to occur, and therefore from a risk management point of view, resource needs to be directed at fixing these environmental factors.

Fixing latent conditions needs to be undertaken with caution, since experience from industries such as nuclear power and air transport shows that, when it comes to making systems safer and secure, more can often end up meaning less — or the so-called "security paradox" (Sagan, 2004). For example, investing money in adding duplicate, or "redundant", back-up processes or systems that take over when something going wrong only works if the new components are truly independent of the existing ones. They seldom are, and accident after accident demonstrates the "common mode" problem, where the failure of one takes out all the supposedly redundant systems because they are all intrinsically, but non-obviously, linked. For example, adding more engines to the wings an airplane to prevent crashes due to engine failure only works up to a certain point. If there are more engines then it is more likely that one of them will fail. This is usually due to catastrophic circumstances such as fire, with a fire in one engine ultimately destroying all the others and indeed the rest of the plane.

The same thing can happen with seemingly redundant processes: they can compromise performance and actually increase the risk of failure. Organizations are suffering from an onslaught of corporate governance regulation with huge amounts of time and money being spent on upgrading weak or vulnerable processes. But as they struggle to avoid being submerged by all this regulation, companies are in danger of throwing too many processes and controls at the problem and, paradoxically, increasing risk. One only has to look at the current state of suspect money laundering reporting, where a "defensive disclosing" procedural backlash is flooding the investigating authorities with irrelevant material that hardly counts as useful intelligence.

The most recent "Banking Banana Skins" survey conducted by CSFI, the independent City of London think tank, found that senior bankers around the world cited liquidity and credit spreads as two of the top three risks facing the global financial sector. The top ten risks also included the prospect of regulatory over-reaction as politicians and regulators prepare to "fix" the problem. Regulatory overkill has featured strongly in previous versions of this survey, in particular the fear that banks may be becoming too process-driven and the current box-ticking and form-filling mentality may be creating a false sense of security. It is ironic that regulation aimed at better managing risk can also be one of the biggest risks facing banks (Lascelles, 2008).

"Target hardening", a term frequently used in the world of physical security, is another method of fixing latent conditions. In simple terms it means "strengthening our defenses" but is often applied inappropriately. All too often organizations who have suffered a security breach respond on the basis of the most recent experience. This engenders a "do-it-yourself" attitude towards security that fails to address the bigger picture or even anticipate the next criminal event. Doomed to failure, the approach quickly takes on a "fool me once, shame on you, fool me twice, shame on me" quality as soon as the next loss occurs. Now more determined than ever, the organization fixates on the latest breach of security to dictate the next response. With its perspective narrowing, the organization becomes more interested in prevailing against a specific kind of previous attack than preventing the next occurrence and has descended into the "target hardening trap" (McKay, 1998).

A similar phenomenon occurs in the information security world in the form of the "penetrate and patch" approach to security. Software developers attack a computer system (e.g. a piece of software, a firewall or a website) from the outside, identify a flaw in it, fix the flaw and then carry on looking for holes. The flaw in this short-term approach is that it does not make the computer system better by design but simply toughens random parts of it by trial and error (Ranum, 2005).

Cultural and Behavioral Shifting

The "people" dimension of security should never be overlooked. A lot of investment is focused on technology-based prevention and detection systems aimed at the minority of hard fraudsters. While this is important, people are often the weakest link, not technology.

When trying to fix the processes that give rise to latent and active conditions, especially in the counter-fraud environment, most organizations fixate on the concept of "enforced compliance". This means creating an environment where those individuals who knowingly set out to defraud either do not, or cannot, act on their intent and where, should they be successful, they are rapidly caught and dealt with accordingly. However, "enforced compliance" processes are not enough by themselves. Most experts in the field agree that in any population, 10% of the people are completely honest, 10% are completely dishonest and 80% are somewhere in between, relying on a flexible morality and their perceptions of risk, reward and opportunity (Dorrington, 2004).

A complementary strategy of "voluntary compliance" focuses on changing the cultural mindset of the 80% (customers, suppliers or employees) who may not knowingly intend to defraud an organization but do not actively support counter-fraud activities either. This modern-day sentiment is echoed by the following quotations that date back to the eighteenth century:

- Edmund Burke, the Anglo-Irish statesman, who said *"The only thing necessary for the triumph of evil is for good men to do nothing"* (Burke, 1770);
- Johann Wolfgang von Goethe, the German novelist, who said *"Misunderstandings and neglect occasion more mischief in the world than even malice and wickedness. At all events, the two latter are of less frequent occurrence"* (von Goethe, 1774).

Some individuals might be unaware of their responsibilities and obligations and therefore unknowingly support fraud. Others may "work around" a cumbersome compliance or security process without realizing why the process exists or what its objectives are. Firms may become overly reliant on documented procedures without truly knowing whether the procedures are being followed or even work. All of these can give rise to the "latent conditions" discussed above and therefore need to be addressed. This strategy has some similarities to the enforced compliance strategy. However, it has proactive measures designed to not only prevent fraud, but to increase levels of compliance. It also recognizes that some cases of non-compliance will "self-correct" if appropriate action is undertaken — especially important if the non-compliance was accidental.

Both enforced and voluntary compliance share a similar sequence of steps that span the gap between creating a culture for compliance through to seeking redress from non-compliant parties. Each will however differ in the detail. For example, cases of deliberate fraud will be investigated whereas incidents of non-compliance due to accident or ignorance will be escalated (Dorrington, 2004). The key steps are summarized in Figure 2.

Voluntary Compliance in Action

A voluntary compliance strategy is particularly relevant for the new breed of young employees or "digital natives" who have been brought up with broadband Internet and to whom "Web 2.0" technologies such as blogs, instant messaging, wiki pages, file sharing and social networking websites are a normal, collaborative, way of life. Through these channels they may, accidentally or intentionally, make disparaging comments about their employers, disclose company secrets, make libelous remarks or make binding contracts. They may also introduce viruses by downloading files, share copyrighted data and lose company-sensitive data. Many make use of personal electronic devices such as cell phones, MP3 players and digital cameras, not to mention the now ubiquitous USB memory stick, to carry documents and other confidential data back and forth. As well as the potential for third parties gaining access to confidential data on these removable media devices, they also provide a backdoor for viruses and other forms of malware wanting to bypass company firewalls. However, these younger employees see the restrictions placed on Internet access and personal electronic devices by security or IT departments as petty and bureaucratic (Financial Times, 2007).

Customers can be similar weak links in the security chain, the migration from magnetic stripe to Chip-and-PIN credit cards being a recent example. In principle, a PIN code should be a more secure means of authenticating a transaction; however the approach taken by many customers can undermine security. In theory, people should memorize different PIN numbers for each credit and debit card they have. However, the potential flaw in this plan is that, as research has shown, cardholders already have to remember an average of five PINs or security codes and of those cardholders who use more than one code, 50% can only remember three or fewer (Detica, 2004). Among those who have more than one PIN or security code to remember, almost half (47%) use the same PIN for two or more things requiring a code, from burglar alarms, car radios and cell phones to ATM, debit and credit cards. At least a third of those surveyed base their PIN on their birthday or that of someone close to them, or alternatively a home or business phone number.

Once they have obtained a "shared PIN" through social engineering techniques, criminals have unchallenged access to a range of valuable assets from bank accounts to physical assets like cars and houses. As for those who do use different PINs for different cards, many of them write their codes down and keep them in their handbags or wallets "just in case". And very few people, apart from security experts, ever bother to change their PINs on a regular basis. So although Chip-and-PIN is a good idea in principle, banks need to educate their customers more effectively on how to select their PINs, manage them properly and effectively take PIN security as seriously as the physical security of their other possessions.

Figure 2. Enforced and voluntary compliance

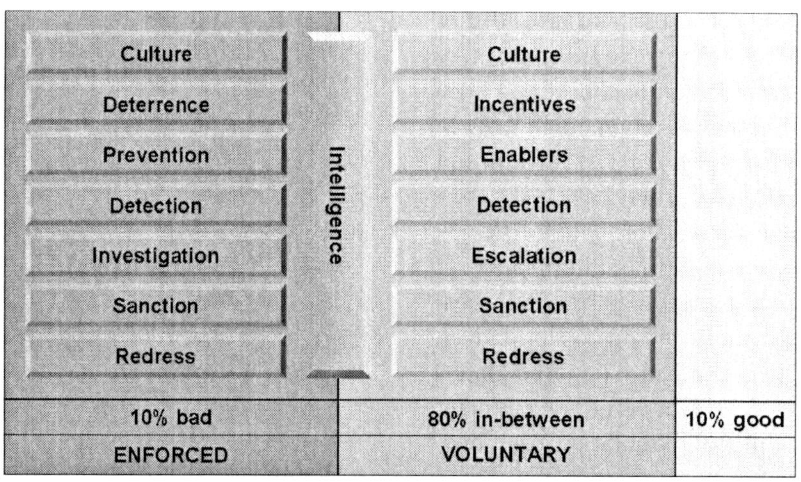

Another area of vulnerability is the susceptibility of consumers to online phishing schemes. These social engineering attacks are, in essence, con tricks that use e-mail messages to fool victims into handing over personal confidential information so that criminals can commit identity fraud. Because hackers are making increasing use of Internet messaging systems to propagate their attacks, a number of sub-categories have developed. "Pharming" is the manipulation of Domain Name Server records to redirect victims, "spear phishing" is a highly targeted attack, "smishing" uses cell phone Short Message Service (SMS) text messaging and "vishing" uses Voice over Internet Protocol (VoIP) telephone calls.

Phishing attacks succeed largely because of human fallibility ranging from haste, distraction, fear and stupidity through to gullibility and sheer greed. Ironically, despite their success rate, most phishing e-mails are easy to spot since they contain poor grammar, spelling mistakes and totally inappropriate language for a conservative, professional financial institution. People should, in principle, be more challenging and less trusting of these kinds of e-mails and should take the time to spot the telltale signs rather than fall into the trap of blindly following instructions from a perceived authority. Unfortunately many people fail to spot the warning signs and are easy prey for the phishing industry.

The situation is not helped by significant levels of adult functional illiteracy, i.e. the inability to understand and employ printed information in daily life. The most recent detailed survey in the UK revealed that between 20-24% of UK adults are functionally illiterate, rising to nearly 40% in some areas (Moser, 1999). In the US the 1998 National Adult Literacy Survey report revealed that over 90m US adults (out of 191m, i.e. nearly one in two) were functionally illiterate (Reder, 1998). A new survey released in 2003 showed there were no statistically significant changes in these figures (Kutner, 2007).

The soaring popularity of social networking websites is a further behavioral problem area. Identity is not confined to personal attributes such as biometric features, passwords and PIN numbers: it is also about a person's biographical attributes (e.g. date of birth, home, school, qualification, job and marital status) and personal relationships (e.g. spouse, partner, children, pets, next of kin, friends, colleagues and employer). Such "memorable" or "cherished" data underpins the vast majority of online security protocols such as passwords and PIN numbers. It is therefore nothing less than amazing that, once online, people drop their guard and disclose details about their lives, loves, jobs and hobbies to the entire world that they would not dream of sharing with a stranger in a bar. In an age where information and identity is the new criminal currency, social networking sites are goldmines for criminals who are determined enough to assemble the "jigsaw pieces" of information strewn around the Internet to penetrate personal or corporate defenses. It remains to be seen whether the high-profile loss of confidential personal data—such as that which occurred in November 2007 by the UK's Revenue and Customs government department—will lead to consumers re-thinking their approach to password selection.

Although social networking websites provide basic privacy controls, there is always the danger of personal data that you have shared with an online "friend" being forwarded by that "friend" to other people who you do not know. Many criminals masquerading as "false friends" will set up fake accounts and use social engineering techniques to gain the friendship of strangers. Once they gain access to an individual's private profile they can strip out personal information for the purposes of fraud or spamming. Permanently deleting the contents of personal profiles can be difficult, if not impossible, to do. Pages from visited websites are frequently duplicated ("cached") and stored on other people's computers, making it almost impossible to "destroy the negatives".

Online sharing of information relating to one's occupation is also an area of concern. There is a growing trend for individuals to disclose job titles, work e-mail addresses and phone numbers in their online profiles. Even the most innocuous information about a business—people and the departments they work for, day-to-day processes, jargon and codes—can be valuable stepping stones for persistent criminals who want to infiltrate corporate security by trickery and subterfuge. It is now possible to type a company's name into a social networking website and acquire an extensive list of employees and, in many cases, a full insight into their private and professional lives. As a result, data which would otherwise remain restricted and confidential can become widely available and vulnerable to criminals and fraudsters. For example, fraudsters can trawl social networking sites for disgruntled employees who complain about their employer online so they can bribe or coerce them into giving out corporate information.

As these examples show, people are often the weakest links in security. However, there is often a difference of opinion regarding the best solution. Many will adopt a "blame and train" approach, insisting that people (responsible for "active failures") need to wise up and take responsibility for protecting their data, maintaining their anti-virus/firewall/encryption software and revolving their passwords and PIN codes. Others say that the onus should be on organizations to design more secure processes and systems in the first place (eliminating "latent conditions") so that fallible human beings can use their services safely. The answer lies somewhere between these two extremes.

Psychological Factors

Related to the "more is less" security paradox are human psychological factors which information security designers ignore at their peril. Take, for example, what psychologists refer to as "diffusion of responsibility". The more people that are asked to make checks on a system, for compliance or security purposes, the less thorough any individual will be since they will assume that others will spot the problem. Such shirking of responsibility is similar to the phenomenon of "bystander apathy", whereby the more people that witness, for example, an automobile accident, the less likely it is anyone will actually call an ambulance.

Another psychological factor is the "overcompensation effect" whereby the more security features that are added to a system, the riskier people's behavior will be. Just as adding seat belts to cars makes people drive faster, or adding child-proof caps to medicine bottles makes parents put them within easy reach of curious, industrious, time-rich infants, so adding a secondary file deletion check in a computer system makes people skip the first check and more likely to delete a valuable file.

This is similar to what economists call "moral hazard", whereby if you compensate people when bad things happen they can become careless. In the case of a car insured against theft, the driver might park it wherever they can find a space, even on a deserted street that does not look entirely safe. Or they may not even bother to lock the vehicle. Moral hazard arises because one of the parties in a transaction does not bear the full consequences of their actions and therefore has a tendency or incentive to act less carefully than would otherwise be the case. Another party in the transaction is left to bear some responsibility for the consequences (Harford, 2007).

There is a similar problem with "workarounds", whereby office workers will view poorly designed, poorly implemented or disproportionate security measures as obstructions to getting the day's work done that must be bypassed or defeated. Long, hard-to-guess passwords are written down on sticky notes and left on computer screens. Self-closing fire doors that obstruct the free flow of people are wedged open. Security is perceived as a low-probability risk, not a reality like getting the work done on time.

These are all important lessons for those responsible for designing new fraud, compliance and security systems. Process and technology are key elements of security; however we must not underestimate the psychological factors that come into play.

Social Network Analysis

A number of innovative technical countermeasures are now being deployed by organizations to counteract the increase in criminal sophistication. Social network analysis is one such example of what is known as "information intelligence" technology. It has been developed to explicitly address the way criminal behavior has evolved over recent years, in particular the increasingly fragmented, distributed and networked nature of the perpetrators' schemes that involve collusion with insiders and the exploitation of false identities. Existing systems, predominantly based on relatively rigid behavioral profiling rules, are unable to identify fragmented schemes where each entity or activity alone is too small to appear "on the radar". Such systems are also highly susceptible to error and degradation when confronted with poor quality input data.

Social network analysis enables investigators to identify, understand and evaluate networks of collaborating individuals across disparate and often unconnected sources of data. Taking fraud as an example, criminals will always try to cover their tracks by having no obvious connection to other members of their network. However, by pooling data from multiple sources — phone numbers, addresses, known relationships, transactions, historic data and third party data — it is possible to use fragments of these records to link groups of people with suspicious transactions. By looking at the resultant graphical networks, and the way they evolve over time and geography, it is then possible to spot large-scale organized fraud.

As a complement to existing analytical approaches, social network analysis moves away from record-level analysis to identify, understand and evaluate higher-level, often embryonic, networks of collaborating individuals. With social network analysis the characteristics of criminal networks, including the emerging sub-groups and key players involved, can be identified. Both machine and human play a key part in the process: the machine performing a quantitative, mathematical based analysis, whilst human investigators bring a qualitative, visual analysis of the machine's results.

Being based on facts rather than hypotheses, social network analysis does not try to guess associations and therefore relies more on data volume than data quality. In fact, the more data it is given to process the better. Because it is immune to data quality and format issues, this means that it is no longer possible for fraudsters to avoid detection using variations in identity.

The result of the quantitative analysis is a list of identified networks, each assigned a score indicating the degree of potential risk. These are then handed over to human investigators to perform a qualitative analysis. The system provides investigators with an instant graphical visualization of each network, including both geographical and temporal views, enabling them to make a rapid visual judgment. Investigators can easily traverse the network, dive down into detail at any point of interest and perform searches on the networks and the underlying data. Figure 3 shows an example of an organized network identified during a recent banking fraud detection assignment.

The best way to detect organized fraud is therefore not to profile a fraudster down to his shoe size, or try to match two unmatchable records, but instead identify networks of collaborating individuals. In other words, it is not the shape of the dots that matters, but the shape of the network that joins them together. This highly effective approach lies at the heart of a number of criminal detection initiatives in the UK and U.S., including insurance fraud, sleeper fraud, rogue trading, tax evasion and benefit fraud. This is promoting a step change in the way that large-scale fraud — and other threats such as terrorism — is detected and investigated.

Latest developments in this area include the use of this approach to identify credit abuse networks which are a growing problem in light of the ongoing "credit crunch". Variously known as "first party lending fraud", "sleeper fraud" and "bust-out fraud", credit abuse involves organized fraudsters making false statements on application forms in order to gain credit which they have no intention of paying back. There is also a growing trend in credit applicants being manipulated by organized fraudsters even though they may not have made any material falsehoods. This high risk activity currently falls between the "organized first party fraud" and "bad debt" definitions

Figure 3. A detected organized criminal network

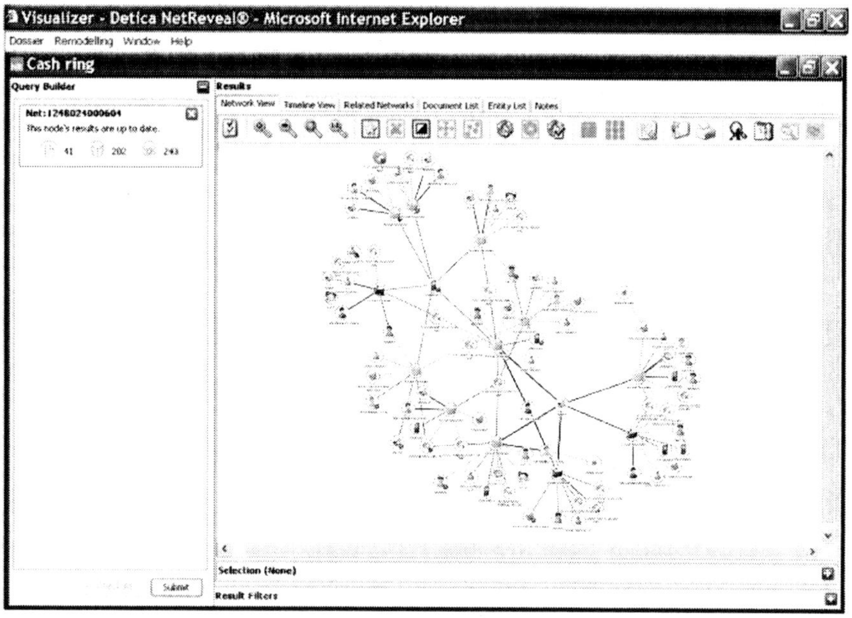

being debated by the banking industry. Social network analysis is now being used to make high-speed checks of credit applicants' details against pre-scored criminal networks during the live application process. It is also being applied in the "back office" where existing customers are scored as they request additional credit facilities. Banks can therefore "shut out" and decline any applications that hit these networks.

Unstructured Data Analysis

Organizations around the world are producing an increasing amount of what is termed "unstructured data". Whereas structured data is data that has been modeled, organized, validated and stored in a relational database, unstructured data has not been treated in this way and is consequently not readily readable or understood by machines. Examples of unstructured data include pictures, video, audio and natural language text. The latter is particularly prevalent, being found in the body of emails, word processor documents, web pages, cell phone text messages, MSN chat messages, PDF files and the free text fields inside databases and other applications.

The explosion of unstructured data is one of the biggest challenges facing business today. It currently accounts for 80% of a company's overall data and the amount of unstructured data in a company is doubling every two years (Accenture, 2006). However, at the same time as presenting a considerable data management challenge, unstructured data also represents a potential intelligence goldmine if the right tools are used.

The four cornerstones of unstructured data analysis are retention, search and retrieval, structuring and intelligence generation. The key challenge for intelligence analysts is that they are faced with a growing volume of unstructured data of varying formats and origins that make analysis a potentially complex and laborious task. However, information intelligence tools are now becoming available that allow analysts to explore large repositories of unstructured data and generate actionable intelligence. They provide the following capabilities:

- fast, relevance-ranked search on millions of documents;
- visual query building for the simple construction of powerful queries;

- automatic discovery of entities mentioned in the text of documents;
- multiple visualizations of search result sets, such as text summaries, timelines, calendars, entity networks, significant terms and geo-spatial images;
- augmentation and enrichment of existing data through the creation of synonyms, taxonomies and saved queries;
- drag-and-drop refinement of search results—such as time, space or significant terms—in order to generate new insights.

In essence these new tools enable analysts who have found a potential "thread" in the data to "pull" that thread out and find the missing links. Figure 4 shows an example of an unstructured data analysis toolset being used to examine the statistical significance of key terms in a large repository of documents. Now the challenge is for organizations to think about the really hard security and intelligence problems that could be solved if they had an unlimited army of people to read and analyze unstructured content.

REALIZING SECURITY IN THE BUSINESS ENVIRONMENT

Getting the Vision and Strategy Right

As we have seen, criminals are becoming more sophisticated by applying "softer" techniques in a highly pervasive manner. Let us now move our focus from the criminals to those responsible for devising and deploying countermeasures. What shifts in technique and approach do they need in today's business environment?

Most importantly, they need to get their strategy right. Too many information security and fraud containment departments have either no strategy in place or one that is way past its shelf life and does not recognize today's rapidly changing threat environment .To develop an effective strategy, we first need a vision of what we are trying to achieve. Even if the driver for change is the need to "fight the current fires", there must be a longer-term view of where we want to be in, say, three years' time.

Figure 4. Analyzing unstructured document content

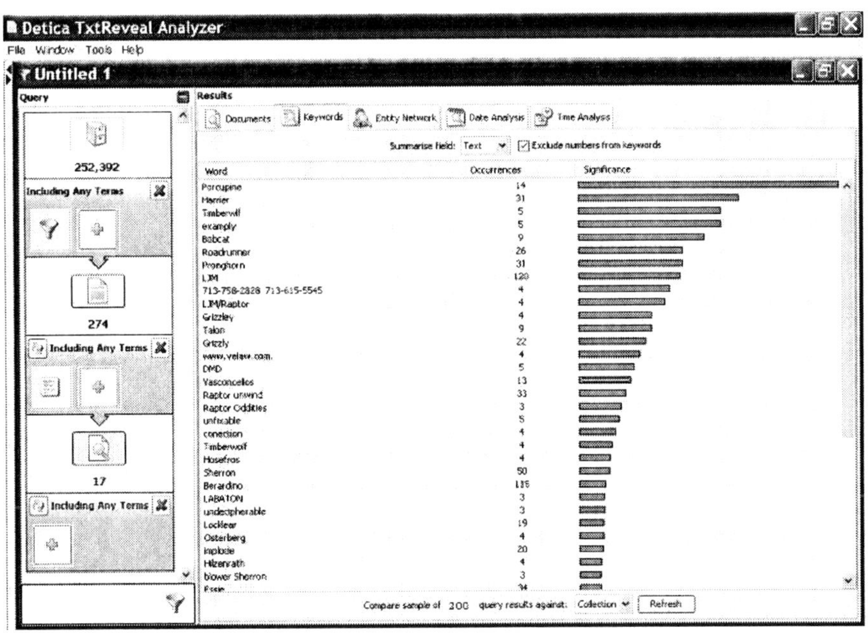

In simple terms, a vision:

- is a relatively succinct picture of a transformed organization once a program of work has delivered (usually in three to five years' time);
- is an outward-facing statement which establishes a clear imperative to change and (with an associated business case) acts as a means of gaining buy-in from all stakeholders;
- acts as an essential communication vehicle and serves as a common reference point throughout the program;
- represents the "end point" and hence gives rise to the strategy required to achieve it.

Taking fraud as an example, given the shifting nature of the threat landscape, and the realization that organizations must improve their fraud risk management capabilities, an example vision statement might be: *"The industry's leading counter-fraud group, working with colleagues and stakeholders to mitigate risk, protect reputation and enhance customer service"*. With a suitably-defined vision we can then create a strategy. A best practice approach is to draw up a "transformation map" that indicates the key milestones that will occur as the organization moves from the "as-is" situation to the goal vision. These milestones are then arranged across a number of dimensions, for example, governance, people, process, technology and data.

Once the key milestones are arranged across the dimensions a number of development phases will become obvious, each phase often corresponding to a year of elapsed time. For example, these phases might be:

- in the short-term, **regain control**—e.g. identify and contain the most significant new threats, implement a "horizon scanning" capability, start cleaning-up data, improve internal communications and deliver similar "quick wins";
- in the medium-term, **stabilize capability**—e.g. improve internal controls, define key performance indicators, upgrade staff training, exploit external market expertise, deploy social network analysis, align with organizational IT strategy and set up a data stewardship program;
- in the long-term, **optimize capability**—e.g. implement predictive and real-time data analysis, deploy an integrated Financial Crime division and launch risk management process improvement initiatives across the organization.

Figure 5 provides an overview of a typical vision and strategy map.

Once defined, the strategy provides a definitive statement of "what" is required to take the organization from the "as-is" state to the goal state. The next step is to draw up a roadmap (or the "how") of the activities needed to execute this strategy

Realizing True Business Benefit

The fundamental reason for undertaking any project is to realize benefits for the organization and its customers. In addition to gaining a better appreciation of vision and strategy development, information security and fraud containment practitioners also need to understand the discipline of benefits realization management.

This reflects an increased focus across the industry on this topic. All too often the traditional approach is to concentrate on the IT system or new process to be developed. However, changing an organization's capability or infrastructure will not produce benefits in itself. For example, delivering a new security system will not produce any benefits if people make no use of it; it may even cause large-scale disbenefits if its transition into operations is badly handled. Very often security departments "fight fires" by implementing a range of reactive, bottom-up, tactical initiatives without any sense of what benefits they are meant to be delivering, nor how these contribute towards the realization of the department's vision, let alone the corporate vision.

Figure 5. Example vision and strategy map

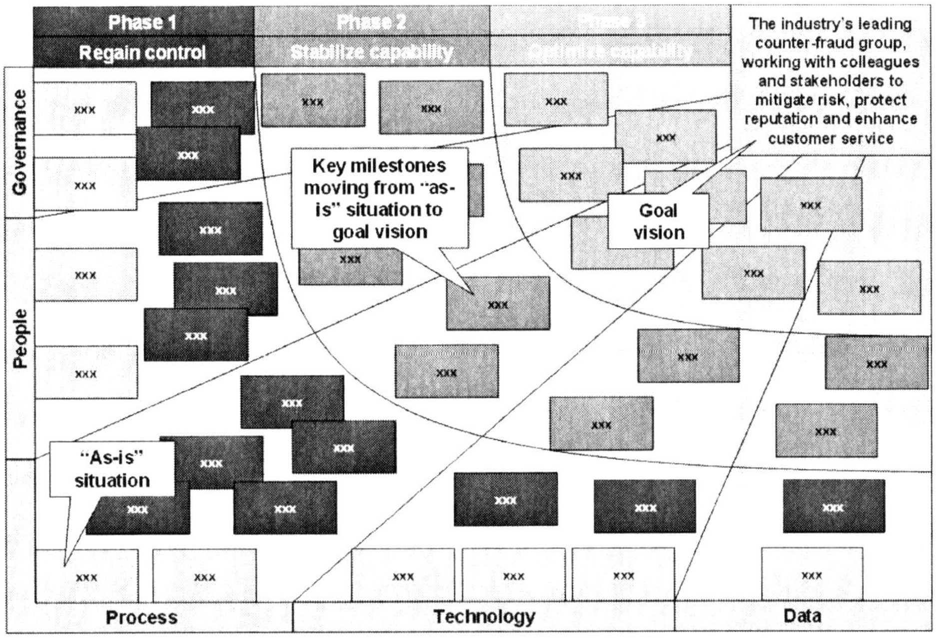

Benefits realization management is the process of identifying, recording, tracking and delivering project benefits. The aim is to ensure that the identification, definition and realization of benefits are placed at the absolute core of any security project in order to ensure its success. This will ensure that this and other projects are selected according to their claimed benefits and that the acquisition of benefits will drive all aspects of the project including the actions of those in 'business as usual' who will receive and use its outputs.

By "benefit" we simply mean "any outcome which is perceived as positive by a stakeholder" (and, by the same token, a "disbenefit" is "any outcome which is perceived as negative"). Any benefit delivered to the business must be capable of being measured and quantified in financial terms since this allows easy comparison and cost benefit analysis. There are three top-level categories of financial benefits, namely cost avoidance, cost reduction and revenue generation — known as "quantifiable financial benefits". Clearly measurement is less easy with less tangible benefits — such as "improved morale" or "high customer satisfaction score" — otherwise known as a "quantifiable non-financial benefits". However, direct measures can be identified in many cases and where they cannot then indirect (or proxy) measures should be found. If it is not possible to derive a method of measuring the benefit then it should not be used as a key justification within the business case.

A key output from a benefit management exercise is the benefits map. This is a "value chain" of cause and effect that exists (or should exist) between the project outputs and the benefits they will bring to satisfy a strategic objective. A benefits map contains the following features:

- technology enablers, which are the physical outputs of projects such as IT systems, buildings, equipment, people, new policies and new processes;
- business changes are the people-oriented outputs of projects such as attitudes, culture, policies, working practices and training;
- technology enablers and business changes in turn provide the business with new or improved capabilities;

- the business uses these capabilities to achieve outcomes;
- these outcomes lead to a set of benefits being realized;
- the benefits in turn satisfy a strategic objective.

At the heart of this approach is the belief that benefits should be the key focus from the outset and that not only will information security projects be selected based upon their claimed benefits but the acquisition of those benefits drives all aspects of the project. This includes the consequent actions of those receiving the outputs (a new or modified capability) in the "business as usual" environment.

Making Change Really Happen

Studies of major IT projects have shown that 80–90% of IT investments fail to meet their performance goals while approximately 40% of IT projects are abandoned. There are a number of theories behind this lack of take-up and most of them settle on the following themes (Porter, 2003):

- projects are too technology-led — users at the "sharp end" have little involvement in or impact upon the system development process;
- most of the time, energy and resources are invested in the change project itself and very little in supporting the people expected to make the (unsolicited) change happen in practice;
- change projects are treated as stand-alone projects rather than as part of the day-to-day running of the business;
- employees fail to recognize what is driving the change and the value it can bring to them and the business as a whole;
- people are not given sufficient time to go through the psychological steps of giving up old ways before embracing new ones.

Change management is no longer the exclusive preserve of the business: information security must also be effective at change management in order to ensure security is applied consistently across the business with the ability to evolve over time and retain the buy-in of all staff. Information security managers need to understand that the secret of effective corporate security rests less on their technical expertise (though this is clearly still important) and more on their ability to respond to human complexities (Briggs & Edwards, 2006).

If the information security vision is about promoting a more widespread, proactive involvement in security amongst employees then the old-fashioned "command and control" approach to change management quickly reaches its limits. People's behavior is altered only by convincing, persuading, influencing and explaining why a new way of working more securely is in everyone's interest. Information security managers need to work through trusted social networks which place greater emphasis on people, management and social skills than security experience. The power of the information security function should therefore be directly proportionate to the quality of its relationships, not the depth of its content knowledge (Briggs & Edwards, 2006).

Organizations change only when individuals within them do, which is usually because they are enthusiastic about the idea. One of the most useful and pragmatic observations on organizational change is the comparison between the spread of ideas — and changed practices — within companies to the spread of the influenza virus (Shapiro, 2003). Three things must be present:

- **"stickiness"** — or the value of the change being suggested;
- **carriers** — or advocates for change;
- **context** — or having the right environmental support and incentives in place to sustain the change.

Taking this idea forward, key factors affecting the spread of influenza include the virulence of the flu strain, contacts between contagious people and environmental factors such as levels of sanitation and medical care. Similarly, key factors affecting the spread of organizational change include the intrinsic value of the organizational change, contacts between advocates and apathetics, and environmental factors such as bonuses for successful implementation.

Earlier we discussed the strategy of changing the cultural mindset of the 80% semi-honest majority who may not knowingly intend to defraud an organization but do not actively support counter-fraud activities either. Creating enthusiasm for change amongst these people is critical and requires the information security function to open itself up to the rest of the company. Information security functions have traditionally used secrecy to build up their credibility and authority. However, as long as security remains a "dark art" then the function will never make its mark on the organization (Briggs & Edwards, 2006).

From Security to Resilience

In addition to secrecy, security has also traditionally suffered from an excess of "silo thinking". With the growing number of data breaches, corporate frauds and terrorist atrocities it is inevitable that organizations will seek to protect themselves from severe or even catastrophic harm by implementing measures to maximize security. But is security enough?

An increasing number of organizations are now moving beyond conventional security practices towards "business resilience", or a level of security more normally associated with critical national infrastructure. On both sides of the Atlantic, critical national infrastructure is defined as those services and systems that support the political and social life of a country. They are so important that any loss or compromise could cause a large-scale loss of life or have a serious impact on the national economy, thereby making their resilience to attack a top priority for any national government. However, the concept of the critical national infrastructure is changing from the classic list drawn up during Cold War days that includes ports, energy, emergency services and the military. It now extends in breadth and depth across our society — in fact across national boundaries — because the threat environment has changed beyond all recognition. There is therefore an increasing need for commercial organizations to think beyond conventional security practices and embrace the concept of resilience.

"Resilience" is an important word: "security" can engender complacency and a false sense of security whereas "resilience" acknowledges the increasing likelihood that high impact events — whether frequent or infrequent — will occur. Organizations need to be able to move from a reactive standpoint to something much more proactive so that they can "roll with the punch" and absorb the shockwaves, whether these are predictable or strike without warning. Business resilience goes beyond traditional "business continuity". It is about being agile, capitalizing upon opportunities and maximizing growth in quickly changing markets. It is also fundamentally about "trust". How does a business gain and maintain shareholder, market and consumer trust? Loss of trust in any of these areas can be just as detrimental to a business as a natural or man-made disaster.

A major impediment towards achieving business resilience, however, is that traditional organizational structures manage the various dimensions of security in a silo-based manner. Generally speaking, organizational security systems divide into three categories:

- **business systems** — policy, processes, culture, organization and people;
- **physical systems** — guards, dogs, CCTV, fences, locks, alarms, disposal;
- **technical systems** — firewalls, anti-virus, biometrics; detection systems and data management.

The situation is further complicated by the organizational reporting line. For example, operational risk is separate from credit and market risk, disaster recovery and information security sit in IT, business continuity sits in operations, physical security sits in facilities, compliance risk sits in finance and reputation risk sits in the CEO's office. Faced with an increasingly complex risk environment the challenge of coordinating these activities becomes increasingly difficult and leads to gaps being created where a risk is not owned or managed by any one department. Internal boundaries are created as subject matter experts and budgets develop distinctly from one another. Organizations are unable to respond in a balanced, holistic manner in order to counter today's new threats. The result is an incomplete threat picture which masks significant vulnerabilities and promotes an illusion of security. Like the Maginot Line of the Second World War, today's security measures could be outflanked and overwhelmed through a combination of surprise and technique (Allcorn, 2003).

We see a similar situation in National Security. For example, the US National Security Act mandated that information be shared up the chain of command but not horizontally with other agencies. When the act was passed, little thought was given to the need for a national-level intelligence apparatus in Washington that could synthesize information horizontally to inform policymakers and support real-time tactical decisions. The subsequent "stovepiping" of intelligence arrested the growth in information sharing, collaboration and integration (McConnell, 2007).

More enlightened organizations are realizing that security initiatives, be they hard technical countermeasures or softer process changes, cannot remain isolated from one another. Information security has to evolve into something much more comprehensive and "joined up". This means integrating risk across the enterprise by bringing together business systems, technical systems and physical systems into a holistic resilience architecture. Four categories of resilience solutions (comprising policies, procedures and technology) can then be applied across the architecture in a consistent manner, namely:

- **assure:** solutions which provide insight into the level of security actually in place and allow legislative or policy conformance to be assessed;
- **enable:** solutions which are focused on allowing the business to operate in new areas or ways whilst ensuring adequate security is in place;
- **control:** solutions which ensure the continued protection of those assets which are seen as of value to the organization;
- **respond:** solutions which ensure the organization is prepared for security incidents (real-world and digital) and can respond when an incident has occurred.

Business resilience is therefore not about looking down into silos but looking laterally across them. The traditional protective functions are still highly relevant but they are connected together in a matrix. Importantly, there is a blending of "hard" and "soft" issues which encourages the understanding and development of cultural, process and technical innovation without loss of detail or functionality.

This also reflects the way leading corporate security professionals are embracing and contributing towards their company's key business concerns and as a result are expanding the security portfolio significantly. Corporate security departments now have responsibilities in areas such as corporate governance, information assurance, business continuity, reputation management and crisis management. They are now exploiting more sophisticated information intelligence tools capable of rapid data capture, retention, evaluation and presentation. This is causing many to question the relevance of the term "security" to describe what they do. The term "resilience" now more accurately reflects the range of their responsibilities.

Returning to the National Security example, there is a call for old cultures and practices to be changed so that today's intelligence community can exchange information more rapidly and effectively. Most important, the long-standing policy of only sharing intelligence on a "need to know" basis should be abandoned. A new mindset is required, namely "responsibility to provide" while still protecting sources and methods. Those who collect data need to be convinced that they not "data owners" so much as "data providers" (McConnell, 2007).

The business resilience approach therefore acknowledges that security requirements should be business-driven and that organizations need an overall umbrella of resilience. This can be achieved by looking at the whole organization and identifying business drivers for security across the piece, not just within silos. The objective is to enable the business to rapidly adapt and respond to internal or external dynamic changes—opportunities, demands, disruptions or threats—and continue operations with limited impact. CEOs can then make the tough business decisions with the confidence that their organization will operate in a highly secure manner without becoming so bureaucratic that they lose agility in dynamic marketplaces.

CONCLUSIONS AND FUTURE DIRECTIONS

A New World of Complexity

Looking to the next decade of technological and social change, a number of important developments are influencing the next stage of criminal evolution. Firstly, the digital revolution is fuelling a huge explosion in data. A decade ago very little was digital. Now, the vast majority of information is digitized: not just words and numbers but photos, music, movies, radio, television and phone calls. The trend seems unstoppable: every day, something else moves from the analogue to the digital world. In 2007, IDC's sizing of the digital universe—data that is either created or captured in digital form and then replicated—was 281 exabytes (10^{18}). IDC has predicted that by 2011 the digital universe will have grown to 1800 exabytes (or 1.8 zettabytes), representing a compound annual growth rate of almost 60%. To put it another way, the digital universe in 2007 was roughly equivalent to one stack of books wrapped three times round the Earth's orbit. By 2011 that stack of books could easily reach from the sun to the edge of our solar system and back (Gantz, 2008). This immense proliferation of data shows no sign of slowing down and there is now concern that the explosion of data is outstripping our ability to protect, control and make sense of it (Black, 2007).

Not only is data growing in volume, it is also growing in complexity. Organizational infrastructures are now composed of a vast and complex network of social, technological and physical elements. Through the combined effects of globalization and the revolution in information and communications technology, a single organization now connects with a diverse, international community of businesses, suppliers, partners, customers, citizens and government departments. Meanwhile, social networking websites have fuelled an explosion in social connectivity, with huge numbers of people linking through common interests, goals and affiliations.

In a world where everything and everyone is becoming interconnected, particularly though data, the counter-intuitive "Pareto effect" comes into play: seemingly inconsequential events can quickly propagate and amplify through the network. While this might be good news for industries such as viral marketing, the "Pareto effect" is creating a much more complex risk environment as seemingly remote disruptive events ripple through networks like seismic shocks through geological fault lines. These impacts can be virtual or physical, or any combination of the two. In the UK, the "run" on the Northern Rock bank in 2007 and the Buncefield oil depot explosion in 2005 are both examples of network-amplified complexity in action. So too, from 2007, are the alleged cyberattacks made by protagonists dotted around the world against Western European government and commercial computer systems. And in the US, a failure by contractors in 2003 to undertake the seemingly inconsequential task of trimming three medium-sized trees led to a cascade of disruption in the closely-knit North American electricity grid, which eventually caused power loss to more than fifty million people on the US East Coast (Lewis, 2007).

In addition to the increase in data volume and complexity, a broad and unpredictable spectrum of "asymmetric threats" is now making the world a more dangerous place. Traditional nation-state protagonists have been supplanted by organized criminals and terrorists with a dramatically increased range of methods for inflicting harm. We are now seeing a consolidation of parties involved in fraud, money laundering and terrorism who are increasingly working in collusion with corrupted or threatened insiders. Criminals are exploiting the increasing volume and complexity of digital data (both structured and unstructured), as well as lax data management policies and practices, in order to camouflage their activities. The Internet is now a potent channel for facilitating not just cyberfraud but crimes such as disruption, sabotage, abuse, counterfeiting, tax evasion, drug trafficking, illegal immigration, money laundering and terrorism.

Security used to be easy. The good people were on the inside and the bad people were on the outside of a well-defined organizational boundary. Today, that boundary has become blurred and diffuse because of advances in information and communications technology and changes in business practices that have led to outsourcing, insourcing, extranets and remote working. It is almost as though inside and outside have ceased to exist and all that is left is a "one sided" threat environment. A suitable metaphor for this is the Mobius strip: a seemingly impossible loop of material which only has one side and only one edge (Spivak, 1979). Furthermore, the stark black-and-white differentiation between "good guys" and "bad guys" has been replaced by people in various shades of grey connected together by collaborative networks. This new threat environment is summarized in Figure 6.

In this new world of one-sided networked complexity, organizations are going to need to implement radically different approaches to security and resilience. If organizations do not model the network of connections centered on them then they cannot fully understand the dangers they face. Failure to take this wider "risk network view" will make organizations much more vulnerable to unexpected disruptions or catastrophic failures that originate from either outside or inside their rapidly vanishing organizational boundaries. In a similar vein, those involved in detecting fraud need to move beyond the obvious profiles and start connecting up social networks that link compromised insiders with shadowy professional criminals circling around the organization's perimeter defenses. There is no longer any excuse for not knowing "what we don't know we don't know".

Consider the recent control failures and rogue trader incidents (such as the one that occurred early in 2008 at Société Générale) which have sent shockwaves throughout the investment banking industry. The traditional reaction of tightening up the control framework is not the answer. Not only does it impose an ever-increasing burden of cost and complexity but it also generates a false sense of security. Recognizing the increasing sophistication of the rogue trader and the complexity of monitoring across multiple silos, a number of banks are now moving beyond conventional risk management practices towards a more integrated approach based on a networked operational risk model. In practical terms this means that a fraudster is no longer confronted by a series of independent controls but a tight network of interconnected defenses, each one reinforcing and being reinforced by its neighbors. These defenses in turn utilize advanced information intelligence analytics to detect previously unknown patterns of suspicious activity (Asplen-Taylor, 2008). This state-of-the-art approach to information security means banks and other organizations will be in a position to better confront and deal with today's threats — and those of tomorrow.

Figure 6. A one-sided networked threat environment

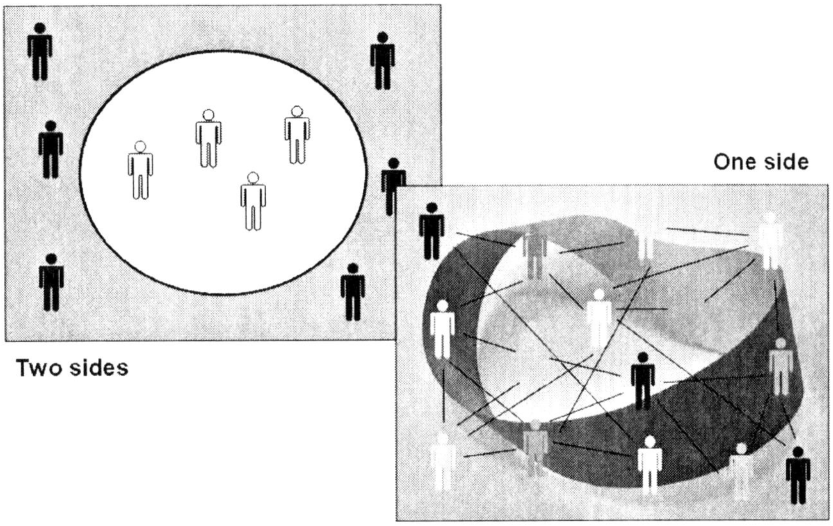

A Surveillance Society?

A final point to consider when predicting future developments in information security and fraud containment is the "Big Brother" factor. Our working, socializing, banking, shopping and traveling habits are routinely monitored by a variety of government, police and commercial agencies that collect, store and analyze digital transactions and CCTV camera images. Although this often done for the reasons of increasing security and reducing fraud, it has fuelled public and media concern about the dawn of the "surveillance society".

However, the debate is blurred by a lack of distinction between surveillance and the information that private individuals consent to provide. Many citizens will accept surveillance when there is true personal benefit, whether this is money off their supermarket shopping or greater protection from terrorists. While it is important we remain vigilant about state surveillance, political scrutiny, legal safeguards and the sheer volume of data mean that the state's "Big Brother" ability to monitor individuals is much less than most perceive it to be. More worrying is "Incompetent Brother": large, bureaucratic organizations – both public and private-sector – that store poor-quality data, use it for making poor-quality decisions, re-use it for purposes for which it was not collected and—as recent well-publicized events have shown—mislay it.

It is likely that within several years we will all be living in a "surveillance society" but we may not call it by that name. It is likely that our feelings towards this society will be complicated. No doubt we will have come to accept that almost everything we do beyond the privacy of our own homes (and sometimes even there) is likely to be recorded and stored somewhere. But by whom?

Consider the tremendous pace of technological change since 1993, when, in the space of a year, a host of new ground-breaking developments began to emerge from the technical laboratories: web browsers, webcams, online photo trading, wireless LANs, computer vision, cell phone text messaging, MPEG digital video, GPS and digital cameras. Today these technologies had evolved, become intertwined and given rise to MP3 players, camera cell phones, Internet telephony, WiFi mesh networks, number plate and facial recognition, satellite navigation, blogs, Amazon, eBay, MySpace, FaceBook and YouTube. An increasing amount of data is now being captured, stored and shared by individuals working and socializing online. In many cases this data is much more personal and sensitive than anything governments or large corporations keep on us.

Given the public's embrace and appetite for new technologies, and the increased awareness and fear of physical crime, financial crime and global terrorism, it is not hard to imagine a future scenario where individuals, equipped with highly advanced miniature devices, record most of what they see and hear and stream the footage to the highest bidder, be they journalist or security agency. George Orwell's novel *Nineteen Eighty-Four* and its character of "Big Brother" have become symbolic shorthand for people's fear of a surveillance society in which the state observes the minutiae of the day-to-day life of every citizen. However, unlike Orwell's novel, in which the all-seeing being was the state apparatus, we may see the day when the collective action of technology-wielding individuals creates that capability (Black, 2008; Porter, 2008). Move over Big Brother – meet Big Citizen.

It is likely that this collective action may rekindle a sense of personal responsibility and break down attitudes to the state as "them versus us". With the enlistment of people in the 80% "semi-honest" majority acting as "community observers", some aspects of physical and information security may well improve and criminals will be displaced once more. Whatever the outcome, technology is certain to redefine our definitions of "personal", "corporate", "state" and "secure", with far-reaching implications for 21st century human society.

REFERENCES

Accenture (2006). *The rising importance of enterprise content management.* New York, NY: Accenture.

ACFE (2006). *Report to the nation on occupational fraud and abuse.* Austin, Texas: Association of Certified Fraud Examiners.

Allcorn, W. (2003). *The Maginot Line 1928-45.* Oxford, England: Osprey Publishing.

Asplen-Taylor, S. (2008). *Preventing operational losses: Are tighter controls really the answer?* London, England: Detica.

Black, T. (2007). *The data explosion: how to survive its impact.* Homeland Defence & Resilience, Issue 1, pp. 72-75. London, England: Newsdesk Communications Ltd.

Black, T. (2008). *In my opinion.* Management Today. London, England: Haymarket Specialist.

Briggs, R., & Edwards, C. (2006). *The Business of Resilience: Corporate security for the 21st century.* London, England: Demos.

Burke, E. (1770). *Thoughts on the cause of the present discontents.* (Note: the referenced quotation is often attributed to Burke but has never been found in his works. It is probably a paraphrase of Burke's view that *"When bad men combine, the good must associate; else they will fall one by one, an unpitied sacrifice in a contemptible struggle".*)

Detica (2004). *Don't put all your PINs in one basket! Consumer PIN-sharing undermines Chip & PIN scheme.* Retrieved May 21, 2008, from http://www.detica.com/index.php?option=com_articlemanager&Itemid=266&task=display&artid=199&year=2004&category=none

Dorrington, P. (2004). *A strategic approach to reducing losses.* Cary, NC: SAS Institute.

Financial Times (2007). *A generation waiting to play havoc with company security.* The Financial Times, March 28 2007. London, England: Financial Times Ltd.

Gantz, J., Chute, C., Manfrediz, A., Minton, S., Reinsel, D., Schlichting, W., & Toncheva, A. (2008). *The diverse and expanding digital universe: an updated forecast of worldwide information growth through 2011.* Framingham, MA: IDC.

von Goethe, J. (1774). *Die Leiden des jungen Werther.* Translated into Hulse, M. (1989), *The*

Sorrows of Young Werther, London, England: Penguin Books.

Harford, T. (2007). *The Undercover Economist.* London, England: Abacus.

Kutner, M., Greenberg, E., Jin, Y., Boyle, B., Hsu, Y., Dunleavy, E., & White, S. (2007). *Literacy in everyday life: Results from the 2003 National Assessment of Adult Literacy.* Washington, DC: National Center for Education Statistics.

Lascelles, D. (2008). *Banking Banana Skins 2008: the CSFI's annual survey of the risks facing banks.* Centre for the Study of Financial Innovation. Huddersfield, England: Portal Publishing.

Levi, M., Burrows, J., Fleming, M., & Hopkins, M. (2007). *The nature, extent and economic impact of fraud in the UK.* London, England: Association of Chief Police Officers.

Lewis, H. (2007). *Cracks in the dam: The network view of risk.* Business Resilience Forum. London, England: AKJ Associates.

McConnell, M. (2007). *Overhauling intelligence. Foreign Affairs, 86*(4). New York, NY: Council on Foreign Relations.

McKay, T. (1998). *Can CPTED tunnel vision be cured?* Security Management magazine. Alexandria, VA: American Society for Industrial Security.

Monahan, M. (2007). *2007 Identity fraud survey report.* Pleasanton, CA: Javelin Strategy & Research.

Moser, C. (1999). *Improving literacy and numeracy: A fresh start.* London, England: DfEE Publications.

Porter, D. (2003). E-Business sector analysis. In Clark, A. & Burrell, P. (Eds), *A practitioner's guide to international money laundering law and regulation* (pp. 395-413). London, England: City & Financial Publishing.

Porter, D. (2006). *Businesses beware: protection from identity thieves.* Paper presented at the Association of Certified Fraud Examiners 17th Annual Fraud Conference & Exhibition, Las Vegas, Nevada.

Porter, D. (2007). The evolution of fraud intelligence. In Gupta, M. (Ed.), *Managing Information Assurance in Financial Services* (pp. 261-283). Hershey, PA: IGI Publishing.

Porter, D. (2008). *Soft, pervasive and complex: The new world of fraud containment.* Paper presented at the Association of Certified Fraud Examiners European Fraud Conference, London, England.

Ranum, M. (2005). *The six dumbest ideas in computer security.* Retrieved May 21, 2008, from http://www.ranum.com/security/computer_security/editorials/dumb/

Reason, J. (2000). Human error: models and management. *British Medical Journal, 320*, 768-770. London, England: BMJ Publishing Group.

Reder, S (1998). *The state of literacy in America: estimates at the local, state, and national levels.* Washington, DC: National Institute for Literacy.

Sagan, S. (2004). The problem of redundancy: why more nuclear security forces may produce less nuclear security. *Risk Analysis, 24*(4), 935-946. Stanford, CA: Center for International Security and Cooperation.

Shapiro, A. (2003). *Creating contagious commitment: applying the tipping point to organisational change.* Hillsborough, NC: Strategy Perspective.

Spivak, M. (1979). *A comprehensive introduction to differential geometry.* Wilmington, Delaware: Publish or Perish.

KEY TERMS

Benefits Realization Management: The process of identifying, recording, tracking and delivering benefits to ensure the ultimate success of a project.

Business Resilience: The move to a level of security more normally associated with critical national infrastructure which involves integrating business, technical physical security systems into a single holistic framework.

Digital Revolution: The widespread diffusion of telecommunications and computer technology that is creating entirely new ways of working and socializing as well as challenging, and even destroying, many others.

Financial Criminal: A term used to describe thieves, fraudsters, money launderers and other criminals who steal money, usually by deception, from financial institutions and other organizations or alternatively use them to launder the proceeds of serious crime.

Identity Fraud: Where someone knowingly assumes a false identity (fictitious, living or dead), with or without consent, in order to apply fraudulently for some kind of credit, service, asset or benefit, or else masquerade as the legitimate holder of an account and steals the account funds.

Information Intelligence: The technique of turning large volumes of complex data into relevant and actionable intelligence in order to better manage risk and increase profitability.

Networked Operational Risk Model: The move to a level of operational risk management that addresses an increasingly complex operational environment through the deployment of a network of interconnected, mutually-reinforcing defenses that utilize advanced information intelligence analytics to detect previously unknown patterns of potentially suspicious activity.

Social Engineering: A collection of techniques used to manipulate people, often via a computer or telephone, into performing acts or divulging confidential information to facilitate the execution of a fraud.

Social Network Analysis: An analytical tool used by investigators to identify, understand and evaluate networks of collaborating individuals across disparate and often unconnected sources of data.

Chapter III
Employee Surveillance Based on Free Text Detection of Keystroke Dynamics

Ahmed Awad E. Ahmed
University of Victoria, Canada

Issa Traore
University of Victoria, Canada

ABSTRACT

In recent years, many studies have highlighted the unprecedented growth in security threats from multiple and varied sources faced by corporate, as well as governmental organizations. People inside the organization with ready access to confidential or proprietary data can easily violate the organization security policy, maliciously or inadvertently, without being caught. In order to protect their reputation and valuable assets, many organizations take the dramatic but necessary step of deploying and operating employee surveillance and monitoring tools within their network perimeters. In this chapter, we discuss employee surveillance schemes from both technological and legal perspectives. We argue that keystroke dynamics could be used to fight effectively against insider threat, and as such it could play an important role in employee surveillance. We present a keystroke recognition scheme based on free text detection that goes beyond the traditional approach of using keystroke dynamics for authentication or employee performance evaluation, and consider using such information for dynamic user profiling. The generated profiles can be used to identify reliably perpetrators in the event of security breach. Such form of user profiling provides a very effective way of combating insider threat that is less intrusive to individual privacy.

INTRODUCTION

In recent years, many studies have highlighted the unprecedented growth in security threats from multiple and varied sources (Denning, 1987). Traditional protection mechanisms such as firewall and intrusion detection systems primarily focus on hacking threats originating from outside the organization network perimeter, whereas people inside the organization with ready access to confidential or proprietary data can easily violate the organization security policy, maliciously or inadvertently, without being caught (Ahmed, 2003; Ahmed, 2005). Hence, insiders pose the greatest challenge to data protection. It has been reported that insiders represent the sources of over half of the security and privacy breaches faced by most organizations. Malicious activity by an insider may expose his organization to credibility lost, or significant financial lost related to lost business or lawsuits.

In order to protect their reputation and valuable assets, many organizations take the dramatic but necessary step of deploying and operating employee surveillance and monitoring tools within their network perimeters (Zimmerman, 2002). The rationale behind such approach is that secure management of organization information assets largely depend on the behavior of the employees. Employees are typically involved in all aspects of information flows within an organization. They are producers or end-users of the organization information asset, and have easier access to it compared with outsiders. So mismanagement or misuse of such information by an employee can have devastating impact on the company.

One class of tools that have gained in popularity in the realm of employee surveillance technologies is keystroke monitor. Keystroke monitors can be used to generate and analyze two different kinds of information: the keystrokes data and the keystroke dynamics. The keystrokes data can be used to reconstruct the actual information typed by the user such as the commands or programs run, or the messages typed etc. Keystroke dynamics have so far been used, in existing surveillance technologies, only for employee work performance monitoring purpose by determining and logging, for instance, the employee typing speed. Prior research has shown that keystroke dynamics can also be used for protection. However, the focus of these research works has mostly been on using keystroke dynamics for authentication (Bleha et al., 1990; Brown, 1993; Bergadano, 2002).

We argue that keystroke dynamics could be used to fight effectively against insider threat, and as such it could play an important role in employee surveillance. To achieve this goal we need to go beyond the traditional approach of using keystroke dynamics for authentication or employee performance evaluation, and consider using such information for dynamic user profiling. The generated profiles can be used to identify reliably perpetrators in the event of security breach. Such form of user profiling provides a very effective way of combating insider threat that is less intrusive to individual privacy.

Although a rich body of research work has been accomplished in the area of keystroke dynamics biometrics, the focus has mostly been on fixed-text detection, which requires typing a fixed or known string (Gaines et al. 1980; Bleha et al., 1990; Legget, 1991; Brown, 1993; Bergadano, 2002). This restricts the applicability of most existing keystroke dynamics technologies to access control, and eliminates the possibility of using them for dynamic and passive user monitoring. In this context, dynamic and passive monitoring requires free-text detection. Free-text detection of keystroke dynamics is a challenging area in which few works have been published so far. In this chapter, we present a new technique for free-text detection of keystroke that can be used for passive and dynamic user monitoring. By allowing dynamic and passive user monitoring, the proposed technology can be used to track reliably and continuously legitimate and illegitimate users throughout computing sessions. By collecting only user keystroke dynamics instead of actual keystrokes data, our technique limit the amount of personal information gathered. This protects to some extent the privacy of the monitored individuals, compared with existing surveillance technologies.

While the case for employee surveillance can be made, most of the technologies used so far infringe significantly on the privacy of the employees. Existing surveillance technologies record sensitive information such as telecommunications records, logs of web usages, email messages, details about employees computer usage or work habits etc. Such sensitive information is stored in organization servers exposing them to possible theft by hackers and identity fraudsters. Privacy advocates and many other critics argue that existing employee surveillance technologies simply violate the privacy of employee, which is a fundamental personal right. In this context, there is a need to balance on one hand the need for organizations to protect their information assets against insider threat and on the other hand the right for privacy of employees.

In Section 2, we discuss insider threat and give a general overview of existing employee surveillance technologies. We also discuss the use of biometrics technologies for workplace surveillance and take the opportunity to discuss the privacy issues involved in employee surveillance. In Section 3, we give an overview of keystroke dynamics recognition technology and review related work on free-text detection of keystrokes. We also introduce a new approach for free-text detection of keystrokes, and discuss its use in the context of employee surveillance. In Section 4, we discuss future trends, and finally in Section 5, we make some concluding remarks.

BACKGROUND

In this section we give an overview of insider threat and discuss employee surveillance which represents the most widely used countermeasures against such threat. We also discuss biometrics technologies which form part of many surveillance strategies, and we end the section by discussing the privacy considerations underlying employee surveillance.

Insider Threats

Previous attempts have been made to study and characterize insiders' threats. In this regard, the Secret Service National Threat Assessment Center (NTAC) and the CERT Coordination Center of Carnegie Mellon University's Software Engineering Institute (CERT/CC) conducted a more comprehensive study examining insiders' threats from both behavioral and technical perspectives (Randazzo et al., 2004; Keeney et al. 2005). The Insider Threat Study (ITS) produced through these joint efforts, analyzed insider threats across various sectors, including banking and finance, information and telecommunications, government, and critical infrastructures, and suggested some remedies. Some of the findings of this study include the following:

- Most insider incidents involve little technical sophistication or complexity.
- Most of the insider incidents are planned in advance, and do not just happen as random isolated actions.
- Most of the incidents are driven by financial motives rather than the will to harm the organization.
- Perpetrators have various profiles and background, and may hold various positions in the organization.
- Incidents are detected using various methods or technologies.

It is important to understand the motives and the psychology of insider criminals in order to be able to design effective countermeasures. Insider threat may originate from the people who design, maintain or operate the target systems. The growing reliance on computing systems increases the dependence on people such as developers, system administrator and operators. As a result, secure operation of sensitive systems relies to a large extent on how trustworthy these individuals are. An insider attack originating from such individuals can have dramatic consequences.

Insider attack may originate from disgruntled employees who have been fired or transferred, or who are angry at their management for various reasons. Insider crimes may also be committed by employees who take advantage of their position to achieve financial gains by, for instance, facilitating or participating in the activities of an established hacker group or an organized crime ring. There are also many reported cases of insider crimes committed by the so-called "moles", who are individuals who get them hired by an organization with the specific intent of conducting espionage or other fraudulent activities.

In order to limit the occurrence or the impact of insider acts a broad range of measures are currently being studied or used by organizations. These measures can broadly be categorized into behavioral and technological. Behavioral measures are based on the assumption that insider acts are based on a combination of predisposing traits of the individuals as well as specific characteristics or context of the organization environment. Such measures involve establishing psychological profiles of perpetrators which can be used in pre-employment screening as well as in monitoring the activity of technology specialists.

Technological measures consist of implementing and deploying in the organization hacker monitoring devices or software. We discuss in detail these technologies in the next section.

Employee Surveillance Technologies

The primary reasons for electronic surveillance of workers include the following:

- Legal liability
- Security concerns
- Legal compliance
- Employee productivity and performance reviews

In order to achieve these objectives, several features are required in typical surveillance technologies. Common features of employee surveillance technologies include:

- Monitoring how employees use their computers by logging, for instance, which sites they visit, how often they visit specific sites, and how much time they spend surfing the web.
- Greater control over employees' computers by enforcing strict policies, for instance, by restricting which programs they can run, or by filtering out certain web sites or blocking certain emails.

Employee surveillance technologies broadly fall into three categories: computer surveillance, camera surveillance, and tracking surveillance. Camera surveillance includes technologies such as closed circuit television (CCTV), facial recognition systems etc. Tracking surveillance includes technologies such as global positioning systems (GPS). Popular examples of computer surveillance include email or web monitoring systems. We are interested in this chapter primarily in computer surveillance technologies. For this kind of technologies, the main monitoring targets include:

- Web connections
- E-mail communications
- Storage and reviews of computer files
- Video recording of job performance
- Storage and review of voice-mail messages

Computer surveillance programs can broadly be classified into two categories according to their scope and target: host-based technologies and network-based technologies (Wakefield, 2004).

Network-based programs are deployed on the employer's network, and as such they typically monitor and log network activities such as email communications and web surfing. The recorded data can be used to profile individual users, and the derived profiles can be used to identify individual employees in case of security breach. Some surveillance technologies allow managers to randomly access employee computer screens, and inspect them or take snapshots. E-mail monitoring represents a significant component of surveillance technologies in use in most organizations. Organizations are legally liable for all communications originating from their networks. This put organizations at risk of lawsuits if employees are involved in unlawful activities such as harassment or discrimination. E-mail monitoring software parses e-mail messages for keywords that may refer to unacceptable or illegal activities.

A good example of network-based surveillance technology is the Vontu data loss prevention software developed by Vontu Inc (Vontu). Vontu data loss prevention software prevents data confidentiality breach from inside by monitoring inbound and outbound network traffic, and blocking web, email or FTP communications that violate the organization security policy. Another example of network-based surveillance product is the e-mail and web monitoring systems developed by Elron Software (Elron). The E-mail module monitors the presence of certain keywords, files or attachments that, when detected, forward the corresponding message to the security or system administrator for review. The web module filters out or blocks blacklisted sites such as porn sites.

Network-based surveillance systems are practical and cost-effective because they allow the employer to monitor several users simultaneously. They are, however, limited in the sense that they cannot monitor local activities occurring on employees' computers, which do not require network connections.

Host-based technologies are needed to monitor and report such local activities. Some host-based surveillance technologies record the programs installed and run by the employee, the amount of time the employee is away from his desk or the computer remains idle. Other products allow the employer to monitor keystrokes on employees' computers. Keystroke monitoring can be used to assess employees' performance by measuring their typing speed and comparing this against company standards. Keystroke logging can also be used to reconstruct the actual information generated through the employees computing sessions. Keystroke logging addresses a key limitation of network-based technologies, which is their inability to deal with encrypted traffic.

It is important to note that the fact that host-based surveillance technologies are deployed on an employee's machine doesn't necessarily indicate that the employee is aware of it. Quite often the program runs passively without knowledge of the user. Sebek, a popular kernel-based key logger developed by the honeynet project, provides an effective illustration of how a host-based surveillance technology works (Sebek). The Sebek distribution consists of two modules: the client module, which is installed on the monitored machine, and the server module, which is located on a separate secure server machine. The Sebek client resides in the kernel space instead of the user space where the shell is running. So it evades detection by the user. The Sebek client captures the keystrokes without the user noticing it, and transmits them to the Sebek server, which logs them. In doing that, it ensures that the system cannot block the transmission. Sebek provides the capability of capturing and decoding encrypted activity whether local or over SSH and SS connections or capturing and decoding passwords used to login locally or remotely etc.

Biometrics Recognition Systems

Biometrics recognition systems form part of the surveillance technologies deployed in many organizations. Biometrics is commonly used for access control to secured facilities or in conjunction with monitoring systems such as closed circuit television. These allow employers to verify employees work time and attendance, but at the same time protect employees against employers' manipulations or mistakes in maintaining such records.

Recent years have seen an increasing interest in biometric systems; the underlying technology has improved and the costs involved have been reduced considerably. Biometrics technologies are widely used in various security applications, and are considered among the most accurate and efficient security systems in the market.

In the Oxford dictionary, the definition of the noun "biometrics" is given as the "the application of statistical analysis to biological data" (Pearsall, 2001). In the particular field of computer security, biometrics is defined as the automated use of a collection of factors describing human behavioral or physiological characteristics to establish or verify a precise identity (Matyas, 2003).

Biometrics technologies are commonly categorized into two different classes: physiological and behavioral. Examples of physiological characteristics include hand or finger images, facial characteristics, speaker verification, and iris recognition. Behavioral characteristics are traits that are learned or acquired. Dynamic signature verification and keystroke dynamics are two examples of behavioral characteristics. Not all biometrics technologies are appropriate or being used for employee surveillance. Voice and Face recognition systems are the most appropriate physiological biometrics for this application. However, several implementation attempts faced a number of privacy concerns. A (legal) case concerning the use of biometrics for authentication was initiated when four Telus (a Canadian Telephone Operator) employees complained that the company forces them to consent to the collection of their voice biometrics to gain access to a number of services. The employees refused the idea of converting their recorded voice to a biometric template. The case was closed to the favor of the company when the court found that the process is appropriate with regards to the company's business interests and that the consent meets the Personal Information Protection and Electronic Documents Act requirements (PIPEDA). Keystroke dynamics is one the most suitable behavioral biometric for employee surveillance (more details are given later).

Biometric recognition requires comparing an enrolled biometric sample (biometric template) against a newly captured biometric sample (for example, finger scan provided at an access attempt). A three-step process (*Acquire, Process, and Store*) should be executed every time the user presents his biometric sample to the system as follows:

1. *Acquire*: Raw biometric data is acquired by a sensing device, such as the image produced by a fingerprint scanning device, or the data collected by a keystroke event logger. Raw biometric data usually contains noise and cannot be used as is to automatically compare between users.
2. *Process*: The raw data is processed to build a biometric model (template). This model consists of a number of extracted distinguishing features which are represented in a mathematical format.
3. *Store*: The biometric template is stored in a database with all other collected information, (like claimed identity, date, time). This process is required in order to secure enough data for the user enrollment process. Some of the biometric systems implementations don't permanently store the generated template during recognition process. This is usually the case for non-audited access control systems. However storing such data increases the accountability of the system. Since the biometric template contains all the data representing the user biometric characteristics to the system there is no need to store the raw data. It is also not possible to reconstruct the raw data from the generated biometric template.

Biometric systems operate in one of three modes: Enrollment, Verification, and Validation modes. In most of the implementations the same hardware is used for the three modes.

During enrollment mode, a reference biometric model is generated for the user. This model can be developed using number of the templates already stored in the database for the same user or it can be based only on one template. The reference model is stored in the database for future comparisons.

In the verification mode a 1 to 1 matching process is performed by comparing the calculated biometric template to the enrolled user reference model. In this mode the user will provide other information to the system to claim a specific identity. The decision will be made based on the comparison result. If the two samples are highly deviated from each other, this will indicate that the user is not who he claimed to be.

In identification mode a 1 to *N* matching process is performed by comparing the calculated biometric template to the reference models for all of the enrolled users. The matching process should be able to detect the similarities in the compared models and select the closest reference model to the collected sample. The result of this process is either an identity confirmation or a non-match. This mode is mainly used in forensic applications where a proof of the identity of a suspect is not known in advance.

In order to evaluate the accuracy of a biometric system, the following metrics should be computed:

1. *False Acceptance Rate (FAR):* the ratio between the number of occurrences of accepting a non-authorized user compared to the number of access trials.
2. *False Rejection Rate (FRR):* the ratio between the number of false alarms caused by rejecting an authorized user compared to the number of access trials.
3. *Failure to Enroll (FTE):* the ratio characterizing the number of times the system is not able to enroll a user's biometric features; this failure is caused by poor quality samples during enrollment mode.
4. *Failure to Capture (FTC):* the ratio characterizing the number of times the system is not able to process the captured raw biometric data and extract features from it; this occurs when the captured data does not contain sufficient information to be processed.
5. *Mean Time to Enroll (MTTE):* the mean time needed to build a reference template for a user. This includes the time needed to collect the biometric samples and the time needed to process the samples and build the reference template.
6. *Mean Time to Detect (MTTD):* the mean time needed to detect or verify user identity after presentation of the user data to the system. This includes the time needed to acquire the biometric sample, build the template and compare it to the reference template/templates to make the decision.

FAR and FRR values can vary significantly depending on the sensitivity of the biometric data comparison algorithm used in the verification/identification mode; FTE and FTC represent the sensitivity of the raw data processing module. In order to tune the accuracy of the system to its optimum value, it is important to study the effect of each factor on the other. In particular the relation between the achieved FAR and FRR when changing main system parameters is important in tuning the system. If the system is designed to minimize FAR to make the system more secure (e.g., for access control systems and intrusion detection systems), FRR will increase. On the other hand, if the system is designed to decrease FRR (e.g., for forensic applications) by increasing the tolerance to input variations and noise, FAR will increase. The optimal tuning point is calculated based on the application requirements and the aimed level of security.

Privacy Concerns

Employee surveillance technologies raise a lot of privacy concerns, heating the debate between privacy advocates and proponents of employee surveillance practices (GAO, 2002). Proponents argue that observing and tracking employee behavior is necessary to reduce the risks to which organizations are exposed. In opposition to this view, critics claim that surveillance technologies violate fundamental personal rights of employees, and that quite often too much information about workers are collected, without any oversight of regulatory bodies over how the data are used, stored or secured. In this debate, one of the arguments that give an edge to employers is the need to comply with standards set by regulatory bodies such as the US Federal Trade Commission (FTC) for the administrative, technical and physical safety of customer records. The FTC's standards set three main objectives for organizations:

- Ensure security and privacy of customer records.
- Protect against external as well as internal threats to the security and integrity of customer records.
- Protect against unauthorized access or use of customer records that may result in substantial damage to the reputation, health, or wealth of the customer.

In this context, data security laws consider that privacy and safety concerns of customer information have higher priority than any privacy expectations of employees. Most employers use this as the legal ground to monitor their employees.

Prior court rulings consider that reasonableness is the standard for electronic surveillance of workers. The employer needs to show that there is a business purpose, and also that there is an electronic monitoring policy in place for which employees have given informed consent. Legal experts advise that, through such policy, the employer should inform employees of the purpose of monitoring activities and related rules, and make sure to remove any privacy expectations in the workplace. The business case for electronic surveillance made by most employers is the need to comply with regulatory statutes and to reduce other employees' risks.

Under such considerations, employers must provide all employees with prior notice indicating the type of surveillance and when it will take place, whether it is intermittent or continuous, and whether it is impending or ongoing. Employers must also take appropriate measures to ensure the protection of the collected data, and avoid improper disclosure or use.

KEYSTROKE DYNAMICS RECOGNITION SYSTEMS

In this section, we review related work on free text detection of keystrokes, and present a new approach that uses neural networks for biometrics analysis.

State of the Art

Since the early 1980's a rich body of research has been produced in the area of keystroke dynamics recognition (Gaines et al. 1980; Bleha et al., 1990; Legget, 1991; Brown, 1993; Bergadano, 2002). Most of these works focus on using this technology for user authentication or access control. Keystroke dynamics recognition systems measure the dwell time and flight time for keyboard actions. The raw data collected for keystroke includes the time a key is depressed and the time the key is released. Based on this data, the *duration* of keystroke (i.e., length of time a key is depressed), and the *latency* between consecutive keystrokes are calculated and used to construct a set of digraphs, tri-graphs or *n*-graphs producing a pattern identifying the user. Because of the time limitation of the identification process, the user is asked to type a pre-defined word or a set of words in order to get reasonable amount of data for the identification. During the enrollment process, the user is also required to enter the same fixed text.

For dynamic and passive monitoring, we need to be able to detect the user without requiring him to enter a predefined message or text. So free text detection is essential for our purpose. However, free text detection presents huge challenges, which explain the limited number of related work available in the literature.

Monrose and Rubin authored one of the earliest works on free text detection of keystrokes (Monrose, 1997). They collected typing samples from 42 users over a period of 7 weeks, during their routine computing usage, without any particular constraint. The collected timing data consist of keystroke durations and latencies. To recognize individual users, they cluster the data using a clustering algorithm to partition the data into cluster domains. The typing speed or number of words typed per minute in a given profile is used as the clustering criteria. Various distance measures were studied along with the clustering scheme, including Normalized Euclidian distance, and weighted and non-weighted maximum probability measures. Although the authors obtain 90% correct classification for fixed text detection, they obtain at best (using the weighted probability measure) only 23% correct classification for free text detection.

In the experimental approach adopted by Dowland et al., typing samples are collected by monitoring users during their regular computing activities, without any particular constraints imposed on them (Dowland et al., 2002). A user profile is determined by calculating the mean and standard deviation of digraph latency and by considering only the diagraphs occurring a minimum number of times across the collected typing samples. By collecting and analyzing data for five users they achieve correct acceptance rates in the range of 60%.

More recently, Guneti and Picardi used the degree of disorder of an array to discriminate between two different typing samples (Guneti, 2005). The degree of disorder of an array is computed by summing the distances between the positions of its elements, with respect to the positions of the same elements in the ordered array. The only timing information considered in their experiments is the time at which a key is depressed. Given two typing samples, they extract the n-graphs commonly occurring in both samples with corresponding timing information, and compute the distances between these samples. The distance $d_n(S_1, S_2)$ between samples S_1 and S_2, with respect to their common n-graphs, is computed. Based on these basic distance measures, they define some more sophisticated distance measure that they use to compare different typing samples. They evaluated their technique through a set of experiments involving 205 individuals, achieving a FAR of 0.00489% and a FRR of less than 5%.

We propose in this work a new approach for free text detection of keystroke dynamics, which introduces and uses a digraph approximation technique based on sorted time mapping. Although our approach is different from the one proposed by Guneti and Picardi, it achieves comparable performance.

Proposed Approach

The enrollment process in any keystroke dynamics detection system requires the existence of an enrollment sample, which is used to compute the behavior of the user. This sample should contain all possible key combinations in order to efficiently detect based on expected or unexpected set of user input. The first challenge facing a free text detection system is the ability to enroll a user using a non-predefined set of data. This allows both monitoring the user on the fly and non-intrusively by totally hiding the detection process from the user. Another challenge is to be able to provide information about the user identity based on a minimal amount of non-deterministic input. This is very important in practice as in most cases it will not be possible to force an attacker to provide more data and a decision should be made based only on this data.

The detection approach we introduce for free text detection addresses those challenges by utilizing a digraph approximation technique, which is based on sorted time mapping. The approach utilizes neural networks to simulate and analyze the user behavior based on the encoded set of digraphs.

Figure 1 illustrates the enrollment process. Raw data collected from a specific user's sessions are processed and converted to a digraph format. A digraph represents a typing action performed by the user from a specific key to another key on the keyboard. The time calculated in each digraph consists of the sum of the dwell times (the time needed to click on the key) and the flight time (the time required to move from one key to another). Generated digraphs are sent as a batch to the digraph-sorting module, which computes a mapping table. In order to calculate the mapping table for the provided set of digraphs, digraphs are sorted twice. The first time, they are sorted according to the average of the times of all digraphs with the same code in the *from*-key. The second time, they are sorted according to the average of the *to*-key. A key code is mapped to its sort order according to whether it is *to* or *from*. The output-mapping table is stored for each of the enrolled users. The next step of the enrollment process consists of training a neural network with collected digraphs after applying the mapping order calculated in the previous step on each of the digraphs. Mapped *(from, to)* key combinations are sent as inputs to the neural network, while the elapsed time is used as the training output.

Figure 2 shows the neural network architecture used. The network is a feed forward multi layer perceptrons (MLP). The number of input nodes is

Figure 1. User enrollment process

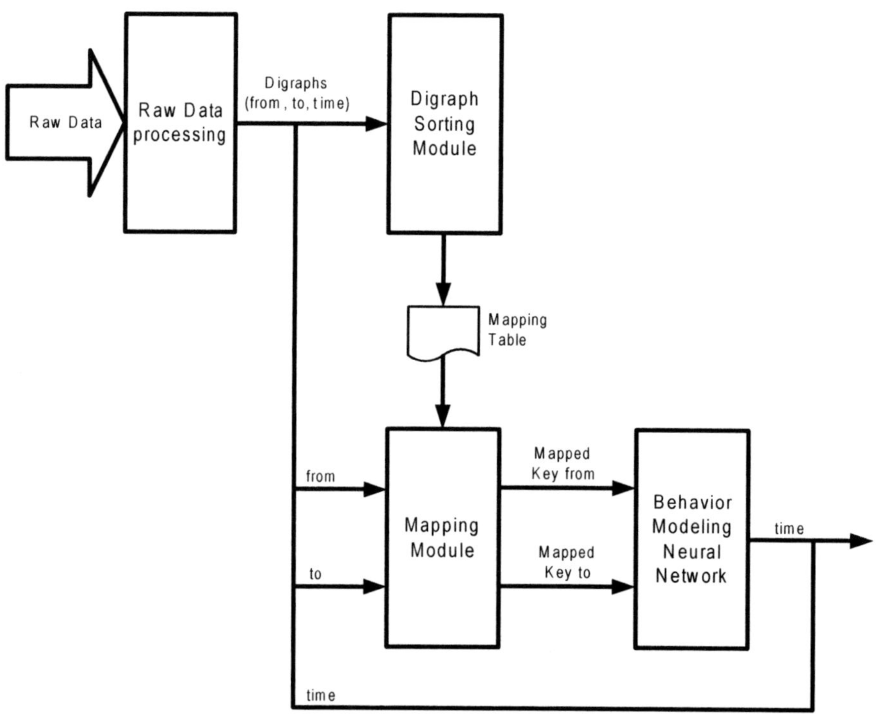

Figure 2. Digraph behavior modeling neural network

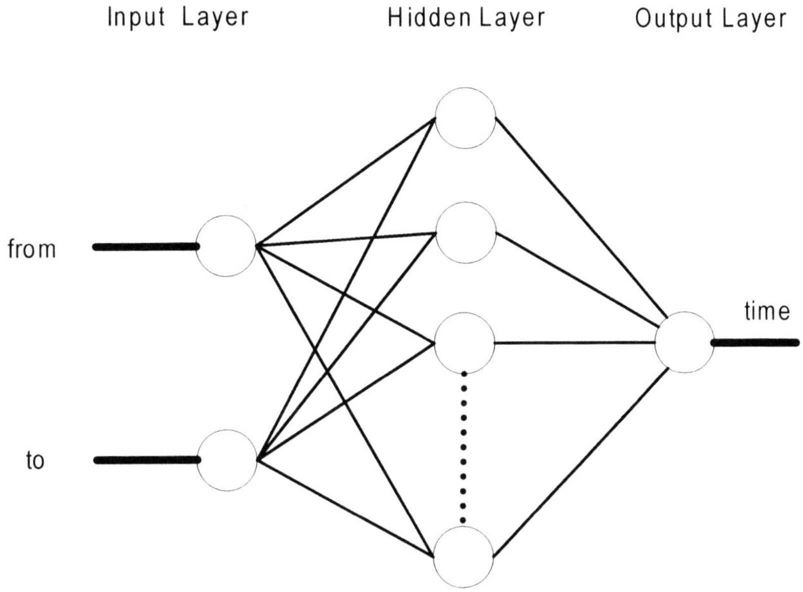

2 representing the *from* and *to* mapped keys. The output layer consists of one node, which represents the time needed to perform the digraph. The hidden layer consists of 20 nodes. The back propagation technique is used to train the network.

A neural network is trained for each of the enrolled users. The weights of the trained networks for all users are saved in a repository for future use during the detection process.

The user signature consists of the mapping table and the weights of the trained neural network. This signature is stored and used for identity verification process; Figure 3 describes this process. In this mode the neural network will be

Figure 3. Identity verification process

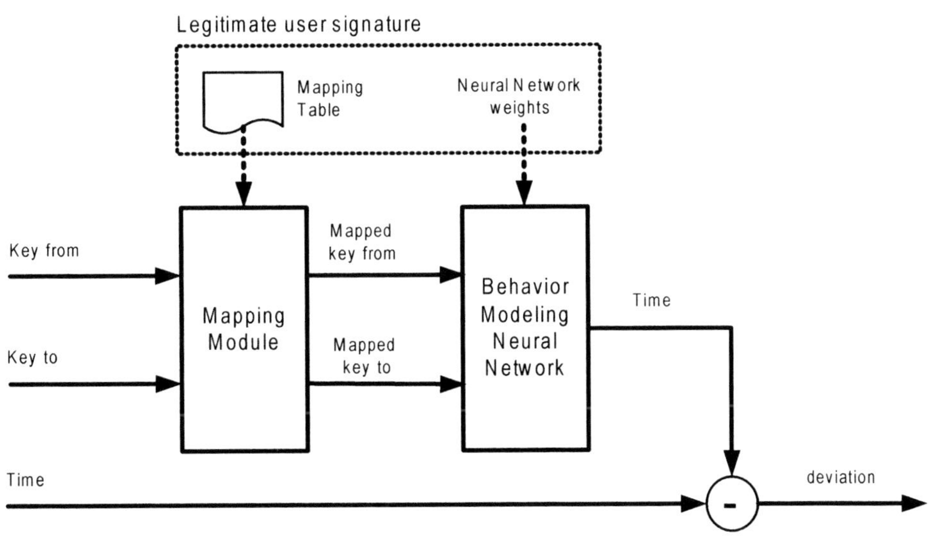

loaded with the weights stored in the legitimate user's signature. Each digraph in the monitored session will pass through the mapping component, which utilizes the mapping table provided by the legitimate user's signature. The output of this digraph will be passed as inputs to the trained neural network, which will provide the time needed for the legitimate user to perform this action. The difference between this time and the original time of the monitored digraph represents the deviation from the legitimate user's behavior. The average of this deviation for all of the digraphs in the monitored session will represent how close the behavior calculated in this session is to the legitimate user's behavior. The lower this number the more confident the system is that this session belongs to the same user.

In case of 1 to *N* identification application, the whole process can be repeated for all of the enrolled users, in each cycle one of the enrolled signatures will be applied, and the signature, which achieves the lowest deviation, will be considered as the closest match to the attacker's identity. If the deviation is low (below a specific threshold) this indicates that this sample belongs to the owner of this signature.

Figure 4 illustrates the behavior comparison process for two sessions belonging to two different users when compared to the reference signature of one of them. The figure shows the relation between the key code (according to the sorting order), and the time needed to move from this key to the "A" key on the keyboard. The Y axis represents the output of the neural network after it has been trained with the sorted key order.

Figure 4a shows the data collected from one of User 1's sessions compared to his reference signature. Notice that the two curves are close to each other; this indicates similarity of the typing behavior. Figure 4b shows one of User 2's sessions compared to the reference signature of User 1. In order to do this comparison it is mandatory to apply User 1's mapping to the session data prior to passing the data to User 1's neural network. The noticeable deviation between the two curves represents the difference in behavior.

Evaluation

We implemented the above recognition system as a distributed client/server application and conducted a wide range experiment involving twenty-two participants. Figure 5 illustrates the hardware setup for the experiment. 16 males and 6 females, with varying computer skills and ages ranging from 13 to 48 years, were involved in this experiment. Each user was asked to install our client software on his workstation and to use the workstation for his daily use throughout the duration of the experiment. The client software was a transparent application with no user interface. The software caches all keystroke dynamics and sends the data to a central server which is located in our lab. The server processes and stores the data in the database for future analysis. The experiment lasted for 9 weeks and we were able to collect an average of 119979 digraphs per user. Figure 6 shows the receiver operating characteristic curve for the main experiment. The curve shows the relation between the false acceptance rate and the false rejection rate for the different possible values of the threshold limit. The optimal threshold limit can be selected from the curve based on an optimization criterion which involves minimizing (FAR, FRR) and giving FAR a priority over FRR. Based on this criterion, as shown by Figure 6, the optimal performance achieved by our detector was a false acceptance rate (FAR) of 0.0152% and a false rejection rate (FRR) of 4.82%.

FUTURE TRENDS

According to a survey conducted by the American Management Association (AMA), over three-quarters of major US companies use some form of employee surveillance technologies. According to the same survey the current trend is to conduct

Figure 4. (a) User 1's session compared to his own reference signature; (b) One of User 2's sessions compared to User 1's reference signature

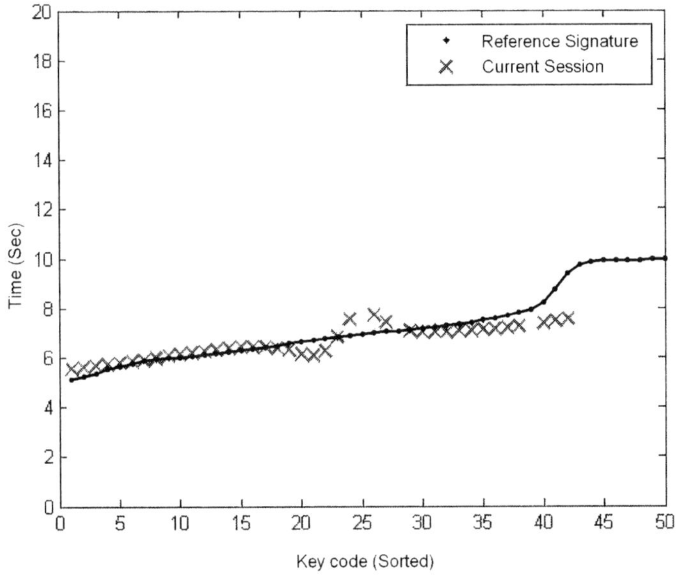

(a)

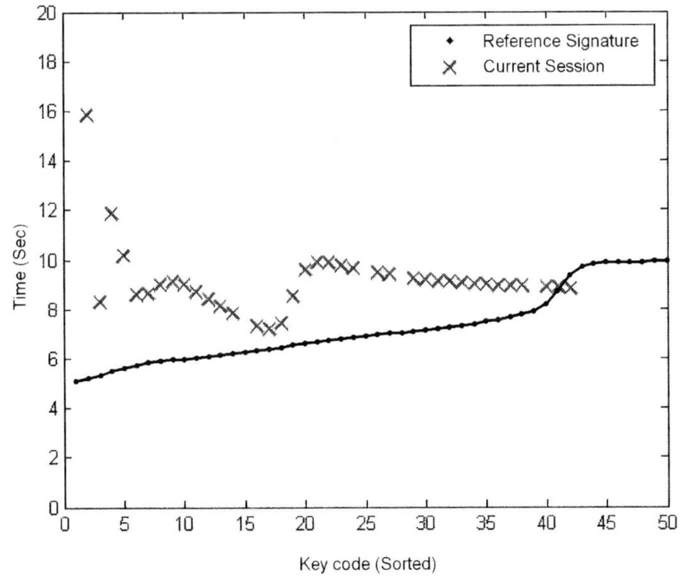

(b)

Figure 5. Experiment environment

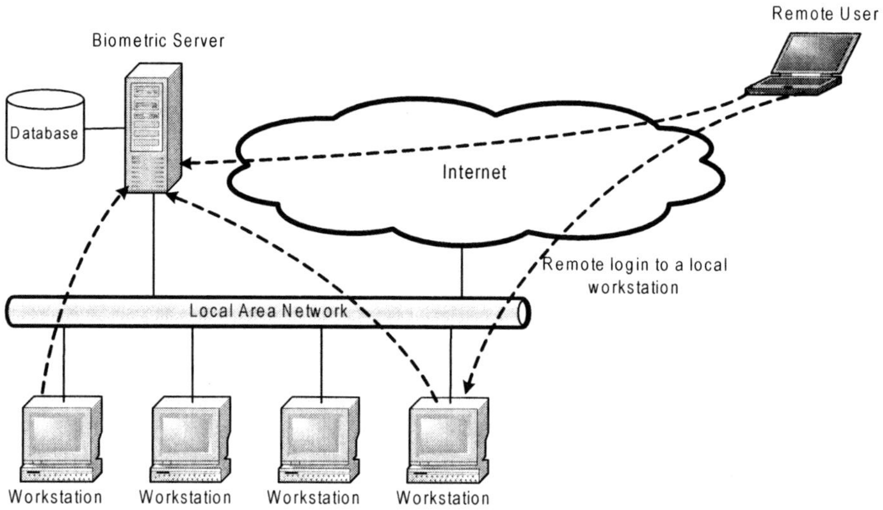

Figure 6. Receiver Operating Characteristic curve for the main experiment

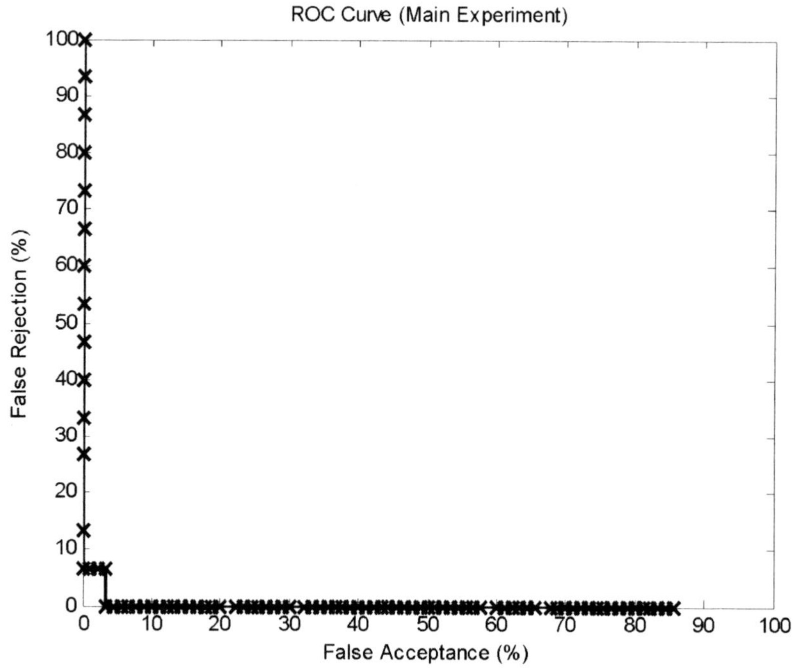

surveillance on an ad hoc basis under the form of random spot checks or as a response to a specific situation rather than in a continuous or systematic way. An explanation for such trend is that spot checking involves less overhead and privacy concerns compared with systematic monitoring. Although continuous monitoring raises more privacy concerns than spot checks, there is a growing interest in systematic monitoring due to the realization that the biggest security challenges are posed by knowledgeable insiders rather than random outsiders. With the decreasing cost of storage and the increasing processing power of computing systems, systematic and continuous monitoring becomes a realistic and affordable possibility for organizations. In this regard, we have developed a prototype client/server application named BIOTRACKER[1], which implements mouse and keystroke dynamics recognition for the purpose of systematic and continuous monitoring. During the experiment described above we collected (through our client software) mouse dynamics data for the participants (in addition of the keystroke dynamics); the collected data was processed and analyzed to study the biometrics in such data. Mouse dynamics biometrics can be very effective in employee surveillance and monitoring. We refer interested readers to (Ahmed, 2007) for more details about mouse dynamics biometrics. Our current goal is to combine mouse and keystroke dynamics biometrics in a high-performance multimodal biometrics framework which can be used to conduct efficiently and effectively monitoring tasks such as the one described in this chapter. We are currently studying various integration architectures with the purpose of improving significantly the accuracy of the multimodal detector. Future trends will be toward the adoption of ubiquitous, continuous monitoring technologies that combine cost-effective storage and processing capabilities and mitigate privacy concerns at the same time. We intend to meet this challenge through the development of BIOTRACKER.

CONCLUSION

Privacy is an important right of any human being. Considering that we spend most of our lives at work, such right should be applicable in some way in the workplace. On the other hand, employers have the legitimate right to take any appropriate measures to ensure safety and productivity in their organizations. Employees' surveillance must strike a balance between privacy and technology effectiveness. To achieve such balance, least invasive or intrusive surveillance technologies should be used, and the information collected should be necessary and not beyond the business purpose.

In this chapter, we have discussed the main issues underlying employee surveillance monitoring. We demonstrated the factors characterizing this process and looked at it from different angle to cover privacy and legal issues. We presented a new framework for free-text detection based on keystroke dynamics which is suitable for passive monitoring and identity verification. The use of this framework allows the balancing between surveillance and privacy since all the generated factors are based on the typing dynamics not on the written contents. The presented approach utilizes neural networks to model the user behavior. Our experimental results demonstrate high accuracy of this approach. The framework allows companies to verify or detect the identity of their employees while they are performing their routine work. The evidence collected from this process is very reliable since the decision is based on strong behavioral biometric characteristics.

REFERENCES

Ahmed, A. A. E., & Traore, I. (2007, July-September). A New Biometrics Technology based on Mouse Dynamics. *IEEE Transactions on Dependable and Secure Computing*, *4*(3), 165-179.

Ahmed, A. A. E., & Traore, I. (2005, October). Detecting Computer Intrusions Using Behavioral Biometrics. *Proceedings of Third Annual Conference on Privacy, Security and Trust* (pp. 91-98), St. Andrews, New Brunswick, Canada.

Ahmed, A. A. E., & Traore, I. (2003). System and Method for Determining a Computer User Profile from a Motion-based Input Device. *PCT patent application with the World Intellectual Property Organization*, filed by the University of Victoria (PCT/CA2004/000669) filing date: 3 May 2004 priority date: May2, 2003.

Bergadano, F., Guneti, D., & Picardi, C. (2002). User Authentication through Keystroke Dynamics. *ACM Transactions on Information and System Security, 5*(4), 367-39.

Bleha, S., Slivinsky, C., & Hussein, B. (1990). Computer-access Security Systems using Keystroke Dynamics. *IEEE Transactions on Pattern Analysis and Machine Intelligence, PAMI-12, 12*, 1217-1222.

Brown, M., Rogers, S. J. (1993). Identification Via Keystroke Characteristics of Typed Names Using Neural Networks. *International Journal on Man-Machine Studies,* Vol. 39, pp. 999-1014.

Denning, D. (1987). An Intrusion Detection Model. *IEEE Transactions on Software Engineering, 13*(2), 222-232.

Dowland , P., Furnell , S., & Papadaki, M. (2002). Keystroke Analysis as a Method of Advanced User Authentication and Response. *IFIP TC11 17th International Conference on Information Security: Visions and Perspectives* (pp. 215-226).

Elron Sofware's Internet Manager. http://www.lansafe.com/elron.html

Gaines, R., Lisowski, W., Press, S., Shapiro, N. (1980). *Authentication by Keystroke Timing: Some Preliminary Results.* Rand Report R-256-NSF. Rand Corporation.

Guneti D., & Picardi, C. (2005). Keystroke Analysis of Free Text. *ACM Transactions on Information and System Security,* 8(3), 312-347.

Keeney, M., Cappelli, D., Kowalski, E., Moore, A., Shimeall, T., & Rogers, S (2005, May). *Insider Threat Study: Computer System Sabotage in Critical Infrastructure Sectors.* U.S. Secret Service and CERT Coordination Center/SEI (Tech. report)

Legget, J, Williams, G. (1991). Dynamic Identity Verification via Keystroke Characteristics. *International Journal on Man-Machine. Studies, 35*, 859-870.

Levitt H. (2004, October). *Employee Surveillance and Workplace Investigations.* Presented at "Demystifying Employee Privacy" Lang Michener Privacy Law Seminar, Toronto, Ontario, Canada.

Matyas, V. Jr., Riha, Z., (2003). Toward Reliable User Authentication through

Biometrics. *IEEE Security & Privacy Magazine, 1*(3), 45-49.

Monrose, F., & Rubin, A. (1997). Authentication Via Keystroke Dynamics. *Proceedings of Fourth ACM Conference on Computer and Communications Security* (pp. 48-56).

Pearsall, J., & Trumble, B. (Eds), (2001). *The Oxford English Reference Dictionary.* Oxford University Press, Great Clarendon Street, Oxford oX2 6DP.

PIPEDA. http://www.privcom.gc.ca/legislation/02_06_01_01_e.asp

Randazzo, M. R., Cappelli, D., Keeney, M., Moore, A., & Kowalski, E. (2004, August)). *Insider Threat Study: Illicit Cyber Activity in the Banking and Finance Sector.* U.S. Secret Service and CERT Coordination Center/SEI (Tech. Report).

Sebek. http://www.honeynet.org/tools/sebek/

United States General Accounting Office (GAO) (2002). *Employee Privacy: Computer-Use Monitoring Practices and Policies of Selected Companies*. Report to the Ranking Minority

Member, Subcommittee on 21st Century Competitiveness, Committee on Education and the Workforce, House of Representatives (No. GAO-02-717).

Vontu Data Loss Prevention Software. http//www.vontu.com

Wakefield, R. L. Employee Monitoring and Surveillance—The Growing Trend (2004). *Information Systems Control Journal, 1*.

Yanushkevich, S. N., Stoica, A., Shmerko, V. P., & Popel, D. V. (2005). *Biometric Inverse Problems*. Taylor & Francis: CRC Press.

Zimmerman, E. (2002). HR Must Know When Employee Surveillance Crosses the Line. *Workforce*. pp 38-45.

KEY TERMS

Biometric Technologies: systems which process and analyze biological or behavioral characteristics of a human in order to recognize or verify user's identity.

Behavioral Biometrics: a set of features acquired over time which describes the human behavior in performing specific category of actions.

Employee Surveillance Technologies: methods and procedures used to monitor and record data collected from employees at work, and detect any misuse of resources.

Free Text Detection of Keystrokes: the process of measuring keystroke dynamics of a stream of previously undetermined keystroke actions.

Keystroke Dynamics: a behavioral biometric which describes the user typing rhythm while using a computer keyboard.

Human-Computer Interaction (HCI): is the study of human behavior when interacting with a computer. Such study can lead to computer UI enhancement for better user experience.

Insider Threat: a potential risk caused by a trusted individual misusing the given privileges to compromise system security.

ENDNOTE

1 See http://www.isot.ece.uvic.ca/projects/biotracker for more about BIOTRACKER.

Chapter IV
E-Risk Insurance Product Design:
A Copula Based Bayesian Belief Network Model

Arunabha Mukhopadhyay
Indian Institute of Management Lucknow, India

Samir Chatterjee
Claremont Graduate University, India

Debashis Saha
Indian Institute of Management Calcutta, India

Ambuj Mahanti
Indian Institute of Management Calcutta, India

Samir K. Sadhukhan
Indian Institute of Management Calcutta, India

ABSTRACT

An online business organization spends millions of dollars on firewalls, anti-virus, intrusion detection systems, digital signature, and encryption, to ensure minimal security breach. Nonetheless, a new virus or a clever hacker can easily compromise these deterrents, resulting in losses to the tune of millions of dollars annually. To minimize the financial loss, we propose that online businesses should invest in e-risk insurance products as a complementary alternative, above the network security appliances. In this work, we develop a Copula aided Bayesian Belief Network (CBBN) model, to assist insurance companies to design e-insurance products. The CBBN model does an e-vulnerability assessment (e-VA) and e-risk quantification (e-RQ). We first draw a casual diagram (BBN) stating the probable reason for security failure in an organization. We assume the marginal distributions for each of the nodes of the diagram. Using the CBBN model we compute the joint probability of the constituent nodes of the BBN. Next the conditional probability of each of the occurrences of the malicious event is arrived at. We then assume a loss distribution, and using the principles of collective risk modeling, we arrive at the expected severity of the attack. The e-risk insurance companies compute the premium, by charging an extra (i.e., overloading and contingency loading), over the expected severity of attack.

INTRODUCTION

E-risk is defined as the possibility of a malicious electronic event, whose occurrence causes loss to e-business. These consists of (i) comprise of network security components (such as firewall, proxy servers, anti virus), (ii) the compromise of the organization web server, and incorrect or indecent material posted on the web site (commonly called graffiti), (iii) service providers (i.e., Application Service Provider (ASP) or Internet Service Provider (ISP)) failing, (iv) identity theft (i.e., confidential customer information is hacked from an organizational database; example, pin numbers of credit cards from a bank), (v) attacks by disgruntled employees, (vi) cyber-extortion ,(vii) Denial of Service (DoS) by making malicious calls to the router, (viii) attack by wireless devices (such as PDAs, mobile phones etc). CSI/FBI 2004 report (Gordon, Loeb, Lucyshyn & Richardson, 2004) states that the most vital e-risk in USA is virus attack (loss of $55 Million). It is followed by DoS attack (loss of $26 Million), and theft of proprietary information (loss of $11 Million).

Organizations spend millions annually for deployment of sophisticated technical defenses (such as encryption, access control and firewalls) (Gordon, & Loeb, 2002) and intrusion detection systems to guard against malicious attacks. CSI/FBI report (Gordon et al., 2004) states most organizations in USA have deterrents such as (i) antivirus software (99%), (ii) firewalls (98%), (iii) proxy servers (71%), and (iv) intrusion detection systems (68%). Yet security breaches are very common.

Anderson (2001) opines that the chance of a clever hacker breaking into the system is much higher than the chance that the CTO would detect it. This can be sustained with the following example. Assume there are n vulnerabilities in an organizational network. In a given period of time, the hacker needs to find only one as opposed to the CTO who has to be aware of all the n vulnerabilities to protect the system from malicious attacks. Thus, it is a win–win situation always for the intruder. Schneier (2001) notes, that a new virus can easily comprise the perimeter security devices, as there is no signature available in the anti-virus engine to track it down. The CSI/FBI report (Gordon et al., 2004) corroborates this fact, as loss due to virus attack in USA alone was $55 Million in 2004.

To supplement the existing security measures and to reduce the monetary loss, an effective alternative mechanism is insuring (Gordon, Loeb, & Sohail, 2003; Grzebiel, 2002; Mukhopadhay, Chatterjee, Saha, Mohanti 2005a; Mukhopadhyay, Chatterjee, Saha, Mohanti, Chakrabarti and Podder, 2005b, 2005c; Mukhopadhyay, Chatterjee, Saha, Mohanti, and Sadhukhan,2006 ; Mukhopadhyay 2007, Mukhopadhay, Chatterjee, Saha, Mohanti, Roy and Sadhukhan,2007a; Mukhopadhay, Chakrabari Saha, Mohanti 2007b) against these risks. This would help reduce the financial burden on the organizations, as the insurance company would indemnify the loss. In effect, the organizations risk is being passed on to another party at the cost of a premium. This reduces the companies concern about "self insuring" (i.e., keeping aside huge amount for contingency purposes). This, in turn, is a good corporate strategy, as huge amounts are not locked away for contingency provisions and security breaches.

In this work we develop a Copula aided Bayesian Belief Network (CBBN) model, to assist insurance companies to design e-insurance products (Mukhopadhyay 2007, Mukhopadhay et al., 2005a). The CBBN model does an e-vulnerability assessment (e-VA) and e-risk quantification (e-RQ). We first draw a casual diagram (using Bayesian Belief Networks (BBN)) stating the probable reasons for security failure in an organization. We assume the marginal distributions for each of the nodes of the diagram and simulate various security breach scenarios and noted the probabilities (i.e., loss frequency) at each of the causal node(s). The marginal probability data can be obtained from the log files of organizational computer network. Using the CBBN model we compute the joint probability of the constituent nodes of the BBN. Next the conditional probability of each of the occurrences of the malicious event is arrived at. We then assume a loss distribution, and using the principles of collective risk modeling, we arrive at the expected severity of the attack. For each of the nodes the loss distribution is assumed to be binomial (i.e., Binomial (1000, 0.2)).The e-risk insurance companies compute the premium, by charging an extra (i.e., overloading and contingency loading), over the expected severity of attack. Expected severity (or risk premium) is defined as the product of loss frequency and loss amount distributions. Here we have assumed that the expense loading to be 10% of the risk premium and contingency loading as 10% of standard deviation respectively.

This is in contrast to Gordon's (2002) work, which is focused on finding out an optimal investment on security apparatus to reduce security breaches. Our paper supplements Gordon's (2003) work by assessing and quantifying e-risk, which he considers, as the most important component of cyber-risk management by e-business organizations.

E-RISK

ATM and Internet banking have fast evolved as the backbone of the banking system. A customer transaction through a bank's window costs about $1USD in the USA, but an online transaction cost just $0.02 USD (Kellermann, 2002). It improves the bottom line for the bank and also increases customer satisfaction. The retail business and the services sector today primarily use the Internet for their day to day operations. A study by Forester Research (Johnson et al., 2006) states that online retail sales are expected to grow to $329 Billion in 2010, from $172 billion in 2005, registering a 14% compound annual growth rate (CAGR) for the next five years. The success of an automated supply chain management or a virtual online organization (such as Amazon.com, e-bay) is solely dependent on the Internet/network channels. But, the communication channel or the Internet till date is prone to virus attacks, snooping, sniffing and DoS by malicious intruders. A hacker or a virus attack can affect the top line of an organization and in the long run have affects on the bottom line too. Three approaches for quantifying operational risk are listed in Table 1 (Smithson, & Paul, 2004).

The ***process approach*** focuses on the modeling the chain of activities that comprise an operation or transaction and finding out the exact risk for each process. The ***factor approach*** aims to determine a mathematical equation that relates the level of operational risk for institution or business or process to a set of factors as follows:

$$\text{Operational risk} = a_0 + \sum_{i=1}^{n} a_i * \text{factor}_i \qquad (1)$$

Methods of regression and discriminant analysis are used to determine the values of a_i. The ***actuarial approach*** aims to identify the loss frequency and the loss amounts distribution associated with an event using past data.

Table 1. Methods for operational risk quantification

Process approach	Factor approach	Actuarial approach
Causal	Risk Indicators	Empirical Loss distributions
Bayesian belief networks		
Fuzzy logic	Capital Asset pricing Model (CAPM)	Explicit distributions parameterized using historical data.
Statistical quality control and reliability analysis		
Connectivity	Predictive models	Extreme Value theory
System dynamics		

In this work, we have used a copula aided Bayesian Belief Networks (CBBN) to model e-risk for online organizations. We choose the process approach, as it is easy to visualize the chain of activities that mostly lead to a security failure, based on past data and expert opinion. Further BBN, has the ability to train itself based on observed data, supplied to it, and identify conclusively the factors that are responsible for a security breach. Modeling e-risk through, the factor approach is difficult, as identifying the causal factors isn't easy. While actuarial approach is constrained by availability of data points, in case of e-risk modeling.

BAYESIAN BELIEF NETWORKS AND COPULA

Bayesian belief network (BBN) (Jensen, 2001) is a graphical relationship between causal variables. BBNs enable reasoning under uncertainty and combine the advantages of an intuitive visual representation with a sound mathematical basis of Bayesian probability. A BBN graph is made up of nodes and arcs. Nodes are random variables and represent an uncertain event. The arcs indicate causal relationship between the variables. Each node has a probability table associated with it. The root node(s) have only marginal probability associated with it, while the child nodes have conditional probabilities tables associated with it. Initially, each of the nodes is populated using a belief (i.e., either an expert view or results from empirical study). If an event in the BBN graph is observed with certainty, it causes each of the probabilities at the nodes to be recalculated, thereby providing a better understanding of the process being modeled. The full joint probability is joint distribution over all the values in the domain and is computed as a product of conditional probabilities for every node-parent combination as follows in equation (2):

$$P(X_1,X_2.........X_n)=\prod_i (X_i \mid Parents(X_i)) \qquad (2)$$

For example, say we have a BBN as shown in Figure 1.

The joint probability of all the nodes is as follows:

$$P\,(D,\,N,\,F,\,T)=P\,(D)*P\,(N|D)*P\,(F|D)*P\,(T|F,\,N) \qquad (3)$$

The essence of the copula approach (Clemen & Reilly, 1999) is that a joint distribution of random variables can be expressed as a function of marginal distributions. This is explained by Sklar's Theorem ((Clemen et al., 1999) The theorem states that given a joint cumulative distribution $F(x_1,x_2,$ $............,x_n)$ for random variables X_1, X_2, ..., X_n with marginal cumulative distribution functions (CDFs) $F_1(x_1),F_2(x_2),.........,F_n(x_n)$, F can be

Figure 1. A BBN

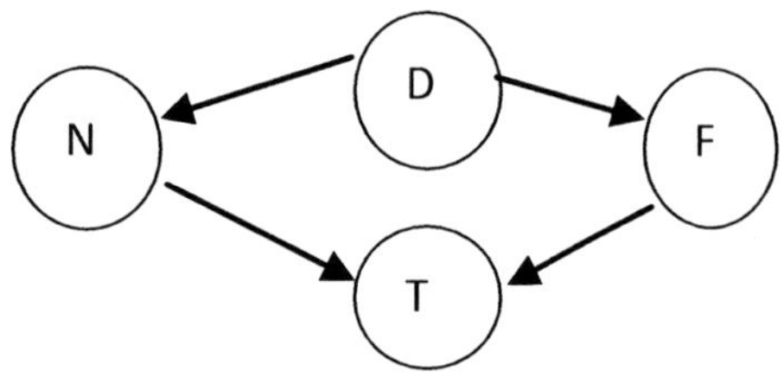

Note: D=Daily, N=Nature of monitoring, F=Frequency of update, T=Techno Policy Failure.

written as a function of marginals:

$$F(x_1, x_2, \ldots\ldots\ldots\ldots, x_n) = C[F_1(x_1), F_2(x_2), \ldots, F_n(x_n)] \quad (4)$$

where $C(u_1, u_2 \ldots u_n)$ is a joint distribution function with uniform marginals. Moreover, if each F_i is continuous, then C is unique, and if each F_i is discrete, then C is unique on the Ran (F_1) X Ran(F_2) .... X Ran(F_n), where Ran(F_i) is the range of F_i. The function C is called a copula.

Given that F_i and C are differentiable, the joint density $f(x_1, x_2, \ldots\ldots, x_n)$ can be written as

$$f(x_1, x_2, \ldots\ldots x_n) = f_1(x_1) \text{ X } \ldots\ldots\ldots \; f_1(x_1) \text{ X } (C(F_1(x_1), F_2(x_2), \ldots\ldots\ldots\ldots\ldots\ldots F_n(x_n)] \quad (5)$$

E-VULNERABILITY ANALYSIS (E-VA)

Figure 2 is the directed acyclic graph (DAG) representing the causes of security breach in an organization. The DAG consists of 12 nodes. We assume that a security failure can occur primarily due to (i) technology failure or (ii) improper non-technology policy implementation. Technology failure occurs if any of these are compromised namely, (i) IDS, (ii) the proxy server, (iii) the firewall, (iv) anti-virus (v) radius authentication server. We ascribe to the fact that the compromise of the network security elements is primarily due to improper technology policy implementation. For example, the improper sequence of ports be-

Figure 2. A BBN of security failure

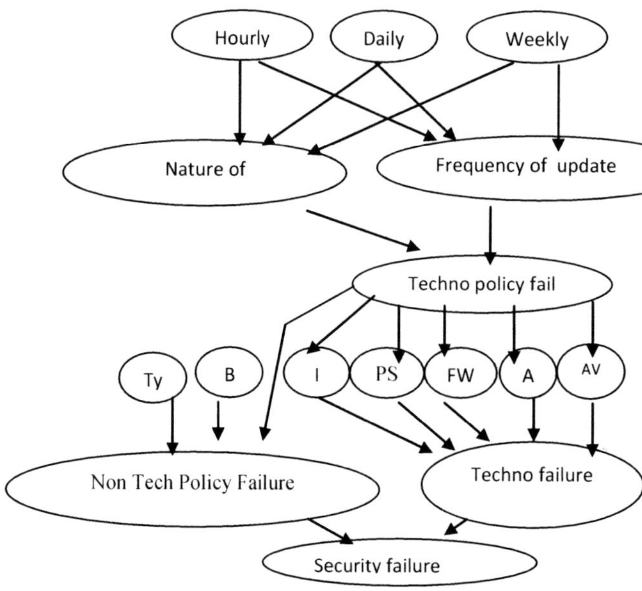

Ty=Type,
B=Budget availability,
I=IDS compromised,
PS=Proxy-Server compromised,
FW=Firewall compromised,
A=Authentication compromised,
AV= Anti-Virus failure.

ing left open in a firewall. The effectiveness of a techno-policy implemented on security appliances can be enhanced based on the (i) frequency of update and (ii) nature of monitoring. This in turn calls for review or monitoring of the log files of the security appliances on an hourly, daily or weekly basis. Non-technology policy issues comprise of (i) availability of budget and (ii) type of policy formulation (i.e. centralized or local). In case of a very centralized decision making process, approvals for implementing security technologies and policies would even need prior approval from higher authorities. For localized e-disaster mitigation at the branch level, the top management intervention is needed. For example, let's assume in a centralized organizational structure, the branch office needs prior approval from the top management for the purchase of an anti-virus engine. Then, the branch office then acts as the weakest link to the overall organizational security and makes it vulnerable for attacks.

For this study, we have kept ourselves restricted to 4 nodes only (techno policy failure, FW, V and Techno failure). Each node has 7 states each (very low, low, low- medium, medium, high- medium, high, very high). The inputs to CCBN model are (i) simulated marginal probability for each of these 4 nodes, using a uniform distribution function, (ii) correlation (R) between the nodes, and (iii) type of copula. We made the following assumptions in this study (i) each of the nodes has normal distribution, (ii) R matrix is symmetrical and diagonals all having ones, and (iii) normal copula. Then using CCBN model we arrived at the joint distribution of the 4 nodes. The output of the model is a joint distribution table comprising of the 4 nodes. From which we generated the conditional distribution for each of the nodes of the DAG. We next provided evidence to the CCBN model and from it inferred the actual vulnerable points in the system. For this study we assumed that we observed moderate frequency of techno-failures. We used our CCBN model to investigate whether the (i) firewall or (ii) antivirus failure was the prime cause of it, in our system. From the simulated data we got the following two outcomes:

(a) *P (Firewall failure=moderate| Techno failure =moderate) =0.49*
(b) *P (Anti-Virus failure=moderate | Techno failure =moderate) =0.38*

From this investigation, it is clear that the policies set in the firewall are enhancing the vulnerabilities in the system. Similarly, we can find out the causal effect for any of the 12 nodes present in Figure 2. Thus BBN provides an effective mechanism for vulnerability analysis.

E-RISK QUANTIFICATION (E-RQ)

We suggest that insurance company use Collective Risk Model (Hossack & Pollard, 1983) for e-RQ. In this study, we assume that the loss frequency (N) and loss amount(X) of an e-risk are both stochastic variables. E (N) denotes the expectation of the loss frequency distribution and E(X) is the expectation of the loss amount distribution. The expected loss or claim severity E (S_N) is the product of claim size and claim amount. The expected loss or claim severity (i.e., E (S_N)) and its variance (i.e., Var (S_N)) are obtained using equation (6).

$$E(S_N)=E(N)*E(X)$$
$$Var(S_N)=E(N)*Var(X)+\{E(X)\}^2*Var(N) \qquad (6)$$

The CBBN model provides us the claim frequency (E (N)). We assume all the nodes have a similar loss amount (E (X). For this study we assume the loss to be Binomial (1000, 0.2).So, the mean (E (X)) of 200 and variance (V (X)) 160. We now compute the e-RQ for our study.

Case I: P (Firewall failure=very high| Techno failure =very high) =0.49

Mean = E (S) =expected loss
= 200*8
=1600.
Variance = Var (S) = 200*8
+ $(2)^2$*160=81,280.

Case II: P (Anti-Virus failure=very high | Techno failure =T). =0.38

Mean = E (S) =expected loss
= 200*9=1800.
Variance = Var (S) =200* 8
+ $(2)^2$*160=81,440

PREMIUM COMPUTATION

The premium for e-risk insurance is arrived at by using equation (7):

$$Premium= (1+q)* E(S_N)+ k* \sqrt{Var(S_N)} \quad (7)$$

where q is the loading factor (profit and overhead charges) and k is the contingency loading. Overhead charges include the administrative and operational cost needed to run an e-risk insurance business. It also factors into account the profit component needed by the e-risk insurance company. Contingency loading implies the provision made by e-risk insurance companies to cope with any sudden variation of the e-risk from its mean. This acts as a cushion for the e-risk insurance companies. It ensures that the e-risk insurance company does not face bankruptcy, due to a sudden rise in claim amount due to an e-disaster. We assume an expense loading of 10% of the risk premium and a contingency loading, of 10% of standard deviation, for premium calculation.

The premium the insurance company would charge the e-business organization for insuring its firewall and anti-virus failure are computed using equation (7). The premium works out to be as follows:

Case I: P (Firewall failure=very high| Techno failure =very high) =0.49

Premium= $(1+0.10)* 1600+ 0.10*√81,280
= $ 9,888.

Case II: P (Anti-Virus failure=very high | Techno failure =T) =0.38

Premium = $(1+0.10)* 1800+ 0.10*√81,440
= $ 10,124.

CONCLUSION

The study was aimed to identify the e-vulnerability (e-VA) of online business and to quantify the associated e-risk (e-RQ). We developed a CBBN model for this purpose. The inputs were simulated marginal distributions at each of the nodes. Then using the CCBN model we calculated the joint distribution of the entire DAG. Subsequently we arrived at the conditional distribution for each of the nodes. The CBBN provides us with the frequency of loss for each of the nodes, based on our observation. Using collective risk model we arrived at the expected loss. Finally, we also arrived at the gross premium the e-insurance products.

ACKNOWLEDGMENT

We would like to thank Mr. A.K Podder, Regional Manager (Actuary), LIC, India for his help to us.

REFERENCES

Anderson, R. (2001). Why information security is hard—An economic perspective. In *Proceedings of 17th Annual Computer Security Applications Conference (ACSAC)* (New Orleans).

Burner, E. R. (2003). Forrester Sees Strong Ecommerce Growth Continuing. Forrestor Web site.

Clemen, T. R., & Reilly, T. (1999). Correlations and Copulas for decision and risk Analysis. *Management Science*, 45(2), 208-224.

Jensen, F. V. (2001). *Bayesian Networks and Decision Diagrams*, Springer.

Johnson, C. A., & Tesch, B. (2006). US E-Commerce: 2005 To 2010: A Five-Year Forecast and Analysis of US Online Retail Sales. Forrestor Web site.

Gordon, A. L., & Loeb, P. M. The economics of information security investment. (2002). *ACM Trans on Inf Sys Sec*, *5*(4), 438-457.

Gordon, A. L., Loeb, P. M., & Sohai, I. T. (2003). A framework for using insurance for cyber-risk management. *Communications of the ACM, 46*(3).

Gordon, A. L., Loeb, P. M., Lucyshyn, W., & Richardson, R. (2004). CSI/FBI Computer Crime and Security Survey, GoCSI.com.

Hossack, B. I., Pollard, J., & Zehnwirth, B. (1983). *Introduction to Statistics with applications to general insurance*, Cambridge University Press.

Kellermann, T. (2002). Mobile risk management: E-Finance in the Wireless Environment. World Bank.

Mukhopadhyay, A., Chatterjee, S., Saha, D., Mahanti, A., Chakrabarti, B. B., & Podder, K. A. (2005a). Security breach losses in e-commerce through Insurance. *Proceedings of 4th Security Conference*, Las Vegas, Nevada.

Mukhopadhyay, A., Chatterjee, S., Saha, D., Mahanti, A., and Podder, K. A. (2005b). E-Risk: A case for insurance. *Proceedings of the Conference on Information Systems and Technology*, New Delhi, India.

Mukhopadhyay, A., Saha, D., Mahanti, A., & Podder, K. A. (2005c). Insurance for cyber-risk: A Utility Model. *Decision, 32*(1), 153-170.

Mukhopadhyay, A., Chatterjee, S., Saha, D, Mahanti, A., and Sadhukhan, K. S. (2006). *E-Risk Management with Insurance: A framework using Copula aided Bayesian Belief Networks. Proceedings of the 39th Hawaii International Conference on System Sciences,* Hawaii, USA.

Mukhopadhyay, A., Chatterjee, S., Saha, D., Mahanti, A., Roy, R., & Sadhukhan S. K. (2007). Insuring big losses due to security breaches through insurance: A business model. *Proceedings of the 40th Hawaii International Conference on System Sciences,* Hawaii, USA.

Mukhopadhyay, A., Chakrabarti, B. B., Saha, D., & Mahanti, A. (2007a). E-Risk management through self-insurance: An option model. *Proceedings of the 40th Hawaii International Conference on System Sciences* , Hawaii, USA.

Mukhopadhyay, A. (2007b). A novel framework for mitigating e-risk through insurance. *Phd Thesis*, Indian Institute of Management Calcutta.

Schneier, B. (2000). *Secrets and Lies: Digital security in a Networked World*: John Wiley & Sons.

Grzebiela, T. (2002). Insurability of Electronic Commerce Risks, *Proceedings of the 35th Hawaii International Conference on System Sciences,* Hawaii, USA.

Smithson, C., & Song, P. (2004). Quantifying Operational Risk, www.risk.net.

KEY TERMS

Actuarial Approach: Identifies the loss frequency and the loss amounts distribution using past data.

Bayesian Belief Network (BBN): A graphical relationship between causal variables. BBNs enable reasoning under uncertainty and combine the advantages of an intuitive visual representation with a sound mathematical basis of Bayesian probability.

BBN Graph: It is made up of nodes and arcs. Nodes are random variables. The arcs indicate causal relationship between the variables. Each node has a probability table associated with it. The root node(s) have only marginal probability associated with it, while the child nodes have conditional probabilities tables associated with it.

Collective Risk Model: It assumes that the loss frequency and loss amount of an e-risk are both stochastic variables. The expected loss or claim severity is the product of claim size and claim amount.

Copula: Joint distribution of random variables can be expressed as a function of marginal distributions. It also takes into account correlation amongst the marginal distributions.

E-Risk: Defined as the possibility of a malicious electronic event, whose occurrence causes loss to e-business. These consists of (i) comprise of perimeter network security components, (ii) graffiti, (iii) Application Service Provider or Internet Service Provider failing, (iv) identity theft, (v) attacks by disgruntled employees, (vi) cyber-extortion ,(vii) Denial of Service, (viii) attack by wireless devices.

Factor Approach: Aims to determine a mathematical equation that relates the level of operational risk for institution or business or process to a set of factors.

Operational Risk: It arises due to failure of process, people, systems or external events. Basel II mandates that operational risk is quantified and a capital allocation done for it.

Premium: It is the product of the expected loss times the loading factor (i.e.,, profit and overhead charges) plus contingency loading times the variance of the loss.

Process Approach: It models chain of activities that comprise an operation or transaction and finding out the exact risk for each process.

Chapter V
E-Commerce Security and Honesty-Credit

Guoling Lao
Shanghai University of Finance & Economics, China

Liping Wang
Shanghai University of Finance & Economics, China

ABSTRACT

E-commerce mode aggravates information asymmetry so that honesty-credit problems become more serious. This chapter discusses the honesty-credit issue and honesty-credit system construction in e-commerce. It argues that the honesty-credit issue belongs to e-commerce security problems to some extent since it also destroys information integrity, confidentiality, and availability. The study of honesty-credit issue in e-commerce will help to promote social culture development as well as improve e-commerce security. Basing on analysis of three game models, the article suggests the construction of social honesty-credit system mainly include four aspects: cultivate citizens' sense of honesty-credit, strengthen legislation, build mechanism of third-party authentication and regulate third-party service industry. At the end of the chapter, the case of Shanghai honesty-credit system construction of is introduced to describe China honesty-credit status.

INTRODUCTION

With the trend of globalization and rapid growth of e-commerce, the credit crisis in e-commerce has quietly hit. As e-commerce belongs to a kind of virtual and non-contact economy, the mode of information communication between the trade parties becomes the major difference from the traditional ecommerce. The information communication in traditional business is face-to-face or at least can be perceived, such as voice and documents, while information communication in e-commerce can be realized only through electronic information, resulting in serious information asymmetry. Such way of information communication provides circumstances for the possible default and decrease the expectation of trust between trade parties engaged in commercial activities. In recent years, security risks, particularly credit risk, false trading, counterfeiting, Internet theft and other illegal behaviors occur frequently. The security problems triggered by the lack of honesty-credit greatly constrains the development of e-commerce. Compared with the traditional business, e-commerce needs a higher degree of Honesty-credit to maintain the normal transactions.

Moreover, the cost of e-commerce transactions is also raised virtually as the honesty-credit is not effectively protected. In order to prevent risks and improve transaction security, enterprises and customers have to make confirmation through traditional means, such as telephone, fax, and even face-to-face meeting. For example, in 2000, in order to solve the distrust between bargainers, eBay China launched a program called "free communication site". Customers can freely use the shooting equipments and other tools provided by eBay in the designated location to confirm the quality of products. This approach seems back to the prototype of C2C – offline flea market. Whereas the offline transactions only need face-to-face transactions, when transferred to the Internet, there needs more procedures of registration and placing order (Wang and Shen, 2002). It is obvious that the advantages of e-commerce are dying away because of the honesty-credit problem.

E-commerce as a business model entirely dependent on the virtual network has indeed brought great convenience, but the prerequisite to realize this benefit is that parties engaged in the transaction must maintain honesty-credit. No honesty-credit, e-commerce will be impossible. So it is of great importance and significance to study the reasons of absence of honesty-credit and analyze how to strengthen construction of honesty-credit system to protect the security and authenticity in e-commerce transactions.

The article studies the current status of e-commerce security and honesty-credit in China, and tries to provide useful suggestions about how to promote the integration of China's e-commerce honesty-credit system with the international practice and to guarantee the development of e-commerce.

BACKGROUND

Definition of Honest-Credit

The so-called honesty-credit, defined from the literal interpretation is "honest and trustworthy". Narrow definition for the honesty-credit is the definition composition of honesty and credit, which can be interpreted as honesty and compliance with the commitments. Generalized definition of honesty-credit involves almost all of contents of "honesty" and "credit", giving a broader and more comprehensive content to honesty-credit from the inner moral virtues to the outer behaviors of the entity. In e-commerce, honesty-credit mechanism includes honest behavior and credit system two aspects, among which, honest behaviors promise the basis and premise for various economic activities to carry out smoothly and orderly (Yu et al, 2006).

Honesty-credit as a virtue has a long history in China. The ancient people think honesty-credit is an important character for man to be a man. The Analects of Confucius and Mean as well as other famous works all refer to the concept and some also give explanations and clarifications, thinking man should consciously accept this moral constraint and try best to adhere to ethics. Honesty-credit, as a favorable moral atmosphere, has close relationship with the enterprise's commercial reputation and value as well as personal values and moral cultivation in modern society. Which reflected to the market environment is orderly, transparent and reliable transaction relationship among trade parties. Here the essential meaning of honesty-credit contains sincerity, honesty, honoring commitments and no fraud.

Modern market economy is a credit economy, in which successful transactions depend on the debt moratorium agreement between traders, so by this means honesty-credit becomes the basic rule in market economy. Once lack honesty-credit, the transaction chain will be suspended and even the overall economic development may be affected. In the market economy, the analysis about honesty-credit is clearly divided into two phases: first is the moral level, including honesty, trust, reliability, integrity (Bloch, 2005), which mainly emphasize dealers' own moral qualities; second is the credit level, which is relative to contract, and bases on the whole package of laws, regulations, rules and systems designed to manage credit relationship between market participants and on the effective form of credit market (Liao & Zhao, 2004). There is a clear boundary between these two levels. However in China practice the difference has been confused. Moral dimension of the concept "honesty" wrongly replace the economic dimension meaning of "credit". The enterprise's aim of credit management is distorted to be awakened moral consciousness. And influenced by this incorrect thought, the credit management in some enterprises becomes the evidence of good company image and degrades to the propaganda tool.

Study of Honest-Credit

The studies about honesty-credit cover the scopes of system, law, philosophy and so on.

Gao (2006) states that honesty-credit involves but does not limit to the individual virtue and it has profound social background and cause of formation. Tian (2007), Xia and Liu (2006) discuss honesty-credit problems in China and gives some advice. Cheng (2003) gives a description about the meaning of honesty-credit from the aspect of law. He believes that honest and kindly atmosphere can provide contracting parties with greater security and more flexible transaction mode. Traditional legal constraints can partly solve this problem but fail to reduce the risk of speculation and keep entities maintain the optimistic attitudes to reasonable interest. The principle of honesty-credit minimizes risk of speculation, establishes good relationship of mutual trust, and guarantees the achievement of maximum benefits for the contracting parties. The introduction of the principle of honesty-credit precisely embodies the spirit of party autonomy and promotes the commercial development.

The trust relationship between counterparties is prerequisite for the transactions to proceed smoothly. According to the structure, trust can be categorized as personal trust and system trust (Zheng, 2001). Personal trust refers the specific trust of some person, such as relatives, natives. Along with the expansion of transaction radius and individual flows, the costs of confidence identification and monitor rise sharply so that it must turn to system trust. System trust means the confidence to a system composed of anonyms. Generally, the social trust system corresponding to personal trust belongs to relation-based governance, while the legal structure based on system trust is a kind of rule-based governance (Li, 1999). The emergence of the Internet has led to time and space separation as well as continuous growth of anonymous and virtual community, which accelerated the transformation from the "society of acquaintance" to a "society of stranger". Mechanism of system trust becomes more and more important while the function of personal trust diminishes gradually.

Li and Li (2005) analyze the honesty-credit problem using game theory. In their opinions, the credit scope in honesty-credit is a kind of information factor; credit transactions attach more importance to information acquirement as well as analysis and understanding of information to facilitate transaction parties to make judgement. They also consider that credit will cut down transaction cost because honesty-credit can reduce the "contracting cost" and "compliance cost" caused by "uncertainty". Lu (2007) analyzes how to establish fabricated community to raise trust in e-commerce using game theory.

As the arrival of the era of e-commerce, socio-economic environment, transaction mode, and the people's behaviors and thought all change a lot compared with the past. In the virtual economic conditions, it will help to reduce transaction costs, lower transaction risks and improve economic efficiency if all parties could keep honest and credible manners. Therefore, it is of great significance to study how to establish a social credit system and promote construction of social honesty-credit and ethics in e-commerce. And this will greatly contribute to the foundation of new economic order as well as social relationships.

Honest-Credit and E-Commerce Security

E-commerce security problems induced by Lack of honesty-credit mainly refer that dealers suffer economic loss because of the dishonesty of counterparties. Generally speaking, information authenticity, credit problems, and other violations of law (such as fraud and trafficking in contraband, etc.), should be all included in the area of e-commerce security. Therefore, the e-commerce honesty-credit problems indeed belong to e-commerce security problems caused by the lack of honesty-credit, since these problems ultimately affect the financial information and asset security in e-commerce transactions, and have no essential difference with definition of e-commerce security only except that main factors turn from network technology to the issue of honesty-credit.

Problems of Current E-Commerce Security Risk Management Strategy

E-commerce Security Problems Brought by Lack of Honesty-Credit

E-commerce transactions are conducted by support of the network virtual platform. Parties in the transactions may never meet each other. So there are less practical constraints, information asymmetry becomes more serious, network fraud problems arise frequently, and Internet users in e-commerce transactions lack of sense of safety. Problems led by of dishonesty have become the crucial obstacle and bottleneck to the development of e-commerce.

According to the data released by the China Consumer Association, from 2003 to 2005, among the complaints with fastest growth in the services category, Internet service complaints are always keeping the first place. The numbers of complaints are shown in Figure 1. And in first half year of 2006, volume of complaints compared with the same period of last year has increased 53.9%, still ranking top of the list. The complaints concentrate mainly on network security and online shopping. Since the current laws do not explicitly stipulate online trading platform to examine status of

Figure 1. Numbers of complaints about China's Internet services (Data source: according to historical statistic data provide by China Consumer Association)

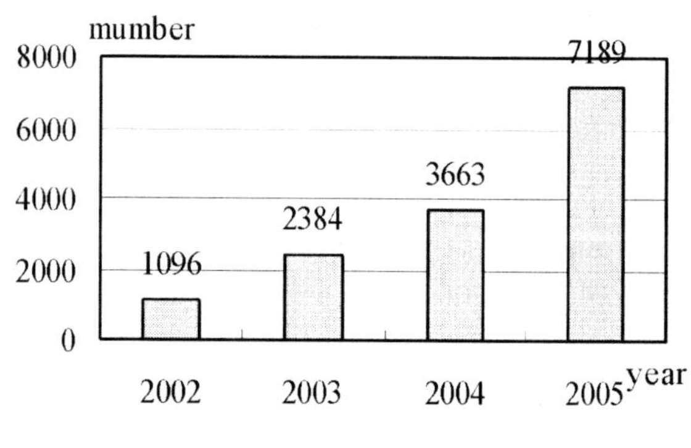

sellers and keep transaction records, it is very difficult for consumers to safeguard their rights in the event of disputes.

In view of this situation, China Electronic Commerce Trust evaluation Center (EC Trust China) and the Electronic Center of Beijing Normal University carried out a survey about status of China e-commerce honesty-credit in 2006 and 41,500 valid questionnaires are collected. The results showed that worries about e-commerce security occupy the mainstream. Survey results showed that 71.1% of respondents have doubt some websites' authenticity and legality; 62.1% claim that the personal information have been abused by websites; 56.4% have experienced problems of inauthentic information. The survey also contains the feedback of netizens about service problems. The result is in Figure 2. Survey results show that in the area of e-commerce in China, the seller's honesty-credit is still worrisome.

At the same time, in June 2006, the China E-commerce Association and other institutions jointly launched a series survey including the "Investigation on China's E-commerce Honesty-credit Situation", "Investigation on China's E-commerce Development and Application", "Investigation on Social Function and Impact of E-commerce in China", the main results are shown in Table 1.

According to the statistic data, it is evident that honesty-credit has become the general concern of both public and enterprises. If we say the results of first survey only state the anxiety and concern of buyers who in e-commerce transactions at a competitive disadvantageous position, then these data fully demonstrate in Chinese all groups engaged in e-commerce activities dissatisfy and worry about the current situation. According to the findings of the survey, although these participants realize the importance of credit rating, only a few will assess the credit after the completion of the transaction. This suggests that the public have no sense of participation in maintaining honesty-credit of e-commerce. If such situation continues, it will be difficult to establish a positive mechanism for honesty-credit evaluation, and may leave some bad business opportunity.

In summary, from these nationwide surveys, we can see the development of e-commerce has been confronted with serious challenges from lack of honesty-credit. Honesty has become most concerned issue of all parties in e-commerce. The honesty-credit atmosphere of e-commerce transaction has not yet taken shape. This constrains the e-commerce further healthy development.

Honesty-credit problems in e-commerce transaction can be summarized mainly as following categories.

Figure 2. Feedback to e-commerce service by China netizens

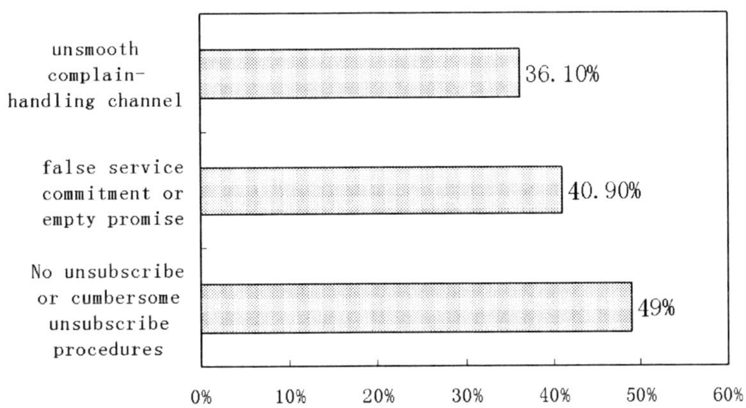

Table 1. Statistic result of China e-commerce honesty-credit status survey

Question	Enterprise (%)	Public (%)
Distrust e-commerce	36.3	13.3
The most worried is e-commerce honesty-credit problem	23.5	26.34
Check the seller's credit evaluation when conduct transaction	64.2	71.1
Assess seller's credit status timely after transaction	16.7	23.5

False Information Overflowing

Information publication through Internet has less constraint than through the traditional media. Because of virtual features of Internet, consumers have difficulty to find the disseminators when aware of the false information. Many websites and trading platforms constantly simplify the procedures for registration and verification in order to attract dealers. Thus it gives opportunities for some enterprises to fraud unscrupulously on the Internet. Some sellers exaggerate functions of commodities, including product quality, sounds, colors, shapes, and so on, to deceive the buyer to order, resulting in poor status of information authenticity and validity; others fabricate news, such as false sales list and so-called promotions to attract consumers so that expand their impacts and obtain economic benefits. If such situation continues, consumers would no longer trust information published online.

The "phishing" on the Internet is most popular in recent years as means of false information publication. Phishing tends to be more targeted and is clearly tied to make financial gains. According to the Symantec's survey, nine of the top ten brands phished are in the financial sector. There are two most typical kind of phishing. One is through e-mail to cheat user's account and password information; the other pretends to be the real bank website to intercept customer input of information. Recently, the Bank of China, Industrial and Commercial Bank of China as well as China UnionPay all suffered "cloned" websites.

Breach of Contract Occurring Frequently

Breach of contract referred here is a relatively broad concept, including not only the default that parties in transaction fail to fulfill their commitments but also non-compliance to provisions of contracts. And the contracts in e-commerce mainly take the electronic form.

In B2C and C2C, the most common ways of breach of contract include registration with untrue information, placing false orders and auction to manipulate transactions. The difficulty of identity authentication is the main reason. When transactions carried out, there still some other honesty-credit problems, for instance the delivery time and mode as well as after-sales services are not in accordance with the terms or online commitment. As commodities are usually distributed by a professional third party, it is very difficult to recognize responsibility when products are damaged or spoilt during delivery. Another familiar honesty-credit problem is delayed delivery. Sometimes it is because of the force majeure. But mostly the seller's weak awareness of honesty-credit is the key.

Payment Problems

As e-commerce transactions respect concept of "shopping the world at home", credit and payment problems become more important in e-commerce transactions. Traders must offer some credit for counterparties, otherwise the transaction will be forced to terminate and return to the traditional trading patterns. However, at present the area of e-commerce is full of frauds and compared to traditional transactions relative laws are insufficient, so customers do not want to provide account information to websites. Moreover, consumers in e-commerce generally distrust enterprise's security methods, so up to now enterprises engaged in the B2C e-commerce choose the more reliable way for customers, i.e. pay on delivery, to solve the mistrust between two sides.

Other Violations of the Laws and Regulations

Other violations of laws and regulations include website's (businessmen) violation of consumer privacy protection commitments such as selling personal information or disturbing consumers with junk mails; illegal tax evasion; violations of network "intellectual property", including violations of copyrights, domain names, trademarks, e-mail, etc.; and the sale of illegal goods as well as fake and shoddy commodities. Such behaviors not only harms the interests of consumers, but also violated the relevant laws and regulations.

Causes of Lack of Honesty-Credit in E-Commerce Transaction

In this section, we will discuss the causes of Honesty-credit lack in e-commerce transactions through classic game models.

E-Commerce Transactions Game Model

Basic one-off game model

The perfect information static game is the simplest method. Here we use the classic model of "Prisoner's Dilemma" to describe the basic game model to describe honesty-credit problem in e-commerce.

Not considering the supervision, there are only two agents in e-commerce transactions: buyer and seller. Both agents have limited rationality and make single simultaneous choice with perfect market information. Each agent has the choices of Honesty and Fraud (hereafter simplified as H and F). And we also suppose following conditions keep in the game model:

Ss= Sb = {H, F}, where Ss is the strategy set available to seller and Sb is buyer's set;

Us (H, H) =W, Us (H, F) =0, Us (F, H) =2W, Us (F, F) =0, and Ub (H, H) =W, Ub (H, F) =2W, Ub (F, H) =0, Ub (F, F) =0,

Where Ui (·, ·) is player i's payoff as a function of the strategies chosen by all players.

We need to explain the reason why Us (H, F) =0, Us (F, H) =2W. Because this is a one-off game and the cheater receives no penalty, the payoff of strategy of "fraud" will obviously exceed that of "honesty", we define the payoff of dishonest player

Table 2. Matrix form of the basic game

S	H	F
H	W, W	0, 2W
F	2W, 0	0, 0

as 2W. And since the player can end transactions once he finds the counterparty's dishonesty, we define the payoff of honest player not negative but 0. The game is described in Table 2.

Whether from the buyer's or the seller's point of view, "fraud" is always the strictly dominant strategy no matter what the other agent chooses. The pure strategy Nash equilibrium of e-commerce transactions will be (Fraud, Fraud), and both payoff is zero. That is, without outer supervision and credit information service, the rational buyer and seller will choose fraud to seek maximum benefits so that e-commerce transactions will not occur. This result is not economically effective and the strategy (Honesty, Honesty) should be more attractive. Thus we draw the conclusion that without supervision mechanism the one-off simultaneous-move game with perfect information between e-commerce traders will easily result in the "Prisoner's Dilemma" and come to an invalid equilibrium.

But in fact for a real dealer, he cannot achieve the maximum profit entirely only through one transaction and the long-term business is necessary. And when the precondition of "one-off" is abandoned, things may change.

Repeated Game Model

Based on the above analysis, we now suppose that both agents hope for long-term cooperation so the transaction is conducted more than once. Other assumptions are presented based on reality: if agent A selects Honesty strategy previously and the other agent B never chooses Fraud, then A will keep honesty sequentially; once B cheats, A will choose Fraud certainly so that transactions end. The payoff function and strategy sets of agents keep the same as above. Here another discount factor d $(0 \leq d \leq 1)$ is introduced to convert payoffs of each game to current value for the convenience of comparison. This variable contains not only the time value of money (discount rate) but probability of the game's termination. It can be regarded as an agent's patience. Closer to 1 is it, more patient the agent is. The factors influencing d are very complicated, including social culture, tradition, qualities of traders and so forth.

At the beginning, we suppose buyer select Honesty at the first time after seller keep honest, then according to sequential game theory, if buyer similarly chooses Honesty, the his payoff will be W and the transactions will go on. As long as both parties choose Honesty, they will gain W definitely each time and the transactions will continue infinitely. Thus the total payoff of seller (it holds for buyer too) will be:

$$U = W + \delta W + \delta^2 W + \delta^3 W + \ldots + \delta^n W,$$

Where $n \to \infty$, $U = W/(1-\delta)$.

If seller chooses Fraud after buyer selects Honesty strategy the first time, then buyer will stop trade immediately and seller's short-term payoff will be "$V = 2W$".

If $\delta \geq 1/2$, then $W/(1-\delta) \geq 2W$, that is, $U \geq V$. As a rational person, seller will not choose Fraud. The same analysis is also applicable to buyer.

Now we discuss the effects of parameters changes basing on this inequality. When other factors keep the same, the larger is the value of d, the greater the payoff of Honesty and the smaller the payoff of Fraud, the more possible agents will choose long-term partnership and keep honest. Conversely speaking, if participants in e-commerce lack of patience and do not expect stable cooperation relationship, or there no effective penalty to dishonesty, the honesty-credit problems will appear. Therefore some mechanisms should be introduced in e-commerce to increase the corresponding cost of fraud and encouragement to honesty as well as improve each party's confidence to honesty-credit.

Model with Reward and Penalty

In the above discussion, the participation of supervision is neglected, and parties in market choose their own strategy according to the principle of maximizing profit in the condition of a spontaneous credit mechanism. In order to simulate reality more accurately, we introduce the supervision mechanism in the above model. If one agent chooses Honesty and his strategy is discovered, his payoff will be W plus R as an reward; if one agent chooses Fraud and his strategy is discovered, his payoff will be W minus P as an penalty; if one agent cheats and his strategy is not discovered, his payoff will be W plus C as an additional revenue; else his payoff will still be W. We also assume that R, P and C are all greater than zero. The probability that agent's strategy is observed is defined as p ($0 \leq p \leq 1$), and the probability that strategy not discovered is $1-p$. The set of payoffs for both parties is showed in Table 3.

In this mixed game, because we do not know the agent's beliefs (i.e. p), we can only calculate his expected utility:

$U_H = p \times (W + R) + (1 - p) \times W$, U_H presents the expected payoff when agent's strategy is Honesty.

$U_F = p \times (W - P) + (1 - p) \times (W + C)$, U_F presents the expected payoff when agent's strategy is Fraud.

When $U_H \geq U_F$, agent will choose Honesty and vice verse.

Above inequality can be simplified as:

Table 3. Payoffs of the game with reward and penalty for both parties

	Discovered (p)	Not discovered ($1-p$)
H	W+R	W
F	W−P	W+C

$$p \geq C / (R + P + C)$$

Next we discuss the influences of parameters changes to the game basing on this inequality. When other factors keep the same, the larger is the value of p, the greater the reward of Honesty as well as the penalty of Fraud and the smaller the revenue of undiscovered Fraud, the more possible this inequality holds and agents will keep honest. Conversely speaking, if there in e-commerce lack of effective supervision, or there no sufficient penalty to dishonesty, the agents will choose cheat regarding the considerable profits resulting from fraud and honesty-credit problems will emerge. The conclusion does not change a lot: powerful supervision mechanisms should be introduced in e-commerce to increase the corresponding cost of fraud and encouragement to honest parties as well as the possibility that cheat is discovered.

However, the honesty-credit mechanism created by repeated games should satisfy the following preconditions:

Firstly, the transaction must be a continuous process and traders are patient so that it is possible to create honesty-credit relationship. Secondly, the information transparency is indispensable in the transactions. The historical actions are the crucial factors to determine whether trust counterparties or not. Thirdly, the parties must have sufficient enthusiasm and possibilities to punish the fraud (Lin, 2004). Of course, other third party can also help to achieve this goal.

Reasons for Frequent E-Commerce Honesty-Credit Problems

Based on the above analysis of the game model, and combining the practice of e-commerce security and honesty-credit, we can infer the following reasons of honesty-credit problems in e-commerce:

E-commerce exacerbates the information asymmetry and increasing security risks.

E-commerce is a form of virtual economy. In most cases, traders cannot affirm counterparty's real identity; commodity and capital flows do not keep synchronous in terms of time and space; contract takes the electronic form. All of these increase the cost of information identification, making the game between traders more complicated and leading to inadequate sense of security. The "information overflow" on the Internet may decrease the information credibility and further exacerbate the information asymmetry, so honesty-credit issue is in fact the information issue (Wang and Yi, 2002). In the above game model, if there is information asymmetry and the cheater's action cannot be discovered, the transaction will continue and he will repeat again and again to pursue more profit. This is why people choose breach of honesty-credit.

Currently, China's commercial information industry has already taken shape. But supervision system of this industry is relatively backward and effective management to credit institutions and credit activities is scarce. Many credit institutions snatch the market by the means of low-price, high rebates and high ratings. The results of credit rating lose objectivity and credibility. Additionally, some employees in this industry are not professionally qualified to provide valuable information.

Lack of laws and regulations increases fraud in e-commerce

Because of the lack of laws and regulations to provide constraint and supervision, the probability of successful fraud in e-commerce increases and dealers have greater sense of insecurity. Qu and Zhang (2006) think that system as the rule of game is the key to establish and maintain the trust relationship. If the system arrangement makes it more profitable to keep honesty-credit than fraud, people will have impetus to resist temptation and pursue long-term interest. Law and regulation are the key factors of this system. Unless powerful laws or industry criterions can stop it, the breach of honesty-credit is inevitable (Li, 2001).

China's e-commerce laws and regulations are promulgated in succession in recent years. In very long time before e-commerce legislation drew attention, the victims of fraud could not receive compensation even they held the relevant evidence. It is just because of the legal vacuum. Currently, China's e-commerce legislation is still far from perfect and needs improvement urgently.

It must be pointed out that even if in the developed countries e-commerce regulations cannot be as sound as the laws dealing with offline business. Some factors will influence the level of legislation as well as the effect of implementation. First, the speed of information technique and e-commerce development is too fast to keep up with and legislation need time to be presented and amended; secondly, some e-commerce disputes such as intellectual property and taxation can not be resolved merely by certain country's laws, it needs cooperation of other countries to promote implementation of e-commerce regulations.

Lack of coordinated measures made it more difficult to keep honesty-credit in e-commerce transactions

The completion of e-commerce transactions also requires other supporting services providers, such as network operators providing transaction platform services and network infrastructure, merchants providing identity authentication and financial services, banks providing payment gateway, and distribution enterprises providing shipment and delivery service, and so on. The actions of these service providers also contribute the honesty-credit system of e-commerce.

We take the distribution service as example. At present there are mainly two kinds of distribution of e-commerce commodity in China. One depends on the enterprise's own transport network, and the other depends on mature distribution network provided by the third party. Depending on third party's network, enterprise and customer are likely to be confronted with problems such as delayed delivery and unreliable services, which become the hotspots among e-commerce complaints. In this process, the principal-agent relationship between the enterprises engaged in e-commerce and express company, as well ad between the express company and delivery people is established by contract. These two relationships create more complex trust problems.

Construction of E-Commerce Honesty-Credit System

The development of e-commerce demands a favorable social environment and a perfect honesty-credit system. According to the analysis on above game model, in the next part we will discuss the construction of e-commerce honesty-credit system from the aspects of ethics, laws and regulations, and other factors influencing implementation of honesty-credit mechanism.

Cultivate the Sense of Honesty-Credit in Whole Society

Enterprise operating business with honesty-credit

As the main body of e-commerce, enterprises must have the sense of self-discipline to keep honesty-credit. E-commerce is a kind of credit economy, and reputation is quite crucial to the survival and development of enterprises. Because of the virtual nature of Internet, consumers always prefer those enterprises with good reputation and well-known brand. And the excellent record of honesty-credit is also important for an enterprise to maintain long-term relationship with business partners.

In order to create the honesty-credit environment, enterprises should make the sense of honesty-credit penetrate each part of the business and consider honest-credit as the core of enterprise culture. Additionally enterprises should specify the business principle of honesty-credit in their management rules, carry out moral educations to raise the staff's consciousness of honest-credit, and then turn the concept of honest-credit into initiative actions.

The following three aspects should be emphasized when enterprises implement honesty-credit operations:

a. **Fulfill commitments faithfully.** The ability to fulfill its commitments is the best interpretation to an enterprise's honesty-credit in the process of e-commerce transactions. Enterprise should deliver goods on time, properly handle complaints and product return, and provide perfect after-sale service according to the e-contract. During performance of e-contract, customers' private information must be kept secret.
b. **Increase brand image.** The brand image of the enterprise is the key factor that influences online shoppers' choices. Fulfillment of commitment is just the first step for an enterprise to establish reputation and its long-term development must depend on brand image. As a commitment to keep honesty-credit, famous brand can attract more costumers with consciousness of honesty-credit and increase customers' loyalty to the enterprise.
c. **Improve network technology.** Perfect security technique and the transaction convenience are also the important factors for establishing trust relationship between partners. E-commerce enterprises should improve technology to provide friendly and convenient services as well as security for consumers so as to build long-term relationship with customers.

Consumption with honesty-credit

With a long history of over 5,000 years, China has an excellent moral tradition. Improving public morality should serve as the first step towards the establishment of honesty-credit system. Formation of honesty-credit and law-abiding ethics of public will facilitate the construction of social atmosphere of honest trading.

Costumers should comply with the principle of honesty-credit, keep flawless credit records, do not register in fake information or place a fake order. The mode of electronic credit payment should be adopted, because this mode not only increase the efficiency of e-commerce transactions but also improve public awareness of honesty-credit.

In the process of online shopping, consumers should cultivate the habit of rating credit for websites. This action can make credit information about these websites available to more costumers. Once the website breaks honesty-credit in one transaction, through this mechanism it becomes the fraud to all the consumers. The cost of fraud is greatly amplified so the possibility of cheat may decrease. On the other hand, consumers should have enough consciousness of self-protection to discern fake information and consumption trap. When rights are infringed, consumers should keep electronic evidence, and make complaint in time. By this mean, those dishonest businessmen will take punishment they deserved.

Provide Legal and System Protection for E-Commerce Honesty-Credit

Improve the legislation

The establishment and improvement of legal system will ensure the implementation of social honesty-credit system. The unique authority, preciseness and mandatory of law are incomparable by any other means of constraints.

Legislation in the domain of international e-commerce has become a hotspot in recent years, mainly concentrating on the regulation of electronic signatures, electronic contracts, and electronic records. From 1995 to now, many countries and regions have promulgated laws related to e-commerce, such as: "Digital Signature Act" (1995) by Utah State of America, "Federal Law on Information, Informatization, and the Protection of Information" (1995) by Russia, "Model Law on Electronic Commerce" (1996) and "Uniform Rules on Electronic Signature"(2000) by UNCITRAL(United Nations Commission on International Trade Law), "Direction on Community Framework for Electronic signatures" (1999)by EC (European Community, now as EU, European Uion), "Information and Communication Services Act'"(1997) by Germany, "Singapore Electronic Transactions Act" (1998) by Singapore, "Electronic Signatures in Global and National Commerce Act" (2000) by the United States, and so on.

In general, the e-commerce legislations have two obvious common characters. Firstly, the process is very quick. The emergency of e-commerce is just in 1990s, while at present there are dozens of countries, regions and organizations that have constituted laws or regulations related to e-commerce. This quick process is unusual in the history of legislation in the world. Secondly, compatibility is the main character. Given the background that the legislation of e-commerce gradually breaks up the border of countries, compatibility is one of the most important principles to take account in the domestic e-commerce legislation for each country. And this principle brings up a unique phenomenon that the international regulations are promulgated before the domestic laws in e-commerce legislation (Alamus, 2005).

China's e-commerce legislation has made remarkable progress although some problems still exist. The various legal areas of e-commerce honesty-credit have been involved in different degree.

a. **Amended law:** Some laws including "Contract Law of the People's Republic of China" and "Intellectual Property Law" have taken the legal relationships of e-commerce as their targets when make adjustments and amendments.
For example, in the Contract Law promulgated in 1999 there are three points involving e-commerce contracts. Firstly, extend the traditional paper contract form to include electronic document. As stated in the Article 11 of General Provisions: "The written forms mean the forms which can show the described contents visibly, such as a written contractual agreement, letters, and data-telex (including telegram, telex, fax, EDI and e-mails)." (China's National People's Congress, 1999) Secondly, specify the time of arrival of the e-contract. Thirdly, define the place of the receipt in e-commerce.
b. **Internet-related law and regulation:** In recent years, some national ministries have issued several regulations to resolve disputes on Internet issues, including "Provisions on the Administration of Internet Electronic Bulletin Services" (2000), "Internet Information Services Management Regulations" (2000), "Provisions on the Administration of Internet News Information Services" (2005), etc. There are also some rules and industry regulations such as "Domain Name Dispute Resolution Policy" (2002) and "Public Pledge of Self-Regulation and Professional Ethics for China Internet Industry".
c. **Specialized e-commerce regulation:** The e-commerce laws and regulations recently issued in China mainly include "Electronic Signature Law of the People's Republic of China" (2004), "Opinions of the General Office of the State Council on Accelerating the development of Electronic Commerce" (2004), "Electronics Identification Service Management Methods" (2005), and so on. On March 1, 2006, "Administrative Measures on Electronic Banking" and "Guidelines on Security Valuation of Electronic Banking" issued by the China Banking Regulatory Commission come to be effective. And another rule of "Criterions for E-commerce Credit Management of SMEs(Small and Middle Enterprises)" is being developed.

In order to provide favorable and effective protection for e-commerce honesty-credit construction, China should further broaden the coverage of e-commerce legislation. Through the online court, online arbitration, online notarization and other support mechanisms, create the flexible legal environment as the helpful supplement of traditional legal system. Moreover, administrator should recognize the function of commercial practices in e-commerce transactions, and combine law, institution, commercial practice, technique and management as an organic system to complete the construction of legal environment and effectively protect the operation and development of e-commerce.

But it must be pointed out that the severe punishment to fraud such as laws and regulations is unlikely to achieve long-term effects according to the theory of "incentive paradox". The theory believes: the dealers may feel it not profitable to cheat because of the increased penalty and reduce fraud in the short term, but the reduction of fraud can make other parties slacken their vigilance, which in turn will increase fraud. So there must be other effective measures to maintain the e-commerce honesty-credit.

Establish honesty-credit supervision system through coordination and cooperation of various social parties

As an afterward punishment, law cannot work during the process of fraud unless the fraud is discovered. It is important to establish effective management and professional supervision approaches. Government should coordinate and combine all the functional public sectors including banks, industry and commerce management administration, taxation bureaus, bureau of public security and technology departments to achieve cross-sector, cross-industry, cross-regional credit information sharing, and then establish an honesty-credit supervision system covering the whole society, laying a good foundation for an open, fair and justice market environment.

Supervision and assessment of honesty-credit is a long-term and dynamic process. During the course of credit supervision, the administrator should adjust and amend the mechanism of assessment continuously, integrate honesty-credit information, give authoritative valuations and publish the credit status without privacy information for public inquiry. For the enterprise and individual who breaks honesty-credit principle, special monitoring and inspection is necessary. In a word, what the administrator should do is to eliminate honesty-credit problems in the bud.

Build Sound Mechanism of Third-Party Authentication

Besides the laws and regulations system on e-commerce transaction monitoring honesty-credit, a professional third-party authentication is also essential to investigate the social credit information. Independent third-party evaluation and authentication organizations can provide true credit information and reliable credit reports, authenticate the trader's identity and qualifications, guarantee non-repudiation in electronic commerce transactions and provide protection and supervision mechanism for the e-commerce honesty-credit system. Third-party authentication includes credit authentication providing credit information investigation services and technical authentication offering technical support for honesty-credit transactions. Third-party evaluation and authentication organizations are independent of the participants of transactions so that they can ensure the impartiality, objectivity and integrity of their certification results. The third-party authentication mechanism can serve as useful supplement of the social credit system. Certainly the proper supervision and management to these organizations is necessary to make the above conclusion sound.

Professional credit authentication

In traditional commerce the most common way to establish direct trust relations is making use of the third-party credit company to make credit investigation and credit rating. E-commerce similarly needs an approach of authentication to build mutual trust relationship between transaction counterparties. The answer is third-party credit investigation.

The specific meaning of credit investigation is investigating personal or other's credit information and authenticating credit, it is also called "credit check". In order to meet the demands for information service in credit activities, credit investigation legally collects, processes, sorts and delivers information to provide reference for decision-making and to solve the problem of asymmetric information. People's Bank of China defines credit investigation system as: "a system constituted by the credit laws and regulations, organizations, market management, culture cultivation, publicity and education which are related to credit investigation activities. Its main function is to serve the credit market. It can also serve the commodities market and the labor market because of its strong extension."

Credit investigation can enhance credit information transparency between counterparties and lower transaction costs. The objective and impartial information and assessment are in favor of the supervision and restriction mechanism of social credit. More important, the credit investigation can lay the foundation for construction and improvement of social honesty-credit system.

There are two major kinds of credit companies: the American mode and the European mode

(Alamus, 2005). In the American mode, credit information is provided totally be independent third party and information service is not free. The core competitive power of the credit company is the capacity to provide accurate and comprehensive credit information. On the contrary, in the European mode, credit organization is non-profit and only "pure intermediary". The quality of credit information provided has no direct influence to the organization. The organization lacks of motives to enforce the strict information authentication. And for the similar reason, it can not afford the high costs to investigate and check all the information to determine whether there are omissions or frauds.

At present, China has owned a number of third-party credit information companies. China Chengxin International Credit Rating Company, Dagong Global Credit Rating Company, and China Lianhe Credit Rating Company are all well-known credit agencies in China. In 2004, China Financial Certification Authority, eBay Each, Sina, Taobao and other known network companies and institutions jointly founded the "China's E-commerce Honesty-credit Union (EC315)". The union supplies the authoritative disclosure, authentication and assessment of the website and enterprise's information including basic registration information, qualification, credit status and history of transactions and services. In addition to the reliable and dynamic information, the union also provides other value-added services such as network notarization and online arbitration, etc.

Meanwhile, the China E-commerce Association set up the Honesty-credit Assessment Center (hereinafter as Center). On March 10, 2006, the Center promulgated "Basic Honesty-credit Criterion for E-commerce Enterprise". This criterion involves the content in three aspects: enterprise's authenticity and legitimacy, protection of consumer's personal information and requirements for enterprise's online business. The promulgation of this regulation indicates that the construction of China's e-commerce honesty-credit system has made substantial progress.

According to the criterion, the Center identifies and assesses to what extent the enterprise's online business accords with the honesty-credit criterion through 12 first-level indicators and 60 second-level indicators. Enterprise can freely choose to accept the assessment of the center or not. In this way, a number of enterprises with good status of honesty-credit would be cultivated and in turn facilitate the honesty-credit system construction of e-commerce industry.

Professional technical authentication

Along with the popularization of Internet shopping and network transaction, more and more security risks emerge: seller publishes false product information; buyer places fraudulent orders; trader denies e-contract; and so on. These special e-commerce security issues caused by the breaches of honesty-credit can be resolved through technical means. Information technique promises to restrain and confirm the behaviors of participants in e-commerce transactions.

E-commerce Certification Authority (CA) is a kind of third-party agency proving online authentication, digital certification issuance and management and other services for participants of electronic transactions. It identifies the participants in the virtual network, guarantees information authenticity and transaction non-repudiation. In the process of certification issuance, CA is able to assess the enterprise's basic status and recognize false information so that protect the security and honesty-credit of e-commerce environment. As the indispensable part to smooth e-commerce transactions, the third-party certification authority technically maintains the honesty-credit in e-commerce.

In China, there are some well-known third-party technical authentication companies, including: China Telecom Certification Authority (CATA), through which China Telecom provides e-commerce participants with personal certificates, enterprise certificates and server certificates; China Financial Certification Authority (CFCA), which is founded jointly by 12 commercial banks including the People's Bank of China, the Industrial and Commercial Bank of China, Agricultural Bank of China, an so on, and is responsible for the certification issuance for various network transactions; Guofu'an Certification Authority; Shanghai Electronic Certificate Authority (SHECA). Since the competitions between these companies become more and more severe, China's Ministry of Information Industry issued the "electronic certification service Management Measures" to regulate qualification requirements and certification services of the certification authorities.

In western countries, Public Key Infrastructure (PKI) is regarded as something with public product attributes and controlled by government. The country will set uniform standards and design the integrated framework of PKI. This kind of experiences will contribute to China's construction of CA to enhance the authority and independence of CA and resolve cross-certification problems.

Regulate the Behaviors of Third-Party Service Providers

E-commerce honesty-credit system regulates not only the activities of e-commerce entities but also the responsibility and behaviors of the third parties involved in the transactions, such as merchants providing trading platform services and network infrastructure, and distribution enterprises proving transportation and delivery services. These service providers participate in the e-commerce transactions indirectly and their status of honesty-credit will influence whether the transactions succeed or not. The breach of honesty-credit by any party is doom to destroy the confidence of e-commerce traders and influence future development of e-commerce. It is the important component of e-commerce honesty-credit to regulate the enterprises' behaviors. Besides laws and regulations, we can employ the bundling agreements to integrate the responsibilities of direct transaction participants and supporting services providers. Thus for the consumers, the contract relationship turns simple and straightforward. The self-discipline of industry also plays a key role to help create honesty-credit environment.

Analysis of Shanghai E-Commerce Honesty-Credit System Construction

Shanghai is one of the Chinese cities in which e-commerce achieves rapid development. Thus the study on the construction of Shanghai e-commerce honesty-credit system can reflect the status of China e-commerce honesty-credit.

In recent years, breaches of honesty-credit in e-commerce transactions emerge continuously. In 2006, the Shanghai Administration for Industry and Commerce published the handling results of consumer complaints through hotline 12315. Complaint for Internet services (3846 times) listed number 5. And among complaints of the service and sales which listed number 1.

The issue of honesty-credit has drawn attention of Shanghai government. As early as in 2000, the government started to build the credit system, which is the important infrastructure for e-commerce honesty-credit construction.

The construction of Shanghai honesty-credit system can be divided into "three stages": First, from 2003 to 2005, improve personal and enterprise credit information service system, promote industry credit information management and services, accelerate enterprises' own credit management, enact corresponding credit regulations and industry standards and form the honesty-credit environment for the city. Second, before late 2007 realize the "four basic forms": that is, form the corresponding credit laws and systems to effectively regulate the credit industry and provide legal basis for credit management and credit activities; form scaled credit intermediary service industry and make credit information services become the important base of the market economic order; form the demands for credit market and universal use of credit instruments by government, enterprise and individual in most social and economic activities; form the comparative perfect social restraint mechanism. Third, until 2010, establish the social honesty-credit system firstly in China to meet the market demand and form healthy and orderly economic and social environment.

Construction of Credit Information System

Shanghai individual credit information system was put into use in July 2000. The system provides individual credit reports and through its 279 terminals linked to 15 local banks it can present these banks with credit information inquiry services. The individual credit reports contain the identity information, bank credit record, non-bank credit record, special records and so on. Until 2003, the system had collected 3,230,000 credit records and issued 840,000 individual credit reports. At the end of April 2005, the individual credit information system had possessed credit information over 5,590,000.

Shanghai enterprise credit information system began its trial run in March 2002. Until the beginning of 2005, the enterprise system had collected 590,000 enterprise credit information, whose data source included administration for industry and commerce, customs, taxation institution, quality and technical supervision agency, statistic bureau, State-owned assets management committee, as well as the People's Bank branch in Shanghai and the Shanghai Credit Corporation.

Individual and enterprise credit information system, these two joint credit information systems promote and complement each other, develop coordinately and form an elementary framework of social credit system. At present, information collection in Shanghai social honesty-credit system has essentially realized "two kind of coverage". The so-called "two kinds of coverage" on one hand refers that in Shanghai individual credit information system the sum of personal records has reached 6,180,000 and basically covered resident populations in Shanghai; on the other hand, it refers that the number of enterprise records has broke 600,000, and almost covered basic information of enterprises registered in recent years in Shanghai.

Additionally, through the "Industry and Commerce Supervision System" which in accordance with e-dictionaries of related laws and rules, near 900,000 enterprises and individual businesses are classified as law-abiding and law-breaking and managed respectively. In the system, the city's enterprises are divided into four ranks, enterprises without law-breaking records are ranked as Class One, with records of a slight, general and serious violations of law are ranked as Class Two, Class Three, Class Four respectively. The system has also introduced the "vertical classification" to classify enterprises as "hot and key industries or enterprises" and "warning enterprises".

Besides the improving credit information collection, the application of credit information products becomes more and more broad. At present, the individual information reports issued each day in Shanghai exceed 7,200. The credit information products are widely used in the areas of business cooperation between enterprises and government supervision and services institutes, such as functionary selection, government purchase, enterprise loan, funding approval and construction project bidding, and other social areas. The utilization increases steadily.

Legislation

In order to develop e-commerce in Shanghai and provide legal and institutional guarantees for social honesty-credit system construction, Shanghai has promulgated a series of rules and regulations related to e-commerce and policies, including "Interim Measures for Shanghai E-commerce Prices Management (part of digital certificate)" (1999), "Shanghai Digital Authentication Management Measures" (2002), "Trial Measures of Shanghai Municipality for the Administration of Enterprise Credit Investigation" (2005) and others. These regulations and rules establish legal and system protection for the e-commerce honesty-credit transactions.

Currently, the relevant agencies and individuals in Shanghai are actively promoting the issuance of local e-commerce regulation and trying to innovate in the enforcement of e-commerce law. In first half of 2005, the legislative researches of the "Shanghai Electronic Transactions Ordinance" began. The aim of this ordinance is not handling e-commerce relationship from a technical perspective but to create a safe legal environment to ensure healthy development of e-commerce.

Construction of Honesty-Credit Environment

Besides laws and regulations, industry supervision and self-regulation are also important means to ensure e-commerce honesty-credit and safeguard consumers' interest.

The E-commerce Complaint Center is founded by Shanghai E-commerce Industry Association in 2004. The center mainly handles e-commerce disputes to protect consumers' right and interest. The center will periodically publish "online shopping warnings" and "blacklist" of dishonest websites and announce cases of complaint in public. These measures aim at improving the operational credit environment of e-commerce and providing consumers with constructive and advisory guidance.

In December 2004, the Shanghai E-commerce Association launched online seller's registration of honesty-credit commitment, intending to protect the online legitimate rights of consumers and merchants and accelerate the construction of online honesty-credit environment. The contents of online seller's honesty-credit commitment include the seller's identity (such as name, address, etc.), history transactions, and pre-sale, on-sale and after-sale service commitments to honesty-credit. Seller's commitments are published in the website of Shanghai E-commerce Association, and online seller will accept mediation and adjudication of the association. Once a seller makes serious fraud, the association will cancel its honesty-credit sign.

In addition, the E-commerce Industry Association plans to guide the establishment of mutual compensation fund. In this way the association can make the "collective compensation" to the consumer victims.

FUTURE TRENDS

Honesty-credit issue is not a new topic, but e-commerce honesty-credit has something different because of the unique characteristics of e-commerce transactions. In e-commerce, information asymmetry is aggravated and the breach of honesty-credit is frequent. Therefore the study of e-commerce honesty-credit issue is necessary and meaningful.

According to classical game theory, infinite repeated game will achieve equilibrium of cooperation. While in the finite repeated game, the traders may choose cheat with the precondition that the one-off payoff of fraud is greater than that of honesty. When there lack of effective and strictly punishment for fraud and reward for honesty, the precondition still holds and breaches of honesty-credit will not cease. As the carrier of e-commerce, Internet possesses the virtual nature and aggravates the information asymmetry. Fraud and cheat can survive under the cover of Internet unless information identification mechanism functions, and the cheat actions can not be identified, let alone the punishment to the cheater.

In future, hot spots of study in this field will still concentrate on the aspects of legislation and information sharing.

E-commerce activities break the bound of national boundaries. Usually one transaction will concern several countries. If breach of honesty-credit causes loss of property, the determination of the trail location and applicable law as well as other legal problems will seriously influence the solution of the e-commerce honesty-credit problems, because the legal systems and practices vary in different countries and will lead to huge disparity of the result. Therefore the study on harmonization and universality of laws and regulations between different countries is a future research trend. Moreover, the legislation needs comparatively long time so that it fails to respond to the latest issues of honesty-credit. So how to employ management system and practice as helpful supplements is another issue deserving focus.

Availability of credit information is a fundamental aspect of the honesty-credit system construction. In current stage, China government plays the role of information provider to a large extent because the government has special administrative power to acquire information that the owners are unwilling to share with others. But since the government itself has also been confronted with honesty-credit issue, its independence is doubtable and questionable to some extent. China's third-party information investigation companies are still not mature enough to replace the position of the government. So how to exploit the functions of third-party information providers is another research direction.

CONCLUSION

E-commerce transactions have incomparable superiority over the traditional trading patterns and occupy a more and more important position in the economic life. It brings issue of honesty-credit as well as convenient transactions and the cost saving. E-commerce is a kind of virtual, interregional and anonymous business mode, so the issue of honesty-credit in e-commerce has more complicated influence and is more difficult to control. The breaches of honesty-credit in e-commerce seriously affect the security of individual and enterprise's information and assets. E-commerce honesty-credit has become the crucial factors to e-commerce security and social honesty-credit system construction.

The construction of e-commerce honesty-credit system should first start from social moral building to raise universal awareness of honesty-credit. Enterprises should conduct business legally and individuals consume honestly. When ethics constraints fail to work, the social regime and legal system is needed to standardize behaviors of traders. The honesty-credit system need coordination of industry and commerce departments, taxation institutions, banks and other sectors of society to collect credit information. And basing on the information system arrangement regulations should formulate the appropriate incentive and punitive measures. The independent third parties providing authentication and identification services are also necessary. The credit information companies can offer objective credit information and information certification, while the Certificate Authority organizations can technically provide authentication services for the integrity, authenticity and non-repudiation of online information. In addition, the construction of e-commerce honesty-credit system cannot succeed unless the enterprises providing supporting services for e-commerce transaction chains enhance their sense of honesty-credit.

Favorable honesty-credit environment cannot be created only depending on legislation and government supervision. It is a slow evolving process of ethics, practice and custom. Only through the organic combination of material basis, ethics construction and the system constraint can e-commerce honesty-credit system become comprehensive and effective to provide a safe and reliable business environment for e-commerce and promote healthy and orderly development of society and economy.

REFERENCES

Alamus. (July 30, 2005). From the International E-Commerce Legislation to China's Environment of E-commerce Policy and Regulation. Retrieved April 3, 2007, from http://www.cyberlawcn.com/Get/lfdt/lfyj/20051005296.htm.

Bloch, A. (2005). Business Relationships Built on Trust, Reliability, Honesty and Integrity. Retrieved April 5, 2007, from http://ezinearticles.com/?Business-Relationhips-Built-On-Trust,-Reliability,-Honesty-and-Integrity&id=98374.

Cheng, Z. (2003). Discussion about the Honesty-credit Principle and the Inspiration of British and American Laws. *Journal of Taiyuan University of Technology (Social Sciences Edition)*, *21*(1), 9-12.

China's National People's Congress. (1999). Contract Law of the People's Republic of China.

Gao, Z. (March 1, 2006). Credit Ethics Study—the Ethics Explanation of Economic Credit Crises. Retrieved April 3, 2007, from http://www.ethics.com.cn/Html/Article/133.html

Li, S. (1999, January). *Relation-based versus rule-based governance: an explanation of the East Asian miracle and Asian crisis.* Paper presented at the American Economic Association Annual Meeting, New York.

Li, S., & Li, X. (2005). Game Analysis on Mechanism of Credit Transaction. *China Economist*, November, 15-16.

Li, Z. (2001) *Ethics based enterprises.* Shanghai: Shanghai Social Sciences Publishing House.

Liao, J., & Zhao, D. (2004). *Honesty-credit and Social Development.* Chengdu, Chongqing: Southwestern University of Finance & Economic Press.

Lin, H. (2004). A Game Analysis on Effect of Information Transparency to Enterprises' Credit Behavior. *Journal of Chongqing University (Social Sciences Edition)*, *110*(23-25), 35.

Lu, X. (2007). Game Model of Credit of Fabricated Community in E-commerce. *Journal of Wuhan University of Technology Information & Management Engineering Edition*, 29(3), 96-98.

Qu, Y. & Zhang, Q. (2006). A Game Analysis of Credit Mechanism. *Journal of ShanXi Finance and Economics University*, *28*(6), 117-122.

Tian, J. (2007). Research on Credit Problem in C2C Commerce——Based on Gambling Mode. *Electronic Ecommerce*, March, 62-66.

Wang, L., & Shen, Y. (2002). *Credit and China's E-commerce*(Tech. Rep. No. 1). Peiking University E-business Research Center.

Xia, G., & Liu, X. (2006). Electronic Commerce and Honesty-credit Problems in China. *Information Network Security*, May, 3-6.

Yu, Z., Shi, B., & Liu, X. (2006). Game Analysis on the Honesty of Transaction Parties in E-commerce. *Business Study*, *339*(7), 67-69.

Zheng, Y. (2001). *On Trust.* Beijing: Trust China Broadcasting and Television Press.

KEY TERMS

Breach of Contract: Breach of contract referred here is a relatively broad concept, including not only the default that parties in transaction fail to fulfill their commitments but also non-compliance to provisions of contracts.

Credit Information Investigation System: Refers a system constituted by the credit laws and regulations, organizations, market management, culture cultivation, publicity and education which are related to credit investigation activities.

E-Commerce Certification Authority (CA): Is a kind of third-party agency proving online authentication, digital certification issuance and management and other services for participants of electronic transactions.

E-Commerce Honesty-Credit Problems: These problems indeed belong to e-commerce security problems caused by the lack of honesty-credit, since these problems ultimately affect the financial information and asset security in e-commerce transactions, and have no essential difference with definition of e-commerce security only except that main factors turn from network technology to the issue of honesty-credit.

Honesty-Credit: Narrow definition for the honesty-credit is the definition composition of honesty and credit, which can be interpreted as honesty and compliance with the commitments. Generalized definition of honesty-credit involves almost all of contents of "honesty" and "credit", giving a broader and more comprehensive content to honesty-credit from the inner moral virtues to the outer behaviors of the entity.

Personal Trust: Refers the specific trust of some person, such as relatives, natives. Personal trust limits to a relatively small interpersonal area, and along with the expansion of transaction radius and individual flows, the costs of confidence identification and monitor rise sharply so that it must turn to system trust.

System Trust: Means the confidence to a system composed of anonyms. The legal structure based on system trust is a kind of rule-based governance.

Chapter VI
Towards a Scalable Role and Organization Based Access Control Model with Decentralized Security Administration

Zhixiong Zhang
The College Board, USA

Xinwen Zhang
Samsung Information System America, USA

Ravi Sandhu
University of Texas at San Antonio, USA
TriCipher Inc., USA

ABSTRACT

This chapter addresses the problem that traditional role-base access control (RBAC) models do not scale up well for modeling security policies spanning multiple organizations. After reviewing recently proposed Role and Organization Based Access Control (ROBAC) models, an administrative ROBAC model called AROBAC07 is presented and formalized in this chapter. Two examples are used to motivate and demonstrate the usefulness of ROBAC. Comparison between AROBAC07 and other administrative RBAC models are given. We show that ROBAC/AROBAC07 can significantly reduce administration complexity for applications involving a large number of organizational units. Finally, an application compartment-based delegation model is introduced, which provides a method to construct administrative role hierarchy in AROBAC07. We show that the AROBAC07 model provides convenient ways to decentralize administrative tasks for ROBAC systems and scales up well for role-based systems involving a large number of organizational units.

INTRODUCTION

With the wide Internet usage in our society, the security and privacy issues become more important than ever. In the last decade, role-based access control (RBAC) had been generating considerable interests among the researchers and practitioners. In RBAC, roles are defined based on job functions, permissions are associated with roles, and users are made members of appropriate roles, thereby acquiring the roles' permissions. This indirect association between users and permissions greatly simplifies users' permission management. RBAC has several attractive features, such as policy neutrality, principle of least privilege, and ease of management. Several well-known RBAC models, such as RBAC96 (Sandhu et al, 1996), the role graph model (Nyanchama & Osborn, 1999), and NIST model (Ferraiolo et al., 2001), have been developed during the last decade. Those models form the basis for the ANSI RBAC standard (ANSI INCITS 359-2004). As a powerful alternative to traditional discretionary and mandatory access control, the adoption of RBAC in commercial software and enterprises has rapidly increased in recent years (RTI International, 2002).

The complexity of an RBAC system can be defined on the basis of the number of roles, the number of permissions, the size of the role hierarchy, the constraints on user-role and permission-role assignments, etc. (Sandhu et al, 2000). For existing large-scale RBAC systems, the number of roles and the number of permissions are in the order of 1000s. Beyond that magnitude, the performance of RBAC may degrade and its management becomes too difficult to handle correctly. Several approaches (Giuri & Iglio, 1997; Thomas, 1997; Perwaiz & Sommerville, 2001; Park et al, 2004) have been proposed to scale up RBAC systems by extending the RBAC model from various perspectives. To achieve decentralized administration of RBAC, some role-based administrative models have been proposed (Sandhu et al, 1999; Crampton & Loizou, 2003; Oh et al, 2006; Bhatti et al, 2004). Most of the previous work address RBAC in the context of a single organization and are mainly motivated by B2E (Business to Employee) applications. On the other hand, B2B (Business to Business) and B2C (Business to Consumer) applications often involve a large number of organizations such as corporations, schools, families, etc. Typically, users from different organizations with the same role name have slightly different access privileges due to privacy consideration. For example, a user with parent role in family A has permission to view the progress records of Family A's kids but not the progress recodes of other families' kids. Using standard RBAC naively in these situations can result in an enormous number of roles and permissions, well into the order of millions.

This chapter tries to address the scalability problem when applying RBAC to applications involving many organizational units. The rest of this chapter is organized as follows. Section 2 gives background and two motivating examples. Section 3 reviews Role and Organization Based Access Control (ROBAC) models. Section 4 presents a decentralized administrative ROBAC model called AROBAC07 (administrative ROBAC '07) to control administrative tasks in ROBAC systems. Section 5 discusses the implementation perspective of ROBAC. Section 6 concludes the chapter.

BACKGROUND

ANSI RBAC reference model includes core RBAC (no role hierarchy), hierarchy RBAC (has role hierarchy), and constrained RBAC (has Separation of Duty constraints). Figure 1 shows a classic (standard) RBAC which is based on the well-known RBAC96 and permission definition from ANSI RBAC.

Here we use the term classic RBAC to refer the typical RBAC models proposed in (Sandhu et al, 1996; Nyanchama & Osborn, 1999; Ferraiolo et al,

Figure 1. Classic (standard) RBAC

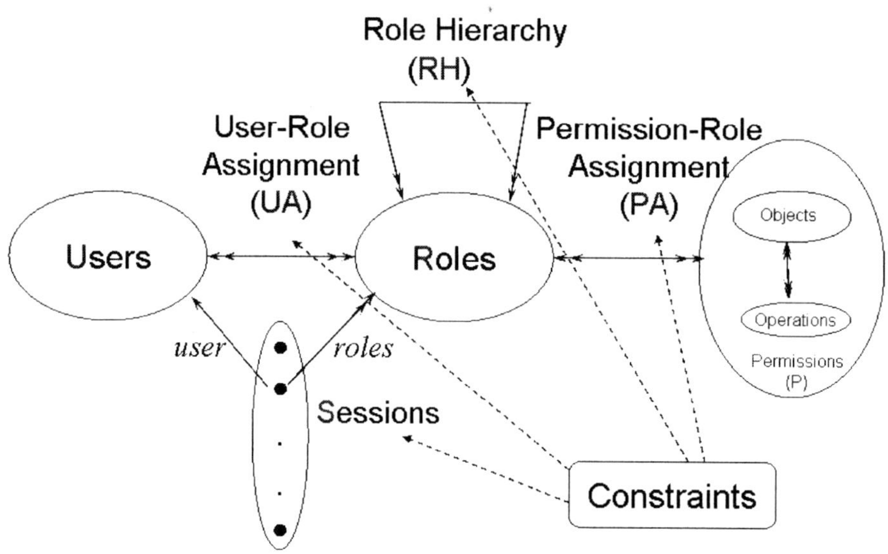

2001). As you can see, permissions are assigned to roles and users are assigned to roles. Users acquire permissions via their memberships in roles during session. The permissions in standard RBAC are defined as operations over objects. Here objects represent any resources need to be protected in the system. Assigning permissions to roles and assigning roles to users are two separate administrative tasks. How to define roles and permissions depends on desired security policy in an organization. RBAC models have been extended from various aspects (temporal, spatial, or context-aware) to better meet the needs in real world (Bertino et al, 2001; Joshi et al, 2005; Bertino et al, 2005, Covington et al, 2001; Kumar et al, 2002). Due to indirect assignment between users and permissions, RBAC based system is more flexible and scales up better than traditional MAC and DAC based system with respecting to the number of users. But RBAC does not scale up well with respecting to the number of roles and permissions. Beyond the magnitude of thousand roles, the management of RBAC is very error prone. Several approaches have been proposed to scale up RBAC systems. Giuri and Iglio (1997) extend RBAC by introducing the concept of role templates with parameterized privileges to achieve content-based access control. Thomas (1997) proposes Team Based Access Control (TMAC) to scale up permission assignment with fine-grained run-time permission activation at the level of individual users and objects. Perwaiz and Sommerville (2001) describe a mechanism for viewing role-permission relationships in the context of organizational structures, which reduces the number of roles in an RBAC implementation. Park et al. (2004) propose a composite RBAC for large and complex organizations. Most of these existing models address problem in the context of one organization. Many B2B and B2C applications involve a large number of organizations and often have some privacy requirements such as users in one organization are only allowed to access the resources related to the organization and are not allowed to access other organizations' resources. We discuss two examples from B2B and B2C context, respectively, to show the motivation of our new models. These are abstracted from our experience with similar real-world applications.

B2B example: Consider access control policies for a web based report delivery system, which only allows authorized users to access specific reports. Users are educational professionals from schools, districts, and states in USA. There are on the order of 10,000 schools participating in the system. Reports are classified into types based on the sensitivity and nature of the content. Because some report types include privacy-sensitive data such as student test results and personal information, only an authorized user, say, School_1's official, can view School_1's reports but cannot view School_2's reports. There are many different types of reports, each of which may have up to three different levels of information (state level, district level, and school level). Some sample report types are listed in Table 1.

States, districts, and schools usually form a management hierarchy. Figure 2 shows an example of a possible management hierarchy among states, districts, and schools.

Informal security policies of the system may include:

- Users from a school are only allowed to access the reports related to this school.
- Users from a district education office are allowed to access the reports related to this district and the schools under it.
- Users from a state education office are allowed to access the reports related to this state and the districts and schools under it.
- School principles can view type A and type B reports.
- School teachers can view type B and type E reports.
- Officials from a district's board of education offices can view type A and type B reports but cannot view type D reports

Table 1. Sample report types in B2B example

Type A Report (school level, district level, and state level)
Type B Report (school level only)
Type C Report (school level only)
Type D Report (school level only)
Type E Report (school level and district level)
...

Under the above policies, an authorized school level user (say School_1 teacher) can only access certain types of the user's own school's reports, but is not allowed to access other types of reports, and, further, cannot access other school's or any district or state level reports. Here we assume that an access not explicitly allowed by the stated policies is denied. An authorized district level user can access certain types of the user's own district's reports (district level) and may also access the same types of its subordinate schools' reports. For example, an authorized District_1 official can access District_1's district level Type_A reports and school level Type_A report for School_1 and School_2 since the School_1 and School_2 are under District_1.

Assuming there are 10,000 organizations and 10 types of reports, if we use standard RBAC to model this problem directly, we have to define about 100,000 (10,000 x 10) permissions because viewing School_1's Type_A report is different from viewing School_2's Type_A report. We also need to define 100,000 different roles because a role that can view a School_1_Type_A report is different from a role that can view a School_2_Type_A report. Table 2 and Table 3 show some samples of the possible permissions and roles in this example.

The goal here is not to define a complete and coherent policy for this example but rather to illustrate the issues and complexities involved.

B2C example: Consider an online subscription-based tutoring system, where customers are families that have children in elementary schools. Parents pay subscription fees for their children and are authorized to create/update the family's profile and view their children's progress reports. Students that have subscribed to the service can take classes on the web and view their progress

Figure 2. A sample organization hierarchy

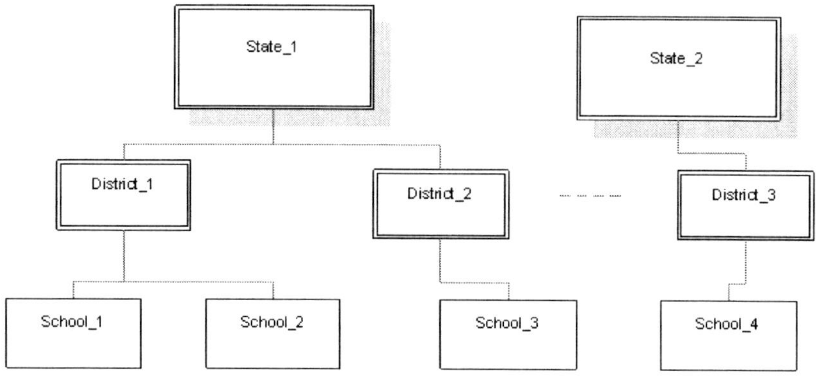

reports and family profiles. Here, family profiles and student's progress reports need to be protected against unauthorized access. There are potentially millions of families, and even 10s or 100s of millions. The informal description of some security policies of this system may include:

- Parents can only view their own children's progress reports.
- Parents can create/update/view their family's profile.
- A student can view his/her own progress report and view his/her family's profile.

Suppose we use standard RBAC to model these policies. Because Family_1's parent is only allowed to access Family_1's profile and Family_1's children's progress reports, the Family_1's parents have slightly different permissions from that of Family_2's parents. Table 4 and Table 5 show some samples of the possible permissions

Table 2. Sample permissions in B2B example (with RBAC)

p1: View School_1 Type A Report
p2: View School_2 Type A Report
p3: View District_1 Type A Report
...

Table 3. Sample roles in B2B example (with RBAC)

r1: School_1 Type A Report Viewer with permission p1.
r2: School_2 Type A Report Viewer with permission p2.
r3: District_1 Type A Report Viewer with permission p3.
...

Table 4. Sample permissions in B2C example (with RBAC)

p1: Update Family_1's Profile
p2: View Family_1's Kids' Progress Reports
p3: View Family_1's Profile
p4: Update Family_2's Profile
p5: View Family_2's Kids' Progress Reports
p6: View Family_2's Profile
......

Table 5. Sample roles in B2C example (with RBAC)

r1: Family_1 Parents with permission p1 and p2.
r2: Family_1 Student with permission p2 and p3.
r3: Family_2 Parents with permission p4 and p5.
r4: Family_2 Student with permission p5 and p6.
...

and roles when using classic RBAC in this B2C example.

We can see that the administrative complexity is very high in applying RBAC directly to the above two examples. These scenarios are quite typical for B2B and B2C applications. In practice, security and application engineers usually work around this problem by combining RBAC with other access control mechanisms such as context-based or attribute-based access control. The result is an ad hoc access control model with a specialized administrative tool for each application (Georgiadis et al, 2001; Schaad et al, 2001).

ROBAC MODELS

To address the issue that classic RBAC does not scale up well for applications involving multiple organizations where privacy issue is the main concern, a family of extended RBAC models called Role and Organization Based Access Control (ROBAC) models has been proposed by the authors (Zhang et al, 2006).

The central idea behind ROBAC is quite simple. Instead of only using role related information, ROBAC utilizes both the role information and the organization information during the authorization process. Specifically, in ROBAC, a user is assigned to role and organization pairs instead of roles only. The permissions in ROBAC are defined as operations over object types instead of operations over objects. A user can access an object if and only if the user is assigned to a role and organization pair, and the role has the right to access the object's type and the object is related to the organization. In the following sections, we show that the number of roles and permissions for the above B2B and B2C examples can be reduced significantly if we use ROBAC to model them.

ROBAC models consist of four models ($ROBAC_0$, $ROBAC_1$, $ROBAC_2$, $ROBAC_3$) based on the increasing security functionality in direct correspondence with the four models of well-known RBAC96 family ($RBAC_0$, $RBAC_1$, $RBAC_2$, $RBAC_3$). $ROBAC_0$ is a base model. $ROBAC_1$ is $ROBAC_0$ plus role hierarchy and organization hierarchy. $ROBAC_2$ is $ROBAC_0$ plus constraints. $ROBAC_3$ is $ROBAC_0$ plus role hierarchy, organization hierarchy and constraints. Figure 3 shows their essential characteristics.

To make the chapter concise, we only review the formal definitions for $ROBAC_0$ and $ROBAC_1$ here.

Definition 1: $ROBAC_0$ has the following components:

- U -- a set of users (same as U in RBAC96);
- S -- a set of sessions (same as S in RBAC96);
- R -- a set of roles (same as R in RBAC96);
- O -- a set of organizations;
- Op -- a set of operations;
- A -- a set of assets;
- At -- a set of asset types;
- $P \subseteq Op \times At$ -- a set of permissions;
- $RO \subseteq R \times O$ -- a set of applicable role and organization associations;
- $PA \subseteq P \times R$ -- a many-to-many permission-to-role assignment relation;
- $UA \subseteq U \times RO$ -- a many-to-many user-to-role-and-organization assignment relation;
- *user*: $S \rightarrow U$ -- a function mapping a session s_i to a single user $user(s_i)$ (same as *user* in RBAC96);
- *atype*: $A \rightarrow At$ -- a function mapping an asset to its type;
- *aorg*: $A \rightarrow O$ -- a function mapping an asset to the organization is related to;
- *assigned_role-orgs*: $U \rightarrow 2^{RO}$ -- a function mapping a user to a set of role-organization pairs assigned to the user; formally: $assigned\_role\text{-}orgs(u) = \{ (r,o) \mid (u, (r,o)) \in UA \}$;

- *active_role-orgs*: $S \rightarrow 2^{RO}$ -- a function mapping a session s_i to a set of active role-organization pairs such that *active_role-orgs*(s_i) $\subseteq$ *assigned_role-orgs*(*user*(s_i));
- *can_access*: $S \times Op \times A \rightarrow$ {true, false} -- a predicate defined as *can_access*(*s*, *op*, *a*) is true iff $\exists$ (r, o) $\in$ *active_role-orgs*(*s*) $\wedge$ *aorg*(*a*) $= o \wedge$ ((*op*, *atype*(*a*)), *r*) $\in$ PA ;

where the operations (Op) are similar to the operations or actions in classic RBAC; the assets (A) are similar to objects; the *active_role-orgs* is used to model activation of role-organization pairs inside a session and it returns a subset of the role and organization pairs that the *assigned_role-orgs* returns. Because certain roles are only meaningful for certain organizations, such as School Principle role is only meaningful for school type organizations, we introduce the set of applicable role and organization pairs (RO) to model that requirement. Briefly, $ROBAC_0$ extends $RBAC_0$ by:

- introducing new sets: Organizations(O), Asset Types (At), and Role-Organization pairs (RO);
- introducing new functions: *atype, aorg;*
- extending *assigned_role* and *roles* (*session_role*) to *assigned_role-orgs* and *active_role-orgs*;
- redefining permissions (P) and user to role assignment (UA);
- introducing a predicate *can_access(s, op, a)*.

Any access control system needs to answer the following question: Can a subject perform an operation over an object?

The newly introduced predicate *can_access* serves this purpose in ROBAC. The definition of *can_access* in $ROBAC_0$ indicates that a user (*user(s)*) in a session *s* can perform an operation *op* over an asset *a* if and only if that the user has an active role and organization pair (*r*, *o*) in that

Figure 3. A family of ROBAC models

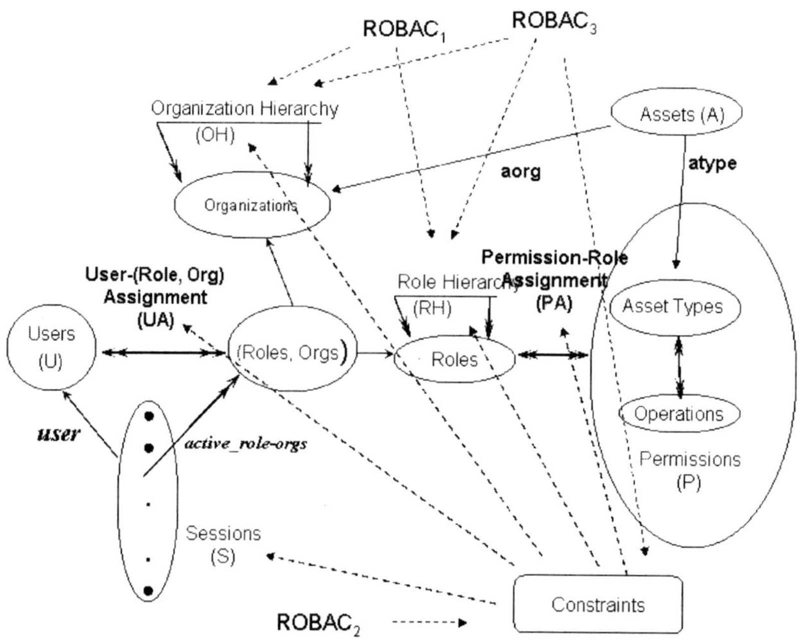

session and the r has a permission to perform the *op* over *a*'s type and *a* is related to *o*.

Definition 2: $ROBAC_1$ has the following components:

- U, S, R, O, Op, A, At, P, RO, PA, UA, *user, atype, aorg* are same as those from $ROBAC_0$.
- $OH \subseteq O \times O$ -- a partial order relation on O called organization hierarchy;
- $RH \subseteq R \times R$ -- role hierarchy (same as RH in RBAC96);
- *assigned_role-orgs*: $U \rightarrow 2^{RO}$ -- a function mapping a user to a set of role-organization pairs assigned to the user; formally: $assigned\_role\text{-}orgs(u) = \{ (r,o) \mid \exists r' \geq r \wedge \exists o' \geq o \wedge (u, (r',o')) \in UA \}$;
- *active_role-orgs*: $S \rightarrow 2^{RO}$ -- a function mapping each session s_i to a set of active role-organization pairs such that $active\_role\text{-}orgs(s_i) \subseteq assigned\_role\text{-}orgs(user(s_i))$;
- *can_access*: $S \times Op \times A \rightarrow \{true, false\}$ – a predicate defined as $can\_access(s, op, a)$ is true iff $\exists(r, o) \in active\_role\text{-}orgs(s) \wedge aorg(a) \leq o \wedge (\exists r' \leq r, ((op, atype(a)), r') \in PA)$;

$ROBAC_1$ adds OH (organization hierarchy) and RH (role hierarchy) and changes *assigned_role-orgs* function and *can_access* predicate from $ROBAC_0$.

The definition of *can_access* in $ROBAC_1$ means that a user *user(s)* in a session *s* can perform an operation *op* over an asset *a* if and only if that the user has an active role and organization pair (*r, o*) in that session and the role *r* or any of its junior roles has a permission to perform the operation *op* over the asset *a*'s type, and the asset *a* is related to the organization *o* or any of its subordinate organizations.

For the aforementioned B2B example, we can use $ROBAC_1$ to model it very conveniently. We show some ROBAC elements differing from those in RBAC as follows.

- O={State_1, State_2, District_1, District_2, District_3, School_1, School_2, School_3, School_4, …}
- OH = {(State_1, District_1), (State_1, District_2), (District_1, School_1), (District_1, School_2), (District_2, School_3), (State_2, District_3), (District_3, School_4), …}
- At = {Type_A_Report, Type_B_Report, …}
- RO = { (r1, District_1), (r2, District_1), (r1, School_1), (r2, School_2), (r3, School_1), (r4, School_1), … }

Possible permissions and roles are listed in Table 6 and Table 7.

In this B2B example, ROBAC only creates one role called Type_A_Report_Viewer which has one permission called View_Type_A_Report for viewing type A report, but a classic RBAC needs to

Table 6. Sample permissions in B2B example (with ROBAC)

p1: View Type A Report
p2: View Type B Report
p3: View Type C Report
p4: View Type D Report
…

Table 7. Sample roles in B2B example (with ROBAC)

r1: Type A Report Viewer which has permission p1.
r2: Type B Report Viewer which has permission p2.
r3: Type C Report Viewer which has permission p3.
r4: Type D Report Viewer which has permission p4.
…

create a role for each organization's type A report viewer, such as School_1_Type_A_Report_Viewer which has View_School_1_Type_A_Report permission, and School_2_Type_A_Report_Viewer which has View_School_2_Type_A_Report permission, etc.

Based on the security policies, r1 and r2 can have role-organization pairs with all levels of organizations but r3 and r4 can only have role-organization pairs with school level organizations.

For the aforementioned B2C example, we can use $ROBAC_0$. Possible permissions and roles are listed in Table 8 and Table 9.

In this B2C example, ROBAC only creates two roles (parent and student) instead of a parent role and a student role for each family in the classic RBAC.

Permissions in ROBAC are defined as a subset of Op × AT while permissions in classic RBAC are defined as a subset of Op × A. Usually, |AT| is much smaller than |A|. In the above B2B example, |A| ≈ 10,000 × |AT|

Comparing to RBAC, the number of roles and permissions in RODBC are reduced dramatically in the above B2B and B2C examples. The set of applicable role and organization pairs (RO) is a newly introduced concept in ROBAC. The size of RO may become large when there are a large number of organizations involved. Instead of creating RO explicitly, we can define RO implicitly by using some rules. For example, in the aforementioned B2B example, we use the following rules to establish RO implicitly:

- r1 (Type A Report Viewer) and r2 (Type B Report Viewer) can associate with any organizations.
- r3 (Type C Report Viewer) and r4 (Type D Report Viewer) can only associate with school type organizations.

For the B2C example, we allow any role associate to any organization. While the size of RO may be large, the administrative work for RO is small.

Because the number of roles and permissions in ROBAC is much smaller than that in RBAC under the situations similar to the above two examples, the administrative complexity in Permission-to-Role assignment is significantly reduced. Therefore, using ROBAC to model the problems similar to the above B2B and B2C examples is more succinct and intuitive than using RBAC.

The organization concept in ROBAC introduces a powerful abstraction that can be coupled quite naturally with the traditional concept of roles. For example, we can treat the divisions or project teams in an enterprise as organizations. So ROBAC can also be used in many B2E applications. A user with an assigned role and organization pair *(r, o)* indicates that the user can act as role *r* within the organization *o* and its subordinate organizations. Because ROBAC performs access control based on both roles and association relations between users and protected resources (assets), it is suitable to model privacy-related policies in applications involving a large number of similar organizational units. A detail comparison between ROBAC and other RBAC extensions can be found in Zhang et al, 2006.

Table 8. Sample permissions in B2C example (with ROBAC)

p1: Update Family Profile
p2: View Kid's Progress Reports
p3: View Family Profile
…

Table 9. Sample roles in B2C example (with ROBAC)

r1: Parent which has permission p1 and p2.
r2: Student which has permission p2 and p3.
…

ADMINISTRATIVE ROBAC

In any security systems, administrative actions need to be controlled. Using role-based method to control RBAC administrative tasks is often a preferred way because it can share the underline authorization mechanism. There are two main approaches to perform RBAC administration. One is centralized such as Gavrila and Barkley's NIST model (1998) and Nyanchama and Osborn's role graph model (1999), where one or more security administrators perform all administrative tasks. Another is decentralized such as Sandhu et al's ARBAC97 model (1999), Crampton and Loizou's SARBAC model (2003), Oh et al's ARBAC02 model (2006), and Bhatti et al's X-GTRBAC admin (2004), where administrative tasks are distributed among many different administrators in a controlled manner. Those role-based decentralized approaches usually add a separate administrative role hierarchy in the original RBAC model. Figure 4 shows an example of regular role hierarchy and administrative role hierarchy created in ARBAC97 model for an engineering department within an organization.

Department Security Officer (DSO) can perform administrative tasks on the department level and Project Security Officer (PSO) can perform administrative tasks on the project level. Each project not only has its own instance of Project Leader role, Production Engineer role, and Quality Engineer role in the regular role hierarchy, but also has its own instance of Project Security Officer role in the administrative role hierarchy. If there are a large number of projects, say in the degree of 100s or more, in an enterprise, both the regular role hierarchy and administrative role hierarchy will become very clumsy and hard to manage correctly. Many classic administrative RBAC models, such as ARBAC97, do not scale up well when a large numbers of similar organizational units are involved.

As we mentioned earlier, the organization concept in ROBAC should not be treated literally.

Figure 4. Examples of role hierarchy using classic administrative RBAC

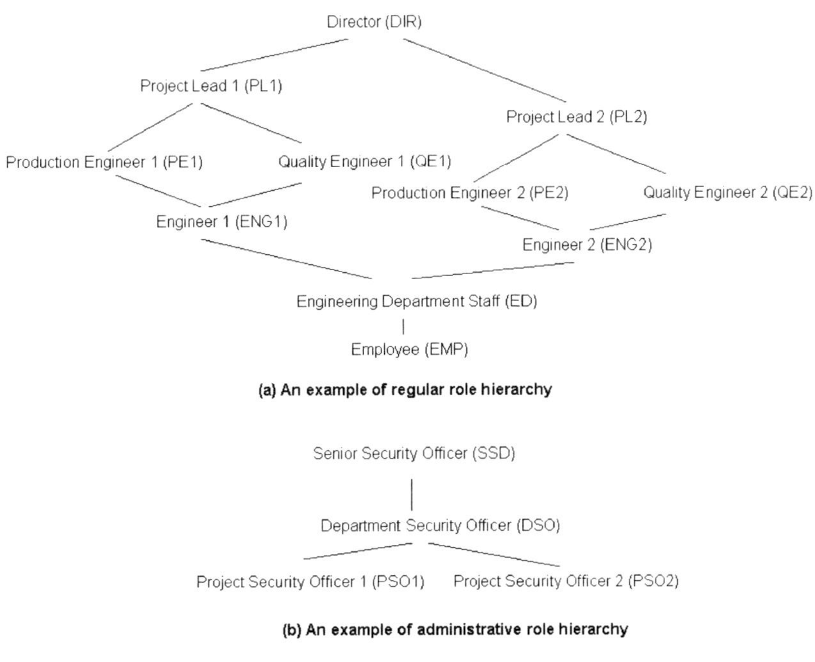

For business to employee (B2E) applications, we may treat the divisions or project teams in an enterprise as organizations. ROBAC model is suitable to be used in large enterprises where there are many similar organizational units. A decentralized administrative approach is preferred for large enterprises. Based on the observation that administrative tasks are very similar in many enterprises, we believe that it is an effective approach to utilize the role and organization based access control concept to manage administrative tasks in ROBAC. The main topic of this section is to present a comprehensive model for role and organization based administration of ROBAC.

In classic RBAC, major administrative tasks include assigning users to roles, assigning permissions to roles, and adjusting role hierarchy. So some role-based administrative model, such as ARBAC97, has three separate sub-models: URA97 (user-role assignment), PRA97 (permission-role assignment), and RRA97 (role-role assignment), to deal with these three major administrative tasks. There are more components in ROBAC than those in RBAC, making the administration of ROBAC more multifaceted than RBAC. Following the ARBAC97 approach, we divide administrative tasks into the following categories: assigning users to role-organization pairs, assigning permissions to roles, managing roles and role hierarchy, managing organizations and organization hierarchy, and managing role and organization association. The reason is that these administrative activities in ROBAC affect user's access rights in different ways. Our administrative model is called AROBAC07 (administrative ROBAC '07). It has five components.

1. UROA07 (user to role and organization pair assignment '07) is concerned with user to role and organization pair assignment;
2. PRA07 (permission to role assignment '07) deals with permission-role assignment;
3. RRA07 (role to role assignment '07) manages roles and role hierarchy;
4. OOA07 (organization to organization assignment '07) handles organizations and organization hierarchy; and
5. ROA07 (role to organization assignment '07) controls applicable association between roles and organizations.

The development of AROBAC07 was heavily influenced by ARBAC97, SARBAC, and ARBAC02. Our AROBAC07 model is presented in the context of $ROBAC_1$. Its interpretation for $ROBAC_0$, $ROBAC_2$ and $ROBAC_3$ is straightforward.

AROBAC07 adds some additional sets, relationships, and functions to ROBAC model. Similar to ROBAC, an administrative user is assigned to administrative role and organization pairs instead of administrative role only. An administrative decision is made based on both role and organization information. The common elements of AROBAC07 are described in Definition 3 and Figure 5 shows some relationship among the elements of AROBAC07.

Definition 3: AROBAC07 has the following components:

- U, S, O, OH, Op, A, At, P, RO, PA, UA, *user, atype, aorg, assigned_role-orgs, active_role-orgs, can_access* are same as those from ROBAC;
- RR -- a set of regular roles (renamed R in ROBAC);
- $RRH \subseteq RR \times RR$ – regular role hierarchy (renamed RH in ROBAC);
- AR -- a set of administrative roles (same as AR in ARBAC97), where $RR \cap AR = \emptyset$.
- $ARH \subseteq AR \times AR$ -- administrative role hierarchy (same as ARH in ARBAC97);
- $R = RR \cup AR$ -- the set of all roles;
- $ARRA \subseteq AR \times RR$ -- a many-to-many administrative role to regular role assignment;

- RH = RRH ∪ ARH -- a combined role hierarchy;
- UO ⊆ U × O -- a set of user-organization affiliations;
- PO ⊆ P × O -- a set of applicable permission-organization associations;
- CRU – a set of applicable prerequisite condition for users;
- CRP – a set of applicable prerequisite condition for permissions;
- CAN_ASSIGN_USER ⊆ ARRA × CRU - an association defines the constraints when assigning users to role-organization pairs;
- CAN_REVOKE_USER ⊆ ARRA × CRU - an association defines the constraints when revoking users from role-organization pairs;
- *can_assign_user*: S × U × RO → {true, false} – a predicate which indicates that if *can_assign_user(s, u, (r,o))* is true then user *u* can be assigned to the role-org pair *(r,o)* within the session *s* (the definition is described in UROA07);
- *can_revoke_user*: S × U × RO → {true, false} – a predicate which indicates that if *can_revoke_user(s, u, (r,o), c)* is true then user *u* can be revoked from role-org pair *(r,o)* within the session *s* (the definition is described in UROA07);
- CAN_ASSIGN_PERMISSION ⊆ ARRA × CRP - an association defines the constraints when assigning permissions to roles;
- CAN_REVOKE_PERMISSION ⊆ ARRA × CRP - an association defines the constraints when revoking permissions from roles;
- *can_assign_permission*: S × P × RR → {true, false} – a predicate which indicates that if *can_assign_permission(s, p, r)* is true then the permission *p* can be assigned to the regular role *r* within the session *s* (the definition is described in PRA07);
- *can_revoke_permission*: S × P × RR → {true, false} – a predicate which indicates that if *can_revoke_permission(s, p, r)* is true then the permission *p* can be revoked from the regular role *r* within the session *s* (the definition is described in PRA07);
- *can_modify_R*: $S \times 2^{RR} \rightarrow$ {true, false} -- a predicate which indicates that if *can_modify_R(s, rset)* is true then the user *user(s)* can modify the roles and their relationship inside the role set *rset* within the session *s* (the definition is described in RRA07);
- *can_modify_O*: $S \times 2^{O} \rightarrow$ {true, false} -- a predicate which indicates that if *can_modify_O(s, oset)* is true then the user *user(s)* can modify the organizations and their relationship inside the organization set *oset* within the session *s* (the definition is described in OOA07);
- *can_modify_RO*: S × R × O → {true, false} -- a predicate which indicates that if *can_modify_RO(s, r, o)* is true then the user *user(s)* can associate or disassociate role *r* with organization *o* within the session *s* (the definition is described in ROA07);

In AROBAC97, UO defines user's organization affiliation. A user may be affiliated with multiple organizations. UO is usually pre-determined by Human Resource (HR) departments of individual organizations. The applicable permission-organization association set PO defines permissions applicable to organizations. Similar to permission set P, PO is pre-determined via joined efforts between HR and Information Technology (IT) departments. So we do not include the management of UO, P, and PO in our model. The set ARRA can be considered as the administrative role's permission over the regular roles. Some constraints need to be enforced when creating or modifying the role hierarchy (RH) or organization hierarchy (OH) such as no circular reference. The detailed descriptions of the prerequisite condition sets CRU and CRP, the predicates *can_assign_user, can_revoke_user, can_assign_permission, can_revoke_permission, can_modify_R, can_modify_O,* and *can_modify_RO* are discussed in the following corresponding subsections.

Figure 5. AROBAC07 model

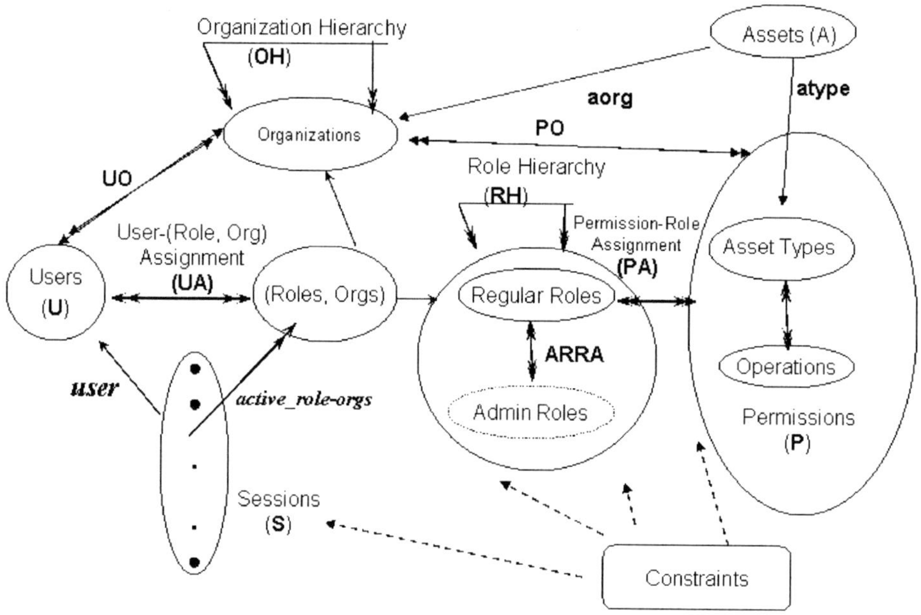

The UROA07 Model

The UROA07 model deals with managing user to role-organization pair assignment. It provides two predicates to determine whether the current session can grant a user membership in a role-organization pair (or simply role-org pair) or revoke a user membership in a role-org pair. Before introducing the details of UROA07 model we need some definitions.

user prerequisite condition (upc) - a *upc* is a boolean expression using the usual $\wedge$ and $\vee$ operators on terms of form of $(r, ?)$, $\neg(r, ?)$, (r, o), and $\neg(r, o)$ where (r, o) is a role-org pair belongs to RO. A *user prerequisite condition* is evaluated for a user u by interpreting (r, o) to be true if $(\exists r' \geq r, \exists o' \geq o)\ (u, (r', o')) \in$ UA and $\neg(r, o)$ is true if (r, o) is not true. Here "?" is a place holder for any $o \in$O, and $(r, ?)$ is true for user u if $(\exists r' \geq r\ ,\ \exists o' \geq ?,\ (u, (r', o')) \in$ UA) and $\neg(r, ?)$ is true if $(r, ?)$ is not true. CRU is a set including all applicable *upc*s plus a *null* element. The *null* is interpreted as true for any user.

Note: The $(r, ?)$ expression represents a condition template where the value of "?" is set to o when the system is asked whether a user can be assigned to a role-organization pair (r, o). We will explain it in an example later.

omembers: O → 2^U, is a function mapping an organization to a set of users who affiliated with the organization; formally, $omembers(o) = \{ u \mid (u, o) \in$ UO $\}$; $omembers^*(o) = \{ u \mid \exists o' \leq o, (u, o') \in$ UO $\}$

Note: *omembers*(o) is the set of all users affiliated with organization o and *omembers**(o) is the set of all users affiliated with organization o or its subordinate organizations.

apermissions: AR → 2^{RR}, is a function mapping an administrative role to a set of regular roles which the administrative role has administrative privilege over;

formally, *apermissions*(*ar*) = { *r* | *(ar, r)* ∈ ARRA }; *apermissions**(*ar*) = {*r* | ∃*ar'* ≤ *ar*, *(ar', r)*∈ARRA }

Note: *apermisions*(*ar*) is the set of regular roles which the administrative role *ar* has administrative privilege and *apermissions**(*ar*) is the set of regular roles which administrative role *ar* or its junior administrative roles has administrative privilege.

may_manage_user: AR × U × RO × CRU → {true, false} - a predicate defined as *may_manage_user(ar, u, (r,o), c)* is true iff (*r* ∈ *apermissions**(*ar*)) ∧ *c* ∧ (*u* ∈ *omembers**(*o*)).

Note: The definition of *may_manage_user(ar, u, (r,o), c)* indicates that a user with administrative role *ar* may manage the user *u* with respect to the role-org pair *(r, o)* if and only if the user *u* satisfies the user prerequisite condition *c* and is affiliated to the organization *o* or its subordinate organizations and the administrative role *ar* or its junior administrative roles can perform administrative tasks on role *r*. The *may_manage_user* predicate is used as a sub-routine in the following UROA07 Grant Model and UROA07 Revoke Model.

Definition 4: The UROA07 Grant Model – *can_assign_user* predicate controls whether a user can be assigned to a role-org pair within a session. Formally, *can_assign_user(s, u, (r,o))* is true iff (∃*o'* ≥ *o*, ∃*(ar, o')* ∈ *active_role-orgs*(*s*)) ∧ (∀*c*∈CRU, *((ar, r),c)* ∈ CAN_ASSIGN_USER ∧ *may_manage_user(ar, u, (r,o), c)*).

The definition of *can_assign_user(s, u, (r,o))* in UROA07 indicates that a user (*user(s)*) in a session *s* can assign a user *u* to a role-org pair *(r, o)* if and only if *user(s)* has an active role-org pair *(ar, o)* (explicitly or implicitly via organization hierarchy) in that session and user *u* satisfies all related user prerequisite conditions defined in CAN_ASSIGN_USER and is affiliated to the organization *o* or its subordinate organizations and the administrative role *ar* or its junior administrative roles can perform administrative tasks on role *r*.

The user prerequisite condition in UROA07 is likely to be empty in most cases. It may be used to model some complex policy, so we include it in the model.

To appreciate the benefit behind the UROA07 model, let us remodel the aforementioned engineering department example in Figure 4 using AROBAC07. Figure 6 shows the AROBAC07 model for the engineering department problem in Figure 4. Here we treat a project team as an organization. We further assume that roles in different project teams within the engineering department perform similar tasks and a team member only can access the resource related to the team he/she is in. This assumption will usually hold because most enterprises need to enforce unified security policy across multiple teams.

We can see that both the regular role hierarchy (Figure 6(a)) and the administrative role hierarchy (Figure 6(c)) in AROBAC07 are simpler. For the moment please ignore the *Greatest Administrative Role* (*gar*) and the *Greatest Organization* (*go*). We will explain these later. Here we prefix "@" in the front of organizations to distinguish them from roles. For example, a user with an active role-org pair (PSO, @PT1) is a security administrator in project team 1. *may_manage_user*(PSO, *u, (*PE, @PT1*)*, ¬(QE, ?)) is true if user *u* is affiliated with project team 1 (@PT1) and *u* is not a QE inside the project team 1. Based on the UROA07 grant-model, the user with active role-org pair (PSO, @PT1) can assign membership of roles: PL, PE, QE, and ENG within project team 1, to users affiliated with the project team 1 but he/she cannot assign these users to roles within project team 2 and cannot assign users not affiliated to project team 1 to any roles. He/she also cannot assign both (PE, @PT1) and (QE, @PT1) to the same user because of the user prerequisite conditions, ((PSO, PE), ¬(QE, ?)) and ((PSO, QE),

Figure 6. Role and organization hierarchies using administrative ROBAC

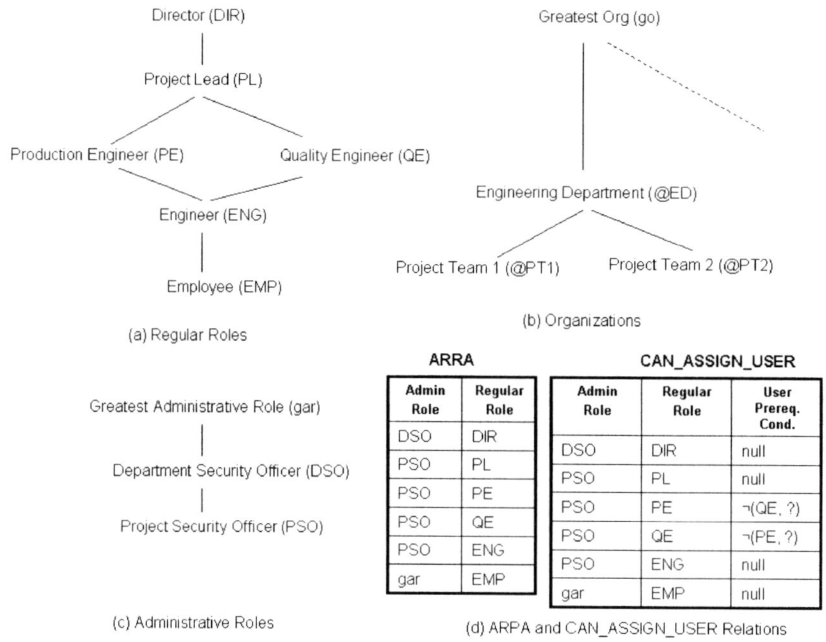

ARRA

Admin Role	Regular Role
DSO	DIR
PSO	PL
PSO	PE
PSO	QE
PSO	ENG
gar	EMP

CAN_ASSIGN_USER

Admin Role	Regular Role	User Prereq. Cond.
DSO	DIR	null
PSO	PL	null
PSO	PE	¬(QE, ?)
PSO	QE	¬(PE, ?)
PSO	ENG	null
gar	EMP	null

(d) ARPA and CAN_ASSIGN_USER Relations

¬(PE, ?)) , defined in CAN_ASSIGN_USER at Figure 6(d), which represents a global separation of duty constraint in ROBAC.

If there are more project teams in the engineering department or there are more engineering departments, we only need to add them in the organization set O and organization hierarchy OH but do not need to change other settings in ROBAC. Even with 100s or more project teams, the UROA07 model will scale up very nicely whereas previous models will become incomprehensible.

To complete the definition of the UROA07 model we define the Revoke Model as follows.

Definition 5: The UROA07 Revoke Model – *can_revoke_user* predicate controls whether a user can be revoked from a role-org pair within a session. Formally, *can_revoke_user(s, u, (r,o))* is true iff (∃*o'* ≥ *o*, ∃*(ar, o')* ∈ *active_role-orgs*(*s*)) ∧ (∀*c*, *((ar, r), c)* ∈ CAN_REVOKE_USER ∧ *may_manage_user(ar, u, (r,o), c)*).

The PRA07 Model

The PRA07 model deals with managing permission to role assignment. Similar to UROA07, it also provides two predicates to determine whether a session can assign or revoke permission to or from a role. We give the following definitions in analogy to similar definitions for UROA07.

permission prerequisite condition (ppc) – a *ppc* is a boolean expression using the usual ∧ and ∨ operators on terms of form of *r* and ¬*r* where *r* is a role in RR. A *permission prerequisite condition* is evaluated for a permission *p* by interpreting *r* to be true if (∃*r'* ≤ *r*, (*p*, *r'*) ∈ PA) and ¬*r* is true if (∀*r'* ≥ *r*, (*p*, *r'*) ∉ PA. CRP is a set which includes all applicable *ppc*s plus a *null* element. The *null* is interpreted as true for any permission.

opermissions: O → 2^P, is a function mapping an organization to a set of permissions which applicable to the organization;

formally, *opermissions*(o) = { p: P | $(p, o) \in$ PO }; *opermissions**(o) = { p: P | $\exists o' \leq o, (p, o') \in$ PO }

Note: *opermissions*(o) is the set of all permissions applicable to the organization o and *opermissions**(o) is the set of all permissions applicable to the organization o or its subordinate organizations.

can_manage_permission: RO × P × RR × CRP → {true, false} – a predicate defined as *can_manage_permission((ar, o), p, r, c)* is true iff ($r \in$ *apermissions**(ar)) $\wedge\ c \wedge$ ($p \in$ *omembers**(o)).

Note: The definition of *can_manage_permission((ar, o), p, r, c)* indicates that a user who is a member of administrative role-org pair *(ar, o)* can manage the permission p for the role r if and only if permission p satisfies the permission prerequisite condition c and is applicable to the organization o or its subordinate organizations and the administrative role ar or its junior administrative roles can perform administrative tasks on the regular role r.

This leads to the following Grant Model.

Definition 6: The PRA07 Grant Model – *can_assign_permission* predicate controls whether a permission can be assigned to a role within a session. Formally, *can_assign_permission(s, p, r)* is true iff $\exists(ar, o) \in$ *active_role-orgs*(s) $\wedge$ ($\forall c$, *((ar, r), c)* $\in$ CAN_ASSIGN_PERMISSION $\wedge$ *can_manage_permission((ar, o), p, r, c)*.

The definition of *can_assign_permission(s, p, r)* in PRA07 indicates that a user (*user(s)*) in a session s can assign a permission p to a role r if and only if *user(s)* has an active role-org pair *(ar, o)* in that session, and the administrative role ar or its junior administrative roles have administrative right over the regular role r, and the permission p is applicable to the organization o or its subordinate organizations, and the permission p satisfies all specified permission prerequisite conditions defined in CAN_ASSIGN_PERMISSION. The permission prerequisite condition in PRA07 is optional.

Finally we have the following Revoke Model.

Definition 7: The PRA07 Revoke Model – *can_revoke_permission* predicate controls whether a permission can be revoked from a role within a session. Formally, *can_revoke_permission(s, p, r)* is true iff ($\exists(ar, o) \in$ *active_role-orgs*(s) $\wedge$ ($\forall c$, *((ar, r), c)* $\in$ CAN_REVOKE_PERMISSION $\wedge$ *can_manage_permission((ar, o), r, c)*).

The RRA07 Model

The RRA07 model deals with managing roles and role hierarchy. It provides one predicate called *can_modify_R* to determine whether the current session can add/remove a role or change role hierarchy during the session. To define *can_modify_R* predicate, we need to introduce some definitions.

rjuniors: R → 2^R, is a function mapping a role to its junior roles; formally, *rjuniors*(r) = { r': R | $r' < r$ }

rseniors: R → 2^R, is a function mapping a role to its senior roles; formally, *rseniors*(r) = { r': R | $r' > r$ }

rfamily: R → 2^R, is a function mapping a role to a set of roles including itself and its junior role and senior roles; formally, *rfamily*(r) = $\{r\} \cup$ *rjuniors*(r) $\cup$ *rseniors*(r)

rfamilies: 2^R → 2^R, is a function mapping a set of roles to a set of roles including all families of its members; formally, *rfamilies*($\{r_1, r_2, \ldots r_n\}$) = *rfamily*(r_1) $\cup$ *rfamily*(r_2) $\cup \ldots \cup$ *rfamily*(r_n)

It is worth noting that *rfamily* and *rfamilies* only include recursive direct family members and do not include siblings.

permissible administrative role set, parset: AR $\rightarrow 2^{RR}$, is a function mapping an administrative role to a set of regular roles in which the administrative role can modify the regular role hierarchy. Formally,

$parset(ar) = \{ r : RR \mid (ar, r) \in ARRA \wedge rfamily(r) \subseteq apermissions^*(rfamily(ar)) \}$.

The above definition indicates that *parset* for an administrative role *ar* includes all of the regular roles it has administrative privilege such that the regular role's family is a part of the regular roles the *ar*'s family has administrative privilege over. For example *parset*(PSO) = { PL, PE }.

Because modifying role hierarchy affects all organizations in ROBAC, we should only allow the users at the highest organization level to perform these actions. We introduce an artificial organization called *greatest organization* (*go*) which is the ancestor for all organizations in O (see Figure 3). Now let us define the *can_modify_R* predicate.

Definition 8: *can_modify_R*: $S \times 2^{RR} \rightarrow$ {true, false} -- a predicate defined as *can_modify_R(s, rset)* is true iff $\exists(ar, go) \in active\_role\text{-}orgs(s) \wedge rset \subseteq parset(ar)$.

The definition of *can_modify_R* means that a user *user(s)* in a session *s* can modify the relationship within the role set *rset* if and only if that the user has an active administrative role *ar* and paired with the greatest organization *go* in that session and the role set *rset* is a subset of the *permissible administrative role set* of *ar*. Here the modification within a set of roles means adding/deleting an edge or adding/removing a role. For example, according to Figure 6, PSO can remove the edge between PL and PE but cannot remove the edge between ENG and QE because QE and ENG are not in its *permissible administrative role set*.

The OOA07 Model

The OOA07 model deals with managing organizations and organization hierarchy. Similar to RRA07, it provides one predicate called *can_modify_O* to determine whether the current session can add/remove an organization or change organization hierarchy during the session. To define *can_modify_O* predicate, we also need to introduce some definitions.

ojuniors: O $\rightarrow 2^{O}$, is a function mapping an organization to its subordinate organizations.

Formally, $ojuniors(o) = \{ o' : O \mid o' < o \}$

oseniors: O $\rightarrow 2^{O}$, is a function mapping an organization to its parent organizations.

Formally, $oseniors(o) = \{ o' : O \mid o' > o \}$

ofamily: O $\rightarrow 2^{O}$, is a function mapping an organization to a set of organizations including itself and its subordinate organizations and parent organizations. Formally, $ofamily(o) = \{o\} \cup ojuniors(o) \cup oseniors(o)$

permissible administrative organization set, paoset: O $\rightarrow 2^{O}$, is a function mapping an organization to a set of organizations. Formally, $paoset(o) = \{ o' : O \mid o' < o \wedge ofamily(o') \subseteq ofamily(o) \}$

For example, *paoset*(@ED) = { @PT1, @PT2 } according to Figure 6(b).

Because modifying organization hierarchy has some global effects on the access right in ROBAC, we should only allow the most senior administrative role to modify the organization hierarchy. We can pre-define a most senior administrative role called *gar* (*greatest administrative role*) in

AR. Here is the definition for *can_modify_O* predicate.

Definition 9: *can_modify_O*: $S \times 2^O \rightarrow$ {true, false} -- a predicate defined as *can_modify_O(s, oset)* is true iff $\exists(gar, o) \in active\_role\text{-}orgs(s) \wedge oset \subseteq paroet(o)$.

The definition of *can_modify_O* means that a user *user(s)* in a session *s* can modify the relationship within the organization set *oset* if and only if that the user has the greatest administrative role *gar* in an organization *o* in that session and the organization set *oset* is a subset of the *permissible administrative organization set* of *o*. For example, a user assigned (gar, @ED) can remove @PT1 from the organization hierarchy or add a new organization say @PT3 under it.

The ROA07 Model

The ROA07 model deals with managing role and organization association in ROBAC. Similar to other models, it provides one predicate called *can_modify_RO* to determine whether the current session can associate / disassociate a role with an organization.

Definition 10: *can_modify_RO*: $S \times R \times O \rightarrow$ {true, false} -- a predicate defined as *can_modify_RO(s, r, o)* is true iff $(\exists o' \geq o, \exists(ar, o') \in active\_role\text{-}orgs(s)) \wedge r \in apermissions^*(ar)$.

The definition of *can_modify_RO* means that a user *user(s)* in a session *s* can associate or disassociate the role *r* with the organization *o* if and only if *user(s)* has an active role and organization pair *(ar, o')* in that session and *o* is *o'* or a subordinate of *o'* and the administrative role *ar* or its junior administrative roles can perform administrative tasks on the role *r*. For example, a user assigned (PSO, @PT1) can associate PE with @PT1 but cannot disassociate PE from @PT2.

The five sub-models in AROBAC07 decentralize the administrative tasks along the administrative role hierarchy and organization hierarchy. They control administrative tasks based on both administrative role permissions and organization hierarchy. This is a ROBAC approach to perform administrative work on ROBAC systems.

Discussion and Related Work

ROBAC models require that organizations have similar roles. Administrator roles across organizations tend to have greater similarity than the underlying regular roles may have. So the ROBAC concept is particularly well suited to administrative tasks. A user assigned an administrative role and organization pair *(ar, o)* can perform administrative tasks the *ar* allowed within the organization *o* and its subordinate organizations. Administrative tasks in AROBAC07 can be delegated not only along the administrative role hierarchy but also along the organization hierarchy.

As we mentioned earlier, AROBAC07 model is inspired by the following three role-based administrative models: ARBAC97, ARBAC02, and SARBAC.

ARBAC97 is one of the most comprehensive role-based administrative models. It uses *role range (encapsulated range)* concept to define the scope of administrative permission. The *user prerequisite condition (upc)* and *permission prerequisite condition (ppc)* in AROBAC07 are extended versions of the corresponding prerequisite conditions in ARBAC97.

ARBAC02 enhances ARBAC97 by incorporating two external organization structures: *user organization structure* (OS-U) and *permission organization structure* (OS-P). URA02 and PRA02 sub-models in ARBAC02 modify the prerequisite conditions in URA97 and PRA97 of ARABC97 by using memberships of organizations to avoid some weakness, such as multi-step assignments, redundant assignment information, restricted hierarchy etc., in ARBAC97. ARBAC02 uses the organization structures only for constructing user pool and permission pool in prerequisite conditions but does not use it to control administrative permissions. UROA07 and PRA07 in AROBAC07 use the build-in organization hierarchy and implicitly enforce the user pool and permission pool constraints with respect to *can_assign_user* and *can_revoke_user* and *can_assign_permission* and *can_revoke_permission* predicates. So UROA07 and PRA07 have similar benefits of user pool and permission pool concepts used in URA02 and PRA02 models without putting the user pool or permission pool as a part of the prerequisite conditions. Similar to ARBAC02, AROBAC07 avoids the weakness of ARBAC97 by using the build-in organization hierarchy, the user-organization affiliation information, and the applicable permissions and organization association information.

SARBAC introduces a concept called *administrative scope*, which can be calculated for each role-based on the role hierarchy. SARBAC tends to be simpler, more flexible, and more permissible than ARBAC97. The ARRA relation in AROBAC07 is similar to the **can_admin** relation in SARBAC. The current construction of *permissible administrative role set (parset)* concept in RRA07 is similar to the *administrative scope* concept in SARBAC. From that perspective, RRA07 is very similar to RH_4 sub-model in SARBAC. So RRA07 has some similar benefits, such as flexibility, that SARBC enjoys. Unlike RH_4, RRA07 enforces strict separation between regular roles and administrative roles because we believe the separation of administrative duty from regular duty is a desired security policy in most cases. It is possible that we can construct *parset* differently, such as using the *encapsulated range* concept in RRA97 or other criteria. The OOA07 applies the similar concept on the role hierarchy.

X-GTRBAC admin (Bhatti et al, 2004) is a decentralized administrative model for the XML-based Generalized Temporal Role-based Access Control (X-GTRBAC) framework (Bhatti et al, 2003). It uses a concept called *admin domain* to tire roles (admin roles and regular roles), permissions (admin permissions and regular permissions), and users (admin users and regular users) together. It uses hard-coded Eligible Role (ER) for users in admin domain to put constraint on user to role assignment task. It uses Admin Permissions to model the possible administrative tasks. An administrator in an Admin Role is authorized to handle assignment of users to regular roles within a given domain. Both administrative roles and admin domains in X-GTRBAC admin are flat. If considering an admin domain as an organization, X-GTRBAC admin's impact on X-GTRBAC framework is similar to the UROA07's impact on $ROBAC_0$ based system. It is hard for X-GTRBAC admin to achieve similar functionality AROBAC07 has when organization hierarchy or/and administrative hierarchy exist.

The first three of aforementioned role-based administrative models control administrative tasks based on roles only while AROBAC07 controls administrative tasks based on both roles and organizations. From the perspective of administrative units, the admin domain concept in X-GTRBAC admin is similar to the organization concept in UROA07 for $ROBAC_0$ based systems, but AROBAC07 has more functionality that the X-GTRBAC admin seems hard to achieve.

In AROBAC07, we use the same ARRA relation across all sub-models. It may be desirable that we use a different version of ARRA in each sub-model when finer-grain control is needed. The administrative role hierarchy in AROBAC07 tends to be simpler than these existing models when there are many organizational units, such as lots of branches or project teams, in an enterprise. With ROBAC/AROBAC07, security policies can be defined in a small scope first and then applied to all organizations.

Practical Consideration when Applying ROBAC to Web Applications

In real world, an authorization service needs to support many applications in an enterprise. AROBAC07 model not only can decentralize the administrative tasks along organization hierarchy, but also can decentralize the tasks along the administrative role hierarchy. Creating appropriate administrative roles and administrative role hierarchy is critical to achieve decentralized administration in ROBAC system.

ACom Based Delegation Model

Each application normally has its own set of roles and these roles are only applicable to the application. So the regular role set may be partitioned based on which application the roles belong to. Here we introduce the concept of application compartment. We denote **App** as a set of all applications controlled by a ROBAC system.

Definition 11: An Application Compartment (ACom) for an application $app_i \in$ **App** in a ROBAC system is a tuple: (U_i, R_i O_i, P_i, RO_i, RH_i, OH_i, PA_i, UA_i), where:

- $U_i = U$ -- the same set of users as in ROABC;
- $R_i \subseteq R$ -- a subset of roles applicable to this application;
- $O_i \subseteq O$ -- a subset of organizations applicable to this application;
- $P_i \subseteq P$ -- a subset of permissions applicable to this application;
- $RO_i \subseteq R_i \times O_i$ -- a set of applicable role and organization association in this application;
- $RH_i \subseteq R_i \times R_i$ -- a partial order relation on R_i called role hierarchy;
- $OH_i \subseteq O_i \times O_i$ -- a partial order relation on O_i called organization hierarchy;
- $PA_i \subseteq P_i \times R_i$ -- a many-to-many permission-to-role assignment relation;
- $UA_i \subseteq U_i \times RO_i$ -- a many-to-many user-to-role-and-organization assignment relation;

Let's use *acom*(app_i) to represent the ACom corresponding to application app_i and denote ACOM as a set of all application compartments in the ROBAC system. We can think of *acom*(app_i) as being controlled by a sub ROBAC system. Here we define a dominate relation DOM in ACOM.

Definition 12: DOM $\subseteq$ ACOM $\times$ ACOM -- is a partial order relation on ACOM such that (*acom*(app_i), *acom*(app_j)) $\in$ DOM iff $U_i \subseteq U_j \wedge R_i \subseteq R_j \wedge O_i \subseteq O_j \wedge P_i \subseteq P_j \wedge RO_i \subseteq RO_j \wedge RH_i \subseteq RH_j \wedge OH_i \subseteq OH_j \wedge PA_i \subseteq PA_j \wedge UA_i \subseteq UA_j$.

For administration purpose, we can create an administrative role ar_i for each *acom*(app_i). That requires adding ar_i in AR, adding $\{ ar_i \} \times R_i$ into ARRA, and adding (ar_i, ar_j) in ARH iff (*acom*(app_i), *acom*(app_j)) $\in$ DOM.

The partitioning process may continue within an application. In general, we can form a hierarchy in AR based on the DOM relationship. The senior administrative role can delegate the administrative tasks to its junior administrative roles safely. ACom concept not only provides a way to partition the regular role set (and construct administrative role hierarchy) in AROBAC07, but also can be used to enforce application boundary. For example, when a user *u* enters an application, say app_i, the ROBAC system only actives the role-org pairs applicable to this application. That is,

if a user *u* is inside app_i then *active_roles-orgs(u)* $\subseteq$ *assigned_role-orgs(u)* $\cap$ *acom*(app_i).RO_i.

where *acom*(app_i).RO_i represents the role-org pairs applicable to the application app_i. You may notice that AROBAC07 does not explicitly talk about how to assign / revoke users to/from administrative role and organization pairs. In practice, a user with administrative role and organization pair *(ar, o)* can assign (or revoke) users to (or from) administrative role and org pair *(ar', o')* such that $ar' \leq ar$ and $o' \leq o$. It is not hard to develop a formal sub-model similar to the UROA07 model if more complex constraints are needed. So a user assigned with *(gar, @go)* can act like a super user in a ROBAC system. The syntax of assigning user to role and organization pair is same regardless a role is a regular role or an administrative role. This feature makes AROBAC07 easy to implement in practice.

A partial implementation of a $ROBAC_1$ model has been successfully used as an authorization engine, which provides authorization services for multiple web applications (https://epl.collegeboard.com/epl/goHome.do).

CONCLUSION

A family of extended RBAC models called Role and Organization Based Access Control (ROBAC) models is reviewed and its corresponding administrative model called AROBAC07 is presented and formalized in this chapter. The motivation behind ROBAC is to scale up RBAC for B2B and B2C applications where a large number of organizational units are involved. The advantages of ROBAC models over traditional RBAC models are shown via two examples. We claim that ROBAC is more intuitive and succinct than many RBAC variants when used for scenarios involving a large number of similar organizational units and the privacy issue is a major concern.

The AROABC07 is a decentralized role and organization based administrative model for ROBAC. It has five sub-models: UROA07 is concerned with user to role and organization pair assignment; PRA07 deals with permission-role assignment; RRA07 manages roles and role hierarchy; OOA07 handles organizations and organization hierarchy; and ROA07 controls applicable association between roles and organizations. UROA07 and PRA07 obtain the benefits of user pool and permission pool concepts in ARBAC02 without specifying user pool and permission pool explicitly. RRA07 has the similar advantage of RHA_4 in SARBAC over RRA97 in ARBAC97 without sacrificing the separation of duty between administrative roles and regular roles. OOA07 and ROA07 provide ways to decentralize the administrative tasks on organization hierarchy and applicable role and organization association. We claim that AROBAC07 scales up well and is better than using existing role-based administrative models by providing more controlled and decentralized approaches to perform administrative tasks on ROBAC.

Many serious security breaches are due to internal users. So it is very important to restrict and control administrative actions on access control systems. ROBAC/AROBAC07 scales up classic RBAC systems for situations where many similar organizational units are involved. It inherits the RBAC's good features and provides a way to restrict access control within specified organizational units without introducing too much administrative burden on access control systems. It is quite suitable for modeling privacy related security policy.

The implication of *can_modify_R*, *can_modify_O*, and *can_modify_RO* predicates on different administrative tasks such as add/delete nodes or edges need to be detailed and studied further. How to manage other aspects of ROBAC such as integrating general constraints and defining *atype* and *aorg* functions may also merit further study.

REFERENCES

American National Standard Institute. ANSI INCITS 359-2004 for Role-based Access Control. 2004

Bertino, E., Bonatti, P. A., & Ferrari, E. (2001, August). TRBAC: A temporal role-based access control model. ACM Transactions on Information & System Security, 4(3), 191-233.

Bertino, E., Catania, B., Damiani, M. L., & Perlasca, P. (2005, June). Access control model I: GEO-RBAC: a spatially aware RBAC. *Proceedings of the tenth ACM symposium on Access control models and technologies.*

Bhatti, R. (2003). *X-GTRBAC: An XML-based Policy Specification Framework and Architecture for Enterprise Wide Access Control.* Masters thesis, Purdue University, May 2003.

Bhatti, R., Joshi, J., Bertino, E., & Ghafoor, A. (2004, June). Role administration: X-GTRBAC admin: a decentralized administration model for enterprise wide access control. *Proceedings of the ninth ACM symposium on Access control models and technologies.*

Crampton, J., & Loizou, G. (2003, May). Administrative Scope: A Foundation for Role-Based Administrative Models. *ACM Transactions on Information and System Security, 6*(2), 201-231.

Covington, M. J., Long, Srinivasan, S., Dev, A. K., Ahamad, M., & Abowd, G. D. (2001, May). Securing context-aware applications using environment roles. *Proceedings of the sixth ACM symposium on Access control models and technologies.*

Ferraiolo, D. F., Barkley, J. F., & Kuhn, D. R. (1999, February). A role-based access control model and reference implementation within a corporate intranet. *ACM Transactions on Information and System Security (TISSEC), 2*(1).

Ferraiolo, D., Sandhu, R., Gavrila, S., Kuhn, D., & Chandramouli, R. (2001). Proposed NIST standard for role-based access control. *ACM Transactions on Information and System Security (TISSEC), 4*(3).

Gavrila, S., & Barkley, J. (1998, October). Formal Specification for RBAC User/Role and Role/Role Relationship Management. *Proceedings of Third ACM Workshop on Role-Based Access Control.* Fairfax, VA, USA.

Giuri, L., & Iglio, P. (1997). Role Templates for Content-Based Access Control. *Proceedings of Second ACM Workshop on Role-Based Access Control*, Fairfax, VA, USA, November 1997

Georgiadis, C. K., Mavridis, I., Pangalos, G., & Thomas, R. K. (2001). Flexible Team-Based Access Control Using Contexts. *Proceedings of Sixth ACM Symposium on Access Control Models*, May 2001, Fairfax, Virginia, USA.

Joshi, J. B. D., Bertino, E., Latif, U., & Ghafoor, A. (2005). A generalized temporal role-based access control model (GTRBAC). *IEEE Transaction on Knowledge and Data Engineering 17*,1 (Jan. 2005).

Kumar, A., Karnik, N., & Chafle, G. (2002, July). Context sensitivity in role-based access control, ACM SIGOPS Operating Systems Review, 36(3),.

Nyanchama, M., & Osborn, S. (1999, February). The Role Graph Model and Conflict Of Interest, ACM Transactions on Information and System Security, 2(1), 3-33.

Oh, S., Sandhu, R., & Zhang, X. (2006, May). An Effective Role Administration Model Using Organization Structure. *ACM Transactions on Information and System Security, 9*(2), 113-137.

Park, J. S., Costello, K. P., Neven, T. M., & Diosomito, J. A. (2004). A Composite RBAC Approach for Large, Complex Organizations. *Proceedings of Ninth ACM Symposium on Access Control Models*, June 2004, Yorktown Heights, New York, USA.

Perwaiz, N., & Sommerville, I. (2001). Structured Management of Role-Permission Relationships. *Proceedings of Sixth ACM Symposium on Access Control Models*, May 2001, Fairfax, Virginia, USA.

RTI International. (2002). The Economic Impact of Role-Based Access Control. March 2002. Retrieved from http://www.nist.gov/director/prog-ofc/report02-1.pdf

Sandhu, R., Bhamidipati, V., & Munawer, Q. (1999, February). The ARBAC97 Model for Role-Based Administration of Roles, *ACM Transactions on Information and Systems Security, 2.*

Sandhu, R., Coyne, E., Feinstein, H., & Youman, C. (1996, February). Role-Based Access Control Models. *IEEE Computer, 29*(2).

Sandhu, R., Ferraiolo, D., & Kuhn, R. (2000). The NIST Model for Role-Based Access Control: Towards A Unified Standard. National Institute of Standards and Technology, December 2000, http://csrc.nist.gov/rbac/sandhu-ferraiolo-kuhn-00.pdf

Schaad, A., Moffett, J., & Jacob, J. (2001). The Role-Based Access Control System of a European Bank: A Case Study and Discussion. *Proceedings of Sixth ACM Symposium on Access Control Models*, May 2001, Fairfax, Virginia, USA.

Thomas, R. K. (1997). Team-Based Acccss Control (TMAC): A Primitive for Applying Role-Based Access Controls in Collaborative Environments. *Proceedings of the Second ACM workshop on Role-based Access Control*, Fairfax, VA, USA, 1997.

Zhang, Z., Zhang, X., & Sandhu, R. (2006). ROBAC: Scalable Role and Organization Based Access Control Models. *Proceedings of CollaborateCom-2006/TrustCol-2006*, Atlanta, Georgia, USA, November 2006.

KEY TERMS

Administrative RBAC: Refers to approaches of controlling administrative tasks in RBAC. It usually provides ways to control the following major administrative tasks: assigning users to roles (user to role assignment), assigning permissions to roles (permission to role assignment), and adjusting role hierarchy (role to role assignment).

Administrative ROBAC: Refers to approaches of controlling administrative tasks in ROBAC. It usually provides ways to control the following major administrative tasks: assigning users to role-organization pairs, assigning permissions to roles, managing roles and role hierarchy, managing organizations and organization hierarchy, and managing role and organization association.

Application Compartment (ACom): An *ACom* of an application is a subset of a ROBAC where only the users, permissions, roles, and organizations applicable to the application are included.

Permissible Administrative Organization Set (PAOSET): A *paoset* of an organization is a set of organizations in which the greatest administrative role (gar) in the organization can modify the organization hierarchy.

Permissible Administrative Role Set (PARSET): A *parset* of an administrative role is a set of regular roles in which the administrative role can modify the regular role hierarchy.

Permission Prerequisite Condition (PPC): A condition a permission needs to be met before the permission can be assigned to roles.

Role-Based Access Control (RBAC): A method to restrict user's access to system resources based on the user's roles. In RBAC, roles are defined based on job functions, permissions are associated with roles, and users are made members of appropriate roles, thereby acquiring the roles' permissions.

Role and Organization Based Access Control (ROBAC): An extension of RBAC. In ROBAC, access is based on user's roles and the indirect association between users and system resources via organizations.

User Prerequisite Condition (UPC): A condition a user needs to be met before the user can be assigned to roles or role-organization pairs.

Chapter VII
Enterprise Information System Security:
A Life-Cycle Approach

Chandan Mazumdar
Jadavpur University, India

Mridul Sankar Barik
Jadavpur University, India

Anirban Sengupta
Jadavpur University, India

ABSTRACT

There has been an unprecedented thrust in employing Computers and Communication technologies in all walks of life. The systems enabled by Information Technology are becoming more and more complex resulting in various threats and vulnerabilities. The security properties, like confidentiality, integrity, and availability, are becoming more and more difficult to protect. In this chapter, a life-cycle approach to achieve and maintain security of enterprises has been proposed. First, enterprise information systems are looked at in detail. Then, the need for enterprise information system security and problems associated with security implementation are discussed. The authors consider enterprise information system security as a management issue and detail the information security parameters. Finally, the proposed security engineering life-cycle is described in detail, which includes, Security Requirement Analysis, Security Policy Formulation, Security Infrastructure Advisory Generation, Security Testing and Validation, and Review and Monitoring phases.

INTRODUCTION

There has been unprecedented thrust in employing Computers and Communication technologies in all walks of life including business, education and governance in almost all the countries. This is a one-way trend in the sense that there is no going back. While, this means lower cost, operational efficiency and client satisfaction, on the flip side, the systems enabled by Information Technology are becoming more and more complex resulting in various vulnerabilities. Also, there are innumerable threats which exploit those vulnerabilities. More importantly, due to global connectivity through the Internet, threats are not confined to a particular area or region; they are omnipresent. These threats pose problems to the economic and administrative independence.

In the context of Information Security, as our information infrastructures are becoming more and more complex, and connected, the properties like confidentiality, integrity and availability are becoming more and more difficult to protect/achieve. The adoption of Information Technology Act in different countries provides the legal framework for acceptance of electronic documents in business and governance, as well as to deter the wrong-doers. Also, the international community is adopting Standards such as ISO 27001 (Snare, 2005) and ISO 17799 (Plate, 2005) for best practices in security management. All these standards have evolved from the knowledge, experience and expertise of international experts. It has been recognized that the security of enterprises has to be tackled from the point of view of a management structure than from purely technological angle.

The rest of this chapter is organized as follows. Section 2 presents some background information and defines an enterprise and its functionality. It also details enterprise information systems and discusses the need for enterprise information system security. Section 3 lists the issues, controversies and problems associated with security implementation. It describes enterprise information system security as a management issue and details the information security parameters. Section 4 describes our proposed security engineering life-cycle. Section 5 lists few future research areas in enterprise information system security. Finally, our conclusions are in section 6.

BACKGROUND

Enterprise and its Functionality

The *Compact Oxford English Dictionary* (Weiner, 1991) defines an "enterprise" as "a project or undertaking, especially a bold one"; "bold resourcefulness"; or, "a business or company". *Webopedia* states that an enterprise is "a business organization. In the computer industry, the term is often used to describe any large organization that utilizes computers". Combining these, we define an enterprise as an organization (Industry/ Govt./Academic) created for business or service ventures. From the Information Security point of view, an enterprise is characterized by its business goals, business activities, organizational structure, and assets and infrastructure.

The *Compact Oxford English Dictionary* (Weiner, 1991) defines "information" as "facts or knowledge provided or learned; what is conveyed or represented by a particular sequence of symbols, impulses, etc". The Wikipedia entry for information is "the result of processing, manipulating and organizing data in a way that adds to the knowledge of the receiver". Thus, information can be viewed as data that is organized and accessible in a coherent and meaningful manner. The generation and use of information has some commonalities in different types of enterprises. For example, all of them rely on user and operator interactions, reliable storage and retrieval, correct processing, as well as timely and good quality dissemination of information. More and more enterprises are becoming dependent on the efficiency and quality of generation and processing of information. Information has become the prime mover in the growth and sustenance of all kinds of enterprises. Information and the technology supporting the creation, and management of information act as important assets of any enterprise. Thus there is a specific need to protect these assets.

Enterprise Information System

Various information resources which are building blocks of any enterprise information system are typically classified into five categories (not necessarily disjoint): containers, transporters, sensors, recorders, and processors (Denning, 1999).

Containers are physical media that hold information. Examples include human memories, computer memories, print media, tapes, disks, and containers for the above. Objects and communication systems that carry information from one location to another are *Transporters*. Examples include human messengers, who carry the information whenever they move from one place to another; physical transportation systems, i.e. trucks, planes, and postal systems; point-to-point telecommunications systems; broadcast media; and computer networks. *Sensors* extract information from other objects and the environment. Examples are human sensors, cameras, microphones, scanners, and radar. Devices like printers, tape recorders, and disk writers that place information in containers are called *Recorders*. Finally, objects that manipulate information are *information processors*. Examples include humans, computer hardware, and software.

All these resources in an information system work in unison enabling information flow from one container to another and over a variety of transporters. Sensors extract information from the physical environment, which is then computerized, processed, broadcast over radio and television, transmitted over telecommunications systems, computer networks, and fed into devices that control processes in the environment such as heating and cooling. This interconnectivity of resources also paves the way for hackers to initiate operations that affect resources other than those explicitly hit.

Need for Enterprise Information System Security

To get a feeling of the urgent need for information system security in the present day scenario, we have to look back at the age of purely paper-based enterprises. In those days, security of valuable information was primarily provided by means of physical and administrative means. But the widespread use of sophisticated data processing equipments in day-to-day enterprise activities necessitated a face change for enterprise information security. This also became evident with the introduction of distributed transaction systems such as railway reservation systems, ATM networks, enterprise WAN etc. Here the main concern is the security of data during transmission over private or public network (Hassler, 2001).

Documents play a key role in most of the human activities ranging from commerce, foreign policy, military action, and personal interactions etc. and success in most of the cases depend on all the parties involved, having confidence over the integrity of the documents involved. Documents typically carry signatures and dates which require protection from disclosure, tampering, or destruction. With information systems becoming ever more pervasive and essential to our day-to-day activities, electronic information is taking over many of the roles traditionally performed by paper documents. These call for efficient technologies for electronic documents to replace functions traditionally performed with paper-based documents.

To survive in the present day competitive business scenario, enterprises are often driven to provide their services online. But security of online transactions becomes a major issue for enterprises which need to take such a decision. Also the security requirements of individual transactions vary widely from one type to another. For example, a million-dollar commercial construction loan being approved by all the parties involved has a much stronger security requirement than basic consumer transactions such as purchasing a CD or a customer service request. Additionally, confidential documents such as financial or health records when put online, requires enhanced security to ensure personal privacy.

In the light of the above discussion, we are now in a position to answer the question: "Why is information security important?", as it is crucial for enterprises to define why they want to achieve information security, in order to determine how they will achieve it. Information security is important for the following reasons:

- *To protect enterprise assets:* This is one of our primary goals. By "assets" we mean the hardware, software, and information assets of an enterprise. Hardware assets (Casar, 2004) consist of computing systems, communication links, and IT sites (or, rooms) in which computing systems are installed. Software assets are the automated and manual applications that process information. Information asset pertains to input, processed, output and stored data.
- *To gain a competitive advantage:* Developing and maintaining effective security measures can provide an enterprise with a competitive advantage over its peers. Information security is particularly important in the area of e-commerce and financial services provided over the Internet. It can mean the difference between wide acceptance of a service and a mediocre customer response. For example, how many people do you know who would use a bank's Internet banking system if they knew that the system has been successfully hacked in the past? Not many. They would rather go to the competitors for their Internet banking services. Enterprise security practices instill confidence in customers and employees. This, in turn, makes potential customers' decision of doing business with an enterprise easier, knowing that best security practices are adopted by the enterprise.
- *To comply with regulatory requirements and fiduciary responsibilities:* Information Security officers of every enterprise have a responsibility to ensure the safety and soundness of the enterprise, which also includes the continuing operation of the enterprise. As a result, enterprises that rely on computing elements for their business must develop policies and procedures that address not only the protection of information assets but also protection of the enterprise from liability. For example financial organizations must protect shareholders' investments and maximize return. In addition, organizations are often subject to government regulations, which generally stipulate safety and security requirements of an organization. Severe penalty is imposed on those enterprises which fail to comply with regulations. In some cases, corporate officers who have not properly performed their regulatory and fiduciary responsibilities are personally liable for any losses incurred by the financial institution that employ them.

ISSUES, CONTROVERSIES AND PROBLEMS OF ENTERPRISE INFORMATION SYSTEM SECURITY

Present Scenario

Information infrastructure consists of technologies for gathering, handling, and sharing information. As the dependence on information infrastructure is significantly increasing there are also rising cases of vulnerability breaches, threats, cyber attacks and cascading or pervasive failures. They are caused due to lack of inherent security in new technologies and protocols, flaws in commonly used products, failures to address security concerns in system design and use, lack of management commitment and approach, and lack of user awareness about security.

Organizations such as banking, finance, telecommunication, transportation and energy have infrastructures that are highly interdependent. Attacks on one infrastructure can damage other infrastructure as well. Concentrated infrastructure attacks could thus have a significant effect on our national security and economy.

A look at the information security requirements of organizations reveal that the amount of IT assets, employees and clients using those assets, nature of their use and geographic distribution of all these are huge. Even for a medium sized enterprise, the task of security management is too complex. Access to critical assets must be controlled after considering their specific security needs (like confidentiality, integrity, and availability needs, as discussed later in this chapter). Other factors like the dynamic nature of the security requirement and business context, combined with the technological infrastructure, patch management, and security testing, complicate matters.

For years, network security was based upon three primary products: firewalls, Vitual Private Networks (VPNs) and anti-virus software, but this security triad has reached its limit. Automated Internet worms, viruses, and Distributed Denial of Service (DDOS) attacks are more prevalent and virulent than ever before causing billions of dollars in worldwide damage and impacting companies like Bank of America, Continental Airlines, eBay, and Yahoo. Also, new technologies like IP telephony, WLANs, and Instant Messaging are gaining rapid acceptance opening up another potential avenue for attacks.

The Future

For the past 10 years, security managers have focused their efforts on the network perimeter with the belief that all external users are 'untrusted' while internal users are trusted. This kind of approach to security is no longer sufficient. The reasons are:

- The network perimeter is no longer static; remote users, contractors, partners, suppliers, even web services-based applications are all allowed network access regardless of physical location.
- Automated attacks often enter the network through legal TCP ports before creating havoc on internal systems.
- Many attacks come from disgruntled employees, not outside hackers. According to the CSI/FBI 2003 survey (Richardson, 2003), 77% of companies claim that employees are the most likely to commit security crimes.

As business requirements blur the perimeter between internal and external users, network availability is more important than ever. Thus worm and virus-driven interruptions must be minimized and contained. To do so, security managers are contemplating to apply new technologies to segment and protect internal networks including end-point security, network behavior modeling, Intrusion Detection/Prevention Systems (IDS/IPS), and internal firewalls.

Today's reactive network security strategy brings heartburn to security staff while leaving enterprises vulnerable to attacks. Fortunately, this situation faces extinction. Business executives now realize that security is an important and necessary component of their overall business infrastructure and must be comprehensive and sound. Over the next few years, companies will invest heavily in network security technology while they formalize policies and improve procedures. At the same time, security features will aggregate and integrate into network hardware and management software. These efforts will help companies establish an enterprise security view while lowering operating costs – a major bottleneck of security technology today.

Enterprise Information System Security is a Management Issue

Enterprise information system security is not absolute. All security measures are relative. Information security should be thought of as a spectrum that runs from very insecure to very secure. The level of security for an information system is dependent on where it lands along that spectrum relative to that point. There is no such thing as an absolutely secure information system. Information security is a balancing act that requires the deployment of "proportionate defense". The defenses that are deployed or implemented should be proportionate to the threat. Enterprises determine what is appropriate in several ways like balancing the cost of security against the value of the assets they are protecting; balancing the probable against the possible; balancing business needs against security needs.

Enterprises must determine how much it would cost to have each system or network compromised – in other words, how much it would lose in monetary terms owing to un-authorized access to the system or information theft. By assigning a monetary value to the cost of having a system or network compromised, enterprises can determine the upper limit they should be willing to pay to protect their systems. For many enterprises this exercise is not necessary, because information systems are lifeblood of the business. Without them there is no business. Enterprises also need to balance the cost of security against the cost of a security breach. Generally, as the investment in security increases, the expected losses should decrease. Companies should invest no more in security than the value of the assets they are protecting. This is where **cost benefit analysis** comes into play.

Moreover, enterprises must balance possible threats against probable threats, as it is not possible to defend against every possible type of attack. Therefore it is necessary to determine what types of threats or attacks have the greatest probability of occurring and then protect against them. For example, it is possible that an organization could be subjected to a van Eck monitoring or a high-energy radio frequency (HERF) attack, but the probability is low. It is also important to balance business needs with the need for security, assessing the operational impact of implementing security measures. Security measures and procedures that interfere with the operation of an organization are of little value. Those types of measures are usually ignored or circumvented by company personnel, so they tend to create, rather than plug, security holes. Whenever possible, security measures should complement the operational and business needs of an enterprise.

In other words, enterprise information system security is a management issue where, a fine balance is to be drawn between system efficiency, security expenses and information protection.

Enterprise Information System Security Parameters

The goal of enterprise information system security is to "enable an organization to meet all of its mission/business objectives by implementing systems with due care consideration of IT-related risks to the organization, its partners and customers". The security goal can be met through the following security parameters (Stoneburner, 2001).

Availability (of Systems and Data for Intended Use Only)

Availability (Yu, 1990) is a requirement intended to assure that systems work promptly and service is not denied to authorized users. This objective protects against:

- Intentional or accidental attempts to either perform unauthorized deletion of data or otherwise cause a denial of service or data.
- Attempts to use system or data for unauthorized purposes.

Availability is frequently an organization's foremost security parameter.

Integrity (of System and Data)

Integrity (Biba, 1975; Clark, 1989; Goguen, 1982 ; Mayfield, 1991) has two facets:

- Data integrity (the property that data has not been altered in an unauthorized manner while in storage, during processing, or while in transit) or
- System integrity (the quality that a system has when performing the intended function in an unimpaired manner, free from unauthorized manipulation).

Integrity is commonly an organization's most important security parameter after availability.

Confidentiality (of Data and System Information)

Confidentiality (Bell, 1976; Lampson, 1974) is the requirement that private or confidential information not be disclosed to unauthorized individuals. Confidentiality protection applies to data in storage, during processing, and while in transit. For many organizations, confidentiality is frequently behind availability and integrity in terms of importance. Yet for some systems and for specific types of data in most systems (e.g., authenticators), confidentiality is extremely important.

Accountability (to the Individual Level)

Accountability is the requirement that actions of an entity may be traced uniquely to that entity. Accountability is often an organizational policy requirement and directly supports non-repudiation, deterrence, fault isolation, intrusion detection and prevention, and after-action recovery and legal action.

Assurance (That the Other Four Parameters Have Been Adequately Met)

Assurance is the basis for confidence that the security measures, both technical and operational, work as intended to protect the system and the information it processes. The other four security parameters (integrity, availability, confidentiality, and accountability) have been adequately met by a specific implementation when:

- Required functionality is present and correctly implemented,
- There is sufficient protection against unintentional errors (by users or software), and
- There is sufficient resistance to intentional penetration or by-pass.

Assurance is essential; without it the other parameters are not met. However, assurance is a continuum; the amount of assurance needed varies between systems.

The five security parameters are interdependent (Stoneburner, 2001). Achieving one parameter without consideration of the others is seldom possible. This is depicted in Fig. 1 below. **Confidentiality** is dependent on Integrity, in that if the integrity of the system is lost, then there is no longer a reasonable expectation that the confidentiality mechanisms are still valid. **Integrity** is dependent on Confidentiality, in that if the confidentiality of certain information is lost (e.g., the super-user password), then the integrity mechanisms are likely to be by-passed. **Availability** and **Accountability** are dependent on Confidentiality and Integrity, in that:

- If confidentiality is lost for certain information (e.g., super-user password), the mechanisms implementing these parameters are easily by-passable; and

- If system integrity is lost, then confidence in the validity of the mechanisms implementing these parameters is also lost.

All of these parameters are interdependent with **Assurance**. When designing a system, an architect or engineer establishes an assurance level as a target. This target is achieved by both defining and meeting the functionality requirements in each of the other four parameters and doing so with sufficient "quality". Assurance highlights the fact that for a system to be secure, it must not only provide the intended functionality, but also ensure that undesired actions do not occur.

Security Services

Security services (Stoneburner, 2001) used in implementing an information technology security capability can be classified into following three broad categories.

- **Support:** Comprises mainly of generic services which underlie most information technology security capabilities.
- **Prevent:** Comprises of services which prevents security breaches from occurring
- **Recover:** Comprises of services which focus on the detection and recovery from a security breach.

Supporting Services

Supporting services (Stoneburner, 2001) are, by their very nature, pervasive and inter-related with many other services. The supporting services are:

- **Identification (and naming)**: This service helps in uniquely identifying users, processes, and information resources. Typically this service in turn is used by other services to identify subjects and objects.
- **Cryptographic key management:** This service enables secure key management which plays a key role in implementing other services where cryptographic functions are used.
- **Security administration**: This service enables efficient administration of security features of an information system to meet the security requirements of a specific installation and also to account for constantly evolving operational environment.
- **System protections:** This service is based on the notion of confidence in the technical implementation of various security functional capabilities. The quality of the implementation is measured from both the perspective of the design processes used and the specific manner in which the imple-

Figure 1. Security parameter dependencies

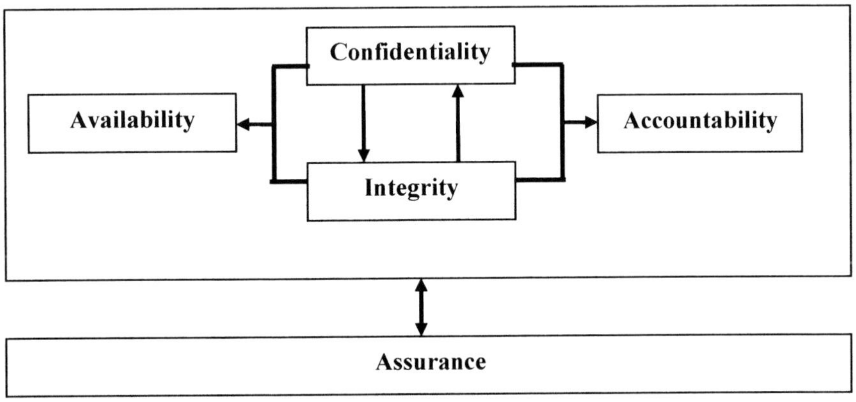

mentation was accomplished. Examples of system protections are: residual information protection, least privilege, process separation, modularity, layering, and minimization of what needs to be trusted.

Prevention Services

These services (Stoneburner, 2001) aim at preventing the security breaches from ever happening.

- **Protected communications:** In a distributed system, the ability to accomplish security objectives is highly dependent on secure communications which helps in achieving integrity, availability, and confidentiality of information while in transit.
- **Authentication:** This service helps in ensuring that a claimed identity is valid.
- **Authorization:** This service enables specification and subsequent management of the allowed actions of a given information system.
- **Access control enforcement:** This service enables enforcement of defined security policy of the enterprise, when any subject requesting access to particular object has been validated. The level of security obtained in any information system depends not only on the correctness of the access control decision, but also the strength of the access control enforcement. A common access control enforcement mechanism is to check identity and requested access against access control lists. File encryption is another example of an access control enforcement mechanism.
- **Non-repudiation:** This service enables the ability to ensure that senders cannot deny sending information and that receivers cannot deny receiving it. This service is treated as a prevention service because it prevents the ability to successfully repudiate an action.
- **Transaction privacy:** This service helps in maintaining the privacy of individuals transacting with information systems. This has become an essential requirement for enterprises both in government and private sectors.

Detection and Recovery Services

Because no system can be made absolute secure, it is necessary to both detect security breaches and to minimize their impact (Stoneburner, 2001).

- **Audit:** This service enables auditing of security relevant events for intrusion forensics and recovery from security breaches.
- **Intrusion detection and containment:** This service provides ability to timely detect signs of intrusions into information systems and also to take counter measures to confine it and minimize the effect.
- **Proof of Wholeness:** This service provides the ability to determine that integrity of an information system has been compromised.
- **Restore 'secure' state:** This service provides a way to restore the system state to a known secure state in the event of a security breach.

SOLUTIONS AND RECOMMENDATIONS

Enterprise Information Security Engineering Lifecycle

Information Security (IS) of Enterprises depends on several factors. The major determinant is the Business Goal; besides, the operation context, technology used, organizational structures and connectivity also play important roles in determining the approach towards IS. The other important concern is that the IS need of an Enterprise is not static, but depends on the dynamics of operation, changing business goals, technological upgrades, etc. The process of developing and deploying a proper IS infrastructure for an Enterprise is not a one-time affair; rather it is a continuous process of analysis, design, monitoring and adaptation to changing needs. In many enterprises, the changes encountered are frequent. This calls for structured representation of the different specification documents and automatic analysis and generation of them with interoperable representation.

This leads to the concept of Information Security Engineering Life-Cycle, or simply "Security Engg. Life-Cycle" (Anderson, 2001; Sengupta, 2005). Following phases are considered to be of prime importance for this Life-cycle concept (refer Figure 2).

Security Requirement Analysis

The very first step in building up a (somewhat) secure system is to understand and correctly specify the requirement. In this phase, information regarding the business modalities and IT assets of an enterprise are extracted.

The categories of information extracted from the enterprise are:

- The modes of activity of the business.
- The assets including the information asset, software asset, hardware asset and service asset and their security requirements vis-à-vis confidentiality, integrity, availability, authentication, non-repudiation, legal and contractual obligation and the perceived security threats to the assets.
- The connectivity details.
- The access control requirements on the basis of "need-to-know" and "need-to-use".

Based the on the above information provided by the enterprise, an analysis is performed to identify the required security controls (this includes technical as well as managerial controls, as suggested by security standards such as ISO 17799 (Plate, 2005)). An overall Risk Analysis (Peltier, 2005) is also performed to categorize the assets into high, medium and low risk zones for implementation of the security controls. During risk analysis, an attempt is made to identify the threats to which an IT system is exposed due to existing security weaknesses. The probability of each of these threats occurring is then estimated and combined with the protection requirements to rate the existing risks.

For any risks which are unacceptable a set of IT security measures is then selected so as to reduce the probability of occurrence and/or the extent of the potential damage. The OCTAVE Method (Alberts, 2001) and the TEN STEP Process are two well-known risk analysis methodologies.

The reports generated in this phase are:

- A structured Security specification format
- The Risk Analyses Report

Security Policy Formulation Phase

The goal of the security policy is to translate, clarify and communicate management's position on security as defined in high-level security principles. A security policy manual (Peltier, 1999) is a set of high level statements describing the objectives, beliefs and goals of the organization as far as security is concerned, but not how these solutions are engineered and implemented. Security policies define the overall security and risk control objectives that an organization endorses. The policy should be implement-able and enforceable; they should assign responsibility and accountability. They must be documented, distributed, and communicated. They should be technology-independent as much as possible and should not change often.

In this phase, the Security requirement Specification document is parsed to determine the security needs of an enterprise. Based on these security needs, a model policy manual is

Figure 2. Security Engineering life cycle

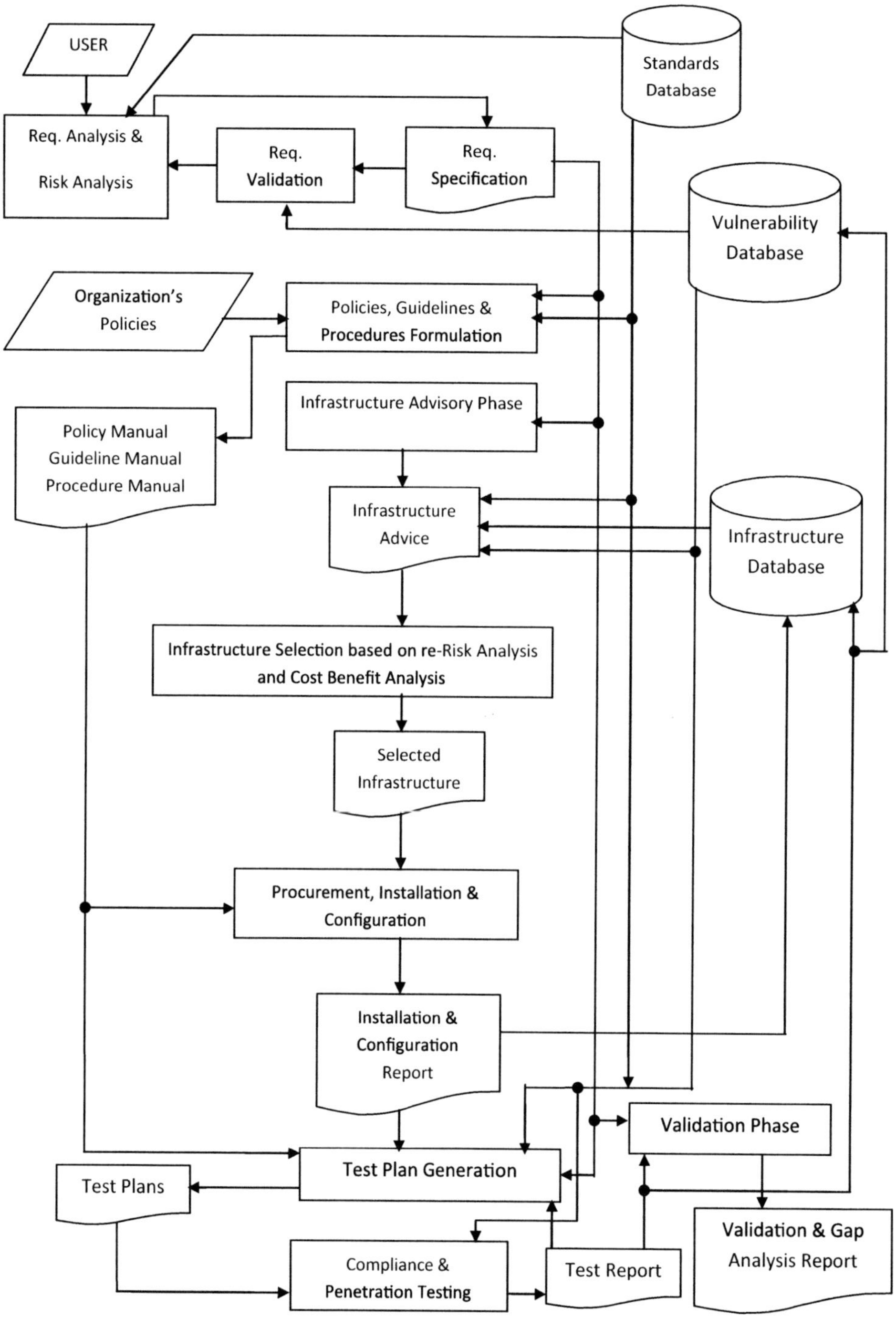

generated which, should conform to a particular information security standard like ISO 17799 (Plate, 2005). Guidelines and procedures, required to implement the policies, are also generated. Procedures consist of detailed steps to implement the policies, while guidelines are optional guidance provided to an enterprise to help in the implementation of policies and procedures. The model policy document should be analyzed by the management in conjunction with the non-security enterprise policies in place to finalize the Security Policy document.

The reports generated in this phase are:

- The policy manual
- The guideline manual
- The procedures manual

Security Infrastructure Advisory Phase

Security infrastructure advisory is a specified set of entities, both physical as well as software, in order to implement the set of identified security controls. It tells an enterprise the details regarding the software necessary, the access rights of individuals, the exact location of security tools, etc., required to mitigate the security risks of the enterprise. This phase will parse the security requirement specification document to identify the security needs of an enterprise and generate a security infrastructure advisory. The advisory will list the security tools required by the organization in order to protect its assets. The exact installation location and configuration advice are also included in the advisory. The report generated in this phase is

- The security infrastructure advisory

Some information security standards suggest probable security tools which are to be installed in an enterprise in order to protect its assets. For instance, ISO 17799 (Plate, 2005) consists of security controls which detail the types of assets and corresponding security parameters (confidentiality, integrity, etc.) to be protected, and the security tools needed for the same.

After getting the security infrastructure specification, a cost-benefit and detailed risk analysis is performed by the management of the enterprise concerned. Based on this, the enterprise decides on the particular infrastructure that it would like to implement. This is stated in the form of a security infrastructure selection document. This selection will take into account all kinds of Policies of the enterprise. Finally, the enterprise implements the security infrastructure as decided by it.

Security Testing and Validation

The main objective of security testing is to ascertain that the proposed security infrastructure is in place and working. Other than this, the system can be tested for faulty combination of software, known security holes and potentially dangerous applications that can be compromised to breach the security infrastructure. An integrated security testing tool may be visualized to automate the objective of security testing as described above.

The security testing phase can be further divided into several sub-phases as described below.

- *Test Case Generation* - A test case can be viewed as a collection of information based on which the security test is conducted. The preparation of a test case requires input from a requirement specification, valid *security infrastructure selection*, database (vulnerability database) containing information on known security holes and inputs from the security analyst. The test plan would be generated in a domain-specific format. Test cases are generated from the test plan templates.
- *Compliance Test* - In this sub-phase the security test tool determines whether the

specified security infrastructure is in place with proper configuration. The security analyst would have the provision on deciding whether to proceed with the later sub-phases of the security test if the security infrastructure is found to be *not implemented, partially implemented* or *fully implemented.*

- *Common Vulnerability Test* - After testing the existence of the *security infrastructure* in a corresponding domain, several tests would be conducted to find out the presence of known vulnerabilities that may be used to compromise the system even in the presence of a security infrastructure.
- *Validation Report Generation* - It is the last sub-phase in the security test mechanism. It is used to generate a validation report for the security requirement in the form of compliance and gaps in the implemented system. This is carried out by applying the Risk Analysis methodology on the security infrastructure in place, to see how far the risks are mitigated, thus, justifying the ROI. The reports generated in this phase are:
    - Compliance test report
    - Vulnerability test report
    - Validation report

Review and Monitoring

The different phases of activities may have to be monitored and the reports may have to be reviewed. The Monitoring process is continuous and may need certain tools and procedures to generate monitoring reports. The Review process involves the review of the requirement, policy, infrastructure and testing methodologies, so that the different entities do not become outdated and, consequently, create holes in the security framework. The review may be triggered by changes in the organizational structure, business goals and activity, technology, legal obligations, etc. Even in the absence of such triggers, review may be done periodically, the period being fixed by a policy. The other important thing triggering a review is the report of a security incident, which may affect, or have already affected, the enterprise security.

The outcome of the Review and Monitoring may re-initiate the activities of the Requirement analysis, Policy Formulation, Risk Analysis, Infrastructure updation and Testing & Validation phases. This is how the Security Engg. Life-cycle is expected to work.

FUTURE TRENDS

The future trend in Enterprise Information Security approach is to overlay the Plan-Do-Check-Act (PDCA) Cycle on the Security Engineering Life-cycle. In fact the various Information Security Management Standards are trying to spell out the activities to be taken up in different phases of the PDCA Cycle and their outcome. A major paradigm shift is happening from the qualitative approach to the monitoring with quantitative measures. The quantitative measures are being proposed to judge the quality of security management solutions in a more objective manner. This would help also in justifying the ROI. As already mentioned, the technology trend is to integrate security functionalities with the operational functionalities of components and subsystems – both hardware and software. This would cater for allowing secure transactions only in order to secure rather open enterprises, where the boundaries are becoming fuzzier, because of the globalization of economy in the cyber space.

CONCLUSION

This chapter looks at different aspects of Enterprise Information System Security. We began by defining an enterprise and its information systems and discussed the need for securing the same. Then the problems associated with the implementation of enterprise information security were discussed. The various security parameters, and their interdependencies, were stated. Finally, a management approach to securing an enterprise was proposed and a security engineering life-cycle methodology to achieve the same was discussed.

ACKNOWLEDGMENT

The authors acknowledge the role of over a dozen students and researchers in the Centre for Distributed Computing, Jadavpur University, for their contributions over the years in shaping and clarifying the concepts presented in this chapter. Most of the work related to the concepts presented in this chapter has evolved during the execution of a couple of R&D Projects sponsored by the Dept. of IT, Ministry of Communications and IT, Govt. of India, and a number of consultancy projects taken up by the Centre.

REFERENCES

Alberts, C., & Dorofee, A. (2001). *An Introduction to the OCTAVE Method*, Software Engineering Institute, Carnegie Mellon University. Retrieved October 11, 2001, from http://www.cert.org/octave/methodintro.html.

Anderson, R. (2001). *Security Engineering: A Guide to Building Dependable Systems*. New York, NY: John Wiley & Sons, Inc.

Bell, D. E., & LaPadula, L. J. (1976). *Secure Computer Systems: Unified Exposition and Multics Interpretation*, ESD-TR-75-306, MTR 2997 Rev. 1. Bedford, Massachusetts: The MITRE Corporation.

Biba, K. J. (1975). *Integrity Considerations for Secure Computer Systems*, MTR-3153. Bedford, MA: MITRE Corporation.

Casar, E., Scheer-Gumm, G., & Simons-Felwor, P. (2004). *IT Baseline Protection Manual*. Germany: BSI.

Clark, D., & Wilson, D. (1989). Evolution of a Model for Computer Integrity, in *Report of the Invitational Workshop on Data Integrity*, Gaithersburg, Maryland, A.2-1A.2-13. Gaithersburg, MD, National Institute of Standards and Technology, NIST Special Publication 500-168: NIST.

Denning, D. E. (1999). *Information Warfare and Security*. Singapore: Addison Wesley.

Goguen, J. A., & Meseguer, J. (1982). Security Policies and Security Models, *Symposium on Security and Privacy*, pp.11-20. Menlo Park, CA: IEEE.

Hassler, V. (2001). *Security Fundamentals for E-Commerce*. Norwood, MA: Artech House Inc.

Lampson, B. W. (1974). Protection. *Proc. Fifth Princeton Symposium on Information Sciences and Systems*. Princeton University, reprinted in *Operating Systems Review, 8*(1), 18-24. Palo Alto, CA.

Mayfield, T., Roskos, J. E., Welke, S. R., & Boone, J. M. (1991). Integrity in Automated Information Systems. *Prepared for National Computer Security Center (NCSC)*. Alexandria, Virginia: NCSC.

Peltier, T. R. (1999). *Information Security Policies and Procedures*. Boca Raton, Florida: Auerbach Publications.

Peltier, T. R. (2005). *Information Security Risk Analysis*. Boca Raton, Florida: Auerbach Publications.

Plate, A., & Weissmann, O. (Ed.). (2005). *Information Technology – Code of practice for information security management*, ISO/IEC 17799:2005. Berlin, Germany: ISO.

Richardson, R. (2003). *CSI/FBI Computer Crime and Security Survey*. Hayward, CA: Computer Security Institute.

Sengupta, A., Mukhopadhyay, A., Ray, K., Roy, A. G., Aich, D., Barik, M. S., & Mazumdar, C. (2005). A Web-Enabled Enterprise Security Management Framework Based on a Unified Model of Enterprise Information System Security : (An Ongoing Project Report), *First International Conference on Information Systems Security*, ICISS 2005. Kolkata, India, Pages 328 – 331: LNCS.

Snare, J., & Kuiper, E. (Ed.). (2005). *Information technology - Security techniques – Information security management systems - Requirements*, BS ISO/IEC 27001:2005 BS 7799-2:2005. Geneva, Switzerland: ISO.

Stoneburner, G. (2001). Underlying Technical Models for Information Technology Security. *NIST Special Publication 800-33*. Gaithersburg, MD: NIST.

Weiner, E. S. C., & Simpson, J. A. (Eds.). (1991). *The Compact Edition of The Oxford English Dictionary*. USA: Oxford University Press.

Yu, C-F., & Gligor, V. D. (1990). A Specification and Verification Method for Preventing Denial of Service. *IEEE Trans. on Software Engineering*, 16(6), 581-592. IEEE.

KEY TERMS

Asset: Asset means anything that has value to an organization. With respect to security, asset may imply physical resources, or information contained within the organization.

Information Asset: Databases, data files, system documentation, user manuals, training material, operational and support procedures, intellectual property, continuity plans, fallback arrangements, archived information.

Hardware Asset: Computer equipment (processors, monitors, laptops, modems), communication equipment (routers, hubs, PABXs, fax machines), magnetic media (tapes and disks), other equipment, cabinets, safes.

Risk Analysis: This term defines the process of analyzing a target environment and the relationships of its risk related attributes. This analysis will identify threat-vulnerabilities, associate those vulnerabilities with affected assets, identify the potential for and nature of an undesirable result and specify risk mitigating controls.

Risk Management: This includes the process of assigning priority to, budgeting, implementing and maintaining the appropriate risk-reducing measures.

Safeguard: This term represents a risk reducing measure that acts to detect, prevent or minimize loss associated with the occurrence of a specified threat.

Security Concern: Security concern of an asset is a function of threat and vulnerability of that asset.

Severity: Level of exploitation of vulnerability on a qualitative scale is defined by the severity value.

Software Asset: Application software, System software, development tools, and utilities.

Threat: Threats are any unwanted activities or events that under certain conditions could jeopardize either the integrity, confidentiality or availability of information and other assets.

Vulnerability: This is an inherent weakness associated with an enterprise asset. It is a condition that has the potential to allow a threat to occur with greater impact and greater frequency or both.

Chapter VIII
An Alternative Model of Information Security Investment

Peter O. Orondo
Acclaim Consulting Group, Inc., USA

ABSTRACT

Most companies would agree that securing their information assets is worth some investment. It is thus plausible to assume that low levels of IT security investment indicate that only a small portion of the firm's business is IT asset value driven. It could also point to a misaligned corporate investment policy. Conversely, some firms may be investing more than is warranted given the value of their information asset holdings, thereby wasting shareholder resources. The question then becomes: What level of IT security investment is enough? Several models exist to help companies set their IT spending in general and Information Security spending in particular. The leading model out there is the Information Technology Portfolio Management (ITPM) model. This is really nothing more than financial portfolio management theory applied to the information technology realm. Thus ITPM tries to optimize IT spending based on a number of factors like business value, efficiency and cost reduction among others. Despite current vigorous research at esteemed institutions like the Center for Information Systems Research (CISR) at MIT and at the Free University of Amsterdam, ITPM is still in its infancy and the field would benefit from alternative models. In this chapter, we propose an alternative model of IT security spending that firms may readily apply when setting their Information Security budgets. The model is analytical and starts by developing a model for the business value of information. It then develops a model for the cost of an information security breach. Finally, we find the relationship between the value model and the cost model from.

INTRODUCTION

The global spending on IT may only be considered as leviathan – \$1.5 trillion in 2007 according to Forrester (Bartels, 2007), and is the driver for a very large segment of the global economy, especially in the western industrialized countries. At any individual firm, the \$1.5 trillion figure typically translates to between 1% and 8% of revenues. Since any firm's spending is a balancing act amongst multiple competing priorities, it becomes critical for CIOs and IT managers to justify every penny spent on IT.

As we mentioned earlier, the most common model appears to be the ITPM model which views IT spending as an investment just like any other that the firm makes. ITPM then creates metrics, processes and monitoring tools that ultimately measure Return on Investment (ROI) for each IT dollar spent (Symons, 2005).

The Forrester Research cited (Symons, 2005) also reveals that firms are most likely to optimize their IT spending around Business Value. In other words, the firms surveyed decided that the business value of IT spending outweighed other considerations like financial return, cost reductions and even efficiency (see Figure 1).

This validates a key premise of our model, namely that IT Security Spending is integral to the firm's value chain. We shall return to this notion of "Business Value" driven IT Security Spending later when we formulate our model.

ITPM however, is still in its infancy, and is fairly complicated to apply, monitor and measure in any given company. Additionally:

- ITPM is ultimately based on financial theory of portfolio optimization. While it is plausible that the basic concepts of Modern Porfolio Theory (MPT) – see for example (*Markowitz, 1952)* - should apply to IT spending, the two problems are sufficiently different that substantial conceptual modifications to MPT are in order before it can make sense to the IT Line Manager. At the very least, it is not clear that MPT is the best approach to model IT Investment Portfolios. For example, the IT Investment portfolio is not as liquid as a stock portfolio, if at all.
- ITPM is complicated and thus not easily accessible except to generally larger firms with a fair amount of resources devoted to IT process and operations modeling. This is evident from the Forrester study (Symons, 2005): of the mostly large firms surveyed, only 33% indicated that they had some form of an ITPM process. Combined with its immaturity as a practical model, we speculate that ITPM will not be accessible to a vast majority of firms as a practical tool to use when setting IT spending levels.

Figure 1. IT portfolio optimization criteria (Symons, 2005)

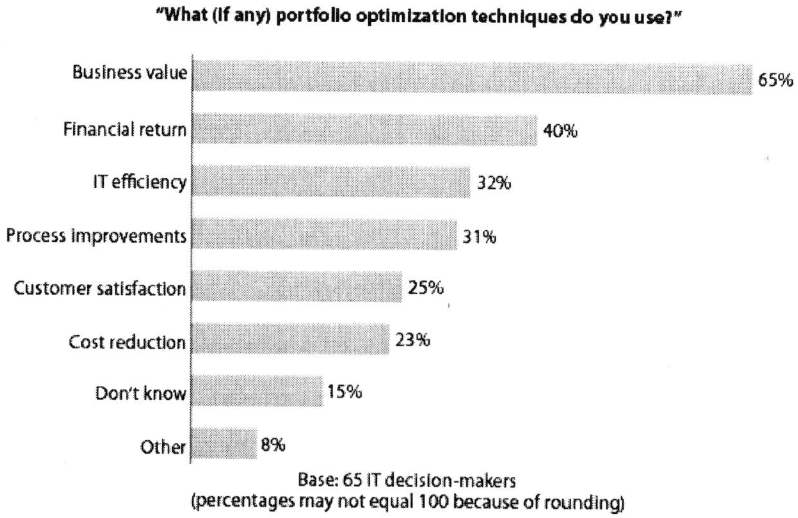

- Even more ominous, the mentioned Forrester survey found that a vast majority of those firms with an ITPM process (82%) considered it to be an IT initiative. In other words, ITPM was not pervasive enough in the firm to be of any meaningful or lasting value beyond just another IT initiative.

Anecdotal evidence from our Identity and Access Management (IAM) consulting in a wide array of industries from financial services, pharmaceuticals and health care services industries also supports Forrester's results: most firms we work with, small and large, don't have any consistent way to model or allocate their IT spending. Rather, they tend to focus on broad goals or generalities, for example:

- Most firms know that they need to make a mandatory investment in IT to operate – the so called 'keep the lights on' IT spending. This IT spending includes basic IT infrastructure like desktop computing and telecommunications, and network and application security, amongst others.
- IT spending mandated by governmental regulations like Sarbanes Oxley in the financial industry or HIPPA in health care; see for example (Orondo, 2007).
- IT spending for competitive advantage – also called 'Keeping up with the Acmes' IT spending. For example, it is not uncommon for firms in the same industry to implement enterprise IT infrastructure systems like portals, ERP or IAM at about the same time. Usually, they perceive an advantage being gained by a competitor as a result of such implementations, and it is the fear of being left behind that drives these IT projects.

Clearly, a more accessible alternative model of IT spending is in order. Note that we focus on IT security spending for simplicity, however, the model we present here may be extended to encompass overall IT spending with only minor modifications.

It turns out that the appropriate model for the level of IT security investment within any firm is fairly easy to determine. In the next section we will focus on creating a simple yet accurate model for IT Security Spending by focusing on the business value of a firm's information assets.

MODELING IT SECURITY SPENDING

The first consideration for a firm when determining IT security investment level is obviously the value of the information being protected. If the value of the firm's information assets is relatively small, there is really no need to spend a large (or any) portion of it in IT security; the firm is better off investing its earnings elsewhere. Conversely, firms should consider an IT security investment level commensurate with how much those IT assets drive sales or some other measure of business value creation. This principle is not new; historically, firms have used it to allocate marketing dollars by, for example, setting aside 5% of revenues to fund sales activities.

Let's call the firm's information asset value ***Va***.

In an information-based economy, it is reasonable to assume that ***Va*** has some relationship to some measurable company financials like total sales or revenues (for if such a relationship did not exist, then the firm should not be spending precious dollars to protect or manage its information assets). We will discuss the exact manner of dependence momentarily.

Note that as a matter of practicality, there will exist an IT Security Investment floor in any given firm. This is the so-called 'keep the lights on' IT Spending we mentioned earlier. We are not particularly interested in this investment floor since we seek an optimal level that may be above or below it.

The second major consideration in determining a firm's IT Security Investment is the cost to the firm of an information security breach. The cost of a breach aggregates several factors. These mainly consist of breach response costs, regulatory fines levied, the costs of defending and/or settling law suits, and the value of lost business or goodwill.

Let's call the total cost to the firm of a breach *Vc*.

Obviously (or plausibly, depending on one's perspective), ***Va*** and ***Vc*** are related. We will revisit this later.

In the next sections, we develop models for ***Va*** and ***Vc***.

Information Asset Value (Va):

Of what value to a firm is information that needs protection? Again ignore the un-interesting "floor" spending and instead focus on the as yet unknown optimal IT Security Investment level.

At a glance this is a very difficult question to answer generally. However, it is a little bit easier to wrap ourselves around it by zeroing in on the business value of the information:

Model Basis:

*An information asset is valuable to the firm solely because of the asset's ability to generate **future** revenues for the enterprise. Present or Past value of the information asset is not of interest to the firm except its contribution to goodwill which the firm may capitalize.*

To arrive at the information asset value as it relates to future income generation, thus, we simply take the current sales of the firm, factor in the contribution from the information assets in question, and then capitalize it using the firm's 'multiple' – the ratio that the market applies to earnings of the firm - the firm's Price to Earnings (PE) ratio. If the firm is private, PE ratios for similar public firms or the firm's industry PE may be utilized.

The factor of sales contributed by the information assets will obviously differ from firm to firm, but should be fairly straightforward to determine in some cases, but not others.

We also need to subtract the investments needed to secure and otherwise 'enable' the information asset, since we realize that information assets must be unlocked before they can become valuable to the firm. The enablement is considered value added – for example, data sitting on a database somewhere within the firm is not really valuable until it is protected, mined and applied to marketing activities or used in a product.

It is critical however not to define enablement so widely as to be useless for the purposes of a model – for example, we should only include activities that make the information usable to the business to generate income. Such activities include IT functions like data/application protection, perhaps data mining and modeling, but should not include activities like marketing or customer acquisition that only leverages information asset's value.

In short hand:

Va = Vs - Ve

whereby:

Va = information asset value

Vs = capitalized value of sales driven by the information asset

Ve = information value added which includes IT security investments and related spending as outlined above

In the following sections, we provide two examples that illustrate the relationship between information asset value and IT Security Spending.

We begin by using the well known Coca Cola's secret ingredient. Note that these examples are for illustration purposes only. The examples also use publicly available financial information at the time of writing.

Example 1: Coca Cola's Secret Ingredient:

The huge sales and global market dominance of Coca Cola's Coke soft drink are reasonably based in part on the firm's famous 100 year old information asset, namely secret ingredient that makes the drink unique. If you are the VP of Sales for Coca Cola, you could perhaps determine pretty accurately what portion of Coca Cola Company's overall \$25B (2006) in sales came from Coke (Google search seems to indicate the fraction is a little over 55%).

We will assume Coke sales are 55% of Coca Cola's total sales of \$25B or \$14B.

It is probably also pretty easy to figure out the secret ingredient attribution to this sales figure.

We will assume the fraction is 25%.

Using these assumptions, the Information Asset value of Coca Cola's secret ingredient is about \$250B (after factoring in a forward PE of 18)

In this hypothetical Coca Cola scenario, and considering just the secret coke ingredient only,

Va = 250 - Ve (in Billions)

Example 2: TJX Companies

According to press accounts, sometime in early 2003, an innovative but wholesomely criminal enterprise planted what may be described as a listening bug on TJX Company's systems and stole credit and debit card data for some staggering 45.7 million TJX customers!

The credit card information per se can and should be considered an information asset since retailers long realized that swiping the card (as opposed to paying cash or writing a check) leads to increased sales. TJX may also leverage the credit card information in its marketing, further adding sales value above the 'credit card' effect.

Note that whether the credit card information was stored in TJX's systems or not does not matter to our model. It only matters that TJX had custody of the information for some duration of time.

Nonetheless, the factor of sales attributable to credit card information asset should be determinable – let's say the effect is 20%. With sales of \$17B and a PE of 17 and assuming ½ of all sales are done via credit or debit cards, the hypothetical TJX Companies scenario with regards to credit card information asset value is:

***Va = 29 - Ve* (Billions)**

Finding a Cost of Breach Model

The cost of a security breach is relatively easy to estimate once a breach occurs. However, we are more interested in creating a model for estimating the cost of a potential breach, i.e. before one occurs.

To estimate potential costs of a security breach, we break it down to its main components: economic losses by affected parties, regulatory payments and lost business. We discuss each in turn in the following sections.

Economic Losses by Affected Parties

Since the firm is most often a custodian, not the owner of information assets, the economic losses by affected parties deals with potential losses incurred by the proper owners of the data after a breach, including company shareholders. This may include losses suffered by credit card holders, the issuing banks or financial losses resulting from identity theft. It may also include loss in shareholder value from theft of trade secrets or intellectual property.

To estimate economic losses from a security breach, we add up their entire capitalized value. For example, the economic loss resulting from a breach of credit card information is the sum of all unused balances (assumes that credit card companies enforce some kind of limit on each card). Presumably this is also the cost of defending and settling the inevitable law suits from a breach.

In the case of intellectual property theft, it is the reduction in shareholder value arising from the assets being used to hurt the firm's future sales or competitiveness.

Similarly, the economic value of a lost identity may be determined based on the value of fraud that may be perpetrated using the stolen identities before the fraud is detected and stopped.

Alternatively, we may simply estimate the cost of defending and settling resulting customer or shareholder lawsuits. This approach may be accurate albeit morally hazardous. For example, the firm may come to the conclusion that defending consumer lawsuits is cheaper that setting the proper IT Security Spending Level necessary to prevent a breach.

Regulatory Penalties

The payments for regulatory penalties are normally spelt out in applicable laws (see Orondo, 2007), and may simply be added up.

Loss of Business

The Lost Business resulting from a breach is not easy to estimate or model. Empirical studies, for example, have shown that publicly traded companies lose an average of 25% in market capitalization for at least one year after an information asset breach. Empirical studies may however be misleading and hard to apply to any particular firm.

Instead of relying on empirical data, we have to go back to the value of the breached information to the business and estimate the extent of the potential business loss based on media publicity and Internet buzz.

Since we already have a basis for capitalized information asset value, the only missing component is what we may call the "business loss index" – the percentage of the firm's business that is lost – and this can be 100% in some cases.

A key metric for determining the loss index is media saturation – note that even though several privacy regulations require client notification in case of information breaches, individual notifications have less impact than the 10 PM news or a determined blogger.

To measure media impact, thus, a firm has to consider where the trigger points for the business loss are – for credit card losses, the trigger points are consumers choosing to shop at competitors' stores. These consumers will most likely watch the adverse news on the evening bulletins or read about it on the Internet, thus a metric or scale may be devised accordingly (a media consulting firm or an Internet buzz firm may need to be engaged).

For a business-to-business relationship, the media saturation point will be business partners and the firm can safely assume the media saturation will be 100%; how much business is lost will be determined by other factors like ease of switching to competitor products or services, etc.

There are obviously other factors, but we can use the business loss index multiplied by the capitalized information asset value as the approximate value of lost business.

Putting everything together, the cost to a business of a security breach is indicated as:

$$Vc = Le + Rp + Li \times Va$$

whereby:

Vc = cost of an information security breach
Le = Economic loss of affected parties
Rp = Regulatory penalties
Li = Business loss index
Va = Value of information asset

Since ***Va = Vs - Ve*** from above, then:

Vc = Le + Rp + Li x (Vs - Ve) where:
Va = information asset value
Vs = capitalized value of sales driven by information asset
Ve = information value added which includes IT security spending

Cost of Breach, Information Asset Value Relationship

The cost of an information security breach must be discounted by the likelihood of a successful breach occurring. The insurance model seems appropriate for this case. In other words, the firm should invest no more than the modeled cost of the breach multiplied by the likelihood of the breach materializing. If that likelihood or probability of a breach is labeled ***Pb***, then the discounted cost, labeled ***Vd***, is

Vd = Pb x Vc

Or

Vd = Pb x [Le + Rp + Li x (Vs - Ve)]

Using the insurance model, then, ***Vd*** is exactly the amount of investment that the firm should be willing to make in order to avoid paying a substantially higher cost, ***Vc*** – we have assumed that the fractional likelihood of a breach occurring is not close to certainly.

But ***Vd*** is exactly the Information Asset Value added, ***Ve***, the amount of investment that the firm should be willing to make to safeguard its information assets.

Putting things together, we get the following:

Ve = Pb x [Le + Rp + Li x (Vs - Ve)]

Or

Ve = Pb/(1 + Pb x Li) x [Le + Rp + Li x Vs]

Note that the likelihood of a breach given adequate information security resources (***Pb***) should be quite low, but not nil. So we can simplify the above relationship as follows:

Ve ~ Pb x [Le + Rp + Li x Vs]

Where:

Ve = information asset value added which includes IT security spending
Pb = the likelihood of an information asset breach
Le = Economic loss of affected parties resulting from information asset breach
Rp = Regulatory penalties from the information asset breach
Li = Business loss index (based on breached information assets)
Vs = capitalized value of sales driven by breached information assets

In this relationship, all factors are referenced to the same information assets.

This result is exactly what we would expect: IT security investment or spending should be no more than the discounted value of any potential losses from breaches, plus the discounted value of the potential loss of value driven sales. This means that as the firm's sales get more dependent on information assets, more resources should be allocated to ensuring those assets don't fall into the wrong hands.

Conversely, as your firm's sales increasingly depend on IT, lack of commensurate information security investment is risk that your firm cannot afford to carry.

Note:

In practice, the above relationship is not linear. Each component is related to other variable factors within the firm, thus:

Ve(x,y,z,..) ~ Pb(x) x [Le(y) + Rp(z) + Li(x,y) x Vs(x,y,z)]

Where:

x, y, z,... are the dependent parameters whose nature of dependence will vary from firm to firm.

SUMMARY

In this article, we have formulated an alternative framework model that may be easily used by firms to determine the level of IT Security investment. Our model ties IT Security investment to the business value generated by information assets being protected, and yields a result that is significantly simpler to understand and implement than the models based on ITPM.

REFERENCES

Bartels, A. (2007). IT Spending and Forecasting. *Forrester Research.*

Symons, C. (2005). Optimizing the IT Porfolio for Maximum Business Value. *Forrester Research.*

Markowitz, H. (1952). Portfolio Selection. *Journal of Finance*, *7*(1), 77-91

Orondo, P. (2007). Unified Identities in Complex Financial Organizations. *Managing Information Assurance in Financial Services.* Rao et al (Editors), 190-207

KEY TERMS

Business Loss Index: The percentage of an organization's business that is lost due to information security breach.

Identity and Access Management: Managing digital identities, of stakeholders such as employees, partners, suppliers, contractors, etc, and access to information resources that are required to perform and support business functions of an organization.

Information Asset Breach: Compromise of security, in terms of confidentiality, integrity or availability, of assets that support business functions by providing secure access to information.

IT Asset Value: Value of an asset that stores, processes or transmits information in terms of value added to business by deploying and supporting it.

IT Economics: It is a concept that related to understanding and applying knowledge of costs and benefits of managing IT assets from a monetary terms.

IT Portfolio Management: Process of defining and managing combination of different types of IT resources such as applications, infrastructure, personnel as portfolio; and aim to optimize their utility in terms of business value add.

IT Security: Securing different components of information technology by ensuring confidentiality, integrity and availability of information stored, processed and transmitted by them.

Security Economics: Field of study and area of application that analyzes and evaluates costs and benefits, in financial terms, of acquisition, deployment and maintenance of resources such as systems and personnel to provide security of information and informational assets.

Section II
Privacy and Social Engineering

Chapter IX
Avoiding Pitfalls in Policy-Based Privacy Management[1]

George O.M. Yee
NRC Institute for Information Technology, Canada

Larry Korba
NRC Institute for Information Technology, Canada

ABSTRACT

The growth of the Internet is increasing the deployment of e-services in such areas as e-commerce, e-learning, and e-health. In parallel, the providers and consumers of such services are realizing the need for privacy. The use of P3P privacy policies on Web sites is an example of this growing concern for privacy. Managing privacy using privacy policies is a promising approach. In this approach, an e-service provider and an e-service consumer each have separate privacy policies. Before an e-service is engaged, the provider's policy must be "compatible" with the consumer's policy. However, beyond compatibility, the policies may face pitfalls arising from improper specification, misapplication, and improper maintenance (e.g. failing to keep a personal privacy policy up-to-date). This can result in the lost of privacy and even lead to serious safety issues in certain cases. This chapter gives examples of how such pitfalls can arise and suggests ways to avoid these pitfalls.

1. INTRODUCTION

1.1 The Privacy Problem

The rapid development of the Internet has been accompanied by a growth in the number of e-services available to consumers. E-services, and in particular, web services, are available for banking, shopping, learning, healthcare, and Government Online. However, each of these services requires a consumer's personal information in one form or another. This leads to concerns over privacy. Indeed, the public's awareness of potential violations of privacy by online service providers has been growing. Evidence affirming this situation include a) the use of P3P privacy policies (P3P, 2002) by web server sites to disclose their treatment of users' private information, b) the enactment of privacy legislation and directives by major jurisdictions as a sort of owners' "bill of rights" concerning their private information, and c) the appointment of privacy commissioners or officials who can assist the consumer in addressing violations of privacy (Canada has a federal privacy commissioner as well as provincial level privacy commissioners). In order for e-services to be successful, privacy must be protected. An effective and flexible way of protecting privacy is to manage it using privacy policies. The objectives of this chapter are a) to show that such use of privacy policies can lead to pitfalls and b) to propose ways to eliminate or mitigate these bad outcomes. This work is based on Yee & Korba (Oct. 2005).

1.2 Approaches for Solving the Privacy Problem

Various approaches have been used to protect personal information, including data anonymization (Iyengar, 2002; Kobsa & Schreck, 2003) and pseudonym technology (Song et al., 2006). Approaches for privacy protection that are in the research stage include treating privacy protection as an access problem and then bringing the tools of access control to bear for privacy control (Adams & Barbieri, 2006), treating privacy protection as a privacy rights management problem using the techniques of digital rights management (Kenny & Korba, 2002), and considering privacy protection as a privacy policy compliance problem, verifying compliance with secure logs (Yee & Korba, 2004). This work is concerned with the latter approach, i.e. the management of privacy using privacy policies. In this approach, the e-service provider and e-service consumer each has a privacy policy that stipulates how personal information is to be handled. The consumer's policy states how the personal information about the consumer is to be handled by the provider, for example, what the information can be used for, how long the provider can retain the information in its possession, to which parties the information may be disclosed, and so on. The provider's policy states how the provider will handle the consumer's personal information, in terms of the same ways of handling information as in the consumer's policy. Naturally, the e-service can only proceed if both policies agree with each other. Once this agreement is reached, privacy protection relies on the provider upholding the agreed upon privacy policy.

1.3 The Privacy Policy Pitfalls Problem

The use of privacy policies in privacy management can have pitfalls or unexpected negative outcomes. Pitfalls can arise from a) how the matching of policies between consumer and provider was carried out, b) improperly specified policy content, c) whether or not the consumer privacy policy was a good fit for the e-service, and d) whether or not the privacy policy was properly maintained or kept up-to-date. For example, a policy allowing a drug prescription to be given to a provider is unlikely to be a good fit if the provider's service sells books instead of drugs. In such a scenario, a pitfall could arise if the provider inadvertently discloses the prescription to an individual who is not to receive such information according to the consumer's wishes (e.g. a mother who the consumer would not wish to worry, if the prescription was for a serious illness).

1.4 Map to the Chapter

The rest of this chapter is organized as follows. Section 2 discusses recent privacy legislation, and further explains what we mean by e-services and privacy management, application, and maintenance. Section 3 explains privacy policies, including their specification, application, and maintenance. Section 4 discusses privacy pitfalls that could arise from improper policy matching (between consumer and provider policies) and inadequate policy specification (creation). In addition, this section also deals with pitfalls arising from misapplication and poor maintenance of privacy policies. Section 5 explains how to avoid the pitfalls uncovered in Section 4. Section 6 presents related work. Section 7 discusses future trends and gives some suggestions for future work. Finally, Section 8 summarizes the key results from the chapter.

2. BACKGROUND

2.1 Privacy Legislation

In Canada, privacy legislation is enacted in *PIPEDA (Personal Information Protection and Electronic Documents Act)* (Government of Canada) and is based on the Canadian Standards Association's *Model Code for the Protection of Personal Information (Canadian Standards Association) recognized as a national standard in 1996.* This Code consists of ten Privacy Principles that for convenience, we label as CSAPP. We will examine the CSAPP below.

Data privacy in the European Union is governed by a very comprehensive set of regulations called the Data Protection Directive (European Union Directive, 1995).

In the United States, privacy protection is achieved through a patchwork of legislation at the federal and state levels. Privacy legislation is largely sector-based (Banisar, 1999). At the Federal level there are presently more than a dozen privacy laws. Some of these laws are: Privacy Act of 1974 as amended (5 USC 552a), Electronic Communications Privacy Act of 1986, and Right to Financial Privacy Act of 1986. Laws applicable to the private sector include: Family Educational Rights and Privacy Act of 1978, Privacy Protection Act of 1980, and Video Privacy Protection Act of 1988. As can be seen, the laws typically apply to specific technologies or privacy threats to, for example, bank records, government databases, or video rental history. The laws serve as operational boundaries rather than requirements and there is no national all encompassing code for privacy protection. As such, the US laws are less effective at protecting personal privacy than either the legislations of the European Union or Canada. The United States is not the leader in privacy protection (Banisar, 1999; Hurley, 1999; Milberg et al., 1995).

2.2 E-Service Model

It is useful to describe what we mean by e-services. An e-service is a service that is offered by a provider to a consumer across a computer network. This includes web services that are characterized by the use of XML and SOAP in a Service Oriented Architecture. A stock quotation service is often used as an example of an e-service. Here a consumer would logon to the service from a computer, and after appropriate user authentication, would make use of the service to obtain stock quotes. Accessing one's bank account through online banking is another example of an e-service. Here the provider is the bank and the service consists of allowing the consumer to check the balance, transfer funds, or make bill payments. The network is usually the Internet, but could also in principle be a private enterprise network. At any point in time, one provider may be serving many consumers and many providers may be serving one consumer. For the purposes of this chapter, the business relationship between provider and consumer is always one-to-one, i.e. the service is designed for one consumer and is provided by one provider, payment for the service is expected from one consumer. In addition, service providers may also be service consumers, and service consumers may also be service providers.

2.3 Privacy Management Model

An effective and flexible way to protect privacy is to manage it using privacy policies. A provider has a privacy policy stating what private information it requires from a consumer and how the information will be used. A consumer has a privacy policy stating what private information the consumer is willing to share, with whom it may be shared, and under what circumstances it may be shared. An entity that is both a provider and a consumer has separate privacy policies for these two roles. A privacy policy is attached to a software agent that acts for a consumer or a provider as the case may be. Prior to the activation of a particular service, the agent for the consumer and the agent for the provider undergo a privacy policy exchange, in which the policies are examined for compatibility. Each agent examines the other's policy to determine if there is a match between the two policies. If each agent finds a match, the agents signal each other that a match has been found, and service is initiated. If either agent fails to find a match, that agent would signal a mismatch to the other agent and service would then not be initiated. In this case, the consumer (provider) is free to exchange policies with another provider (consumer).

In our model, the provider requires private information from the consumer for use in its e-service and so reduces the consumer's privacy by requesting such information. This reduction in consumer privacy is represented by the requirements for consumer private information in the provider's privacy policy. The consumer, on the other hand, would rather keep her private information to herself, and so tries to resist the provider's attempt to reduce her privacy. This means that the consumer would only be willing to have her privacy reduced by a certain amount, as represented by the privacy provisions in her privacy policy. There is a *match* between a provider's privacy policy and the corresponding consumer's policy where the amount of privacy reduction allowed by the consumer's policy is at least as great as the amount of privacy reduction required by the provider's policy. Otherwise, there is a *mismatch*. Where time is involved, a private item held for less time is considered less private. A privacy policy is considered *upgraded* if the new version represents more privacy than the prior version. Similarly, a privacy policy is considered *downgraded* if the new version represents less privacy than the prior version. Figure 1 illustrates our privacy management model. For the purposes of this chapter, it is not necessary to consider the details of service operation. However, the provider is expected to comply with the consumer's privacy policy if service is initiated.

3. PRIVACY POLICIES

3.1 Requirements from Privacy Principles

In this section, we identify some attributes of private information collection using the CSAPP as a guide. We use the CSAPP because it is representative of principles behind privacy legislation in many countries, including the European

Figure 1. The exchange of privacy policies (PP) between consumer agent (CA) and provider agent (PA)

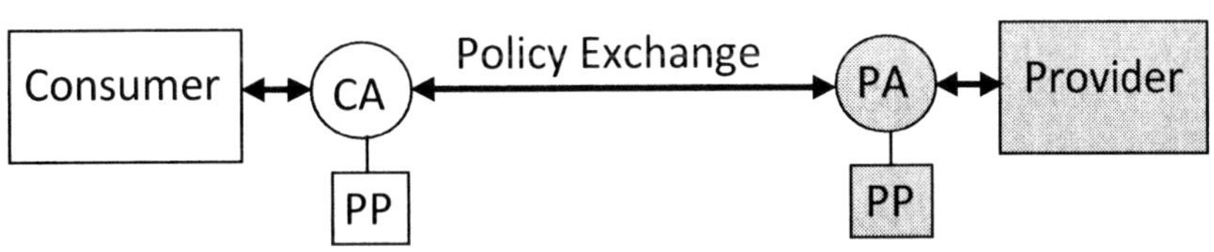

Table 1. CSAPP - The ten privacy principles from Canadian Standards Association (n.d.)

Principle	*Description*
1. Accountability	An organization is responsible for personal information under its control and shall designate an individual or individuals accountable for the organization's compliance with the privacy principles.
2. Identifying Purposes	The purposes for which personal information is collected shall be identified by the organization at or before the time the information is collected.
3. Consent	The knowledge and consent of the individual are required for the collection, use or disclosure of personal information, except when inappropriate.
4. Limiting Collection	The collection of personal information shall be limited to that which is necessary for the purposes identified by the organization. Information shall be collected by fair and lawful means.
5. Limiting Use, Disclosure, and Retention	Personal information shall not be used or disclosed for purposes other than those for which it was collected, except with the consent of the individual or as required by the law. In addition, personal information shall be retained only as long as necessary for fulfillment of those purposes.
6. Accuracy	Personal information shall be as accurate, complete, and up-to-date as is necessary for the purposes for which it is to be used.
7. Safeguards	Security safeguards appropriate to the sensitivity of the information shall be used to protect personal information.
8. Openness	An organization shall make readily available to individuals specific information about its policies and practices relating to the management of personal information.
9. Individual Access	Upon request, an individual shall be informed of the existence, use and disclosure of his or her personal information and shall be given access to that information. An individual shall be able to challenge the accuracy and completeness of the information and have it amended as appropriate.
10. Challenging Compliance	An individual shall be able to address a challenge concerning compliance with the above principles to the designated individual or individuals accountable for the organization's compliance.

Union. We will then apply these attributes to the specification of privacy policy contents. Table 1 shows the CSAPP.

We interpret "organization" as "provider" and "individual" as "consumer". In the following, we use CSAPP.n to denote Principle n of the CSAPP. Principle CSAPP.2 implies that there could be different providers requesting the information, thus implying a *collector* attribute. Principle CSAPP.4 implies that there is a *what* attribute, i.e. what private information is being collected. Principles CSAPP.2, CSAPP.4, and CSAPP.5 state that there are *purposes* for which the private information is being collected. Principles CSAPP.3, CSAPP.5 and CSAPP.9 imply that the private information can be disclosed to other parties, giving a *disclose-to* attribute. Principle CSAPP.5 implies a *retention time* attribute for the retention of private information. Thus, from the CSAPP we derive 5 attributes of private information collection, namely *collector*, *what*, *purposes*, *disclose-to*, and *retention time*.

The Privacy Principles also prescribe certain operational requirements that must be satisfied between provider and consumer, such as identifying purpose and consent. Our service model and the exchange of privacy policies automatically satisfy some of these requirements, namely Principles CSAPP.2, CSAPP.3, and CSAPP.8. The satisfaction of the remaining operational requirements depends on compliance mechanisms (Principles CSAPP.1, CSAPP.4, CSAPP.5, CSAPP.6, CSAPP.9, CSAPP.10) and security mechanisms (Principle CSAPP.7). Security and compliance mechanisms are outside the scope of this chapter.

3.2 Specification of Privacy Policies

Based on the above examination of CSAPP, the contents of a privacy policy should, for each item of private data, identify a) *collector* - who wishes to collect the information, either an organization or a specific person, b) *what* - the nature of the information, c) *purposes* - the purposes for which the information is being collected, d) *retention time* – the amount of time for the provider to keep the information, and e) *disclose-to* – the parties to whom the provider will disclose the information. A privacy policy can be considered as a machine-readable document that lists each item of private information with corresponding description of *collector*, *what*, *purposes*, *retention time*, and *disclose-to*.

The attribute grouping <collector, what, purposes, retention time, disclose-to> is called a *privacy rule*. A privacy policy then consists of a header section followed by one or more privacy rules. This header consists of the fields: *Policy Use* (for what e-service?), *Owner* (name of the provider or consumer who owns the policy), *Proxy* (Yes or no – yes if a proxy will act for the consumer to give the information), and *Valid* (period of time during which the policy is valid). Figure 2(a) shows an example provider privacy policy for e-learning; Figure 2(b) shows the corresponding consumer privacy policy.

The above method of specification results in a minimal policy in the sense that the policy is the minimum required to satisfy privacy legislation. Additional provisions can be added but are not necessary for the purposes of this work.

As an aside, with reference to the Privacy Management Model of Section 2.3, the policies in Figure 2 match, since 2 years retention time offered by the consumer for course marks is less private than the 1 year required by the provider, i.e. the consumer allows a privacy reduction that is greater than the reduction required by the provider. Privacy policies need to be expressed in a machine-readable policy language such as APPEL (W3C, 2002) which is XML-based. The investigation of suitable policy languages for privacy policies is ongoing research and outside the scope of this chapter.

3.3 Application of Privacy Policies

According to the Privacy Management Model, a consumer's privacy policy is used to express how the provider is to handle the consumer's personal information. A provider requests the consumer's personal information for use in its e-service. The consumer therefore needs to ensure that the provisions in her privacy policy are targeted for the personal information requirements of the e-service that she wishes to engage from the provider. In practice, this means that the consumer needs to specify a new policy if the personal information requirements of the e-service changes, or the policy is being used for a new e-service with different personal information requirements. There is a one-to-*n* correspondence between the consumer's privacy policy and the corresponding e-service(s), where *n* is the number of e-services that have the same personal information requirements.

3.4 Maintenance of Privacy Policies

As time passes, the personal information needs of an e-service can change, e.g. the provider may decide to offer a new feature that would require additional personal information. For example, an e-learning service may offer to sell reference material to its clients requiring new personal information on which material a client wishes to purchase. The consumer's preferences for the handling of her personal information can also change with time, e.g. change in who may receive disclosure of medical condition due to a change in physician. Thus, for a particular consumer privacy policy – e-service pair, the consumer needs to be cognizant of such changes and keep her policy updated and maintained accordingly.

Figure 2. Example provider (a) and corresponding consumer (b) privacy policies

a)

Header	*Policy Use:* E-learning *Owner:* E-learning Unlimited *Proxy:* No *Valid:* unlimited
Privacy Rule	*Collector:* E-learning Unlimited *What:* name, address, tel *Purposes:* identification *Retention Time:* unlimited *Disclose-To*: none
Privacy Rule	*Collector:* E-learning Unlimited *What:* Course Marks *Purposes:* Records *Retention Time:* 1 year *Disclose-To*: none

b)

Header	*Policy Use:* E-learning *Owner:* Alice Consumer *Proxy:* No *Valid:* unlimited
Privacy Rule	*Collector:* Any *What:* name, address, tel *Purposes:* identification *Retention Time:* unlimited *Disclose-To*: none
Privacy Rule	*Collector:* Any *What:* Course Marks *Purposes:* Records *Retention Time:* 2 years *Disclose-To*: none

4. PRIVACY POLICY PITFALLS

We are interested in pitfalls that result from the use of privacy policies with e-services. These pitfalls arise from a) how the matching policy was obtained, b) the content of the matching policy, and c) the misapplication or poor maintenance of the user's policy for a particular e-service. Note that misapplication and poor maintenance have been combined into one category due to their common effect of causing bad privacy rules or missing privacy rules in the privacy policy. Pitfalls from a) and b) require a more in depth analysis before they can be uncovered, whereas pitfalls from c) follow readily from the privacy rule or rules being incorrectly specified or missing for the application at hand. We examine each of these categories in turn.

4.1 Pitfalls from How the Matching Policy was Obtained

The matching policy can be obtained through policy upgrades or downgrades. These policy changes can occur while the policy was being formulated for the first time or after a mismatch had occurred in an attempt to obtain a match (e.g. during policy negotiation (Yee & Korba, Jan. 2003; Yee & Korba, May 2003)). Recall from Section 2.3, that an upgraded policy reflects a higher level of privacy. On the other hand, a downgraded policy reflects a lower level of privacy.

Policy Upgrades

Given our privacy management model that the provider reduces the consumer's privacy, it is possible that the policy non-match was due to the provider's policy requiring too much privacy reduction. Suppose then that the match occurred after the provider upgraded its privacy policy to represent more privacy, i.e. require less privacy reduction. This could mean that the provider is requiring less information that is private. In this case, the provider or consumer may not realize the extra costs that may result from not having access to the private information item or items that were eliminated through upgrading. For example, leaving out the social insurance number may lead to more costly means of consumer identification for the provider. As another example, consider the provider and consumer policies of Figure 3. In this figure, suppose All Books Online upgraded its privacy policy by eliminating the credit card

Figure 3. Example online book seller provider (left) and consumer (right) privacy policies

Provider	Consumer
Policy Use: Book Seller *Owner:* All Books Online *Proxy:* No Valid: *unlimited*	*Policy Use:* Book Seller *Owner:* Alice Consumer *Proxy:* No Valid: *December 2004*
Collector: All Books Onl. *What:* name, address, tel *Purposes:* identification *Retention Time:* unlimited *Disclose-To*: none *Collector:* All Books Onl. *What:* credit card *Purposes:* payment *Retention Time:* until payment complete *Disclose-To*: none	*Collector:* any *What:* name, address, tel *Purposes:* identification *Retention Time:* unlimited *Disclose-To*: none

requirement. This would lead to a match with Alice's privacy policy, but may cost Alice longer waiting time to get her order, as she may be forced into an alternate slower means of making payment (e.g. mail a cheque), if payment is required prior to shipping.

Policy Downgrades

Since the consumer resists the provider's privacy reduction, it is possible that the policy non-match was due to the consumer's policy allowing too little privacy reduction. Suppose then that the match occurred after the consumer downgraded her privacy policy to represent less privacy, i.e. allow for more privacy reduction. This could mean that the consumer is willing to provide more information that is private. Then the provider or consumer may not realize the extra costs that may result from having to safeguard the additional private information item or items that were added through downgrading. For example, the additional information might be a critical health condition that the consumer does not want anyone else to know, especially her employer, which could result in loss of her employment. The provider had better add sufficient (costly) safeguards to make sure that the condition is kept confidential. The provider may not have fully realized the sensitivity of the extra information.

4.2 Pitfalls from the Initial Specification of the Privacy Rules

We give here some example pitfalls due to the content of the matching policy. We examine the content of the header and privacy rules in turn, as follows.

Proxy

If the consumer uses a proxy to provide her private information, the consumer needs to make sure that the proxy is trustworthy. Otherwise, the consumer's private information may be divulged against her wishes.

Valid

If the valid field of the consumer's policy is not carefully specified, the provider may become confused upon expiry if there is not another consumer policy that becomes the new policy. In this state of confusion the provider could inadvertently disclose the consumer's private information to a party that the consumer does not want to receive the information.

Collector

Specification of who is to collect the consumer's private information needs to consider what happens if the collector is unavailable to receive the information. For example, consider the privacy policies of Figure 4. The policies are not compatible, since Alice will reveal her medical condition only to Dr. Smith whereas the provider would like any doctor or nurse on staff to take the information. Suppose the provider upgrades its policy to satisfy Alice by allowing only Dr. Smith to receive information on Alice's condition. Then a pitfall is that Alice cannot receive help from Nursing Online because Dr. Smith is not available (he might have been seriously injured in an accident), even though the policies would match and the service could theoretically proceed. There are various ways to solve this particular situation (one way is simply to have an overriding condition that in an emergency, Alice *must* give her condition to any doctor or nurse on staff) but we make our point. An improperly specified collector attribute can lead to unexpected serious consequences.

Retention Time

Care must also be taken to specify the appropriate retention time for a particular information item. The responsibility for setting an appropriate retention time lies with both the provider and the consumer. For example, consider once again the policies of Figure 4. Suppose Alice changes her privacy rule for medical condition from "Dr. A. Smith" to "any" and from "unlimited" to "2 years". Then the policies match and the service can proceed. At the end of 2 years, the provider complies with the consumer's privacy policy and discards the information it has on Alice's medical condition. But suppose after the 2 years, medical research discovers that Alice's condition is terminal unless treated with a certain new drug. Then Nursing Online cannot contact Alice to warn her since it no longer knows that Alice has that condition. Poor Alice! Clearly, both the provider and the consumer are responsible for setting the appropriate retention time. One could conclude that in the case of a medical condition,

Figure 4. Example medical help provider (left) and consumer (right) privacy policies

Policy Use: Medical Help *Owner:* Nursing Online *Proxy:* Yes *Valid:* unlimited	*Policy Use:* Medical Help *Owner:* Alice Consumer *Proxy:* No *Valid:* December 2004
Collector: Nursing Online *What:* name, address, tel *Purposes:* contact *Retention Time:* unlimited *Disclose-To*: pharmacy	*Collector:* any *What:* name, address, tel *Purposes:* contact *Retention Time:*unlimited *Disclose-To*: pharmacy
Collector: Nursing Online *What:* medical condition *Purposes:* treatment *Retention Time:* 1 year *Disclose-To*: pharmacy	*Collector:* Dr. A. Smith *What:* medical condition *Purposes:* treatment *Retention Time:*unlimited *Disclose-To*: pharmacy

the retention time should be "unlimited". However, "unlimited" can also have its risks, such as retaining information beyond the point of when it no longer applies. For example, Alice could one day be cured of her condition. Then, retention of Alice's condition could unjustly penalize Alice if it somehow leaked out when it is no longer true.

Disclose-To

If the *disclose-to* attribute of the consumer's privacy policy is not specified or improperly specified, providers can share the consumer's private information with other providers or consumers with resulting loss of privacy. Consider the following examples.

Suppose Alice has a critical health condition and she does not want her employer to know for fear of losing her job (the employer might dismiss her to save on sick leave or other benefits – this really happened! (Kumekawa, n.d.)). Suppose she is able to subscribe to Nursing Online as in the above examples. Then through the execution of the service, Nursing Online shares her condition with a pharmacy in order to fill her prescription. Suppose the company that Alice works for is a pharmaceutical supplier, and needs to know contact information of patients in the area where Alice lives in order to directly advertise to them about new drugs effective for Alice's condition. Suppose the pharmacy with which Nursing Online shared Alice's condition is a consumer of the pharmaceutical supplier and the pharmacy's privacy policy does not restrict the sharing of patient information that it receives second hand. Then the pharmaceutical supplier, Alice's employer, can learn of her health condition from the pharmacy and Alice could lose her job – a pitfall with serious consequences. A possible solution to this situation is for Alice to specify "pharmacy, no further" for disclose-to. Then to comply with Alice's policy, Nursing Online, as a consumer of the pharmacy, in its privacy policy with the pharmacy would specify "none" for the disclose-to corresponding to Alice's condition, thus preventing Alice's employer from learning of her condition and preserving her privacy.

As another example, suppose Alice, as a consumer, uses graphics services from company A and company B. Her privacy policy with these companies stipulate that the rates she pays them is private and not to be disclosed to any other party. Suppose she pays company A a higher rate than company B. Now suppose companies A and B are both consumers of company C, which provides data on rates paid for graphics services. In order to use company C's services, companies A and B must provide company C with de-identified information regarding rates they are paid. This does not violate the privacy policies of consumers of companies A and B because the information is de-identified. However, company B now learns of the higher rate paid company A and seeks a higher rate from Alice. There does not appear to be any solution to this situation, since Alice has already specified disclose-to as "none". This example shows that there can be pitfalls that may not be preventable.

We have presented a number of pitfalls arising from how the policy match was obtained and how the content of the policy was specified. Our outcomes are all negative ones because they are the ones we need to be concerned about. There are also, of course, positive unexpected outcomes, which are outside the scope of this work.

4.3 Pitfalls from the Misapplication or Poor Maintenance of Privacy Policies

Misapplying a privacy policy to an e-service means the use of a privacy policy that was put together for a different e-service. This may occur simply for the sake of convenience, where there is perhaps no time to specify a new policy. The associated pitfalls can be serious and far ranging.

At worst, it is tantamount to having the wrong information for each of the parameters *collector*, *what*, *purposes*, *retention time*, and *disclose-to* for each privacy rule, or required privacy rules may be missing altogether. Another possibility is that there may be too many privacy rules, e.g. two rules covering the same information item. At best, perhaps only one or two privacy rule parameters are misapplied and these parameters are only slightly different from their intended content.

Poor maintenance of a privacy policy can lead to similar consequences as misapplying a privacy policy. The causes of the consequences are similar to the misapplication case, arising from having wrong information (by not keeping the information up-to-date) for the parameters *collector*, *what*, *purposes*, *retention time*, and *disclose-to*, or stemming from privacy rules that are missing or superfluous.

To have a feel for the consequences of misapplication or poor maintenance, suppose *collector* and *what* are incorrect. This could lead to personal information that the user had not intended to share ending up in the hands of a party that the user had not intended as the information recipient. If the information in question is the user's credit card number and expiry date, the financial consequences could be disastrous. One could envisage similar bad consequences for incorrect information in the other privacy rule parameters. These consequences are fairly evident and will not be discussed further. In the case of missing or too many privacy rules, the consequences may not be so bad. According to the above Privacy Management Model, a policy with missing or excessive rules will be identified during the policy matching as being incompatible with the provider's policy. The user will then be informed on the causes of the incompatibility and learn that her policy is missing some privacy rules or has too many privacy rules.

5. AVOIDING PRIVACY POLICY PITFALLS

The pitfalls discussed in Section 4 can be further classified as those that arise through improper privacy policy creation and those that arise from improper policy application (improper use of a privacy policy once created). Pitfalls from how the matching policy was obtained and pitfalls from the initial specification of the privacy rules fall under improper policy creation. Pitfalls from the misapplication or poor maintenance of privacy policies fall under improper policy application. In the following, we show how these pitfalls can be avoided.

5.1 Avoiding Pitfalls During Policy Creation

The problem at hand is how to detect and prevent the pitfalls. Since all pitfalls derive from the privacy policy (at least in this work), it is necessary to ensure "well-formed" policies that can avoid pitfalls. Further, if a non-well-formed policy matches the first time and leads to pitfalls, it is too late to do anything about it. Based on the discussion of Section 4.2, we define a "well-formed" privacy policy after defining "privacy pitfall":

Definition 1

A privacy pitfall is a negative outcome of the use of privacy policies per the Privacy Management Model (Section 2.3) such that a) the outcome is unexpected by both the provider and the consumer, and b) the outcome leads to either the provider or the consumer or both experiencing some loss, which could be private information, money, time, convenience, job, and so on, even losses that are safety and health-related. A privacy pitfall may be referred to simply as a "pitfall" in the context of this work.

Definition 2

A *well-formed (WF)* privacy policy (for either consumer or provider) is one that does not lead to privacy pitfalls. A *near well-formed (NWF)* privacy policy is one in which the attributes *valid*, *collector*, *retention time*, and *disclose-to* have each been considered against all *known* misspecifications that can lead to privacy pitfalls.

In Definition 2, the misspecifications can be identified through experience (e.g. trial and error) or by scenario exploration (as above). We have already presented a number of misspecifications in Section 4.2. A NWF privacy policy is the best that we can achieve at this time. Clearly, such a policy does not guarantee that pitfalls will not occur – it just reduces the probability that a pitfall will occur. Also, we do not include "proxy" in the above definition. We assume that if a proxy is used, that proxy is reliable and will represent the interest of the consumer to the best of her ability.

Rules for Specifying Near Well-Formed Privacy Policies

Let us consider once more the content of a privacy policy by looking at the header and the privacy rules.

The header (Figure 2) consists of *Policy Use*, *Owner*, *Proxy*, and *Valid*. *Policy Use* and *Owner* serve only to identify the policy and assuming they are accurately specified, they are unlikely to lead to pitfalls. That leaves *Proxy* and *Valid*, and we have already disposed of *Proxy* in the previous section. As discussed in Section 4.2, *Valid* must be specified so that it is never the case that the provider is in possession of the consumer's private information without a corresponding valid consumer policy (i.e. with the policy expired). Another way to look at this is that it must be true that the provider is no longer in possession of the consumer's information at the point of policy expiration. Hence a rule for specifying *Valid* is the following:

Rule for Specifying *Valid*

The time period specified for Valid must be at least as long as the longest retention time in the privacy policy.

This rule ensures that if the provider is in possession of the consumer's private information, there is always a corresponding consumer privacy policy that governs the information, which is what is needed to avoid the pitfalls from an improperly specified *Valid*.

Let us now consider the content of a privacy rule. The privacy rule consists of the attributes *Collector*, *What*, *Purposes*, *Retention Time*, and *Disclose-To* (Figure 2). *What* and *Purposes* serve only to identify the information and the purposes for which the information will be put to use. Assuming they are accurately specified, they are unlikely to lead to pitfalls. That leaves *Collector*, *Retention-Time*, and *Disclose-To*, which we discussed in Section 4.2. We now formulate specification rules for them, based on the discussion of Section 4.2.

Rule for Specifying *Collector*

When specifying an individual for Collector, the consequences of the unavailability of the individual to receive the information must be considered. If the consequences do not lead to pitfalls (as far as can be determined), proceed to specify the individual. Otherwise, or if there is doubt, specify the name of the provider (meaning anyone in the provider's organization).

Rule for Specifying *Retention Time*

When specifying Retention Time, the consequences of the expiration of the retention time (provider destroys corresponding information) must be considered. If the consequences do not lead to pitfalls (as far as can be determined), proceed to specify the desired time. Otherwise, or if there is doubt, specify the length of time the service will be used.

Rule for Specifying *Disclose-To*

When specifying Disclose-To, the consequences of successive propagation of your information starting with the first party mentioned in the Disclose-To must be considered. If the consequences do not lead to pitfalls (as far as can be determined), proceed with the specification of the Disclose-To party or parties. Otherwise, or if there is doubt, specify "none" or "name of receiving party, no further".

These rules address the problems discussed in Section 4.2 that lead to pitfalls. Except for *Valid*, in each case we require the consumer or provider to consider the consequences of their intended specification, and propose specification alternatives, where the consequences lead to pitfalls or there is doubt. By definition, application of these rules to the specification of a privacy policy will result in a near well-formed policy. Undoubtedly, mathematical modeling of the processes at play together with state exploration tools can help to determine whether or not a particular specification will lead to pitfalls. Such modeling and use of tools is part of future research.

Approach for Obtaining Near Well-Formed Privacy Policies

We propose an approach to obtain NWF privacy policies, applied during the initial privacy policy specification process and during the subsequent privacy policy negotiation process when there is a mismatch.

Initial Specification

We propose that the above rules for obtaining near well-formed policies be incorporated during initial policy specification. This is best achieved using an automatic or semi-automatic method for specifying privacy policies, such as the approach for consumer policies given in Yee & Korba (Jan. 2005). The Rule for *Valid* is easy to implement. Implementation of the remaining rules may employ a combination of artificial intelligence and human-computer interface techniques to assist the human specifier to reason out the consequences. Alternatively, the rules may be applied during manual policy specification in conjunction with a tool for determining possible consequences of a particular specification, as noted above.

Policy Mismatch

Near well-formed policies may still not match. At a policies mismatch, the consumer or the provider upgrades or downgrades her/its individual policy to try to get a match. In so doing, each could inadvertently introduce new values into the policy or remove values from the policy that result in pitfalls or loss of NWF-ness. We propose the use of privacy policy negotiation (Yee & Korba, Jan. 2003; Yee & Korba, May 2003; Korba, 2002) between consumer and provider agents to guide the policy upgrading or downgrading to avoid undoing the values already put in place for NWF-ness in the initial specification. Alternatively, negotiation may expose a needed application of the above rules. This is also a consequences exploration, but here both provider and consumer do the exploration while negotiating in real-time. For example, in the All Books Online example of Section 4.1 where Alice does not need to provide her credit card, negotiation between Alice and All Books Online could have identified the consequence that Alice would need to wait longer for her order and direct her to another more viable alternative, such as agreeing to provide her credit card. Similarly, in the example of Section 4.1 where the provider has to introduce more costly safeguards to protect the consumer's added highly sensitive information, negotiation could have uncovered the high sensitivity of the new information and possibly result in a different less costly alternative chosen (e.g. the new information may not be needed after all).

Table 2 illustrates how negotiation can detect and prevent the pitfall of Alice having no access to medical service when it is needed (read from left to right and down). The result of this negotiation is that Nursing Online will be able to provide Alice with nursing service whenever Alice requires it, once she makes the change in her privacy policy reflecting the results of negotiation. If this negotiation had failed (Alice did not agree), Alice will at least be alerted to the possibility of a bad outcome, and may take other measures to avoid it. This example shows how negotiation may persuade the consumer to resolve a mismatch by applying the above rule for specifying "collector".

Table 3 gives another example of negotiation at work using Alice's Book Seller policy in Figure 3. This policy mismatched because Alice did not want to provide her credit card information. At the end of the negotiation, Alice modifies her privacy policy and receives service from All Books Online.

We have assumed that either the consumer or the provider will want to inform the other about changes to a policy that could lead to pitfalls. We believe this is a reasonable assumption given that it is in their mutual interest to avoid the pitfalls.

5.2 Avoiding Pitfalls During Policy Application

Pitfalls arising from the use of a privacy policy that was created for a different e-service may be avoided by ensuring that the policy to be used fits the e-service. This assurance is already provided partly by the Privacy Management Model of Section 2.3, which calls for a policy exchange and matching between user and provider policies. Thus, any discrepancy between user privacy rules and provider privacy rules will

Table 2. Preventing pitfalls—Nursing Online

Nursing Online (Provider)	Alice (Consumer)
OK if a nurse on our staff be told your medical condition?	*No, only Dr. Alexander Smith can be told my medical condition.*
We cannot provide you with any nursing service unless we know your medical condition.	*OK, I'll see Dr. Smith instead.*
You are putting yourself at risk. What if you need emergency medical help for your condition and Dr. Smith is not available?	*You are right. Do you have any doctors on staff?*
Yes, we always have doctors on call. OK to allow them to know your medical condition?	*That is acceptable. I will modify my privacy policy to share my medical condition with your doctors on call.*

Table 3. Preventing pitfalls—All Books Online

All Books Online (Provider)	Alice (Consumer)
OK if you provide your credit card informa-tion?	*No, I do not want to risk my credit card number getting stolen.*
If you do not provide your credit card information, you will need to send us a certified cheque before we can ship your order. This will delay your order for up to 3 weeks.	*I still don't want to risk my credit card number getting stolen.*
Your credit card information will be encrypted during transmission and we keep your information in secure storage once we receive it. You need not worry.	*OK, I will modify my privacy policy to share my credit card information.*

be identified and result in negotiation. However, a user policy that was created for a different e-service may still be compatible with the provider policy of the new service and at the same time not reflect the privacy wishes of the user for the new service. For example, consider the retention time for a particular information item. Suppose the provider's policy requires a retention time of 1 year. If the user policy that was created for a different e-service states a retention time of 2 years, this policy would be compatible with the provider policy of the new service, but suppose the user only wishes a retention time of 1.5 years for the new service. This would not be caught by the policy matching and could lead to a pitfall. To remedy this and provide more assurance of avoiding pitfalls caused by such use of policies, we propose that the user agent taking part in the policy matching also interactively review the privacy rules of the user's policy with the user before the matching. Each rule can be displayed and the user asked to approve the rule before going on to the next rule. After all rules have been reviewed, the user can be asked to approve the policy as a whole before proceeding to the policy matching. Prior to giving this last approval the user should be allowed to go back and re-review a rule or edit it at any time.

The pitfall avoiding provisions mentioned in the previous paragraph, namely policy matching and interactive review, may also be used to avoid pitfalls arising from poor maintenance.

6. RELATED WORK

Apart from the authors' earlier work (Yee & Korba, Oct. 2005), there does not appear to be references in the literature that directly concern themselves with pitfalls arising from the use of privacy policies. However, related work can be found by reinterpreting the problem as a feature interaction problem (discussed below), as conflict resolution in other non-privacy domains, and as other aspects of privacy policies. We discuss each of these related works next.

Pitfalls arising from privacy policies may be regarded as a feature interaction problem, where policies "interact" and produce pitfalls or unexpected negative outcomes (Yee & Korba, June 2003). Traditionally, feature interactions have been considered mainly in the telephony or communication services domains (Keck & Kuehn, 1998). More recent papers, however, have focused on other domains such as the Internet, multimedia systems, mobile systems (Blair & Pang, 2000), and Internet personal appliances (Kolberg et al., 2002). In this work, we have chosen not to frame pitfalls from privacy policies as a feature interaction problem. In so doing, we have obtained new insights and results.

Another related area has to do with resolving conflicts in access control and mobile computing (e.g. Jaeger et al. (2004), Capra et al. (2002)). However, it is believed that these methods and similar methods in other domains will not work for privacy due to the subjective nature of privacy, i.e. personal involvement to consider each privacy rule is necessary. Looking at these other methods for possible application to privacy is another topic for future research.

Related works on privacy policies concern their normal specification (but not to avoid pitfalls) and their processing. In terms of specification, Stufflebeam et al. (2004) discuss lessons learned in the specification of privacy policies using the policy languages P3P (P3P, 2002) and EPAL (IBM, n.d.). In addition, Cranor et al. (2006) discuss user interfaces for privacy agents that facilitate user understanding of privacy policies. Still in the area of specification, Karat et al. (2006) present an evaluation of interfaces for the authoring of privacy rules. In terms of privacy policy processing, Backes et al. (2004) discuss the comparison of enterprise privacy policies using refinement. In addition, Brodie et al. (2006) describe an empirical study of the natural language parsing of privacy policy rules using a workbench. Finally, an interesting related work by Zannone et al. (2005) discusses the preservation of privacy for semi-personal information that is derived from personal information. This is not too unlike this work's requirement of original privacy policy compliance for personal information that is sequentially disclosed from one party to another.

7. FUTURE TRENDS

As mentioned in the Introduction, the concerns for privacy are escalating, as evidenced by the growing deployment of privacy policies, privacy legislation, and privacy commissioners. This trend, along with the use of privacy policies to manage privacy, can only continue and increase as more and more e-services are deployed. In such an environment, works on the proper use of privacy policies are very timely and needed. We suggest that this work also falls under the latter category, and is therefore very timely and needed. In the broader context of this book, we believe that this work discusses a very important issue in the social and human elements of information security: that of safety in the specification and application of privacy policies.

The following topics can be considered for future research: a) identify other pitfalls arising from the use of privacy policies, b) design tools to help users and providers do consequences exploration; these tools could be used to identify pitfalls and/or a pitfall's impact or seriousness, c) identify methods to avoid or mitigate pitfalls, and last but not least, d) implement the approach of this work to ensure near well-formed-ness at initial policy specification time, to experiment with automatic creation of well-formed user privacy policies.

8. CONCLUSION

The Canadian Privacy Principles impose legislative conditions to protect the rights of individuals (consumers) to privacy. They imply that the collection of private information may be done under the headings of *collector, what, purposes, retention time,* and *disclose-to*. Privacy policies may be constructed using these headings to specify each private information item to be shared. In an online community, consumers and providers of electronic services specify their privacy preferences using privacy policies. The provider specifies the private information items it requires from the consumer. The consumer specifies the items she is willing to share with the provider. Software agents for consumers and providers exchange and compare these polices to see if they match. The service is initiated only if the policies match. The content of the matching privacy policies can lead to pitfalls. Examples of pitfalls arising from policy upgrades or downgrades, from malformed policy content, and from improper application and maintenance were given. An approach was proposed to avoid pitfalls, involving (1) the application of rules to construct near well-formed policies at initial policy specification time, (2) the negotiation of mismatched policies between consumers and providers to agree on private information items and to construct near well-formed policies through consequences exploration and the application of the rules of Section 5.1, and (3) the interactive review and sign-off of the user's privacy policy conducted by the consumer agent prior to policy matching. Item 1 can be used right away without any computer tools. Items 2 and 3 require computerization (part of future research) to be effective.

We have based our work on our particular formulation of a privacy policy. An obvious question is whether our approaches apply to other formulations of privacy policies. We believe the answer is yes, for the following reasons: a) privacy policy formulations (i.e. contents) cannot differ too much from one another since they must all conform to privacy legislation and our policy is a minimal policy that so conforms, b) the privacy legislation of Canada, the European Union, and the United

States are all very similar (Yee et al., 2006), and c) if necessary, we can fit our approach to any formulation by applying the same logic we used in this work. There is much future research to be done on the subject of this work (see Section 7). We hope that we have provided useful insight into the pitfalls that can accrue from the use of privacy policies, and have given practical suggestions on how these pitfalls can be mitigated.

REFERENCES

Adams, C., & Barbieri, K. (2006). Privacy Enforcement in E-Services Environments. Chapter in *Privacy Protection for E-Services*, edited by Yee, G., Idea Group, Inc.

Backes, M., Karjoth, G., Bagga, W., & Schunter, M. (2004). Efficient Comparison of Enterprise Privacy Policies. *Proceedings of the 2004 ACM Symposium on Applied Computing*, pp. 375-382.

Banisar, D. (1999). Privacy and Data Protection Around the World. *21st International Conference on Privacy and Personal Data Protection*, September 13.

Blair, L., & Pang, J. (2000). Feature Interactions – Life Beyond Traditional Telephony. *Proceedings of the 6th International Workshop on Feature Interactions in Telecommunications and Software Systems*, pp.83-93, Glasgow, Scotland, May.

Brodie, C. A., Karat, C.-M., & Karat, J. (2006). An Empirical Study of Natural Language Parsing of Privacy Policy Rules Using the SPARCLE Policy Workbench. *Proceedings of the Second Symposium on Usable Privacy and Security*, pp. 8-19, Pittsburgh, Pennsylvania, USA.

Canadian Standards Association (n.d.). Model Code for the Protection of Personal Information. *Available as of Sept. 5, 2003 at: http://www.csa.ca/standards/privacy/code/Default.asp?articleID=5286&language=English*

Capra, L., Emmerich, W., & Mascolo, C. (2002). A Micro-Economic Approach to Conflict Resolution in Mobile Computing. *Proceedings of the 10th ACM SIGSOFT Symposium on Foundations of Software Engineering*, November.

Cranor, L. F., Guduru, P., & Arjula, M. (2006, June). User Interfaces for Privacy Agents. *ACM Transactions on Computer-Human Interaction (TOCHI), 13*(2), 135–178.

European Union Directive (1995). Directive 95/46/EC of the European Parliament and of the Council of 24 October 1995 on the protection of individuals with regard to the processing of personal data and on the free movement of such data. *Unofficial text available as of Sept. 5, 2003 at: http://aspe.hhs.gov/datacncl/eudirect.htm*

Government of Canada (n.d.). Personal Information Protection and Electronic Documents Act. *Available as of February 28, 2005 at: http://www.privcom.gc.ca/legislation/index_e.asp*

Hurley, D. (1999). A Whole World in One Glance: Privacy as a Key Enabler of Individual Participation in Democratic Governance. *21st International Conference on Privacy and Personal Data Protection*, September 13.

IBM (n.d.). Enterprise Privacy Authorization Language (EPAL). Available as of May 31, 2007 at: http://www.zurich.ibm.com/security/enterprise-privacy/epal/

Iyengar, V.S. (2002). Transforming Data to Satisfy Privacy Constraints. *Proceedings, The Eighth ACM SIGKDD International Conference on Knowledge Discovery and Data Mining*, Edmonton, Alberta.

Jaeger, T., Sailer, R., & Zhang, X. (2004, June). Resolving Constraint Conflicts. *Proceedings of the Ninth ACM Symposium on Access Control Models and Technologies*.

Karat, C.-M., Karat, J., Brodie, C., & Feng, J. (2006). Evaluating Interfaces For Privacy Policy

Rule Authoring. *Proceedings of the SIGCHI Conference on Human Factors in Computing Systems*, pp. 83-92, Montreal, Quebec, Canada.

Keck, D., & Kuehn, P. (1998, October). The Feature and Service Interaction Problem in Telecommunications Systems: A Survey. *IEEE Transactions on Software Engineering*, 24(10).

Kenny, S., & Korba, L. (2002, November). Adapting Digital Rights Management to Privacy Rights Management. *Computers & Security*, 21(7), 648-664.

Kobsa, A., & Schreck, J. (2003, May). Privacy Through Pseudonymity in User-Adaptive Systems. *ACM Transactions in Internet Technology*, 3(2), 149-183.

Kolberg, M., Magill, E., Marples, D., & Tsang, S. (2002). Feature Interactions in Services for Internet Personal Appliances. *Proceedings of IEEE International Conference on Communications 2002 (ICC 2002), 4*, 2613-2618.

Korba, L. (2002). Privacy in Distributed Electronic Commerce. *Proceedings of the 35th Hawaii International Conference on System Science (HICSS)*, Hawaii, January 7-11.

Kumekawa, J. K. (n.d.). Health Information Privacy Protection: Crisis or Common Sense? *Available as of Sept. 7, 2003 at: http://www.nursingworld.org/ojin/topic16/tpc16_2.htm*

Milberg, S. J., Burke, S. J., Smith, H. J., & Kallman, E. A. (1995, December). Values, Personal Information, Privacy, and Regulatory Approaches. *Communications of the ACM, 38*(12).

P3P (2002). The Platform for Privacy Preferences 1.0 (P3P 1.0) Specification. W3C Recommendation, April 16, 2002. *Available as of May 31, 2007 at: http://www.w3.org/TR/P3P/*

Song, R., Korba, L., & Yee, G. (2006). Pseudonym Technology for E-Services. Chapter in *Privacy Protection for E-Services*, edited by Yee, G., Idea Group, Inc.

Stufflebeam, W. H., Anton, A. I., He, Q., & Jain, N. (2004). Specifying Privacy Policies with P3P and EPAL: Lessons Learned. *Proceedings of the 2004 ACM Workshop on Privacy in the Electronic Society*, pp. 35-35.

W3C (2002). A P3P Preference Exchange Language 1.0 (APPEL1.0). W3C Working Draft 15 April 2002. *Available as of August 12, 2002 at: http://www.w3.org/TR/P3P-preferences/*

Yee, G., & Korba, L. (2003, January). Bilateral E-services Negotiation Under Uncertainty. Proceedings, *The 2003 International Symposium on Applications and the Internet (SAINT2003)*, Orlando, Florida, USA.

Yee, G., & Korba, L. (2003, May). The Negotiation of Privacy Policies in Distance Education. In *Proceedings of the Information Resources Management Association International Conference 2003 (IRMA 2003)*, Philadelphia, Pennsylvania, USA.

Yee, G., & Korba, L. (2003, June). Feature Interactions in Policy Driven Privacy Management. *Proceedings, Seventh International Workshop on Feature Interactions in Telecommunications and Software Systems*, Ottawa, Canada.

Yee, G., & Korba, L. (2004). Privacy Policy Compliance for Web Services. *Proceedings, 2004 IEEE International Conference on Web Services (ICWS 2004)*, San Diego, California, July.

Yee, G., & Korba, L. (2005, January). Semi-Automatic Derivation and Use of Personal Privacy Policies in E-Business. *International Journal of E-Business Research, Vol. 1, No. 1*, Idea Group Publishing.

Yee, G., & Korba, L. (2005, October). Specifying Personal Privacy Policies to Avoid Unexpected Outcomes. *Proceedings, Third Annual Conference on Privacy, Security and Trust*, St. Andrews, New Brunswick, Canada.

Yee, G., Korba, L., & Song, R. (2006). Legislative Bases for Personal Privacy Policy Specification. Chapter in *Privacy Protection for E-Services*, edited by Yee, G., pp. 281-294, Idea Group Inc., March.

Zannone, N., Jajodia, S., Massacci, F., & Wijesekera, D. (2005). Maintaining Privacy on Derived Objects. *Proceedings of the 2005 ACM Workshop on Privacy in the Electronic Society*, pp. 10-19, Alexandria, VA, USA.

KEY TERMS

e-Service: An e-service or electronic service is a service that can be accessed by users of the service through a network such as the Internet. Two examples of e-services are 1) an online broker such as etrade.com that allows users to obtain stock quotations and trade stocks, and 2) an online book seller such as amazon.com. Web services comprise an important class of e-services that is characterized by the use of XML and SOAP in a Service Oriented Architecture.

Pitfall: A pitfall in the context of privacy policies is an unexpected negative outcome (see "unexpected outcome" below) resulting from the application of a privacy policy.

Privacy: Privacy refers to the ability of individuals to control the collection, use, retention, and distribution of information about themselves.

Privacy Policy: A user's privacy policy is a statement that expresses the user's desired control over an e-service's collection, use, retention, and distribution of personal information about the user. A service provider's privacy policy is a statement that expresses the provider's desired control over the collection, use, retention, and distribution of personal information about the user.

Privacy Policy Matching: Before a user invokes an e-service, the user's privacy policy should agree with the provider's privacy policy. Privacy policy matching is the process of comparing these polices to determine if there is such agreement.

Specification of Privacy Policy: This refers to the process of constructing the privacy policy. This can best be done through the use of a computer application that guides the user or service provider in constructing the policy and results in a machine readable form of the policy that is amenable to further computer processing (e.g. for privacy policy matching).

Unexpected Outcome: An unexpected outcome in the context of privacy policies, is an event or result from the application of a privacy policy that was unexpected or unintended. Unexpected outcomes can be positive (e.g. the application of the privacy policy resulted in unexpected financial savings that would not have accrued in the absence of the policy), or negative (e.g. the application of the privacy policy resulted in some unexpected personal loss such as loss of a job – see examples in this chapter).

ENDNOTE

1 NRC Paper Number: NRC 49848

Chapter X
Privacy and Banking in Australia

Supriya Singh
Smart Internet Technology Cooperative Research Centre/RMIT University, Australia

Margaret Jackson
Smart Internet Technology Cooperative Research Centre/RMIT University, Australia

Jenine Beekhuyzen
Smart Internet Technology Cooperative Research Centre/RMIT University, Australia

ABSTRACT

Enabling customers to influence the way they are represented in the bank's databases, is one of the major personalization, responsiveness, and privacy issues of banking. In this chapter we draw on the results from a qualitative study of the ways in which Australians think of privacy, security, and money. We find that changes in life stages, residence, and relationships motivate people to share additional personal information with their bank, in order to receive personalized services. The chapter proposes ways in which privacy rights management can help customers better represent themselves in a flexible manner, reflecting the changes in their lives.

INTRODUCTION

In industrialized countries, the use of electronic money has increased. From the customers' perspective, electronic payments instruments and channels have made money impersonal and virtual (Singh, 2004). Seeing the same changes from the organizational point of view, it is the customer who has become impersonal and virtual. As a bank manager said, "I'm actually seeing very, very few of my own... customers... we never see them. We've never even heard of them..." (Hughes et al., 1999, p. 31). The challenge for the bank is to align the "customer in the machine" with the real customer. As Hughes et al. say, banking technologies help represent this customer 'in the machine'. They say these technologies

... appear to be routinely deployed as an integral aspect of cooperating with the customer; as a factor in the configuring and reconfiguring of customer behaviour; and as an element in relationship management (Hughes et al., 1999, p. 30).

So from the bank's perspective it is the customer who has become information, with money remaining "real". This is the reverse picture when seen from the users' perspective, where the customer is "real", but the money is virtual.[1]

One of the contributions of our study will be enabling the customer to influence the way the "customer in the machine" is represented. Privacy Rights Management technologies could enable the customer to personalize how he or she wants to be treated by ensuring that the relevant information is included in the way the customer is "configured" within the organization.

In this paper we are reporting on the results of a qualitative study on Banking, Personal Communications and Financial Decision Making. This research is part of a wider project focusing on Security, Trust, Identity and Privacy in the Smart Internet Technology Cooperative Research Centre. We are studying these issues from the users' perspective so that users can be central to the design of financial services and bank strategy.

We conducted a qualitative study between April 2005 and July 2006, covering 108 people in Melbourne, rural Victoria and Brisbane in Australia. We conducted 84 open-ended interviews, two 'yarning' circles (these are like group interviews) with six Indigenous people in Brisbane and three focus groups with 18 people with disabilities. Our sample had:

- 62 persons who used Internet banking and 46 who did not.
- 45 men and 63 women. This dominance of women was partially explained because women manage money particularly in the lower income households;
- Four participants were aged between 18-24; 24 aged 25-34; 28 aged 35-44; 21 aged 45-54; 18 aged 55-64; and 13 aged 65 or over.
- We had a range of annual household income levels: 23 had an income below $25,000 (all dollar values are in Australian dollars); 25 between $25,000-49,999; 20 between $50,000-$74,999; ten between $75,000-$100,000; and 21 had over $100,000 a year. Nine participants did not want to disclose their household income.
- 43 participants had a Certificate or lower educational qualification, 64 had a BA or higher degree, and one did not say. Of those who had a BA or higher degree, at least 11 were in IT. This reflected our personal networks also participants' interest in issues of privacy, security and identity.

We chose the qualitative approach for we needed to understand how people manage their financial information across life stages. We also wanted to go beyond attitudes to behavior. The study had at its centre the perspectives of user-centered design where the users' activities within their social and cultural context are at the centre of design (Singh et al., 2004; Vredenburg, Isensee, & Righi, 2002). It was a 'grounded' study in that there was a fit between data and emerging theory, rather than a testing of hypotheses (Glaser & Strauss, 1967).

The interviews were transcribed. We used N6, a computer program to assist with qualitative analysis. This meant we first broadly coded the data, then organized the data into matrices to check emerging themes in a transparent manner. We also used the N6 program to identify negative cases so that the study was rigorous. As Morse and Richards (Morse & Richards, 2002) say

The key to rigorous qualitative inquiry is the researcher's ability ... of being constantly aware and constantly asking analytic questions of data, which, in turn, constantly address the questions

asked. Qualitative inquiry constantly challenges assumptions, constantly challenges the obvious, reveals the hidden and the overt, the implicit and the taken for granted, and shows these in a new light (p. 170).

Once the different facets of money, banking and privacy were understood, these insights were translated to personas and scenarios so that they could be better communicated to bankers as well as to computer scientists working on the technical implementation of Privacy Rights Management in the Smart Internet Technology Cooperative Research Centre.

PRIVACY, MONEY AND BANKING

Lawyers, technologists, sociologists and psychologists have defined the concept of privacy in different ways. These definitions have little connection with the way people speak about privacy, making it problematic to connect privacy, money and banking.

Different Approaches to Privacy

Legal debate about the need for a right of privacy is relatively recent, first raised in a seminal article, 'The Right to Privacy', published in the Harvard Law Review in 1890 (Warren & Brandeis, 1890). At that time, the issue about privacy concerned intrusions by media and invasions of individuals' rights by government. Warren's family had been hounded by newspaper exposure of private matters and the Warren and Brandeis paper called for controls on invasion of private and domestic life and the right to protection of the private personality (Cowen, 1976).

Later American writers, such as Alan Westin, were to offer different definitions of the concept of personal privacy. Westin adopted a view of personal privacy that was more concerned with control over information about an individual than with intrusions into personal life. This view reflected a growing European debate in the 1960s and 1970s about the protection of personal data, led by organizations such as the Organisation for Economic Co-operation and Development ('the OECD') and the Council of Europe. Westin defined the right of privacy as "the claim of individuals, groups or institutions to determine themselves when, how and to what extent information about them is communicated to others" (Westin, 1967). This definition has been thought too narrow by some, including Professor William Morison who conducted a review in New South Wales on privacy in 1973, because it excluded people's concerns about intrusions such as unsolicited mail and telephone calls, and intrusive surveillance (Morison, 1973). Westin's definition arose, however, in the context of the use of new technological methods of recording and disseminating information. The growth of computer technology allowed for the collection, use and disclosure of personal information in computer databases, leading to vast amounts of information about people being able to be collected, manipulated and transferred easily. It became possible to capture electronically all the facts that could identify a person in one file and to share it internationally.

In much of computer science and engineering literature – and in some science fiction – the ultimate horror is that of stolen identity. In everyday language, this equates to the ultimate crime of annihilation (See (Lambert, 2002; Saunders & Zucker, 1999; Vinge, 2001)). Identity fraud is primarily a security issue, and is spoken of in the language of defense. Become as anonymous as possible, withhold personal details, and it will be more difficult to steal your identity. Anonymity becomes the best way of achieving privacy.

There have been few user studies concentrating on how people want to control personal information and manage their identities while engaged in different activities. Existing policy studies for the main part focus on attitudes to privacy rather than behavior in activity contexts (see (Federal

Privacy Commissioner, 2000)). In the user studies on the control of personal information conducted in the Smart Internet Technology CRC, we have found that privacy is seen as the control of the sharing of personal information and control over the representation of ourselves. Privacy did not equate with anonymity. It also did not mean being left alone (Supriya Singh & Cassar-Bartolo, 2004).

This approach to privacy shares much with the literature in sociology and social psychology where identity is seen more in terms of the construction of different versions of the self, depending on context (see (Altman, 1975, 1977; Kroger, 2000). It also connects with the post modern approach to a multiplicity of identities (Turkle, 1995) and the ethnographic approach of a continuity of identity between the real and virtual worlds (Miller & Slater, 2000).

Money and Privacy

Money is one of the most private aspects of life for Anglo-Celtic couples in Australia. Salary, bonuses, savings, assets, debts are private information. Having them disclosed without your choice could lead to a loss of money or an inappropriate presentation of self. The privacy of personal money is so entrenched in Australia that even when there is little money involved, the principle of privacy is accepted. Money is private but people talk about it with people within "their circle of care". This circle in Australia nearly always includes the partner and sometimes is confined to the marital unit. People also talk about money with one or more parents, maybe adult children, siblings and close friends, who are of the same socioeconomic status (Singh & Cassar-Bartolo, 2004).

There are at least three important points in a person's life when the privacy boundaries change. Firstly, there is a greater exchange of money information within the family when there is a need for support. Family support in terms of loans or gifts of money are particularly important for families with a low annual household income (under $50,000). In middle-income families we expect a greater flow of money between parents and children with the rise in housing prices. In Anglo-Celtic Australia, unlike Asia and Africa, money seldom flows from children to parents. This can be explained because of the presence of an adequate welfare net and also because parents pride themselves on their ability to manage. Secondly, though money does not get transferred, it is not unusual for children to help manage the financial affairs of their parents, most often of the mother after she has been widowed. And thirdly, the sharing of information between partners stops when there is a breakdown in relationship.

In our qualitative study people spoke at length about the sharing of information about money. The data substantiated previous qualitative and quantitative studies in the Smart Internet Technology Cooperative Research Centre that most people discussed money with their partners. There were exceptions to this general pattern in the following situations:

- In de facto relationships where the money was separate but equal, there may be little discussion of money.
- There could be partial information sharing when a person had commitments to their natal family or a previous marital family. This was true for blended families, but also true for families where one or both partners were recent migrants and sent money home.
- Information about money was not wholly shared in families where the husband controlled and managed money, and the husband was the major earner in the household.

Not sharing information about money with the partner went together with a pattern of separate rather than joint accounts. It has to be noted that not all separate accounts were accompanied by secrecy. The mix of separate and joint accounts in relationships more often reflected the symbolic meanings of financial independence and/or jointness, rather than the use of money. Frequently, separate accounts were used for joint family expenditure. At times joint accounts were used as a transactional account only by one partner.

PRIVACY, SECURITY AND IDENTITY IN BANKING

In our study, the issues of privacy, security, identity and banking came to the fore mainly for the middle and higher income participants.For nearly two-thirds of low-income persons in our sample, issues of the Internet and privacy or the wider issues of privacy in a cyber world were not at the centre of their banking. Only 13 of the 36 people without a disability (36%) who said their annual household income was below $50,000, used the Internet for banking.. On the other hand, 36 of 47 (76%) persons without disability with a household income above $50,000 said they used Internet banking.

Household income is not as important a determinant of Internet use by people with disabilities. In our sample of the 12 persons with disability with a household income under $50,000, seven persons (58%) used Internet banking

Issues of privacy in banking spill over to issues of security and identity theft. The common link in the banking context is the risk of losing money via the fraudulent use of the credit card and/or information related to Internet banking. Drawing on our qualitative research we found that the participants who commented, saw privacy and security as different concepts. Privacy and security however were increasingly linked in a digital world. A security breach would lead to people having information about you that they are not authorized to have and thus breach privacy as well.

The people in our sample who commented on banking and privacy were comfortable with the bank knowing copious details about their financial affairs. This was seen as inevitable even though it was the accountant who was the professional with whom money matters were more often discussed. As Ingrid, a fulltime PhD student, 35-44, says,

Privacy I tend to equate more with the information I have allowed the bank in order to do my banking. That is going to be related to actual private details like my name, address, phone number. But it also relates to things like my bank balances, what accounts I have...

She notes "there is nothing private about your dealings with the bank. Everything is reported. Cash transactions are reported. Loans are reported." She thinks the aspect of privacy and banking that is most important is that banks "not ...sell my details to marketers".

Bridgette, 55-64, (all the names are pseudonyms) an academic with a household income of between $75,000 and $99,999, says, she doesn't "have a greatly developed sense of privacy" She says that being on the Internet is not a private activity. And "electronic banking is a way of just stepping outside and shouting to the world". She says,

I don't care about what people know about me. It wouldn't worry me if people would get onto my bank account online as long as they couldn't do anything with it. If they could then take money out of it, that would worry me.

The privacy issues that arose for people were more about the bank disclosing details of separate accounts to a person with whom you have a joint account. This disclosure of information was greatly resented. We had two cases of such privacy infringement. In Faroukh's case (45-54 years of age, an IT professional with more than $100,000 in annual household income), the bank showed his wife a separate account that he had with the bank. This was when he and his wife went to visit the branch about their joint home loan. He says he was able to explain it, but felt the bank had not kept his details private.

The other case was Erin, 25-34 whose husband had a joint bank account with his father. She said when she and her husband changed their contact details, the bank also changed her father-in-law's contact details. It meant that her father-in-law's account statements were coming to them.

Identity issues were more connected with credit card fraud and email spam, than the actual theft of a personal identity such as depicted in Hollywood films. In the United States, it was reported that 86 percent of people had changed their behaviour in at least one way because they were concerned someone could steal their identity from personal information on the Internet (Princeton Survey Research Associates International, 2005). In our sample, awareness of the possibility of identity theft, that is credit card fraud and email spam, led to some people changing their behaviour, as detailed in the section below.

Privacy, Identity, Security and the Credit Card

Issues of money being fraudulently spent by misuse of a credit card have been directly experienced by at least three of our 108 participants. Anita, now a housewife, 55-64 with a household income between $55,000 and $74,000, says $300 was withdrawn from her husband's credit card. When he rang the bank – for he was the primary cardholder – the money was returned. This experience left Anita cautious about checking statements and she does not use the credit card on the Internet – choosing to use BPAY. However, she regularly uses the Internet to monitor her accounts, transfer money and pay bills. She uses the Internet but worries about the security and keeps a constant eye on her finances. Her only strategy to lessen the risk is that of constant monitoring. She says, "I just hope that... nothing will happen. I just put .. full trust on...the banks that...they are doing their best...".

Amber, 28, with a household income below $50,000 says her partner had money taken from his credit card. He rang the bank and they put the money back. This experience of fraud with the credit card and its subsequent solution has gone to enhance the feeling of trust in the bank.

Dora, 35-44, an academic also had a problem with the fraudulent use of her credit card when in South East Asia. Worried also about media reports relating to security breaches, she decided to stop using Internet banking.

Little You Can Do About Privacy in the Cyberworld

Most of the participants were not totally satisfied with the security and privacy of the Internet. Trust, convenience, usefulness and habit over-rode their concerns. In some cases, they tried not to think of the risks because they could not do much about them. In other cases, they used risk minimization strategies such as using credit cards with low limits, using a computer and network they saw as secure (avoiding public and/or shared computers), regularly using and updating spyware and anti-virus software on their personal computers, and assuring themselves that the site had the sign of a lock to symbolize security.

Ellen, 35-44, an academic in part time work and with a household income of over $100,000, says she likes the convenience and the immediacy of the Internet. She buys groceries online and does all her banking on the Internet. She thinks that hackers are going to be able to steal their money one day, "but at this stage I don't see it as a security problem". She tries to be careful by keeping the passwords secure, and making sure she is on a secure site. She sees the university server as secure. In the end she tries to stop being anxious by saying nothing is totally secure. And if anything happened she has the confidence to follow up and get the money back.

Laura, 25-34, with her own business in health services, has always banked using the Internet.

Replying to questions about trust, privacy and security, she says, "I don't know that I think about it a lot, because I think I don't understand it enough. So I don't think about it... It's completely hiding your head in the sand."

Henry, 45-54, an academic on a household income of between $75,000 and $99,999 says "In terms of privacy, I don't think we actually have a lot of control over it". The banks have more data on us than we know. He is not sure whether they would sell this data.

There is an underlying assumption that ...there are controls and mechanisms ... in place to stop it. .. I am nearly sure most of them aren't there... The only time that you actually find out that there is a huge problem is when it hits you in the arse.

Only 18 of the 62 Internet users in our sample read the privacy policy even in a cursory manner. Kevin for instance does not read the privacy policy

...because I know it has more outs than ins.....I know that all that information is shared. Fundamentally, it's all available. Now, whether I read or acknowledge that privacy statement or not, is not going to stop them from making that information available across... institutions.

Peter, 25-34, with a small IT consulting business and a household income of more than $100,000 believes the privacy policy is usually a copy of someone else's privacy policy. Amber, 28, with a household income below $50,000 occasionally reads the privacy policy. She says she is a habitual "checker". Gillian concedes that the privacy policy is important to a certain degree. Ingrid, 35-44, a PhD student, says the privacy policy does not tell what is important. She says,

Almost every organization will have a privacy policy you have to tick to say that you have read it and understood the conditions, but no-one reads it. The only people that read those kinds of things are people who are new to the Internet, or compulsive people. I don't read them half the time. I tend to be more careful when it comes to things like the financial organizations and I will always scan something to see whether it says we won't sell your details to marketers.

Neither Secure Nor Private

For five participants with a household income above $50,000, issues of privacy and security are worrying enough for them to not use Internet banking, though they use the Internet and sometimes also buy on the Internet.

Callie, 55-64, in accounting with a household income of $50,000 to $74,999, says Internet banking is essentially insecure. She says, no one can guarantee its security. It is not a question of a lack of trust. "I just don't think... you can build a foolproof system." She says, "I just don't think that organizations are in a position to guarantee ... that they've got the safeguards to ensure privacy of information and safeguard it".

An academic with a household income of more than $100,000, Dora, 35-44, says she used Internet banking but stopped after the security breaches reported in the media. She was also worried because she had troubles with her credit card when she was overseas. She says "I just decided that I'd like to know that it was a bit safer before I went back to it."

She continues to occasionally buy tickets and books online but for banking uses the telephone and ATMs. Dora hopes that in five years time Internet banking will be more secure so that she can feel comfortable using it. She is naturally risk adverse and in this decision she has been influenced by her husband who is worried about the privacy aspects of online personal information. She is sufficiently worried that she is one of the three who occasionally reads privacy policies.

Alice, 62, a part time teacher, with a household income between $50,000 and $74,999 has used the Internet for work. The most useful part of the Internet for her is to be able to get to the catalogue of the local library. She abhors the Internet, particularly its lack of privacy, while at the same time being enthralled by it. She doesn't use Internet banking and has used telephone banking once when the credit card payment was due, but they were uncomfortable about it. Her husband too feels adamant about not using Internet banking. She at times gives her credit card details over the phone to buy something or sends them off by mail. But in similar situations, her husband sends a check. Media reports of security and privacy breaches seem to confirm their attitude for themselves. They do not consider that the security and privacy situation will ever be comforting enough for them to use the Internet for banking transactions.

Olivia is 25-34, an academic and consultant with a household income of between $75,000 and $99,999. She uses the Internet but does not use Internet banking, She says she is uncomfortable with the idea of her data being used for telemarketing. Moving to security issues she says, "I just feel that my data is not safe." She tolerates banks rather than trusts them. They make mistakes and "are always out to get money off you for fees." The fearful scenario for her is "what if you are putting through a transaction and something happens and it shuts down and then people steal your details..."

Gay, also 25-34, with a household income over $100 000 also has reservations. She says,

I'm not really up with all the security, so I'm a little bit hesitant to use the banking when I'm not sure I have enough security on my computer to...I don't understand the dangers of the internet that well. So I'm happy to email, look at stuff or whatever, but I'm not prepared to put my bank details on there at this stage.

Convenience Overrides Concerns of Security and Privacy

Sixty-two of our 108 participants currently use Internet banking. Of these 62, only two did not use it routinely. Thirteen were greatly concerned about privacy and security, while the other 47 valued convenience over concerns about privacy and security.

Convenience here refers to flexibility in banking. Internet banking has made it possible to do banking outside of branch hours, such as at night when the children are asleep or on the weekend. Internet banking makes visiting a branch unnecessary for most transactions. It has always been difficult to bank at a branch in remote Australia. With many bank branches closing over the past years in Australia, it has become more onerous even in rural Australia.

But ironically we may now have a more frequent relationship with our bank than we did before Internet banking. Many of those who use Internet banking use it with high frequency (regularly), sometimes daily.

Customers are now making decisions about when to visit the branch, and for what purposes. Just like Hester, who runs his own small business, customers are now ensuring that any physical contact with the branch is valuable to them. Hester visits the branch when he has specific questions about his exports or has papers to sign. Otherwise he daily monitors his "five or six accounts online".

Privacy and Responsiveness in the Bank

In our sample four people saw the bank's use of the Privacy Policy as a way to restrict customer access to information. This was particularly the case with joint accounts, where there was a hierarchical structure of the primary and secondary account or cardholder.

Kevin, 45-54, with an annual household income of more than $100,000, says it's a pain "primarily when one or the other has set up the account or done something and we need to change and we're not the original signatory, or were not."

Alice was in a similar situation and felt dismissed as she is not the primary account holder of the joint account. She manages the money but did not bring the account number with her and found the bank would not give it to her. She does not know why she did not give them her credit card. Her husband had to ring up the bank but they said the rules are that only the primary account holder can have particular kinds of information.

Gillian, 35-44, a full-time PhD student with a household income between $75,000-$99,999 said she and her husband found themselves in the awkward situation where the bank would not accept her changing the contact details for the credit card for both herself and her husband. She is the one who has the online log-on for the credit card. This is so that they can minimise the number of passwords they have. She says she emailed and asked

...to change our address, our postal and home address because we had moved. They changed mine but they wouldn't change his, even though I'm a secondary cardholder. They said it had to be the primary cardholder even though he doesn't have a log-on. So we had to physically ring the bank and change it, which was really not as secure as it could have been.

This meant her husband had to ring the bank to give Gillian permission to change the credit card details. She tried to find out if she could change the details in the future and the bank said "No. Every time you want to make any changes, he has to ring and authorize you to talk to me again".

Gillian says,

All we had to do was tell his name, his date of birth, his mother's maiden name and the account number....If you knew the person you could quite possibly know the mother's maiden name. ...To me that is not as secure as being able to send an encrypted email through a banking system. There is no point fighting them. They don't listen.

Erin, a mother of two and a full-time personal assistant, also faced similar restrictions when faced with the rules enforced by the privacy policy. She talked about the problem of her husband being the primary account holder and how this restricted her from connecting the kids' accounts with their main account with Internet access. She says, ""It takes longer because I have to get (my husband) to do it".

SCENARIOS: CHANGES IN LIFE STAGES, RESIDENCE, AND RELATIONSHIPS

We draw on our qualitative study to sketch personas and scenarios, which illustrate users' problems with money, privacy and the bank.

Scenarios have been successfully used to bridge the different perspectives of users, providers of services and policy makers, while keeping the user at the centre (Carroll, 2000). The stories themselves become a 'boundary object'(Star & Griesemer, 1989), around which people of different perspectives can come to a shared understanding of user needs. Through the use of personas and scenarios we ensure that we translate insights into user needs to viable strategy and design of technologies. The strategy and design has to be sustainable from three perspectives – the consumers, the providers and the designers. As Norman (1998) said when speaking of the design of technologies, all three legs of the tripod have to work together for success (Norman, 1998).

In the following section we present scenarios that connect with fears over the leakage of personal information; changing relationships and information requirements; and being able to control the way we are represented in the bank through our personal details and financial arrangements.

Ensuring that Personal Information Does Not Leak Out

Barry is an IT professional and knows that the PC was not designed for secure money transactions. He also goes to great lengths to ensure he minimizes the possibility of spam. He would like to use Internet banking because of its immediacy and convenience. He feels he could from his side make his PC and networks sufficiently secure for the low-level money transactions he has in mind. But he would like to be assured that the bank will not sell his personal details to telemarketers. At present he does not believe their privacy policies and wonders whether privacy is achievable in a digital world.

User problem: Barry wants proof that the bank's privacy policy is an enforceable contract and that the bank be held accountable if his personal details leak outside the organization.

Design solution: In a reverse form of digital rights management, consumers should be able to track the flow of their personal information. This visual record of how information has not gone outside the organization will help engender trust and boost its brand.

Banking, Gender, Privacy and Joint Accounts

Tom and Helen are highly paid professionals in their late 50s. Their children have moved out and their mortgage has been paid. They have a relationship with three banks – their salaries and main payments are with one; savings go into the second and financial investment is done through the third.

Over the years, their mix of individual and joint bank accounts has changed, as has their individual financial status. However their banks continue to see Helen as subsidiary to Tom. Helen continues to note with unease that even when the bank communication is for her, it is addressed to Mr and Mrs... But then information about a personal loan was also sent to her husband. She says,

I went to borrow money for a holiday house and I was aghast that the bank sent the information to Tom. He had had nothing to do with it. It is not that I did not want him to know, but it was my loan application, not his.

There are some accounts, where Tom is the only account holder. Helen wanted to inform the bank about a change in their address, but they would not accept it from her, as she was not named on that particular account. Helen says, "We would like to tell the bank how it should deal with our financial information, rather than them assuming that all the decisions are made by Tom."

User problem: The bank is keeping to old stereotypes about money and gender built into banking products and not keeping up-to-date with changes in social norms and within Tom and Helen's family. The bank needs to find a way to honor the individual's preferences for the giving and receiving of financial information.

Design solution: When Tom and Helen open accounts, the bank asks them to specify how they want their personal information treated through the Privacy Rights Management (PRM) system. This is so that they can influence how they are represented in the bank's information bases. The default choices are the traditional ones. There can be at least two additional choices allowing Tom and Helen to personalize the way they want to receive and give information. This is also an approach that can be taken to deliver information when it is a community, rather than an individual that owns the money and/or property.

Caring for the Mother's Finances

James, 45-54 has been caring for his mother's finances since his father died. James' mother used to leave the banking to her husband. At 72, she is wary of the new technologies and the lack of personal contact. In the beginning James would go with his mother so that she could do her weekly banking. She now is used to the local branch. However he would like to pay bills and transfer money on his mother's behalf. His mother would appreciate the help but does not want to sign a third party agreement for it is irrevocable. She trusts James but does not want to cede all control.

User problem: An aged parent would like help with the money management, while at the same time keeping some control over the sharing of information.

Design solution: The parent should be in control of access to information about money and the money in her or his account. However, the parent should also have an easy way of sharing this information so that she can get the help needed.

Stranded When Changing Country

Jane and her husband moved recently from the United Kingdom to Australia. Before leaving, they informed the bank about their change of address and contact details.

Soon after they arrived in Australia they rented an unfurnished house and bought an unusual number of goods. To their horror they found the bank had cancelled their credit card, after it was unable to contact them at their old address.

Jane tried to call and tell the bank that they indeed were using the card in Australia and here were the new contact details. However the bank insisted that Jane's husband call and make the complaint.

User problem: parts of the bank's information base do not communicate with each other. Hence the bank has different personal data on the customer that remains unconnected.

Design solution: Users should be able to control the input of a change of details, which then is communicated to all parts of the bank.

Stuck because of Direct Debit and Credit

Ian is a plumber and has been with the bank for 20 years. He is livid because they dishonoured a cheque without trying to contact him. In order to move his account, he has to keep two accounts going for a considerable period to make sure that the direct debit and direct credit instructions have been successfully changed.

User problem: The convenience of direct debit and credit is negated by users' lack of control over changes or stoppages of direct debit and credit.

Design solution: Ian should be in control of his direct debit and credit instructions so that he can give the information to his new bank, who then can affect the transfer.

DESIGN OF PRIVACY RIGHTS MANAGEMENT

Privacy Rights Management (PRM) can be used to protect and manage the privacy rights of customers. It has to be a two-tier system. The first level is to ensure that customers' information does not go outside the bank and its designated agents. This level of PRM could give additional comfort to people who at present are not users of Internet banking because of concerns with security and privacy. The second level of PRM ensures that people's privacy preferences are honored. This will ensure that separate account transactions are not revealed to others without explicit permission and those that have permission will be shared accordingly. It means that people can articulate the way they want their rights on joint accounts to be handled by the bank.

Technologically we see PRM as the mirror image of Digital Rights Management systems (DRMs) that are used to protect and manage the rights of digital copyright owners and manage access to digital information. Rather than protecting digital copyright, the technology could be used to shape the sharing of information and thus protect consumers' privacy.

Individuals generally do not object to providing personal information for the purpose of obtaining a service or a product. Their broad concerns relate to whether the information provided is used for the purposes advised by the data acquirer and whether it is disclosed to others inappropriately, without consent. The other more immediate concern is that the customers themselves should be able to set the rules about the sharing of information with partners and family.

Privacy Rights Management (PRM), therefore, gives people the ability to control how far their personal information is disseminated and by whom it is viewed. PRMs can work in a number of ways, such as operating as Trusted Third Parties or as central government agency. What is important is that the controller of the PRM is trusted by individuals. This lack of trust is one reason why government proposals to establish national identity databases meet with suspicion. The approach selected by the SITCRC is for the organization requiring access to personal information, in this case, a bank, to be the provider of the PRM. We see that there will be substantial benefits for the bank in providing the PRM in respect of identity verification of customers and in differentiating themselves from competitors.

Bank customers will be able to set a few basic rules to be followed by the bank. These rules might cover the way customers want their information shared; and the ways in which they want their information communicated. These could include:

- Rules about a third party's right to information about a customer's accounts
- Rights to change details or report changes on a joint credit card and account; The sending of marketing information to customers
- Preferred ways to contact the customer – email, mobile telephone, fixed line telephone, post.

CONCLUSION

We have conducted a qualitative study of the way 108 people bank and conduct their money relationships. We have focused on how privacy, security, trust and identity influence customers' choices, particularly in regard to Internet banking.

It is important to note that 43 per cent of our sample does not use Internet banking. This is because of low income, security concerns and lack of perceived usefulness. Most of the Internet banking users remain concerned about privacy and security. They trust the bank will look after their interests and choose to rate convenience over the risks, or try not to think of the dangers.

There is also a feeling that banks are unresponsive and do not help consumers personalize their information and the ways in which they would like to receive and share information.

We translated these consumer insights into personas and scenarios, so that the user can be at the centre of business strategy and the design of services. We think PRM, suitably designed has a role to play in the user-centred design of personalized financial services.

Acknowledgment

We would like to gratefully acknowledge the support of the Smart Internet Technology Cooperative Research Centre for making this research possible. We are also grateful to the participants of the *Privacy-Enhanced Personalization* Workshop at CHI 06, where a preliminary version of this paper was first presented.

REFERENCES

Altman, I. (1975). *The environment and social behaviour: Privacy, personal space, territory and crowding.* Monetery: Brooks/Cole.

Altman, I. (1977). Privacy regulation: Culturally universal or culturally-specific? *Journal of Social Issues, 33*(3), 66-84.

Carroll, J. M. (2000). Five reasons for scenario-based design. *Interacting with computers, 13*(1), 43-60.

Cowen, Z. (1976). *Opening address.* Paper presented at the *Symposium on Privacy*, Sydney.

Federal Privacy Commissioner. (2000). *Community attitudes towards privacy in Australia.* Retrieved 18 June, 2004, from http://www.privacy.gov.au/publications/rcommunity.html

Glaser, B. G., & Strauss, A. L. (1967). *The discovery of grounded theory: Strategies for qualitative research.* Chicago: Aldine.

Hughes, J., O'Brien, J., Randall, D., Rodden, T., Rouncefield, M., & Tolmie, P. (1999). Getting to know the 'customer in the machine'. In the Proceedings of the international ACM SIGGROUP conference on *Supporting group work*, Phoenix.

Kroger, J. (2000). *Identity development: Adolescence through adult.* Tromso, Norway: Sage.

Lambert, L. (2002). Asian underground banking scheme: A field note. *Journal of Contemporary Criminal Justice, 18*(4), 358-369.

Miller, D., & Slater, D. (2000). *The Internet: An ethnographic approach.* Oxford: Berg.

Morison, W. (1973). *Report on the Law of Privacy*, New South Wales Parliament, para 4.

Morse, J. M., & Richards, L. (2002). *Readme first for a user's guide to qualitative methods.* Thousand Oaks, Calif.: Sage Publications.

Norman, D. A. (1998). *The invisible computer.* Cambridge, Mass: MIT Press.

Princeton Survey Research Associates International. (2005, October 26). *Leap of faith: Using the Internet despite the dangers- Results of a National Survey of Internet Users for Consumer Reports WebWatch.* Retrieved 30 January, 2006, from http://www.consumerwebwatch.org/pdfs/princeton.pdf

Saunders, K. M., & Zucker, B. (1999). Counteracting identity fraud in the information age: The identity theft and assumption deterrence Act. *International Review of Law, Computers & Technology, 13*(2), 183.

Singh, S. (2004). Impersonalisation of electronic money: Implications for bank marketing. *The International Journal of Bank Marketing, 22*(7), 505-521.

Singh, S., & Cassar-Bartolo, K. (2004, November 21-24). *The privacy of money and health.* Paper presented at the OZCHI, Wollongong.

Singh, S., Zic, J., Satchell, C., Bartolo, K. C., Snare, J., & Fabre, J. (2004, 29 June- 2 July 2004). *A reflection on translation issues in user-centred design.* Paper presented at the 7th International Conference on Work with Computing Systems, WWCS 2004, Kuala Lumpur.

Star, L. S., & Griesemer, J. R. (1989). Institutional ecology, 'translations' and boundary objects. *Social Studies of Science, 19*(3), 387-420.

Turkle, S. (1995). *Life on the screen: identity in the age of the Internet.* New York: Simon and Schuster.

Vinge, V. (2001). Introduction. In J. Frenkel (Ed.), *True names and the opening of the cyberspace frontier* (pp. 15-23). New York: Tom Doherty Associates.

Vredenburg, K., Isensee, S., & Righi, C. (2002). *User-centered design: An integrated approach.* Upper Saddle River, NJ: Prentice Hall.

Warren, S., & Brandeis, L. (1890). The Right of Privacy. *Harvard Law Review, 4*(193).

Westin, A. (1967). *Privacy and freedom.* New York: Atheneum.

KEY TERMS

Grounded Study: The focus is on the fit between data and theory.

Identity: Representation or representations of self.

Personalization: People shaping services to suit their information preferences.

Privacy: Control of personal information.

Privacy Rights Management: Managing and implementing users' privacy preferences.

Security: Fear of loss.

User Centered Perspective: Placing the user and his or her activities at the center of the study.

ENDNOTE

1 We are indebted to Anuja Cabraal for this insight.

Chapter XI
A Multistage Framework to Defend Against Phishing Attacks

Madhusudhanan Chandrasekaran
SUNY at Buffalo, USA

Shambhu Upadhyaya
State University of New York, USA

ABSTRACT

Phishing scams pose a serious threat to end-users and commercial institutions alike. E-mail continues to be the favorite vehicle to perpetrate such scams, mainly due to its widespread use combined with the ability to easily spoof them. Several approaches, both generic and specialized, have been proposed to address this growing problem. However, phishing techniques, growing in ingenuity as well as sophistication, render these solutions weak. To overcome these limitations, we propose a multistage framework – the first stage aims at detecting phishing based on their semantic and structural properties, whereas in the second stage we propose a proactive technique based on a challenge-response technique to establish the authenticity of a Web site. Using live e-mail data, we demonstrate that our approach with these two stages is able to detect a wider range of phishing attacks than existing schemes. Also, our performance analysis study shows that the implementation overhead introduced by our tool is negligibly small.

INTRODUCTION

Phishing is a form of Web based attack where attackers employ deceit and social engineering to defraud users of their private and confidential information such as password, credit card number, social security number (SSN), and bank account number. As the Internet is becoming the *de facto* medium for online banking and trade, phishing attacks are gaining notoriety, especially amongst hacker communities. Anonymity over the Internet, coupled with the potential for large financial gains serves as strong motivation for attackers to perpetrate such seemingly low risk, yet high return scams. The first recorded mention of phishing attacks was in AOL forums ("Phishing - Wikipedia,") wherein attackers posing as system administrators tricked the registered users into disclosing their account information. Since then, phishing attacks growing in sophistication and ingenuity have affected millions of users causing heavy monetary damage. For example, in the year 2006 alone, phishing attacks cost $2.8 billion in losses to consumers and commercial organizations worldwide (Gartner Press Release, 2006).

Due to its widespread adoption and ability to be easily spoofed, email continues to be the favorite vehicle to perpetrate such scams. Email based phishing attacks are usually carried out as a three step process: (i) In the first step, phishers harvest email addresses of their potential victims from Web pages, online forums and by other social engineering mechanisms; (ii) For the second step, a large volume of specially crafted emails appearing to originate from legitimate domains is dispatched to the assimilated list using open SMTP servers and compromised machines. These emails contain hyperlinks which redirect the users to a fake Web site similar in appearance to the legitimate domain; (iii) Finally, account details and other personal information are collected from the users who unsuspectingly provide them into the fake Web site thinking it to be a legitimate one. Phishing attacks, like other social engineering attacks, for their success depend upon users' lack of system knowledge. Phishers adopt a variety of visual deception agents to imitate the legitimate Web site's look-and-feel (Drake, Oliver, & Koontz, 2004). The mimicry of a legitimate Web site is usually achieved through spoofing the URLs with non-ASCII Unicode characters using customized images to mask fake URLs and embedding the fake Web sites within images that resemble a browser window. Recent studies (Dhamija, Tygar, & Hearst, 2006) show that naïve users are inept in identifying common browser based cues such as address bar, status bar, SSL certificates, and toolbar indicators and often fall prey to such imitation sites.

Until recently, anti-spam techniques were employed to detect phishing emails. However as phishing emails closely resemble their legitimate counterpart, they do not share similar features as that of spam emails. Also, there exist a vast number of readily available tools that can bypass both the statistical and rule based spam filters. Several browser extensions and plug-ins have been proposed to detect phishing attacks. Although these techniques act as a first line of defense, they suffer from many limitations. First, as these approaches operate on the fake Web site, they take the users a step closer to the attack giving little leeway for suspicion. Second, most of the existing defense mechanisms are not automated and delegate the onus of decision making onto the users. Third, as these tools embrace the authenticity of the IP address as an important classification criterion, they fail to protect from attacks that are launched within the realm of legitimate domain. For example, an attacker could compromise a Web server and launch phishing pages from the domain itself[1].

To overcome these limitations, we leverage on our prior works (Chandrasekaran, Chinchani, & Upadhyaya, 2006; Chandrasekaran, Narayanan, & Upadhyaya, 2006) and present a two-stage solution to protect users against email based phishing attacks. The first stage aims at detecting phishing emails based on their semantic and structural properties, whereas in the second stage a proactive approach using the *challenge-response* technique is presented to test the authenticity of links present in the email. The essential driving force for this two-stage approach is that cleverly fabricated emails can evade even the most smart spam filters which are put in place for phishing detection. In the first stage, the existing phishing email corpus are analyzed and *context models* are constructed which encapsulate the underlying meaning of the emails using their syntactic and semantic properties. These context models then serve as discrimination indicators, and are used to distinguish the legitimate and the phishing emails apart. The context models are constructed from various language specific features such as usage of certain emotional words, patterns of vocabulary usage, unusual language usage, underlying content, and also other stylistic features that appear frequently across the phishing emails. These feature vectors constitute the message carried out by the phishing emails, which is used primarily to trick the recipients. Since there exist a large number of such relevant features, to reduce the curse-of-dimensionality, Simulated Annealing (SA) (Debuse & Rayward-Smith, 1997) is employed to identify the set of relevant features. Once the relevant features are identified, for the testing phase, Support Vector Machine (SVM) (Drucker, Wu, & Vapnik, 1999) is used to classify the phishing emails even before it reaches the users' inbox.

Although most of the present day phishing emails can be detected using our first stage solution, phishing emails, similar to spamming, can be cleverly devised omitting the relevant features that are used for training in our scheme. In the second stage, to detect such outliers a more proactive standpoint is adopted by using fake responses which mimic real users, essentially reversing the role of the victim and the adversary. The key idea behind our approach is to protect the real user's identities by providing fake information to the Web sites requesting critical information, until their authenticity is verified. Here, the detection leverages on the premise that just as an end user cannot tell legitimate and spoofed emails apart, similarly phishers cannot tell the responses of legitimate and phantom users apart. As the mail user agent (MUA) receives emails, their content are analyzed for the presence of embedded links and attached HTML forms. If the email contains no such suspicious characteristics, further investigation is discarded. Otherwise, it parses the appropriate tokens and supplies fake values to the information requested by the Web site. Based on our assumption, we note that the fake Web site cannot verify the credibility of the supplied information, and is indifferent to both the real and the contrived response. Using live email data it can be demonstrated that this two-stage approach is able to detect a wider range of phishing attacks than other existing schemes. Also, preliminary performance analysis study reveals that the implementation overhead introduced by the proposed tool is negligible.

The remainder of this chapter is organized as follows: First, we briefly discuss the existing antiphishing techniques and give out their strengths and weaknesses. Then we talk about commonly adopted phishing attack vectors that are used by the attackers to successfully launch phishing attacks. As classification algorithms rely on identifying invariant features intrinsic to the phishing emails, we dissect the phishing email structure for the purpose of extracting such features. This also helps in training the classifier to detect phishing emails even before it reaches the user inbox. Next, a two-stage approach is presented which can detect both phishing emails and Web sites. Finally, In order to bring out the efficacy of our approach, we evaluate both stages against live phishing sites and emails and give out their performance details.

Readers may note that the flavor of our exposition is rather technical; for a terminological, business and legal exposition of phishing and pharming, one could refer to (Kierkegaard 2007).

EXISTING DETECTION TECHNIQUES

A large number of defense efforts have been undertaken in academia and industry to tackle the phishing scourge. AntiPhishing Working Group (APWG) ("Anti-Phishing Working Group,") is a consortium of pan-industrial and law enforcement agencies formed to record and analyze the trends in current day phishing attacks. It comprises of more than 1600 companies worldwide, including 8 of the top 10 US Banks. From the academia front, to date, CMU Usable Privacy and Security Laboratory (CUPS), Stanford computer security lab and Indiana University's anti-phishing work group have been involved with projects that focus on antiphishing efforts. In this section, we summarize these existing defense solutions depending on the functionality they offer to detect and eliminate phishing attacks.

Browser Plug-ins and Antiphishing Toolbars

Several commercial and open source toolbars have been proposed to test and validate the Web sites visited by users. Spoofstick (Spoofstick, 2004) is one such browser add-on which displays the IP address of the connecting Web site in its toolbar, even if the URL displayed in the browser is spoofed. As Spoofstick requires human to know the IP address of legitimate Web sites, it does not provide an automated solution to detect phishing attacks. NetCraft antiphishing toolbar (NetCraft, 2004) is another monitoring tool that employs client-server architecture. Each toolbar subscriber acts as a client and is responsible for reporting suspicious Web sites to a central server. The server then processes every incoming request by checking the domain age, hosted location and URLs, and then puts the reported Web sites either into a whitelist or a blacklist. These lists are propagated to other clients to assist them with their decision making. A disadvantage with such an approach is that as phishing Web sites are ephemeral, it might not be possible to propagate the generated blacklists to the clients in time. SpoofGaurd (Chou, Ledesma, Teraguchi, & Mitchell, 2004) is a browser plug-in that examines the visited Web site using *stateful* and *stateless* evaluation. The stateless evaluation includes check for invalid links, URL obfuscation attacks, valid https connection and authenticity of SSL/TLS certificates. It also checks to determine whether the images present in the legitimate sites are imported by unknown suspicious domains. Unlike stateless evaluation, the stateful page evaluation monitors every outgoing data using site specific *salts* so that a user does not provide his username and password into a site he has never visited before. In most cases, the final result of these toolbars is either binary (phishing or safe) or ternary process (where a score/color is displayed on the toolbar to warn users about the sites' suspiciousness). Despite their advantages, a recent study (Zhang, Egelman, Cranor, & Hong, 2007), experimented with 10 popular antiphishing toolbars revealed that the toolbars failed to identify 15% of the phishing Web sites used for testing. Also, as discussed earlier, these toolbars depend on the validity of IP as an important detection criterion and fail to protect from attacks launched from the legitimate Web sites. Lastly, these toolbars ignore the weak human factor and require users to make the final decision, i.e., to trust a suspicious Web site or not.

Digital Signing and PKI Based Schemes

Digital signing and trust propagation schemes have been proposed to make email secure and reliable. These schemes employ publicly available standards such as S/MIME, PGP and GPG to encrypt, decrypt and validate email messages. The main purpose of digital signing is to guarantee two basic security properties: non-repudiation and integrity (Kapadia, 2007). Non-repudiation is used to ensure that the sender and the recipient are, in fact, the parties who claimed to have sent or received the message, respectively. On the other hand, integrity is used to verify that a part or whole of the message is not modified during transit. Spam protection framework (SPF), Certified Sender Validation (CSV) and DomainKeys have also been proposed as an alternative mechanism to authenticate emails based on their sender's domain name. DomainKeys uses digital signatures to authenticate domain name and the entire content of a message, whereas SPF and CSV look at the email headers to identify forgery. Even though these schemes act as an effective anti-spoofing solution, they suffer from several disadvantages. First, adoption of these techniques necessitates steep learning curve which might be elusive to everyday users. Second, these techniques require installation of additional software to support S/MIME, PGP, GPG, etc. These provisions are not readily available in most of the popular Web based email clients such as Yahoo Mail, Hotmail and Gmail. Finally, these techniques suffer from key distribution problem, where a trusted medium is needed to exchange keys needed to sign and encrypt/decrypt messages. In the case of PGP/GPG schemes, as there is no central authority server, a phisher can infiltrate the Web of trust by digitally signing his emails. Another drawback of this PKI-based and authentication based approaches is that both the sender and the receiver need to have the same signing and verification mechanisms.

Hardware Tokens and Session Based Authentication

Strong token based authentication mechanisms can be enforced using physical devices like smartcards, Bluetooth devices, USB tokens, and other devices that generate onetime passwords. As these generated passwords expire after a single logon, it is not possible for the phisher to impersonate the user at a later point in time. Some commercial implementations of such hardware tokens are RSA's SecurID, Aladdin's eToken, ActivIdentity tokens. Even though these schemes provide multi-way authentication by having an out-of-band (OOB) authentication channel, they are vulnerable to man-in-the-middle attacks where phishers, to avoid detection, replay the obtained password in the legitimate Web site and then present the received information back to the users. Moreover, these approaches incur high set-up and management costs and their large scale adoption is not always feasible. Other session based authentication mechanisms include email sequence numbering and email personalization. Unfortunately, similar to hardware tokens, they also impose additional burden on the users to manually verify the validity of sequence number and personal information. Moreover, these session-based authentication schemes also suffer from *man-in-the-middle* attacks.

Content Based Phishing Attack Detection

Several research efforts employing machine learning and pattern recognition techniques have been proposed to classify phishing emails. Most of the earlier algorithms were tailored to detect spam emails and did not perform well when applied in the context of phishing attacks. These approaches were *naïve* in the sense that they essentially focus on detecting the presence of uncommon words that appear in the spam emails. As phishing emails closely imitate their legitimate counterpart, unlike spam, they do not contain such random and *junk* words. In order to classify phishing emails, Fette et al. (Fette, Sadeh, & Tomasic, 2007) employ a set of 16 different machine learning algorithms operating on a predefined feature set. The feature set consists of structural elements that indicate presence of illegitimate hyperlinks, IP based URLs, non-matching URLs and other characteristics intrinsic to phishing emails. CANTINA (Zhang, Hong, & Cranor, 2007) is another tool which uses term frequency and inverse document frequency (tf-idf) to identify commonly appearing words in phishing Web pages. These words along with other structural elements are used as features for classification. Wenyin et al. (Wenyin, Huang, Xiaoyue, Min, & Deng, 2005) propose a technique to detect phishing Web pages by evaluating their resemblance with other Web pages previously visited by the users. Normally, as two Web pages do not share the same content and layout, three metrics based on block level, layout level and overall similarity are used to tell the fake and the legitimate apart. The main drawback of these approaches is that they fail to consider the underlying message conveyed in the phishing emails using which an attacker lures his victims to visit the fake Web site. Here, we also argue that, to decrease the true negative rates and to promote the overall awareness about phishing attacks, it is important to also include the messages' *tone* as an essential classification feature.

COMMONLY ADOPTED ATTACK VECTORS

Attack vectors are the means by which an attacker can gain access to a computer or network server for malicious purposes. Attack vectors enable hackers to exploit system vulnerabilities, and also the human element which is regarded as the 'weakest link' in the security chain. Attack vectors include viruses, email attachments, spoofed URLs, pop-up windows, instant messages, and deception. In this section, we review some of the commonly adopted phishing attack vectors used by the phishers to trick the user into visiting the fake Web site.

URL and Host Name Obfuscation Attacks: Phishing attacks use spoofing techniques to conceal such that an unsophisticated user cannot distinguish them from legitimate ones. One trivial deception method is to register a fake domain that is a misspelled variant of the legitimate one. For example, a phisher can host the phishing site from www.paypai.com to forge www.paypal.com (replace lower case 'L' with 'i'). Third party service exists that can shorten URLs so that it can be compatible with existing email and Web application systems. Such shortened URLs lose their identity and are represented as if hosted within their providers' domain. For example, www.google.com/accounts and http://moneycentral.msn.com/banking/accounts are mapped to http://tinyurl.com/8ydws and http://tinyurl.com/2lmgd2 respectively. Other form of visual deception is brought about by replacing ASCII characters with special encoded characters that use DWORD, HEX, UTF-8 encoding ("How to obscure any URL - How Spammers And Scammers Hide and Confuse," 2002).

Browser Vulnerabilities: Browsers in their quest to support extended features and functionalities provide hooks to install unauthorized third party plug-ins and add-ons. As these add-ons usually operate with the same security privilege as the browser, attackers can essentially exploit vulnerabilities present in them to hijack the browser. With new vulnerabilities being discovered and patches released, it is extremely difficult for a naive user to constantly update and protect against the attacks. Poorly configured browsers installed with third party plug-ins are susceptible to homographic attacks like International Domain Name (IDN) spoofing and pop-up hijacking attacks. Also, vulnerabilities in ActiveX controls and browser helper objects (BHO) can install trojans which can modify the system's host file to redirect the users to a fake Web site. Disabling the features like ActiveX controls, unauthorized third party plug-ins, IDN support is often viewed as a trade-off between extended functionality and security.

Cross-site Scripting (XSS) and Session Hijacking Attacks: Phishers exploit the security loopholes in Web applications and Web server's software to make the users unknowingly execute malicious scripts. These scripts are usually embedded through encoded characters in the URL for the purpose of redirecting the users to a malicious server. For example, a user might click on the www.legit.com/account? URL=*www.fakebank.com* assuming it to be a part of the legitimate bank itself. Here the user is first directed to the legit.com Web site. But due to the coding flaws, the account accepts arbitrary URLs and redirects the control over to the www.fakebank.com. Also, by installing packet sniffers and extracting session ID from the server side exploits, it is possible for the phishers to hijack the user's current session.

Pharming and Host Redirection Attacks: Pharming is a domain redirection attack wherein an attacker modifies the victim's Domain Name Service (DNS) (Kerner, 2005) infrastructure so that the users are redirected to a fake Web site even when the legitimate URLs are keyed in correctly. "DNS Cache Poisoning", exploitation of vulnerabilities in DNS software, surreptitious modification of host files in victims' computer and router can be used to achieve pharming attacks. Phishing attacks that use domain redirection are difficult to detect as they do not depend upon obfuscation techniques that trick the users into visiting the fake Web site.

Botnets and Malware based Phishing Attacks: Botnets are a collection of compromised machines that act under the attackers' command-and-control. These machines are then used to send out spam and host phishing Web sites through the dynamic DNS service. As these botnets do not directly root back to an attacker, they can be used to surreptitiously send out phishing emails and launch fake Web pages. Malware, other than recording the users' keystrokes and input data, can capture the users' browsing history to send out targeted phishing attacks known as 'spear phishing.'

STRUCTURE OF PHISHING EMAILS

In order to devise defense solutions that can detect phishing emails, it is important to chart out invariant properties that are present in most, if not all, of the phishing emails. These invariant properties are mostly visual deceptive agents employed by the phisher to trick the users. Identifying these invariant properties also helps in building discriminators that are accurate and less prone to false positives.

Spoofing of Online Banks and Retailers: Phishing emails closely imitate online banking and retailers to gain the trust of the users. The companies spoofed most often are Citibank, eBay, and PayPal. Also, the targeted industries are financial services, Internet retailers and Internet Service Providers. Phishers adapt quickly and target organizations such as Internal Revenue Service (IRS) and charity organizations that are not safeguarded. Usually, the company's image and links referring to the company's Web site are spoofed in the fake email to deceive its customers.

Non-Matching URLs: In spoofed email messages, the link text seen in the email is usually different from the actual link destination. In the following example, though the email refers to "http://www.chase.com" it redirects the user discretely to the site http://www.climagro.com.ar/agro/chase.htm which is the actual referred Web site <a class="m1 "target="_blank" title="LOGIN" ahref= "http://www.climagro.com.ar/agro/chase.htm">http://www.chase.com</a>.

Age of Referred Domains: Most of the phishing Web sites are hosted using free Web hosting services or from compromised machines that are running dynamic DNS service. In general, these fake sites are short-lived; they are detected automatically by monitoring bots or taken down as a result of users' complaint. Hence, active uptimes of most of the phishing domain are less when compared to their legitimate counterpart. WHOIS query on a domain gives out the date at which it was registered along with their location information. The date and location can then be used to determine whether it is a phishing site or not. For example, Fette et al. (Fette et al., 2007) mark the domains registered in the past 60 days as phishing.

Using IP Addresses instead of URLs: Frequently, phishers attempt to conceal the destination Web site by scrambling the URLs so that it is hard for normal users to tell it fake. One method of concealing the destination is to use the IP address of the Web site, rather than the hostname. An example of an IP address used in a fraudulent email message's URL is "http://210.14.228.66/sr/."

Generalization in Addressing Recipients: As the success of email based phishing attacks depend on their reachability to vast number of recipients, most of the phishing emails do not contain personalized content while addressing their potential victims. Unlike legitimate business communication, they do not address the customers using their names for identifiers, and lack embedded scrambled information such as 'last four digits of account information', which is used to establish authenticity. Although, it might be possible for a phisher to include this information, by employing social engineering and other malpractices, the success rate of such attacks is limited; it is hard to target wide range of users.

Usage of Well Defined Situational Contexts to Lure Victims: As the objective of phishing emails is to trick the users into divulging their confidential information, phishers modify the tone and underlying meaning of the message body to (i) invoke a sense of false urgency – an user may be instructed to revalidate his account information in the masqueraded Web site within the 24 hour period, (ii) invoke a sense of threat – phishing messages may threaten the users into divulging their confidential information to prevent account revocation, (iii) invoke a sense of concern – in their emails, phishers may imply false security promises such as weak password change to trick the users in changing the passwords in the fake Web site, (iv) invoke a sense of opportunity/reward – phishers might lure victims to reveal their information as a part of the survey which credits money to their accounts.

A TWO STAGE APPROACH TO DETECT PHISHING ATTACKS

In this section, we present a two-stage approach to mitigate phishing attacks. The first stage aims at detecting phishing based on their semantic and structural properties, whereas in the second stage we propose a proactive technique based on a challenge-response technique to establish the authenticity of a Web site. Unlike traditional solutions that focus either on detecting phishing emails or Web sites, our approach is encompassing as the combination of these proactive or reactive approaches can be used to protect the users from falling prey to both fake emails and Web sites. Here, we discuss the workings of these stages in detail and analyze their performance.

Stage I: Detecting Phishing E-mails through Structural Properties

For our first stage, we perform a linguistic analysis of the phishing email content in order to detect the 'tone' or the implied message of the email. We consider the identification of implied sense of threat/lure, or more generally, the 'tone' of the email, a critical factor towards not only identifying phishing emails, but also communicating the importance of the email to the end user. Consider the phishing emails that get past the standard phishing filter: if our framework can provide a meaningful communication to the user regarding the intentions of the email originator, it would not only be an effective methodology to defeat the attack, but also educate the naïve user to the potential harmful effects, which, after all, is the key to defeating these attacks. An important issue is to use characteristics such as language, layout, and structure of phishing emails so that it is able to capture all different contexts of phishing emails, with a high degree of confidence. For this purpose, we propose using certain features relevant to language, composition and writing, such as particular syntactic and structural layout traits, patterns of vocabulary usage, unusual language usage, stylistic and sub-stylistic features that are present in most of the phishing emails. The identification and learning of these features with a sufficiently high accuracy is the most difficult challenge during automated phishing email classification. Although, the identification process is time consuming, it is a one-time effort and can be achieved with the help of domain experts. Furthermore, we use feature selection and ranking metrics that assists in pruning away the unwanted features that do not have any significance in actual classification. These derived features, together with one-class Support Vector Machine (SVM) are used to stop phishing emails even before it reaches the users' inbox, essentially reducing the human exposure.

Feature Selection

One of the main issues during classification of phishing emails is improving the accuracy of the underlying algorithm by pruning the unwanted features that do not contribute towards accurate prediction. Therefore, the trivial and weak features termed as 'classification noise' have to be removed for proper functioning. Formally, feature selection is defined as follows. Given a set of labeled data points $\{(x_1, y_1), \ldots, (x_l, y_l)\}$ where each $x_i \in \mathbb{R}^n$ and $y_i \in \{\pm 1\}$, choose a subset m (m < n) features that achieve the lowest classification error. As deterministic selection of m-best features is an expensive task, which is exponential in the number of features, many heuristic search based algorithms are used for feature selection. Here, we apply simulated annealing for feature selection, which is a well suited approximation measure for locating global optimum in a large search space. A subset of features identified by the domain experts is randomly chosen and evaluated as a part of the algorithm. A control parameter is varied to narrow down the random selection of the features such that the classification error is reduced. Thus, the algorithm converges to yield a subset of features that performs near accurate classification.

Classification

Support vector machine is very well suited for linear binary classification. The concept of SVM is based on the idea of structural risk minimization which minimizes the generalization error. Suppose we have N training data points $\{(x_1, y_1)\ldots(x_l, y_l)\}$ where each $x_i \in \mathbb{R}^n$ and $y_i \in \{\pm 1\}$, we would like to learn a linear separating hyperplane classifier that separates the positive and negative examples. The points which lie on the hyperplane satisfy $w \cdot x + b = 0$, where w is normal to the hyperplane, $|b| / \|w\|$ is the perpendicular distance from the hyperplane to the origin and $\|w\|$ is the Euclidean norm of w. Let d+ (d-) be the shortest distance from the separating hyperplane to the positive (negative) example. The margin of the separating hyperplane is defined as (d+) + (d -). Therefore, suppose that all the training data satisfy the following constraint:

$$y_i (x_i \cdot w + b) - 1 \geq 0 \; \forall i$$

The support vector machine attains better classification by maximizing this margin. We adopted SVM as our underlying algorithm because it has been successfully used in text classification applications, and especially in the field of computer security in the context of spam detection, hidden email construction, authorship attribution and masquerade detection. The main advantage of using SVM as a learning algorithm is that it is completely oblivious to the number of input features, and rather focuses on increasing the separable margin.

Evaluation

***Dataset*:** The dataset used for evaluation consists of 400 emails out of which 200 were phishing emails and the rest normal emails, also known as ham emails in the information retrieval (IR) community. These phishing emails were collected over a period of six months. In order to maintain uniqueness in the dataset, redundant copies of phishing emails were discarded. The ham email set consists of two parts: (i) 140 of the ham emails were collected from postings on public newsgroups, bulletin boards, and users' inbox; (ii) The remaining 60 emails were obtained from eight users who volunteered to provide emails sent to them from legitimate business organizations such as credit card statements, online purchase receipts from Amazon, and so on. In order to abate privacy concerns, we provided the participants a cleaning tool to sanitize all identifying information such as account numbers, account balance, etc.

***Experimentation*:** A total of 25 features consisting of a mixture of style marker and structural attributes are used as shown in tables 1 and 2. Here, we explain how some of these features are derived. All words of length less than 2 are omitted for the sake of sanity. The total number of words (W) is calculated as the sum of all the words from both header and body of the email document. A similar method is adopted for the calculation of the features C and U as shown in Table 1. Also, we have chosen 18 different functional words as features for classification. These words are collected by observing repositories of phishing emails and then extracting their common properties. As the existing emails intend to model or capture the characteristic that are unique to phishing emails such as a sense of threat, concern or urgency, we select several keywords that are associated with this context such as risk, suspended, identity, etc. A complete listing of such commonly used words is provided in Table 3. We believe that all such functional words put together would closely give rise to a character that is not very likely to be the one exhibited by authentic emails.

Two simple structural properties described in Table 2 are used as features. The first one is derived from the subject line of the email by checking if it exhibits a certain pattern that makes it more suspicious of being a phishing email. The second one is derived in a similar way by looking at the salutation/greeting used in the first line of the email body. In both cases, binary classification is performed and only the presence or absence of the pattern is used as the feature. The experimentation was carried out in two steps. In the first step, emails were pre-processed to remove all the blank lines. In the second step, style marker and structural features were extracted.

We have used SVMlight, the support vector machine classifier developed by Joachims (Joachims, 1998). Since SVM is a linear classifier that provides only a two-way categorization, it directly maps to our purpose. A total of 200 emails, 100 phishing and 100 non-phishing emails were used in the training phase. The confusion matrix obtained as a result of applying multiple runs of the experiment is documented in Table 4. In runs I and II, all 18 function words were used. The only difference between the two runs is the usage of 2 structural features. Inclusion of the structural features results in 100% detection accuracy. In runs III & IV, the total number of function words used as features was reduced to 5 from 18 and five most frequent words that appear in the phishing email were picked. In run III, both structural attributes were used and in run IV no structural attributes were used. Result shows that the classification tends to get better when the words that are unique to phishing emails are carefully picked and used as features. Removal of structural attributes from the training set has resulted in the drop of accuracy by 20%. This is a good indication of the fact that studying the structural properties of phishing emails and employing them in classification will have a positive effect. Runs V & VI follow the same methodology as runs III & IV but with a different set of function words. This type of experiment was conducted to highlight the point that the function words feature selection bears a profound impact on the obtainable accuracy level. The experiment was conducted multiple times by varying the number of styles and structural attributes used. Also, we applied simulated annealing to select a proper subset of most relevant features. This was done a number of times until a particular feature configuration was repeated during simulated annealing. We believe this will provide a complete analysis of the role played by several functional words and attributes that are unique to phishing in classifying them apart from the genuine ones.

The performance of our model was measured using the common techniques used in information retrieval and text categorization, namely, the calculation of the *Precision (P)* and *Recall (R)* metrics (Baeza-Yates & Ribeiro-Neto) as show in Table 5. Precision gives out the proportion of documents retrieved that are relevant, whereas Recall indicates the proportion of relevant documents that are actually retrieved. Formally, precision and recall are calculated as follows:

$$\text{Precision } (P) = \frac{\text{\# phishing emails classified}}{\text{\# phishing emails classified + \# ham emails classified}}$$

$$\text{Recall } (R) = \frac{\text{\# phishing emails classified}}{\text{\# phishing emails classified + \# phishing emails not classified}}$$

In other words, Precision is the number of relevant documents retrieved divided by the total number of retrieved documents and Recall is the number of relevant documents retrieved divided by the number of irrelevant documents retrieved. In addition, we use two metrics *Accuracy* and *Combined F_1 Statistic* which are defined below. Accuracy is calculated as:

$$\text{Accuracy} = \frac{\text{total \# of emails classified correctly}}{\text{total \# of emails to classify}}$$

$$\text{Combined } F_1 \text{ Statistic} = \frac{(2RP)}{(R+P)}$$

The emails used in our experiments had little relation among each other. The topics picked/used were vastly independent of one another. This fact coupled with the results we obtained above is a clear indicator of the fact that phishing emails have characteristics which when identified and isolated could be used to demarcate them from genuine emails. Challenge lies in the ability to pick features that will distinguish a phishing email from the closely resembling non-phishing one it spoofs. Results of our experiment aim to present that appropriate choice of structural and style attributes can aid towards such finer classification via the application of Support Vector Machines.

Stage II: Mimicking User Response to Detect Phishing Attacks

Most of the present day phishing emails can be detected using our first stage, yet phishing emails,

Table 1. Style marker attributed extracted from the email document; total of 23 style marker features are used

Style Marker Attribute
Total number of words (W)
Total number of characters (C)
Total number of unique (distinct) words (U)
Vocabulary richness i.e., W/C
Function word frequency distribution (18 features) (see Table 3)
Total number of function words/W

Table 2. Two structural attributes extracted from the email document

Structural Attribute
Structure of the Email Subject line
Structure of the Greeting provided in the email body

Table 3. List of 18 functional words used in the experiment

Keywords
ACCOUNT
ACCESS
BANK
CREDIT
CLICK
IDENTITY
INCONVENIENCE
INFORMATION
LIMITED
LOG
MINUTES
PASSWORD
RECENTLY
RISK
SOCIAL
SECURITY
SERVICE
SUSPENDED

similar to spamming, can be cleverly devised by omitting the relevant features that are used for training the classifier. To detect such outliers, a more proactive standpoint is adopted in the second stage by using fake responses which mimic the real users, essentially reversing the role of the victim and the adversary. Here, a phishing attack is viewed as a two-round game between the user and the adversary. In the first round, the attacker sends email messages pretending to represent legitimate business domains for tricking the users into divulging their personal information. The success of the attack lies in the phishers ability to craft the attack in a manner that a naive user is unable to differentiate between the legitimate and the masqueraded messages, as shown in Figure 1. As a first step, the incoming messages are analyzed for the presence of embedded links and attached HTML forms. If the email does not contain such features, further investigation is safely discarded. Otherwise, a set of "phantom" users, are assigned to actively communicate with these Web sites with appropriate random values as shown in Figure 2. The random/fake information supplied to the Web sites act as active honeytokens (Spitzner, 2003) and the Web sites' responses are forwarded to the decision engine for further

Table 4. 2-Way Confusion Matrix between the actual and predicted categories

Experiment Run	Actual Category	Predicted Category	
		Phishing	Not phishing
I	Phishing	90(A)	10 (B)
	Not phishing	0 (C)	100(D)
II	Phishing	100	0
	Not phishing	0	100
III	Phishing	60	40
	Not phishing	0	100
IV	Phishing	80	20
	Not phishing	0	100
V	Phishing	50	50
	Not phishing	0	100

Table 5. Results of SVM classification

Run No.	Precision (P)	Recall (R)	Accuracy	Combined Statistic (F1)
I	100%	90%	95%	94.7%
II	100%	100%	100%	100%
III	100%	60%	80%	75%
IV	100%	80%	90%	88.8%
V	100%	50%	75%	66.7%

analysis. The key idea here is to shield the user from giving out critical personal information until authenticity of the Web site is verified. Since the attacker cannot distinguish between the fake and legitimate responses, his response is indifferent to both real and contrived responses.

The detailed working of Stage II is as follows: First, the preprocessor probes the mail server for incoming messages. Once an email arrives, its content is examined for the presence of embedded links and HTML forms. Emails with HTML forms that request sensitive information are directly tagged malicious. In the presence of an embedded URL, the control is passed to the content parser which constructs the HTML document object model (DOM) (W3C, 1998) tree of the referred Web page. HTML DOM tree is the commonly used standard to encapsulate the HTML documents in a hierarchical structure and to provide interfaces for accessing and manipulating them. The DOM tree is traversed to determine if it has forms containing variables with names as *user-name, password, credit card numbers, social security number, password,* etc. Depending on the nature and type of these variables, appropriate honeytokens are supplied to the Web site by phantom users. The behavior of the Web site to the honeytokens is recorded and analyzed for any activities not conforming to reasonable response. The decision engine is formalized as a rule based system, which relies on set of pre-determined propositions and inference rules to deduce whether the process has terminated in any of the known attack instances.

Case Studies

To illustrate the efficacy of Stage II, we have evaluated it against 200 different phishing emails. At the time of testing, however, only 87 of these emails contained links referring to live phishing Web sites. In order to measure the false positive rates, we also tested against emails that contain embedded URLs of legitimate domains. Based on

Figure 1. Defense-centric view: Who is the real sender - legitimate or adversary?

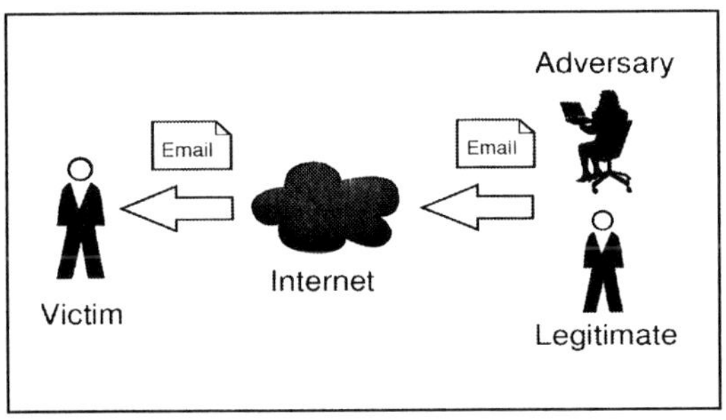

Figure 2. Offense-centric view: Who is the real respondent - the real or Phantom USER?

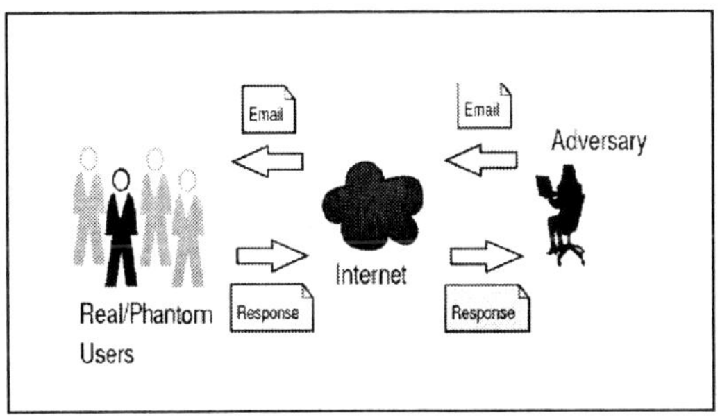

the tests, we show that Stage II was able to successfully detect all email based phishing attacks with zero false alarms. Furthermore, to the best of our knowledge, we can claim that our tool can detect most of the email based attacks listed on the www.antiphishing.org archive. For illustrative purposes, we show three different scenarios which exemplify the working of our tool. The interaction between the phantom user and the phisher's Web site is captured by hooking the detection engine, as an ActiveX control in Internet Explorer.

***Scenario 1*:** In the first example, we look at a simple email based phishing attack against the Regions Bank. First, the phisher sends an email in HTML format, requesting the users to verify their account data by following the embedded link. Here, the visible link in the email https://secure.regionsnet.com/EBanking/logon/user?a=defaultAffiliate masks the reference to the phisher's Web site http://www.club-daich.com/.checking/regions/. Such attacks can be easily determined by the preprocessing engine as shown in Figure 3, which bases its decisions solely based on the visual differences. Also, to further validate our claim, the phisher's Web site is supplied with fake information. Upon automatic submission of fake authentication values, as shown in Figure 4, the site predictably refers to a page asking credit card related information, thereby triggering our tool to raise an alarm. As most of the observed email based phishing scams adopts similar attack model, these can be easily detected.

***Scenario 2*:** In the second example we show the working of our tool on an email mimicking eBay Web site. The email had a URL which redirected the users to the phishing Web site http://www.cba.or.th/member/. There were two noticeable differences in this phishing site: (i) This site attempted to spoof its URL as a legitimate site using an IE vulnerability. On our test machine, this spoofed URL was clearly detected since the machine was patched. (ii) Also, the behavior of this site was different from the other cases. Upon submission of any value, the user was asked to enter his/her information again. Only when the submission was made a second time in the same browser session, the user was directed to another page asking for more information. This is an excellent social engineering tactic where the phisher assumes that the naive user on receiving an email about account suspension would hastily type in wrong credentials. However, as the Web site acccpts the

Figure 3. Preprocessor analyzing the referred Web page and auto submitting with fake random values

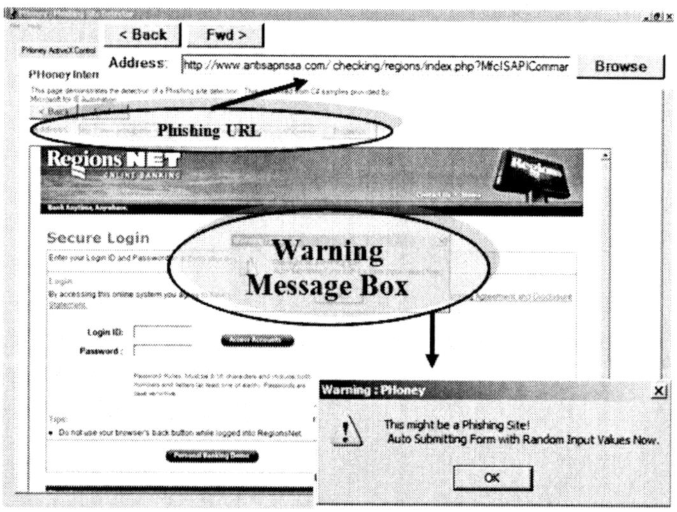

Figure 4. Redirection to a page asking for more information even after submission of fake values

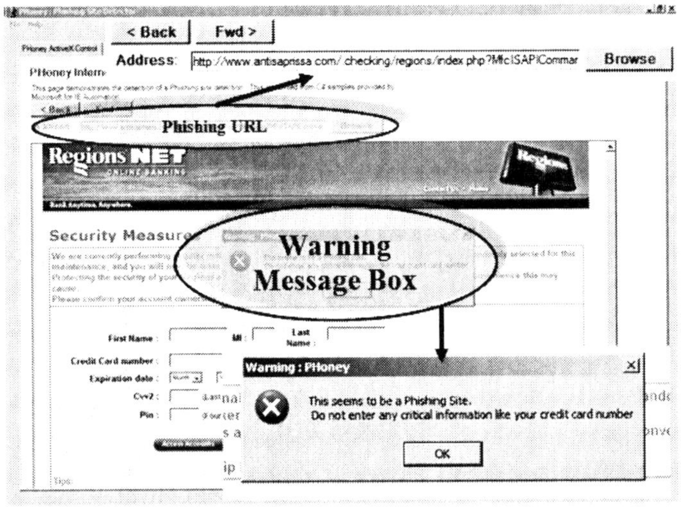

typed information the second time, we can repeat the same process of supplying honeytokens to the fake Web site to ensure correctness.

***Scenario 3*:** The third example is to show the working of our system against emails received from the legitimate domains. Here, we test our tool with an email containing the URL referring to the hotmail login page. Though our tool correctly identified this to be legitimate email, there are two caveats in hotmail. Usually, when users type in their user name in hotmail and move to the password field, a script automatically fills in the '@hotmail.com'. However with our tool, no such action happens. Submission of these contrived values resulted in a pop-up Java script box asking the information to be entered again. Our tool nevertheless detects that fake inputs lead to the same behavior and infers that this is a legitimate site. We again would like to note in passing, that it is trivial to maintain a list of such domains, to appropriately random values. While being able to detect legitimate domains correctly, it is possible that an attacker launch denial-of-service attacks by sending emails with URLs of real domain. Though this poses a serious threat, during real-time deployment we can force the traffic through our own server, which maintains the list of all the tested Web sites thereby eliminating the need to test for previously tested domains.

Evaluation

An evaluation of the second stage was conducted to quantify the performance overhead incurred during detection. The overhead introduced by our detection system highly depends upon two parts: (a) phantom user instantiation overhead; (b) response analysis overhead. We performed our experiments on an Intel Pentium M, 1.3 GHz processor with 512Mb RAM. The five attacks illustrated in the www.antiphishing.org archive were replicated on an Intel Pentium 4, 2.60GHz processor running Apache HTTP Server version 1.3.33. The operating system is Redhat Linux running kernel version 2.4.20. We also benchmarked the execution time of each of the subcomponents, using customized auditing scripts.

***Phantom User Instantiation Overhead*:** The overhead involved in instantiation of phantom user is the aggregation of the time taken by the preprocessing component plus the time needed to generate the fake values. However, generation of the fake values on-the-fly can be preempted by storing the probable variable names along with their values beforehand. Instantiation of phantom users, on an average took 1.2secs with a standard deviation of 510msecs for its operations.

***Response Analysis Overhead*:** The total time taken by the response analysis subsystem is the time taken to post the response of phantom users plus the time taken for analysis. The average delay time because of response analysis was of the order of 2.35secs with an exception that links whose Web site did not exist took far longer because of the timeout policy. From our observations, we can conclude that our detection framework does not introduce any significant computation overhead in the system. Also, the modular nature of the individual subcomponents provides hooks to replace existing modules with efficient variants, without affecting the overall performance.

Limitations

The technique given in stage II has a few limitations. First, if this tool is widely adopted, the phishers can circumvent the given defense mechanism by replaying the response of the legitimate site for spurious inputs. However, such behavior is disastrous from the phisher's standpoint, as it may invoke suspicion in users, if they consistently observe invalid data error despite providing authentic information. Second, phishers can include robot detecting schemes like CAPTCHA (completely automated public Turing tests to tell computers and humans apart) in their Web sites to subvert the tool's effort to enact the responses of the legitimate users. Currently, this is not a problem, as CAPTCHA is widely used for preventing automated registration rather than user validation. Finally, there might also be legal ramifications of our tool consuming the sites bandwidth and computation power for its detection purposes. Though the traffic can be contained by the use of distributed lists, like Web crawlers they also should operate with caution, to not violate any Web site's terms of usage.

CONCLUSION

Several antiphishing toolbars and browser extensions have been proposed to address the phishing scourge. Although these techniques provide a first-line of defense in preventing phishing attacks, they suffer from several limitations. Most of these tools require server-side assistance for functioning, incurring high setup and operational cost. Existing client-side defenses also have the burden of keeping up server-side IP changes making them vulnerable to server level exploits. Also, phishing techniques, growing in ingenuity as well as sophistication, render these solutions weak. Unless new solutions are devised to defeat phishing attacks, this scourge will continue to hurt unsuspecting Internet users in their day-to-day lives. To address these deficiencies, in this chapter, we present a two-stage approach which employs a combination of content analysis and challenge-response mechanism to detect phishing attacks. In the first stage, emails are identified using the linguistic and structural properties present in the content. As the number of such features is usually large, we employ simulated annealing as a feature selection heuristic. Furthermore, actual classification is performed by using SVM. Experimental results show that our technique is effective in identifying phishing emails with minimum errors. Since the first stage is purely based on content analysis, it is possible for an attacker to fabricate phishing emails which can bypass the content analysis filter. Hence, in our second stage, we designate phantom users to mimic the responses of legitimate users. The response obtained back from the site is analyzed to check if it is able to tell the phantom user and the legitimate user apart. Lack of such discerning capability is used as an imperative to deem the site phishing. Even though when deployed in isolation these stages have some limitations, it is their tandem working that can detect the most sophisticated phishing attacks.

REFERENCES

Anti-Phishing Working Group. Retrieved July, 11, 2007, from http://www.antiphishing.org/

Baeza-Yates, R., & Ribeiro-Neto, B. *Modern Information Retrieval.*

Chandrasekaran, M., Chinchani, R., & Upadhyaya, S. (2006). *PHONEY: Mimicking User Response to Detect Phishing Attacks.* Paper presented at the World of Wireless, Mobile and Multimedia Networks (WoWMoM), Niagara Falls, Canada.

Chandrasekaran, M., Narayanan, K., & Upadhyaya, S. (2006). *Phishing Email Detection Based on Structural Properties.* Paper presented at the New York State Cyber Security Conference (NYS), Albany, NY.

Chou, N., Ledesma, R., Teraguchi, Y., & Mitchell, J. (2004). *Client-Side Defense Against Web-Based Identity Theft.* Paper presented at the 11th Annual Network and Distributed System Security Symposium (NDSS), San Diego, CA.

Debuse, J., & Rayward-Smith, V. (1997). Feature subset selection within a simulated annealing data mining algorithm. *Journal of Intelligent Information Systems.*

Dhamija, R., Tygar, D., & Hearst, M. (2006). *Why Phishing Works.* Paper presented at the SIGCHI conference on Human Factors in computing systems, ACM Special Interest Group on Computer-Human Interaction.

Drake, C., Oliver, J., & Koontz, E. (2004, July). *Anatomy of a Phishing Email.* Paper presented at the First Conference on Email and Anti-Spam Mountain View, CA.

Drucker, H., Wu, D., & Vapnik, V. (1999). Support vector machines for Spam categorization. *IEEE-NN, 10,* 1048--1054.

Fette, I., Sadeh, N., & Tomasic, A. (2007). *Learning to detect phishing emails* Paper presented at the 16th international conference on World Wide Web (WWW), Banff, Alberta, Canada.

Gartner Press Release. (2006). Gartner says number of phishing e-mails sent to U.S adults nearly doubles in just two years. from http://www.gartner.com/it/page.jsp?id=498245

How to obscure any URL - How Spammers And Scammers Hide and Confuse. (2002). Retrieved July, 11, 2007, from http://www.pc-help.org/obscure.htm

Joachims, T. (1998). *Text Categorization With Support Vector Machines: Learning With Many Relevant Features.* Paper presented at the 10th European Conference on Machine Learning {ECML}-98.

Kapadia, A. (2007, March/April). A Case (Study) For Usability in Secure Email Communication. *IEEE Security and Privacy, 5,* 80-84.

Kerner, S. M. (2005). DNS-Based Phishing Attacks on the Rise Retrieved July, 11, 2007, from http://cws.internet.com/article/2792-.htm

NetCraft. (2004). NetCraft Anti-phishing Toolbar. Retrieved July, 11, 2007, from http://toolbar.netcraft.com/

Phishing - Wikipedia. Retrieved July 10, 2007, from http://en.wikipedia.org/wiki/Phishing

Slashdot. (2006). Phishing in Yahoo! Geocities? Retrieved from http://ask.slashdot.org/article.pl?sid=06/07/12/0028254

Spitzner, L. (2003). Honeytokens: The Other Honeypot. Retrieved July, 11, 2007.

Spoofstick. (2004). Spoofstick Toolbar. Retrieved July, 11, 2007, from http://www.spoofstick.com/

W3C. (1998). HTML Document Object Model (DOM). from http://www.w3c.org/DOM

Wenyin, L., Huang, G., Xiaoyue, L., Min, Z., & Deng, X. (2005). *Detection of phishing webpages based on visual similarity.* Paper presented at the Special interest Tracks and Posters of the 14th international Conference on World Wide Web (WWW), Chiba, Japan.

Zhang, Y., Egelman, S., Cranor, L., & Hong, J. (2007, 28 February--2 March, 2007). *Phinding Phish: Evaluating Anti-Phishing Tools.* Paper presented at the 14th Annual Network and Distributed System Security Symposium (NDSS 2007), San Diego, CA.

Zhang, Y., Hong, J., & Cranor, L. (2007). *Cantina: a content-based approach to detecting phishing web sites* Paper presented at the 16th international conference on World Wide Web (WWW), Banff, Alberta, Canada.

KEY TERMS

Challenge-Response Analysis: Challenge-response analysis is an authentication mechanism where either one or both the communicating parties adhere to a pre-agreed protocol used in verifying their identities. The party which desires to prove its identity has to provide correct response to the challenge posed by the opposite party with which it desires to communicate.

Context Models: Context models encapsulate the messages conveyed in the phishers' emails to attract the potential victims into the fake Web sites. Phishers usually employ some kind of threat, fake reward, and false pretext in their email message to trick the users.

Email / Web site Spoofing: Email/Web site spoofing is the process by which the look-and-feel and the behavior of fake Web sites/emails is forged to mimic their legitimate counterpart.

Feature Selection: Feature Selection is a process of selecting a subset of relevant features so that the net performance of underlying classifier is increased. Feature selection helps to minimize the presence of "noise" that adversely affects the model building.

Linear Binary Classification: The process of separating a set of m examples $\{(x_1, y_1)\ldots(x_m, y_m)\}$ into two regions by a linearly separable hyperplane parameterized by w such that $y_i (x_i . w + b) > 0$ for all i = 1...m. Such a hyperplane is called as separating hyperplane.

Phishing: Phishing is a form of Web based identity theft where attackers employ deceit and social engineering to defraud users of their private and confidential information such as password, credit card number, social security number (SSN), and bank account number.

Phishing Email Structural Properties: Phishing email structural properties represent the set of invariant features that are present in most, if not all, of the phishing emails. These invariant properties are mostly visual deceptive agents employed by the phisher to trick the users. These invariant properties also helps in building discriminators that are accurate and less prone to false positives.

ENDNOTE

1 A recent phishing attack on Yahoo Inc. (Slashdot, 2006) showed that phishing attacks could be launched within the same domain. The phisher had actually hosted the fake login page in www.geocities.com/login_group_auth, where geocities.com is Yahoo Inc.'s Web hosting service and login_group_auth is a Yahoo account created by the phisher.

Chapter XII
A New Approach to Reducing Social Engineering Impact

Ghita Kouadri Mostefaoui
Oxford University Computing Laboratory, UK

Patrick Brézillon
LIP6, Paris 6, France

ABSTRACT

In recent years, the security research community has been very active in proposing different techniques and algorithms to face the proliferating security vulnerabilities. However, social engineering remains an alarming threat to the most secured networks. Security administrators are certainly aware of the gravity of the human factor, whatever is the strength of the technological measures. The human factor is still a difficult-to-surround notion and a difficult to quantify concept. It is rarely considered in the early stages of the development lifecycle of software, assuming traditional security considerations have been taken into account. In this chapter, we discuss the added-value of context as a way to deal with social engineering. Based on a case study describing a typical attack, we provide a first attempt to model this parameter.

INTRODUCTION

Most of us have already been the target of social engineering attacks, whatever they succeeded or not. Emails asking for bank accounts passwords, grabbing user credentials by directing him to fake websites, or extracting passwords by false pretext phones are all examples of social engineering attacks. Kevin Mitnick in his book "*The art of deception: controlling the human element of security*" states that "*Social engineering uses influence and persuasion to deceive people by convincing them that the social engineer is someone he isn't, or by manipulation. As a result, the social engineer is able to take advantage of people to obtain information with or without the use of technology.*" (Mitnick & Simon, 2003). Even if some application like medical systems and bank websites are more targeted than others to such attacks, social engineering is gaining ground in other fields. Curiosity, trust and intimidation are all examples of human weaknesses the social engineer takes advantage of. For example, the well-known "ILoveYou" virus email exploited the weakness that curious people would click on an e-mail attachment with such an attractive subject was one of the factors that allowed this virus to have such a big impact (Edmead, 2002) even if it also used technological tools. A worsening factor for social engineering impact is the discrepancy with the technical dimension i.e. the evolution of ICT (Information and Communication Technology) often left an increasing number of persons on the side. The social-technical gap is the difference between social needs/expectations and computer system capability. It is the degree software fails to meet social requirements. Additionally, the fact that duration of work with others is limited, and the turnover is increasingly important and that on the Internet one is not always sure of the identity of the other (use of pseudo), trust becomes a key element in all transactions.

In this chapter, we discuss the added-value of context as a way to deal with social engineering. Two things are worth developing, the focus and its context of validity. Generally in security one is concerned by the focus only. Our claim is to learn how to recognize the context of the current focus, to identify it and to determine what the legal actions are authorized in relationships to the focus in the current context. For example, some attacks use URLs or Web pages very close from those of enterprises. One example is "BankOfAmerica" instead of "Bank_of_America". Another example is to write the real URL on a web page and hide another link when the user clicks.

As social engineering is now admitted to be the weakest link in the security chain, several efforts have been made in order to study its different ways of operation and to try finding defenses against this threat. From these contributions, users' awareness to information security and training emerge as the agreed upon ways for facing the attacks. Related work includes (Lafrance, 2004) which considers psychology as a valuable security tool. The author argues on the understanding of employees' psychology in order to be able to face their potential attacks. He proposes a set of 'psycho-security tips' and shows how they can apply to real situations. More focused on information security awareness, (Manjak, 2006) examines the various social engineering tactics targeting employees that an InfoSec Awareness campaign is designed to counter.

In this chapter, we will first define context and show how it can be considered as an operational factor for modeling the human element in security. Based on a case study of an attack preparation and execution, we show how the previous list of countermeasures (user's awareness, training) can be extended. A list of best practices is derived for the sake of reducing the impact of human element on information security. Then, a summary of previous contributions on the use of context in security is presented. Finally, the last section concludes the paper with a summary of future research.

BACKGROUND ON CONTEXT

This Section is intended to provide a summary of theoretical study of context.

The term context has been extensively defined and commented in recent research. However, there is not yet a commonly accepted definition of context (Bazire & Brézillon, 2005). Nevertheless, a consensus begins to appear around "*Context is what constrains a problem solving without intervening in it explicitly*" (Brézillon & Pomerol, 1999). This definition suggests that the context is always let implicit and tacit, and is rarely mentioned explicitly.

Then, the authors consider it by extension as the focus of an actor. Several elements justify this definition, the three main elements being that:

1. Context is relative to the focus,
2. As the focus evolves, its context evolves too, and
3. Context is highly domain-dependent. As a consequence, one cannot speak of context in an abstract way.

In a recent publication, Brézillon (2007) shows that the focus at a given stage, allows the division of the context into external knowledge and contextual knowledge. The latter constitutes a kind of tank where the contextual elements are to some extent related to the focus in a flat way, whereas the former has nothing to do with the focus. At this conceptual level, the focus acts as a discriminating factor on knowledge in a similar way as for social networks. The focus evolves because a new event occurs (e.g. an unpredicted event) or as a result of a decision made at the previous stage of the focus. The notion of context impacts more on the relationships between knowledge pieces than upon the pieces themselves. The following publication (Brézillon & Brézillon, 2007) provides greater detail about the relationship between a context and a focus.

A context-based formalism has been developed and is introduced in (Brézillon, 2005). This formalism known as contextual graphs allows a uniform representation of elements of reasoning and of contexts. A contextual graph is a representation of a task execution. Contextual graphs are oriented, acyclic, without circuits, with exactly one input and one output, and a general structure of spindle. A path (from the input to the output of the graph) represents a type of execution of the task with the application of selected methods. There are as many paths as practices. Different solutions can be associated with the unique output corresponding to the current context. A contextual graph is an acyclic graph because user's tasks are generally in ordered sequences. For example, the activity "Make the train empty of travelers" is always considered at the beginning of an incident solving on a subway line, never at the end of the incident solving. A more drastic divergence in the type of output (e.g. the execution of the task is stopped like "Error 104" in information retrieval) must be considered at a upper level in which the contextual graph at hand is a branch of an alternative (a contextual element such as "Are the conditions required for the task execution present? If yes got to the contextual graph otherwise does not consider this contextual graph). In contextual graphs, the two types of context identified earlier can be easily distinguished. Namely, contextual knowledge, which is represented in the graph by a set of contextual elements, and proceduralized context which is an ordered set of instantiated contextual elements.

In this chapter, we point out that the consideration of context in security is getting importance. The need for taking into account the *security context* has been dictated by the need for changing policies according to changes into the environment. In a previous work, we define a security context as *"set of information collected from the user's environment and the application environment and that is relevant to the security infrastructure of both the user and the application."* (Kouadri, 2004) The word relevant means that has direct or indirect effect on the security policy. What is really relevant is application-dependent. This information may include user's identity, membership, resource location, date, time, the user's interaction history with the system, social situation, etc.

Wireless applications and on-demand services have been the main consumers of security context as we will show in Section "Related Work". As a result, context-based access control and adaptive authentications schemes emerged as solutions to the security requirements of these specific environments.

In our previous work on context-based security (Kouadri, 2004), we noted that it should be considered as *"a new trend that may face future more subtle security attacks."* We also stated that *"the force of a good security system should not rely only on the force of security protocols but also on the way it copes with new and completely unpredictable situations or at least learn from new situations and updates its behavior accordingly.*"

In prior contributions related to this idea, we mainly concentrate on context-based access control solutions and proposed in (Kouadri & Brézillon 2006) the contextual graphs formalism discussed earlier as a model for security contexts. Contextual Graphs have been used in various real-world applications. They allow a uniform representation of elements of reasoning and of contexts for describing different human tasks such as troubleshooting and interpretation. In our situation, a contextual graph represents a security task realization. These tasks include access to remote services, establishing a secure communication between heterogeneous communicating parties, etc. Its paths represent the different ways of reaching this realization, each way corresponding to a practice developed by an actor realizing the task. Our focus was on expressing fine-grained requirements for dynamic security policies.

In this chapter, we extend the other aspect of security context and discuss its role in reducing the impact of social engineering in information systems.

CONTEXT PROFILE IN SOCIAL ENGINEERING

In order to demonstrate the relevance of our claim, we stress in the following the typical modus operandi of a hacker for realizing a security attack. It should be noted that the described scenario represents a generic case-study with an internal environment protecting some assets and served by actors with different roles.

We summarize the process into four steps. The next sections show how context is used to grab this process and then, how it can be used for profiling social engineering attacks.

Attack Preparation and Execution

- First, the attacker tries to get closer to an actor in the target enterprise in order to get familiar with the different aspects of the enterprise. Such actor may represent an employee or any tier person involved into the activities of the enterprise. This step aims at developing a shared context by establishing privileged relationships with the tier. This shared context may be based upon common and general interests such as political/ideological preferences, sport, etc.

  In an alternative way, the focus could be pushed on a specific topic in order to find an agreement (e.g. I like science-fiction, political men are all the same, TV is boring, etc.). The aim of manipulating the shared context is to develop strong ties with the other, the attacker looking for a tie of which the nature will be important for the tier as discussed in the area of social network (Granovetter, 1983). Note that here the shared context is not related to the hacker's focus but tries exhibits some general ties between the two actors.
- The hacker than tries to shrink this shared context into a more restrained one around professional interests by exploiting some of the various psychological approaches. For instance, by establishing a neophyte-expert relationship (i.e. I don't have enough knowledge in this field but you do). Or, by pretending the need for help to solve a given problem. This is achieved by establishing a community of practice between peers (i.e. we are both in the same domain, so if I have a problem you can help me solve it) always embedded in the general shared context established previously. In the second step, the hacker begins by moving the shared context by introducing contextual elements related to the hacker's focus (I have a problem that

is certainly a toy problem for you because I know that from our shared context building).

- The hacker then tries dragging the tier person along to the focus of the shared context developed earlier. In practice, this is equivalent to the hacker getting closer to the focus of interest (i.e. the target asset to attack). Here the goal is to introduce in the shared context a foreigner element in a way apparently normal, when in a usual situation the tier will react against it. This situation is very close from medicine and biology with virus. This third step is a kind of synthesis of the two first steps by introducing the focus (i.e. hacker's focus) in the initial shared context, that is in the opposite way that two normal actors interact (with first agreeing on the common focus, and then developing a shared context around this focus).
- When the attack is launched, the hacker locks the system in a way that prevents the abused tier from establishing a connection with the information he/she provided (i.e. the context focus) and which are for the tier a set of unrelated contextual information given in an extra-professional circumstance. In this fourth step, the hacker puts the tier to accept that the "sensible" focus in the shared context is naturally explainable in term of the shared context elements, when in the real context of the focus; the tier will react in a totally different way.

While the presented scenario can be seen as an industrial-espionage attack, it actually, represents a pattern for attacks in any information-based system. The differences are mainly the assets: business documents, credit card numbers, healthcare private information, etc. The tier may represent respectively: a business partner, an employee, a nurse in a hospital, etc. Also, most of these domains make use of computer-based systems, so even if they take benefit of human weaknesses, the assets are typically stored as digital data, so the attacks are mainly performed using technological means as discussed earlier.

Defenses

The main approach to reduce the number and/or the impact of social engineering attacks is to break the process described in the previous section. This can be achieved by following the set of countermeasures described in the following. Where some of them are technical, others are more social-oriented.

- ***Information Security Awareness***: A common error made by actors is to think that as long as the two "individual" contexts (related to the enterprise and the hacker respectively) are not intersecting, the risk of attacks is small. In fact, this risk is increased using his/her own context. Indeed, the actor's context intersects with both other contexts and constitutes the shared one which connects the two others. It is thus, important to establish an effective users' awareness of the context of their tasks within the enterprise, especially the different changes of this context as a consequence of external events. With the notion of shared context, one needs to develop a notion of exclusive contexts. As a concrete example, a nurse should be aware of the different cases (context) where information about patients is likely to be disclosed. A concrete precaution is to prevent copying patients' records to personal devices or sending it outside the hospital network. In practice, it is important to learn how to maintain disjoint contexts and how to identify any new contextual element that may provoke a shift of the working context.
- ***Managing Internal Actors***: Statistics show that most of the social engineering attacks are performed by internal actors or through their help. The enterprise should be aware of

conflicts and dissatisfaction of actors within the enterprise in order to avoid expressing their dissatisfaction outside the enterprise boundaries causing the internal context to flood outside.

- ***Minimum Processes Principle***: This principle suggests running the minimum set of computer processes for a specific task within the enterprise. This implies blocking unnecessary ports and assigning minimal privileges on assets for users. This is equivalent to reducing the context attached to each task, reducing this way the type of attacks that can be performed. A special attention should be given to the underlying sub-tasks, the data they handle and the information they send over the internet.
- ***Fine-Grained Security Solutions***: to constraint the actor context with fine-grained security in a way that make the latter an integral part of its tasks. An example of fine-grained security is context-based access control where access is no longer *only* dependent on users' credentials but also constrained by the time of the access, geographical location of the requester, the frequency of access requests, etc. This approach helped several banks to detect credit cards frauds by comparing the geographical locations of a requester during a short time interval. Here a short time is relative to the reasonable time a credit card owner needs to travel from a location to another. Thus, a use by the same card in France and than in China in a day interval is somehow suspicious and leads to alerting the issuing bank for a potential problem.
- ***Prepare the coming of new ICT in the enterprise***: The increase need for higher computer performance and more complicated software functionalities leads enterprises to continually adopt new technologies. It is of primordial importance to prepare the actors (employees) to these new technologies in order to give them the right information about potential threats on the software and how to face them.
- ***Use a modeling of actors' activities in a formalism allowing a uniform representation of elements of reasoning and of contexts***: This guideline suggests an explicit consideration of contextual information in controlling actors' actions on assets. An example of such formalism is contextual graphs. Information on contextual graphs may be found on the web site dedicated to it (CxG's Software, 2007).
- ***Consider the context of a focus like a dressing of this focus:*** which allows the identification of differences between the behavior prescribed by security policies and the effective behaviors of actors. A detailed discussion of this aspect with an example in road safety domain is given in (Brézillon & Brézillon, 2007).
- ***Contextualize identities instead of trying to personalize the users*** A possibility could be to reinforce the technology-mediated approach of social systems.

A similar work to our current contribution is presented in the paper by (Gragg, 2002) which proposes a multi-level defense against social engineering. The author discusses the psychological triggers leading to a successful social engineering attack. He then lists a set of defense measures to handle these weaknesses. While the objective is the same, this specific work aims at incorporating social psychological research into the task of resisting social engineering.

RELATED CONTRIBUTIONS: CONTEXT IN SECURITY

The first attempts to integrate context into security systems put the focus on context-based RBAC (Role-Based Access Control). A related contribution was made by (Masone, 2002) who designed and implemented a simple programming language RDL (Role Definition Language) to describe roles in terms of contextual information. The strong characteristics of RDL are simplicity of use and extensibility. An extended form of authorization policies where conditions corresponding to context are represented using programs rather than expressions is proposed by (McDaniel, 2003). (Georgiadis & al., 2001) propose TMAC which stands for team-based access control. It provides an access control model that supports collaborative activity being accomplished by teams of users and includes contextual information.

Another related contribution is C-TMAC; a hybrid access control model that takes advantage of role-based permission assignment of RBAC and yet provides the flexibility for fine-grained activation of permissions for individual users on individual object instances. This fine-grained access control is dictated by a set of constraints (or context). For example, in a healthcare setting a doctor may have the permission to prescribe certain medications. However, the doctor should not be allowed to prescribe for anyone. Rather, he/she should be allowed to prescribe only for the patient's he/she is taking care of.

In the same direction, (Covington et al., 2001, 2002) propose an approach to design security services that use security-relevant "context" in order to provide flexible access control. The main application of their approach is intelligent home environments such as the Aware Home described in (AHRI, 2007). The authors make use of the context toolkit (Dey, 2000) a software that aims at leveraging the development of context-aware applications and provides software components for collecting environment variables and interpreting their associated values. Access policies are based on environment roles (Covington et al., 2001) and encoded into the eXtensible Markup Language (XML). The contributions towards integrating context with a security service other than access control are fewer. It is worth mentioning the work by (Pierson et al., 1999) which introduces context-agile encryption as a technique that provides a different encryption (in terms of key lengths, type of encryption algorithm, etc) according to the applications needs and to hardware capabilities. For example, some web services in high speed communication networks may be able to tolerate long times to encrypt/decrypt information, but may also need to protect that information for a long period of time. Other types of web services, dealing with data that is sensitive while useful, but quickly becomes stale, might benefit from short encryption/decryption times that may accompany a less cryptographically robust algorithm.

Bellavista et al. propose a context-centric access control middleware for mobile environments called COSMOS (Bellavista et. al., 2003). The middleware dynamically determines the contexts of mobile proxies, and rules the access to them based on a set of data such as user profile and system/user-level authorization policies. COSMOS has been tested in the design and implementation of a context-centric movie assistant which aim is to allow mobile users to find nearby cinemas and to exchange opinions about cinema characteristics such as seat comfort, air-conditioning, sound and screen resolution.

As one can deduce from the previous summary of earlier work, the consideration of context in security has been mainly encouraged by the need for security to fit within the very nature of emergent applications. Adaptability to users' needs and preferences and to hardware capabilities has imposed a need for security solutions following the same pattern of flexibility. However, these contributions towards integrating context into security have been proposed without being explicit about its broader use.

CONCLUDING REMARKS AND FUTURE WORK

In this chapter, we presented a novel approach to understanding social engineering using context as an operational parameter. Our aim was two-fold: a) to give a generic view over the diverse social engineering attacks. This is approached by looking at a common parameter – context -, and b) to help giving the abstract nature of a social attack a concrete face so further investigations can be pursued in order to reduce the impact of these attacks.

As stated in the chapter, the definition of *context* is tightly related to the application domain. For example, in an e-health application, the role of the user within the hospital (i.e. treating physician, nurse, administrator, etc) is a relevant contextual information used to regulate the access to patients' records. In the other hand, it is difficult to exhaustively enumerate its content. However, a good practice is to identify the maximum of this context by learning from similar applications before setting up a security solution so it becomes possible to block most attacks or, a least not create back doors to hackers.

It is interesting to note the interest of the security community in social engineering and in the same time the lack of effective solutions. Daily news and technical publications are full of real stories describing security attacks where human deception is the main tool. In the other hand, and apart from users training, there is no concrete parameters the security community can use to model and thus to study and evaluate proposed solutions. In the current chapter, we sketched the context profile during an attack and deduced a list of countermeasures.

This new approach is a first attempt to quantify the social aspect of security for the sake of a better understanding and management. In the following we summarize the main research directions that may be pursued as a future work.

- Developing techniques for the automatic discovery of relevant security contexts. For example, in the credit card fraud scenario discussed earlier, data mining techniques and case-based reasoning can be used to devise what context is worth taking into account. The location from where the user uses his card for e-transactions, his buying preferences, are examples of common elements emerging in fraud scenarios. They can be used to profile the use of a card by a hacker.
- Developing tools for the visualization of context evolution during an interaction scenario (e.g. access to a resource). This may help for a better understanding of the role of context. The tool can be used as a training mean for information security awareness.
- Devising techniques for the formal verification of the completeness of security context for a given application i.e. to devise the percentage of the contextual information already taken into account in the establishment of the security solution and thus deducing the percentage of missing context.
- Devising ways for establishing trust with context providers. Since a security context is built from a set of information (e.g. user' location, interaction history with the system) gathered from different sources, the system to secure should be able to gather context only from trusted sources.
- Proposing a uniform way for documenting social engineering attacks and their corresponding involved context for each specific application. These reports can be used to help similar applications to develop a defense against these attacks. This is equivalent to antivirus that needs to update its virus definition file regularly.

Having presented our proposal in considering context as a key element in profiling social engineering attacks, we believe that further investigations may shed the light on other factors that can be combined with context, for the sake of better understanding of social engineering and thus, being able to face the proliferating attacks. It is our hope that this first step provides a starting point for further advancements.

REFERENCES

AHRI. (2007). *Georgia Tech aware home research initiative (AHRI).* Retrieved September 11, 2007, from http://www.chia.org/programs/2000/prg_oct00.htm.

Bazire, M., & Brézillon, P. (2005). Understanding context before to use it. *Modeling and Using Context (CONTEXT-05),* A. Dey, B.Kokinov, D.Leake, R.Turner (Eds.), Springer Verlag, LNCS 3554 (pp. 29-40).

Brézillon, J., & Brézillon, P. (2007). Context modeling: Context as a dressing of a focus. In: *Modeling and Using Context (CONTEXT-07),* LNAI 4635, Springer Verlag, (pp. 136-149).

Brézillon, P. (2005) *Task-realization models in Contextual Graphs. Modeling and Using Context (CONTEXT-05*), A. Dey, B. Kokinov, D. Leake, and R. Turner (Eds.), Springer Verlag, LNCS 3554, (pp. 55-68).

Brézillon, P. (2007). Context Modeling: Task model and model of practices. In: Kokinov et al. (Eds.): *Modeling and Using Context (CONTEXT-07),* LNAI 4635, Springer Verlag, (pp. 122-135).

Brézillon, P., & Pomerol, J.-Ch. (1999). Contextual knowledge sharing and cooperation in intelligent assistant systems. *Le Travail Humain, 62*(3), 223-246. Paris: PUF.

Covington, M. J, Long, W., Srinivasan, S., & Dey, A. K., Ahamad, M. & Abowd, G. D. (2001). Securing Context-Aware Applications Using Environment Roles. In *Proceedings of the sixth ACM symposium on Access control models and technologies*, Chantilly, Virginia, United States, (pp. 10-20), ACM Press.

Covington, M., Ahamad, M., & Srinivasan, S. (2001). *A security architecture for context-aware applications*, Technical Report GITCC-01-12, College of Computing, Georgia Institute of Technology.

Covington, M., Fogla, P., Zhan, Z., & Ahamad, M., (2002). *A context-aware security architecture for emerging applications.* In *Proceedings of the Annual Computer Security Applications Conference (ACSAC).*

CxG's Software (2007). *Contextual Graphs Homepage.* Retrieved September 11, 2007, from http://cxg.fr

Dey, A. (2000). *Providing Architectural Support for Building Context-Aware Applications.* PhD thesis, College of Computing, Georgia Institute of Technology.

Edmead, M. T. (2002) *Social engineering attacks: What we can learn from Kevin Mitnick.* Retrieved September 11, 2007, from http://searchsecurity.techtarget.com/tip/1,289483,sid14_gci865450,00.html

Georgiadis, C. K., Mavridis, I., Pangalos, G., & Thomas, R. K. (2001). Flexible team-based access control using contexts. In *Proceedings of the sixth ACM symposium on Access control models and technologies*, (pp. 21–27).

Gragg, D. (2002). *A Multi-Level Defense Against Social Engineering.* Retrieved on September 11, 2007 from http://www.sans.org/rr/papers/51/920.pdf.

Granovetter, M., (1983). The Strength of Weak Ties: A Network Theory Revisited. In *Sociological Theory,* 1, 201-233. Michigan, American Sociological Association.

Kouadri Mostefaoui, G. & Brézillon, P. (2006). *Human-centric network security management: A comprehensive helper.* In *Proceedings of the 4th international Workshop on Wireless Mobile Applications and Services on WLAN Hotspots* (Los Angeles, CA, USA, September 29 - 29, 2006). WMASH '06. ACM Press, New York, NY, (pp. 47-52).

Kouadri Mostefaoui, G. (2004). *Towards a Conceptual and Software Framework for Integrating*

Context Based Security in Pervasive Environments. Ph.D. Thesis No. 1463, University of Fribourg, Switzerland, October 2004.

Lafrance, Y., (2004). *Psychology: A Precious Security Tool.* Retrieved on September 11, 2007 from http://www.sans.org/reading_room/whitepapers/engineering/1409.php?portal=611fd7dad659f7fefb9f79f9b33edc58.

Manjak, M. (2006). *Social Engineering Your Employees to Information Security.* Retrieved on September 11, 2007 from http://www.sans.org/reading_room/whitepapers/awareness/1686.php

Masone, C. (2002). *Role definition language (RDL): A language to describe context-aware roles.* Technical report, Dartmouth College, Computer Science. Hanover, NH.

McDaniel, P. (2003). On context in authorization policy. In *Proceedings of the eighth ACM symposium on Access control models and technologies*, (pp. 80–89).

Mitnick, K. D., & Simon, W. L. (2003). *The Art of Deception: Controlling the Human Element of Security.* John Wiley & Sons, Inc

P. Bellavista, R. Montanari and D. Tibaldi, (2003). *COSMOS: A Context-Centric Access Control Middleware for Mobile Environments, MATA'2003*, (pp. 77–88).

Pierson, L., Witzke, E., Bean, M., & Trombley, G., (1999). *Context-agile encryption for high speed communication networks*, ACM SIGCOMM Computer Communication Review, 29(1): (pp. 35-49).

KEY TERMS

Case-Based Reasoning: A technique that helps solving a specific problem based on past similar ones.

Data Mining: A set of techniques that analyze data for the sake of finding patterns and relationships.

E-Health: Electronic health is the result of the involvement of electronic in providing health services such as patient record and health plan description.

Human Factor: Influence of human behavior on information security.

Security Asset: Any valuable resource protected by a computerized infrastructure.

Security Context: Set of information collected from the user's environment and the application environment and that is relevant to the security infrastructure of both the user and the application.

Trust: The degree of confidence an entity has in another entity.

Chapter XIII
Privacy-Enhancing Technologies

Yang Wang
University of California, Irvine, USA

Alfred Kobsa
University of California, Irvine, USA

ABSTRACT

Privacy-enhancing technologies (PETs), which constitute a wide array of technical means for protecting users' privacy, have gained considerable momentum in both academia and industry. However, existing surveys of PETs fail to delineate what sorts of privacy the described technologies enhance, which in turn makes it difficult to differentiate between the various PETs. Moreover, those surveys could not consider very recent important developments with regard to PET solutions. The goal of this chapter is two-fold. First, we provide an analytical framework to differentiate various PETs. This analytical framework consists of high-level privacy principles and concrete privacy concerns. Secondly, we use this framework to evaluate representative up-to-date PETs, specifically with regard to the privacy concerns they address, and how they address them (i.e., what privacy principles they follow). Based on findings of the evaluation, we outline several future research directions.

INTRODUCTION

Privacy has been recognized as a fundamental human right at least since the seminal treatise of Warren and Brandeis (Warren & Brandeis, 1890). However, it is only in recent decades that privacy issues have attracted substantive attention in society, due to the proliferation and advancement of innovative information technologies such as computers, the Internet, and recently mobile and ubiquitous computing applications. Despite its importance, the concept of privacy is difficult to grasp. Privacy is a truly multi-dimensional notion. It involves, but is not limited to, cultural, social, legal, political, economic and technical aspects.

Privacy-enhancing technologies (PETs), which constitute a wide array of technical means for protecting users' privacy, have gained considerable momentum in both academia and industry. A number of overviews of the PET landscape have already been published (Blarkom, Borking, & Verhaar, 2003; Burkert, 1997; Camp & Osorio, 2003; Goldberg, 2002; Senicar, Jerman-Blazic, & Klobucar, 2003; Tavani & Moor, 2001). However, most of these studies fail to delineate what sorts of privacy the described technologies enhance, which makes it difficult to differentiate between the various PETs. Moreover, those surveys could not consider very recent important developments with regard to PET solutions. We will therefore focus on these newer solutions here (specifically on privacy policy languages and systems aimed at empowering users in their privacy decisions), and conduct an in-depth examination of the privacy landscape in which these PETs are supposed to make meaningful contributions. More classical PETs such as authentication and identity management systems as well as systems that provide authorization and access control will only be briefly mentioned in the passing. So does another class of very specialized PETs, namely privacy-preserving personalization methods, which have been described in (Y. Wang & Kobsa, 2008).

The goal of this chapter is to provide an analytical framework upon which to chart past, present and future research on PETs. It is our belief that a deeper understanding of their underpinnings will enable us to identify gaps that may still exist, and research directions in developing next-generation PETs.

The remainder of the chapter is organized as follows. Firstly, we provide a review of current privacy-related regulatory requirements and users' privacy concerns and preferences. Secondly, we introduce our analytical framework consisting of privacy principles and privacy concerns. Thirdly, we use this framework to evaluate representative PETs, specifically with regard to the privacy concerns they address, and how they address them (i.e., what privacy principles they

Figure 1. The hierarchy of potential privacy constraints

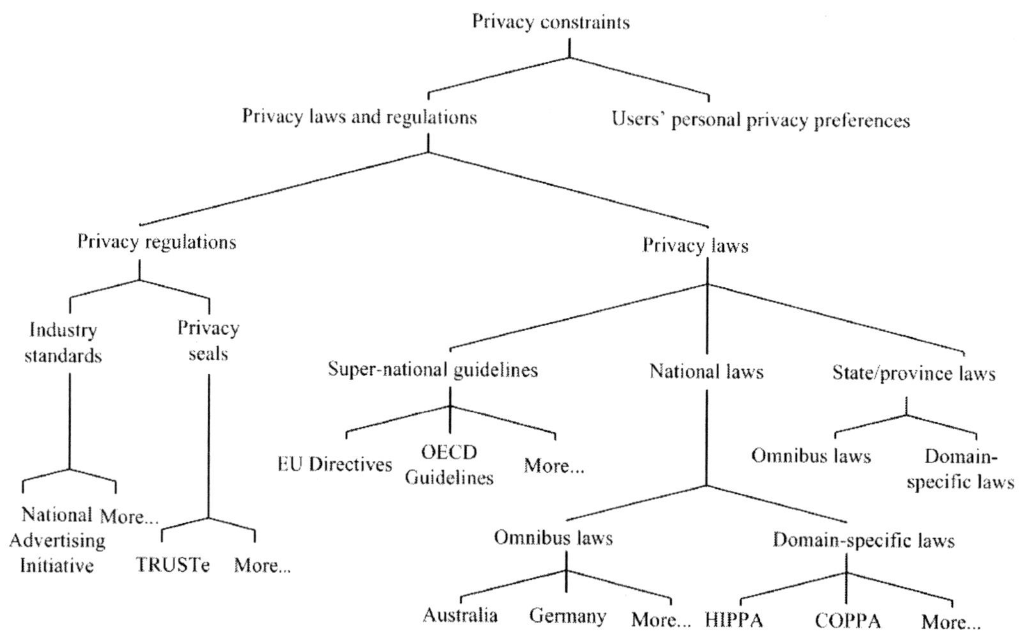

follow). Fourthly, we further discuss the findings. Finally, we conclude with an outline of promising future research directions.

THE PRIVACY LANDSCAPE

Privacy has been studied for decades, and many different definitions of privacy have been proposed. This is largely due to the fact that privacy is "an overwhelmingly large and nebulous concept" (Boyle & Greenberg, 2005). Young (Young, 1978) wittedly commented that "privacy, like an elephant, is ... more readily recognized than described". In essence, privacy is personal, nuanced, dynamic, situated and contingent (Dourish & Anderson, 2006; Palen & Dourish, 2002).

If privacy considerations are taken into account in the design of computer systems, they restrain the possible design space for such systems. Solutions that violate privacy constraints cannot be considered any more. Privacy constraints for computer systems stem primarily from two sources, namely from privacy laws and regulations and from personal privacy expectations of the computer users. Figure 1 shows the hierarchy of these constraints with a focus on privacy laws and regulations.

Privacy Laws and Regulations

We have witnessed a proliferation of privacy laws and regulations during the past 30 years. More than 40 countries currently have national privacy laws enacted. In addition, numerous other types of privacy regulations, industry seal programs and company self-governing policies have been introduced as well.

Privacy laws and regulations generally apply when personal data of people are being processed who can be identified with reasonable means. These laws and regulations usually lay out organizational and technical requirements for ensuring the protection of personal data that is stored and/or processed in information systems. These requirements include, but are not limited to, proper data acquisition, notification about the purpose of use, permissible data transfer (e.g., to third parties and/or across national borders) and permissible data processing (e.g., organization, modification and destruction). Other requirements prescribe user opt-ins (e.g., asking for their consent before collecting their data), opt-out (e.g., of data collection and/or data processing) and user inquiries (e.g., regarding what personal information was collected and how it was processed and used). Other stipulations mandate the establishment of adequate security mechanisms (e.g., access control for personal data), and the supervision and audit of personal data processing.

Historically, Europe and the U.S. launched parallel initiatives in privacy and data protection (Westin & Gelder, 2003). In the 1970s, the U.S. inaugurated legislation for the protection of citizen and consumer information databases, with the Fair Credit Reporting Act of 1970 and the Privacy Act of 1974. The Fair Information Practice Principles that were first formulated by the U. S. Department of Health, Education and Welfare in 1973 became the basis for many privacy laws and regulations worldwide. A number of Western European countries, such as Sweden, Germany and France followed the move in the early 1970s and early 1980s.

In 1980, the Organisation for Economic Cooperation and Development (OECD) drafted *Guidelines on the Protection of Privacy and Transborder Flows of Personal Data* (OECD, 1980) These guidelines are however not binding for its currently 30 member countries, which include the U.S.. The European Union issued two privacy-related directives (EU, 1995, 2002) that set out the minimum standards for its member states to implement in their respective national privacy laws. The Asia-Pacific Economic Cooperation (APEC) recently also drafted a privacy framework (APEC-FIP, 2004), serving as recommendations for its currently 21 member countries including the U.S.

In the U.S., several sector-specific laws have come into effect such as the Health Insurance Portability and Accountability Act of 1996 (HIPAA) for medical privacy, the Children's Online Privacy Protection Act of 1999 (COPPA) for protecting children under the age of 13, the Gramm-Leach-Bliley Act of 1999 for financial privacy, and the Sarbanes–Oxley Act of 2002 for accounting and financial reporting. In 2000, the Federal Trade Commission (FTC) published a widely known report to Congress on Fair Information Practice Principles (FTC, 2000b). In the same year, the FTC also issued the so-called Safe Harbor Principles (FTC, 2000c) to meet the adequacy standard imposed by the EU. In 2006, the Association for Computing Machinery (ACM), the world's largest computer science association, announced recommendations of privacy principles drafted by its U.S. Public Policy Committee (USACM, 2006).

Users' Personal Privacy Preferences

While privacy laws and regulations are on the normative side of privacy, personal privacy attitudes represent its subjective aspect. Numerous opinion polls and empirical studies have revealed that Internet users harbor considerable privacy concerns regarding the disclosure of their personal data to websites, and the monitoring of their Internet activities. These studies were primarily conducted between 1998 and 2003, mostly in the United States but also in other countries. In the following, we summarize a number of important findings (the percentage figures indicate the ratio of respondents from multiple studies who endorsed the respective views). For more detailed discussions we refer to (Kobsa, 2007; Teltzrow & Kobsa, 2004).

Personal Data

1. Internet users who are concerned about the privacy or security of their personal information online: 70% - 89.5%;
2. People who have refused to give personal information to a web site at one time or another: 82% - 95%;
3. Internet users who would never provide personal information to a web site: 27%;
4. Internet users who supplied false or fictitious information to a web site when asked to register: 6% - 40% always, 7% often, 17% sometimes;
5. People who are concerned if a business shares their data for a purpose that is different from the original purpose: 89% - 90%.

User Tracking and Cookies

1. People concerned about being tracked on the Internet: 54% - 63%;
2. People concerned that someone might know their browsing history: 31%;
3. Users who feel uncomfortable being tracked across multiple web sites: 91%.
4. Internet users who generally accept cookies: 62%;
5. Internet users who set their computers to reject cookies: 10% - 25%;
6. Internet users who delete cookies periodically: 53%.

Behavioral experiments moreover show that Internet users also follow up on their privacy concerns to some extent, and supply more data about themselves, make purchases more frequently, and are willing to pay a small premium when interacting with e-commerce sites that noticeably have good privacy practices (Gideon, Cranor, Egelman, & Acquisti, 2006; Kobsa & Teltzrow, 2005; Metzger, 2006; Tsai, Egelman, Cranor, & Acquisti, 2007).

ANALYTICAL FRAMEWORK FOR EVALUATING PRIVACY-ENHANCING TECHNOLOGIES

To evaluate the effectiveness of various PETs, we propose an evaluation framework that analyzes solutions along two dimensions:

1. What high-level principles the privacy solution follows
   We identify a set of fundamental privacy principles from various privacy laws and regulations, and treat them as high-level guidelines for enhancing privacy. Other principles that are desirable for privacy enhancement (e.g., usability) are also included.
2. What privacy concerns the privacy solution addresses
   While privacy principles are high-level guidelines to enhance privacy, privacy concerns are more concrete and mundane. Ideally one would need user studies to examine how effectively solutions address users' changing and contingent privacy needs and preferences. Since running such studies for every evaluated solution is barely realistic, we instead chose to investigate privacy concerns that are somewhere in between high-level privacy principles and low-level contingent privacy needs of users.

Furthermore, to be better able to assess the privacy protections that privacy-enabling technologies afford, we propose to group them into the following three categories:

- Protection of identity: this type of privacy protection aims to prevent users' true identities from being revealed (i.e., who they are).
- Seclusion: this type of privacy protection attempts to prevent users from being bothered by unwanted contact or solicitation (e.g., spam emails).
- Control over data: this type of privacy protection allows users to have control over their data, e.g. regarding what data can be collected or disclosed for what purpose, how the data will be used, and with whom the data may be shared or to whom it may be transferred.

Principles

Privacy legislation and regulations are usually instantiations of more fundamental privacy principles. We select a core set of privacy principles that are frequently addressed in privacy laws and regulations, and add other principles/properties that are also desirable for privacy enhancement. This list of principles is by no means exhaustive, but meant to initiate a discussion on what principles are desirable for enhancing privacy effectively. The principles are grouped by their origin in the listing below.

Privacy principles from privacy laws and regulations

1. Notice/Awareness
   - Privacy policy: *Make [...] privacy policy statements clear, concise, and conspicuous to those responsible for deciding whether and how to provide the data* (USACM, 2006);
   - Notice upon collection: *Whenever any personal information is collected, explicitly state:*
     - *the precise purpose for the collection,*
     - *all the ways in which the information might be used,*
     - *all the potential recipients of the personal data,*
     - *how long the data will be stored and used;* (USACM, 2006)
2. Data minimization
   Before deployment of new activities and technologies that might impact personal

privacy, carefully evaluate them for their necessity, effectiveness, and proportionality: the least privacy-invasive alternatives should always be sought (USACM, 2006).

3. Purpose specification
   The purposes for which personal data are collected should be specified not later than at the time of data collection and the subsequent use limited to the fulfillment of those purposes or such others as are not incompatible with those purposes and as are specified on each occasion of change of purpose (OECD, 1980).
4. Collection limitation
   There should be limits to the collection of personal data and any such data should be obtained by lawful and fair means [...] (OECD, 1980).
5. Use limitation
   Personal data should not be disclosed, made available or otherwise used for purposes other than those specified (OECD, 1980).
6. Onward transfer
   Personal data should not be transferred to a third country/party if it does not ensure an adequate level of protection (EU, 1995; FTC, 2000c).
7. Choice/Consent
   Where appropriate, individuals should be provided with clear, prominent, easily understandable, accessible and affordable mechanisms to exercise choice in relation to the collection, use and disclosure of their personal information (APEC-FIP, 2004). The two widely adopted mechanisms are (FTC, 2000a):
   - Opt-in: *requires affirmative steps by the consumer to allow the collection and/or use of information*;
   - Opt-out: *requires affirmative steps to prevent the collection and/or use of such information.*
8. Access/Participation
   An individual should have right to:
   - *know whether a data controller has data relating to her (OECD, 1980),*
   - *inspect and make corrections to her stored data (USACM, 2006).*
9. Integrity/accuracy
   A data controller should ensure the collected personal data is sufficiently accurate and up-to-date for the intended purposes and all corrections are propagated in a timely manner to all parties that have received or supplied the inaccurate data (USACM, 2006).
10. Security
    Personal data should be protected by reasonable security safeguards against such risks as loss or unauthorized access, destruction, use, modification or disclosure of data (OECD, 1980).
11. Enforcement/Redress
    - Effective privacy protection must include mechanisms for enforcing the core privacy principles. At the minimum, the mechanisms must include (FTC, 2000c):
    - Recourse mechanisms for customers: *readily available and affordable independent recourse mechanisms by which an individual's complaints and disputes can be investigated and resolved and damages awarded where the applicable law or private sector initiatives so provide;*
    - Verification mechanisms for data controllers: *follow-up procedures for verifying that the attestations and assertions businesses make about their privacy practices are true and that privacy practices have been implemented as presented*;
    - Remedy mechanisms: *obligations to remedy problems arising out of failure to comply with these principles by organizations announcing their adherence to them and consequences for such organizations.*

Anonymity-Related Principles

12. Anonymity
    Anonymity means that users cannot be identified nor be tracked online.
13. Pseudonymity
    Pseudonymity also means that users cannot be identified, but they can still be tracked using a so-called alias or persona. The German Telemedia Law (DE-TML, 2007) mandates that profiling necessitates the use of pseudonyms or the prior consent of the user.
14. Unobservability
    A data controller cannot recognize that a system/website is being used or visited by a given user.
15. Unlinkability
    A data controller cannot link two interaction steps of the same user.
16. Deniability
    Deniability means that users are able to deny some of their characteristics or actions (e.g., having visited a particular website), and that others cannot verify the veracity of this claim.

Other Desirable Principles for Privacy Enhancement

17. User preference
    Different users can potentially have different privacy preferences. A data controller should tailor its privacy practices to each individual user's preferences.
18. Negotiation
    This principle calls for the support of negotiation between a user and a website, during which they can reach an agreement on privacy practices that the website may employ for the respective user.
19. Seclusion
    Seclusion means that users have the right to be left alone. Violations of this principle in the electronic world are popup ads and junk emails.
20. Ease of adoption
    Oftentimes privacy protection mechanisms rely on the presence of other infrastructures or technologies, and this fact may pose significant barriers for adoption. This principle relates to the readiness of *organizations* to adopt the examined privacy protection (e.g., whether the solution relies on special protocols or technologies that are proprietary or not readily available).
21. Ease of compliance
    This principle is concerned with the ease of fulfilling legal requirements by adopting a specific privacy protection solution.
22. Usability
    The privacy protection solution should be easy for *users* to adopt (e.g., the efforts required from users to utilize the solution should be reasonable).
23. Responsiveness
    The privacy protection solution should respond promptly to changes in users' privacy decisions.

Privacy laws and regulations typically only include subsets of the above principles. For a comparison, Table 1 shows a group of representative privacy laws and regulations in its columns, and the privacy principles discussed above in its rows. An "X" in a cell means that the framework includes the respective principle.

Applying Our Privacy Protection Taxonomy to the Principles

We now categorize the 23 identified principles based on the type of privacy protection they relate to. Note that the general category contains principles that pertain to all three types of privacy protection. Table 2 represents which category each privacy principle falls into.

Table 1. Privacy guidelines/frameworks and privacy principles

Specification / Principle	OECD Guidelines (OECD, 1980)	EU Directive on Data Protection (EU, 1995)	German Telemedia Law (DE-TML, 2007)	APEC Privacy Framework (APEC-FIP, 2004)	FTC Safe Harbor Principles (FTC, 2000c)	FTC Fair Info Practice (FTC, 2000b)	ACM Principles (USACM, 2006)
Notice/Awareness	X	X	X	X	X	X	X
Minimization							X
Purpose specification	X	X	X	X	X		X
Collection limitation		X	X	X	X		
Use limitation	X	X	X	X	X		X
Onward transfer		X	X		X		
Choice/Consent	X	X	X	X	X	X	X
Access/Participation	X	X	X	X	X	X	X
Integrity/accuracy	X	X	X	X	X	X	X
Security	X	X	X	X	X	X	X
Enforcement/Redress		X	X		X	X	
Anonymity-related principles							
Anonymity							
Pseudonymity		X	X				
Unobservability							
Unlinkability							
Deniability							
Other desirable principles for privacy enhancement							
User preference							
Negotiation							
Seclusion							
Ease of adoption							
Ease of compliance							
Usability							
Responsiveness							

Privacy Concerns

Whereas privacy principles are high-level guidelines for enhancing privacy, users' privacy concerns are more concrete and down to the earth. We discuss and analyze them here in order to also be able to evaluate the effectiveness of privacy enhancements from a subjective stance. Privacy concerns usually arise from characteristics of a specific application domain. To illustrate this, we will focus on the potential privacy concerns that may arise in web personalization (Brusilovsky, Kobsa, & Nejdl, 2007), such as Amazon's personalized book recommendations.

Wang et al. (H. Wang, Lee, & Wang, 1998) present a taxonomy of privacy concerns in Internet

Table 2. Categorization of principles based on the type of privacy protection

Principle \ Protection	General	Protection of Identity	Seclusion	Control over data
Notice/Openness	X			
Minimization				X
Purpose specification				X
Collection limitation				X
Use limitation				X
Onward transfer				X
Choice/Consent	X			
Access/Participation				X
Integrity/accuracy				X
Security				X
Anonymity		X		
Pseudonymity		X		
Unobservability		X		
Unlinkability		X		
Deniability		X		
Enforcement/Redress	X			
User preference	X			
Negotiation	X			
Seclusion			X	
Ease of adoption	X			
Ease of compliance	X			
Usability	X			
Responsiveness	X			

marketing that includes improper access, improper collection, improper monitoring, improper analysis, improper transfer, unwanted solicitation and improper storage. These high-level concerns as well as concerns about improper merging of data also apply in web personalization. Table 3 shows what privacy concerns (columns) can arise from typical web personalization activities (rows).

EVALUATING PETS

In this section, we will review major privacy-enhancing technologies, namely privacy policy languages, anonymity techniques, authentication and identity management, authorization and access control, usable security and privacy mechanisms. We will contrast them against the two evaluative elements of our framework, namely what principles they follow and what privacy concerns they address. This close examination of existing PETs will allow for a more comprehensive view of their pros and cons as well as their current gaps, and thus point out future research avenues.

Privacy Policy Languages

The U.S. Federal Trade Commission (FTC) defines a privacy policy as a comprehensive description of a company's information practices, accessible by

Table 3. Potential privacy concerns in typical web personalization activities

	Control over data							Seclusion	Protection of identity
	Improper acquisition			Improper use			Improper storage	Unwanted solicitation	Identity fraud/theft
	Improper access	Improper collection	Improper monitoring	Improper analysis	Improper merge	Improper transfer			
Tracking		XX	XX						
Profiling		X	X	X	X	X			X
Cross-website recommendation		X	X	X	XX	XX	X	X	
Single-website recommendation		X	X	X	X	X	X	X	
Third-party data sharing				XX	X	XX	X	X	X
Direct mailing				X				XX	

Legend: xx = very likely; x = likely

clicking at a hyperlink on the company's website (FTC, 1998). Its aim is to enhance users' awareness of the privacy practices of the website. Privacy policies thus are directed at human readers.

Privacy policy languages, in contrast, are intended to be machine-readable. They can be roughly divided into two types: external policy languages to describe websites' public privacy policies or users' privacy preferences, and internal ones to specify companies' or websites' internal rules for privacy practices. In general, external privacy policy languages are declarative without enforcement mechanism, while internal privacy policy languages are normative with support for enforcement.

External Privacy Policy Language

P3P: The Platform for Privacy Preferences

Developed by the World Wide Web Consortium (W3C), the Platform for Privacy Preference (P3P 1.1) (L. Cranor et al., 2006) aims at increasing the transparency of websites' privacy practices in such a way that users can easily decide whether or not these websites meet their privacy expectations. Technically, P3P consists of two parts: (1) a standard machine-readable (XML) language/syntax that allows websites to describe their privacy practices regarding the collection, use, and distribution of personal information, and (2) a "handshake" protocol built on top of the HTTP protocol that enables P3P-enabled user agents (e.g., web browsers) to retrieve websites' P3P privacy policies automatically (Garfinkel & Cranor, 2002). Agents can also be configured to inform users about the sites' privacy policies, to notify them when those change, to warn them when those deviate from their pre-specified privacy preferences (expressed in languages like APPEL (L. Cranor, Langheinrich, & Marchiori, 2002) or XPref (Agrawal, Kiernan, Srikant, & Xu, 2003)), and to semi-automate or automate the decision whether or not to disclose the requested information on users' behalf.

A P3P policy file can be applied to a whole website or certain parts of it such as web pages, images, cookies, forms and even a single form field[1]. Every P3P policy contains a description of the legal entity responsible for the privacy policy, whether the site allows users to have access to the information collected about them, (optional) information regarding dispute resolution and remedy, and at least one statement. Each statement describes the data being collected (physical contact information, online contact information, purchase information, click stream data, etc.), the purpose(s) for collection (web site administration, research and development, profiling, etc.), whether the site supports user opt-in or opt-out for those purposes, what organizations will have access to the collected data (primary service provider only, delivery services, unrelated third parties, etc.), the retention of the collected data (single session, stated purpose, indefinitely, etc). Personalization can be considered as one type of purposes dubbed as "individual decision"[2] and similarly anonymous personalization as "pseudo decision".

P3P was designed as part of a broader privacy protection framework (including privacy legislation and enforcement) and is applicable to any web-based systems. P3P implementations include

- P3P user agents (such as Internet Explorer 6 (Microsoft, 2000) that supports cookie management as well as websites' privacy policies disclosure,
- AT&T Privacy Bird (L. Cranor, 2002), an add-on to the Internet Explorer, that utilizes differently colored bird icons in the corner of the browser window to indicate whether or not a site's P3P policy matches the user's preferences,
- Privacy Bird Search Engine (Byers, Cranor, Kormann, & McDaniel, 2004) that annotates regular search results with an indication to what extent the P3P policy of each site matches the user's requirements,
- P3P policy generators/editors/checkers (e.g., P3PEdit), and
- server-side P3P support (e.g., IBM Tivoli Privacy Manager For E-business that can enforce privacy policies internally in a system).

P3P's official website currently lists about 2900 websites worldwide that have adopted P3P 1.0[3]. The latest P3P adoption study conducted in the summer of 2005 (Egelman, Cranor, & Chowdhury, 2006) estimates the overall P3P adoption rate at about 10% using a list of "typical" search terms taken from AOL users' queries, and the government adoption rate roughly at 36% (this is by far the largest sector to adopt P3P, which is probably due to the P3P adoption mandate of the E-Government Act[4] (USA, 2002)). The usage of P3P has also been proposed in the context of ubiquitous computing (Langheinrich, 2002).

Despite its relative popularity, P3P has a number of limitations. First, P3P does not include any technical mechanism for enforcing privacy policies. It is totally up to the websites to follow their stated privacy policies, and users cannot verify whether a site acts as promised.

Second, P3P (even the latest version 1.1) does not support different policies for different users, albeit offering users a choice of P3P policies is mentioned in P3P's future plan. Nevertheless, several proposals for individual negotiation of P3P policies have been made (Buffett, Jia, Liu, Spencer, & Wang, 2004; Preibusch, 2006).

Third, P3P might not be expressive enough to be able to fully encode the nuances of websites' privacy practices. For example, P3P cannot handle cases where privacy concerns crosscut more than one statement (e.g., that personal data that were obtained for different purposes may not be grouped (CZ, 2000)). Because of this lack in expressiveness and enforcement, it is difficult for websites to keep their P3P privacy policies, human-readable privacy policies and actual practices all consistent. P3P allows sites to further explain those nuances in the human-readable fields, which are not technically analyzable though.

Furthermore, P3P is not able to accurately capture the subtleties of privacy laws and regulations, nor does it develop a minimum set of privacy or security standards that web sites should follow. Therefore, websites cannot rely on P3P as a technical means to comply with relevant privacy provisions, and discrepancies might exist between the P3P policies and the applicable privacy laws which in turn can expose the websites to legal jeopardy (L. F. Cranor & Reidenberg, 2002).

Last but not least, P3P has been criticized for facilitating websites' data collection, rather than protecting users' privacy (Coyle, 1999). A convincing example is that the default value for data retention is "indefinitely" instead of "no retention" or "stated purpose". Besides, P3P makes it difficult for users to protect their privacy (for instance, users find changing defaults for cookie settings to be burdensome and confusing (EPIC & Junkbusters, 2000). P3P could also effectively excludes non-compliant sites (e.g., websites without P3P compact policies would be blocked by IE6) and P3P-compliant sites do not make themselves more trustable (a study has shown that among the top 500 companies, only nine out of the 65 sites that adopted P3P have P3P satisfactory to a pragmatic user who wants some privacy protection (Ashrafi & Kuilboer, 2005)).

In order to gauge P3P's expressiveness, we attempted to describe six representative privacy provisions that have the biggest impact on the internal operation of web personalization (Y. Wang & Kobsa, 2006). The results show that P3P can express most of the provisions, with the following deficiencies: First, it needs more fine-grained expressiveness (e.g., retention time cannot be set in a continuous time scale; this can be easily solved by introducing an "expiry"-like sub-element for the retention element). Secondly, perhaps the biggest issue with the P3P language, it cannot express interactions across different statements; a potential solution is to introduce logic operators in the statement-group element so that different relationships between statements can be captured. Thirdly, the overall P3P framework is short of an interface with systems that enforce P3P privacy policies.

APPEL: A P3P Preference Exchange Language

APPEL (L. Cranor, Langheinrich, & Marchiori, 2002) was designed to complement P3P by allowing users to express their privacy preferences in terms of rules that specify certain conditions under which user information may be collected and used, so that P3P-enabled agents are able to check users' preferences against a website's P3P policy to make automated or semi-automated decisions whether or not users' data may be released to the website. A rule includes a behavior, an optional persona, optional explanation and prompt messages, and a number of expressions (L. Cranor, Langheinrich, & Marchiori, 2002). An expression is used to match a full XML element or a single attribute and its value in an XML element in the evaluated P3P policy.

APPEL only allows logical operations at nodes corresponding to P3P elements. The matching scheme of APPEL is problematic: a P3P policy can contain multiple statements, and a rule will fire and then stop being further evaluated against the policy if any of the statements satisfies the rule. Therefore, the remaining statements will be ignored. Because of this deficiency, APPEL only works correctly when rules express what is unacceptable rather than what is acceptable (Agrawal, Kiernan, Srikant, & Xu, 2003).

XPref

XPref (Agrawal, Kiernan, Srikant, & Xu, 2003) is another preference language for P3P and is based on the XPath language (Clark & DeRose, 1999), a W3C Recommendation for navigating and matching the hierarchical structure of an XML document. The biggest difference between XPref and APPEL is that APPEL uses the sub-elements of a rule to specify acceptable and unacceptable combinations of P3P elements, while XPref utilizes XPath expressions for the same purpose.

XPref outweighs APPEL in that it can specify what is acceptable as well as what is unacceptable, and combinations of both. Agrawal et al (Agrawal, Kiernan, Srikant, & Xu, 2003) show that XPref subsumes APPEL, and that APPEL can be programmatically translated into XPref.

Individual Privacy Policy Negotiation

Buffet et al (Buffett, Jia, Liu, Spencer, & Wang, 2004) present a framework for the negotiation between users and websites about the disclosure of user information for compensation. It relies on utility theory to allow users to express the value associated with each piece and combination of personal data. The proposed PrivacyPact protocol enables the transmission of messages for negotiation. Preibusch (Preibusch, 2006) identified relevant privacy dimensions (recipient, purpose, retention, and data) for negotiation and proposed a simple extension of P3P to allows for the expression and implementation of such negotiation processes.

Internal Privacy Policy Language

EPAL: Enterprise Privacy Authorization Language

EPAL (Ashley, Hada, Karjoth, Powers, & Schunter, 2003) is a formal language developed by IBM that allows enterprises to write their internal privacy policies, so that those can be enforced across IT applications and systems in an automated manner. To take advantage of EPAL, an enterprise first defines an EPAL vocabulary (i.e., concrete element types) that caters to its own needs, and then specifies its EPAL privacy policies. Applications that aim to share an EPAL policy obviously must agree on the vocabulary and interpret it in the same way.

An EPAL policy contains a set of privacy authorization rules that allow or deny requests. Rules have the following constituents (Ashley, Hada, Karjoth, Powers, & Schunter, 2003):

- the action for which authorization is requested (e.g., disclose or read)
- the data categories upon which these actions are going to be performed (e.g. medical records or contact info),
- the user categories that are affected (e.g., a department or a particular employee),
- the usage purposes (e.g., direct marketing or auditing),
- associated conditions (e.g., the purpose category must be billing purpose), and
- associated obligations (e.g., delete data after 7 days or obtain consent).

An authorization request contains a user category, an action, a data category, and a purpose.

An authorization result is a statement that includes a ruling (allow or deny), a user category, an action, a data category, and a purpose. A rule may also contain conditions and obligations. Authorization results are used to determine if a request is allowed or denied. At first sight, EPAL policies seem quite similar to P3P policies since both describe privacy practices. However, they differ in the following ways:

- P3P is data-centric (i.e., a P3P statement covers different aspects of a specific type of data), while EPAL is access-centric (i.e., a EPAL rule refers to an instance of information access) (Stufflebeam, Anton, He, & Jain, 2004);
- EPAL aims to describe the internal privacy practices of an enterprise, which are probably not to be shared with the public, while P3P is used to describe public privacy policies;
- unlike P3P that predefines the elements of a privacy policy, EPAL elements (such as actions or user categories) are abstract types which are mapped to actual instances of elements during the implementation;

- the design of EPAL takes privacy legislation and regulations into account, by including an obligation element;
- EPAL policies are machine enforceable: they are akin to access control policies in the security domain. An authorization engine parses the EPAL policies to generate a ruling given a request, and subsequently an enforcing environment/software will execute the ruling;
- Conflicting EPAL rules are allowed and solved by prioritizing rules, to allow for general rules and exceptions;
- P3P policies are always formulated in a positive manner (i.e., what is acceptable, not what is unacceptable), whereas EPAL can express both via the ruling element (allow or deny).

Although EPAL was designed to be expressive and flexible so as to capture evolving privacy legislation and customized privacy policy, we observe that it fails to express some privacy provisions, for example, that personal data that were obtained for different purposes may not be grouped (CZ, 2000). Essentially, as with P3P, EPAL cannot express the interactions between different rules.

EPAL's current abstraction of actions is not sufficient for privacy authorization purposes. Actions need to be modeled with finer granularity (e.g., modeled as hierarchyType like data categories). For example, in the case of the action "personalization/inference", we believe that it should be further categorized into different specific personalization techniques (such as collaborative filtering and incremental machine learning). Our justification is based on the observation that if privacy laws apply to a personalized website, they may affect the methods (i.e., actions) that may be used for processing them (Kobsa, 2002). Or in other words, different specific actions may lead to opposite privacy authorization results. For instance, one-time machine learning methods that rely on a record of raw data from several user sessions are not permitted without the user's consent under the German Telemedia Law (DE-TML, 2007). In contrast, incremental machine learning methods that discard the raw data of each user session and only retain the learning results may be employed. However, in the current language both types of machine learning methods/actions are modeled as an abstract "inference" action and thus the critical distinction in authorization results is lost.

XACML: eXtensible Access Control Markup Language

XACML[5] (OASIS, 2005) is a general-purpose access control policy language. XACML can be used to describe not only general access control policies/rules, but also access control decision requests and responses. The root element of an XACML policy document is a Policy or PolicySet element (a container for a set of policies). A Policy contains a set of access control Rules. A Rule includes a Condition (that can be nested) and the Rule's effect (Permit or Deny). If the Condition evaluates to true, the Rule's effect (Permit or Deny) is returned. If the Condition evaluates to false, it means the Rule is not applicable (NA is returned). If an error occurs during the evaluation, "Indeterminate" is returned.

When a user/subject wants to perform some action on a resource, she will make a request to the so-called "Policy Enforcement Point" (PEP) that protects the requested resource (e.g., a file system or web server). The PEP will generate a request that includes Subject, Resource, Action and optionally Environment attributes (values). The PEP will then submit the request to a Policy Decision Point (PDP), which will identify all policies that apply to the request by evaluating their Targets. A Target is a set of conditions associated with a PolicySet or Policy or Rule. When the Target evaluates to true, the corresponding PolicySet/Policy/Rule applies to the request. The PDP will then evaluate the request against the applicable policies, yielding a response that consists of an access control decision regarding whether or not the request should be allowed, and optionally a list of obligations (i.e., actions that the PEP is obligated to perform before granting or denying access). Since each Rule and Policy may evaluate to yield different access control decisions, the XACML utilizes a collection of Combining Algorithms (e.g., Deny Overrides Algorithms) to derive a single final access control decision. Finally, the PDP returns the final decision back to the PEP, which can then enforce the decision (namely either allow or deny the access).

XACML also comes with an approved OASIS Standard profile for privacy policies, for modeling how personally identifiable information is collected and used. An attribute of "resource: purpose" defines the purpose for which the data resource was collected. Another attribute of "action:purpose" indicates the purpose for which access to the data resource is requested. A Rule element mandates that access shall be denied unless the purpose for which access is requested matches, by regular-expression match, the purpose for which the data resource was collected.

A thorough comparison of the latest versions (EPAL 1.2 and XACML 2.0) shows that XACML is a functional superset of EPAL 1.2 and outweighs EPAL in expressing not only access control policies but also privacy policies. Specifically, XACML provides the following important features that EPAL lacks (Anderson, 2005):

- the ability to combine results of multiple policies developed by different policy issuers;
- the ability to reference other policies in a given policy;
- the ability to specify conditions on multiple subjects that may be involved in making a request;
- the ability to return separate results for each node when access to a hierarchical resource is requested;
- support for subjects who must simultaneously be in multiple independent hierarchical roles or groups;
- policy-directed handling of error conditions and missing attributes;
- support for attribute values that are instances of XML schema elements; and
- support for additional primitive data types (including X.500 Distinguished Names, RFC822 names, and IP addresses).

Summary of Privacy Policy Languages

Table 4 shows a summary of various privacy policy languages and their characteristics. Two

Table 4. Privacy policy languages and their characteristics

	External privacy policy	Internal privacy policy	User preference	Expressiveness	Negotiation	Enforcement
P3P	+			+		
APPEL			+	+		
XPref			+	++		
PrivacyPact	+		+		+	
EPAL		+		++		+
XACML	+	+	+	+++		++

Legend: +++: Very strong support ++: Strong support +: Support

observations can be made in this table. First, negotiation and enforcement still call for wider support. Second, XACML seems to surpass all other existing privacy policy languages, although it lacks support for negotiation.

An Integrated Privacy Management System Based on Privacy Policy Languages

The IBM Tivoli Privacy Manager is a comprehensive enterprise privacy management system that aims at supporting a variety of privacy enhancement functionalities (IBM, 2006):

- centralized authorship and management of an enterprise's privacy rules,
- a natural language interface to author and manage privacy policies,
- translation of privacy policy from prose to P3P,
- enforcement of privacy policies across the enterprise's IT infrastructure,
- monitoring access to personal information and generating detailed audit logs,
- notification and consent preferences for information sharing across the enterprise, and
- automatically generation of reports detailing compliance to corporate policies.

This solution focuses on privacy protection in the sense of "control over data". It marginally addresses "seclusion and barely touches the protection of identity. In other words, the Tivoli Privacy Manager cannot protect end users' identities, which is understandable since it is geared towards enterprise privacy management.

Anonymity Techniques

Anonymity of a user means that she cannot be identified nor tracked online. One way to improve anonymity is what Goldberg et al. (Goldberg, Wagner, & Brewer, 1997) called "strip identifying headers and resend" approach. This approach has been used in anonymous email remailers (Gülcü & Tsudik, 1996) and anonymous web browsing tools like Anonymizer (ConneXion, 1996), a web proxy that strips off identifying headers and source addresses from the web browser.

Another approach is "onion routing" which is built upon the notion of "mix network" (Chaum, 1982). A mix network is essentially a chain of proxy servers (called mixes). In onion routing, a message or packet is encrypted to each mix node using public key cryptography. The resulting encryption is like a layered "onion" with the original message in the innermost layer. As the message traverse over the network, each mix node strips off its own layer of encryption to reveal where to send the message next. Untraceability can be achieved unless all mix nodes are compromised. For example, Tor (Tor), a concrete onion routing system can provide anonymous communication such as web browsing, remote login sessions, instant messaging and other applications that rely on the TCP protocol.

The third major approach is centered on the concept of "k-anonymity" (Sweeney, 2002). It is concerned with a practical problem of releasing data about individuals without revealing identifying information about them. In a k-anonymized release, each individual's record is indistinguishable from at least k-1 others' records. A myriad of policies and techniques (e.g., clustering (Aggarwal et al., 2006)) have been proposed to achieve k-anonymity.

Authentication and Identity Management

Authentication seeks to ensure that a user is actually the person who she claims to be. This is usually achieved by employing a username in combination with a password, where the username is considered as a digital identity of the bearer and the password as her authentication. A more sophisticated and thus more secure scheme is the so-called two-factor authentication, which involves two independent ways for verifying identity. It may include a user having something (e.g., a bank ATM card or a time-dependent token card) and the user knowing something (e.g., a PIN).

One of the goals of the emerging identity management systems is to allow users to have more than one digital identity and be able to freely choose which identity to use. For example, Google allows its users to use different identities/accounts in its various applications (so that, for instance, one's interactions with Google Calendar will not be combined and used in Google's personalized search).

Another recent industry example is Microsoft's CardSpace (Microsoft), an "identity metasystem" that allows users to create multiple virtual ID cards. Each virtual card created by the user would only contain the minimum amount of information (retrieved from an identity provider) that individuals will need to divulge to carry out the transaction to which the card applies. CardSpace thereby uses the metaphor of the various cards that we use to identify ourselves in the physical world, such as business cards, driver's licenses and credit cards. With these virtual cards, users no longer have to hassle with daunting passwords. CardSpace has been integrated into Microsoft's operating system Vista.

OpenID (OpenID) is an open specification of a truly distributed identity system. OpenID providers are essentially authentication brokers between users and OpenID-enabled websites. They allow users to log into an OpenID-suported website without registration, using a URI as a username that belongs to the user (e.g., the URL of her homepage or blog). Users' passwords and other credentials are safely stored by OpenID (which can be run by the user or by a third-party identity provider). Because of its open and distributed nature, ease of use, and easy adoption for websites (free libraries are available in most web programming languages), OpenID is gaining more and more momentum and emerges as the de-facto industry standard.

Authorization and Access Control

Authorization involves granting or denying specific access rights. In a classic access control model, an access matrix specifies what permissions each subject has on the resources the system retains. In a role-based access control model, permissions are assigned to roles instead of subjects directly (subjects can take on multiple roles, and multiple subjects can take on the same role). In a directory-based access control model, subjects are managed and organized in directories (e.g., in an LDAP server), and permissions are granted based on these different directories (Cannon, 2005).

Privacy policy languages such as P3P and XACML have an access control aspect since they prescribe who can access what information under what condition for what purpose.

Systems for Empowering Users in their Privacy Decisions

Security has long been primarily regarded as a technical and theoretical problem. It is well known though that many established security mechanisms are barely used in practice since they pose usability problems. A growing number of security researchers have therefore shifted towards so-called "usable security and privacy", which studies the usability of security and privacy mechanisms. This emerging field aims at uncovering the reasons behind the mismatch between technical security mechanisms and their practical usage by end users, and on ways of bridging the gap to better meet users' security needs.

Whitten and Tygar's conducted a seminal usability analysis of PGP 5.0 (Whitten & Tygar, 1999), to find out why users failed to achieve their security goals (encrypting and decrypting email messages in this case). They found that this is largely due to interface design problems, causing a mismatch between users' needs and the structure of the encryption technology. Bellotti and Sellen (Bellotti & Sellen, 1993) identified two primary sources for a number of potential security and privacy problems, from their experiences in ubiquitous computing: disembodiment (the actors are invisible in actions) and dissociation (actions are invisible to actors), both of which are visibility issues.

In the light of rendering the invisible visible (privacy threats in this case), Ackerman and Cranor (Ackerman & Cranor, 1999) proposed privacy critics that are semi-autonomous agents and can monitor users' online actions, warn users about potential privacy threats and suggest available countermeasures. Gideon et al. (Gideon, Cranor, Egelman, & Acquisti, 2006) and Tsai et al. (Tsai, Egelman, Cranor, & Acquisti, 2007) confirmed the effectiveness of such awareness mechanisms empirically.

de Paula et al. (Paula et al., 2005) moved one step further. Instead of simply examining the usability of secure mechanisms, they framed security as an interaction problem (a practical, situated and contingent problem of decision making) and looked at a broader concern: "how security can manifest itself as part of people's interactions with and through information systems". In other words, security cannot be confined within components of a system specifically designed to attain security, but is an intrinsic and pervasive aspect of a broader context that includes end users, work practices and information systems. They argued that in practice the key issue is not how theoretically secure the underlying security mechanisms are, but rather to what extent end users can understand and make effective use of the secure mechanisms. They deliberately turned their "attention away from traditional considerations of expression and enforcement and towards explication and engagement". They designed Impromptu, a peer-to-peer file-sharing application based on supporting informed decision-making via two design principles: (1) the dynamic real-time visualization of system state, and (2) the integration of configuration and action. The former principle aims at helping users comprehend and assess the consequences of their actions when making privacy decisions. The later is based on the observation that "the separation of configuration and action may result in either overly rigid or ineffective control over security".

In short, these solutions underlie the strategy dubbed as "user empowerment" – helping users make informed privacy decisions.

DISCUSSION

Table 5 below presents how a set of representative PETs address the privacy concerns, and Table 6 shows in what ways these solutions follow the privacy principles. We now discuss some observations from these tables, and then propose implications for future research in the next section.

Two observations can be made in these two tables. First, privacy protection solutions form clusters. Solutions of the same type tend to address almost identical privacy concerns by following similar privacy principles, while different types of solutions address different but not necessarily disjoint concerns, and follow different but not necessarily disjoint principles. For example, P3P-enabled user agents such as Privacy Bird, PrivacyPact and Ackerman and Cranor's (Ackerman & Cranor, 1999) privacy critics address all listed privacy concerns except improper access. They do this by applying general principles (e.g., Notice/Openness) and data principles (e.g., purpose specification) but not identity principles. In contrast, identity management tools (such as CardSpace and OpenID) and anonymizers (e.g., Anonymizer) attend to concerns such as improper monitoring and improper use (e.g., improper merge) by observing identity principles (e.g., pseudonymity) but not data principles. This phenomenon indicates that research in data protection and identity management is still somewhat fragmented, albeit some

Table 5. How PETs address privacy concerns

	Control over data							Seclusion	Protection of identity
	Improper acquisition			Improper use			Improper storage	Unwanted solicitation	Identity fraud/theft
	Improper access	Improper collection	Improper monitoring	Improper analysis	Improper merge	Improper transfer			
Privacy Bird		+	+	+	+	+	+	+	
Privacy Pact		+	+	+	+	+	+	+	
IBM Tivoli privacy manager		+	+	++	++	++	++	+	++
PGP	++								
CardSpace			+	+	++	+			+
OpenID			+	+	++	+			+
Anony-mizer			++	+	+	+			+
History/ cookie man-ager	+	++	++	+	+		+		+
Popup blocker/ Antispam								++	
Privacy critics		+	+	+	+	+	+	+	+

Legend: ++: Effective +: Partially effective

overlap exists. Since both form integral parts of privacy enhancement, collaborations between the two research communities to integrate the two types of PETs would be desirable.

Second, no current PET effectively addresses all privacy concerns, nor follows all privacy principles. The IBM Tivoli privacy manager is the most comprehensive solution among those examined in this section. However, since it is designed and implemented as a server-side enterprise privacy management system, principles like usability (i.e., a PET solution should be easy for *end users* to adopt) are inevitably hard to achieve. Rather than mulling over whether one can develop a technical solution that effectively addresses all privacy concerns, our pragmatic strategy is to merely highlight directions that deserve more attention. For example, principles such as responsiveness, enforcement and ease of compliance are barely supported by the discussed solutions, except for the IBM Tivoli privacy manager.

CONCLUSION AND FUTURE DIRECTIONS

We proposed and applied a multi-faceted approach to the investigation and evaluation of privacy-enhancing technologies, which considers both privacy principles and individuals' privacy concerns. Privacy principles thereby serve as high-level guidelines for the conceptual evaluation of technical solutions, while privacy concerns constitute user needs that privacy mechanisms need to address. Our analysis reveals trends, identifies deficiencies, and suggests future directions in this research area.

Table 6. What privacy principles PETs follow

Principle \ Solution	Privacy Bird	Privacy Pact	IBM Tivoli privacy manager	PGP	Card Space	Open ID	Anony-mizer	History/ cookie manager	Popup blocker/ Antispam	Privacy critics
GENERAL										
Notice/Openness	+	+	+							+
Choice/Consent	+	+	+					+		
Enforcement/Redress			+							
User preference	+	+	+					+	+	
Negotiation		+								
Ease of adoption	+	-	-		-	+				+
Ease of compliance			+							
Usability	+					+				+
Responsiveness	+	+	+							
IDENTITY										
Anonymity							+			
Pseudonymity					+	+	+			
Unobservability							+			
Unlinkability					+		+	+		
Deniability										
SECLUSION										
Seclusion			+						+	
DATA										
Minimization		+								
Purpose specification	+	+	+							+
Collection limitation										
Use limitation	+	+	+							+
Onward transfer	+	+	+							+
Access/Participation										
Integrity/accuracy										
Security			+	+			+			+

Legend: ++: Strong support +: Support -: negative impact

Based on our investigation of existing privacy enhancing technologies, we suggest the following directions for future research:

- Privacy needs to be treated as a first-class requirement from the early onset in the design of an information system since, like for security and usability, it is extremely difficult if not impossible to "retrofit" a completed system to make it more privacy-friendly.
- While compliance has long been technically framed and treated as a server-side problem, we believe that the "user empowerment" strategy has a great potential for compliance

since the "expression and enforcement" paradigm seems too rigid to accommodate users' changing and context-dependent privacy desires.

- Since users' privacy needs and preferences are inherently dynamic and contingent, solutions need to cater to users' individual privacy needs. We start to see solutions like negotiable privacy policies that follow this promising direction.

REFERENCES

Ackerman, M., & Cranor, L. (1999). Privacy Critics: UI Components to Safeguard Users' Privacy. *In proceedings of the CHI '99 Extended Abstracts on Human Factors in Computing Systems* (pp. 258-259).

Aggarwal, G., Feder, T., Kenthapadi, K., Khuller, S., Panigrahy, R., Thomas, D., et al. (2006). Achieving anonymity via clustering. *In proceedings of the Symposium on Principles of Database Systems* (pp. 153 - 162).

Agrawal, R., Kiernan, J., Srikant, R., & Xu, Y. (2003). An XPath-based Preference Language for P3P. *In proceedings of the 12th Int'l World Wide Web Conference* (pp. 629 - 639) Budapest, Hungary.

Anderson, A. (2005). *A Comparison of Two Privacy Policy Languages: EPAL and XACML*: Sun Microsystems Laboratories. Retrieved from http://research.sun.com/techrep/2005/smli_tr-2005-147/ TRCompareEPALandXACML.html

APEC-FIP. (2004). *APEC Privacy Framework* (No. 2004/AMM/014rev1): Asia-Pacific Economic Cooperation.

Ashley, P., Hada, S., Karjoth, G., Powers, C., & Schunter, M. (2003). Enterprise Privacy Authorization Language (EPAL 1.2). W3C Member Submission 10 November 2003.

Ashrafi, N., & Kuilboer, J.-P. (2005). Privacy Protection via Technology: Platform for Privacy Preferences (P3P). *International Journal of E-Business Research, 1*(2), 56-69.

Bellotti, V., & Sellen, A. (1993). Design for Privacy in Ubiquitous Environments. *In proceedings of the Third European Conference on Computer-Supported Cooperative Work (ECSCW'93)* (pp. 77-92) Milan, Italy.

Blarkom, G. W. v., Borking, J. J., & Verhaar, P. (2003). PET. In G. W. v. Blarkom, J. J. Borking, & J. G. E. Olk (Eds.), *Handbook of Privacy and Privacy-Enhancing Technologies: The Case of Intelligent Software Agents.* College bescherming persoonsgegevens.

Boyle, M., & Greenberg, S. (2005). The Language of Privacy: Learning from Video Media Space Analysis and Design. *ACM Transactions on Computer-Human Interaction (TOCHI), 12*(2), 328-370.

Brusilovsky, P., Kobsa, A., & Nejdl, W. (2007). *The Adaptive Web: Methods and Strategies of Web Personalization.* Heidelberg, Germany: Springer Verlag.

Buffett, S., Jia, K., Liu, S., Spencer, B., & Wang, F. (2004). Negotiating Exchanges of P3P-Labeled Information for Compensation. *Computational Intelligence, 20*(4), 663-677.

Burkert, H. (1997). Privacy-Enhancing Technologies: Typology, Critique, Vision. In P. E. Agre, & M. Rotenberg (Eds.), *Technology and Privacy: The New Landscape* (pp. 126-143). Boston, MA: MIT Press.

Byers, S., Cranor, L., Kormann, D., & McDaniel, P. (2004, May, 2004). Searching for Privacy: Design and Implementation of a P3P-Enabled Search Engine. *In proceedings of the 2004 Workshop on Privacy Enhancing Technologies (PET2004)* (pp. 26-28) Toronto, Canada.

Camp, J., & Osorio, C. (2003). Privacy-Enhancing Technologies for Internet Commerce. In *Trust in the Network Economy*. Berlin: Springer-Verlag.

Cannon, J. C. (2005). *Privacy: What Developers and IT Professionals Should Know*: Addison-Wesley.

Chaum, D. (1982). Blind Signatures for Untraceable Payments. *In proceedings of the CRYPTO 82* (pp. 199-203).

Clark, J., & DeRose, S. (1999). XML Path Language (XPath) Version 1.0, W3C Recommendation 16 November 1999. Retrieved from http://www.w3.org/TR/1999/REC-xpath-19991116

ConneXion, C. (1996). *Anonymous Surfing*. Retrieved from http://anonymizer.com

Coyle, K. (1999*). P3P: Pretty Poor Privacy? A Social Analysis of the Platform for Privacy Preferences* (P3P) [Electronic Version]. Retrieved from http://www.kcoyle.net/p3p.html

Cranor, L. (2002). *Web Privacy with P3P*. O'Reilly.

Cranor, L., Dobbs, B., Egelman, S., Hogben, G., Humphrey, J., Langheinrich, M., et al. (2006). The Platform for Privacy Preferences 1.1 (P3P1.1) Specification. W3C Working Draft 10 February 2006. Retrieved from http://www.w3.org/TR/2006/WD-P3P11-20060210/

Cranor, L., Langheinrich, M., & Marchiori, M. (2002, April 15). *A P3P Preference Exchange Language 1.0 (APPEL1.0): W3C Working Draft.*.

Cranor, L. F., & Reidenberg, J. R. (2002). Can User Agents Accurately Represent Privacy Notices? *In proceedings of the 30th Research Conference on Communication, Information and Internet Policy*, Alexandria, VA. from http://articles.ssrn.com/sol3/articles.cfm?abstractid=328860

CZ. (2000). Czech Republic Act of 4 April 2000 on the Protection of Personal Data and on Amendment to Some Related Acts (Vol. 101).

DE-TML. (2007). *German Telemedia Law*. Retrieved from http://www.gesetze-im-internet.de/tmg/

Dourish, P., & Anderson, K. (2006). Collective Information Practice: Exploring Privacy and Security as Social and Cultural Phenomena. *Human-Computer Interaction, 21*(3), 319-342.

Egelman, S., Cranor, L., & Chowdhury, A. (2006). An Analysis of P3P-Enabled Web sites among Top-20 Search Results. *In proceedings of the 8th International Conference on Electronic Commerce* (pp. 197 - 207).

EPIC, & Junkbusters, Pretty Poor Privacy: An Assessment of P3P and Internet Privacy. (June 2000). from http://www.epic.org/reports/prettypoorprivacy.html

EU. (1995). Directive 95/46/EC of the European Parliament and of the Council of 24 October 1995 on the Protection of Individuals with Regard to the Processing of Personal Data and on the Free Movement of such Data. *Official Journal of the European Communities* (23 November 1995 No L. 281), 31ff.

EU. (2002). Directive 2002/58/EC of the European Parliament and of the Council Concerning the Processing of Personal Data and the Protection of Privacy in the Electronic Communications Sector.

eXtensible Access Control Markup Language (XACML), Version 2.0; OASIS Standard, February 1, 2005. (2005). from http://www.oasis-open.org/committees/tc_home.php?wg_abbrev=xacml

FTC. (1998 June 1998). Federal Trade Commission. Privacy online: A Report to Congress.

FTC. (2000a). Online Profiling: A Report to Congress.

FTC. (2000b, May 2000). Privacy Online: Fair Information Practices in the Electronic Marketplace. A Report to Congress.

FTC. (2000c). The Seven Safe Harbor Principles.

Garfinkel, S., & Cranor, L. (2002). P3P: Privacy Primer.

Gideon, J., Cranor, L., Egelman, S., & Acquisti, A. (2006). *Power* Strips, Prophylactics, and Privacy, Oh My! *In proceedings of the Second Symposium on Usable Privacy and Security* (pp. 133-144) Pittsburgh, Pennsylvania.

Goldberg, I. (2002, April 2002). Privacy-Enhancing Technologies for the Internet, II: Five Years Later. *In proceedings of the Workshop on Privacy Enhancing Technologies 2002.*

Goldberg, I., Wagner, D., & Brewer, E. (1997). Privacy-Enhancing Technologies for the Internet. *In proceedings of the 42nd IEEE Spring COMPCON.* San Jose, CA.

Gülcü, C., & Tsudik, G. (1996). Mixing Email with BABEL. *In proceedings of the 1996 Symposium on Network and Distributed System Security (SNDSS '96)* (pp. 2).

IBM. (2006). *IBM Tivoli Privacy Manager for E-Business.*

Kobsa, A. (2002). Personalization and International Privacy. *Communications of the ACM,* (5), 64-67.

Kobsa, A. (2007). Privacy-Enhanced Web Personalization. In P. Brusilovsky, A. Kobsa & W. Nejdl (Eds.), *The Adaptive Web: Methods and Strategies of Web Personalization* (pp. 628-670). Springer-Verlag.

Kobsa, A., & Teltzrow, M. (2005). Contextualized Communication of Privacy Practices and Personalization Benefits: Impacts on Users' Data Sharing Behavior. In D. Martin & A. Serjantov (Eds.), *Privacy Enhancing Technologies: Fourth International Workshop, PET 2004, Toronto, Canada* (Vol. LNCS 3424, pp. 329-343). Heidelberg, Germany: Springer Verlag.

Langheinrich, M. (2002). *A Privacy Awareness System for Ubiquitous Computing Environments* In proceedings of the 4th International Conference on Ubiquitous Computing (pp. 237-245) Göteborg, Sweden.

Metzger, M. J. (2006). Effects of Site, Vendor, and Consumer Characteristics on Web Site Trust and Disclosure. *Communication Research, 33*(3), 155-179.

Microsoft. CardSpace [Electronic Version]. Retrieved 2006, from http://cardspace.netfx3.com/

Microsoft. (2000). Microsoft Announces Privacy Enhancements for Windows, Internet Explorer. Retrieved 21 June 2000, from http://www.microsoft.com/PressPass/press/2000/jun00/ p3ppr.asp

OASIS. (2005). eXtensible Access Control Markup Language (XACML), Version 2.0; OASIS Standard, February 1, 2005. from http://www.oasis-open.org/committees/tc_home.php?wg_abbrev=xacml

OECD. (1980). Recommendation of the Council Concerning Guidelines Governing the Protection of Privacy and Transborder Flows of Personal Data.

OpenID. OpenID: An Actually Distributed Identity System [Electronic Version]. Retrieved 2006, from http://openid.net

Palen, L., & Dourish, P. (2002). *Unpacking "Privacy" for a Networked World.* In proceedings of the CHI-02 (pp. 129-136) Fort Lauderdale, FL.

Paula, R. r. d., Ding, X., Dourish, P., Nies, K., Pillet, B., Redmiles, D. F., et al. (2005). In the Eye of the Beholder: A Visualization-based Approach to Information System Security. *International Journal of Human-Computer Studies, 63*(1-2), 5-24.

Preibusch, S. (2006). Personalized Services with Negotiable Privacy Policies. *In proceedings of the PEP06, CHI 2006 Workshop on Privacy-Enhanced Personalization* (pp. 29-38) Montreal, Canada.

Senicar, V., Jerman-Blazic, B., & Klobucar, T. (2003). Privacy-Enhancing Technologies: Approaches and Development. *Computer Standards & Interfaces, 25*(2), 147-158.

Stufflebeam, W., Anton, A. I., He, Q., & Jain, N. (2004). *Specifying Privacy Policies with P3P and EPAL: Lessons Learned.* In proceedings of the 2004 ACM Workshop on Privacy in the Electronic Society (pp. 35-36).

Sweeney, L. (2002). K-anonymity: a model for protecting privacy. *International Journal on Uncertainty, Fuzziness and Knowledge-based Systems, 10*(5), 557-570.

Tavani, H., & Moor, J. (2001). Privacy Protection, Control of Information, and Privacy-Enhancing Technologies. *ACM SIGCAS Computers and Society, 31*(1), 6-11.

Teltzrow, M., & Kobsa, A. (2004). Impacts of User Privacy Preferences on Personalized Systems: a Comparative Study. In C.-M. Karat, J. Blom & J. Karat (Eds.), *Designing Personalized User Experiences for eCommerce* (pp. 315-332). Dordrecht, Netherlands: Kluwer Academic Publishers.

Tor. (2004). from http://tor.eff.org/

Tsai, J., Egelman, S., Cranor, L., & Acquisti, A. (2007). The Effect of Online Privacy Information on Purchasing Behavior: An Experimental Study. *In proceedings of the Sixth Workshop on the Economics of Information Security*, Pittsburgh, PA.

USA. (2002). *The E-Government Act.* Retrieved from http://thomas.loc.gov/cgi-bin/bdquery/z?d107:HR02458:| TOM:/bss/d107query.html

USACM. (2006). *USACM Policy Recommendations on Privacy.* Retrieved from http://usacm.acm.org/usacm/ Issues/Privacy.htm

Wang, H., Lee, M. K. O., & Wang, C. (1998). Consumer Privacy Concerns about Internet Marketing. *Communications of the ACM, 41*(3), 63-70.

Wang, Y., & Kobsa, A. (2006). Impacts of Privacy Laws and Regulations on Personalized Systems. *In proceedings of the PEP06, CHI06 Workshop on Privacy-Enhanced Personalization* (pp. 44-46) Montréal, Canada.

Wang, Y., & Kobsa, A. (2008). Technical Solutions for Privacy-Enhanced Personalization. In Mourlas, C. & Germanakos, P. (Eds.), *Intelligent User Interfaces: Adaptation and Personalization Systems and Technologies*: IGI Global.

Warren, S., & Brandeis, L. (1890). The Right to Privacy. *Harvard Law Review, 4*(5), 193-220.

Westin, A., & Gelder, V. v. (2003). Privacy & American Business: Special Issue on Consumer Privacy in Japan and the New National Privacy Law. Retrieved from http://www.privacyexchange.org/ pab_japanissue.pdf

Whitten, A., & Tygar, D. (1999). *Why Johnny Can't Encrypt. A Usability Evaluation of PGP 5.0.* In proceedings of the Ninth USENIX Security Symposium. from http://www.cs.berkeley.edu/~tygar/papers/Why_Johnny_Cant_Encrypt/OReilly.pdf

Young, J. (1978). Introduction: A Look at Privacy. In J. Young (Ed.), *Privacy.* New York: John Wiley & Sons.

KEY TERMS

Anonymity: The property that a user cannot be identified within the total user population, nor her interactions be tracked.

APPEL: A P3P preference language that allows users to express their privacy preferences.

Authentication: A process for verifying the digital identity of users or processes.

Authorization: A process for verifying whether an identified user or role enjoys specific access rights to certain resources.

Identity Management: The management and provisioning of information about users across different applications (sometimes users may entertain different identities with partially different characteristics).

P3P: A machine-readable (XML) language that allows websites to describe their privacy practices and P3P-enabled user agents (e.g., web browsers) to retrieve these privacy policies automatically and potentially analyze them.

Privacy Policy Language: A machine-readable language for expressing the privacy policies of organizations.

Pseudonymity: The property that a user cannot be identified within the total user population, but her interactions nevertheless be tracked.

XACML: A general-purpose access control language that can be used to describe access control decision requests and responses as well as access control rules and policies.

ENDNOTES

1 The P3P 1.1 specification provides a new mechanism that binds a P3P policy to an XML element that does not have to be associated with a URI.

2 Information may be used to determine the habits, interests, or other characteristics of individuals and combine it with identified data to make a decision that directly affects that individual.

3 http://www.w3.org/P3P/compliant_sites.php3

4 The act mandates that government agencies post machine-readable privacy policies on their web sites.

5 At the time of writing, XACML 3.0 is being drafted.

Chapter XIV
Social Engineering and its Countermeasures

Douglas P. Twitchell
Illinois State University, USA

ABSTRACT

This chapter introduces and defines social engineering, a recognized threat to the security of information systems. It also introduces a taxonomy for classifying social engineering attacks along four dimensions: who or what the targets are, what media are used, how the attacks fit in an attack cycle, and the techniques used to execute the attacks. Additionally, the chapter discusses current social engineering countermeasures and how to map attack types to these countermeasures. Finally, the chapter ends with a discussion of future trends and technologies for defending against social engineering attacks. Use of the taxonomy should help security professionals and researchers understand social engineering attacks, and implementation of the discussed current and future countermeasures should help professionals reduce the risks associated with social engineering attacks.

INTRODUCTION

In 1970, Jerry Schneider took part in an early example of social engineering. While dumpster diving the local Pacific Telephone office, Jerry found the procedures for making internal equipment orders and charging them to company accounts. Posing on the phone, or pretexting, as company employees he was able to get the correct account numbers and eventually stole and resold about $250,000 in computer equipment (Whiteside, 1979). Twenty-five years later, in 2005, Hewlett-Packard's board discovered that sensitive information from a board meeting had been leaked to the media. The chairman of the board decided to determine the culprit and hired a security consulting firm for the job. Private investigators from the firm called the phone company and, posing as the victims, or pretexting, obtained the phone records of members of the media without their knowledge (Kersetter, 2006; Shankland, 2006). Recently, many people with email accounts have been recipients of yet another social engineering attack, *phishing*, the use of deceptive emails to encourage users to input sensitive identifying data. These three cases are specific examples of a more general information security phenomenon: social engineering.

Social engineering is the use of deception and other non-technical means to gain unauthorized access to information or information systems. Social engineering has been used to describe a number of attacks ranging from widespread phishing for identity information to targeted pretexting for corporate or governmental espionage. Social engineers rely on psychological triggers (e.g., fear, kindness, and greed) and cognitive biases (e.g., truth bias, anchoring, and miscalculation of risk) to gain unauthorized access and evade detection. For the most part, current countermeasures against social engineering attacks rely on people for prevention by educating users through awareness programs and by policy implementation, enforcement and auditing, although new technical countermeasures are emerging.

This chapter has the following objectives:

- Define social engineering
- Provide a taxonomy of social engineering attacks
- Discuss emotional triggers and cognitive biases on which social engineers rely
- Describe current social engineering countermeasures and how they map to techniques
- Discuss future trends in social engineering research and countermeasures

DEFINITION

Social engineering has been used to describe a number of attacks ranging from widespread phishing for identity information to narrow pretexting for specific records. It is unclear who first coined the term "social engineering," but several have attempted to define it. Some definitions are as simple as "the art and science of getting people to comply to your wishes" (Harl, 1997) to much more complex definitions. For the purposes of this chapter, social engineering will be defined as follows:

Social Engineering is the exploitation of psychological triggers and cognitive biases as a means to gain unauthorized access to information or information systems.

Phishing and pretexting are only two examples of social engineering attacks that manipulate or deceive targets to obtain information. Table 1 contains some additional examples of social engineering attacks.

The celebrity ex-hacker Kevin Mitnick best described the effectiveness of social engineering to the U.S. Congress in these terms (Mitnick, 2000):

I was so successful in that line of attack that I rarely had to resort to a technical attack. Companies spend millions of dollars toward technological protections, and that's wasted if somebody can basically call someone on the telephone and either convince them to do something on the computer that lowers the computer's defenses or reveals the information they were seeking.

Attackers with good social skills who don't have to resort to technical attacks represent a grave and continuing danger to information security. To aid in better understanding them and understand

Table 1. Examples of social engineering techniques

Asking for Favors (Lively Jr., 2003)	Pretexting
Dumpster Diving	Reverse Social Engineering
Cold Calling	Reconnaissance
Contriving Situations (Silltow, 2001)	Shoulder Surfing
Giving out free software	Simple Requests
Impersonation	Surveys
Photography	Tailgating
Pharming	Theft
Phishing	Trojan Horses

their attacks, next section introduces a taxonomy for categorizing these types of attacks.

A TAXONOMY OF SOCIAL ENGINEERING ATTACKS

By classifying social engineering attacks using a taxonomy, defenders can determine which kinds of attacks to which their organization is vulnerable. Depending on the organization's exposure, it may be possible to identify social engineering attacks that have little chance of occurring. For example, an organization that relies little on telephone support may be less vulnerable to pretexting than one that does. Additionally, organizing and categorizing can help ensure that all social engineering threats are covered—not only are the common, broad-based social engineering threats considered, but also the sometimes more devastating, rare targeted attacks. Finally, a taxonomy provides the opportunity to map attack types to attack techniques and potential controls. Social engineering attacks can be classified along a number of dimensions including who or what the targets are, what media are used, how the attacks fit in an attack cycle, and the techniques used to execute the attacks.

Targeting

The first dimension is targeting, meaning the extensiveness of those targeted by the attack. As illustrated in Figure 1, social engineering attacks can be put on a continuum that on one end has widespread attacks with small individual value. The most common and most recognizable of these are phishing attacks. These attacks rely on duping of users into believing they are entering sensitive information into a legitimate web page when they are actually giving the information to a hacker. Phishing attacks often take advantage of the fear of other identity theft attacks to motivate targets to succumb to the attack. Email-borne viruses and

Figure 1. Social engineering techniques placed along a spectrum from targeted to broad

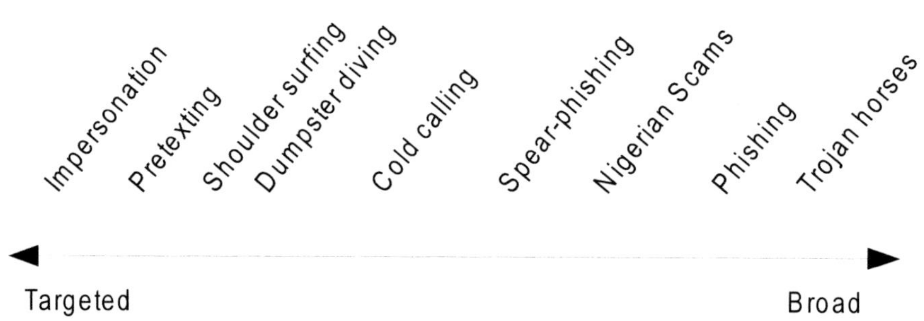

worms use a similar kind of social engineering attack that often includes the enticing promise of pornographic material to lure targets into running programs attached to an email. At the other end, the continuum are the most malicious, rarest, but usually highest value attacks—those where the social engineer uses outright fraud and deception to make his or her way into an organization and obtain specific information (e.g. calls up the technical support office and asks for a password reset).

Media

Another related and not independent dimension for categorizing SE attacks is the media used. Social engineering can be done in face-to-face conversations, on the telephone, through email, and through paper mail. These media use three major modalities: visual, audio, and text—the first conveying the most contextual information (e.g., gestures, facial expressions, and voice tone) and the last conveying the least (e.g., text only) (Daft & Lengel, 1986). Each modality has advantages and disadvantages for attackers and targets. Given good social skills, the attacker can use the increased contextual richness of face-to-face communications to engender more trust in the target and increase the likelihood of an attack's success. On the other hand, a suspicious target may be more likely to determine the attacker's intent based on cues such as nervousness leaked by the attacker through gestures, body movements, and facial expressions.

Related to the media used are the aspects of proximity and synchronicity. Some media, like face-to-face conversations and non-broadcast, one-to-many speeches require proximity to the speaker. Most other technologically advanced media allow communications over a distance, and therefore expand the reach of a social engineer to broader attacks.

Media may also allow for synchronous or asynchronous communications. Synchronous communications give both the attacker and the target opportunity to adjust their communication tactics for either succeeding at the attack or detecting the attack (Buller & Burgoon, 1996). On the other hand, an attacker using a synchronous communication mode must be able to think quickly, possibly arouse suspicion, or abort the attack when suspicion is detected. While asynchronous communication doesn't allow the attacker or the target to adjust tactics quickly, it does give the attacker time to prepare the attack or a response to a previous attack. Preparation time gives the attacker the opportunity to use more sophisticated attacks than they otherwise could have during spontaneous synchronous communication. Table 2 lists some example media that may be used in social engineering attacks and their synchronicity and proximity characteristics.

The most familiar and common proximate and synchronous form of communication is face-to-face conversation. By definition, face-to-face SE attacks must be done at the physical location of the attacker (i.e., they must be proximate), and they allow the target to give and the attacker to receive immediate feedback. Attackers can modify their attack as a face-to-face conversation evolves, which, depending on the skill of the attacker, could make the attack easier or more difficult for the target to detect. Therefore, face-to-face attacks require more skill from the attacker than other, less interactive attacks.

Other forms of visual, synchronous communication such as videophones and videoconferencing are not currently common forms of communication (although their use might become more common in the future), and may be impractical for the social engineer to employ. Asynchronous visual attacks such as television broadcasts could also be employed by the attacker to reach a broad audience and direct them to fraudulent websites similar to phishing attacks, but no such attack has been documented, despite the common use of infomercials for other types of fraud (Ahrens, 2004). Because of proximity and skill require-

Table 2. Characteristics of media used in social engineering

	Media Characteristics			
	Synchronous		Asynchronous	
Media	Proximate	Distant	Proximate	Distant
Face-to-face	X			
1 to many speech			X	
Video conference		X		
Video broadcast				X
Telephone/VOIP		X		
Audio broadcast				X
Chat/Instant messaging		X		
Email				X
Dynamic web pages		X		
Static web pages				X
Software distribution				X
Paper				X

ments, visual channel attacks of any kind will likely be targeted and rare.

Audio channel attacks—mainly using the telephone—do not require the attacker to be physically collocated with the target, allowing a greater number of potential threat agents access to potential targets. In the past, the telephone has been one of the major tools used by social engineers because of its ubiquity, the visual anonymity it provides, and the trust the attacker can build. Phone conversations, like face-to-face conversations, are also synchronous, and therefore allow the attacker and the target continuous feedback and tactical adjustment. However, the audio channel doesn't transmit as much information in the form of non-verbal communication as the visual channel, giving the attacker a shield against possible detection. It is possible, but technically difficult, for attackers to set up automated telephone attacks, though they may use it to boost the legitimacy of another type of attack. For the most part, however, audio channel attacks are also on the targeted and rarer end of the spectrum.

Phreaking is a term associated with telecommunications fraud where an attacker uses technical or social means to gain access to the public switched telephone network and make calls, long-distance and otherwise, without payment. Although phreaking is used to gain access to audio channel communication, the fraud itself need not be done through the audio channel or with social engineering.

Besides "419" fraud or "Nigerian Letter" fraud—which need not be considered social engineering since it doesn't involve information systems—widespread text-based social engineering is a fairly recent phenomenon. A common use of social engineering in text media is the trojan horse. In 2001, users began receiving email with the subject: "Here you have, :o)", the body: ""“Hi: Check This!", and the attachment "AnnaKournikova.jpg.vbs". At the time, Anna Kournikova was a tennis star considered by many a sex symbol. The email was promising the receiver a picture of Anna Kournikova; instead, it executed a script that copied itself to the windows directory, sent itself to others in the victim's address book, and attempted to launch a browser on a specific date each year ("New e-mail virus preys on Anna Kournikova fans", 2001). Although this particular virus did nothing to harm the receiver, it did slow networks and along with others like it provided a model for introducing malware to unsuspecting users.

Text-based social engineering attacks provide the attacker anonymity, a broad geographic reach, and—through automation—a large target pool. Unlike visual or audio attacks, text-based attacks aren't susceptible to physical or vocal recognition. The attacker can impersonate someone the target knows without fear of being recognized, and although using text the attacker doesn't have the social closeness visual and audio provide, he or she can use "official"-looking, html-based messages as shown in Figure 2 to build feelings of trust and legitimacy with the target. Like telephone calls, text-based social engineering attacks are not geographically bound. Geographical freedom vastly increases the number of potential targets for the attacker and the number of potential attackers for potential targets. The number of practical targets increases further when asynchronous techniques such as email are used rather than instant messaging. Phishing is a good example of a broadly targeted, email-based social engineering attack. Although many people are aware of phishing scams, attackers have the ability to send enormous amounts of phishing messages, and only a few targets need to respond for the attacker to perpetrate numerous identity thefts.

In general, then, proximate, synchronous attacks, such as face-to face impersonation attacks, will be rare while distant, asynchronous attacks, such as phishing, will be common. Proximate, synchronous attacks are mostly found at the targeted end of the targeted-broad spectrum in Figure 1, and distant asynchronous attacks are mostly found at the broad end.

Attack Cycle

An additional step to in classifying social engineering attacks is to look at the cycle social engineers follow in most attacks. These attacks follow a pattern that can be depicted as a cycle of four steps. First, the attacker gathers information about the target and the target environment. Information gathered could include, for example, organizational jargon for building trust or key names for invoking authority. The information

Figure 2. An example of a phishing email with identifying information redacted. The URL shown in the email does not match the URL of the page referred to by the hyperlink

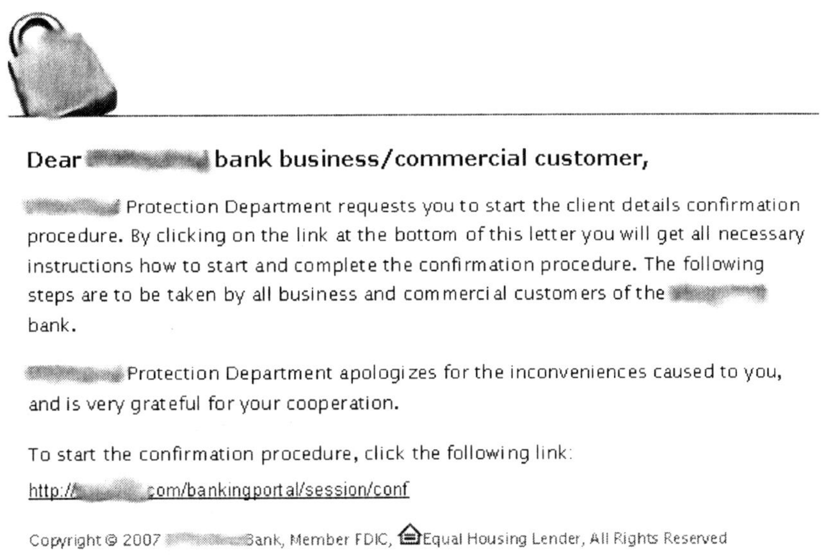

Dear [redacted] bank business/commercial customer,

[redacted] Protection Department requests you to start the client details confirmation procedure. By clicking on the link at the bottom of this letter you will get all necessary instructions how to start and complete the confirmation procedure. The following steps are to be taken by all business and commercial customers of the [redacted] bank.

[redacted] Protection Department apologizes for the inconveniences caused to you, and is very grateful for your cooperation.

To start the confirmation procedure, click the following link:
http://[redacted].com/bankingportal/session/conf

Copyright © 2007 [redacted]Bank, Member FDIC, Equal Housing Lender, All Rights Reserved is gleaned using any of the media described in media section above. The information is then used to build a relationship with the target, a relationship built on either positive or negative emotions, as is described below. The attacker then exploits the relationship by requesting that the target either divulge information or perform some action that gets the attacker closer to his or her goal. As shown in Figure 3 the last step is for the target to execute the request. If the attacker has not yet reached his or her goal, the process starts again.

Attack Techniques

In developing relationships and exploiting them, social engineers rely on the inherent weaknesses in human nature and culture for attacking their targets. These techniques include psychological techniques such as emotional triggers or exploits, and cognitive and cultural biases.

Psychological Triggers and Exploits

Social engineers use both negative and positive emotions to their advantage. Negative emotions include feeling overloaded, urgency, fear, scarcity, and other strong emotions. The negative emotion attack relies on the human tendency to shun these types of unpleasant feelings, which can impede cognitive ability and rational thought and can provoke a *fight or flight* response in the target. When aroused in this manner the target will often do what he or she can to rid themselves of the source, even if that means not following policy and divulging important information. Positive emotions include such feelings as reciprocation, trust, similarity, helpfulness, integrity, legitimacy, authority, conformity, and curiosity. Positive emotions bring build a trusting relationship between the attacker and target, making the target more willing to comply with the attacker's requests. Diffusion of responsibility—giving targets the assurance that a security breach will not be their fault—and carelessness are for the most part neutral in the resulting emotions. Diffusion of responsibility brings the target back to a normal emotional state while carelessness requires no manipulation of the target—it is simply a state the target is in that the attacker exploits. Table 3 lists some of the emotional exploits along with their definitions and sources.

Figure 3. Social engineering attack cycle (Allen, 2006)

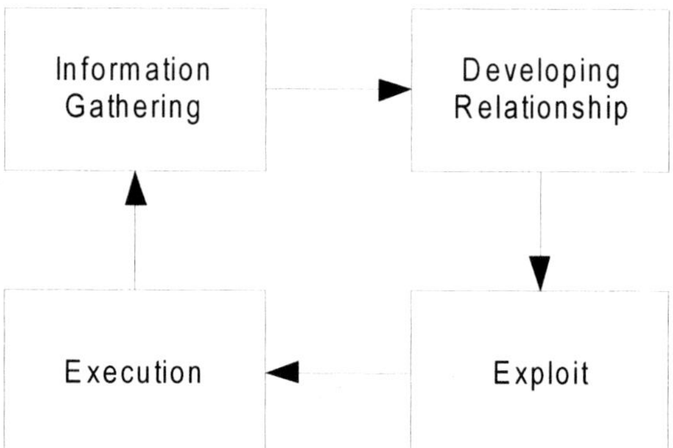

Cognitive and Cultural Biases

In addition to emotions are cognitive and cultural biases that an attacker can exploit in a social engineering attack. These biases are related to the psychological triggers listed above, but aren't necessarily emotionally based. Instead, they are heuristics—mental shortcuts—humans use when making decisions under conditions of uncertainty. Social engineering attacks can be thought of as an attacker influencing a target into making a certain decision. If the social engineer can influence the target's decision-making processes, specifically the heuristics or biases the target uses, he or she can steer the target to the decision the attacker desires (i.e., give out the desired information). These biases and heuristics include, among others, the truth bias, prospect theory, the representativeness heuristic, and anchoring and adjustment. These four, discussed below, represent only a few of

Table 3. Common emotional exploits used in social engineering attacks and their sources

Category	Emotional Exploit	Definition or Example	Sources
Negative Emotion	Strong Affect	The heightening of emotional state in the target	a
	Overloading	Giving the target too much to think about	a
	Urgency	Making the target feel rushed	
	Fear	Fear of repercussions or revenge	b
	Scarcity	Attacker increases target's desire for something based on perceived scarcity	d
Positive Emotion	Reciprocation	Doing something for the target who then feels a responsibility to do something in return	a,b,d
	Building Trust	Establishing a trusting relationship using internal jargon	a,c
	Similarity	Attacker builds trust by finding targets similar to the attacker or becoming similar to the target	d
	Helpfulness	Attack motivates target to "help" the attacker	c
	Integrity	Commit target to action through promises	
	Legitimacy	Attack has characteristics that make it seem to come from a credible, authoritative source	c
	Authority	Communication supposedly from someone with authority	a,b,d
	Conformity	Attack exploits target's desire to fit in	b
	Curiosity	Entice target with a desire to know or see something	
Neutral Emotion	Carelessness	Attacker takes advantage of target's lack of vigilance	b
	Diffusion of Responsibility	Attacker causes target to not feel fully responsible for a breach of security	a

a: *(Gragg, 2003)*
b: *(Lively Jr., 2003)*
c: *(Mitnick & Simon, 2002)*
d: *(Rusch, 1999)*

many heuristics, biases, and theories regarding decision making. For more see (Plous, 1993).

Truth Bias

Truth bias is the belief held by most people in western and other cultures that when a person, especially a person with which the hearer has a trust relationship, says something he or she is telling the truth (Stiff, Kim, & Ramesh, 1992). Social engineers can use the truth bias by building a relationship where the target has no reason to be suspicious of the attacker. For a skilled social engineer, building such a relationship may only take a few minutes of banter, but then, once the relationship is there, he or she moves to exploiting that relationship. Truth bias may serve people well in most social situations (people without a truth bias may be considered "paranoid"), but it should be combated in situations where social engineering attacks would result in valuable data losses.

Prospect Theory

Prospect theory has many aspects, but one that is important to the social engineer is the idea that losses loom larger in decision-making than gains (Kahneman & Tversky, 1979). That is, people are more afraid of losing something they already have. An attacker can combine this tendency with authority and urgency to convince a target that the target might lose his or her job or be demoted. In general, this kind of tactic would be more successful than an attack where the attacker promises the target some kind of a reward such as a job promotion or pay raise, even if the demotion was equal in value to the promotion or pay raise.

The Representativeness Heuristic

To make their stories more believable, social engineers can exploit the representativeness heuristic, the tendency for people to believe a scenario that has more representative detail than one with less (Tversky & Kahneman, 1974). If a story contains details that "should" be in it, then people are more likely to believe it is true than one that has less detail, even though, mathematically, a story with more detail is less likely to be true than one with less detail. For example, an attacker may call a target and, in attempting to impersonate a systems administrator, tell the target that he or she (the attacker) is calling from the server room, is currently seeing strange activity on the network, and needs to use the target's login information for some purpose. Because these details are representative of a systems administrator, the target will be more likely to believe them than if the attacker simply claimed he or she was the systems administrator and wanted the target's login information, even though the latter is, according to probability theory, more likely than the former.

Anchoring and Adjustment

Anchoring and adjustment refer to the tendency of people to establish a baseline and, as new evidence is uncovered, adjust from that baseline (Tversky & Kahneman, 1974). For example, when buying a car, usually the first price mentioned is established as a baseline, and adjustments to it are considered extra costs or savings. In social engineering, attackers can use this to their advantage by initially asking for something somewhat outrageous (e.g., asking directly for a password). Then, if it is rejected, adjusting to something less extreme (e.g., asking what kind of system is being run). Once the more extreme request is established as a baseline, the less extreme case will seem more reasonable.

For the most part, all of the psychological triggers and cognitive biases discussed in this section are simply part of human nature or cultural norms. Organizations cannot easily change the way people think and feel, nor do they usually want to. But, they can put countermeasures in place to prevent human nature or cultural norms from turning into actions that result in security breaches.

COUNTERMEASURES

With attacks categorized according to their targets, their phases, and the techniques used, the next step is to determine the countermeasures for defeating those attacks. Countermeasures to social engineering attacks fall into four broad categories: (1) policy; (2) education, training, and awareness; (3) audit; and (4) technology.

Policy

The most important tool in preventing and detecting social engineering attacks is good policy. Good policy is easy to understand, has well-defined scope, is enforceable, and has clear consequences of violations. Creating good policy for preventing social engineering attacks is not a trivial task. It involves understanding human behavior and anticipating unintended consequences a policy can create that might reduce an organization's flexibility. To combat social engineering, at minimum, an organizations information security policy should address the topic; however, it would be better to have policies specifically directed at social engineering threats. For example, Mitnick & Simon (2005, pg. 238) give the following suggestions involving policy:

- Develop clear, concise security protocols that when they are consistently enforced give employees confidence when facing attacks
- Develop simple rules defining what information is sensitive so that employees know when to question someone requesting information
- Require the requestor's identity when restricted actions are requested

These policy recommendations bolster the defense against social engineering attacks, but there should also be procedures for handling social engineering incidents. Incident reporting should be easy and rewarded. Employees should be able to easily report the following information (Microsoft, 2006):

- Target name
- Target department
- Date
- Attack vector
- Attack description
- Attack outcome
- Attack effect
- Recommendations

Education, Training, and Awareness (ETA)

Once policy is in place, users need to know the content of the policy, why it exists, and what happens when it is violated. Having a good knowledge of policy can give a target the ability to recognize an attack and the confidence to repel it and report it. Knowing why a policy exists helps users feel responsible for the policy, and knowing what will happen if the policy is violated deters the user from ignoring the policy and rendering it useless. These three pieces of knowledge are imparted to the user through education, training, and/or awareness (ETA).

Not all users are equal in their ability to divulge important information to a social engineer; therefore, not all training is given equally to every user. Those who develop security policy, manage security personnel, or administer security technology require education in the form of degrees, certification, or experience to understand the how security, including security from social engineering attacks, works. Other personnel who have access to sensitive data or systems should receive training that ensures they know the sensitivity of the data and the impact of its loss or divulgence. They should also be trained on how to actively resist a social engineering attack by making them aware of the psychological triggers and cognitive biases used by social engineers. These two types of personnel, the systems administrators and the data administrators, should understand attacks from across the target spectrum in Figure 1. The remaining users should have regular security training that includes specific training on those social engineering attacks that are broadly targeted.

Technology

Broadly targeted attacks are also a good place to implement technical controls. Email filtering is a basic technique for preventing such broad-based attacks as phishing and trojan horses. Additionally, a robust technical security architecture that emphasizes defense-in-depth can prevent or prevent the spread of previously unforeseen attacks. For example, the use of two-factor authentication defends against a number of attacks, among them the social engineering attack of requesting a password using any one of the psychological exploits described above. The social engineer may be able to get the password, but without the other authentication factor (e.g., smart card, biometric, etc.), he or she will not be able to get to the desired data or system.

Auditing

With good policy in place, on-going training occurring and technical controls where possible, the organization should ensure that the policy, training, and technology are effective against potential attacks, and that attacks that do happen are detected. Mitnick & Simon (2005) recommend testing employees' susceptibility to social engineering attacks through penetration testing. Penetration testing can indicate to security management where improvement is needed, and, importantly, it can provide a reality check for users who get to see how vulnerable they are. Penetration testing supplements training and awareness and can vividly illustrate to users where their weaknesses are (Gragg, 2003). Systems administrators who emphasize technical security controls such as firewalls, cryptography, and access controls may not be aware of the social and behavioral vulnerabilities to their data and systems, but penetration testing coupled with thorough briefings afterward can ensure that administrators understand the full breadth of their security situation.

In addition to penetration testing, good auditing practice for defending against social engineering will make sure that the policy, training, and technical controls are actually implemented. Policy may dictate that all organizational data be part of a data classification scheme, but an audit will give the assurance that it actually its. Similarly, policy may stipulate that technical controls such as two-factor authentication are used with highly-sensitive data, but an audit will give the assurance that it actually is used and used correctly. Good auditing adds checks and assurances to security practices.

MAPPING TECHNIQUES TO MEDIA, VECTORS, AND COUNTERMEASURES

To determine the countermeasures needed to defend against a specific social engineering attack, security personnel can map the technique to the attack phase, the media used in the attack, and the emotional exploits and biases the attacker employs. This information can help point to effective countermeasures. For example, a common technique used in social engineering attacks is impersonation. An attacker using impersonation may use a number of the emotional exploits shown in Table 3. During the *information gathering* phase of the attack and using the *phone*, an attacker could impersonate a corporate officer to convey *authority* and *fear*, speak with jargon to convey *legitimacy*, and a looming deadline to

Table 4. Mapping impersonation to phase, media, exploit and countermeasures

Technique	Targeting	Attack Phases	Media	Exploits	Countermeasures
Impersonation	Narrow	Information Gathering	Phone (Audio)	Authority Fear Legitimacy Prospect of loss	Call-back policy User training

Table 5. Mapping phishing to targeting, phase, media, exploit and countermeasures

Technique	Targeting	Attack Phases	Media	Exploits	Countermeasures
Phishing	Broad	All	Email and Web page	Fear Legitimacy Urgency Carelessness	Email filters Web browser warnings User training

impose *urgency*. Because the technique is on the narrow end of the targeting continuum, technical countermeasures may not be appropriate. Instead, sensible countermeasures could include a call-back policy to verify the identity of the requester when giving out important information or better user training could counteract this attack. Table 4 illustrates this process

Doing the same kind of mapping with phishing results in the mapping in Table 5. In this example, phishing, a very broad attack, comprises *all* of the phases of social engineering attacks. The attacker uses *email* and a *web page* with a message tailored to arouse *fear*, *legitimacy*, and *urgency* in the target. The target, being *careless*, does as the email message and web page instruct and gives out the desired information. Because it is broad, common, and uses text, organizations can employ technical controls such as *email filters* and automated *web browser warnings*, along with *user training* to counteract the phisher's attempts.

FUTURE TRENDS

Technical means for protecting information systems have improved over the years as has adoption of security technologies such as firewalls, intrusion detection systems, anti-virus systems, and patch management systems. The effect of this increased adoption of security technology has been the decreased effectiveness of many kinds of technical attacks, although the quantity and sophistication of attacks have increased. The Air Force recently confirmed this phenomenon (Herbert, 2005). With the decreasing effectiveness of technical attacks attackers may increasingly turn to social engineering to get the information they seek. Furthermore, social engineering attacks render the most sophisticated technical countermeasures useless: why spend hours developing a sophisticated technical attack when the same information can be had by simply asking for it? Organizations may spend large amounts on technical security infrastructure, but if they neglect the social weaknesses inherent in human nature, their organization will still be vulnerable. Although there haven't been any extensive studies of the prevalence of social engineering attacks, laptop/mobile theft, a non-technical attack, has been ranked the second, third, or fourth most common type of attack for the last eight years (Gordan, Loeb, Lucyshyn, & Richardson, 2007). Even as technology evolves, the human aspect of information security will likely remain a prominent concern for years to come (Twitchell, 2006).

Technical controls that defend against highly targeted social engineering attacks are rare, but two new technologies originally developed for detecting deception in text-based communication could be useful. Message feature mining and speech act profiling are technologies that utilize natural language processing to extract non-content related features from free text, and they could be used to detect social engineering attacks that are common and use the text channel, such as a text-based helpdesk (Twitchell, 2006). The extracted features can be fed to classifiers commonly used in data mining to classify text as containing deception or not containing deception.

Since deception is a major component of social engineering attacks, these technologies could be useful in detecting social engineering attacks. However, because of the complexities of human interactions, it is highly unlikely that automated attack detection will stand on its own. Instead any security system utilizing these technologies would have people at the front lines with the technology as their aid. The system could be used to overcome biases and to give timely reminders to those facing a social engineering threat.

CONCLUSION

It is surprising how effective simple social engineering attacks can be. Recently, researchers from a university in the southeast United States set up a table on a busy street near several banking institutions. The researchers prominently displayed their association with the university and proceeded to hand out a survey. Upon completion of the survey, the respondent received a piece of candy. The survey began by asking some general questions about passwords and security. Toward the end of the survey, the questions were more specific, and, finally, the last question simply asked respondents to write down their passwords. 73% of the respondents gave the researchers their passwords (Cazier & Botelho, 2007). The researchers, of course, destroyed the passwords after the experiment, but there is nothing that the researchers did that a social engineer couldn't do.

This attack can be put into the framework introduced in this chapter. The attack was broad in that it only had a class of people to target, those who worked in the financial district of the city. All phases of the social engineering cycle were represented. The researchers used information gathering to decide the best place and methods, they developed a relationship using their positions at a university and handing out candy, and they exploited the targets using a paper survey, to which 73% complied. They exploited legitimacy, carelessness, and the truth bias to influence the targets into complying. Countermeasures that could have prevented this attack include mainly user training and awareness of the sensitivity of passwords. Otherwise, the attacked organizations would have to rely on further defenses (e.g., two-factor authentication) to mitigate the damage done.

The framework presented in this chapter is a tool for understanding social engineering attacks and putting in countermeasures to those attacks; however, there are other issues concerning social engineering that will need consideration. Culture is a factor that could change the usefulness of the psychological techniques and cognitive biases described. For example, are there cultures where the truth bias does not hold true, where relationships are built around assumed deceit rather than assumed truth? Culture and language are factors not yet adequately considered in the study of social engineering. A factor that has been studied, but was not emphasized in this chapter, is the need to go through the risk management process when deciding to implement countermeasures. The mapping framework can aid in selecting the kinds of countermeasures to use, but a risk management process can tell whether that countermeasure is worth the associated cost.

The survey attack described above, the 1970 attack on Pacific Telephone, and the 2005 incident at Hewlett-Packard illustrate the need for information security specialists to seriously consider social engineering threats and the need for social engineering countermeasures. As technical controls evolve and more effectively deter, prevent, and detect technical attacks, attackers will move into the long-exploited social realm. While security personnel strive to keep up with the ever changing technical realm, they must also be constantly aware of the social threats that will remain as long as humans are part of the security equation.

REFERENCES

Ahrens, F. (2004, September 8). FTC Pulls Plug on Infomercial Giant. *Washington Post,* p. E1.

Allen, M. (2006). Social Engineering: A Means to Violate a Computer System. Retrieved May, 2007, from http://www.sans.org/reading_room/whitepapers/engineering/529.php

Buller, D. B., & Burgoon, J. K. (1996). Interpersonal Deception Theory. *Communication Theory, 6*(3), 203-242.

Cazier, J. A., & Botelho, C. M. (2007). *Social Engineering's Threat to Public Privacy.* Paper presented at the the 6th Security Conference, Las Vegas, Nevada.

Daft, R. L., & Lengel, R. H. (1986). Organizational information, media richness and structural design. *Management Science, 32*, 554-571.

Gordan, L. A., Loeb, M. P., Lucyshyn, W., & Richardson, R. (2007). 2006 CSI/FBI Computer Crime and Security Survey: Computer Security Institute.

Gragg, D. (2003). A Multi-level Defense Against Social Engineering. Retrieved May, 2007, from http://www.sans.org/rr/whitepapers/engineering/920.php

Harl. (1997). People Hacking: The Psychology of Social Engineering. Retrieved May, 2007, from http://library.cyber-punk.cc/files/se10.html

Herbert, A. J. (2005, December). Information Battleground. *Air Force Magazine, 88.*

Kahneman, D., & Tversky, A. (1979). Prospect Theory: An Analysis of Decision under Risk. *Econometrica, 47*(2), 263-292.

Kersetter, J. (2006). Reporters' records accessed in HP probe. *CNET News.com* Retrieved May, 2007, from http://news.com.com/Reporters+records+accessed+in+HP+probe/2100-1014_3-6113362.html

Lively Jr., C. E. (2003). Psychological Based Social Engineering. Retrieved May, 2007, from http://www.giac.org/certified_professionals/practicals/gsec/3547.php

Microsoft. (2006). How to Protect Insiders from Social Engineering Threats. Retrieved May, 2007, from http://www.microsoft.com/technet/security/midsizebusiness/topics/complianceandpolicies/socialengineeringthreats.mspx

Mitnick, K. D. (2000). Cyber Attack: Is the Government Safe? *Senate Committee on Governmental Affairs* Retrieved May, 2007, from http://www.iwar.org.uk/comsec/resources/sa-tools/mitnick-testimony.htm

Mitnick, K. D., & Simon, W. L. (2002). *The Art of Deception: Controlling the Human Element of Security.* Indianapolis, Indiana: Wiley.

Mitnick, K. D., & Simon, W. L. (2005). *The Art of Intrusion: The Real Stories Behind the Exploits of Hackers, Intruders, and Deceivers.* Indianapolis, Indiana: Wiley.

New e-mail virus preys on Anna Kournikova fans. (2001). *CNN.com.* Retrieved May, 2007, from http://archives.cnn.com/2001/TECH/internet/02/12/anna.worm/index.html

Plous, S. (1993). *The Psychology of Judgment and Decision Making.* New York: McGraw-Hill.

Rusch, J. (1999). The "Social Engineering" of Internet Fraud. *INET '99.* San Jose, California.

Shankland, S. (2006). HP chairman: Use of pretexting 'embarrassing'. *CNET News.com* Retrieved May, 2007, from http://news.com.com/HP+chairman+Use+of+pretexting+embarrassing/2100-1014_3-6113715.html

Silltow, J. (2001). Social Engineering, Part 1. Retrieved April, 2007, from http://www.theiia.org/ITAudit/index.cfm?act=itaudit.archive&fid=339

Stiff, J. B., Kim, H., & Ramesh, C. N. (1992). *Truth Biases and Aroused Suspicion in Relational Deception. 19*(3), 326.

Tversky, A., & Kahneman, D. (1974). Judgment under Uncertainty: Heuristics and Biases. *Science, 185*(4157), 1124.

Twitchell, D. P. (2006). *Augmenting Detection of Social Engineering Attacks Using Deception Detection Technology.* Paper presented at the International Conference on i-Warfare and Security, Princess Anne, Maryland.

Whiteside, T. (1979). *Computer Capers: Tales of Electronic Thievery, Embezzlement, and Fraud*: Sidgwick & Jackson.

KEY TERMS

Modality: The type of media used to communicate during a social engineering attack.

Penetration Testing: Use of active hacking techniques to test the effectiveness of information security controls.

Phishing: Using fraudulent emails to direct users to websites that mimic valid websites in order to obtain private information.

Proximity: The closeness of parties to a communication.

Social Engineering: The exploitation of psychological triggers and cognitive biases as a means to gain unauthorized access to information or information systems.

Synchronicity: The turn-taking nature of communications. Synchronous communication requires immediate feedback while asynchronous communication allows time to pass between turns.

Targeting: The extensiveness of the pool of potential targets in social engineering attacks.

Chapter XV
Social Networking Site: Opportunities and Security Challenges

Tom S. Chan
Southern New Hampshire University, USA

ABSTRACT

Social networking has become one of the most popular applications on the Internet since the burst of the dot-com bubble. Apart from being a haven for teenagers and online marketers, social networking sites are increasingly adopted by the corporate community. The trend makes viable many new business models and applications. The popularity of these sites has altered the way society interacts, but it also greatly heightened the threats of cyber crime. Safety and crime issues aside, the massive amount of user-generated content in these Web 2.0-enabled social networking sites are becoming fertile grounds for viruses. Furthermore, these sites pose great challenges on how to protect copyrighted works as they are havens for digital content sharing. Society must learn to balance the benefits of social networking with its drawbacks as the phenomenon is an inescapable global trend, expanding at the speed of light.

INTRODUCTION

A social networking site is a category of websites with user profiles and persistent public commentary forming a traversable networked virtual community. A user profile contains identifiable information about the participant, such as, age, gender, interests and etc. The profiles have unique URLs that can be visited directly. Site visitors can also post comments or other information for everyone to see. Network participants have the ability to list other profiles as "friends", link to friend's profiles, and see comments posted by others. The comments are semi-permanent because they may disappear over a period of time or upon removal. All of the above functions generate a virtual network for social interaction where each node contains a link to the profile of the other person so that individuals can traverse the network through friends of friends.

Social networking sites bring people together in a virtual community to talk, gossip, exchange ideas, share interests and making new friends. The sites typically provide tools for posting messages, sharing photos and creating personal pages. The Internet is made of people, and people are social by nature. Embraced mostly by teenagers and young adults who find it irresistible, MySpace.com, a social networking site, launched only four years ago is now one of the world's most popular. In U.S., it ranks second only to Yahoo in page views, drawing almost 5% of all site visits, ahead of even Google, which drew only a little over 4%. According to a recent web metrics report (Tatham, 2006), one in every twenty U.S. Internet visits went to one of the top twenty social network sites in September 2006.

The popularity of social networking has altered the way society interacts, but it also greatly heightened the threats of cyber crime. Safety issues aside, the massive amount of user-generated contents in the Web 2.0 enabled sites are becoming fertile grounds for viruses. Furthermore, these sites pose great challenges on how to protect copyrighted material as they are now havens for digital content sharing. Society must learn to balance the benefits of social networking with its drawbacks as the phenomenon is an inescapable global trend, expanding at the speed of light.

Social Network Theory and Social Network Analysis

"Social network", a term coined by J.A. Barnes (1954), represents a web of relationships and flows between people, groups, organizations, animals, computers or other information processing entities. Social network theory differs from traditional sociological studies. In traditional theories, attributes of individual actors are assumed to matter the most. Social network theory takes a different approach, where individual attributes are less important than their relationships and ties with others within the network. Social network theory in Social Sciences began with the urbanization studies of the Manchester School (Barth, 2005). Started as an attempt to quantify social relationships, social network theory has been helpful in explaining many real life phenomena, from the success of individual business to the rise of political powers, and from the process of how juries reach consensus to the decision that countries pattern their trade.

Social network theory, deeply rooted in Sociology, has recently found a home in many business applications. Social network analysis helps us to understand the dynamic of informal networks. Social network analysis theory views social relationships in terms of nodes and ties. Nodes are individuals within the networks, ties are the relationships between the individual, and a social network is a map of all of the relevant ties between the nodes being studied (Scott, 1991). The International Network for Social network Analysis, http://www.insna.org/, is an academic association of social network analysts. New visualization tools are constantly being developed and many are available online for scholars to study the patterns of complex social interaction using graphical images of network models. A social networking service is a website specifically focused on providing and supporting online social networks for whatever purpose. As of April 2006, social networking sites claim an estimate of 68.8 million unduplicated unique participants, reaching 45% of active web users (Nielsen, 2006).

A Short History of Social Networking Site

Hammersley (2003) noted, "Given the right knowledge of the people between us, I could probably plot a chain of people between myself and you, wherever you are. If such information was available, and it turned out it might be advantageous for us to chat, then we could ask each of the middlemen in turn for an introduction and get on with it. Or we could skip the middle guys altogether. That's the idea of the growing number of social network sites on the net today."

The non-digital form of social networking has existed as long as human civilization. As the cliché goes, "It is not what you know, but who you know". The Small World Theory, or the Six Degrees of Separation, speculates that there are only six degrees, or levels, of separation between a person and everybody else in the world (Barabasi, 2003). A degree of separation is defined as an acquaintance or friend who separates one from someone else. Thus, zero degree of separation exists between one and one's immediate friends. It is a common human practice to use a network of friends to exchange information, enhance job prospects, or further one's career. With advent of the Internet, it is only natural that the traditional social network ceded the spotlight to digital social network, from contacting friends who might be able to help nearby, to friends in a broader sense on the Internet, i.e., the ultimate "network of networks".

Emerging technology always affects the society around it, and social networking site carries no exception. As technologies become more dynamic and participative, the social networks form around these communication channels also become more complex. The Internet can trace its roots back to the ARPANET, the first computer-mediated communication networks developed in the 1960s (Wellman, et al., 1996). The earliest digital social networks emerged on the ARPANET are small tightly-bounded groups making up of specially trained users. In the 1970s, e-mail mailing lists and bulletin board systems (BBS) were some of the pioneer technologies that enable mass social collaboration and interaction online. UseNet and Internet Relay Chat (IRC) extended the concept of messaging and enable newsgroup of users with common interest to dialogue in relatively unrestricted ad hoc manner. UseNet, the first virtual community in existence, was estimated to have over 8.1 million participants in 2000 (Rheingold, 2002). Instant messaging (IM) emerged in 1996, creating an almost synchronous messaging environment by fusing the functionality of real-time chat and e-mail (Huang & Yen, 2003). Unlike the UseNet which restricts membership to a global list, IM empowers users to define and maintain the social networks themselves. IM users maintain a list of people which they have a relation or desire to communicate, and individually, they can negotiate to add new contacts, restrict or remove the addition of one's name to other's list.

The earliest social networking commercial website was launched in 1995 (Wikipedia, 2007). Classmate.com, http://classmates.com/, was the first website that aimed at assisting members to find past friends and acquaintances from school, work and military throughout the U.S. and Canada using the Internet. Members were searchable by name, age, hometown, and institutions. The site provided a vehicle for friends to re-connect and keep-in-touch with tools such as personal websites, message boards and other tools for event planning and email exchange. With the success and growing popularity of Classmate.com, a new movement was spawned towards initiating and cultivating new relationships online. SixDegrees.com, from 1997 to 2001, followed Classmate's lead, but with added dimension of allowing members to meet their friends' friends. Modeled after the "Six Degrees of Separation" concept, members could send and post messages to people in their first, second, and third degrees, and see their connection to any other users on the site. The first site that really garnered popular appeal was Friendster.com, http://www.friendster.com/, launched in 2002, and it was followed by MySpace.com in 2003. MySpace.com allows users to personalize their profiles by uploading photographs and music as well as personalizing the backgrounds of their pages. Catered to teenage population much more effectively than previous sites, MySpace.com has attracted a huge membership from teens and young adults. It has become such a success that the company was acquired by News Corporation for $580 million in 2005 (Carr, 2007).

Most commercial social networking sites allow everybody to join, but some only allow those who are invited by an existing member. In any case, all the sites have certain mechanism to restrict links that are made with existing members. There are several common features in addition to the registration and invitation process. Each new member is asked to provide a profile of who they are: their interests, hobbies, skills, professional affiliations, and etc. The other members may browse through their personal network of linked members, or search for members within the network by any combination of the user-defined demographic and interest criteria. Members can then make inquiries using an internal interface, a form of anonymous messaging supported within the site's communication framework, to negotiate for unknown but potential relations. Increasingly, social networking sites are focused on providing a multitude of web content presentation supports, including journals and ratings; and the presentation of multimedia including graphics, photos, audio and video.

SOCIAL NETWORKING FOR BUSINESSES AND CORPORATIONS

While young people propel MySpace.com to become the most popular website on the Internet, there are now social networking sites for practically every niche. Some are by invitation only, and some are even for very pragmatic and practical purposes. Fueled by a stagnant job market, online business networking has generated serious attentions. A business professional joins a site by creating a personal profile, then e-mail friends and associates inviting them to set up their own profiles. Each person who accepts the invitation becomes a member of the personal social network. As other members solicit their own friends and colleagues to join, the person's network grows exponentially. These sites provide the benefit of an inherent filtering system and personal privacy is somewhat protected as network memberships are by invitation only (Kandra, 2003). Social networking sites are no longer just for making friends and meeting new people. People are using the sites for professional purposes: searching for jobs, making professional contacts, and expanding one's current business reach.

Social networking has profoundly impacted the corporate world, though most of the current hype and attention are focused on individual Internet users. Companies and organizations can capitalize on the growing trend of meeting people and maintaining relationships online just as much as individuals are benefited from using these sites. A recent study showed the top reasons for business blogging included publishing content and ideas, building community, promoting thought leadership, and getting information and feedback quickly to and from customers (Backbone, 2005). Similarly, a corporation can use social networking internally for applicant and staff research, and team build; and externally for the maintenance of business to consumer (B2C) and business to business (B2B) relationships.

The Internet is a public domain. If one can use the Internet to search for information on others, others can also be searching for one's information online. What if those others are law enforcement, principal, parents, spouse and even current and possible future employers? Social networking sites allow users to search for each other once registered and logged into service. Once an individual is found, their pages, posting blogs, pictures, messages and etc., are essentially open for public viewing. Companies can make certain inferences and stereotypes regarding someone's productivity and potential distractions from these materials. While the practice may be ethical questionable, it would be naïve to assume employers are not using them as a source of information on current and perspective employees (Finder, 2006).

The corporate intranet has long established as a platform for team building and delivering updated information to employees (Bansler, et al., 2000). Social networking allows an organization to broaden the scope of their intranets to encompass more interactive activities and streamline their internal business value chain. Connecting employees in a collaborative manner via an internal network can foster trust and reinforce organizational identification. They promote the company culture, organize events to unite employees, and help them connect in new non-work ways, all of which can boost company morale. Multinationals are at the forefront of applying this innovation because they are facing the challenge of connecting thousands of employees worldwide, who are speaking many different languages.

The popularity of social networking sites has made them magnets for advertising dollars. Corporations are constantly looking for the most efficient manner available to build their brand or push a new product. Web advertising now competes head to head with both print and television ads, and is an important component in any overall campaign. Companies are starting to use social networking and blogs as a way to promote their products and services. Some simply send their marketing people online to participate in blogs and social networking sites masquerading as consumers. Such tactic is unwise and can be serious backfired. They are often discovered and reported, and end up causing serious embarrassments and damages to the company's reputation (Barbaro, 2006). Honesty is always the best approach. A company can create its own social networking site, tell consumers who they are and what they want from them. Ask for opinions from visitors and give them current information about the company's products and services. Companies can get plenty valuable feedbacks by telling their potential customers about their products and new ideas in an open forum.

Apart from the traditional empowerment of employees to share their contacts and build relationships outside of the company, some organizations are using social networking sites for "crowdsourcing". Crowdsourcing is a new business model that delegate internal works to the outside of the company. Unlike outsourcing that is typically done by lower paid professionals, crowdsourcing relies on a combination of volunteers and temporary participants who use their spare time to create content, solve problems, or even research and development. For example, corporations can use their social network to outsource a complex scientific challenge facing the company to leading researchers from around the globe. Rather than invest in expensive research and development, the social network allows companies to build upon the previous, current, or future work of experts from all over the world. Potentially, this approach can produce a huge saving in time and money, and to solve even the most perplexing problems (Howe, 2006). Why reinvent the wheel if someone out there already has the answer?

Social networking sites are also becoming a valuable platform for entrepreneurs and professionals to connect with one another to find new partners, suppliers, and ultimately increase their own customer base. Musicians, celebrities, filmmakers, authors and comedians are already using these sites to promote their work and reach a larger audience or reinforce the fan base they already have. Professionals can network online to grow their current business and their own career network. Entrepreneurs can network to compensate for their lack of resources and remain competitive with larger firms. Small businesses can locate potential partnerships, share experiences, and leverage a global network of opinions and advices online. Several niche social networking sites cater just for such purposes. For example, LinkedIn.com (http://www.linkedin.com/) provides the ability for its members to host a "virtual trade show", overcoming the traditional resource barriers for conducting such events for individuals and small business owners.

Popular social networking sites such as MySpace.com are also creating its own ecosystem. Just like EBay, MySpace.com is populated with small businesses that do everything from helping users to decorate their profiles to creating tools that let advertisers target site members (Rosmarin, 2006). Companies are also developing new technology and business model to take advantage of the social networking phenomenon. For example, wallop.com, http://www.wallopcorp.com/, was started as a research project at Microsoft, which provides users a more lively and vivid experiences with Flash-based applications; eSnips.com, http://www.esnips.com/, is a startup social media sharing site where members can share any digital content they want, including photos, video, text and links. Progressively, people will have more options for interacting with other people. Furthermore, devices will automate an increasing variety and amount of intrapersonal communications. These new technologies have already changed the manner in which people meet, share information, do business and organize their lifestyles.

A NEW PARADIGM FOR SOCIAL INTERACTIONS

Social networking sites have a huge impact on the American society. They change the definition of networking, from that of face-to-face interpersonal event, to virtual meeting on the global village. Rather than meeting someone in person with the traditional physical contact, people are now using technology to interact and network from their very own homes anywhere in the world. Without the face-to-face exchanges that are the hallmark of traditional physical social interaction, computer mediated communication is based only on written text. The complexity and diversity of techno-modern life makes it difficult to evaluate the effect of social networking sites on the society. Some scholars believe virtual communities reinforce existing social ties because they enable easy reach to others. At the same time, others worry the reduction of face-to-face exchanges will have a detrimental effect on interactions between people.

Proponents of social networking sites note the many benefits offered by these sites to their users and to the society. These sites provide opportunities for users to meet new people with similar interests, essentially linking members of society together who may never have gotten the chance to interact (Wellman & Gulia, 1999). Social networking sites are not only valuable sources of information. They are also sources for companionship, social support, and most importantly, a sense of belonging. Because social networking sites provide simple and quick access to many people, these sites encourage more interpersonal interactions instead of lessen them. There are other benefits cited by proponents of these virtual communities. For instance, they provide simple and quick access to people and an endless amount of people to reach. Furthermore, relationships and dialogues can be built upon intellect and common interests, without the assumptions and bias of race or gender (Fernback & Thompson, 1995). Finally, these sites provide the opportunity for individuals to express themselves and preserve their uniqueness despite the conformity constraint imposed upon by the physical society. Such freedom of expression is important because liberty, autonomy and selfhood are the bedrock of any free society.

Traditional approaches to community are perhaps inapplicable to virtual spaces, but urbanization and modernization do threaten the traditional patterns of social life (Bender, 1978). While social networking sites allow one to connect with others more conveniently, they could conceivably encourage people to remain in their homes and away from other people. "Mouse potatoes" will replace "couch potatoes" and people will continue to hide from real life. Not only is there a loss of physicality, but the convenience of the Internet will also discourage people to interact face-to-face. Some scholars argue computer mediated communication is not a legitimate way to socially interact. "True" interpersonal communication explicitly reveals emotion. It is not that empathy, tenderness, reassurance, flirtation, sadness or happiness cannot be expressed in written text. Rather, it is the matter of eye contact, body language, facial expressions, vocalization and hugs that would be sorely missing (Nie, Hillygus & Erbring, 2002).

When one talk about networking, one tends to assume that more connectivity at lower costs are always better than less connectivity at higher costs. Such assumption may be incorrect. A lot of low cost friendships might simply means many low quality friendships. The arrival of online social networks has changed the social landscape by creating a new level of social structure. While the long term impact remains to be determined, oversimplifying and exaggerating of any new phenomenon are without exception dangerous. When telephone first became popular, some researchers suggested that people would no longer leave their houses, thus automobile traffic would be reduced dramatically. Yet, it turned out that people would not only use the telephone to call each other; but also to arrange meeting each other physically. It actually increased the level of face to face social activity.

Social networking has become one of the most popular applications on the Internet since the burst of the dot-com bubble. By serving the needs of a specific population, social networking sites enable advertisers to reach niche audiences. But looking beyond banner ads and page views, online marketers see social networks as free focus groups and social networking sites as treasure troves of consumer data. Big players such as Google have started to add social networking applications on top of the existing features, for example, utilizing existing buddy lists and connecting them to profiles. The scope of social networking is expanding at hypersonic speed. While some people may not be technologically savvy enough or feel comfortable enough to network online. The trend setting demographic of 15 to 40 year old, who have spent most of their lives using the Internet, are undoubtedly avid online social network users. It is unavoidable that the society must come to terms with balancing the benefits of such new networking opportunities verse its inherent risks.

Privacy, Web Safety and Cyber Crime

Social networking can create an illusion of privacy where none actually exists. By not really knowing who is watching, one could easily post more information on one's profile than one would otherwise give to a common stranger. This leaves users, especially younger ones, susceptible to those with ill intentions. The phenomenal popularity of social networking sites has greatly heightened the concerns over sexual predators lurking in them. Parents, educators and police have become increasingly worried that teens are finding troubles at these sites. MySpace.com has gotten the brunt of the publicity given its prominent position and with 20% of its members under the age of 18. In June 2006, the mother of a 14-year-old who said the 14-year-old was sexually assaulted by a 19-year-old user sued MySpace.com, seeking $30 million in damages. The lawsuit, filed in a Texas state court, claims the 19-year-old lied about being a senior in high school in order to gain the child's trust; and MySpace.com is not doing enough to protect minors from sexual predators (Rawe, 2006).

Self-reported identity system is often problematic but reliable verification requires expenditures and restricting access results in a smaller user base. For example, a credit card can be used to demonstrate a user's age, but credit verification incurs cost, and not everyone has a credit card. Although more robust techniques can verify user provided addresses, birth dates and other information against public databases, but minors do not possess as many unique identifiers as adults do, and their records are strictly under guard by states and schools for privacy and security reasons. To create a safer environment, social networking sites can restrict access only to those with a valid e-mail address from a school, college or participating company. It can even require parents to submit identity vouching for their children.

On a positive note, social networking sites can be a helpful tool for law enforcement. For example, police officers can set up sting operations by posing as teens that are targeted online by adult predators (Cressman, 2006). The government is also developing new laws regulating these websites. The Deleting Online Predators Act of 2006, or HR 5319, was brought before the U.S. Congress as an amendment to the Communications Act of 1934 (Fitzpatrick, 2006). The statue requires schools and libraries to limit and monitor a minor's access to social networking sites. Ultimately, parents must be proactive, by setting limits on how much time their children can spend on social networking, what activities they can participate in, and what the appearance and messages are in their profiles.

While the dangers minors facing on social networking sites have been well documented, adults' behaviors on social networking sites could also increase their risk of becoming a victim of cyber crime and identity theft. In a recent survey by the National Cyber Security Alliance, 83% adults who use social network exposed themselves to hackers by downloading and opening unknown files from these sites, 74% have given out some sort of personal information such as their email address, name, birthday, and some even their social security number, 57% received unsolicited or phishing emails asking for money, requesting account information, informing users of lottery winnings, or asking users to download a video. Surprisingly, 31% of those who received such emails actually responded to them (Russell, 2006).

In this Information Age, personal information is a highly valued commodity. It is captured and compiled, bought and sold in ways never imagined before. The level of privacy one can expect from offline activities usually is clear from the nature of that activity. Online activities are less obvious. Many users expect their online activities to be anonymous and private. In reality, they are not. Social networking sites are billboards in cyberspace, so it is important to guard one's financial, personal and other sensitive information with extra care. Since it is hard to judge people by self-posted photos or information, one should be cautious about meeting a new cyber friend in person. Social networking sites are fast becoming the hunting ground for criminals to hack into financial records and compromise personal information to commit identity thefts and frauds. For this reason, people need to beware of the scams and con artists lurking in them.

Creating a safe virtual community has its costs and appeals. Managing a limited population and keep them all safe, instead of looking for a million unique members, can be a viable business model. Safety experts warn that creating too many barriers could drive teens to other social networking sites with fewer controls, or perhaps free-for-all chat rooms. Furthermore, ineffective solutions could give parents and children a false sense of security, ending up increase dangers. While technology alone would not be the solution, it could be very helpful in resolving the dilemma. Perhaps some sort of V-chip technology can be devised just as when violence on television was the hot button issue of the day. Other promising technology may involve blog patrol armed with artificial intelligence that scan and approve every posted word. Parents must also get more involved in what their children are doing. In the end, education is the only way that teaches children to be proactive, which will stay with them forever even when social networking is replaced by the next big fad.

Web 2.0, Hackers and Malwares

Safety and crime issues aside, security experts worry the massive amount of user-generated content in social networking sites make fertile grounds for viruses. It may even make such content sharing sites a more common vehicle than e-mail for virus propagation. As users flocked to social networking sites, it is only a matter of time before these sites attract the interest of hackers. In the past year alone, MySpace's visitors have been the repeated target of attacks, falling prey to everything from cross-site scripting (XSS) to phishing. MySpace.com was forced to shut down hundreds of user profiles after a combination worm and phishing attack that compromises the visitor's "About me" page (Kawamoto, 2006). Last fall, the site was hit by the Samy worm, the first attack to exploit a XSS vulnerability (Mook, 2005). This attack highlights the opportunity for a self-propagating worm to take advantage of the XSS technologies. The malicious code injects itself into sites with the aim of being parsed and/or executed by browser or e-mail clients.

XSS is a type of second generation Internet based software coined as Web 2.0, which emphasizes online collaboration and sharing among users (O'Reilly, 2005). Lacking a precise definition, Web 2.0 is an umbrella term uses to describe a number of technologies that empowered websites to be more than just plain, static pages. The key to Web 2.0 is a programming technique called AJAX, or "Asynchronous JavaScript and XML." AJAX enables web pages to render without a complete page refresh by decoupling user interaction with the browser from the browser's interaction with the web server.

AJAX builds web applications by combining Extensible Hypertext Markup Language (XHTML) and Extensible Stylesheet Language (XSL) standards for presentation; and using Extensible Markup Language (XML) and XSL Transformation (XSLT) for data interchange. AJAX follows the Document Object Model (DOM) to interact with items on a webpage by treating the items as platform and language independent objects. Finally, the XMLHttpRequest (XHR) is used by AJAX to establish asynchronous exchange of data to and from the web server using standard Hypertext Transfer Protocol (HTTP) connection; with JavaScript to bind and tie all these components together (MDC, 2007).

In a standard web application, the interaction between browser and server is synchronous. When a user clicks on a link on the browser, a request is sent to the web server. The server then processes the request and sends data back to the browser while the user waits. Under AJAX, the presentation control logic is embedded as JavaScript code in the webpage. When a page is loaded, AJAX handles most of the basic tasks such as data validation, data manipulation and display rendering. Requests from the user does not necessary have to wait for a request respond cycle to the server. If additional data is needed from the server, AJAX will do so using an asynchronous request without the interrupting the user's interaction with the browser. AJAX allows interaction with the browser and user asynchronously and independently; and the transfer of data between browser and server is not dependent upon actions of the user.

While offers richer user experience, AJAX enables XSS attacks that anti-virus software, intrusion detection system and firewall are ill equipped to protect against. One could lose control of one's site in the rush to create an attractive surfing experience. By exploring poorly designed AJAX code, a hacker can initiate XSS by downloading and running script on the victim's browser. The malicious script might steal cookies, launch phishing attacks or even make request as that user. Such XSS attacks can be activated either by a user unwittingly clicking on a fraudulent link or by simple visiting a webpage with embedded malicious code. Typically, a hacker will create multiple profiles and the links on their sites. Each link can take the unsuspected users to sites that will either download or drive-by download the malware. Websites that permit users to manipulate code is inherently flaw and posting a huge security risk to everyone (Kaplan, 2007).

Rich Site Summary (RSS) is another type of XML document which often used to share web contents. RSS has been adopted by news syndication services, weblogs, webcasting and online information services. RSS is thus also known as "Really Simple Syndication". While around for many years, RSS is now quickly gaining momentum due to its active "content-push" technology. It has become a staple of the Web 2.0 pantheon. However, RSS is susceptible to malicious script being embedded in the XML feeds too, particularly for one with a vulnerable feeder (Microsoft, 2006). Users should refrain from routinely accepting feeds, putting the RSS readers in their Outlook, and downloading content automatically into their mailboxes without security control and validation.

While Internet users can protect themselves to some extent using PC security software, such applications are typically effective only after an attack has surfaced as they are mostly signature based system. Firewalls are not designed to prevent software installed internally from doing what it is supposed to. A firewall's function is to keep external intruders out. The ultimate countermeasure against malicious code has to be security awareness and the practice of safe browsing. At a minimal, browser's Internet Security settings should be set to medium or higher with the following options for ActiveX and plug-in objects:

- Disable initialization and scripting ActiveX controls that are not marked as safe
- Prompt signed and disable unsigned download of ActiveX controls
- Prompt running of ActiveX controls and plug-ins
- Prompt scripting ActiveX controls marked as safe

While AJAX makes web pages and sites more interactive, it also opens ways for hackers to hack into a web server, exploit the site and attack its visitors. If enterprises do not demand basic security capability in Web 2.0 applications and do not adapt existing security processes and controls to the new concepts, waves of security incidents and business interruption will wipe out any increase in productivity or customer value provided by the technology. For Web 2.0 developers, they must be careful not to make security an afterthought in the rush to add features and abilities. The key to security is awareness, training and practices. Like all software development, developers should always address security first and build products with the user's best interests in mind.

On a positive note, deploying fixes should be easier in web applications as downloads are automatic and user actions are typically not required. Web 2.0 sites must also be more proactive and work closer with vendors to ensure security, track down problems and get fixes to users promptly. Adjusting to new technology will be invariably challenging. Developers are facing a learning curve as working inside a browser is a departure from the traditional browser/server development environment. Moreover, business adoption could be a slow and long process. While technological savvy users may love the new technology, less experience workers might resist applications that have different controls, layouts, looks and feels (Hoover, 2006).

Copyright in the Age of MySpace.com

New technological developments always pose challenges on how to protect copyrighted works and how to create new business models to deliver those products to consumers securely, conveniently and cost-effectively. Some argue Internet has marked the end of intellectual property and copyright. Countering the trend of downloading illegal copyrighted material on the Web, the Digital Millennium Copyright Act (DMCA) was enacted. The act criminalized both the development and employing hardware or software that cracks digital copy-protection schemes (USG, 1998). While the development of hardware or software may be in itself legal, the action could facilitate others to access materials that are copyright protected, and thus break the copyright laws. Based on DMCA, the Universal Music Group filed a copyright infringement lawsuit against MySpace.com recently, charging that much of MySpace's content is often "user-stolen" intellectual property of others, and MySpace.com is a willing partner in that theft. It alleges MySpace Videos being a vast virtual warehouse for pirated copies of music videos and songs (Leed, 2006).

Some would argue the current copyright laws, such as DMCA, has become outdated as its provisions never addressed the rampant file-sharing taking place across the Internet. The e-commerce paradigm is both an opportunity and challenge to business. While delivering contents via the Internet can be efficient and economical, content owners risk losing control of their intellectual property. Digital content providers, such as the music industry, are reevaluating their business models, opting to move away from a traditional buy-and-own to a pay-per-use model. Any business that wishes to control access to and use of its intellectual property is a potential user of Digital Rights Management (DRM) technologies. The entertainment industry is leading the charge for DRM adoption as a mean to preserve their copyrights.

DRM refers to protecting the copyright of digital content by restricting the actions a recipient may take with regard to the content. DRM gives owners the ability to securely distribute their valued content and to control the use of this content, preventing it from unauthorized distribution. Whether the content is books, photographs, music or video, DRM can be used to manage access and identify content (Russ, 2001). Encryption is used for setting and automatically limiting user behavior. After downloading the content, one may have the right to use the work, but the user has to authenticate his or her legitimacy whenever and wherever the digital content is used. While DRM does not raise privacy issues in itself, to require server authentication each time digital content is accessed can constitute the worst sort of privacy invasion. Information garnered by DRM systems in our highly networked society can be used to build a dossier of user's preferences and usage patterns. Such information could in turn be sold to online marketers or even obtained by the government to keep a tight watch on its citizens (EPIC, 2002).

Information goods are characterized by negligible marginal costs, making the Internet a perfect medium for their delivery. Few would argue against the right of copyright holders to control how their content is distributed and for how much. Social networking sites put the end-user at the center of the digital universe, but those who wish to consume and share digital media are hamstrung by a pre-digital age copyright law and business model. Content owners need to come up with a digital age business model that discourages piracy but does not alienate consumers.

Undoubtedly, social networking sites and media companies stand to benefit by working together. While a reexamination of the DMCA may be in order, government mandates must be fashioned with great care because they may limit the ability of innovators to introduce new technologies as well as the ability of consumers to purchase goods on the free market (McCullagh, 2006).

FUTURE TRENDS AND CONCLUSION

Society is learning to balance the benefits of social networking with its drawbacks. Apart from security risk, potential problems might include loss of productivity at school or workplace and an overall lack of real human interaction. A knee jerk reaction to social networking sites may be to severely restrict its availability, blocking access from the home, school or corporate networks. This reactive solution is only a band-aid on a much larger problem, as resourceful users can always find ways around access restrictions. Moreover, government regulations will unlikely be enforceable as international companies are not abided by American laws assuming the servers are hosted outside of the U.S.

The Metcalfe's law states that the value of a telecommunications network is proportional to the square of the number of users of the system. Metcalfe's Law can be applied to more than just telecommunications devices. It can be applied to almost any computer systems that exchange data, including telephones, facsimiles, operating systems, applications and even to social networking websites. Society's future consists of a vastly expanding landscape of online social networks. The current phenomenon is only at its infancy. As more people participate in these sites, the more powerful they will become. Although most people are aware of the phenomenon, most participants are relatively young. Will social networking persist as these participants grow older, develop professionally, and start families? Is this a phenomenon just for relationship hungry college kids? Such questions remain awaiting for answers. An inescapable reality is that online social interaction forums are not a U.S. specific phenomenon. As popular as these sites are for Americans, they will have equal appeal abroad. Online social networking is a global trend, happening before our eyes, and moving at the speed of light.

REFERENCES

Backbone (2005). *Backbone Corporate Blogging Survey 2005*. Backbone Media, Inc. Retrieved 1/18/07 from http://blogsurvey.backbonemedia.com/archives/2005/06/_not_a_factor.html

Bansler, J., Damsgaard, J., Scheepers, R., Havn, E., & Thommesen, J. (2000). Corporate Intranet Implementation. *Journal of the Association of Information Systems*, 1(10), 1-39.

Barabási, A.-L. (2003). *Linked: How Everything is Connected to Everything Else and What It Means for Business, Science, and Everyday Life*. New York, NY: Plume.

Barbaro, M. (2006). Wal-Mart Enlists Bloggers in Its Public Relations Campaign. *New York Times*, March 7, 2006, Section C, Page 1, Column 2.

Barnes, J. A. (1954). Class and Committees in a Norwegian Island Parish. *Human Relations*, 7, 39-58.

Barth, F. (2005). The Golden Age, 1945-1970. *One Discipline, Four Ways: British, German, French, and American anthropology*, 32-43. Chicago, IL: University of Chicago Press.

Bender, T. (1978). *Community and Social Change in America*. Baltimore, MD: Johns Hopkins University Press.

Carr, D. (2007). Case Dissection: Inside MySpace. *Baseline Magazine*, 68, 34-49

Cressman, Joe (2006). Elmhurst Police Logging on to Catch Predators. *Liberty Suburban Chicago Newspapers,* November 22, 2006. Retrieved 2/18/2007 from http://www.libertysuburban.com/story.php?pub=4&sid=72741#

EPIC (2002). *Letter to House Judiciary Subcommittee on the Courts, the Internet, and Intellectual Property.* The Electronic Privacy Information Center and the Electronic Frontier Foundation, June 5, 2002. Retrieved 2/16/2007 from http://www.epic.org/privacy/DRM/hjDRMltr6.5.02.html

Fernback, J., & Thompson, B. (1995). *Computer-Mediated Communication and the American Collectivity: The Dimensions of Community Within Cyberspace.* Paper presented at the annual convention of the International Communication Association, Albuquerque, New Mexico.

Finder, Alan (2006). When a Risqué Online Persona Undermines a Chance for a Job. *New York Times*, June 11, 2006, Section 1, Page 1, Column 1.

Fitzpatrick, Michael (2006). *HR 5319 IH, the "Deleting Online Predators Act of 2006".* The US. Congress. Retrieved 2/16/2007 from http://www.techlawjournal.com/cong109/bills/house/hr5319/hr5319ih.asp

Hammersley, Ben (2003). Click to the clique. *The Guardian*, January 9, 2003. Retrieved 2/10/2007 from http://technology.guardian.co.uk/online/story/0,3605,870848,00.html

Hoover, N. (2006). MySpace Beefs up Security. *InformationWeek*, 1119, 31.

Howe, J. (2006). The Rise of Crowdsourcing. *Wired Magazine*, *14*(06). Retrieved 1/18/07 from http://www.wired.com/wired/archive/14.06/crowds.html

Huang, A., & Yen, D. (2003). Usefulness of Instant Messaging among Young Users: Social vs. Work Perspective. *Human Systems Management*, 22, 63–72.

Kandra, A. (2003). Social networking Sites are Hot, and They can be Useful Business Tool. *PCWorld Magazine*. Retrieved 1/18/07 from http://www.pcworld.com/article/id,113738-page,1/article.html

Kaplan, D. (2007). Web 2.0, Emerging Threats. *SC Magazine*, *18*(2), 25-29.

Kawamoto, D. (2006). *Worm Lurks behind MySpace Profiles*. CNET News, July 18, 2006. Retrieved 2/16/2007 from http://news.com.com/Worm+lurks+behind+MySpace+profiles/2100-7349_3-6095533.html.

Leeds, J. (2006). Universal Music Sues MySpace for Copyright Infringement. *New York Times*, November 18, 2006, Section C, Page 3, Column 2.

McCullagh, D. (2006). *Congress Readies Broad New Digital Copyright Bill.* CNET News, April 23, 2006. Retrieved 2/16/2007 from http://news.com.com/2100-1028_3-6064016.html

Microsoft (2006). More on Feed Security. *Microsoft Team RSS Blog*. Retrieved from http://blogs.msdn.com/rssteam/archive/2006/09/09/747111.aspx

Mook, N. (2005). *Cross-Site Scripting Worm Hits MySpace*. BetaNews, October 13, 2005. Retrieved 2/16/2007 from http://www.betanews.com/article/1129232391

MDC (2007). *AJAX Getting Started.* Mozilla Development Center. Retrieved 2/16/2007 from http://developer.mozilla.org/en/docs/AJAX:Getting_Started

Nie, N., Hillygus, D., & Erbring, L. (2002). Internet Use, Interpersonal Relations, and Sociability. *The Internet in Everyday Life*, 215-243, Oxford, UK: Blackwell.

Nielsen (2006). *Social networking Sites Grow 47 Percent, Year over Year.* Nielsen/NetRatings Inc., Press Release: May 11, 2006.

O'Reilly, T. (2005). *What Is Web 2.0, Design Patterns and Business Models for the Next Generation of Software*. O'Reilly Associate. Retrieved 2/16/2007 from http://www.oreillynet.com/pub/a/oreilly/tim/news/2005/09/30/what-is-web-20.html

Rawe, J. (2006). How Safe is MySpace? *Time Magazine,* 168(1), 43.

Rheingold, H. (2002). *Smart Mobs: The Next Social Revolution*. Cambridge, MA: Basic Books.

Rosmarin, R. (2006). The MySpace Economy. *Forbe Megazine*. Retrieved 1/18/07 from http://www.forbes.com/digitalentertainment/2006/04/07/myspace-google-murdoch-cx_rr_0410myspace.html

Russ, A. (2001). *Digital Rights Management Overview*. SANS Information Security Reading Room, July 26, 2001. Retrieved 2/16/2007 from http://www.sans.org/reading_room/whitepapers/basics/434.php

Russell Research (2006). *CA/NCSA Social networking Study Report*. CA and the National Cyber Security Alliance. Retrieved 2/16/2007 from http://staysafeonline.org/features/ncsalibrary.html

Scott, J. (1991). *Social network Analysis: A Handbook*. New York, NY: Sage Publications.

Tatham, M. (2006). *One in 20 US Internet Visits Went to Social networking Websites*. Hitwise. Retrieve 2/16/2007 from http://www.hitwise.com/press-center/hitwiseHS2004/us-08112006cgm.php

USG (1998). *The Digital Millennium Copyright Act of 1998*. US. Copyright Office, Pub. 05-304, 112 Stat. 2860.

Wellman, B., Salaff, J., Dimitrova, D., Garton, L., Gulia, M., & Haythornthwaite, C. (1996). Computer Networks as Social networks: Collaborative Work, Telework, and Virtual community. *Annual Review of Sociology, 22*, 213-239.

Wellman, B., & Guila, M. (1999). Virtual Communities as Communties: Net Surfers don't Ride Alone. *Communities in Cyberspace*, 167-194. London, UK: Routledge.

Wikipedia (2007). *Social network*. Wikipedia. Retrieve 2/16/2007 from http://en.wikipedia.org/wiki/Social_network

KEY TERMS

Cross-Site Scripting (XSS): Cross-site scripting is a type of computer security vulnerability typically found in web applications which allow code injection by malicious web users into the web pages viewed by other users.

Digital rights management (DRM): Digital Rights Management is anti-piracy technology that allows digital copyright owners to control who and how gets to access and copy their work.

Instant Messaging: Instant messaging is the ability to exchange messages in real time with others over the Internet. Typically, it requires one to be connected to the Internet and with access to instant messaging software.

Social Network: Social networks are a way to describe systems as composed of multiple elements. Each element, or node, may or may not have a relationship with the other nodes. The most common social network is a node of people and relation between them.

Social Network Analysis: Social Network Analysis is the techniques used to study social networks. While traditionally sociologists focus on the individual elements in their study, social network analysis emphasizes more on relations between individuals.

V-Chip Technology: V-chip is a technology that blocks objectionable television for younger viewers. The V-Chip reads information encoded in the rated program and blocks programs from the set based upon the rating selected by the parent.

Virtual Community: An online or virtual community is the gathering of people, in an online virtual space where they come, communicate, connect, and get to know each other better over time.

Web 2.0: Web 2.0 is based on the idea of the Web as a platform. Instead of thinking of the Web as a place where browsers viewed data through small windows on the readers' screens, the Web was actually the platform that allowed people to do things.

Section III
Security Education and Awareness

Chapter XVI
Designing Antiphishing Education

James W. Ragucci
Syracuse University, USA

Stefan A. Robila
Montclair State University, USA

ABSTRACT

Fraudulent e-mails, known as phishing attacks, have brought chaos across the digital world causing billions of dollars of damage. These attacks are known for their ability to exploit the human aspect of a computer system by pretending to originate from a source trusted by the victim. While technology defenses have been setup for protection, people are still succumbing to these attacks at alarming rates. Therefore, educational techniques must implement to strengthen the human factor of security. We propose the use of a phishing IQ test that when used in classroom setting can help users build experience needed to identify phishing e-mail during their daily routine.

INTRODUCTION

Phishing is generally described as sending computer users messages claiming to originate from a legitimate entity and attempting to lead the user to provide private information that will be further used for identity theft ("Phishing," 2006). While the nature of the message (and the purported originating entity) varies from with each individual attack, one can notice that the entities continue to diversify and that the sole number of such attacks is staggering. A brief review of phishing related news for the first seven days of November 2006 in chronological order is shown in Figure 1. Such bleak reality is shared by professional reports that suggest that the number of reported phishing attempts has almost doubled between August 2005 and August 2006 ("Phishing Activity Trends Report - September 2006," 2006).

Faced with an increasing threat, software companies, federal agencies, financial and commercial institutions and internet service providers have increased their antiphishing efforts. Statistics are now being compiled monthly monitoring the threat level, and repositories of phishing events have been created (and are publicly available). As the variety of phishing techniques increase, more defense tools/methods are developed. In recent versions of the internet browsers, 'anti-phishing' filters are provided (an application component that checks the website against a list of known phishing sites) (Microsoft, 2006). Log-in procedures have been revamped by requiring multi-step authentication and changing challenge-response pairs (Schechter, Dhamija, Ozment, & Fischer, 2007). Despite all this effort from the IT world, people continue to fall victim to phishing tactics. It is therefore necessary to improve upon previous methods of education to help protect an increasingly vulnerable population. Thus, we present an educational method that can be used to help teach users how to protect themselves from phishing associated identity theft. To better understand how to identify a phishing attack, people need to learn how and why phishing works. Hence, it is imperative to show the reasons phishing is so successful as well as why it has become one of the top cyber threats of the new millennium. With this knowledge people should be able to see their own mistakes in phishing identification and be able to reduce the problem.

In the following, we start by providing a survey of the 'state of the art' in phishing. Next, we describe the current phishing education strategies we developed and implemented. The educational method includes phishing detection tests, as well as an education session that starts by defining the threat and builds that knowledge into means for phish identification. The education module has been already administered to approximately 120 undergraduate students at Montclair State University. Survey results indicate an increased awareness of the issue and an increased ability to detect phishing attempts.

IDENTIFYING THE THREAT

The Diversity in Phishing

The increase in phishing attacks and their diversity can be explained by several factors. First, more and more of the day to day human activities are done online, therefore increasing the number of opportunities for accessing private data. Second, phishing remains an effective attack due to the relatively high response rate from the victims, Third, as online applications themselves diversify, so do the phishing tools. We will next look at some of these factors.

Why Do People Respond to Attacks?

Dhamija et al. surveyed 20 participants in order to determine a reason for why people fall prey to phishing attacks. They categorized three general reasons for phishing success: *lack of knowledge*, *visual deception* and *bounded attention*. When analyzing *lack of knowledge*, one can decompose it into lack of computer system knowledge, lack of knowledge of security and security indicators, lack of knowledge of web fraud, and erroneous security knowledge (Dhamija, Tygar, & Hearst, 2006). This ignorance of security leads to poor decisions when using the internet that can endanger a user's own data. In one situation, Dhamija et al. describes a participant who used her actual username and password to test if the website in question was truly the authentic website. Her logic was that passwords are not as harmful as financial information for phishers to acquire (Dhamija et al., 2006).

Visual cues are also enough to convince a weary user that a website is legitimate or fake.

Figure 1. Survey of phishing related news for the first week of November 2006

- November 1 – Dekalb Medical Center warns its employees of a phishing e-mail that is being sent around the hospital telling employees that they have been fired and they need to check their job status. By going to the website in the e-mail employees unknowingly downloaded a trojan keylogger. (Garretson, 2006)
- November 1 – A California man was re-arrested after being accused of stealing identities of AOL users with phishing tactics. ("Accused AOL Hacker Arrested After Months At Large," 2006)
- November 2 – Softscan reports spam levels rose sharply in October to account for over 89% of the email sent out that month. Within the spam messages, phishing still remains a viable threat. (James, 2006)
- November 2 – The Department of Veterans Affairs (DVA) claims that a stolen laptop containing personal data of millions has been recovered. Unfortunately, DVA is unsure if the data on the laptop was compromised. As a precaution they issued a warning to veterans whose data was on the laptop, to be on to lookout for targeted phishing attacks that may have been generated from their data.(Kent, 2006)
- November 2 – Christian Aid, an international UK based charity agency, issues a warning to its supporters of a fraudulent donation seeking e-mail. ("New warning about fraudulent charity email scams," 2006)
- November 2 – PandaLabs detects and warns of false job offers looking for people to handle wire transfers in exchange for commission. They believe phishers hope to use these 'mules' to help shake the trail of the authorities. ("PandaLabs Warns Users of the Mass-mailing of False Job Offers," 2006)
- November 2 – Better Business Bureau warns Mid-Southerners of a phishing scam from "Heritage Bank." (Hartley, 2006)
- November 3 – The FBI arrests 17 members of an International Phishing gang in Operation Cardkeeper. Arrests were made in both the United States and Poland. (Savvas, 2006)
- November 3 – In an effort to combat phishing, GoDaddy.com announces support of the new Extended Validation (EV) SSL certificate as a way to fight phishing. (DiFalco, 2006)
- November 3 – OpenDNS announced statistics for the first month of its anti-phishing community, "PhishTank". Highlights include 94,602 votes within the month, 7, 312 unique or suspected phishing scams and an average time of 18 minutes to verify a site as a phish. ("OpenDNS Shares October 2006 PhishTank Statistics," 2006)
- November 3 – MSNBC warns of a phish attack in the guise of an IRS refund. (Maranjian, 2006)
- November 4 – eBay announces that to combat phishing they will hide the userID's of bidders who bid over $200 for an item on eBay motors. Only the seller will be able to see who bids on the items. (Steiner, 2006)
- November 5 - CastleCops reports a PayPal phishing e-mail where the phisher disguises the attack as a financial newsletter giving the victim anti-phishing tips (CastleCops, 2006).
- November 6 – PC Tools Limited estimates as the holiday season draws closer, approximately 1 in 10 holiday shoppers who do business online will face some sort of fraudulent internet attack. ("One in 10 Holiday Shoppers Will Face Fraudulent Internet Attacks This Year," 2006)
- November 7 – ITWeek states that 24% of all phishing sites are hosted in the United States. Paypal and eBay are listed as the most popular targets for October. (Nichols, 2006)
- November 7 – The BBC reports a surge in phishing related attacks for the first half of 2006. The number of attacks has shown a 16-fold increase from the previous year causing £23 million worth of financial damage. ("Online Banking Fraud Rises Fast," 2006)
- November 7 – Indiana University researchers announce that per targeted phishing attack approximately 14% of people become victims. This number is considerably higher than the original estimate of 3% a year. (Loechner, 2006)

A poorly made website with numerous spelling errors could easily tip off the most novice user that something is askew. However, obscure details of a well crafted phishing website, with lifted media content like an "animated bear video" in one of the examples tested by Dhamija et al., are enough to lull some people into dropping their guard when examining the websites. This is because some users cannot fathom a phishing attack being detailed. Other visual cues include strategically placed security icons in areas of the webpage near the location they should appear on the web browser (Dhamija et al., 2006).

Evolution and Variation of Attack Strategies

The early roots of phishing traced back to 1996 when hackers coined the term for stealing password from AOL accounts in order to get free internet access (Ollmann, 2004). In the 11 year period since, a variety of methods for creating phishing attacks have been invented and evolved further into more complex attacks.

Basic Phishing Attacks

Simple phishing attacks are conducted with the use a fake website and an official sounding e-mail. To administer these attacks a phisher will use spam tactics to mass mail a database of potential victims. (Berghel, Carpinter, & Jo, 2006) Phishers utilize social engineering techniques as well as URL obfuscation as a way of capitalizing on the reasons that people fall victim to attacks, as mentioned in "Why Do People Respond to Attacks".

Phishing Botnets – Throwing a Larger Net

A botnet is a collection of compromised computers that run a malicious application under a common control ("Botnet," 2006). While botnets have been used for various purposes such as distributed denial of service, spam or misuse of mail relays, reports indicate cases where the end goal was phishing. An analysis of Trojan code by researchers from Tsinghua University discovered some viruses that were in actuality phishing bots attempting to create phishing botnets (Zheng, Xing, Wang, & Duan, 2005). When activated, the phishing botnets send out large numbers of phishing e-mails in an extremely short period of time. The UK experienced this in August 2006 when a botnet containing 20,000 nodes was activated and sent out 8.1 million phishing e-mails in just over a day (Jaques, 2006). This specific attack sent messages disguised as email from NatWest bank and the Bank of Scotland.

Context-Aware Phishing Attacks

When phishing attacks were originally used, they relied heavily on tactics taken from spamming, the general principle being that they need to send out as many phishing messages to as many valid e-mail addresses as possible. If in any given attack 1% of the recipients use the service being spoofed, then the odds of those victims responding to the attack is more likely (Duntemann, 2004). If the accuracy of the attack could be increased while decreasing the range of amount of potential victims, then there is an increased chance in generating a profit from phishing attacks (Ragucci & Robila, 2006b). Furthermore, if the targeted range of e-mail address is decreased, then detection of an attack becomes increasingly difficult.

By first gathering preliminary data on potential victims, a phisher can construct a targeted phishing attack. "Spear-phishing" geared for individual users and "puddle-phishing" geared for companies are both types of attacks that gather information on their victims (Schipke, 2006). Both attacks fall under the category of a targeted or context-aware phishing attacks (Jakobsson, 2005). To the casual observer or nontechnical user, the information required to build a successful context-aware attack might appear near impossible to gain. In reality it is easier than one would imagine. A variety of ways exist for a phisher to acquire this data. In (Ragucci & Robila, 2006b), we mentioned a few of these ways which include data mining of public databases, exploiting browser vulnerabilities, exploiting mentalities of organizations and companies, and taking advantage of the philanthropic nature of people during disasters. Jakobsson (Jakobsson, 2005) also describes monitoring public auctions on eBay as a means to conducting a man in the middle attack.

Philanthropic Phools

Phishers have learned that disasters, whether natural or man-made, create a ideal atmosphere to exploit for their attacks (Ragucci & Robila, 2006b). In the case of Hurricane Katrina, one of the most devastating storms to hit United States in recent times, the Anti-Phishing Working Group (APWG) detected numerous phishing attacks that took advantage of people's generosity in this disaster. These attacks came disguised as appeals from the Red Cross, Salvation Army and other charity organizations ("Phishing Activity Trends Report - September 2005," 2005). Other tragedies that phishers have exploited for personal gain include the Virginia Tech Massacre (Nichols, 2007).

AT&T Speared

In context-aware attacks, phishers need to have advance information about the victim. While in the past methods existed to extract the desired information from an unknowing victim using browser exploits or basic communication with the target, other sources for acquiring the data are emerging. In August 2006, AT&T suffered a security breach that compromised the data of 19,000 customers. Unfortunately for the customers, the breach was only a data reconnaissance phase for an advanced spear-phishing attack. The data stolen encompassed names, e-mail addresses, credit card numbers and other important pieces of information with the exception of social security numbers and birthdays. To fill in the missing information, the phishers laced the stolen data into phishing e-mails. In the eyes of the casual user, these e-mails appeared real. Even advanced computer users with adequate knowledge of phishing have difficulty recognizing these e-mails as fraudulent because of their high quality. (Lazarus, 2006) This phish hatchery of hack and phish attacks could easily be mimicked as data from other organizations is compromised. Thsis is why, with good reason, the Department of Veteran's Affairs issued a phish warning to veterans whose information was contained on the stolen laptop (Kent, 2006).

Technology Defenses and Failures

Because phishing is a problem delivered to victims through technology, it is natural to see numerous groups also using technology as an aid for protecting people from phishing.

Anti-Phishing Toolbar

One commonly proposed defense to phishing is the use of anti-phishing toolbars. An anti-phishing toolbar is a security indicator that generates warnings or displays some sort of security related information on the screen in order to help a user identify a phishing attack. As phishing has become more of a threat, several companies have recently jumped on the bandwagon to produce these toolbars, including the most recent round of the browser wars where anti-phishing toolbars were integrated into the browsers. Despite the effort from these companies, if people do not possess the knowledge of how to properly use these toolbars, then the effectiveness of this security measure is diminished. Furthermore, people who are not aware of the dangers of the internet, including phishing, are not going to seek an anti-phishing toolbar and are very likely to ignore built in browser warnings (Downs, Holbrook, & Cranor, 2006). Wu et al. concluded that users tend to determine a website's authenticity based on web content over use of a toolbar (Wu, Robert, & Simson, 2006). High quality phishing sites, such as those in Wu et al.'s study, showed that even with the toolbar-generated alerts, people still surrender their information to these imitation webpages. Anti-phishing toolbars are also not 100% perfect. Similar to spam filters, anti-phishing toolbars do not identify all phishing attacks. In fact, even the best toolbars may fail to spot over 20% of fraudulent websites used for phishing (Kumaraguru et al., 2007).

However useful anti-phishing toolbars have the potential to be, the fact remains that these toolbars are still software, and as with several other computer programs, they may have vulnerabilities that can be exploited. For instance, the anti-phishing software that Google developed for Firefox was discovered to send some user credentials to the publicly available servers (Claburn, 2007). Additional exploits that have the potential to circumvent phishing toolbar protection include

Page Load Attacks and Content Distribution Network Attacks; both of these attacks are described in detail in (Cranor, Egelman, Hong, & Zhang, 2006).

Certificates and Extended Validation Certificates

Because of the dynamics of both the internet and phishing websites, a perfectly complete phishing blacklist is almost impossible to create. An alternative method is the use of certificates to authenticate websites. Unfortunately, this model has flaws. Many of websites on the internet today do not use certificates authorized by a certificate authority (CA). This is due to the fact certificates from CA's are relatively expensive and public entities do not wish to pay the money for those certificates (Myers, 2007). For example, as of March 2007 Verisign charges $400 for a single year certificate and $1,499 for a one-year Extended Validation (EV) Certificate (VeriSign, 2007). Therefore, people are not aware of the lack of security indicators that browsers give off when a certificate is present. Phishers rely on the fact that the general population is unaware of the lack of security indicators through certificates and therefore only bother to spoof the legitimate sites. The majority of phishing scams make no attempt to use certificates and this would indicate that these attack method is very successful; otherwise, phishers would abandon this attack strategy (Myers, 2007).

One recommendation to help improve the effectiveness of phishing identification with certificates is to make the browser give off more cues to show that a website has a legitimate certificate. EV certificates attempt to apply this idea. An EV certificate is a X.509 certificate that entails a more rigorous background investigation before the CA can issue the certificate. The requirements to obtain an EV are stricter than a regular certificate. An entity desiring an EV must be a legally incorporated body with a registered office. These certificates cannot be issued unincorporated associations, general partnerships, sole proprietorships or individuals (Schneier, 2006). Browsers that support EV certificates will display more information about the certificate than the previous certificates that were available. In the case of IE7, the address bar will turn green and a label will appear that will display either the name of the website owner or the CA. One issue with EV certificates is that small businesses fear that the fact that customers will be afraid to purchase from them because the address bar will not turn green. It is also possible, as seen with regular certificates, that people will learn the indictors are not always reliable and ignore them (Schneier, 2006). In one study that evaluated the effectiveness of EV certificates, researches observed no improvement from EV use (Jackson, Simon, Tan, & Barth, 2007). In fact, they discovered that the group of subjects in their study trained to use IE7 with EV certificates are more likely to categorize real and phishing sites as authentic. Several of these participants relied on warnings generated from EV certificates and anti-phishing toolbars to identify a webpage as a fraud. When these warnings were not generated, users were lulled into a false sense of security that made them think that the website was authentic (Jackson et al., 2007).

Image Site Keys

Image site keys (ISK) are user selected images that are shown to the user upon login to attest that the website is real. The image itself is only known to the user and the entity that the user does business with. If the site key does not appear when the user is logging into the system, then there is a highly probable chance that the website is a phishing attack. The institutions that implement this hope that implementation of the ISK's will curve the fears of using online services caused by phishing. The effectiveness of this security feature was measured in (Schechter et al., 2007).

The researchers had users login to a spoofed version of the website that removed a security indicator each time a user logged in. During one of these logins, the ISK was removed. Of the 60 participants in their study, 97% of them continued to login to the website even after the ISK was removed. Researchers were able to conclude from this that despite repeated instructions from institutions that use ISK's in their login process, a vast majority of banking constituents are still willing to authenticate to the website even in the absence of the ISKs. They do however point out that they selected test subjects who were not security conscious to participate in their study and believe that might have had an effect on the results (Schechter et al., 2007).

What Harm Can Phishing Cause?

Financial Damage

When the topic of phishing damage arises, people tend to think of the monetary harm it causes. In 2003, it was estimated that approximately $1.2 billion was lost due to phishing attacks (Emigh, 2005). Prior to the holiday season in 2006, losses from phishing amounted to nearly $2.8 billion (ICTWorld, 2006). The average person in 2004 suffered $257 in losses compared to $1,244 per victim in 2006 (ICTWorld, 2006). Unfortunately for victims as the amount of damage increase, the amount of money recovered from attacks decreases. Today, the average amount recovered from an attack is about 54% of what is lost; this is a significant drop from 2005 where the average victim was able to recover 80% of phishing loses (ICTWorld, 2006).

Trust Damage

Direct financial damage is the most obvious damage caused by phishing to individual people. However, for businesses it is not the only kind of harm that phishing causes. The indirect losses from phishing are more devastating to businesses than the direct losses. These indirect losses include customer service expenses, account replacement costs and increased online expenses due to lack of trust in online services (Ragucci & Robila, 2006b). The distrust and anxiety have created an increase of false positives in phishing identification among people. For instance, in 2005 it was reported that legitimate html e-mails saw a drop in opening rates of approximately 20-30% (Brandt, 2005). Responses in a 2006 Gartner survey show that 85% of the 5000 questioned delete unfamiliar e-mails without authenticating them first (ICTWorld, 2006). The decrease in trust will only continue as people become more paranoid about suffering financial losses from responding to e-mails.

PREVIOUS WORK IN USER EDUCATION

There is no unique way that humans learn. Various methods and strategies have been developed in order to educate people. Learning the dangers of phishing and how to identify an attack is no exception; a large amount of time and resources have been devoted to developing ways to educate people about the issue.

Educational Websites

With the number of phishing attacks increasing over 271% from October 2004 to November 2006 (see figure 2)("Anti-Phishing Working Group," 2007), the FTC decided to start an identity theft education campaign. Through this program they created the *Fight Back Against Identity Theft* webpage ("Fight Back Against Identity Theft," 2006) that can be used to inform people of the dangers of identity theft. The FTC also partnered with several other government and private organizations, including the Department of Justice, the Department of Homeland Security and the

Anti-Phishing Working Group (APWG) to create an educational website called *OnGuardOnline*, that warns people of the dangers of the internet. The website includes numerous facts about phishing, videos and an interactive e-card that is utilized for educating people how to respond to a phishing attack ("OnGuardOnline," 2006).

Good Guys Pretending to Be Bad Guys

A variety of institutions have attempted to teach their constituents about the dangers of phishing by actually sending them a phishing e-mail first, then alerting them to the fact that they have fallen prey to a phishing attack. Examples of institutions that have adopted such approach include West Point (Ferguson, 2005) and Indiana University (Jagatic, Johnson, Jakobsson, & Menczer, 2005).

The study dubbed the *West Point Carronade* was intended to be a short range exercise conducted solely within the military academy. The goal of the experiment was simple: teach the cadets how vulnerable they can be to a phishing attack without causing harm to the school's network or punishing the cadets. The administrator at West Point sent an e-mail out to cadets that posed as a Colonel who wanted them to log into the system to check their grades. The idea of the e-mail was to exploit the "don't question your order" mentality at West Point. This e-mail was also sent out at the end of the semester when stress was highest among students and concerns for grades would make students overlook simple warning signs that the e-mail was illegitimate. Therefore the timing of this attack was vital to the success of it. In total, there were 512 students randomly selected from the student body of 4,200 people. Of the participants, over 80% of them responded to the attack (Ferguson, 2005).

Indiana University took the proof-of-concept experiment from West Point and exploited a different element of people's trust with the attack: their social networks. By data mining these social networking websites, such as Facebook.com and Myspace.com the researchers at Indiana Univer-

Figure 2. This graph shows the rise in reported phishing attacks to APWG in a 26 month period ("Anti-Phishing Working Group," 2007)

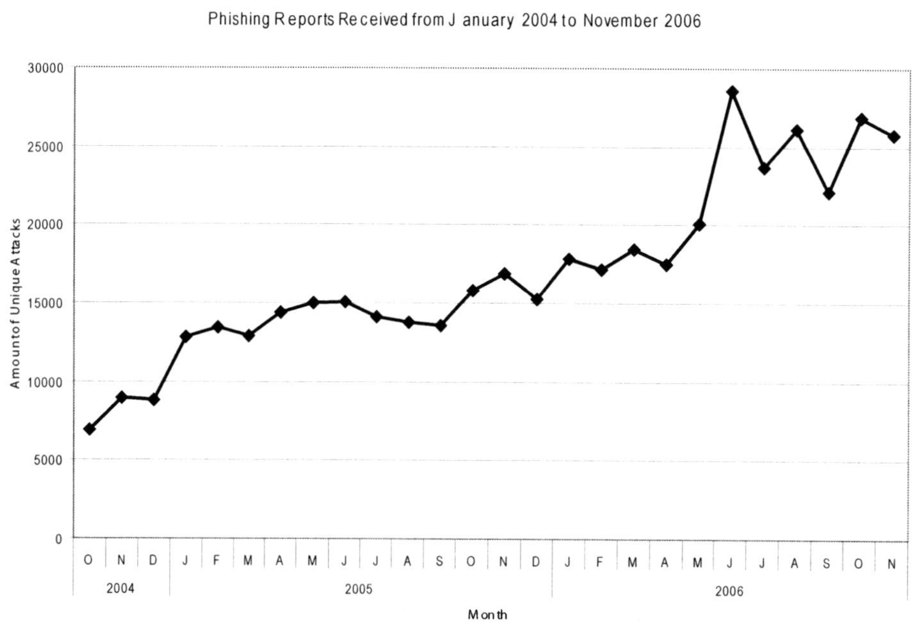

sity were able to map out relationships between their unknowing participants. They were able to use this information to create their own phish database. They focused on two groups for their study. A control case, which received a phishing e-mail from someone they do not know and a context-aware group which received phishing e-mails that were constructed using their phish database. In total, the researchers sent out their own phishing attack to 1,700 unknowing participants that were randomly selected from the student body. The difference in success rates of these two groups varied greatly; the control case had a 16% success rate among participants while the context-aware group had a 72% success rate (Jagatic et al., 2005).

The observations from both of these studies are the same: context-aware and social attacks are extremely successful and can cause people to ignore important clues that may otherwise warn them that they are receiving a phishing attack. In the end of both of these studies awareness of phishing did increase. However, at the end of the day the clearest outcome was university IT departments had to work harder in order to protect the students from phishing attacks. Furthermore, in both cases, use of this scare method created a "Cry Wolf" atmosphere where students lost trust in campus authorities and have the potential to think that future authentic phishing attacks may be the work of their IT department again, causing them to ignore other warning signs and creating more havoc down the road.

An alterative yet similar approach to sending fake e-mails to users is being developed by (Kumaraguru et al., 2007). Parallel to the West Point and Indiana University studies, Kumaraguru et al. focuses on training users to evade phishing attacks by sending them their own phishing e-mails. The different between their work and the aforementioned work in the beginning of this section is that Kumaraguru et al. sends an intervention message to would be victims when they click on the phishing e-mail. In their study, they tested a variety of formats for their intervention messages. This includes a basic security notice intervention, which was a long message that came off as confusing to participants, as many of them were unsure why they were looking at the message as well as didn't scroll down to read the entire warning the security notice provided. The other intervention formats included a short text and graphical message as well as a message that was a comic strip. Both of these formats proved to be more useful to participants as they were now quickly able to read and understand what had happened when they clicked on the phishing attack in the e-mail (Kumaraguru et al., 2007). While this method has the risk of creating a "Cry Wolf" atmosphere that was seen at West Point and Indiana, this study did find a way to preserve the trust between the administrators and the participants while improving the participants knowledge of phishing identification.

Phishing IQ Test

A different approach to educating people how to identify phishing e-mails was developed by MailFrontier. They constructed a phishing IQ test that provides users several legitimate and phishing e-mails to look through. The users were then asked to look through these e-mails and categorize them. When the test was over the user is given a score of how well he or she was able to distinguish between the legitimate and phishing e-mail identification. Results from this Phishing IQ test show that the average user's ability to identify a phishing attack increased in the first year that the test was online; this rose 14 percentage points to an average of 75% of the e-mails identified correctly (Horgan, 2005). A new version of the test was created by Sonicwall using the same quiz style as MailFrontier. Results from this IQ test show that 6.2% of the 755,000 people that have taken the Phishing IQ test have scored a 100%. Furthermore, the results show that 81% of the phishing e-mails are identified correctly whereas 52% of the legitimate e-mails are marked correctly by users ("SonicWALL Phishing IQ Quiz," 2006). This lower outcome of correctly identified e-mails may be a result of users deciding better safe than sorry and marking all e-mails they get as phish(Brandt, 2005).

A CONTEXT-AWARE PHISHING IQ MODULE

A Hybrid Approach

As expressed in "Technology Defense Failures" phishing technologies do not prevent people from handing over their data to phishers. "Why do people respond to phishing attacks" describes, lack of user education is a cornerstone of the success of phishing attacks. People cannot be expected to protect themselves if they do not know what they are protecting themselves from. In addition, even if they have knowledge of the threat, they cannot defend themselves if they do not know how. This lack of knowledge can render technical methods of defense useless. The above section shows various different methods used to educate people how to identify phishing attacks.

MailFrontier and Sonicwall's IQ tests, have a restricted usability in the in the classroom. Given their questions are targeted for the entire country; the questions may appear to be too broad for some people. This broadness makes it very plausible for test takers to have never dealt with the companies being displayed in the questions. This causes problems because of the user's inexperience with the unknown source. In real life, an average person would mark messages from organizations that he or she does not do business with as SPAM, therefore never bothering to verify if the message is legitimate (Emigh, 2005). On the other hand, the experiments conducted by (Ferguson, 2005) and (Jagatic et al., 2005) have a powerful affect on teaching users what to look for, since they used sources familiar to the participants. This approach, although interesting from a research point of view, has a limited affect on education while potentially destroying the relationship between the participants and the administration.

Previously, we explored the issue of user education by creating a phishing lesson plan geared for a targeted group of students (Robila & Ragucci, 2006). This lesson plan implemented a Context-Aware Phishing IQ test, which borrows ideas from the concept of a context-aware phishing attack by gathering information about the target audience and using the information to create a customized phishing identification test that shows users legitimate and phishing e-mails based on companies that they have experience dealing with on a regular basis. The element of inexperience with the source would be eliminated and false classification of e-mails on the test could be attributed to a different set of reasons. These reasons for false identification could include any of the subsequent causes (Robila & Ragucci, 2006): 1) user does not know what phishing is 2) user has knowledge of the issue, but does not know how to identify it and 3) user receives a phishing attack from a source that he or she does not suspect as a likely threat.

In general, there are numerous methods available that will allow one to collect social context information about an individual or group of people. These methods include collecting browser data (through use of the auto-fill properties, browser cache, browser history, etc. – examples of this could be found at ("Stop-Phishing.com(Indiana University)," 2006), exploiting vulnerabilities in browsers (Lemos, 2004), gain access to the user's computer labs and data mine social networking websites (Jagatic et al., 2005).

Customizing the Module for Montclair State University

Using similar techniques to those described above, we designed a customize phishing IQ test with a focus on students at Montclair State University

(MSU). Selecting companies and services that the majority of MSU students use required us to use different methods of data collection in order to meet the specifications addressed above. A significant portion of the data was gathered from the computer laboratory where we later administered our tool, and the campus computer centers. The computers found at those locations underwent browser analysis using resources found at ("Stop-Phishing.com(Indiana University)," 2006). Following this, the browser cache and local history of those computer, was studied to determine if people using these machines visited any other websites of significance. After looking over resources available to students on campus, we added additional websites to this project that used these resources. For example, all the ATM machines on the MSU campus belong to BankX. Because of this, it is logical to presume that a large portion of the student body, if not most of them, have an account with BankX to avoid receiving a surcharge when using the ATM machines.

Once we finished collecting the data of companies and services used by MSU students, we proceeded to create and collect phishing e-mails from various sources including ("Anti-Phishing Working Group," 2007) and ("MailFrontier," 2004). We used these e-mails that we collected to create a Phishing IQ test with 12 questions claiming to originate from financial institutions, social networking sites, web portals, commercial portals, free email providers, wireless phone companies, university and university related sites. Six of the questions in the IQ test are legitimate e-mails and the remaining six are phishing attacks. The survey formed at the end had messages from the following: University registrar (P), Ebay.com (L), BankX (L), University Parking (L), MySpace.com (P), BankY (L), Fastweb.com (L), Amazon.com (P), Paypal.com (P), Yahoo.com (P), Blackboard.com (P), Facebook.com (L) where L and P specify a legitimate or a phishing e-mail, respectively. A sample question is shown in Figure 3 of a phishing attack disguised as MySpace.com e-mail. All the images used in the test can be found (Ragucci & Robila, 2006a)

Beginning with the second administration of the tool, we found it of interest to generate a second version of the test. (For reasoning, see "Educational Appraoch".) As in the first version of the test, we had 12 questions split in half by legitimate and phishing e-mails. The messages given to users in this version were as follows: Facebook.com (P), Yahoo (L), University Parking (L), BankX (P), Gmail (P), Fastweb.com (L), Amazon.com (L), Ebay.com (L), Ebay.com (P), MySpace.com (L), Rave Wireless (P), MSN.com (P).

For the first and second application of our tool, including survey administration and result recording, we used an in-house software package written using JavaScript. In addition, a Sun Solaris box running an Apache Tomcat server

Figure 3. An example phishing e-mail constructed using a confirmation message sent by MySpace.com to a dummy account

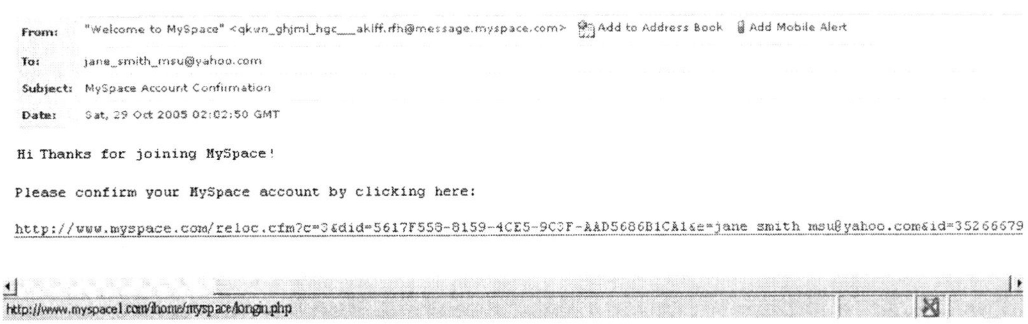

was used to run the software package. During administration, each user would see a single image of an e-mail and would have to classify the e-mail as a phishing attempt or not. Once they selected and submitted their answer, the tool would display the next e-mail in the cycle for the user to classify. Once finished, the software would display a score consisting of the amount of e-mails the user correctly identified. For the third use of our tool, both versions of the IQ test were also ported to a commercial course management system to improve portability.

Educational Approach

Steps in our First Administration

The basic steps we took in educating and testing students about phishing are listed in Figure 4. We began our session by teaching students what phishing is and explaining the implications of a phishing attack. For this step, we started off by giving students a textbook definition of phishing followed by having them look up information about the topic through websites such as APWG, FTC and Wikipedia. Basic facts as emphasized by (Bardzell, Blevis, & Lim, 2007) are taught, including do not click on e-mail or suspicious, do not believe urgent calls to action links and check website for security indicators. Once baseline knowledge was established, we proceeded to discuss the traits of phishing e-mails and the methodologies that are used by phishers to create context-aware messages. With this, we discussed how browser and web vulnerabilities contribute to making these context-aware attacks. A conversation about ways of increasing public knowledge of the phishing followed, which included a debate on aggressive (e-mails used to mimic phishing attacks (Ferguson, 2005; Jagatic et al., 2005)) versus passive (IQ tests("SonicWALL Phishing IQ Quiz," 2006)) educational approaches.

The final two steps in Figure 4 were used to measure the quality of the lesson. For the sixth step an IQ survey was administered to the students per the specifications in the previous section. Step seven was a class assessment survey that gave students the opportunity to rate there feelings on the experience. The overall session is timed to take approximately half an hour. Students were given a control number which they used to show that they took the survey. It is important to note that this number cannot be matched back with the students' answers on the survey, thus preserving anonymity.

Changes Made in Approach of Second and Third Administrations

The results from the first administration are discussed in "Results". We decided to modify the approach of our lesson plan in subsequent applications of our module to better assess how students learned. Given that the average student

Figure 4. Steps used in the first administration of the module (Robila & Ragucci, 2006).

1. Learn what phishing is.
2. Understand the implications of phishing.
3. Discuss the ways phishing can be detected.
4. Discuss the ways phishing information can be collected.
5. Discuss ways to evaluate phishing education.
6. Fill Phishing IQ
7. Discuss general results and evaluate the session.

in the class is assumed not to be from a technical field and not to have any prior knowledge of phishing, we decided to introduce a second version of the module that would be given to students at the very beginning of the session. The new version was given to students prior to step one in figure four. With the addition of the second version we are now able to compare before and after results to measure if our phishing IQ test shows any improvement in helping students better identify phishing attacks. In the subsequent third administration of the tool, we decided to see if how well students were able to retain the knowledge from our lesson after a given period of time. To assess this, we retested students with version one of the quiz a week after the lesson.

Description of the Course

We have currently administered this tool combined with our education strategy a total of three times. Each time we applied our approach, we used two sections of an Introduction to Computing course. The course meets the General Education requirements for computer literacy in a liberal arts college. The format of the course includes one lecture and one lab session every week for a semester. The course lectures are devoted to several different issues in computing including structured programming, computer organization, internet use, privacy and computing ethics. Alternatively, the labs are used to teach basic programming concepts, web development and netiquette. Students who take the course are primarily from non-science majors. Due to spacing limitations, each course section can hold a maximum of 24 students.

Given the arguments provided by (Werner, 2005), it was a natural choice to select the Introduction to Computing course as a target audience for piloting our Phishing IQ test due to the vast majority of students in the course that will have computing knowledge from the point of view of the user. Furthermore, phishing falls under the topic of network security which is one of the topics covered in the course. Lastly, because of the lab component of the course, the educational approach can be administered in a set timeframe with the ability to discuss the general results of the administration afterwards.

RESULTS

First Administration

For the first administration of the phishing module, the 48 students whom attended the session had an average score of 6.87 or 57.29% of the e-mails identified correctly. At this current ratio, for every two e-mails students read they misclassify one. This ratio means that students can either erroneously identify a phishing attack as a legitimate e-mail or legitimate message as a phishing attack.

After looking at the overall scores of the students, we next broke down the results to analyze the results of the correctly identified legitimate and phishing e-mails. Users were able to correctly identified 60% of the six legitimate e-mails on the test compared to the 53% of the six phishing e-mails that were classified correctly. Among the messages in the module, the legitimate message from Fastweb.com was the highest correctly identified e-mail of all the legitimate messages, with a rating of 81%. The authentic e-mail from BankX had the lowest correct identification, only correctly identified 50% of the time. Contrarily, the phishing e-mail that was misidentified the most was a message disguised as a message from MSU's registrar office (35%), while the phishing e-mail most recognized as fraud was another one built from scratch asking students to check their grades on Blackboard.com (75%). It should be noted that at the time the module was administered, MSU revealed that a large amount of personally identifiable information for students was accidentally made available to the public, increasing the risk of identify theft amongst undergraduates. We believe that because students knew of this incident, it affected their decision process in classifying this e-mail. An attack like this would have been hazardous on the student population with a 65% success rate. It should also be noted that approximately a month after this module was used in the classroom, the university sent out a legitimate version of the message to students.

Second Administration

As stated above, a second test was administered to students to help us measure improvement in student's ability to identify phish. Based on the numbers, we were able to see that the average score after the exam rose from 59.2% to 59.4%. We acknowledge this is small. Further breakdown of the results shows that after our lesson students were more likely to have a false negative than prior to it. Figure 5 shows that students were 2.4% more likely to identify a legitimate e-mail correctly after our education module. However, as seen in Figure 6, respondents' ability to correctly identify a phishing e-mail slightly declined by approximately 1.9%.

Third Administration

In the third semester administration of our phishing IQ test in an educational setting, we had students retake the first survey a week later to measure how well students retained what they were taught. Through this administration of the module, we were able to see a larger improvement among students than in the second administration. The average of the 44 students who took the test before they received any knowledge about the subject was rather low; the majority of the students had a score of seven or below with a class average of 50%. After completing the session on phishing, the students showed improvement with a new average score of 53.3%. By looking at the graph in Figure 7, one can see that the general bell curve shifted towards the higher scores in the immediate after test. The week after test results show an increase in the overall average with a class average of 54%. One should note a few absences occurred this day, therefore the number of the students present during the week after retest is not the same. However, when directly compared to the original test given before students had any knowledge on the topic, an increase is seen. Comparably, the students are still retaining the

Figure 5. Percentage of correct and incorrect identification of phishing emails a) Before administration, b) After administration

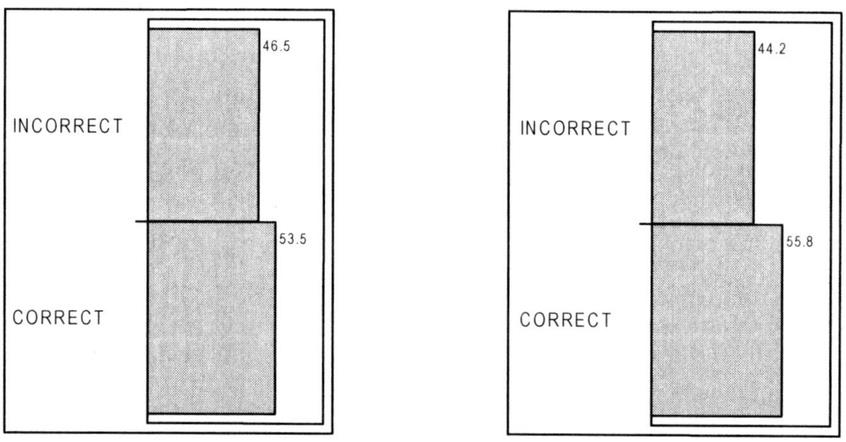

a) b)

Figure 6. Percentage of correct and incorrect identification of legitimate emails a) Before administration, b) After administration

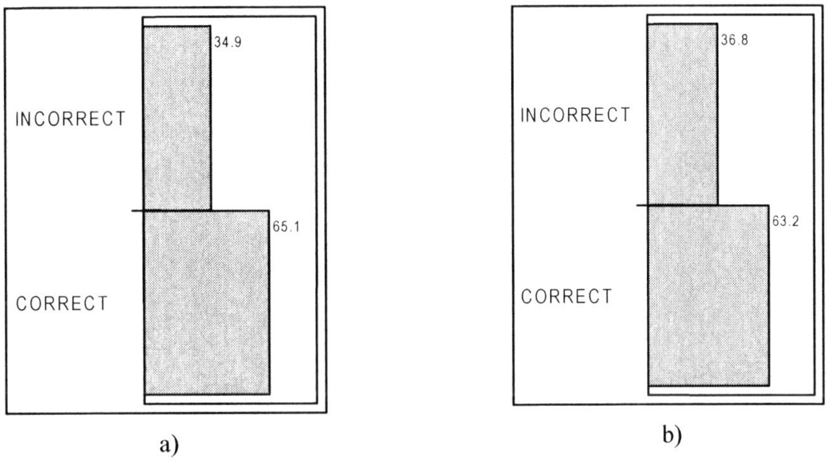

Figure 7. These graphs illustrate the results of the third administration of the tool. The numbers over each bar are the percentage of respondents that received that particular score.

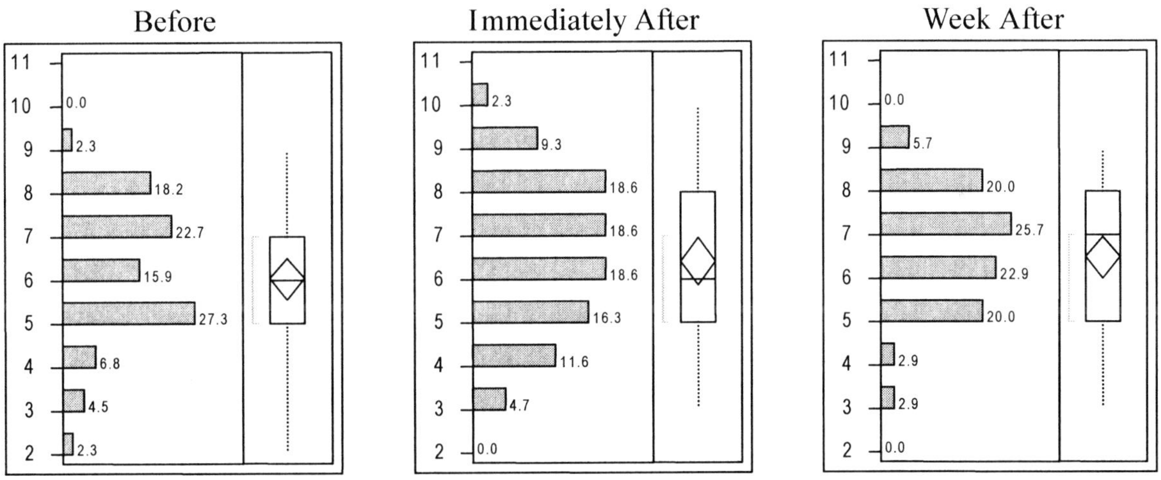

knowledge gained during the lesson. Upon classification of the survey questions, results show an overall improvement between the before and after tests for both legitimate and phishing e-mails. Correct responses to legitimate message went up 3.7% while phishing attackers were identified correctly 2.3% more after the educational lesson than before.

We note that all three administrations were done as anonymous surveys without the students' responses being correlated to a grade value. As such, it is possible some of the students may have provided frivolous or random answers to the tests. To reduce this possibility, we intend future sessions to have the first test as an anonymous survey to be used for training while the second and third will be graded based on correctness and used for assessment.

Educational Assessment Results

The final step in our educational module included an assessment of the activities. This took shape as an additional anonymous survey that was kept the same throughout the three semesters the module was used. We noticed during each semester we administered this lesson, the amount of students who claimed not to know of phishing before our lesson slowly decreased. In the year that we have implemented this lesson, the respondents who were unaware of phishing dropped from 78% to 70%. Neglecting this drop, 91% of the students between all three semesters believe they have received a possible phishing e-mail in the past and an average of 37% of them believe they succumbed to those attacks in the past.

The questions asked in Figure 8 and 9 are instances we used to test students understanding of social context factors being used to generate a phishing attack. As seen in the figures, the majority of students would still consider messages from friends to be authentic. There is a minority that has second thoughts on the issue (on average about 38%). About 75% of the students are now aware of the vulnerabilities that can be used to refine a phishing attack with browser data (see Figure 7). Overall, the students were able to agree that attending the session on phishing helped them become more aware of the dangers on the internet (Figure 10) and, specifically, they found the phishing IQ test as a useful tool to help them understand the topic (Figure 11).

Through the discussions we have had with the students, we found the majority of them place a large amount of trust in social networking websites as well as educational institutions. From this, many students were shocked to learn that attacks from e-mails disguised to originate from these entities are potential hazards they could face in their daily routine.

FUTURE TRENDS

Phishing attacks will continue to evolve and expand as phishers utilize new methods of contacting victims. During the time period we wrote this chapter, we received a phishing attack through use of cell phone text messaging. The message was sent from an IP phone number; it informed

Figure 8. Information stored by the Internet browser can be used to refine a phishing attack

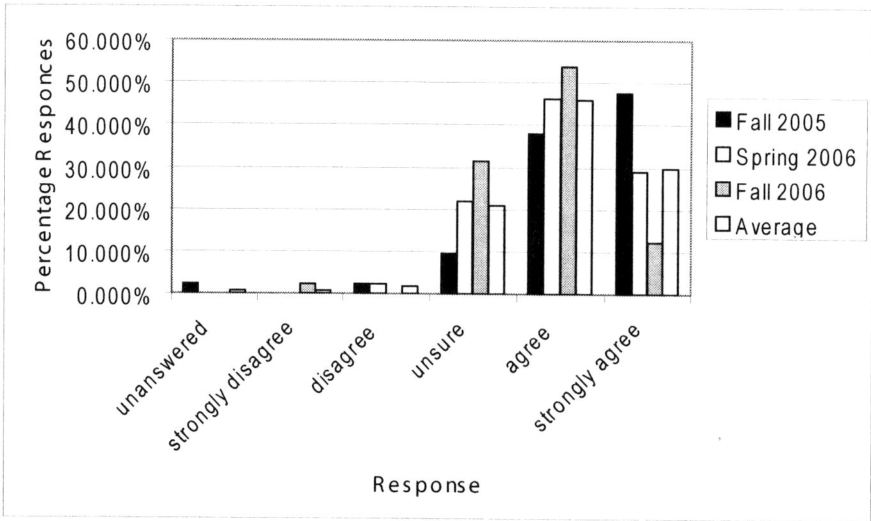

Figure 9. Receiving a message from a friend makes me less likely to assume it is a phishing attempt

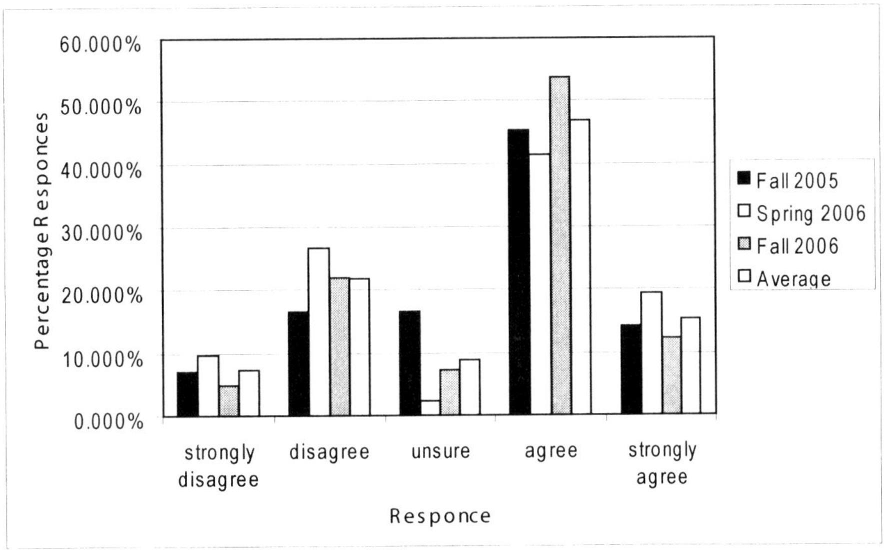

Figure 10. Attending this lab made me more informed about phishing and less likely to fall prey to such an attack

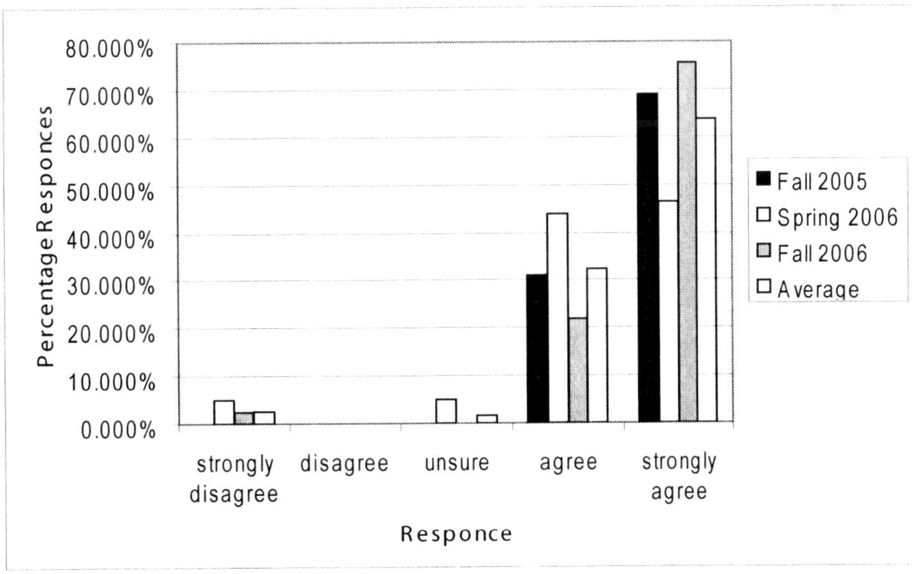

Figure 11. The surveys with examples of phishing were helpful in understanding the Topic

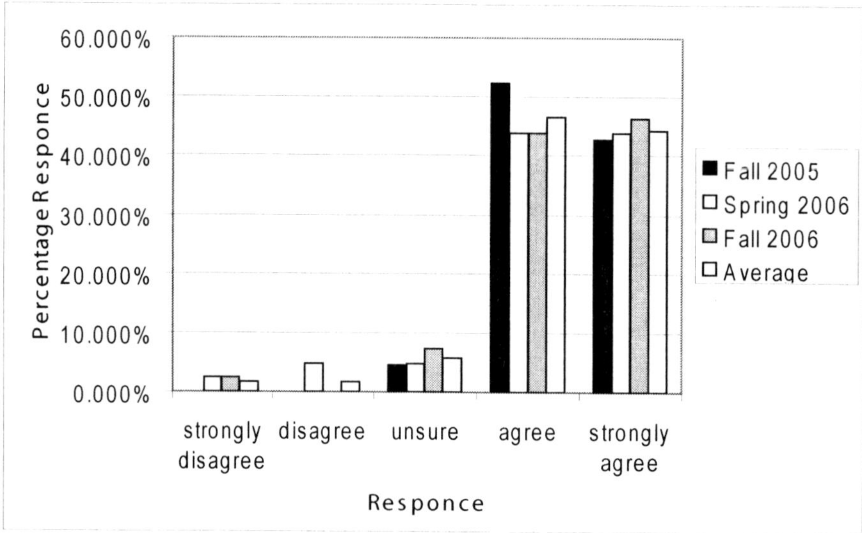

us that we have exceeded our text messaging quota and we should call their toll free number that was supplied in the text message to upgrade the phone plan. Other mediums phishers are making use of to lore victims include the creation of fake weblogs. These phishing weblogs can install Trojan Viruses to redirect users to phishing websites (Evers, 2007). These future trends show that the phishing phenomenon is continuously changing and, as such, require continuous effort in education.

CONCLUSION

Advances in computer and transmission technologies are currently revolutionizing the way we communicate as humans. In many aspects, electronic mail has replaced the traditional mail as a faster and more convenient communication tool. Many individuals and institutions are already using email as the only communication mechanism. While trust in communication is an important aspect of any human's social interaction, providing mechanisms to ensure trust in electronic mail is becoming increasingly important. Phishing is one aspect of trust abuse. Victims respond to phishing attacks mainly because they trust the source of the message to be authentic. In an increasingly electronic world, being able to identify the trusted partners is essential. As such, educating internet users on phishing is worthwhile.

Our educational approach focuses on both the complex aspects of efficient phishing as well as on user training. The module includes two phishing IQ tests customized to the local institution together with supporting discussions and materials on email harvesting, browser reconnaissance and social phishing. The IQ tests are administered anonymously throughout the module. The results obtained suggest an increased ability to discern phishing attacks from legitimate emails. Assessment questions also indicate that education on phishing is needed and is useful. Participants overwhelmingly comment on their previous lack of knowledge on the topic as well as an increased ability to identify attacks. While specific to the institution where it was administered, the surveys can be easily modified to fit other local environments. Local resources such as public computer labs, social networking hubs and campus services are main sources of the customization process.

ACKNOWLEDGMENT

We would like to extend our gratitude to Dr. Carl Bredlau for his invaluable role in the creation of the surveys and as well as hosting the files on his server for the first two administrations of our module. We would also like to thank Keri Flanagan for her invaluable suggestions on improving the readability of this chapter.

REFERENCES

Accused AOL Hacker Arrested After Months At Large. (2006, November 1, 2006). Retrieved November, 2006, from http://cbs2.com/topstories/local_story_305232841.html

Anti-Phishing Working Group. (2007). Retrieved March 17, 2007, from http://www.antiphishing.org/

Bardzell, J., Blevis, E., & Lim, Y.-K. (2007). Human-Centered Design Considerations. In M. Jakobsson & S. Myers (Eds.), *Phishing and Countermeasures: Understanding the Increasing Problem of Electronic Identity Theft* (pp. 241-275). Hoboken, New Jersey: John Wiley & Sons, Inc.

Berghel, H., Carpinter, J., & Jo, J.-Y. (2006, August 28, 2006). Phish Phactors: Offensive and Defensive Strategies. Retrieved November 12, 2006, from http://berghel.net/publications/phishing/phishing.php

Botnet (Eds.). (2006). Wikimedia Foundation.

Brandt, A. (2005). Phishing Anxiety May Make You Miss Messages. *PCWORLD, 34* .

CastleCops. (2006, November 5, 2006). New PayPal Phishing Approach. Retrieved November 6, 2006, from http://www.castlecops.com/article-6680-nested-0-0.html

Claburn, T. (2007, January 22, 2007). Minor Google Security Lapse Obscures Ongoing Online Data Risk Retrieved January 24, 2007, from http://www.informationweek.com/shared/printableArticle.jhtml?articleID=196902585

Cranor, L. F., Egelman, S., Hong, J., & Zhang, Y. (2006, Novemeber 13, 2006). Phinding Phish: An Evaluation of Anti-Phishing Toolbars. Retrieved March 16, 2007, from http://www.cylab.cmu.edu/files/cmucylab06018.pdf

Dhamija, R., Tygar, J. D., & Hearst, M. (2006, Aoruk 2). *Why Phishing Works.* Paper presented at the SIGCHI Conference on Human Factors in Computing Systems, Montreal, Quebec, Canada.

DiFalco, G. (2006, November 7). Web Host GoDaddy Supports Rigorous New Validation SSL. Retrieved November 3, 2006, from http://www.tophosts.com/articles/004087.html

Downs, J. S., Holbrook, M. B., & Cranor, L. F. (2006). Decision strategies and susceptibility to phishing. In *Proceedings of the second symposium on Usable privacy and security* (pp. 79-90). Pittsburgh, Pennsylvania: ACM Press.

Duntemann, J. (2004). *Degunking Your Email, Spam, And Viruses.* Scottsdale, Arizona: Paraglyph Press.

Emigh, A. (2005). *Online Identity Theft: Phishing Technology, Chokepoints and Countermeasures*: Radix Labs.

Evers, J. (2007). Fortinet: Beware of Google's Blogger [Electronic Version], 2007. Retrieved March 15, 2007 from http://news.com.com/8301-10784_3-6167750-7.html.

Ferguson, A. J. (2005, 11/1/2005). Fostering E-mail Security Awareness: The West Point Carronade, 54-57.

Fight Back Against Identity Theft. (2006). Retrieved March 17, 2007, from http://www.ftc.gov/bcp/edu/microsites/idtheft/

Garretson, C. (2006, November 1, 2006). Spam that delivers a pink slip. Retrieved November 6, 2006, from http://www.networkworld.com/news/2006/110106-spam-spear-phishing.html

Hartley, R. L. (2006, Novemeber 2, 2006). Scam Stoppers Alert: Phishing Scam. Retrieved November 7, 2006, from http://www.myeyewitnessnews.com/news/local/story.aspx?content_id=DD5603BF-DDF1-47EA-B73E-A08456EB7E36

Horgan, D. (2005, November 14). *The Phishing Phleet.* Retrieved December 2, 2006, from http://blogs.courant.com/travel_columnists_horgan/2005/11/the_phishing_ph.html

ICTWorld. (2006, November 11, 2006). Number of phishing e-mails has almost doubled in two years. Retrieved November 12, 2006, from http://www.mybroadband.co.za/nephp/?m=show&id=4849

Jackson, C., Simon, D., Tan, D., & Barth, A. (2007). *An Evaluation of Extended Validation and Picture-in-Picture Phishing Attacks.* Paper presented at the Usable Security (USEC'07). from http://usablesecurity.org/papers/jackson.pdf.

Jagatic, T., Johnson, N. A., Jakobsson, M., & Menczer, F. (2005). *Social Phishing: ACM.*

Jakobsson, M. (2005). *Modeling and Preventing Phishing Attacks.*

James, C. (2006, November 2, 2006). Spam levels reach record high. Retrieved November 7, 2006, from http://www.itnews.com.au/newsstory.aspx?CIaNID=41608&src=site-marq

Jaques, R. (2006, August 2, 2006). *Huge botnet swamps UK firms with 8 million phishing emails.* Retrieved November 13, 2006, 2006, from http://www.vnunet.com/vnunet/news/2161530/huge-botnet-swamps-uk-firms

Kent, D. C. (2006, November 2, 2006). *Tricare, Medicare issues at forefront of defense bill.* Retrieved November 7, 2006, from http://www.zwire.com/site/news.cfm?newsid=17405636&BRD=1659&PAG=461&dept_id=8110&rfi=6

Kumaraguru, P., Rhee, Y., Acquisti, A., Cranor, L. F., Hong, J., & Nunge, E. (2007). *Protecting People from Phishing: The Design and Evaluation of an Embedded Training Email System.* Paper presented at the Computer/Human Interaction 2007 Conference. Retrieved March 15, 2007, from http://www.cs.cmu.edu/~jasonh/publications/CHI2007-embedded-training-final.pdf.

Lazarus, D. (2006, September 1, 2006). *Phishing expedition at heart of AT&T hacking.* Retrieved November 15, 2006, from http://sfgate.com/cgi-bin/article.cgi?f=/c/a/2006/09/01/BUGVBKSUIE1.DTL

Lemos, R. (2004). Browser phishing 'flaw' could hook users [Electronic Version]. *CNETNEWs.Com.* Retrieved 15 December, 2005 from http://news.com.com/Browser+phishing+flaw+could+hook+users/2100-1002_3-5484315.html.

Loechner, J. (2006, November 7, 2006). Phishing May Net More Than Previously Thought. Retrieved November 7, 2006, from http://publications.mediapost.com/index.cfm?fuseaction=Articles.showArticleHomePage&art_aid=50686

MailFrontier. (2004). *Phishing IQ* Retrieved 3 Nov. 2005, 2005, from http://www.mailfrontier.com

Maranjian, S. (2006, November 3, 2006). *Toss That IRS Email, Please*! Retrieved November 7, 2006, from http://msnbc.msn.com/id/15546334/

Microsoft. (2006). *Windows Internet Explorer 7* (Version 7.0.5730.11): Microsoft.

Myers, S. (2007). Status Quo Security Tools. In M. Jakobsson & S. Myers (Eds.), *Phishing and Countermeasures: Understanding the Increasing Problem of Electronic Identity Theft* (pp. 139-173). Hoboken, New Jersey: John Wiley & Sons, Inc.

New warning about fraudulent charity email scams. (2006, November 2, 2006). Retrieved November 7, 2006, from http://www.ekklesia.co.uk/content/news_syndication/article_06112scam.shtml

Nichols, S. (2006, November 7, 2006). *US hosts a quarter of all phishing sites*. Retrieved November 7, 2006, from http://www.itweek.co.uk/vnunet/news/2168068/claims-per-cent-phishing-sites

Nichols, S. (2007, April 18, 2007). *Online scammers exploit Virginia Tech shootings*. Retrieved April 30, 2007, from http://www.itweek.co.uk/vnunet/news/2187983/security-firms-brace-virgina

Ollmann, G. (2004, September 9, 2004). *The Phishing Guide: Understanding & Preventing Phishing Attacks*. Retrieved November 12, 2006, from http://www.ngssoftware.com/papers/NISR-WP-Phishing.pdf

One in 10 Holiday Shoppers Will Face Fraudulent Internet Attacks This Year. (2006). Retrieved November 7, 2006, from http://www.earthtimes.org/articles/show/news_press_release,16881.shtml

OnGuardOnline. (2006). Retrieved March 17, 2007, from http://onguardonline.gov/index.html

Online Banking Fraud Rises Fast. (2006, November 7, 2006). Retrieved November 7, 2006, from https://news.bbc.co.ck/2/hi/business/612216.stm

OpenDNS Shares October 2006 PhishTank Statistics. (2006, November 2, 2006). Retrieved November 7, 2006, from http://press.xtvworld.com/article15152.html

PandaLabs Warns Users of the Mass-mailing of False Job Offers. (2006, November 2, 2006). Retrieved November 7, 2006, from http://home.nestor.minsk.by/networks/news/2006/11/0205.html

Phishing. (2006, November 13, 2006). Retrieved November 29, 2006, from http://www.webopedia.com/TERM/p/phishing.html

Phishing Activity Trends Report - September 2005. (2005, October 2005). Retrieved November 19, 2006, from http://www.antiphishing.org/reports/apwg_phishing_activity_report_sept_05.pdf

Phishing Activity Trends Report - September 2006. (2006, October 9, 2006). Retrieved November 29, 2006, from http://www.antiphishing.org/reports/apwg_report_August_2006.pdf

Ragucci, J. W., & Robila, S. A. (2006a, July 7, 2007). Montclair Phish. Retrieved April 30, 2007, from http://csam.montclair.edu/~robila/RSL/Phish/

Ragucci, J. W., & Robila, S. A. (2006b). *Social Implications of Phishing*. Paper presented at the IEEE ISTAS 2006, Queens, NY.

Robila, S. A., & Ragucci, J. W. (2006). *Don't be a Phish: Steps in User Education*. Paper presented at the ITiCSE'06, Bologna, Italy.

Savvas, A. (2006, November 3, 2006). FBI anti-phishing operation leads to Polish and US arrests. Retrieved November 6, 2006, 2006, from http://www.computerweekly.com/Feeds/RSS/Articles/2006/11/03/219637/FBI%2Banti-phishing%2Boperation%2Bleads%2Bto%2BPolish%2Band%2BUS%2Barrests.htm

Schechter, S., Dhamija, R., Ozment, A., & Fischer, I. (2007). *The Emperor's New Security Indicators*. Paper presented at the Usable Security (USEC'07). from http://usablesecurity.org/emperor/.

Schipke, R. C. (2006). *The Language of Phishing, Pharming, and Other Internet Fraud—Metaphorically Speaking*. Paper presented at the IEEE ISTAS 2006, Queens, NY.

Schneier, B. (2006, December 21). Microsoft Anti-Phishing and Small Businesses. Retrieved

March 16, 2007, from http://www.schneier.com/blog/archives/2006/12/microsoft_antip.html

SonicWALL Phishing IQ Quiz. (2006). Retrieved March 18, 2007, from http://www.sonicwall.com/phishing/

Steiner, I. (2006, November 4, 2006). *eBay Reduces Bidding Transparency in Phish Fight*. Retrieved November 7, 2006, from http://www.auctionbytes.com/cab/abn/y06/m11/i03/s01

Stop-Phishing.com(Indiana University). (2006, 15 February 2007). Retrieved March 23, 2007, from http://www.indiana.edu/~phishing/

VeriSign. (2007). Buy SSL Certificates - SSL Certificate from VeriSign, Inc. Retrieved March 16, 2007, from http://www.verisign.com/ssl/buy-ssl-certificates/index.html

Werner, L. (2005). *Redefining computer literacy in the age of ubiquitous computing*. Paper presented at the Proceedings of the 6th conference on Information technology education.

Wu, M., Robert, C. M., & Simson, L. G. (2006). *Do security toolbars actually prevent phishing attacks?* Paper presented at the Proceedings of the SIGCHI conference on Human Factors in computing systems. from http://portal.acm.org/citation.cfm?id=1124863&coll=Portal&dl=GUIDE&CFID=6253896&CFTOKEN=24538716#.

Zheng, H., Xing, W.-L., Wang, D.-Q., & Duan, H.-X. (2005). *Analysis of Malicious Code for Phishing*. Paper presented at the 8th Association of anti Virus Asia Researchers Conference (AVAR 2005). from http://worm.ccert.edu.cn/doc/spark/AnalysisMaliciousCodeForPhishing.pdf.

KEY TERMS

Context-Aware Phishing Attack: A phishing attack that built from information gathered in advance about the target used to harvest additional information needed for identity theft.

Context-Aware Phishing IQ Text: The combination of context information of a target audience and a phishing IQ text that is custom built as a way to optimize the education experience of the end-users.

Content Distribution Network Attacks: A toolbar exploit that appends a blacklisted phishing address to a white listed webpage in an effort to circumvent the toolbar.

Identity Theft: The act of stealing personal information and user credentials, with the intent of using the information for fraudulent purposes.

Page Load Attack: A toolbar exploit that delays a webpage from fully loading in the web browser as a way of preventing the browser from determining the webpage's authenticity.

Phishing: The use of social engineering in e-mails for the purpose of deceiving the recipient into either compromising sensitive information or following a set of instructions that leads to a security breach.

Phishing Botnet: A collection of compromised computers that run with the intent of conducting phishing attacks.

Chapter XVII
Theories Used in Information Security Research:
Survey and Agenda

Serkan Ada
State University of New York, USA

Raj Sharman
State University of New York, USA

Manish Gupta
State University of New York, USA

ABSTRACT

This chapter discusses the recent theories used in information security research studies. The chapter initially introduces the importance of the information security research and why it became so important recently. Following this introduction, "theory" is defined and the importance of the theories in information security research is mentioned. After this discussion, recently used theories (socio-technical systems theory, activity theory, distributed cognition theory, general deterrence theory, grounded theory, social cognitive theory) are listed and basic information about these theories as well as applications from the literature are given. Other recently used theories are also summarized in a table in the next section. The chapter finally ends with concluding remarks on the theories and recommendations to the researchers in the information security area.

INTRODUCTION

In today's global and competitive business environment, organizations are becoming increasingly dependent on information and dissemination of the information. Such being the case, the use of computer-based information systems as well as globally scattered computer networks is of great importance in order to meet these requirements. On the other hand, this dependency makes organizations' information systems progressively more vulnerable to outside attacks and/or internal security breaches which may cause financial losses and disruption of the business activities (Siponen, 2005) (Choobineh et al., 2007).

In order to better comprehend the significance of the problems mentioned above, it is beneficial to take a look at the findings of the recent study conducted by Computer Security Institute. According to this study (CSI Survey, 2007), 46% of the 487 survey respondents reported that their organization was exposed to at least one security incident in the past 12 months. Another very significant statistic shows that organizations' total financial losses due to computer security incidents are approximately $66,930,950 in 2007 (based on the responses from managers of 194 companies). More interestingly, 27% of the respondents also reported that up to 20% of the cyber losses is caused by the people inside the organization, while this proportion is 37% for the cyber losses greater than 20% (Richardson, 2007). In light of the findings, as mentioned above, it is obvious to conclude that proper management of information systems security is vital and inevitable. In addition to this very fact, it is also of great importance for academic environments to attach more importance to the information security related issues in organizations.

How academic environments approached these issues are summarized in a review paper on Information Security Research (Willison & Siponen, 2007). This study reports that there are 1280 security related papers published in 3 IS Security journals and 20 IS journals between 1990-2004. Out of these papers, only 18.51% include a theory as a framework the study. Based on the fact that the application of the theories and appropriate research methods are essential for any research study, it is our belief that academic researchers should attach more importance on the creation, adoption, and/or application of the theories from the literature (Willison & Siponen, 2007). Drake and Clarke (2008) also offer a model to suggest solutions and guidelines to fill the information security research gaps by using social theories, various aspects of which deal with both human and technical issues from the perspective of those involved in the system of concern.

In this chapter, it is our objective to present some of the related theories used in the context of Information Security in order to bring this issue to the academic researchers' notice. As also mentioned by Choobineh et al. (2007), theoretical conceptualizations are necessitated in order to create more effective principles and guidelines for "best practices" in information security management and to develop solutions for the related problems (Choobineh et al., 2007). Because of this, we would like to encourage researchers to utilize these theories or adopt other related theories from the literature for their research studies.

The remaining of this chapter is organized as follows. The next section discusses what the theory is and why the theories are used in research studies. Following this section, we will discuss the related theories used in Information Security Research (Socio-technical Systems Theory, Activity Theory, Distributed Cognition Theory, General Deterrence Theory, Grounded Theory, and Social Cognitive Theory). After discussion of these theories, other recent theories used in the literature will be briefly mentioned. Finally, the chapter will conclude with the conclusion and discussion section.

THEORY AND ITS APPLICATION IN INFORMATION SECURITY

Theory is defined by Kerlinger (1979) as "a set of interrelated variables, definitions, and propositions that presents a systematic view of phenomena by specifying relations among variables, with the purpose of explaining natural phenomena." (Creswell, 2003). Another definition of the theory is done by Babbie (2004) as "a systematic explanation for the observations that relate to a particular aspect of life". According to Babbie, theories are composed of concepts which explain these observations. Concepts, which are "basic building blocks of the theories", are abstract elements that represent classes of phenomena in a field of study (Babbie, 2004).

Theories are of great significance in every field of science, either natural (physics, chemistry, and etc.) and social (economics, sociology, and etc.) or formal sciences (mathematics, statistics, and etc.). In science, theories are needed to explain the characteristics and behaviors of certain phenomena. Based on the theories, researchers develop models which externally and explicitly represent a part of reality (Pidd, 2003). Based on these models, researchers derive hypothesis to test the validation and the proof of the theory under consideration.

In research studies, theories and theoretical issues are sometimes utilized only as a background for the empirical analyses. On the other hand, there are other group of studies which uses empirical data in order to support theoretical arguments. It is obvious that theories have a considerable impact on scientific research, since the research is needed to test the theories and/or as the theories are developed by analyzing the research data (Babbie, 2004).

In addition to most of the study fields in Information Systems Research, theories are also utilized by the information systems security researchers. However, as mentioned in the first section of this chapter, there are not many research studies using theories as a framework in the studies. As also mentioned above, it is our objective in this chapter to present some of the theories used in the context of information systems security, by providing definitions and applications, and to encourage researchers in using, developing, and adopting theories in their research.

It is important to point out that there are certain criteria in developing theories in security research. In order to develop a theory in information security research, researchers need to consider the following (Choobineh et al., 2007):

- *Consistency* – a theory have to be consistent
- *Soundness* – a theory have to make sense
- *Falsifiability* – falsifiable theories are scientific
- *Satisfiability/contingency* – models or frameworks are true for the definitions and the assumptions
- *Experience explication* – A security theory should not merely be an opinion regarding how security have to be in an organization

In the next section, we discuss social and organizational theories that have suggestions for strong applicability to information security research. In conjunction with discussions on a theory, we also present example studies that have used the underpinnings of the theory in their research. The studies show typical applications of the theories within context of information security research.

Socio-Technical Systems Theory

Socio-technical (STS) Systems Theory was initially coined by Eric Trist and Fred Emery, consultants in Tavistock Institute in London, in 1960 (Wikipedia, 2008b). The problem in the middle of 20th century was that businesses were not achieving high level of productivity with their investments in technological systems. Therefore, it was argued that organizations should be approached as socio-technical systems, in which social and technical systems are considered together in order to increase the productivity (Schneberger & Wade, 2008b).

STS Theory is an approach to better explain today's complex organizational systems. The theory basically discusses that organizational systems are composed of social systems and technical systems, which are independent and interactive. As shown in Figure 1, social system component of the theory is concerned with the people and attributes of the people as well as the interactions between people in an organization's structure. Technical system component of the theory is basically deals with the processes and tasks inside the organization as well as the technology that is required to transform the inputs into the outputs (Bostromand & Heinen, 1977).

STS Theory is of great importance for organizations due to the everlasting increase in proportion of technology in organizational processes. Because of this fact, businesses need to jointly optimize their organization's social and technical dimensions and they should pay attention to the interrelatedness of these components for better utilization of the resources (Mitchell & Nault, 2003).

In practice, Socio-technical Systems Theory is being applied in many perspectives in organizational development, such as job design, Information Systems design, and reengineering projects (Appelbaum, 1997). Recently, the theory is becoming more accepted in Information Security area, as the organizations increase their security investments. One of the applications of STS Theory in Information Security area is seen in a study by Fontes and Ballioni (2006). In this study, information security system of an organization, including establishing and maintaining the systems, is described in terms of STS Theory constructs and components. The authors argue that Information security processionals usually perceive the security system from a more technical perspective. However, it is important to point out that organizations also need to consider human needs and perspectives in addition to the technical efficiency and they should integrate both technical and social aspects of the security system for a better security prevention and detection (Fontes & Balloni, 2007).

According to another study, information security system of a company is examined from a socio-technical perspective. In particular, the paper discusses that examining culture, usability problems, security internal controls, and security requirements by combining both technical and social aspects provides a more efficient perspective for modeling and developing Information Systems security systems (Chaula, 2006).

Figure 1. Components of socio-technical systems (Bostrom and Heinen, 1977)

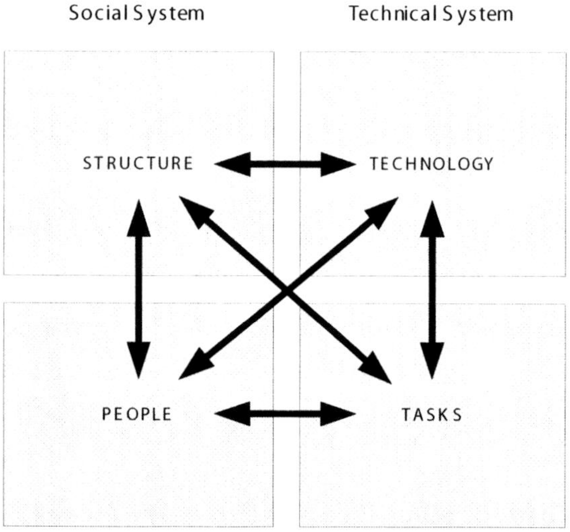

Activity Theory

The inception of Activity Theory dates back to 1920's and 1930's. According to Vygotsky (1978), one of the revolutionary psychologists in Russia, humans do not act with the environment directly, but by means of mediating artifacts (Chen, et al., 2007). Engstrom (1987), one of the second generation activity theoretician, made a further contribution to the theory which became a very powerful tool for the analysis of the social systems.

Activity Theory proposes that human activity aims at accomplishing certain outcomes through the help of artifacts and other resources. Fundamental principles of the theory includes that the activity is the basic unit of analysis, the activities have a history and development process, and the activities includes mediatory artifacts. In accordance with Engestrom's (1987). Activity Theory conceptualization, an activity consists of several elements, including the subjects, objects, and the community and the instruments (or tools), rules, and the division of labor (Figure 2). The main objective of the human activity is to produce certain artifacts in order to transform it into certain outcomes. In order to do so, a community of subjects shares the artifacts with a division of labor toward achieving the objective. These activities are mediated with the instruments and tools and the rules and regulations of the community and the environment that draws the limits in which the activities should be performed (Kuutti, 1995).

Recently, Activity Theory draws the attention of the research community who is involved in systems design and development for individuals and organizations. In particular, the theory provides a framework for the analysis of the computer-mediated activity of a group of people or organizations (Chen et al., 2007).

Activity Theory is also used in the context of Information Security. Show (2007) applies the same model of Engestrom into a payroll processing system. In this system, Show defines payroll processing and issuing payments as objects; employees, staff, amd stakeholders as involving objects; payroll software, information systems, as accounting procedures as mediating artifacts. The subjects in this activity system perform the required functions with a division of labor based on certain organizational policies and legal guidelines to the community. Information Security perspective of this activity system comes to the screen, when contradictory tensions happen in such systems. Furthermore, how non-technical functional workers perform security procedures as well as how contradictions between formal security structures and the actual behaviors affect information security practices in organizations are also articulated in this study (Show, 2007). Another application of activity theory can be found in design of secure RBAC (Role based Access Control) roles and role engineering processes (Gupta, 2008). This study uses constructs of activity theory to explore social and organizational structures and interactions to unravel shortcomings of traditional role engineering processes.

Distributed Cognition Theory

Distributed Cognition Theory is developed by Edwin Hutchins in the middle of 1980's (Wikipe-

Figure 2. Model of activity system (Engestrom, 1987)

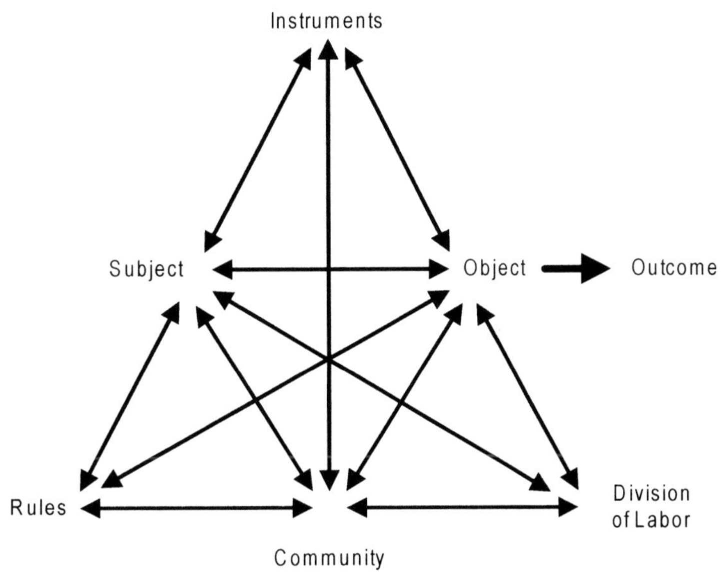

dia, 2008a). In contrast to the traditional cognitive phenomena which explains information processing at individual level, this theory proposes that cognition should be approached as a distributed phenomenon (Rogers, 1997).

Distributed Cognition is a theory in which all aspects of the cognition are covered in terms of cognitive, social, and organizational perspectives. In this theory, cognitive phenomena are explained in a distributed structure in which individuals and interactions among individuals, artifacts, and internal and external representations are jointly considered. Furthermore, it is assumed in this approach that, cognitive properties of a cognitive system consisting of two or more individuals differ significantly from the individuals' personal cognitive properties (Rogers, 1997). Figure 3 shows a simple model of distributed cognition. In this model, it is represented that collaboration of a group of individuals directed toward achieving a common outcome produces a more effective results than individuals' isolated efforts. This collaboration is of course more meaningful with the use of mediatory artifacts (Kittur, 2006).

Today, Distributed Cognition Theory is attracting research community due to its new approach to the social aspects of cognition and its emphasis on individuals and their environments. The theory is usually used in the context of collaborative learning and development efforts (Wikipedia, 2008a). In particular, it is utilized when a group of people design and develop software in a distributed nature (Domino et al., 2004).

It is also important to accentuate that distributed cognitive approach is used in information security research as well. According to a study in which organizations are defined as distributed cognition systems, it is argued that information security management issues should be related to the human cognition and behavior. It is pointed out that information is highly disseminated in the virtual environment in which employees of an organization create security breaches by contradicting the policies of the organization. Since such violating activities make the issue more complex, the author argues that the task of dealing with these problems exceeds the traditional scope of information security management and should be approached in a distributed manner. The proposed solution is to create a corporate awareness, or distributed awareness, in order to build an organization-wide threat recognition and awareness for the information security issues (Lueg, 2001).

Figure 3. Distributed Cognition Model (Kittur, 2006)

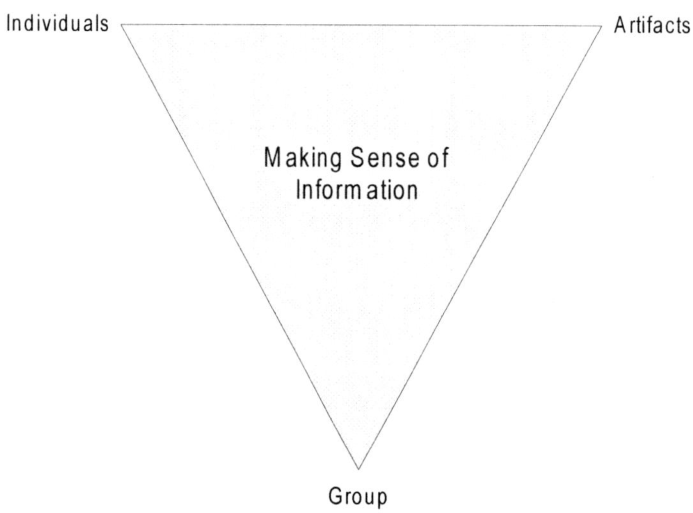

General Deterrence Theory

General Deterrence Theory is basically adopted from the discipline of criminology. The focus of this theory is disincentives and sanctions against a criminal act (Cohen & Nagin, 1978).

According to this theory, information systems security measures and actions are able to deter potential computer security abusers from committing an illegal act (Bagchi & Udo, 2003). As mentioned above, disincentives are an important way of discoursing such activities. The disincentives can be represented as two sub-constructs, which are the certainty of sanctions and the severity of sanctions (Cohen & Nagin, 1978). This means that the risk of the punishment and the harshness of the punishment will inhibit the potential criminals from committing the insecure acts.

General Deterrence Theory is great importance in Information Systems research and Information Security Research in particular. Straub and his colleagues initially used this theory in Information Security context. According to these researchers, the theory is well fit in establishing the security policies and assessing the effectiveness of these policies as well as the assessment of the system's risk (Straub & Welke, 1998). Using similar theories such as the Rational Choice Perspective and Situational Crime Prevention into the IS field have also been suggested to open up potentially new areas for future research and to provide insights into relationship between the offender and the context (Willison, 2006).

As for the applications of the theory in security context, Straub (1986) had examined the theory in his general model of computer security as shown in the Figure 4. This is a multilayer model in which deterrence is the very first layer. As can be seen from the model, the deterrents, which are policies in which the acceptable and unacceptable actions and uses of information systems of organizations are mentioned, discourage the potential computer security abusers from committing a security crime. Such being the case, contemplated abuses turn out to be an unattempted abuse. This model also shows the other layers in computer security such as the preventives and the detectives as the abusers succeed to abuse (Foltz, 2004).

Straub, with other collaborators, has another study in which they examined the cheating behaviors of computer science students in doing their programming assignments. They examined how public and private deterrence sanctions affect the cheating in such assignments. They found in their research based on a field experiment that publicly known deterrence sanctions significantly lower the

Figure 4. Computer Security Model (Straub, 1986)

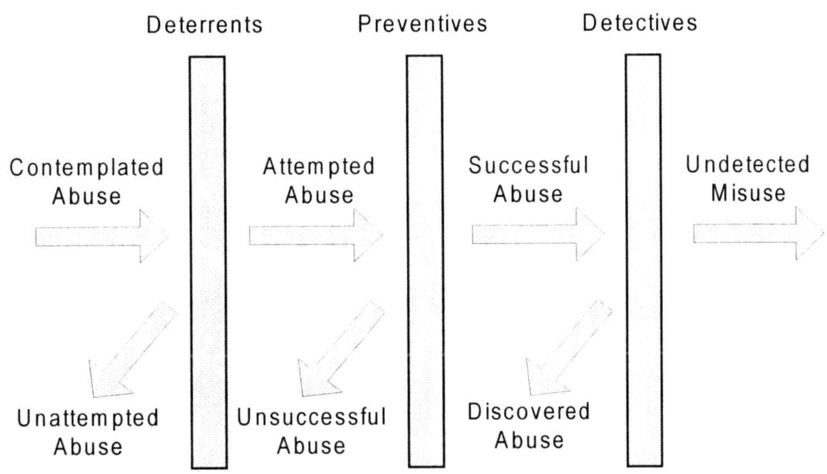

incidence of cheating on unsupervised homework assignments (Straub, et al., 1992). Theoharidoua et. al. (2005) uses General Deterrence Theory to support arguments for a multiparadigm and multidisciplinary approach towards information system security management and insider threat mitigation. They investigate suggestions and measures from ISO17799, the dominant standard in IS security management, to address threats from insider misuse using General Deterrence Theory.

Grounded Theory

Grounded Theory, a systematic and qualitative way of generation of the theories based on the data, is developed by Glass and Starus (1967). Grounded Theory is one of the most effective qualitative research approaches in theory-creating research (Siponen, 2005).

This is a methodological approach which is based on the development of the theories grounded in systematically collected and analyzed data. Martin and Turner (1986) defines this approach as "an inductive, theory discovery methodology that allows the researcher to develop a theoretical account of the general features of a topic while simultaneously grounding the account in empirical observations or data." (Myers, 1997a). In order to create a theory based on this approach, there are some significant steps to be taken. As can be seen in the following figure, based on the theoretical sampling, the data is collected, and then ordered. After this step, the data analysis is done and the theory is developed, if the marginal value of the data is minimum. If theory is still not saturated, then the data is collected again and the same steps are retaken (Pandit, 1996).

Grounded Theory approach has been utilized in Information Systems Research. Baskerville and Pries-Heje (1999), Bowker et al. (1995), and De Vreede et al. (1999) used this approach in their studies (Myers, 1997b). The approach has also been used in the area of information security research where the use and the development of theories is not common.

In one study, Knapp (2005) uses this approach in developing a theoretical model with respect to the managerial constructs on the effective management of information security. In this study, the author initially collects the data by conducting intense interviews based on the open-ended questions. After collection of the data, the author systematically analyzes these data and develops a theoretical model. In this model, he proposes that the variables affecting the effectiveness of information security are top management support, user training, security culture, policy relevance, and policy enforcement (Knapp, 2005).

In another study on the use of Grounded Theory approach in information security context, Adams et al. (1997) investigates the user's perceptions

Figure 5. Steps in Grounded Theory (Pandit, 1996)

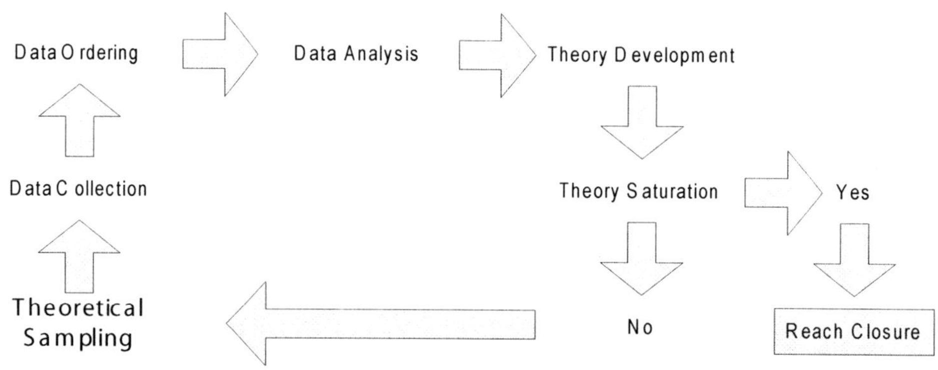

of password mechanisms by questionnaires and interviews. Based on the data collected, they developed a theoretical framework by discovering the variables about the user's password behavior. The authors concluded that the level of conformance of users to the security mechanisms depends on their perception of security levels, information sensitivity and compatibility with work practices (Adams, et al., 1997).

Goodall et al. (2004) present an interesting study in the area of intrusion detection systems using grounded theory analytic protocols. The study was based in transcribed and coded interviews and observations. They find that organizational changes must be combined with improved technical tools for effective, long-term solutions to the difficulties of managing growth of intrusion detection roles and responsibilities. For example, they suggest that monitoring tasks in intrusion detection systems can be separated and staffed by less experienced security analysts when supported by corresponding tool.

Social Cognitive Theory

Social Cognitive Theory (SCT) is developed by Bandura (1986). It is widely accepted and one of the most important models of individual behavior in the literature. The framework provided by this theory is very important in terms of understanding, predicting, and changing human behavior (Schneberger & Wade, 2008a).

According to SCT, environmental influences, personal factors, and behavior are determined reciprocally. Figure 6 shows these reciprocal relationships (Compeau & Higgins, 1995). The relationship between person and behavior includes the personal influences on thoughts and actions; the relationship between person and environment includes the human beliefs and competencies which are developed and modified by social structures and influences; and finally the relationship between the behavior and the environment includes how behavior affects the aspects of the environment and how in turn the behavior is modified by the environment (Schneberger & Wade, 2008a).

Self-efficacy is one of the aspects of the SCT and defined by Bandura (1986) as "People's judgments of their capabilities to organize and execute courses of action required to attain designated types of performances. It is concerned not with the skills one has but with judgments of what one can do with whatever skills one possesses". Self-efficacy concept is commonly used in information systems research, such as in the context of computer self-efficacy (Compeau and Higgnis, 1995; Compeau et al.,1999). This aspect of SCT is also used in information security research in the context of security self efficacy.

Figure 6. Triadic and reciprocal relationships in SCT (Bandura, 1986)

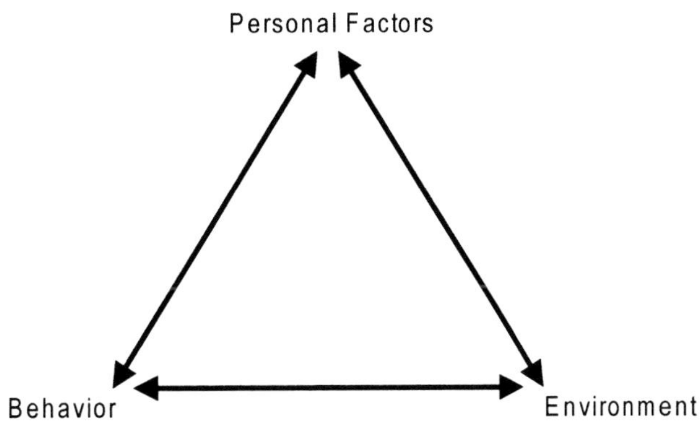

For instance, Phelps (2005) developed and tested a causal model, based on SCT, on the information systems security self-efficacy. In this study, the relationship between systems librarians' educational preparation and effectiveness of their information security implementation is examined. The author found that there is a significant relationship between the previous information technology training, information systems security self-efficacy and the IS security implementation effectiveness (Phelps, 2005).

SCT is also utilized in another study in the context of middle school children's information security behavior. SCT is used to introduce concepts such as information security self-efficacy, perceived information security importance and exposure of information security. The findings of this study indicate that students having high self-efficacy on information security showed a higher level of security behavior, such as updating the antivirus software and not opening the emails coming from the unidentified senders (Chai et al., 2006).

OTHER RECENT THEORIES

In this part of the chapter, we present other recent theories used in Infomation Security literature. Table 1 summarizes these theories.

Table 1. Summary of other theories

Theory	Description	Context used in ISSec
Institutional Theory (Hu, Hart, & Cooke, 2006) (Bjorck, 2004)	Organizations structure depend on their environments and their isomorphism process	- Why formal security structures and actual security behaviors differ - Why organizations create formal security structures and do not attempt to fully apply them
Information Security Management Theory (Finne, 1998)	"a set of systematically interrelated concepts, definitions, and propositions that are advanced to explain and predict phenomena (facts)."	Used in a way to approach costs, economic losses and level of ISEC
Theory of Contextualism (Karydaa, Kiountouzisa, & Kokolakis, 2005)	"an analytical instrument for exploring the relationship and interplay between the content of strategic change, the context of change and the process of managing change in organization studies."	"formulation and implementation of IS security policies and relate these with the context within which they take place"
Cultural Theory (Tsohou, Karyda, Kokolakis, & Kiountouzis, 2006)	"the way people socially interact impinges on the systems of symbols they use to understand the world"	"identifying patterns in the stakeholders' perception of risk and its effect on information system (IS) risk management"
Integrated System Theory (Hong, Chi, Chao, & Tang, 2003)	"Based on contingency management and integrates information security policy, risk management, internal control and information auditing theories to form an Information security Architecture that is consistent with organizational objectives."	Explaining information security management strategies and predicting management outcomes
Gompertz Model (based on Social Conflict Theory) (Bagchi & Udo, 2003)	"the probable causes for the outbreak of such incidents are imitative as well as inhibitive in nature"	"analyzing the growth rates of different types of computer and Internet-related crimes"

DISCUSSION AND CONCLUSION

As mentioned above, the use of theories in information security research is not widespread which prevents a better development of information security management practices. Using that as our motivation, in this chapter, we have surveyed and presented some of the research-relevant theories used in the context of information systems security research to enable researchers to think more on the use of theories in this study field. This chapter does not aim to mention all the theories used in information security research or all the studies in the area that use them. We presented some of the most relevant theories in aspiration that it will stimulate information researchers to apply theories in their research towards contribution to the literature in the field.

In particular, some of these theories are very useful in conducting the social aspects of the information security management. Socio-technical Systems Theory and Social Cognitive Theory are some of these theories which can be used in this context. On the other hand, in some cases, research may require the researcher to consider examining the groups of people and their interactions based on several factors as well as the mediating artifacts of these interactions. Activity Theory and Distributed Cognition Theory can be used in such cases. The abovementioned theories are only a few examples of the use of theories in information systems security. There is of course a considerable need for developing new theories or adopting the existing theories from other study fields in the literature. In order to develop related theories, Grounded Theory approach can be a useful tool as mentioned above as well. Table 2, below, summarizes the constructs of the theories discussed in the previous section.

As a conclusion, we are able to say that researchers should pay more attention to the use of theories in Information Security research in order to facilitate the development of the effective information security practices and policies in organizations. It is of great importance in a world where importance of information and information systems is very increasingly growing. Also, we would like to assert that the Information Systems Security researchers consider the criteria given in the second section (consistency, soundness, falsifiability, satisfiability/contingency, and experience explication) in using these theories in information security research(Choobineh et al., 2007). Thus, the researchers will be able to develop / adapt other useful and valuable theories which can be used by other researchers or use these theories in their research

REFERENCES

Adams, A., Sasse, M. A., & Lunt, P. (1997). *Making Passwords Secure and Usable.* Paper presented at the Proceedings of HCI on People and Computers XII.

Table 2. Summary of theories

Theory	**Theoretical constructs**		
	Social Elements	**Artifacts**	**Norms**
Socio-technical Systems	Structure, People	Technology, Tasks	Improved Efficiency
Activity Theory	Subject, community	Instruments	Rules, Division of Labor
Distributed Cognition Theory	Individuals, group	Artifacts	Interactions
General Deterrence Theory	Individuals	X	Disincentives, Sanctions
Social Cognitive Theory	Personal Factors, environment	Cognition	Self-efficacy

Appelbaum, S. H. (1997). Socio-technical systems theory: an intervention strategy for organizational development. *Management Decision, 35*(6), 452–463.

Babbie, E. (2004). *The Practice of Social Research.* Belmont, CA: Wadsworth/Thomson Learning.

Bagchi, K., & Udo, G. (2003). An Analysis of the Growth of Computer and Internet Security Breaches. *Communications of the Association for Information Systems, 12*, 684-700.

Bjorck, F. (2004). *Institutional theory: A new perspective for research into IS/IT security in organisations.* Paper presented at the Proceedings of the 37th Hawaii International Conference on System Sciences.

Bostromand, R., & Heinen, S. (1977). MIS Problems and Failures: A Sociotechnical Perspective. *MIS Quarterly*, 17-32.

Chai, S., Bagchi-Sen, S., Morrell, C., Rao, H. R., & S.Upadhyaya. (2006). Role of Perceived Importance of Information Security: An Exploratory Study of Middle School Children's Information Security Behavior. *Issues in Informing Science and Information Technology, 3.*

Chaula, J. A. (2006). *A Socio-Technical Analysis of Information Systems Security Assurance A Case Study for Effective Assurance.* Stockholm University, Stockholm

Chen, R., Sharman, R., Chakravarti, N., Rao, H. R., & Upadhyaya, S. J. (2007). mergency Response Information System Interoperability: Development of Chemical Incident Response Data Model. *Journal of the Association for Information Systems.*

Choobineh, J., Dhillon, G., Grimaila, M. R., & Rees, J. (2007). Management of Information Security: Challenges and Research Directions. *Communications of AIS, 20.*

Cohen, A. B. J., & Nagin, D. (Eds.). (1978). *Introduction.* Washington, DC: National Academy of Sciences.

Compeau, D. R., & Higgins, C. A. (1995). Computer self-efficacy: Development of a measure and initial test. *MIS Quarterly, 19*(2), 189.

Creswell, J. W. (2003). *Research Design: Qualitative, Quantitative, and Mixed Methods Aprroaches.* Thousand Oaks, CA: Sage Publications.

CSI Survey (2007). The 12th Annual Computer Crime and Security Survey. Computer Security Institute Survey. Retrived online from http://ccr.i2.nscee.edu/resources/CSISurvey2007.pdf on 6th May, 2008.

Domino, M., Klaus, T., & Collins, R. W. (2004). *An Experiment in Collaborative Programming: How Distributed Cognition Impacts Performance Outcomes.* Paper presented at the Proceedings of the Tenth Americas Conference on Information Systems, New York, New York.

Drake, P., & Clarke, S. (2008). *Social Aspects of Information Security: An International Perspective.* In Gupta, M and Sharman, R. (Eds), Social and Human Elements of Information Security: Emerging Trends and Countermeasures. IGI Publishing. Hershey, PA: Information Science Publishing. September 2008.

Finne, T. (1998). A Conceptual Framework for Information Security Management. *Computers & Security, 17*, 303-307.

Foltz, C. B. (2004). Cyberterrorism, computer crime, and reality. *Information Management & Computer Security, 12*(2), 154-166.

Fontes, E. L. G., & Balloni, A. J. (2007). Security in Information Systems: Sociotechnical Aspects. In *Innovations and Advanced Techniques in Computer and Information Sciences and Engineering* (pp. 163-166): Springer Netherlands.

Goodall, J. R., Lutters W. G., & Komlodi, Anita. (2004). *The Work of Intrusion Detection: Rethinking the Role of Security Analysts.* Proceedings of the Tenth Americas Conference on Information Systems, New York, New York, August 2004

Gupta. M. (2008). Activity Theory Guided Role Engineering. *Proceedings of 14th Americas Conference on Information Systems (AMCIS 2008),* Toronto, Canada, August 14-17, 2008.

Hong, K.-S., Chi, Y.-P., Chao, L. R., & Tang, J.-H. (2003). An integrated system theory of information security management. *Information Management & Computer Security, 11*(5), 243.

Hu, Q., Hart, P., & Cooke, D. (2006). *The Role of External Influences on Organizational Information Security Practices: An Institutional Perspective.* Paper presented at the Proceedings of the 39th Hawaii International Conference on System Sciences.

Karydaa, M., Kiountouzisa, E., & Kokolakis, S. (2005). Information systems security policies: a contextual perspective. *Computers & Security, 24,* 246-260.

Kittur, N. (2006). Cognition, Computation, Design. Retrieved 04/26, 2008 from http://www.kittur.org

Knapp, K. J. (2005). *A Model of Managerial Effectiveness in Information Security: From Grounded Theory to Empirical Test.* Auburn University.

Kuutti, K. (1995). Activity Theory as a potential framework for humancomputer interaction research. In B. Nardi (Ed.), *Context and Consciousness: Activity Theory and Human Computer Interaction* (pp. 17-44): Cambridge: MIT Press.

Lueg, C. (2001). *A Distributed Cognition Approach to Integrate Security Management and Business Processes.* Paper presented at the Proceedings of the 2nd International Conference on Working for e-Business (WeB 2001), Perth, WA.

Mitchell, V. L., & Nault, B. R. (2003). *The Emergence of Functional Knowledge in Sociotechnical Systems.* Calgary, Alberta: Haskayne School of Business University of Calgaryo. Document Number)

Myers, M. D. (1997a). Qualitative Research in Information Systems [Electronic Version], from http://www.qual.auckland.ac.nz/

Myers, M. D. (1997b). References on Grounded Theory. Retrieved 04/26, 2008, from http://www.qual.auckland.ac.nz/grndrefs.htm

Pandit, N. R. (1996). The Creation of Theory: A Recent Application of the Grounded Theory Method [Electronic Version], *2,* from http://www.nova.edu/ssss/QR/QR2-4/pandit.html

Phelps, D. C. (2005). *Information System Security: Self-Efficacy and Security Effectiveness in Florida Libraries.* PhD Dissertation, Florida State University.

Pidd, M. (2003). *Tools for Thinking: Modelling in Management Science*: John Wiley & Sons Ltd.

Richardson, R. (2007). *Computer Crime and Security Survey.* Computer Security Institute, 2007.

Rogers, Y. (1997). A Brief Introduction to Distributed Cognition [Electronic Version], from http://mcs.open.ac.uk/yr258/papers/dcog/dcog-brief-intro.pdf

Schneberger, S., & Wade, M. (2008a, 28 January 2008). Social Cognitive Theory. Retrieved 04/27, 2008, from http://www.fsc.yorku.ca/york/istheory/wiki/index.php/Social_cognitive_theory

Schneberger, S., & Wade, M. (2008b, 28 January 2008). Socio-technical theory. Retrieved 04/27, 2008, from http://www.fsc.yorku.ca/york/istheory/wiki/index.php/Socio-technical_theory

Show, J. (2007). *Information Security in Practice from an Activity-Theoretic Perspective.* Paper presented at the Proceedings of the 6th Annual Security Conference, Las Vegas, NV.

Siponen, M. T. (2005). An analysis of the traditional IS security approaches: implications for research and practice. *European Journal of Information Systems, 14*, 303-315.

Straub, D. W., Carlson, P. J., & Jones, E. H. (1992). *Deterring Highly Motivated Computer Abusers: A Field Experiment in Computer Security.* Paper presented at the Proceeding of the IFIP/Sec '92 Conference.

Straub, D. W., & Welke, R. J. (1998). Coping with Systems Risk: Security Planning Models for Management Decision-Making *MIS Quarterly, 22*(4), 441-469.

Theoharidoua, M., Kokolakisb, S., Karydaa, M. and Kiountouzis E. (2005, September). *The insider threat to information systems and the effectiveness of ISO17799.* Computers & Security, 24(6), 472-484.

Tsohou, A., Karyda, M., Kokolakis, S., & Kiountouzis, E. (2006). Formulating information systems risk management strategies through cultural theory. *Information Management & Computer Security, 14*(3), 198-217.

Wikipedia. (2008a, 28 April 2008). Distributed cognition. from http://en.wikipedia.org/wiki/Distributed_cognition#Applications

Wikipedia. (2008b, 6 April 2008). Socio-technical systems. Retrieved 04/27, 2008, from http://en.wikipedia.org/wiki/Socio-technical_systems

Willison, R. (2006). *Understanding the perpetration of employee computer crime in the organisational context,* Information and Organization, 16(4), 304-324

Willison, R., & Siponen, M. (2007). A Critical assesment ifIS Security Research Between 1990-2004. *Working Paper No. 01-2007.*

KEY TERMS

Activity Theory: An approach which proposes that human activity aims at accomplishing certain outcomes through the help of artifacts and other resources.

Computer Security Model: A multilayer model which shows the steps in computer security including the measures and the next actions of the security abusers after being successful against a security measure.

Distributed Cognition Theory: An approach which considers cognition as a distributed phenomenon.

General Deterrence Theory: A term adopted from the discipline of criminology, which is about the disincentives and sanctions to prevent a criminal act in security.

Grounded Theory: A systematic and qualitative methodology of developing theories based on the systematically collected and analyzed data.

Self-Efficacy: "People's judgments of their capabilities to organize and execute courses of action required to attain designated types of performances."

Social Cognitive Theory: A model on human behavior which argues that environmental influences, personal factors, and behavior are determined reciprocally.

Socio-Technical Systems Theory: An approach that considers organizations as the combination of both social and technical systems in order to increase the productivity.

Theory: "A set of interrelated variables, definitions, and propositions that presents a systematic view of phenomena by specifying relations among variables, with the purpose of explaining natural phenomena."

Chapter XVIII
Information Assurance and Security Curriculum Meeting the SIGITE Guidelines

Samuel Liles
Purdue University Calumet, USA

Reza Kamali
Purdue University Calumet, USA

ABSTRACT

Information assurance education is an interdisciplinary endeavor that only when taken as a holistic and inclusive educational activity can be successful. When considering the design and implementation of a curriculum that is set to meet standards set by outside agencies, the educational institution must use a flexible and repeatable process. Building a curriculum on top of a strong foundation will empower and facilitate success. Meeting outside agencies' requirements, such as accrediting agencies, will close, if not eliminate any credibility gaps within an institution.

INTRODUCTION

There is a dearth within the literature of repeatable and sustainable processes or guidelines on "how to" create a curriculum that meets the requirements of outside or internal agencies making demands on the university for appropriate curriculum (R. Kamali, Liles, Winer, Jiang, & Nicolai, 2006). Further, the balance between the requirements of accrediting agencies and the stake holders in an institution may be in conflict. Preparing and creating a curriculum to meet these coordinate and conflicting requirements is a solvable task.

It is important to make insightful decision in the creation of curriculum. The sustainability of a curriculum going into the future will be predicated on the foundation of the elements and decision used to differentiate it from other curriculums.

When the overall goals and missions of the program of study are considered certain elegance can be found in the creation of a holistic curriculum model. The strength of outcome based objectives within information technology is documented strongly (Melissa J. Dark, 2004; Melissa Jane Dark, Ekstrom, & Lunt, 2005; Hazem et al., 2004; Rigby & Dark, 2006). Information assurance and security is a large interdisciplinary area of study that defies definition. The perspective of the computer scientist finds information assurance and security to be encryption and computational models. The computer engineer might find information assurance and security in the hardware security devices such as firewalls.

Information assurance and security has been defined by many authors as the practices, techniques, methods, of securing information in all of its forms from the various threats and risks that information can be subjected to in the enterprise (McKnight, 2002; National Security Telecommunications and Information Systems, 1997a). As practitioners and educators the primary subjects we deal with are confidentiality, integrity, availability, authentication, and non-repudiation and we define information assurance and security based on those topics (Maconachy, Schou, Ragsdale, & Welch, 2001). There are other ways of defining the breadth of the discipline and as an interdisciplinary area of study there will likely be more ways of defining it in the future.

The Association of Computing Machinery (ACM) and the Institute of Electrical and Electronics Engineers (IEEE) maintain standards bodies that assist the Accreditation Board for Engineering and Technology (ABET) in defining information technology curriculum and the information assurance and security areas required for accreditation (Liles & Kamali, 2006). Of specific interest to faculty and students are the curriculum volumes for accrediting information technology programs and specifically the topical requirements for information assurance and security. The ACM maintains special interest educations groups (SIGS) and these groups define the best curricular practices for a discipline such as computer science and specifically the special interest group for information technology education (SIGITE). ("Computing curricula 2001," 2001) ("Curriculum: Proposed standards for IT curriculum," 2005). It might be easier to split up information assurance and security in a few specific topical areas such as systems, software, networking, and management. These will allow us to look at the topical elements and consider them in our end solution for creating a curriculum.

Systems are all of the computing and logical devices inside the enterprise that are computational or embedded in the way the overall information systems of the enterprise works. The systems can be the sensory devices for the data center that determine the temperature of the cooling systems, or they could be the computer sitting in front of a secretary.

Software is all of the code running on the different machines. This is the code in the internal applications of the enterprise such as patches and scripts. The software we are interested in includes the operating systems of personal communication devices. There are large discussions over the validity and viability of teaching software assurance topics to undergraduates but if the techniques are baked into the first classes instructors will not be un-training students in graduate school.

Networking is the entire associated infrastructure required to make all of the different systems talk to each other. With the increase in wireless infrastructure that does not mean cables and fiber from point "A" to point "B", but it can mean the implementation of wireless local area networks (LAN) trunks between two buildings. The networking side of the information technology budget has matured substantially in the realm of securing and inspecting data flowing on the network. The realistic creation of network redundancy and relative risk mitigation is still a new discipline in the data communication side of networking.

Management of security is often tantamount to dictatorial repression of users or liaise faire' hope for the best and accepting user and supervisory ambivalence. Within the area of management though is found the topics of risk mitigation, risk analysis, and policy and procedure creation.

ASSUMPTIONS

A program is only as good as the faculty who deliver the content. The faculty must be engaged in this process. When creating a curriculum it will be rare that a department or program will be able to simply dissolve an older program and implement a new program (Reza Kamali, Liles, Winer, Jiang, & Nicolai, 2005). It could be suggested that any program will have the associated baggage and skew in interest based on the hosting institution and the faculty's previous experience. Of course those are the very things that make the differentiators in program delivery and it should be welcomed that the faculty will give their own perspectives on how topics should be delivered.

Community participation at the local level should be an expectation. The local community, as well as the larger information assurance and security community, are stake holders in the education of future implementers and designers of security apparatus. Further it would be expected that programs considering security will become active in that community. This could be an issue for a small college with minimal funds for travel, and of no consequence to some faculty. The issue with participation is the rapid and accelerating pace of security curricula and dissemination of information from the knowledge holders to the community. In some cases this is only possible person to person. The literature simply cannot keep up with the winds of change. A simple explanation to the requirements for community is the rapid pace of change considering "Moore's Law". As density of silicon increases, storage capacity increases, size decreases, and the sophistication of technologies increase the impacts on information assurance and security equally increase. Simply put technology evolves at such a rapid pace waiting for a journal article on a bug or attack method will not be prudent.

A CURRICULUM PROCESS

A curriculum process should start with a framework structured by a tapestry of outcome based learning objective guidelines as proposed by a relevant accreditation agency. Each of the outcome based learning objectives are processed for level of skill based on the Bloom Taxonomy (Bloom, Krathwohl, Masia, & Emgelhart, 1956) for education. The objectives are then looked at for area of expertise as applied to individual curricula guidelines. Balance of instructional expectation is attained by insuring that freshman and sophomore classes are balanced strongly towards the lower levels of Bloom taxonomy with fewer upper level objectives. Consequently upper level courses have higher level objectives and significantly fewer lower level objectives with an expectation that prior courses prepared the student sufficiently. As part of the preparation of that expectation course designers should meet and built a map of the course objectives and knowledge requirements.

Before beginning the mapping of objectives, the role of a student completing the course should be discussed as what a successful student form the program do as a career and whether the objective is to create practitioners, scholars, or graduate school aspirants.

Considering the inherent interdisciplinary nature of the Information Assurance Education, there is the burning question of who are the relevant external agencies formulating the learning objectives upon which to build the holistic and inclusive curriculum process. There are many external agencies ranging from educational institutions to governmental agencies and private stakeholders with differing requirements on the parameters defining the boundaries of an information assurance curriculum and it would be difficult, if not impossible, to formulate accreditation standards satisfying all the parties involved.

However, it seems that there is an implicit agreement among different stakeholders in splitting up information assurance and security in a few specific topical areas such as systems, software, networking, and management. These will allow us to look at the topical elements and consider them in our end solution for creating a curriculum model and accreditation standards. This, in turn, may allow us to concentrate ACM and IEEE standards that assist ABET in defining curriculum for accreditation. Also, of specific interest to practical consideration of the accreditation standards would be revising and modifying ABET accreditation standards for systems, software, networking, and management to ensure their compatibility with NTISSI 4011 standards.

REPORTS OF AN IMPLEMENTATION

At Purdue University Calumet, creation of curriculum after adapting and changing the structure became substantially easier when the holistic view was engaged by all participants. The effective learning objectives of one course could be fed into another course as the prerequisites of that course. If the assessment of learning was accomplished then a complete understanding of the capabilities of a student was fairly easy to understand.

The curriculum for Purdue University Calumet was set up to mirror as closely as possible the SIGITE guidelines for ABET accreditation. Within the draft guidelines are located a series of learning objectives and even examples of how classes can be set up. This close mirror meant that in documenting the objectives for a course, a laboratory exercise within a course, or a test questions each element of the course was tied back to the accreditation model. This could be perceived to slow the development of a course, or worse it could be considered to be a restriction on the faculty development process. Quite the opposite was felt by the faculty. With a concrete understanding of the needs of a course, and what the expectations would be the curriculum development process was very smooth and a common base of understanding lead to increasing collaboration across specialties.

The question of what does not work within the curriculum process is easily answered. The structure meant that textbooks that were designed for "topic" based courses and not modified for the SIGITE guidelines do not match even distantly to courses designed for outcome based learning objectives. The topic areas might be found in three or more textbooks but almost never in just one text book. The textbook issue specifically affects the information assurance and security discipline since there are so few books in the first place. The result had faculty using textbooks that had as much information as possible and supplementing that information with papers and documentation from a variety of locations. This did have the added benefit of increasing the number of students enrolling in the ACM student program and the library sought and adopted the ACM library portal as a site wide license.

OVERVIEW OF THE IMPLEMENTATION

As an example of the Purdue University Calumet System, a set of courses was designed that created the core structure of the information assurance and security curriculum. Each of the courses followed the SIGITE ("Curriculum: Proposed standards for IT curriculum," 2005) guidelines exactly and the were copied then into the selected courses in their entirety as the learning objectives of the courses, or as part of the NTISSI (National Security Telecommunications and Information Systems, 1994, 1997b, 1997c, 1997d) standards that were built upon as a foundation. The topics of each course description are also from the SIGITE guidelines numbered as they were found in the draft and found to be topical while being vendor and specific technology neutral.

The introductory course into the information assurance and security track is a fundamentals course and each successive course is laid out with their associated learning objectives from the SIGITE draft guidelines building a cohesive flexible undergraduate curriculum.

ITS 250 Fundamentals of Information Assurance: (Pattern 2 hours lab, 2 hours lecture, 3 hours credit) (Prerequisite ITS 170 (introductory networking course) and ITS 135 (introductory operating systems course)) This course covers security mechanisms, fundamental aspects, operational issues, policy, attacks, security domains, forensics, information states, security services, threat analysis, vulnerabilities, and other topics.

IAS1. FUNDAMENTAL ASPECTS

Topics: History and Terminology; Security Mindset (reasoned paranoia); Design Principles (Defense in Depth); System/security life-cycle; Security implementation mechanisms; (gates, guards, guns; cryptography); Information assurance analysis model by Maconachy, Schou and Ragsdale (MSR Model); Disaster recovery (natural and man-made)

Core learning outcomes:

1. Briefly describe the history of the field of Information Assurance and Security.
2. Explain the relationship between threats, vulnerabilities, countermeasures, attacks, compromises and remediation.
3. Give examples of how IT system components (e.g. servers, routers, people, software) can be countermeasures, vulnerabilities, and also threats.
4. Describe the security mindset and the role of "paranoia" in that mindset.
5. Explain and give examples of why security and assurance must be "built in" to design and architecture from the beginning to be most effective.
6. Outline the system life-cycle and its relationship to security.
7. List the Security Services as defined by the MSR model.
8. List the Information States as defined by the MSR model.
9. List the Countermeasures as defined by the MSR model.
10. Given the MSR model, explain how the components interrelate to categorize threats, vulnerabilities and attacks.
11. Describe a disaster recovery scenario.
12. Define forensics.
13. Describe a situation where a forensic investigation would be necessary.

Elective learning outcomes:

1. Describe the major developments in the field of IAS and analyze the reasons for those developments.
2. Choose a development that has had significant impact on the field of IAS and justify the reason(s) why it is significant.
3. Prepare a threat analysis.
4. Given a threat analysis, recommend the appropriate countermeasures.
5. Demonstrate the ability to preserve evidence necessary for a forensic investigation.

IAS9. SECURITY SERVICES

Topics: Availability; Integrity; Confidentiality; Authentication (source reliability); Non-repudiation

Core learning outcomes:

1. Describe the possible availability levels for a web service.
2. Describe how redundancy and geographic dispersion relate to availability.
3. Define integrity as a security service.
4. Describe how one-way cryptographic functions are used to implement integrity in document transfer.
5. Define confidentiality as a security service.
6. Describe how cryptographic encryption algorithms are used to implement confidentiality in document transfer.
7. Define authentication as a security service.
8. Describe how one-way functions and encryption are used to implement a typical authentication service.
9. Define non-repudiation as a security service.
10. Describe how one-way functions are used to implement a non-repudiation service.

Elective learning outcomes:

1. Describe the sequence of events for a typical challenge hand shake protocol authentication scheme.
2. Describe the sequence of events needed to protect the integrity and ensure non-repudiation of an electronic contract distributed through email to the participants in the contract.
3. Describe what needs to be done in addition to provide confidentiality for the contract in 2 above.

ITS 350 Systems Assurance: (Pattern 2 hours lecture, 2 hours lab, 3 hours credit)(Prerequisite ITS 250) This course covers the implementation of systems assurance with computing systems. Topics include confidentiality, integrity, authentication, non-repudiation, intrusion detection, physical security, and encryption. Extensive laboratory exercises are assigned.

IAS2. SECURITY MECHANISMS (COUNTERMEASURES)

Topics: *Cryptography* {Cryptosystems; Keys: symmetric & asymmetric; Performance; Implementation} *Authentication {Bio-authentication (use of biometrics)};* Redundancy; Intrusion Detection

Core learning outcomes:

1. Describe the three key factors involved in authentication and how they are used to verify identity and grant access to a system.
2. Explain the process and value of two-factor authentication.
3. Describe the characteristics of an effective password.
4. Describe and compare physical access control to logical access control.
5. Identify the key types of biometric information utilized in authentication from the perspectives of accuracy, intrusiveness and efficiency.
6. Describe the differences between symmetric and asymmetric cryptosystems, e.g., number of keys required, the types of algorithms used, etc.
7. Explain what is meant by integrity, confidentiality, and authentication.
8. Describe how cryptosystems offer 1) Confidentiality, and 2) Authentication
9. Describe digital signatures and certificates
10. Describe how a public key infrastructure (PKI) works
11. Describe the data encryption standard (DES) and 3DES algorithms
12. Demonstrate how public-key cryptography works by the use of public and private keys

13. Describe the advanced encryption standard (AES) algorithm
14. Describe the differences between block and stream cryptosystems.
15. Explain the differences in efficiency and performance between software based and hardware based cryptosystems

Elective learning outcomes:

1. Describe the single sign-on authentication process and problem related to using and implementing this technology.
2. Compare key access control and authentication mechanisms to select the one appropriate to specific business contexts (Kerberos, RAS, etc,)..
3. Compare the advantages and disadvantages of centralized access controls to decentralized access controls.

IAS5. ATTACKS

Topics: Social Engineering; Denial of Service; Protocol attacks; Active attacks; Passive Attacks; Buffer Overflow Attacks; Malware (Viruses, Trojan Horses, Worms)

Core learning outcomes:

1. Explain and give examples of the social engineering techniques used to gain access to computing and network assets in an organization.
2. Describe how a Denial of Service attack works against an organization's network.
3. List some different protocol attacks to which TCP/IP is susceptible.
4. Describe how the different protocol attacks (e.g. TCP/IP) works against an organization's network.
5. Explain some techniques used during an active attack.
6. Explain some techniques used during a passive attack.
7. Describe how an active attack might use information from a passive attack to compromise a system.
8. Describe and explain how a Buffer Overflow Attack might be used to compromise a system.
9. Identify and distinguish between the different types of Malware (Viruses, Trojan Horses, Worms).

Elective learning outcomes:

1. Plan a social engineering attack against an organization's network.
2. Perform a penetration test (active attacks/ passive attacks) against an organization's network.
3. Demonstrate the tools and technologies used in passive and active attacks.
4. Demonstrate a Denial of Service attack.

ITS 352 Disaster recovery and planning: (Pattern 2 hours lab, 2 hours lecture, 3 hours credit) (Prerequisite ITS 350) This course covers risk management and business continuity. Topics include disaster recovery strategies, mitigation strategies, risk analysis, and development of contingency plans for unexpected outages and component failures. Extensive laboratory exercises are assigned.

IAS3. OPERATIONAL ISSUES

Topics: Trends, Auditing, Cost / benefit analysis, Management, Standards, Enforcement, issues, Disaster recovery (natural and man-made)

Core learning outcomes:

1. Describe legal and ethical considerations related to the handling and management of enterprise information assets

2. Specify what constitutes admissible evidence in a legal proceeding and how to acquire and maintain this information.
3. Describe the importance of and key elements involved in incident tracking to develop an incident handling and reporting process
4. Identify risks associated with disasters or disruptions and specify key mitigation strategies.
5. Identify the types of company assets to be protected by a security plan.
6. Specify the key aspects of physical site security.
7. Describe the elements contributing to the cost of an organizations security management and operations process and their relation to risks and losses associated with information assurance or security related issues and incidents.
8. Describe and evaluate employment policies and practices that are relevant to safeguarding an organization's information assets.
9. Describe the importance of utilizing standards and key standard processes currently utilized in information assurance and their areas of relevance (i.e. DES – Data Encryption Standard).
10. Describe the purpose and elements of the key types of security audits. Discuss how various security standards (i.e. ISO 177799) impact the direction of these audits.

Elective learning outcomes:

1. Develop an incident handling and reporting process
2. Suggest appropriate operational and managerial processes to mitigate security and information assurance issues based on a BIA (Business Impact Analysis report).
3. Create a financial analysis report BIA (Business Impact Analysis report) hat itemizes costs associated with information assurance and security activities and compares these costs to potential risks and costs associated with incidents in these areas.
4. Describe how key information security and assurance standards are or should be utilized in specific industry contexts.
5. Discuss the role of CASPR (Commonly Accepted Security Practices and Recommendations) forms in defining and approving standard operational and management practices.
6. Specify how changes in technology and the constantly changing methods of attacking systems and attempting to compromise information or access it inappropriately impact operational and managerial practices and policies.

IAS11. VULNERABILITIES

Topics: Perpetrators Inside attacks External attacks Black Hat White Hat, Ignorance,, Carelessness, Network, Hardware (design, implementation, installation, etc.), Software (design, implementation, installation, etc.), access

Core learning outcomes:

1. Explain the differences between a hacker and a cracker. Consider white hat, black hat, culture, community, tools, and technologies used and how they are used by each.
2. Describe the role of the user in information assurance and how they fit into an overall information assurance plan for an organization.
3. Explain how ignorance and carelessness leads to vulnerabilities for an organization.
4. Give an example of how inside and external attacks are similar and are different.
5. List and explain the major network threats and vulnerabilities for an organization.
6. Demonstrate how software contributes to the vulnerabilities for an organization. Consider

design, implementation, and installation issues.
7. Demonstrate how hardware contributes to the vulnerabilities for an organization. Consider design, implementation, and installation issues.

Elective learning outcomes:

1. Demonstrate how you would test a system for vulnerabilities.
2. Do a vulnerability analysis of a system.
3. Develop user education modules to educate users on their role in information assurance.
4. Choose a common vulnerability and describe how an attacker uses this vulnerability to gain access to a system.

ITS 354 Information Assurance Risk Assessment: (Pattern 2 hours, lecture, 2 hours lab, 3 hours credit)(Prerequisite ITS 350) This course covers industry and government requirements and guidelines for information assurance and auditing of computing systems. Topics include risk assessment and implementation of standardized requirements and guidelines.

IAS4. POLICY

Topics: Creation of Policies, Maintenance of Policies, Prevention, Avoidance, Incident Response (Forensics), Domain integration (physical, network, internet, etc.)

Core learning outcomes:

1. Describe the role of policy and procedure in the IAS Model.
2. Explain why policy and procedure are listed as countermeasures.
3. Explain how poorly defined and executed policies can be a vulnerability.
4. Describe how an organization might develop a policy to defend against password vulnerabilities.
5. Describe why a password policy might need to be modified due to changing circumstances.
6. Explain why security policies must consider all aspects of an organization in order to be effective.
7. Give an example of how a vulnerability in one area of an organization might enable a compromise in another area. (Example: weak physical security allows sniffer access to the LAN which allows a password to be read from a POP3 packet. The password is used to gain access to a corporate server. Login access to the server allows a root-kit to be applied and the bad guy has total access to the server).
8. Describe a situation in which an incident would require a full forensic approach including evidence gathering, full chain of custody auditing and expert analysis.
9. Describe how failure to follow good forensic procedures could make prosecution of an attacker impossible.

Elective learning outcomes:

1. Create a set of policies that implement a specified organizational objective.
2. Update a set of policies to reflect a change in organizational objectives.

IAS10. THREAT ANALYSIS MODEL

Topics: Risk assessment Cost benefit

Core learning outcomes:

1. Identify the aspects of a business that may be impacted by a security breach or interruption of operation.

2. Quantify the financial losses associated with potential security breaches and interruption of operations.
3. Identify and describe the nine steps to assess risks associated with security specified by the National Institute of Standards and Technology (NIST).
4. Describe the costs associated with actions that can be taken to mitigate security risks.

Elective learning outcomes:

1. Define an Information Risk Management (IRM) policy for an organization by analyzing its information assets to determine the appropriate financial, managerial and security aspects of this policy.
2. Identify the quantitative and qualitative measures that can be used to assess risk and evaluate the effectiveness of risk management policies and practices.
3. Specify the value of the benefits to be achieved as a result of risk mitigation efforts and relate this benefit to the cost associated with achieving these benefits.

ITS450 Software Assurance: (Pattern 2 hours lecture, 2 hours lab, 3 hours credit)(Prerequisite ITS 352) This course covers defensive programming techniques, bounds analysis, error handling, advanced testing techniques, detailed code auditing, and software specification in a trusted assured environment. Extensive laboratory exercises are assigned.

IAS8. INFORMATION STATES

Topics: Transmission; Storage; Processing
Core learning outcomes:

1. Give an example of a file representing a document in each of the three states.
2. Justify the statement "An electronic document is frequently in more than one state at the same time."
3. Describe a situation where the same document is in all three states at the same instant of time.
4. Give examples of the relationships between the security services and information states.
5. Give examples of different vulnerabilities that apply to specific states.
6. Explain how the concept of "information state" relates to the concept of a "lifecycle".

Elective learning outcomes:

1. Analyze a proposed data storage system describing all of the information objects and their states during the entire object lifecycle.
2. Describe some vulnerabilities of the information objects in each of the states.
3. Describe in detail the security services required to implement a specified security policy given an analysis as described above.

ITS452 Computer Forensics: (Pattern 2 hours, lecture, 2 hours lab, 3 hours credit)(Prerequisite ITS 354) This course covers the techniques used in the forensic analysis of computerized systems for gathering evidence to detail how a system has been exploited or used. Extensive laboratory exercises are assigned.

IAS7. FORENSICS

Topics: Legal Systems, Digital Forensics and its relationship to other Forensic disciplines, Rules of Evidence, Search and Seizure, Digital Evidence,

Core learning outcomes:

1. List three types of legal systems used by countries in the world.
2. Describe how digital forensics fits with the other forensic disciplines.
3. Describe a method for capturing a disk drive as evidence and proving its integrity for legal evidence purposes.
4. Explain the difference between the rules for a corporation seizing its property from an employee and law enforcement's seizing of property from a citizen.

Elective learning outcomes:

1. Explain the concept of "reasonable expectation of privacy", its relationship to corporate policy banners displayed on workstations, and the use of email as evidence in the prosecution of an employee by the corporation.
2. List the areas on a disk that could contain evidence that are not accessible through normal operating system access.
3. List three methods for hiding information on a typical file system.
4. Explain why "free space" often contains interesting data.
5. Capture a forensic image of a disk drive and guarantee the integrity of the image using MD5 or SHA signatures.
6. Perform a basic media analysis of a captured drive using a forensic toolkit.

ITS 454 Assured Systems Design and Implementation: (Pattern 2 hours lecture, 2 hours lab, 3 hours credit)(Prerequisite ITS 450 and ITS 452) This course covers the design and implementation of assured systems in an enterprise environment. Topics include hardening of operating systems, choice of platforms, design criteria within the assured systems domain. Extensive laboratory exercises are assigned.

IAS6. SECURITY DOMAINS

Topics: Human-Computer Interaction, Information Management, Programming, Networking, Program Fundamentals, Platform Technologies, System Administration, System Integration and Architecture, and Professional Issues, Web Systems, Physical plant

Core learning outcomes:

1. Give examples of shared concerns across a specified set of security domains.
2. Give examples of concerns that are specific to specified security domains.

Elective learning outcomes:

1. Describe the aspects of Human-Computer Interactions which must be considered in designing and implementing secure systems.
2. Discuss how Information Management is impacted by security concerns.
3. Explain how Integrative Programming can utilize security and information assurance concepts to ensure the development of secure systems and applications.
4. List several areas of Networking where security must be considered (i.e. access control, authentication, etc.). Discuss several best practices in programming that can prevent security flaws.
5. Describe how security concerns may impact Platform section and operation.
6. Explain key security concerns from a Systems Administration perspective.
7. Discuss policies and practices that may be applied to Systems Integration and Architectures to ensure secure system operation and information assurance.
8. List the impact of ensuring secure systems on society and on ones professional practice.
9. Identify the aspects of Web Systems that must be considered to ensure Web based applications are secure.

10. List the elements of the physical plant that should be considered in preventing security breaches.

ITS 459 Topics in Information Assurance and Security: (Pattern 3 hours, lecture, 0 hours lab, 3 hours credit)(Prerequisite ITS 450 and ITS 452) This course covers special topics and emerging technologies in information assurance and security.

The topics in information assurance and security course have no formal learning objectives. This capstone course is taught by the faculty in an area that is emerging, is something the faculty member is interested in or a special topic that may be brought up by students The idea behind this course was to provide a finishing environment where students could be introduced to new and emerging concepts of faculty research.

CONCLUSION

We have discussed that information assurance and security has been defined by many authors as the practices, techniques, methods, of securing information in all of its forms from the various threats and risks that information can be subjected to in the enterprise (McKnight, 2002; National Security Telecommunications and Information Systems, 1997a). With so many external agencies ranging from educational institutions to governmental agencies and private stakeholders with differing requirements on the parameters defining the boundaries of an information assurance curriculum and it would be difficult, if not impossible, to formulate accreditation standards satisfying all the parties involved.

The approach was to show a series of courses that were designed around a national accreditation model for information technology curriculum. This model was chosen based on a few factors one of the primary factors being the substantial amount of interdisciplinary nature in the realm of information assurance and security.

REFERENCES

Bloom, B. S., Krathwohl, D. R., Masia, B. B., & Emgelhart, M. D. (1956). *Taxonomy of educational objectives : the classification of educational goals.* New York: Longmans, Green.

Computing curricula 2001. (2001). *J. Educ. Resour. Comput., 1*(3es), 1.

Curriculum: Proposed standards for IT curriculum. (2005). from http://sigite.acm.org/activities/curriculum/downloads/IT%20Volume-April%202005.pdf

Dark, M. J. (2004). *Assessing student performance outcomes in an information security risk assessment, service learning course.* Paper presented at the Proceedings of the 5th conference on Information technology education, Salt Lake City, UT, USA.

Dark, M. J., Ekstrom, J., J., & Lunt, B., M. . (2005). *Integration of information assurance and security into the IT2005 model curriculum.* Paper presented at the Proceedings of the 6th conference on Information technology education, Newark, NJ, USA.

Hazem, S., Chaytor, L., Humpert, D., Nyland, J., Schlemmer, R., Stockman, M., et al. (2004). *An implementation of a core curriculum in an information technology degree program.* Paper presented at the Proceedings of the 5th conference on Information technology education, Salt Lake City, UT, USA.

Kamali, R., Liles, S., Winer, C., Jiang, K., & Nicolai, B. (2005). *An implementation of the SIGITE model curriculum.* Paper presented at the Proceedings of the 6th conference on Information technology education, Newark, NJ, USA.

Kamali, R., Liles, S., Winer, C., Jiang, K., & Nicolai, B. (2006). A Curriculum Model Based on the SIGITE Guidelines. *Journal of Information Technology Education, 5.*

Liles, S. P., & Kamali, R. (2006). An Information Assurance and Security Curriculum Implementation. *Issues in Informing Science and Information Technology, 3.*

Maconachy, W. V., Schou, C. D., Ragsdale, D., & Welch, D. (2001). A Model for Information Assurance: An Integrated Approach. *Proceedings of the 2001 IEEE Workshop on Information Assurance and Security, US Military Academy, West Point, NY*, 5-6.

McKnight, W. (2002, July). What is Information Assurance. *CROSSTALK, The Journal of Defense Software Engineering.*

National Security Telecommunications and Information Systems. (1994). *National Training Standard for Information Systems Security (INFOSEC) Professionals.* Retrieved April 20, 2006. from http://www.cnss.gov/Assets/pdf/nstissi_4011.pdf.

National Security Telecommunications and Information Systems. (1997a). *National Information Systems Security Glossary No. 4009.* Retrieved. from.

National Security Telecommunications and Information Systems. (1997b). *National Training Standard for Designated Approving Authority (DAA).* Retrieved April 20, 2006. from http://www.cnss.gov/Assets/pdf/cnssi_4012.pdf.

National Security Telecommunications and Information Systems. (1997c). *National Training Standard for Information Systems Security Officers (ISSO).* Retrieved April 20, 2006. from http://www.cnss.gov/Assets/pdf/cnssi_4014.pdf.

National Security Telecommunications and Information Systems. (1997d). *National Training Standard for System Administrators in Information Systems Secuirty (INFOSEC).* Retrieved April 20, 2006. from http://www.cnss.gov/Assets/pdf/cnssi_4013.pdf.

Rigby, S., & Dark, M. (2006). Using outcomes-based assessment data to improve assessment and instruction: a case study. *SIGITE News, 3*(1), 10-15.

KEY TERMS

Assurance: The act of implementing protection measures against risks. Within the context of information assurance and security it is a holistic concept suggesting a variety of information controls.

Authentication: Protection measures and methods of insuring only authorized entities access information. This is linked to concepts such as need-to-know. Authentication suggests control of communication channels and access to information internally and externally as a security service.

Availability: The ability to access information assets when needed and as needed. This suggests mechanisms that insure that information is there to be accessed even after the original data environment may have been destroyed. Availability suggests control of the inbound communication channel as a security service.

Confidentiality: Keeping information restricted to only those who should have access to it. Information should be controlled from outside interception. Confidentiality suggests control of information on the outbound communication channel as a security service.

Integrity: Insuring that information that is stored or transmitted is not maliciously changed. Protection mechanisms for data while stored or transmitted are important to protect the original meaning of information. Integrity suggests control of information while stored or transmitted internally as a security service.

Non-Repudiation: Also known as authenticity the ability to state that an entity was involved in a communication exchange or prove that an entities credentials are genuine based on the trust established between two entities or using a trusted third entity. Non-repudiation is a mechanism for insuring the relationship of entities involved in the communications channel as a security service.

Security: An evaluation of risk to communication and information and mitigation of those risks through different services.

Chapter XIX
Information Security Awareness

Gary Hinson
IsecT Ltd, New Zealand

ABSTRACT

This chapter highlights the broad range of factors that are relevant to the design of information security awareness programs, primarily by reference to the literature. It emphasizes the need to supplement technical information security controls with security awareness, training and educational activities to address human vulnerabilities. It outlines requirements noted in standards, laws and regulations, and explains the value of motivational employee communications techniques in creating a security culture.

INTRODUCTION

As with health and safety or legal compliance, management can hardly expect employees to comply with corporate information security policies, adopt security standards and follow security procedures if they don't even know of their existence. Information security awareness is therefore an essential component of effective information security management systems, supporting and enhancing the technical and procedural information security controls and contributing to the corporation's overall governance. In order to instill a genuine security culture throughout the organization, the awareness issue goes well beyond simply informing employees of their security obligations. To overcome the inevitable change resistance or inertia, employees have to be both informed and motivated to modify their behaviors, to 'think security and act securely'. This chapter explains the challenges and details information security awareness approaches that work, using quotations from others in the field to illustrate the points made.

BACKGROUND

The Importance and Limitations of Information Security

Information is the lifeblood of organizations, a vital business asset in today's IT-enabled world. IT systems and networks link every internal department and connect us with a myriad of suppliers, partners and markets. Access to high-quality, complete, accurate and up-to-date information improves managerial decision-making by reducing the margin for error.

Protecting and enhancing the value of information assets has become a central strategic objective in most businesses, second only to making profits. Schmidt (2005) said "We need to build security into the core fabric – the DNA – of the computing world."

Regulations and laws such as Health Insurance Portability and Accountability Act (HIPAA, 1996), Financial Modernization Act (GLB, 1999), Basel II (2004), Sarbanes Oxley Act (SOX, 2002), Federal Information Security Management Act (FISMA, 2002), and various privacy/data protection laws such as the Data Protection Act (DPA, 1998) impose a raft of obligations.

Information security is not just a simple matter of having usernames and passwords! Information security controls improve the organization's profitability by reducing both the number and the extent of information security breaches, reducing both the direct and indirect costs (*e.g.* lost productivity through time lost investigating and resolving breaches and hoaxes; irrecoverable loss of data; expenses incurred in recovering and securing compromised data and systems; notification of customers and regulators; fines for breaching laws and regulations; damaged reputation leading to customer defections and brand devaluation). Furthermore, comprehensive and reliable information security controls reduce the organization's overall risk profile. Good information security builds management's confidence and trust, allowing the organization to press ahead with business opportunities (such as eBusiness) that might otherwise be too risky to contemplate. Part of this arises from better knowledge of the extent of security breaches that occur: consistently reporting information about actual and potential (near-miss) security breaches to management is a sign of a mature information security framework.

Despite the self-evident goal of information security, "There is no such thing as security – it is a dream. Security is not an absolute quantity, only a relative commodity," said Cochrane (1997, p.40). Wang (2005) attributed security failure to three factors:

1. People concentrating too much on security itself;
2. Security measures not aligned with business strategy; and
3. The existence of a communication gap between senior management and IT professionals.

Seeing the 'big picture', Wang said, begins with positioning—that is, establishing a security position that suited both company resources and business direction. "It has to be a long-term commitment and sustainable." Corporate culture is important too, according to Wang. He addressed the problem of the communication gap that exists between senior management and the executives proposing the security measures, saying that the problem lay with ineffective explanation of security objectives. Senior management is often not aware or concerned with the measures.

Menta (2005), commenting on research of the top 350 UK companies listed by the Financial Times, said "Four out of five investors indicated that a significant breach in security would have a major impact on share price. Two thirds said it would influence a decision to buy or sell shares. Nearly nine in ten expected board members to be aware of, and to be able to review, their company's infosec vulnerabilities, and 57 percent thought they should know about the company's information risk strategy". Like Wang (2005), Menta (2005) also made a case for keeping stakeholders informed about an organization's information security status - an unusual perspective on security awareness and one that we'll return to later.

Technical Security Controls Alone are Insufficient

Most IT-enabled organizations have invested heavily in firewalls, antivirus and other security technologies in recent years. Every one of those products was no doubt sold on the basis of its effectiveness but still information security breaches are commonplace and the problems seem to be getting worse, not better. Kark *et al.* (2005) said, "Today, organizations spend millions of dollars on technical solutions and process improvements but still feel vulnerable." What is going wrong here?

There comes a point of diminishing returns, when throwing big money and ever more complex technologies at the problem is no longer as effective at improving security. Contos (2006) said "There is no piece of technology that once deployed will solve all of an organization's security problems. Security encompasses people, process, and technology. By finding the right combination of these, an organization can successfully reduce risk." (p. 70).

Byrnes of META Group (quoted in AT&T, 2003) estimated that "30% of IT security relates to technology, and 70% relates to people and practices." COSO (1994) made the point that "Internal control is effected by people. It's not merely policy manuals and forms, but people at every level of an organization." Cochrane (1997, p.40) said "The reality is that most security failures are down to human fallibility, bribery and corruption." "Regardless of the technology in place to protect data, people still represent the biggest threat" said Ryskin (quoted by Green, 2005). McCarthy (2006) said "The primary cause of security breaches—human error—is not being adequately addressed. The person behind the PC continues to be the primary area where weaknesses are exposed." This goes for both the PC user and the system designers, developers, testers and administrators.

There is ample evidence to support these assertions, for example a 'lighthearted and unscientific survey' by Verisign found that most people asked were willing to reveal their passwords for a $3 Starbucks coffee token (reported by Claburn, 2005). "According to the company, one executive who was too busy to respond to questions but still wanted a gift card sent his administrative assistant back to complete the survey. The assistant promptly revealed both the executive's password and her own." An astonishing 90% of office workers using London's Waterloo Station gave away their computer password to a surveyor in exchange for a cheap pen. "No amount of technology will be successful in protecting an organization if employees are naïve, poorly trained or are not made aware of the impact of security violations," says Tamar Beck (quoted in AT&T, 2003). Such informal surveys, generally conducted in connection with marketing for information security trade shows, have become passé: it is depressingly easy for surveyors to persuade members of the public to part with their passwords and other potentially sensitive private information.

Carey (2006) looked at the issue in some depth through a research study sponsored by $(ISC)^2$. "According to more than 4,000 information security professionals from more than 100 countries in the largest study of its kind, the most important elements in effectively securing their organization's infrastructure are (in order of importance):

- Management support of security policies
- Users following security policy
- Qualified security staff
- Software solutions
- Hardware solutions"

According to the $(ISC)^2$ study (Carey, 2006), the top three success factors highlight the need for public and private entities to focus more time and attention on policies, processes and people, all areas which have been traditionally overlooked in favor of trusting hardware and software to solve security problems. Survey respondents said "organizations are now beginning to recognize that technology is an enabler, not the solution, for implementing and executing a sound security strategy." "As headlines continue to report data security breaches at an alarming rate, discussion often focuses on the need for enhanced technical controls, such as two-factor authentication and encryption, to protect sensitive, personally identifiable information," said Sulkin (2006). "The role of the company employee, both as the cause of, and the first line of defense against, security breaches is often lost in the analysis."

THE RÔLE OF SECURITY AWARENESS, TRAINING AND EDUCATION

Even if management accepts the value of information security, there is still an open question of how best to spend the budget. "People would like to be told what they have to do to be secure. However, this is no more realistic than asking you what I have to do to be profitable," said Czekalski (2006).

Many information security investment decisions are made by, or at least on the recommendation of, information technology professionals. IT people have a natural bias towards technological solutions and most tend to shy away from 'soft' sociological issues such as policy and procedural compliance by employees. Awareness, training and education are consequently a neglected area of security investment, compounded by a relatively immature market compared to that for technical security controls. Despite widespread sympathy for the view that "Security is a process, not a product" (Schneier, 2004, p. 273), expenditure on security technologies such as firewalls, antivirus and PKI still dwarfs spending on security processes and the associated training and awareness.

Instead of continually installing and patching the technology, and forever scrambling to deal with security incidents and emerging risks, it's time to take a step back and find a better, more comprehensive approach. "Technology alone is not enough. Sound information security policies and procedures must be in place. Staff must be trained and aware" (McKenzie, 2005). Smith (2007) recommends "We must stop developing increasingly technical solutions for increasingly obscure problems at the expense of the blindingly obvious. Systems malfunctions and human error or ignorance will cost you far more than viruses, cybercrime, phishing or Denial-of-Service attacks." Kark *et al.* (2005) said "Security is a function of people, process, and technology working in concert, but often the people aspect of security is ignored. An effective security awareness program goes a long way to address people security and makes organizations look and feel more secure. Organizations must take a structured approach to develop effective security awareness programs."

According to Gartner's Witty and Wagner (2005), "Information security awareness training is a much-maligned part of a complete information security program. Taken alone—without technology solutions such as malicious code detection and prevention, vulnerability assessments, firewalls, and identity and access management—a training program will not address all IT risks. Users of IT assets must know their responsibility in protecting these assets, as well as customer information, and the consequences if they fail to comply with information security policies. Therefore, Gartner considers an information security awareness training program to be an essential tool for all companies, regardless of size."

"Investing time and money into securing the organization and its customers can be completely undermined if employees don't understand their role in the security plan," said Navarro (2007). But "with the right training, employees can become an organization's strongest security asset. A security awareness program enables organizations to improve their security posture by offering employees the knowledge they need to better protect the organization's information through proactive, security-conscious behavior. To successfully protect information assets, employees at every level - from the top down - need a basic understanding of security policies as well as their respective responsibilities in protecting these assets. Management personnel with security responsibilities require additional training. Without this understanding, organizations cannot hold employees accountable for protecting the organization's resources and ultimately, its profitability."

Johansson and Riley (2005) said, "Helping people understand their own security vulnerabilities and how to, well, 'patch' them is the most effective way we know of to help educate people about computer security vulnerabilities and the need to remain vigilant in protecting corporate and personal information. Typical system administrators have very little understanding of how to do such a thing—indeed, they even lack awareness that it's necessary; what awareness they do have is usually related to laws and regulations requiring only passing knowledge. This lack of awareness often leads to total system compromise as an attacker bypasses all the carefully built technical security controls and goes directly to the most vulnerable part of any network: the people" (p. 128).

Formal security policies, no matter how carefully they are written, are of little value unless employees know about them, understand their obligations and actively comply. Claudia Warwar, managing consultant at IBM BCS Security and Privacy Practice, said "People are becoming the weakest link," (quoted by Hearne, 2006). Warwar continued, "A fluid work force with diminished loyalty to organisations is being exacerbated by the fact that people do not always realise the value of information that they deal with." According to Hearne, Warwar "believes that the rise in internal security attacks has come about because outside criminal gangs realise that recruiting or tricking employees to hand over insider knowledge is less expensive and traceable than other forms of cybercrime."

A report by the State of Texas Department of Information Resources (2001) noted that Internet security requires "more than a 'technology fix': formulating a strategic approach to information security management is a matter of addressing two basic issues: process and technology infrastructure. Ensuring Internet security requires more than simply the right technology resources. Like a bank vault, no amount of technology will provide adequate security in and of itself. To 'keep the money secure' the vault must be used correctly. Security is breached when procedures are not followed, when the wrong people are admitted to the vault, or if the vault is left open and unattended. Often we look to technology to solve business problems when in fact the processes are the more important solutions."

"A building protected by nothing more than a cheap combination lock but inhabited by people who are alert and risk-aware is much safer than one with the world's most sophisticated alarm system whose tenants assume they're living in an impregnable fortress" (Mason and Gruenfeld, 2003). This gets to the heart of the security awareness issue. Whilst locks and other security technologies can help, the most important factor is the security/risk alertness and motivation of the people who tend to the controls. Faced with two shops, one protected by attentive security guards and other alert employees versus one whose staff appear to be in a world of their own, the robber has an obvious choice. Even if the second shop has better security technology, the chances are that staff will not respond as quickly and effectively as the first. In the same way, given two organizations that have both deployed Intrusion Detection Systems but only one of which has qualified and experienced professionals attentively monitoring the alerts and tending to the monitoring rules, it is obvious which is the more vulnerable. Note that security awareness is an issue for IT and information security professionals as well as general staff.

There is evidence that information security adversaries increasingly recognize and deliberately exploit human vulnerabilities. The Honeynet Project and The Honeynet Research Alliance (2004) reported that "The primary threat is changing from machine-focused to human-focused. There is a growing trend towards social engineering, attacking the people using computers. In some cases, it is no longer the computer that is valuable, but the individual's information that resides on it. Also, it is often becoming easier to attack the user as opposed to the system, as newer installations are more secure by default. As a result, considerably more effort is being expended in strategies such as phishing to extract valuable information from targets, or malicious websites and mobile code that compromise client systems."

THE VALUE OF, AND NEED FOR INFORMATION SECURITY AWARENESS

"Arguably the biggest source of security breaches has nothing to do with installing and managing technology. The greatest weakness in the corporate security infrastructure is us" (Tamar Beck, quoted by AT&T, 2003). Alastair Morrison (quoted by Murray-Watson and Dennis, 2005) said "If I were a terrorist or criminal who wanted to disrupt and steal from your company, I would look at your vulnerability through your staff".

The phrase 'To err is human, to forgive divine' encapsulates a fundamental difference between people and computers. People often make mistakes, are sometimes lazy, forgetful or inattentive, and often misunderstand complex situations. We seek shortcuts to avoid boring, repetitive tasks and may cheat, bend or break the rules to get things done. People often forgive minor errors and even perfectionists occasionally have to settle for 'good enough'. We react emotionally, sometimes irrationally. Computers, in contrast, slavishly and precisely follow logical program instructions. Boredom is not a factor - computers simply take proportionally longer to process more data or resolve more complicated problems. If we are to improve information security, we must take these fundamental differences into account.

We need to think holistically: 'systems' are not just the computers but include the users, developers and administrators plus the management and operational processes. Errors are caused by faulty systems, processes and conditions that lead people to make mistakes or fail to prevent them. Even technical system faults have a human element: software bugs that create security vulnerabilities are mostly the result of errors in the development process that failed to take into account the different ways in which software can be used or abused.

It is pointless to put stronger and stronger links in our security chain unless we address the weakest links – the humans. "Inadequate user awareness is the single most important thing we should tackle," said Hackworth (2005). "The first line of defense from insider threats is the employees themselves," said Capelli *et al.*, (2006). "Sure, you have to protect against insider attacks. But, for the most part, insiders are your allies. Enlist their support as much as possible, and as often as possible," said Schneier (2004, p.373).

Technology alone is clearly not enough to ensure information security: it has to be implemented and managed professionally and of course it has to be used properly. The problem lies not so much with technology itself but with the people and processes in the organization. General staff, technologists and managers must actually use the security controls properly in order for them to be effective. People and processes are the weakest links. Until we measure and improve security awareness, this will inevitably remain true.

"A positive security culture provides the single best security defense. Awareness can contribute to building such a culture along with many other elements such as an effective management structure" (Hunter *et al*., 2002). Jan Babiak of Ernst and Young (quoted by Condon, 2006) said, "Companies must make strong and effective security practices part of their culture through awareness, education and accountability. This needs to be enforced by the CEO and the board, with organizations aspiring to implement well designed controls and fostering a security-conscious culture led from above. Without this top-down endorsement, employees will often ignore controls or worse avoid them, placing the entire enterprise at great risk." "If companies properly focus on key employee-related security controls and implement those controls in a reasoned and responsive manner, employees can be powerful assets to data security. Employees can assist companies with compliance requirements and, at the same time, help serve as an important line of defense from insider and outsider threats" (Sulkin, 2006).

However, security surveys consistently show that not all organizations are heeding the advice. The Department of Trade and Industry (2006) noted that "many UK companies are a long way from having a security-aware culture. Security expenditure is either low or not targeted at key risks". Minieri (2004) noted, "The single most important element in developing, implementing and maintaining an ongoing confidentiality program is the education and training of ALL employees in the organization. Information security must be an integral part of the orientation process, of the policy and procedure manual and of the employee handbook. Some excellent lessons in this regard can be taken from occupational health and safety professionals, and a glaring contrast becomes evident. When was the last time you saw posters on the wall reminding employees about protecting information?"

Awareness, training and education are complementary activities. According to NIST SP 800-50 (Wilson and Hash, 2003), *awareness* involves guiding and motivating people on appropriate behaviors, *training* helps people develop specific skills and *education* provides a broad basis through explaining conceptual frameworks and factual information. Information security is normally described in general terms through both awareness and education, with the motivational elements of awareness being a significant objective (*i.e.* not just telling people what they ought to do but encouraging them to do it). Training courses typically focus on particular security topics in more depth and involve students dedicating their time away from the day-job, whereas awareness and educational activities tend to happen in the background or in small segments, often self-directed.

Awareness, training and education help to secure information assets by:

- Informing people about information security risks and controls in a general sense, and providing more specific information and guidance where necessary;
- Emphasizing management's support for, and commitment to, information security;
- Promulgating the organization's information security policies, standards, procedures and guidelines, and externally imposed laws, rules and regulations;
- Motivating people to behave in a more security-conscious manner, for example taking security risks into account in business decision making;

- Improving and speeding up the identification and notification of security breaches.

Not only do awareness, training and education leverage the organization's existing investment in information security technologies, they enhance security in areas where the technology is of little if any use, such as social engineering and phishing attacks. Minieri (2004) said: "As with experts in any endeavor, security practitioners of all specialties study the tactics and techniques of their potential adversaries. In researching the practices of those who seek to obtain corporate secrets, most are surprised at how easy it is to elicit information from unsuspecting employees. The operative word here is 'unsuspecting'. What may seem to be an innocent and common conversation may – in reality – be a carefully crafted pretense to acquire protected information. Personnel in scientific fields tend to work in a culture where sharing research and other information is the norm. Once engaged in a conversation, such as at a tradeshow booth or job interview with a competitor, anyone might inadvertently let slip some tidbit that – added to data assembled from all available sources – makes the difference between who gets an innovative new product to market first."

Rasmussen (2005) said "Establishing a culture of security is critical. Information security managers must be well versed in the breadth of the IT career field and other disciplines as well (*e.g.* physical security, accounting and human resources management). In addition, a security manager must be a passionate advocate and an effective communicator. Interpersonal skills should include the ability to communicate in non-technical terms."

Schneier (quoted by Berinato, 2003) said "Computers and networks might be difficult to secure, but the biggest security vulnerability is still that link between keyboard and chair. People are sloppy with security; they choose lousy passwords, don't properly delete critical files, and they bypass security policies. They're susceptible to social engineering, and they fall victim to phishing attacks. They misconfigure security hardware and software. They accidentally bring worms and Trojan horses into the network. In short, they're a huge security problem ... Most of the time security problems are inherently people problems, and technologies don't help much. Photo IDs are a great example. Technologists want to add this and that technology to make IDs harder to forge, but I worry about people bribing issuing officials and getting real IDs in fake names. Technology that makes the IDs harder to forge doesn't solve that problem." "Always remember: amateurs hack systems. Professionals hack people" (Schneier, quoted by Pentasafe Security Technologies, 2002).

An army training manual (US Army, 2006) states: "People are a crucial factor in ensuring the security of computer systems and valuable information resources. Human actions account for a far greater degree of computer-related loss than all other sources combined. Of such losses, the actions of an organization's insiders normally cause far more harm than the actions of outsiders. The major causes of loss due to an organization's own employees are: errors and omissions, fraud, and actions by disgruntled employees. One principal purpose of security awareness, training, and education is to reduce errors and omissions. However, it can also reduce fraud and unauthorized activity by disgruntled employees by increasing employees' knowledge of their accountability and the penalties associated with such actions. Management sets the example for behavior within an organization. If employees know that management does not care about security, no training class teaching the importance of security and imparting valuable skills can be truly effective. This 'tone from the top' has myriad effects an organization's security program."

AusCERT (2005) noted: "The top vulnerabilities reported closely matched the top security management challenges for organisations. Inadequate staff training in computer security management (47%) and poor security culture within organisation (40%) were among the top vulnerabilities reported. This compares to 61% of respondents who identified changing users' (staff) attitudes and behaviour towards computer security practices a challenge for them." Respondents to the AusCERT survey overwhelmingly acknowledged that they "need to do more to ensure an appropriate level of IT security qualification, training, experience or awareness for general staff, IT security staff and management."

Miller (2001) said "Too many times, the assumption is made that improving cyber security and fighting cyber crime can be done with technology alone. That is wrong. Failures in the 'process and people' part of the cyber crime solution may, in fact, be the majority of the problems we see ... The challenge is to make cyber security a top priority issue. Moving from platitudes to practical action requires the sustained commitment of senior management. The goal is to embed cyber security in the corporate culture ... Organizations must be willing to invest in the development of comprehensive security procedures and to educate all employees--continuously ... The scope of the effort must also take into account the extended organization—supply chain partners, subcontractors, customers, and others that must interact on a routine basis."

GUIDANCE ON INFORMATION SECURITY AWARENESS FROM STANDARDS AND REGULATIONS

For more than a decade, numerous information security-related standards, regulations, laws, professional practice statements, methods, manuals *etc.* have recommended security awareness.

NIST SP 800-12 (1995) says "People, who are all fallible, are usually recognized as one of the weakest links in securing systems. The purpose of computer security awareness, training, and education is to enhance security by: improving awareness of the need to protect system resources; developing skills and knowledge so computer users can perform their jobs more securely; and building in-depth knowledge, as needed, to design, implement, or operate security programs for organizations and systems. Making computer system users aware of their security responsibilities and teaching them correct practices helps users change their behavior. It also supports individual accountability, which is one of the most important ways to improve computer security. Without knowing the necessary security measures (and to how to use them), users cannot be truly accountable for their actions."

HIPAA (1996) recommends that an organization should "implement a security awareness and training program for all members of its workforce (including management)".

The Awareness Principle is one of the fundamental Pervasive Principles defined in the Generally Accepted Systems Security Principles (GASSP, 1999, section 2.1.2): "All parties with a need to know, including, but not limited to, information owners and information security practitioners, should have access to available principles, standards, conventions, or mechanisms for the security of information and information systems, and should be informed of applicable threats to the security of information. Rationale: This principle applies between and within organizations. Awareness of information security principles, standards, conventions, and mechanisms enhances and enables controls and can help to mitigate threats. Awareness of threats and their significance also increases user acceptance of controls. Without user awareness of the necessity for particular controls, the users can pose a risk to information by ignoring, bypassing, or overcoming existing control mechanisms. The awareness principle applies to unauthorized and authorized parties."

The OECD (2002) says "Owners, providers, users and other parties should readily be able, consistent with maintaining security, to gain appropriate knowledge of and be informed about the existence and general extent of measures ... for the security of information systems."

NIST SP 800-53 (Ross *et al.*, 2005) advises that "An effective information security program should include ... security awareness training to inform personnel (including contractors and other users of information systems that support the operations and assets of the organization) of the information security risks associated with their activities and their responsibilities in complying with organizational policies and procedures designed to reduce these risks" (pp. 1-2).

The Standard of Good Practice for Information Security (Information Security Forum, 2005) recommends that "Specific activities should be undertaken, such as a security awareness programme, to promote security awareness to all individuals who have access to the information and systems of the enterprise," (section SM2.4). Also, "Staff should be educated/trained in how to run systems correctly and how to develop and apply security controls," (section SM2.5). Both sections give further, more explicit advice.

FIPS PUB 200 (NIST, 2006) notes: "Awareness and training: organizations must: (i) ensure that managers and users of organizational information systems are made aware of the security risks associated with their activities and of the applicable laws, Executive Orders, directives, policies, standards, instructions, regulations, or procedures related to the security of organizational information systems; and (ii) ensure that organizational personnel are adequately trained to carry out their assigned information security-related duties and responsibilities."

ISO/IEC 27002 (ISO/IEC, 2005) advises "All employees of the organization and, where relevant, contractors and third party users should receive appropriate awareness training and regular updates in organizational policies and procedures, as relevant for their job function. Awareness training should commence with a formal induction process designed to introduce the organization's security policies and expectations before access to information or services is granted. Ongoing training should include security requirements, legal responsibilities and business controls, as well as training in the correct use of information processing facilities *e.g.* log-on procedure, use of software packages and information on the disciplinary process. The security awareness, education, and training activities should be suitable and relevant to the person's role, responsibilities and skills, and should include information on known threats, who to contact for further security advice and the proper channels for reporting information security incidents. Training to enhance awareness is intended to allow individuals to recognize information security problems and incidents, and respond according to the needs of their work role." (section 8.2.2).

PRAGMATIC ADVICE ON MAKING INFORMATION SECURITY AWARENESS MORE EFFECTIVE

"A good security awareness program helps you secure your IT resources – one user at a time. A broad base of informed employees is the most cost-effective way to mitigate all the risks that exist for today's businesses. The trick is to build a great security awareness program" SANS (2003). Unfortunately, though, relatively few advisors, standards *etc.* go much further than saying 'something must be done about awareness': there has been a dearth of pragmatic advice for managers on how to design and deliver security awareness. The following notes promote more effective security awareness programs, emphasizing pragmatism and creativity when developing awareness communications and planning to change the corporate culture for the better. Further assistance is available from Herold (2005), ENISA (2006) and Wilson and Hash (2003).

Identify the Target Audiences and Make it Relevant

According to Ernst and Young (2004), the key to security awareness is "communicating with the entire organization regarding the threats that exist and the countermeasures that are available. Information security places a heavy emphasis on the judgment of individuals at all levels - particularly middle management. However, uninformed judgment, even in the presence of genius or intuition, is no substitute for accurate and timely information about the threats that an organization faces. Awareness also helps ensure that individuals understand security risks and the importance of security in their daily functions." Whilst I would agree with the need to communicate with the entire organization, that does not mean we have to treat them all as one.

With a bit of thought, Information Security should be able to identify distinct audience groups within the organization that have different communications needs and preferences. Take the IT Department for example: the high proportion of technically qualified IT professionals is likely to appreciate more technical security awareness materials than the average employee. They are likely to be more confident with online materials than most.

Another group commonly singled-out for special treatment is 'management'. Busy managers need succinct information and guidance on issues such as oversight of security processes involving their employees, divisions of responsibility and legal compliance. Given widespread concern abut IT governance resulting from the need for legal compliance (*e.g.* SOX, 2002), senior executive management in the C-suite and even the Board of Directors are increasingly interested in the state and effectiveness of information security and risk management at a strategic level. Security awareness and education help them understand the relevance of security metrics and the value of security investments as well as (hopefully!) putting their minds at rest.

Finally, there are narrower audiences – departments, teams and even individuals – for whom particular information security topics have a special significance. The Human Resources and Legal departments, for instance, would appreciate not only hearing about the disciplinary processes associated with deliberate security breaches by insiders, but also being involved in preparing and perhaps even delivering the security awareness messages to employees. Collaborations of this nature on areas of common interest sow the seeds for further cooperation and break down internal barriers.

Make it Accessible

One reason why people sometimes fail to use system security features and functions correctly is that IT is difficult for non-technical people to understand. What's more, even technical people struggle with complex modern technologies and nobody is an expert in every field. Effective security awareness programs need to find a balance between glossing-over important points and getting buried in the jargon, acronyms and fine details all too common in technical manuals. It is vital that awareness materials are written in a clear yet engaging style, and that the information content is interesting, relevant and useful. This is arguably the biggest challenge in security awareness, especially for technical authors with a strong IT background.

To counteract boredom, introduce more creative communications methods into your security awareness program. Organizations need to have information security policies in place but this means more than just writing and circulating policy statements. For various historical and legal reasons, corporate security policy manuals tend to be deadly dull and very stilted in style, making them poor awareness materials in their own right. Case studies, newsletters, presentations and briefings can all help brighten up the message. If your culture is not too conservative and stifling (or perhaps I should say especially if it is!), why not have some fun with security awareness quizzes, competitions and crosswords? As a last resort, consider simply circulating précis of important policies, written in a more accessible and user-friendly language, as a gentle introduction to the heady world of security awareness.

Don't Let the Security Messages Go Stale

If you think security awareness is simply a matter of putting up a few posters, heed the following sound advice (United States Army, 2006): "After a while, a security poster, no matter how well designed, will be ignored; it will, in effect, simply blend into the environment. For this reason, awareness techniques should be creative and frequently changed." People get bored seeing the same old posters, month after month, and soon become oblivious to them - a process known as 'accommodation' in biology and something even Pavlov's dogs exhibited after a while. If you feel you must communicate something repeatedly, at least vary the presentation a little – it's really not that hard.

An effective way to address the problem of staleness is to develop a rolling security awareness program that works its way methodically through a planned series of information security topics, changing month-by-month. Although each awareness topic tackles a different aspect of information security (*e.g.* viruses, email security, passwords *etc.*), branding techniques borrowed from the world of advertising – even something as simple as an awareness program logo - link all the awareness materials into a consistent theme. General information and advice on security, risks, controls, governance, responsibilities *etc.* may be emphasized by subtle repetition and cross-referencing between the topics, yet without the audience feeling they are being brainwashed (or at least that's the plan!).

Make it Captivating and Motivational or, Better Still, Inspirational

"We must inspire a commitment to security rather than merely describing it" (Kabay, 1993). "Organizations must introduce and maintain "motivators" to help their people be ever-vigilant about the security function. Motivators can be both positive and negative - recognition programs as well as penalties and dismissals" (Deloitte, 2005).

A well-informed, strongly motivated and security-conscious workforce (comprising both managers and staff) can be the information security manager's most powerful ally. Although significant proportion of information security incidents occur through people simply not knowing or understanding their security obligations, highly-motivated employees are more likely to follow security procedures, for example reporting and acting upon security incidents and near misses. They are more likely to read-up on security issues and make an effort to comprehend their obligations. Motivation is the key. Without motivation, no amount of knowledge or understanding will change their behavior.

As to *how* to motivate people on information security, well that's not entirely obvious. Think about motivational communications in other contexts, perhaps, for sources of inspiration. Compare impassioned presentations by extroverted speakers with Something Important To Say against those tediously and laboriously delivered by dull speakers following a prescribed script. Look for topics and angles that will capture the audience's imagination, for example relating information security at work to that at home. Almost anything must be better than "Here, read this policy and sign at the bottom to say you've read it"!

An interesting idea is to find opportunities to focus on the positive, such as rewarding people who do follow security procedures and describing security controls that have prevented incidents. This kind of approach counteracts the negativism inherent in information security and risk management. Security metrics showing efficiency savings and significant avoided costs may be just the key to obtaining sufficient budget for the next year's information security efforts!

Other Points to Consider When Designing the Awareness Program

A seminal paper explored the psychological reasons why conventional approaches to security awareness are ineffective (Kabay, 1993). "A couple of hours of lectures followed by a video, a yearly ritual of signing a security policy that seems to have been written by Martians--these are not methods that will improve security. These are merely lip service to the idea of security." The whole concept of an annual or even less-frequent "security awareness/training session" is fundamentally flawed, yet this nonsense is exactly what happens in many blinkered organizations. Kabay's conclusions included the following points:

- "Presenting case-studies is likely to have a beneficial effect on participants' readiness to examine security requirements;
- Security awareness programs should include many realistic examples of security requirements and breaches;
- Emphasize improvements rather than reduction of failure;
- Employees who dismiss security concerns or flout the regulations should be challenged on their attitudes, not ignored;
- Identify the senior executives most likely to succeed in setting a positive tone for subsequent security training;
- Security awareness programs should include repeated novel reminders of security issues;
- Build a corporate culture which rewards responsible behavior such as reporting security violations;
- Develop clearly written security policies and procedures;
- Encourage social activities in the office ... Pay special attention to social outliers during instruction programs ... Work with the outliers to resist the herd's anti-security bias;
- Include small gifts in your security awareness program;
- Start improving security a little at a time and work up to more intrusive procedures;
- Bring in experts from the outside when faced with groupthink."

On that last point, it is worth noting that there is a small but growing market in information security awareness, training and educational services. If your organization is stretched to find the right people to develop creative security awareness materials, there are commercial suppliers who are keen to help in this area. Arguably the best approach is to collaborate, combining external awareness expertise with internal resources. That way, the program is likely to be both cost-effective and self-sustaining. External awareness specialists bring a source of inspiration and best practice, while internal awareness specialists contribute knowledge and understanding of the corporate culture and access to the audience groups.

TRENDS IN INFORMATION SECURITY AWARENESS

Online intranet-based security training packages are all the rage, developing a trend started by first generation non-interactive intranet websites. Learning Management Systems are a convenient way for the organization to disseminate important information to employees and track their access and use of the materials, making them particularly popular for functions such as HR and Legal with requirements to ensure that everyone has seen the regulations. Simple systems, however, typically suffer from poor content and limited workflows, while the better ones are more expensive and require more maintenance. Multiple-choice tests are commonly used to assess students' factual recall, although this style of test is less suitable to assess comprehension. The technological bias of IT professionals (noted earlier) should not be forgotten. IT solutions are not universally welcomed and employee acceptance varies: some people appreciate the convenience of at-your-desk training while others, especially those who are not confident computer users, may prefer personal contact with an experienced trainer who can personally respond to students' needs. For these reasons, online security training systems are best combined with offline means such as security awareness seminars and other high-contact approaches.

There is growing interest in using metrics to measure and drive improvements in the effectiveness of management systems, including information security management systems. Suitable metrics can enhance information security awareness programs, both by identifying security controls that deserve greater attention and as interesting nuggets of information in their own right. Metrics is a complex topic that goes beyond the scope of this chapter but is one to watch closely over the next few years.

Convergence of information and physical security on the one hand, plus governance, risk and compliance areas on the other, is likely to affect security awareness programs in two ways. Firstly, awareness can be used as a communications tool to support the convergence and integration of disparate corporate functions. Secondly, all these functions have their own awareness, education and training needs that benefit from a more coherent and consistent approach. With economies of scale, there are opportunities for more organizations to employ and support dedicated awareness specialists. Perhaps you, dear reader, would be interested in a new career direction?

CONCLUSION

John Worth, CIO of Prudential (quoted by Samuels, 2005), said "It is sometimes forgotten that a motivated, capable workforce delivers faster, smarter, higher-quality work. People should therefore be the emphasis rather than the afterthought." A well-designed and creatively delivered awareness program places the emphasis very firmly on the rôle of people as an essential component of the information security framework. Saving the best 'till last, awareness is extremely cost-effective when compared to more technical security measures, and maximizes the value obtained from other security investments.

REFERENCES

AT&T (2003). Achieving network security – point of view. Retrieved May 13, 2007 from http://www.typex.com/.../bcfbc9acb168ca5380256f71004b363b/$FILE/achieving_network_security_3.pdf

AusCERT (2005). Australian Computer Crime and Security Survey. Retrieved May 12, 2007 from http://www.auscert.org.au/images/ACCSS2005.pdf

Basel II (2004). International Convergence of Capital Measurement and Capital Standards: A Revised Framework.

Berinato, S. (2003). The state of information security 2003. CIO Magazine. Retrieved May 13, 2007 from http://www.cio.com/article/print/29841

Capelli, D., Moore, A., Shimeall, T. J., & Trzeciak, R. (2006). Common Sense Guide to Prevention and Detection of Insider threats, 2nd Edition. Carnegie Mellon University, CyLab.

Carey, A. (2006). 2006 Global Information Security Workforce Study, sponsored by (ISC)^2.

Retrieved May 12, 2007 from http://www.isc2.org/download/workforcestudy06.pdf

Claburn, T. (2005). Workers Trade Password Security For Starbucks. Information Week, May 6. Retrieved May 12, 2007 from http://www.informationweek.com/story/showArticle.jhtml?articleID=162600315

Cochrane, P. (1997). *108 Tips for Time Travellers.* London, England: Orion Business Books.

Condon, R. (2006). Analysis: protecting yourself from an inside job - what are the options? Retrieved May 12, 2007 from http://software.silicon.com/security/0,39024655,39158082,00.htm

Contos, B.T. (2006). *Enemy at the water cooler – Real-life stories of insider threats and enterprise security management countermeasures.* Rockland, MA: Syngress Publishing Inc.

COSO (Committee Of the Sponsoring Organizations of the Treadway Commission, 1994). *Internal control – integrated framework.* New York, NY: American Institute of Certified Public Accountants.

Czekalski, E. (2006). Personal communication.

Deloitte (2005). *Global security survey.* Retrieved May 12, 2007 from http://www.deloitte.com/dtt/cda/doc/content/dtt_financialservices_2005GlobalSecuritySurvey_2005-06-22b.pdf

DPA (1998). Data Protection Act. U.K. Parliament.

DTI (United Kingdom Department of Trade and Industry, 2006). Information security breaches survey 2006 – technical report. Retrieved May 12, 2007 from http://www.dti.gov.uk/files/file28343.pdf

ENISA (European Network and Information Security Agency, 2006). *A user's guide: how to raise information security awareness.* Retrieved May 13, 2007 from http://www.enisa.europa.eu/doc/pdf/deliverables/download.htm

Ernst and Young (2004). Global information security survey. Retrieved May 13, 2007 from http://www.ey.com/global/download.nsf/UK%20/Survey_-_Global_Information_Security_04/$file/EY_GISS_%202004_EYG.pdf

FISMA (2002). Federal Information Security Management Act. U.S. Congress.

GASSP (1999). *Generally Accepted Systems Security Principles*, version 2.0. Retrieved May 13, 2007 from http://www.infosectoday.com/Articles/gassp.pdf

GLB (1999). United States Financial Modernization Act, also known as Gramm-Leach-Bliley.

Green, T (2005). Security chiefs share pains of being caught in the middle. Retrieved May 12, 2007 from http://www.networkworld.com/news/2005/121205-security-interop.html

Hackworth, R. (2005). *Presentation to the Information Systems Security Association*, London, England.

Hearne, L. (2006). The enemy within the firewall. *The Age*, Australia, March 13.

Herold, R. (2005). *Managing an information security and privacy awareness and training program.* Boca Raton, FL: Auerbach Publications.

HIPAA (1996), Health Insurance Portability and Accountability Act. U. S. Congress.

Hunter, R., Girard, J., & Mogull, R. (2002). *Don't fund security awareness until you're secure.* Gartner. Retrieved May 13, 2007 from http://www.gartner.com/resources/109900/109981/dont_fund_security_awareness_109981.pdf

Information Security Forum (2005). *Standard of good practice for information security.* Version 4.1. Retrieved May 13, 2007 from http://www.isfsecuritystandard.com/pdf/standard.pdf

ISO/IEC (International Standards Organization/International Electrotechnical Commission, 2005). International Standard ISO/IEC 27002:2005 - Information Technology – Security Techniques - Code of Practice for Information Security Management.

Johansson, J. M., & Riley, S. (2005). *Protect your Windows network - from perimeter to data.* Addison Wesley Professional.

Kabay, M. (1993). Social Psychology & INFOSEC. Retrieved May 12, 2007 from http://catless.ncl.ac.uk/Risks/15.16.html

Kark, K., Orlov, L. M., & Bright, S. (2005). Five steps to effective security awareness. Forrester Research.

Mason, B., & Gruenfeld, L. (2003). *Confessions of a master jewel thief.* New York, NY: Villard.

McCarthy, B. (2006). Attributed by Swartz, M., in Employees Cause Most Security Breaches, Yet Response Lags - What's the best way to stop users from inadvertently compromising your company's information security?. Retrieved May 12, 2007 from http://www.esj.com/security/article.aspx?EditorialsID=1769

McKenzie, A. (2005, October). *The Enemy is "Us" - What the Surveys tell us.* Paper presented at CACS Oceania Conference, Perth, Western Australia.

Menta, R. (2005). *A need to know.* SCmagazine, UK edition, July.

Miller, H. (2001). *Submission to the Senate Committee on Commerce, Science and Transportation, on behalf of the Information Technology Association of America (ITAA).* Retrieved May 12, 2007 from http://commerce.senate.gov/hearings/071601Miller.pdf

Minieri, M.W. (2004). Protecting corporate secrets - A brief primer on contemporary practices in information security. Kroll Schiff & Associates. Retrieved May 12, 2007 from http://www.becca-online.org/images/Protecting_Corporate_Secrets.pdf

Murray-Watson, A., & Dennis, G. (2005). How to make your company a hard target. *The Telegraph.* London, England. July 10.

Navarro, L. (2007). Train employees - your best defense - for security awareness. *SC Magazine.* US edition. February 27.

NIST (National Institute of Science and Technology, 1995). *An Introduction to Computer Security: The NIST Handbook.* Special Publication 800-12. Retrieved May 12, 2007 from http://csrc.nist.gov/publications/nistpubs/800-12/handbook.pdf

NIST (National Institute of Science and Technology, 2006). Minimum security requirements for federal information and information systems. Federal Information Processing Standards Publication 200 (FIPS PUB 200). Retrieved May 13, 2007 from http://csrc.nist.gov/publications/fips/fips200/FIPS-200-final-march.pdf

OECD (Organization for Economic Co-operation and Development, 2002). *Guidelines for the security of information systems – towards a culture of security.* Retrieved May 13, 2007 from http://www.oecd.org/dataoecd/16/22/15582260.pdf

Pentasafe Security Technologies (2002). *Security awareness index report: The state of security awareness among organizations - worldwide security awareness survey.* Retrieved May 12, 2007 from http://security.ittoolbox.com/pub/AM101502a.pdf

Rasmussen, G. (2005). *Implementing information security: Risks vs. cost.* Retrieved May 12, 2007 from http://www.gideonrasmussen.com/article-07.html

Ross, R., Katzke., S., Johnson, A., Swanson, M., Stoneburner, G., Rogers, G., & Lee, A. (2005). Recommended Security Controls for Federal Information Systems. *NIST SP 800-53.* Retrieved May 13, 2007 from http://csrc.nist.gov/publications/nistpubs/800-53/SP800-53.pdf

Samuels, M. (2005, June 22). CIOs must be business and IT experts. *Computing Magazine*. UK.

SANS (2003). *Newsletter*. Retrieved May 13, 2007 from http://www.sans.org/newsletters/statusupdates/11.php

Schmidt, H. (2005, September). *Keynote address presented at the Information Systems Security Association*. London, England.

Schneier, B. (2004). *Secrets & lies – digital security in a networked world*. Indianapolis, IN: Wiley Publishing, Inc.

Smith, M. (2007). *The importance of security awareness*. Retrieved May 12, 2007 from http://www.thesecurityco.com/kzscripts/default.asp?cid=7

SOX (2002). *United States Public Company Accounting Reform and Investor Protection Act*. Also known as Sarbanes-Oxley.

State of Texas Department of Information Resources (2001). *Statewide information technology security assessment*. Retrieved May 12, 2007 from http://www.dir.state.tx.us/IRAPC/security_assessment/html/DIR.SSA.FinalReport.htm

Sulkin, R. (2006). *First Line of Defense Against Data Security Breaches: Employees*. Retrieved May 12, 2007 from http://www.law.com/jsp/article.jsp?id=1167300410341

The Honeynet Project & The Honeynet Research Alliance (2004). *Know your enemy – trend analysis – trend: Life expectancy increasing for unpatched or vulnerable Linux deployments*. Retrieved May 12, 2007 from http://www.honeynet.org/papers/trends/life-linux.pdf

United States Army (2006). *Army information assurance training program*. Retrieved May 13, 2007 from http://ia.gordon.army.mil/iaso/lesson04.htm

Wang, G. (2005). Keynote speech, IDG World Expo SecurityWorld Conference and Showcase, Singapore. Retrieved May 12, 2007 from http://cio-asia.com/ShowPage.aspx?pagetype=2&articleid=3147&pubid=5&issueid=76

Wilson, M., & Hash, J. (2003). *Building an Information Technology Security Awareness and Training Program*. National Institute of Science and Technology Special Publication 800-50. Retrieved May 12, 2007 from http://csrc.nist.gov/publications/nistpubs/800-50/NIST-SP800-50.pdf

Witty, J. and Wagner R. (2005). *Awareness training is necessary to support your information security program*. Gartner. Retrieved May 12, 2007 from http://www.gartner.com/resources/125800/125896/awareness_training_is_necess_125896.pdf

KEY TERMS

Awareness: Broad appreciation and understanding of concepts (such as information security risks and controls) and obligations achieved through guidance and motivation

Captivating: Characteristic of awareness programs that engage and interest their audiences, therefore increasing the likelihood of changing behaviors for the better

Compliance: Conformance with security requirements and obligations defined through laws, regulations, policies, standards, procedures and/or guidelines

Education: Systematic process of acquiring knowledge and factual information about more or less specific concepts (such as information security risks and controls), usually but not necessarily through formal teaching.

Inspirational: Characteristic of security awareness programs that inspire a commitment to security, for example encouraging audiences to seek out further information and share knowledge with their peers

Motivational: Characteristic of security awareness programs that encourage their audiences to behave securely and avoid insecure practices

Training: Systematic process of bringing students to a level of proficiency in a given topic, acquiring specific skills and competencies.

Chapter XX
Creating a Security Education, Training, and Awareness Program

Nick Pullman
Citigroup, USA

Kevin Streff
Dakota State University, USA

ABSTRACT

Security training and awareness is often overlooked or not given sufficient focus in many organizations despite being a critical component of a layered defense. Organizations often purchase expensive hardware and software to help secure their organization, but fail to allocate resources to train employees who will install and configure the product. Similarly, organizations will devote many hours developing polices and procedures to protect sensitive information, but fail to allocate the appropriate resources to ensure awareness of those policies and procedures. This chapter discusses how to design, create, and implement a formal security education, training, and awareness (SETA) program as a component of a layered defense strategy.

OVERVIEW

Kevin Mitnick, one of the world's most famous hackers, wasn't particularly skilled at exploiting technology, but was notoriously effective at social engineering; he tricked and persuaded individuals into disclosing sensitive information. Mitnick took advantage of individuals' trusting nature by impersonating "trusted" individuals to perform reconnaissance for later attacks. The adage goes that a chain is only as strong as its weakest link, and many security experts would agree that the human element is the weakest link in information security (Hansche, Berti, & Hare, 2004). These threats due to human failures are significant with the theft of intellectual property accounting for a loss of $59 billion a year from American companies (National Security Institute, 2007). A security education, training, and awareness program aims to mitigate the human risk in securing organizations and their assets. The core issue with organizations today, however, isn't whether or not to perform security training and awareness, many organizations have some form of training and awareness, but how to implement a program that it is effective and efficient in providing the additional level of security that was intended.

A security education, training, and awareness (SETA) program is designed to mitigate threats due to human factors such as employees not being properly trained on a specific technology or not being aware of a security policy. There are many facets to information security and organizations tend to try and solve security issues with a technical bias; however, the reality is that humans are typically the first and last line of defense in protecting the organization. Technical-only solutions are insufficient as these defenses are installed and managed by individuals who if not properly trained could leave a system vulnerable to attack. In addition, employees use systems and applications on a daily basis so they are the most likely the first to identify issues or security breaches.

There are three pieces to understand with regard to security education, training and awareness:

- creating an overall security program,
- understanding SETA fundamentals, and
- creating the SETA program.

First, before beginning to create the SETA program, the organization must develop a comprehensive information security program. The overall security program details the approach that the organization will use to secure its assets. Next, the organization must understand the fundamentals behind a SETA program such as which topics are appropriate and what the best methods are for delivering the learning material. Finally, after the organization has an understanding of the appropriate topics, materials, and distribution methods, they can create the SETA program. This includes determining what the needs of the organization are, ensuring that there is an appropriate plan for designing and executing the SETA program, and following appropriate methods to implement and evaluate the SETA program. It is important for an organization to understand its overall security needs so that the SETA program can be developed to meet those needs. In addition, following a defined process for implementing and evaluating the SETA program will ensure that the program is effective, efficient, and continuously improving.

PEOPLE BASED SECURITY BREACHES

Information assurance is the process of protecting the confidentiality, integrity and availability of electronic systems and the information it stores, processes and transacts (McCumber, 2005). There are many different types of security incidents as it relates to compromising information, such as loss or theft of data, unauthorized changes, disclosure of sensitive information, and loss of system availability and these incidents could originate for a number of reasons such as viruses, hackers, insider abuse, and natural disasters. Technical attacks, such as remote exploits and malware, are important to defend against, but equally or more important are the human aspects of information security.

All individuals within an organization need to do their part in defending against information security attacks. Further, because many of the information security breaches are conducted or aided by internal personnel, all individuals need to be on the lookout for anything unusual that could lead to a breach in sensitive customer or financial information. However, the typical employee is likely unaware of the myriad of threats that an organization faces on a daily basis or what their responsibilities are towards protecting the organization. An employee throwing away a document that has the name of the IT manager might not seem like a threat; however, an attacker might find that piece of paper while rooting through the organization's trash, also called dumpster diving. The attacker could then either impersonate the IT manager or use the IT manager's name while masquerading as someone else in order to sound more legitimate and obtain sensitive information. This process of tricking or influencing an individual into providing sensitive or confidential information is called social engineering (Hansche, Berti, & Hare, 2004). In addition to social engineering, there are many other attacks leveraging the trusting tendencies of people, such as shoulder surfing which is where an attacker will watch over the shoulder of an employee in order to see any useful or confidential information or piggy-backing which is the practice of allowing a perceived trusted party to physically enter a secure area without appropriate identification. These threats need to be understood by the organization so that these risks to the organization can be mitigated to an acceptable level.

There are many other incidents that can occur such as an employee not following the change control procedure which leads to a server crash or an employee who doesn't update the firewall rules correctly, allowing an intruder to gain unauthorized access to the internal network. There are many security tools and applications available that assist organizations in securing their environment, such as firewalls, intrusion detection, host monitoring, and many others; however, these applications don't install and configure themselves. In order for these applications to be effective, the organization must employ individuals that are knowledgeable and understand how these applications work.

There are many threats to an organization including threats that attack through both technical and non-technical means. Many organizations don't pay enough attention to the non-technical threats such as social engineering, shoulder surfing, or dumpster diving. In addition, many organizations don't pay attention to other threats such as employees using unauthorized software or not properly securing their laptop. These types of security breaches can be very costly to an organization and so it is critical that organizations implement appropriate safeguards in order to protect their information.

SBS

Secure Banking Solutions, LLC

Human-Based Security Breaches: USB Sticks

Secure Banking Solutions, LLC (SBS) is an information security consulting firm focused on information protection in small and medium-sized financial institutions (www.protectmybank.com). SBS is often hired to test the controls at an institution to determine compliance and adequacy of its information security program. SBS has been a leader in developing innovative human-based tests to determine information protection readiness. One such case is a test where USB sticks are purposefully "dropped" in locations outside and inside the bank to see if employees, contractors, etc. will plug them in to their institution's network. SBS consistently finds that over 50% of the USB drives "dropped" are subsequently attached to the institution's network. These USB drives are empty; however, they could include malware that could delete information on the network or install a Trojan or backdoor for subsequent abuse. SBS performs these tests to provide empirical data to feed the institution's SETA program so that it can be used as real-world examples for the need to improve awareness.

CREATING AN INFORMATION SECURITY PROGRAM

A SETA program provides little value to an organization unless it is implemented as part of an overarching information security program. The information security program outlines the overall strategy and comprehensive management approach that the organization will follow in order to protect its assets ("An introduction to computer", 1995). Security education, training, and awareness is a vital component of an overall security program so before a SETA program can be created, a comprehensive security program must be in place to lay the security foundation for the organization. This section discusses how an organization can create and/or ensure that there is a structurally sound and comprehensive information security program in place.

Layered Security

According to John McCumber, layered security is a key security principle and a fundamental element of an overarching and comprehensive security program (McCumber, 2005). One way to assist an organization with creating an information security program with a layered approach is to follow the defense-in-depth approach. Defense-in-depth is a layered security approach and is widely held as the de facto standard that organizations and government agencies use to protect their organizations from threats (Central Intelligence Agency, 2003). The model was developed by the National Security Agency and purports that a holistic, layered approach is necessary to defend the organization against a variety of threats, including natural disasters, insider, outsider, accidental and intentional attacks by nation states, criminal elements, hackers, corporate competitors, and terrorists (*Defense in Depth*, 2002). This model indicates that even if an adversary breaks through an outer barrier, there are additional barriers, possibly even higher and stronger controls, that the attackers must overtake to compromise the information asset or infrastructure (*Visual Evidence*, 2004).

The defense-in-depth approach includes three complimentary components: people, process, and technology. While many organizations have focused primarily on the technology component, the defense-in-depth model suggests that people and process investments are also necessary to protect critical infrastructures and assets. The model suggests that vulnerabilities and threats should be mitigated based on using a trained workforce that follows clear, explicit security policy that is enforced and augmented with technology. Blakley's research (2001) concluded that the technology-only approach should be revisited if organizations are to significantly mitigate information risk (Blakley, McDermott, & Geer, 2001).

Regardless of the level of sophistication of information assurance technology, asset protection is virtually impossible unless the human element is adequately addressed through planning and policy (Wood, 1995).

In order to create a successful and comprehensive security program a layered security approach to information assurance should be implemented. In addition, ample focus needs to be placed on both people and processes in addition to the technology, and of particular interest to this chapter is the people component of the model. Employees can help protect these critical assets by being aware of the importance of security and of the techniques attackers use to exploit human, process, and technological vulnerabilities. One example of the focus that is being applied to social aspects of the layered defense model is in the food industry. In 2002, the U.S. Department of Agriculture published a fact sheet entitled Keep America's Food and Agriculture Safe and stated "you [people] are the front line of defense in protecting America's food supply system" (*Keep America's Food and Agriculture Safe*, 2002, p. 1). The Ernst & Young 2004 Global Security Survey

Figure 1. Defense-in-depth

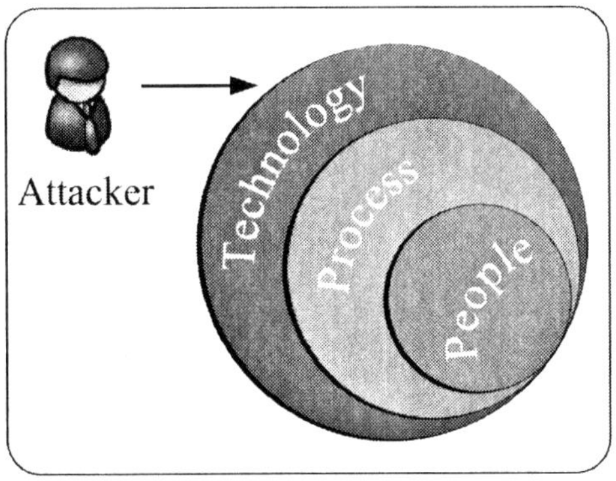

identifies security awareness programs as a vital component of any company strategic plan, clearly stating "Companies should place more emphasis on creating a security-conscious culture" *(Ernest & Young, 2004).* According to Tom Ridge, the past Homeland Security Secretary, "people are the front line of defense" (Stump, 2003). It is clear that there is a push to mitigate the risks due to social aspects of information security. The first step for an organization to address the human aspect of information assurance is the creation of information security policy, which is discussed next.

Policies, Standards, Guidelines, and Procedures

A major artifact of an information security program is the security policies that will be used to guide the organization in securing its assets. According to Thomas Peltier, a well written policy statement is the cornerstone of an effective information security architecture (Peltier, 2004). Security policy is a starting point to define at a high level the strategy of the organization; however, policies alone are not sufficient to complete an information security program. In addition to policies, the organization needs to create procedures, standards, and guidelines to clarify how the organization is going to comply with the security policies (Barman, 2002).

The information security policies are the high-level documents that define the security goals, approach, and strategies of the organization (Barman, 2002).These high level policies define "what" an organization is going to do, but not necessarily how to do it. For example, a policy statement might say, "*Each employee in the organization is responsible for and will protect the confidentiality, integrity, and availability of corporate information and assets*". This statement guides the organization in what the organization is going to do, but not how to accomplish the task (Peltier, 2004). This statement doesn't define how employees are supposed to protect the information, but just that it is their responsibility. The details of how to protect the corporate information is left up to the supporting documentation from the procedures, standards, and guidelines.

Information security policy is supported in more detail by security standards and guidelines. The security standards are documents that describe the mandatory requirements that the organization will implement in order to comply with security policy (Peltier, 2004). For example, a security standard might state, "*All employees must be trained on information security practices and procedures within three weeks of initially being*

Figure 2. Policies, standards, guidelines, and procedures

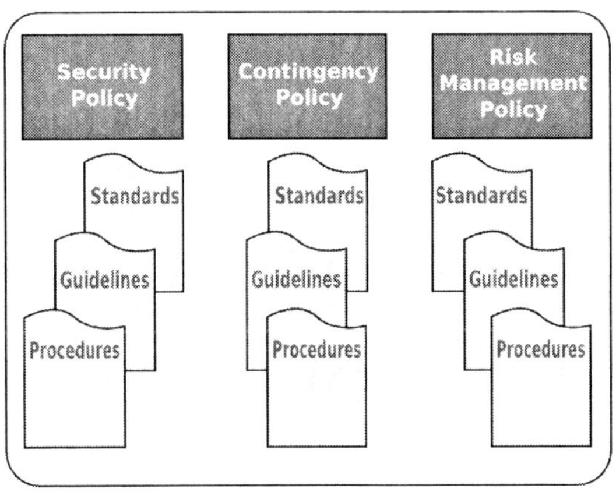

hired and must receive a minimum of 3 hours of security awareness training every subsequent calendar year". This statement as part of the security standard clarifies the organizations stance on how the organization will handle the minimum training and awareness that all employees must receive. Security standards also may detail specific technologies or products that must be used in order to secure the organization. Examples of this would be standards such as which anti-virus application to use or what firewall rules to implement on perimeter firewalls. In addition to standards, guidelines provide additional clarification on how to comply with security policies, but whereas standards are required, guidelines provide a recommendation but not an explicit requirement (Peltier, 2004). Typically guidelines are created to allow some management and individual discretion in deciding whether or not they are appropriate depending on the situation. Together, security standards and guidelines set the foundation for an organization to implement a coherent and complete security program and allow an organization to create its specific procedures.

Information security procedures are documents that support the security policy and standards in a detailed step-by-step manner (Peltier, 2004). The procedures detail exactly how the organization implements the security controls. For example, a very simple procedure for getting a password reset at an organization might look like:

1. Login to corporate help desk website,
2. Authenticate to system with username/password,
3. Click on "Retrieve Password", and
4. Check email to obtain temporary password.

Procedures ensure a consistent implementation of a process throughout an organization and eliminate any uncertainty in the organization's controls. Procedures, in addition to standards, also allow an organization to very simply audit the processes that are being used. Once the procedures are created, it is straightforward for an auditor, internal or external, to review a process and compare the written procedure to what is actually being performed to audit for compliance.

In order for any organization to be successful in securing its assets, it must have a plan. The organization must plan its security goals, what will be done to achieve the goals, and how to execute on those goals. These plans are laid out in its security policies, standards, guidelines, and procedures and lay out the foundation for how security operations will be performed across the organization. In order to be effective, these documents need to be clear, concise, comprehensive, accurate, and approved by management. Once created, these documents can be implemented across the organization to secure the organizations assets.

ISO 27001 Security Standard

The previous section discussed how to create policies, procedures, standards, and guidelines, but ensuring that the security program is comprehensive can sometimes be a challenge. One way that an organization can ensure that their security program is comprehensive is by following a security standard such as the International Standards Organization's (ISO) 17799 standard and ISO 27001 ("ISO/IEC 17799", 2007). These two standards are expected to be used in conjunction with one another, are commonly referred to collectively as ISO 17799 or ISO 27001, and can be used by an organization to create an information security program which is termed by the standard as an Information Security Management System (ISMS) ("ISO/IEC 27001", 2007). The standard provides a comprehensive approach to implementing an information security program and in addition, organizations can become certified to the standard to show compliance. Following this standard provides many benefits for the organization and allows an organization to ensure that they are creating a comprehensive security program.

The ISO 27001 standard provides a model and approach for creating, implementing, operating, monitoring, reviewing, maintaining, and improving a security management system ("Information technology – Security", 2005). The approach taken by the ISO 27001 standard to implement an ISMS is the PDCA (Plan, Do, Check, Act) model. The PDCA model provides a robust and flexible model to be used for risk assessment, security design and implementation, security management, and reassessment ("Information technology – Security", 2005). The PDCA model is summarized below.

1. **Plan:** The organization creates the policies, standards, guidelines, procedures, and other processes or objectives that are used to security the organization's assets.
2. **Do:** The organization implements and operates the processes and controls.
3. **Check:** The organization reviews and measures the performance of the ISMS policy and objectives
4. **Act:** The organization takes preventative and corrective action against the ISMS to keep the program current and to ensure that the program is constantly improving ("Information technology –Security", 2005).

Following the PDCA model provided in the ISO 27001 standard allows an organization to follow a proven and standardized approach for creating, executing, reviewing, and improving an information security program.

The ISO 27001 standard provides the approach and model for creating an information security program and the ISO 17799 standard provides the specific control objectives that should be met by the security program; that is the ISO 27001 standard provides the process and the ISO 17799 standard provides the control objectives to be implemented.

The ISO 17799 standard itself is a guidance on the controls that should be implemented, not necessarily a definitive source, so depending on the organization some of the controls may not be applicable and/or other controls may need to be implemented that aren't currently in the standard ("Information technology – Code of", 2001). The twelve major control objectives in the ISO 17799 standard are:

1. Risk assessment and treatment,
2. Security policy,
3. Organization of information security,
4. Asset Management,
5. Human resources security,
6. Physical and environmental security,
7. Communications and operations management,
8. Access Control,
9. Information systems acquisition, development, and maintenance,
10. Information security incident management,
11. Business continuity management, and
12. Compliance ("ISO/IEC 17799", 2007)

An organization using the ISO 17799 standard in conjunction with the ISO 27001 standard can

Figure 3. PDCA model ("Information technology –Security", 2005)

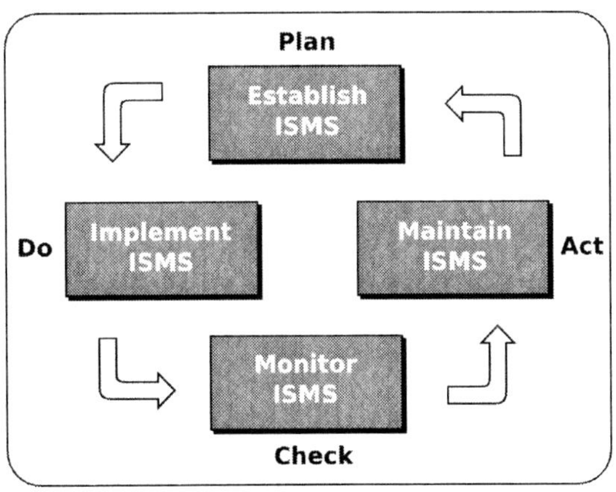

create a comprehensive security program that follows a proven approach and internationally recognized standards in order to protect the organization.

Creating an information security program is essential before trying to create or implement a SETA program. The SETA program must align with and be a component of the overall security program and so an organizational security program must first be implemented. The security program needs to be comprehensive, covering the people, process, and technology components of information security, as well documented with policies, standards, guidelines, and procedures. One way to ensure that an organization's security program is comprehensive enough is to follow a proven and rigorous security standard such as the ISO 17799 and ISO 27001. Overall, the security program provides the framework for which all security functions within the organization are derived so having a comprehensive security program, whether based on industry standards or not, is critical.

FUNDAMENTALS OF A SETA PROGRAM

There are many facets to a SETA program such as how to organize the program, what materials to use, how to determine the correct audience, what distribution or teaching methods to use, and what content is appropriate to be included for training and awareness. There are some basic fundamentals behind a SETA program that should be understood before attempting to create the program. For example, in addition to the security awareness that all employees should have, the organization must train and develop their security and technical staff. Different roles within the organization need different levels of awareness and training so it is important for an organization to understand this as it works towards a comprehensive SETA program.

Security education, training, and awareness are integral parts of creating a comprehensive security program. All employees need to be aware of the organization's polices and they need to understand their role and responsibility in maintaining a secure organization. In addition, depending on the role of the employee in the organization, they may need additional training and education beyond general security awareness in order to effectively secure the organization. This section describes the fundamentals behind security education, training, and awareness so that these foundational concepts are understood before attempting to create a SETA program.

The Learning Model

Security education, training, and awareness are distinct, but connected concepts that are implemented within a SETA program. These concepts can be thought of as a progression or continuum beginning with awareness, building to training, evolving into education, and finally leading to professional development (Dodaro et al., 1998). Each level of the continuum has different goals, strategies, and activities that define how they are implemented within the SETA program. Before an organization attempts to create a SETA program, it must first understand the differences between these concepts and build the program with these specific concepts in mind.

The first level of the continuum is security awareness. Security awareness functions are aimed at everyone in the organization; such as everyone needs to be aware of the security policies, standards, guidelines, and procedures of the organization. Awareness activities highlight and inform all users of the importance of and their responsibilities towards information security so that they can respond appropriately (Dodaro et al., 1998). In general, awareness activities are created to reach a broad audience with specific topics in hopes to change the attitude and culture of the individuals in the organization. These activities ensure that the employees are aware and diligent about their responsibilities towards securing the organization. A recent report from the National Security Institute suggested that repetition is the key to information security awareness (National Security Institute, 2004).

The second level on this model is security training, which is broken down into security basics and literacy and role-based training (Dodaro et al., 1998). Security training activities are aimed at targeted audiences within the organization and the material is targeted specifically for their job functions. With these training activities, the learner is much more involved with the process and the structure of the training is typically a classroom or web-based training course. The first stage of training, security basics and literacy, is really a foundational step to ensure that the users have a basic knowledge of security principles before moving forward with more specific training (Dodaro et al., 1998). Once the user has completed the training on security basics and literacy, they then move forward into training that is specific to their role in the organization. For example, network analysts need to be trained with firewall and intrusion detection systems whereas application developers need to be trained with secure coding techniques. Overall, the training activities are created to reach a targeted audience to train them on specific skills that relate to their job function.

The third level on this model is education. Educational activities are typically completed outside of the organization and with a formal educational institution such as a college or university (Dodaro et al., 1998). Educational activities are aimed at those individuals with specialties in information security and include the entire skill set and major competencies into a common body of knowledge that the individual should learn. In general, educational activities aim to teach the individual not only how to accomplish a security function, but also why it needs to be done and how to be proactive with accomplishing the function in the future.

Professional development is the final step on this security learning continuum. With professional development activities, the individuals obtain industry certification of their skills and competencies within information security (Wilson & Hash, 2003). Obtaining one of these certifications typically requires a study of a common body of knowledge as well as on-the-job experience. Overall, professional development activities provide a certificate of completion which could lead to an opportunity for career advancement and/or merit increases for those individuals.

Overall, the security learning model incorporates four levels of learning which include awareness, training, education, and professional development. These are the main activities that organizations need to keep in mind when creating a SETA program. It is vital to the overall security health of an organization to have staff aware of their information security responsibilities, well-trained technical staff, and educated and certified information security specialists.

Role-Based Learning

There are many different roles within an organization and each role has unique needs in regards to the type of security training that is required. A network administrator has very different needs than a Java developer and both have very different needs than an IT manager. When developing and creating a SETA program, it is important to understand the different needs of the organization's many different roles.

Awareness, educational, and professional development activities are quite straightforward. Awareness activities are meant for every individual within an organization no matter what their role or function may be; everyone should be aware of the organization's policies and procedures. On the other end of the spectrum is security education and professional development. These activities are specific to security professionals such as security administrators, security managers, security officers, or IT auditors (Dodaro et al., 1998). In general, knowing which roles to provide awareness, educational, and professional development activities for should be fairly simple; everybody gets security awareness and only security professionals get security education and professional development.

Whereas determining which roles within an organization to provide awareness, educational, and professional development is fairly straightforward, determining who should get training and what the training should be is much trickier. One way to determine what training to provide and to whom is to follow the process that is laid out by the Nation Institute of Standards and Technology's (NIST) model on role-based training (Dodaro et al., 1998). The NIST model creates a security matrix with three main training categories on the side and six main role categories on the top. This basic model is shown in Table 1.

This is s a very basic model, and in a real implementation, each of the three main training categories would need to be broken down into more specific subject areas; however, the basic process remains the same.

In order to implement this process using a training matrix, the organization needs to create training materials for each of the boxes and then determine which roles are appropriate for each of the boxes (Dodaro et al., 1998). For example, the Chief Security Officer and Chief Information Officer might be appropriate to place in the box for managing an information security program, but not appropriate in the box for implementing and operating laws and regulations. Once the training matrix is complete, it is straightforward to create training courses with only the content that is needed for a specific role within the company.

To ensure that all employees are receiving the appropriate training and awareness, it is important for an organization to consider the roles of its employees within the organization. All employees should receive periodic awareness materials, but only security personnel need to have security education and professional development. Most, if not all, members of the IT department will need to have some training on information security concepts and in addition, they will probably need to have some additional training on topics that directly relate to their job function. Overall, the organization needs to be aware of the needs of the unique roles and tailor the training and awareness materials appropriately.

Learning Styles, Teaching Methods, and Delivery Options

Determining the method that training and awareness material is being distributed is as important as the actual information itself. There are many ways to provide information and different individuals learn in very different ways, so when creating content for security awareness or training the organization needs to be aware of these differences and provide appropriate material in a suitable manner.

Individuals learn in many different ways, but most individuals have a way in which they prefer to learn (Dodaro et al., 1998). For example, some individuals prefer lectures, some individuals prefer

Table 1.

	Manage	Acquire	Design & Develop	Implement & Operate	Review & Evaluate	Use
Laws & Regulations						
Security Program						
Systems Life Cycle Security						

reading material on their own, and yet others prefer to have an involved group discussion (Dodaro et al., 1998). In order to ensure that training and/or awareness sessions are reaching the audience, it is important to use different teaching methods to keep everyone focused on the material. These teaching methods include:

- moving around the classroom;
- having silent reading in addition to lectures;
- include small group problem solving or large group discussions;
- use blackboard diagramming or other visual aids;
- provide hands-on exercises; and
- provide one-on-once coaching and/or mentoring (Dodaro et al., 1998).

Using these different teaching methods allows the students to stay focused on the material and not get too "bored" with a single teaching method. Many people also tend to "tune out" because of information overload. Role playing scenarios are found to have worked to overcome these types of issues (Thomson, M.E. & Von Solms R, 1998). In addition, since individuals all have different preferred ways of learning, using many different teaching methods makes it is more likely that the information will be retained by all students. In addition to the teaching methods, the instructors themselves should be likeable, have good communication skills, and have a have deep technical knowledge in order to relate what they know to the audience.

In addition to the different learning styles and teaching methods, there are many different options for how to actually deliver content to the users. These materials differ greatly depending on whether they are for training or awareness. The more common delivery methods for training are:

- interactive video training,
- web-based training,
- non-web, computer based training, and
- on-site, instructor led training (Dodaro et al., 1998).

These training methods can be used to provide detailed and in-depth material on different security topics. On the other hand, security awareness materials are usually much simpler and to the point so they can be much more creative. There are many different ways to disseminate security awareness information, but a few examples are:

- posters,
- motivational and catchy slogans,
- brochures or flyers,
- pens/pencils or other trinkets,
- post it notes,
- cartoons,
- monthly emails or bulletins, and
- security banners (Hansche, Berti, & Hare, 2004).

These are just a few of the many different options that can be used to deliver awareness materials to the users. It is important to keep the delivery method fresh to ensure that users don't "tune-out" the material. If an organization uses the same delivery option too often, users will have a tendency to ignore those particular materials.

How the material is presented to users is just as important as the material itself. If the material presented isn't in a format that is meaningful and suitable for the target audience, then the material will be ineffective. When developing training or awareness material, it is important to create it using a mix of the teaching methods and deliver options in order to ensure that the broadest audience possible will be reached. It is also important with awareness materials to ensure that the delivery method is periodically changed to keep users interested in what is being presented.

Security Curriculum

In addition to choosing the proper distribution approach, in order for any SETA program to be successful the learning material must also be relevant. If the learning material is too easy, too difficult, or not relevant then it won't be affective in training the user or improving their security awareness. A needs assessment, which is discussed later in this chapter, will provide insight into what topics are appropriate and relevant; however, it is important for an organization to know which topics are important to be included in an awareness and training program.

Security awareness materials are typically short, simple, and have a very narrow scope, usually a single topic. These materials, which can typically be found in the form of posters, banners, and flyers, need to have topics which apply to the broad audience of the organization yet are relevant to security needs. Some of these topics are shown in Table 2.

There are many other awareness topics that could also be included as part of a SETA program, but in general the appropriate topics to include depend on the individual organization and their individual needs. Security training topics are more difficult to identify and depend entirely on the organization and the needs of its employees. Appropriate security training topics include anything within the twelve major control objectives of the ISO 17799 standard such as risk management or access control or any topic within the Common Body of Knowledge (CBK) that is defined by the ISC^2 organization (Hansche, Berti, & Hare, 2004).

Successful training and awareness programs change the way that employees work and think about security (VanWyk, K. R. and Steven, J. 2006). Overall, it is important for the organization to create a security curriculum for both training and awareness that is based on the needs of the organization. The specific needs of the organization will provide insight and direction into the topics and material as well as ensure that the SETA program is obtaining the desired results. It is also important that the curriculum is balanced and not too focused on a single topic to ensure that users are obtaining a broad security knowledge and awareness base.

CREATING A SETA PROGRAM

Any organization can create a SETA program by haphazardly throwing together some posters and maybe a corporate website, but that doesn't make the program efficient or effective. As discussed previously, a good security program starts at the top with policies and procedures; however, policies and procedures aren't effective if they aren't followed. All individuals in an organization need

Table 2.

• Password Management	• Viruses, Worms, Trojans
• Corporate Policy/Procedures	• Social Engineering
• Email Attachments	• Incident Response
• Web Usage	• Shoulder Surfing
• Spam	• Change Management
• Data Backup and Recovery	• Inventory and Property Transfer
• Encryption	• Software Licensing
• Laptop Security	• Allowed Software
• Personal Software	• Access Control Issues
• Patch Management	• Individual Accountability
• Desktop Security	• Physical Access and Security
• Confidentiality	• Email etiquette (Wilson & Hash, 2003)

to follow the policies and procedures in order to keep the organization secure; however, often times users aren't aware or don't fully understand the policies or their responsibilities towards them. Emails are easily deleted and posters can be ignored, so it's important for an organization to develop a SETA program that is comprehensive, targeted, and measurable.

Developing a comprehensive, targeted, and measurable program takes a formal methodology that is rigorously defined in order to ensure that the organization is getting the desired results from the program. The SETA program must be planned, organized, and implemented correctly in order to properly train the organization's workforce and ensure that they are aware of the organization's policies. This section describes an overall approach and methodology that can be used by an organization to create and implement an effective SETA program.

Information Technology Risk Assessment

The basis for developing the SETA program is an information technology risk assessment. Which information assets hold the sensitive information? What controls best protect this information? If I have only $100 to spend on information protection, which control should I implement and on what system(s)? The information technology risk assessment answers these questions and more regarding which controls should be put in place. Similarly, the information technology risk assessment also identifies the threats that are most likely to occur and the content that should be included in the SETA program. For example, if an organization is planning a security awareness poster, would they be better off creating the poster reminding employees not to share their password or better off reminding employees not to prop open doors? The answer depends upon the information obtained in the information technology risk assessment; mainly, which threat represents the greatest risk to the organization: password sharing or physical security? Each organization is unique and only through conducting a thorough information technology risk assessment can an organization truly understand its threats, resulting risks and recommend controls. Several of these recommended controls should be people-oriented controls which are deployed via a SETA program.

Building Relationships and Obtaining Executive Buy in

After conducting a thorough information technology risk assessment and before beginning to develop a SETA program, executive buy-in must be garnered. Obtaining executive buy in is critical in being able to implement a successful SETA program (Swanson & Guttman, 1996). There are a number of challenges when implementing a SETA program such as budgetary constraints, user resistance, legal requirements, bureaucracy, and auditing and without support from executive management, these challenges could prove difficult to overcome (Munley, 2004). Executive management backing will provide the necessary funding and resources to ensure that a security awareness program is implemented successfully. Also, if a member of executive management assumes the role of the program sponsor, then they will have an additional vested interest in ensuring that the program succeeds.

In addition to the financial support that executive management can provide, having the support of upper management also makes obtaining other organizational buy in much easier (Voss, 2003). An organization needs to ensure that all employees are aware of security policies and are trained on security concepts and users may resist the SETA program if there isn't executive level management backing up the program. If upper management has sponsored the program and made it known that he/she supports the program, then users will be less likely to resist the program. For example, a department of 1,000 customer service representatives required to attend a one hour session on email attachments could cost the organization in excess of $10,000 merely in personnel time (without accounting for trainer costs, session material costs, facilities, and other costs associated with awareness/training sessions). In an environment where businesses are attempting to increase productivity and reduce costs, sessions like these could be viewed as time drains and not supported by line management. However, if executives truly believe in information protection and allocate time and money to SETA programs, then line management is less likely to opt out of SETA activities.

Four Step Plan

In order for an organization to successfully implement a SETA program, it should use a formal process to go about creating the program. Following a formal approach is suggested for a number of reasons:

- it is easier to explain to auditors and other outsiders how the program is run and why it is effective;
- it provides milestones that can be reviewed by management to ensure that the program is working as designed and where changes can be made before moving forward; and
- it provides a structured format which lends itself to a complete and organized program (Carlsen, Thingsted, & Thorne, 1993).

One approach that can be used to create a SETA program is the 4-step lifecycle of a security awareness and training program created by the National Institute of Standards and Technology (NIST) special publication (SP) 800-50 (Wilson & Hash, 2003). SP 800-50 is a model that describes four steps to creating and implementing a SETA program: design, development, implementation, and post-implementation. Following this model, an organization can create and implement a

Figure 4. NIST 4-Step Plan (Wilson & Hash, 2003)

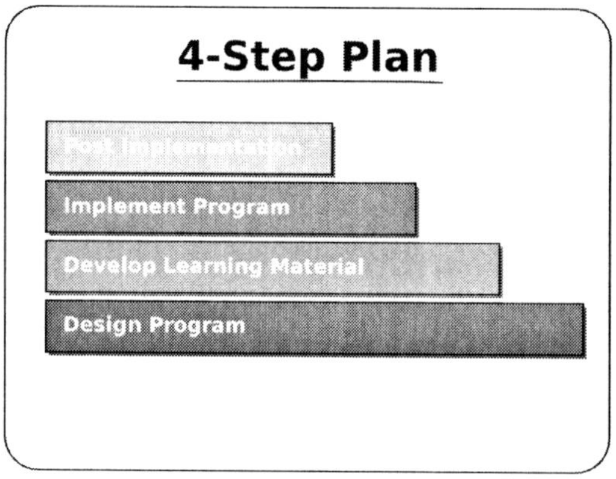

SETA program that is effective and efficient in addition to supporting the organization's needs to be more secure.

The first step in a SETA program's lifecycle is the design phase. During this phase, the organization performs the following tasks:

1. determine organizations needs,
2. develop a SETA strategy and plan,
3. establish priorities,
4. set the goals of the plan, and
5. procure funding for the program (Wilson & Hash, 2003)

The first task, and probably the most important, is to determine the organization's training and awareness needs. This information can be gathered through surveys, interviews, previous audit material, and many other sources (Wilson & Hash, 2003). The information technology risk assessment described in the previous section also serves as input into the program design. Once the needs of the organization have been determined, a strategy and plan can be created to remediate awareness and training deficiencies. Part of creating the plan is to establish the priorities of the plan. Establishing the priorities needs to take into account not only the needs of the organization but also the impact to the organization and the available resources/material that are available (Wilson & Hash, 2003). After the plan is developed, the organization needs to determine the goals of the program; such as how complex and in-depth the materials should be. Finally, after the entire plan and strategy is developed it should be taken to management to be approved and appropriately funded. Overall, the design phase of the SETA lifecycle encompasses determining the organization's needs, developing an appropriate strategy and plan with priorities and goals, and procuring the funding for the program.

The next step in the SETA lifecycle is the development of the awareness and training materials. During this phase of the lifecycle the organization develops, based on the plan developed in the design phase, the materials that will best remediate the deficiencies that were found in the needs assessment. Dessman (2002) suggested that organizations must understand what works and what does not work for your organization and modify policies and procedures accordingly. The needs assessment gains insight into this important information. McCoy and Fowler (2004) determined it is also important to point out that the information relayed in the security awareness program was relevant to the audience. Topics not related to the audience may hurt the integrity of the program (McCoy, C., & Fowler, R., 2004). When developing the materials, the organization should determine which behaviors it wants to reinforce and the skill or skills that the organization wants the audience to learn (Wilson & Hash, 2003). Awareness materials should be developed with the entire organization as the audience. These materials are typically short, simple, and to the point. Training materials, on the other hand, are more in-depth, targeted materials with a specific audience in mind. The audience is typically more technical individuals and the material is tailored directly towards the skills that they need to be able to secure the organization (Wilson & Hash, 2003).

The third step in the SETA lifecycle is the implementation of the plan. During this phase of the lifecycle, the organization communicates and delivers the plan that has been created (Wilson & Hash, 2003). First, before the SETA program is implemented, the program should be communicated to all users in the organization to ensure that they are aware of their responsibilities towards the program, as well as what the expected results and benefits are to the organization. After appropriate communication to the users, the program can be implemented. The information can be disseminated to the individuals as specified in the SETA plan such as through posters, emails, and web-based materials.

The final step in the SETA lifecycle is post-implementation. During this phase of the lifecycle, the organization performs tasks related to continuous improvement of the SETA plan. The organization should begin tracking and monitoring the compliance and effectiveness of the program. The organization can obtain this information in a similar fashion to the needs assessment such as by conducting surveys, taking interviews, and giving voluntary quizzes. Once the organization has this feedback, it can analyze the information and take the appropriate steps to enhance the SETA program. Overall, this phase essentially reviews the effectiveness of the program and performs another needs assessment to determine how to better improve the program.

The NIST 4-step lifecycle model is a way for organizations to develop a comprehensive approach to security education, training, and awareness. Too often, the tasks of training and awareness in an organization are done in an ad-hoc manner and so following the NIST model, an organization can improve the effectiveness and efficiency of their SETA program. The model itself is quite similar to any project lifecycle model in that there is first a design phase, a development phase, an implementation phase, and then post-implementation phase. Once the SETA program has been implemented, the program becomes a matter of gathering metrics and feedback, and then using that information to enhance the overall program.

Organizing Awareness into Campaigns

A SETA program is a continuous process of implementing, reassessing, and then implementing again. Consequently, organizations should break information security awareness activities into individual campaigns (Carlsen, Thingsted, & Thorne, 1993). These campaigns are specific activities that are broken down to be tailed either to a specific audience or towards a specific topic or set of topics (Carlsen, Thingsted, & Thorne, 1993). Unlike an information security program which is continuous, a campaign has a start date and an end date; it is setup more like a project rather than a program. Using this process, it is much easier to measure and track the effectiveness and efficiency of the specific campaign as opposed to tracking and measuring the entire program.

Similar to the overall SETA program, each of the campaigns should go through a structured approach of designing the campaign, building the materials, and executing the campaign (Carlsen, Thingsted, & Thorne, 1993). After the campaign has been completed, the organization can assess the effectiveness of the campaign and then determine any changes that need to be made to the campaign. The scheduling of the specific campaigns is completed as part of the overall SETA program during the needs assessment and program plan. Overall, breaking a SETA program down into smaller campaigns allows an organization to have a more detailed structure that is better tailored towards the specific needs of the organization and also improves the ability of the organization to measure and track the effectiveness of the campaigns and the overall program.

Three Program Models

Depending on the size of the organization, the political landscape, budget allocations, and geographic locations, different SETA program deployment models can be used when funding, creating, executing and maintaining the SETA program. There are three main models that can be used:

- **Centralized:** Centralized policy, strategy, and implementation:
- **Partially decentralized:** Centralized policy and strategy, distributed implementation; and
- **Fully decentralized:** Centralized policy, distributed strategy and implementation (Wilson & Hash, 2003).

In a completely centralized model, all of the functions of the SETA program, policy, strategy, and implementation, are managed at a central authority. This central authority writes the policy, determines the overall strategy, and provides the implementation materials and guidelines to each of the organizations departments. The organization's departments then disseminate the information to the users, collect any feedback, and provide the feedback to the central authority to be analyzed

Figure 5. Program models

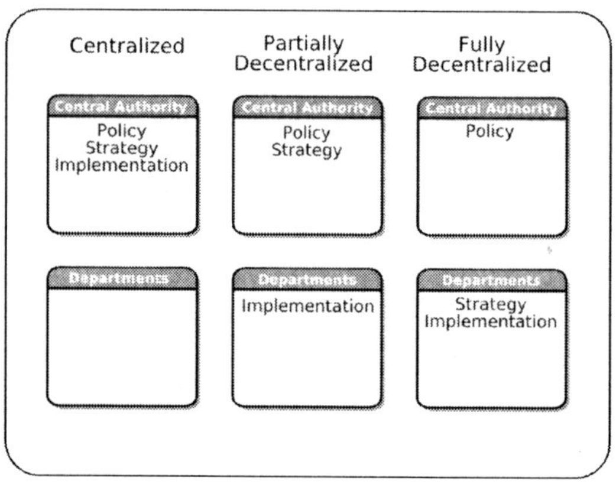

((Wilson & Hash, 2003). This model works well in the following situations:

- small, structured organizations with central IT management;
- organizations with a central authority that has the resources and is knowledgeable of the organization's specific departments; or
- the organization has departments with similar missions and/or objectives (Wilson & Hash, 2003).

Conversely, in large, dissimilar, or geographically separate organizations, this model could be more difficult to implement.

In a partially decentralized model, the policy and strategy of the SETA program are defined by a central authority, but the implementation is managed by the individual departments within the organization (Wilson & Hash, 2003). In this model, the central authority writes the policy, provides the framework, and provides the budget, but the individual departments are responsible for developing the training plans, materials, and implementing the plan. Similar to the centralized model, the individual departments still record any feedback and provide it to the central authority to be analyzed. This model works well in the following situations:

- organizations with a large or decentralized structure that has well-defined responsibilities at both the central and department level;
- organizations that are geographically widespread; or
- organizations that have diverse objectives and missions (Wilson & Hash, 2003).

This model doesn't work particularly well in smaller organizations where departments don't have the resources to implement the plan and depend on the central authority for IT functions.

In a completely decentralized model, the policy is created at the central authority, but the strategy and implementation is performed at the individual departmental level. In this model, the policy is created and disseminated by the central authority, but the individual departments perform their own needs analysis, create the strategy and plans, develop the materials, and implement the plans (Wilson & Hash, 2003). Different from the previous models, in this model the individual departments don't necessarily provide any user feedback to the centralized model since the department determines its own strategy; however, the central authority may request information from the departments regarding the success of their strategy. This model works well in the following situations:

- organizations that are very large;
- organizations with a very decentralized structure that has general responsibilities at the central authority and more specific responsibilities at the departmental level;
- organizations that are geographically widespread; or
- organizations that have discreet departments where their objectives differ greatly (Wilson & Hash, 2003).

This model doesn't work well in smaller organizations or other organizations where there is a need to have a consistent strategy across the organization.

Each of these models is appropriate for different organizations, so each organization must determine the best overall model to use based on their overall structure and specific needs. Smaller organizations should use the centralized or partially centralized model in order to maintain consistency across the organization and have the benefit of economies of scale. Larger or more complex organizations should use the partially decentralized or fully decentralized model to allow for more flexibility with the individual departments. Whichever model is used, it should be chosen while looking at all of the factors of the organization such as political landscape, size, budget, and geographic location. For example, an organization that is geographically dispersed and decentralized will likely elect the fully decentralized model where the information security policy is centralized and the carrying out of this policy is left to the individual business units.

Evaluating Effectiveness of SETA Program

Implementing a SETA program only partially satisfies the needs of the organization. One of the most critical steps in a successful SETA program is determining the effectiveness of the program. If an organization implements a SETA program and never tracks how well it is working, then the program could either be completely ineffective or it could be inefficient. In order to determine how well a SETA program is working, an organization must first implement the program in a formal and structured manner with a plan that states goals and objectives of the SETA program. Secondly, the organization must gather metrics and feedback regarding the SETA program so that it can determine how effective the SETA plan was and adjustments can be made

There are four basic levels of evaluation and they are:

1. End-of-course evaluations;
2. Behavioral objective testing;
3. Job transfer skills; and
4. Organizational benefit.

These levels of evaluation determine how effective the SETA program is from different perspectives. The end-of-course evaluation is to determine how "satisfied" the users were about the material that was presented. The behavioral objective testing is to determine how much knowledge, information, or skill was retained from the learning activity (Dodaro et al., 1998). The job transfer skills evaluation determines how much of the learning activity actually transferred over into the users' daily job activities. Finally, the organizational benefit evaluation determines how much benefit the organization obtained; what was the return on investment (Dodaro et al., 1998). Obtaining these metrics and evaluations can be difficult, but it is very important to have a process in place to capture this information.

There are numerous methods that can be used to capture feedback from the SETA program and a mixture of these will probably be needed in order to capture all of the relevant information. Some of the most common feedback methods are:

- Evaluation forms and questionnaires,
- Focus groups,
- Interviews,
- Independent observation and analysis,
- Status reports, and
- Benchmarking (Wilson & Hash, 2003).

First, some questionnaires and evaluation forms can be used to solicit feedback directly from the users. This form of feedback can help capture the end-of-course and behavioral objective testing evaluations that are needed. Secondly, focus groups and individual interviews can provide feedback for how well the training or awareness directly affects the users' daily job. Finally, independent observation/analysis, status reports, and benchmarking can help determine the organizational benefit from the SETA program.

Overall, tracking the effectiveness and efficiency of the SETA program will ensure that the organization is getting the desired results and that the methods used are efficient. In order to get the best results from a SETA program, the program must be designed with the intent purpose of being able to be tracked and measured. Once the program is created in a way that lends itself to being evaluated, the appropriate metrics and feedback must be obtained so that they can be analyzed to determine the effectiveness of the program. The results from the analysis must then be fed back into the process to ensure that the program is consistently being enhanced and improved. Following this iterative process, the organization will soon have an effective and efficient SETA program.

CONCLUSION

Everyday organizations face many threats, both internal and external, and in order to protect the assets of the organization a layered security approach must be followed. In order to achieve the layered approach an organization must utilize people and processes to compliment the technology-based controls. Many cyber vulnerabilities exist because of a lack of cyber security awareness on the part of computer users, systems administrators, technology developers, procurement officials, auditors, chief information officers (CIOs), chief executive officers, and corporate boards (The National Strategy to Secure Cyberspace, 2003). For example, in addition to buying antivirus software to protect against malware, the organization must fund training for the IT employees to implement the solution properly and security awareness to the employees and contractors to ensure they understand what malware is, what antivirus software is and what they can do to mitigate the threat. Organizations need to ensure that they are securing the organization with a layered approach which includes an adequately trained workforce that is aware of their responsibilities towards security. Implementing a formal and comprehensive SETA program will assist an organization in securing their assets and maintaining the overall well-being of the organization.

REFERENCES

(1995). *An introduction to computer security: The NIST handbook (NIST SP800-12).* National Institute of Standards and Technology.

Barman, S. (2002). *Writing Information Security Policies.* Indianapolis: New Riders.

Blakley, B., McDermott, E., & Geer, D. (2001). *Information security is information risk management.* Paper presented at the ACM Special Interest Group on Security, Audit, and Control, Cloudcroft, New Mexico.

Carlsen, J., Thingsted, P., & Thorne, S. (1993). *Implementation guide: How to make your organization aware of IT security.* European Security Forum.

Central Intelligence Agency. (2003). *The 2002 annual report of the United States intelligence community.* Washington, DC.

Defense in depth. (2002). Retrieved December 27, 2006, from nsa2.www.conxion.com/support/guides/sd-1.pdf.

Desman, M. (2002). Building an Information Security Awareness Program. Florida: CRC Press LLC.

Dodaro, G. L., Zafra, D. d., Pitcher, S. I., Tressler, J. D., & Ippolito, J. B. (1998). *Information technology security training requirements: A role- and performance-based model* (No. 800-16). Gaithersburg, MD: National Institute of Standards and Technology.

Ernest & Young (2004). *Global Information Security Survey 2004.* Retrieved March 5, 2006 from http://www.ey.com/GLOBAL/content.nsf/International/Press_Release_-_2004_Global_Information_Security_Survey

Hansche, S., Berti, J., & Hare, C. (2004). *Official (ISC)² Guide To The CISSP Exam.* New York: Auerbach Publications.

Homeland Security Presidential Directive/Hspd-9, Defense of United States Agriculture and Food, Retrieved January 30, 2004 from http://www.whitehouse.gov/news/releases/2004/02/text/20040203-2.html.

Information technology – Code of practice for information security management (ISO/IEC 17799) (2001). International Standards Organization / International Electrotechnical Commission.

Information technology - Security techniques – Information security management systems – Requirements (ISO/IEC 27001) (2005). International Standards Organization / International Electrotechnical Commission.

ISO/IEC 17799 (2007). Retrieved May 25th, 2007, from http://en.wikipedia.org/wiki/ISO_17799.

ISO/IEC 27001 (2007). Retrieved May 25th, 2007, from http://en.wikipedia.org/wiki/ISO_27001.

Keep America's food and agriculture safe. (2002). Retrieved January 30, 2004, from www.usda.gov/homelandsecurity/fsproc.htm

Marks, P. (2002, February 3). Airport security to grow. *The Hartford Courant*.

McCumber, J. (2005). *Assessing and managing security risk in IT systems*. Auerbach Publications.

McCoy, Carrie, Fowler, Rebecca (October 2004). You are the key to security: establishing a successful security awareness program. *Proceedings of the 32nd annual ACM SIGUCCS conference on User Services SIGUCCS '04*.

Munley, Mary (2004). *Moving from consciousness to culture: creating an environment of cultural awareness*. SANS Information Security Reading Room. Retrieved May 25th, 2007, from http://www.sans.org/reading_room/whitepapers/awareness/1439.php?portal=f48313ae979fda5525 1e768b2dadd2d2.

National Security Institute. (2004). *Improving Security from the Inside Out (A NSI Special Report)*. Medway, MA. URL: http://nsi.org

Peltier, T. R. (2004). *Information Security Policies and Procedures*. Washington D.C.: Auerbach Publications.

Stump, J. (2003). *Food security - protect and prevent*. Retrieved December 29, 2006, from www.vdacs.state.va.us/foodsafety/advisory.html

Swanson, M., & Guttman, B. (1996). *Generally accepted principles and practices for securing information technology systems*. National Institute of Standards and Technology. Retrieved May 25th, 2007, from http://csrc.nist.gov/publications/nistpubs/800-14/800-14.pdf

The National Strategy to Secure Cyberspace (2003). *The President's Critical Infrastructure Protection Board*. Retrieved February 14, 2003, from http://www.whitehouse.gov/pcipb/.

VanWyk, K. R., & Steven, J. (2006). Essential Factors for Successful Software Security Awareness Training. *IEEE Security and Privacy, 4*, 5 (Sept 2006), 80-83. DOI= http://dx.doi.org/10.1109/MSP.2006.119

Visual evidence. (2004). Retrieved December 28, 2006 from www.cr.nps.gov/nr/twhp/wwwlps/lessons/60sanjuan/60visual2.htm

Voss, B. D. (2003). *The ultimate defense of depth: Security awareness in your company*. SANS Information Security Reading Room. Retrieved May 26th, 2007, from http://www.sans.org/reading_room/whitepapers/awareness/395.php?portal=e890567ebf0e64fc81d240d49821e7ba.

Wilson, M., & Hash, J. (2003). *Building an information technology security awareness and training program* (No. 800-50). Gaithersburg, MD: National Institute of Standards and Technology.

Wood, C. C. (1995). Writing infosec policies. *Computers & Security, 14*(8), 667.

KEY TERMS

Centralized Model: A centralized model implements all of the functions of the SETA program, policy, strategy, and implementation, at a centrally managed authority.

Defense-in-Depth: Defense-in-depth is a layered security approach in which people, process, and technology are utilized to protect an organization's assets.

Fully Decentralized: A fully decentralized model implements a centralized policy with distributed strategy and implementation.

Guideline: Guidelines provide additional clarification on how to comply with security policies, but whereas standards are required, guidelines provide a recommendation but not an explicit requirement.

ISO17799 / ISO27001: ISO 17799 and ISO 27001 are complimentary security standards which define a process to create an information security management system and the specific control objects which should be met.

Partially Decentralized: A partially decentralized model implements the policy and strategy of the SETA program by a central authority, but the implementation is managed by individual departments.

Policy: The information security policies are the high-level documents that define the security goals, approach, and strategies of the organization.

Procedure: Information security procedures are documents that support the security policy and standards in a detailed step-by-step manner.

Standard: Security standards are documents that describe the mandatory requirements that the organization will implement in order to comply with security policy.

Chapter XXI
Information Security Within an E-Learning Environment

E. Kritzinger
University of South Africa, South Africa

S.H von Solms
Rand Afrikaans University, South Africa

ABSTRACT

This chapter introduces information security within the educational environments that utilize electronic resources. The education environment experienced a paradigm shift over the last several years, due to the rapid growth in technology. This growth has made it possible for the education environment to utilize electronic services to enhance education methods. It is however vital that all education environments (traditional or new ones) ensure that all resources (lecturers, students and data) are properly protected against any possible security threats. This chapter highlights the importance of securing information within the electronic environment. This is done by providing key aspects that must be addressed and implemented to ensure information security. The chapter also identifies four information security pillars that could assist top management to enhance overall information security management.

INTRODUCTION

Over the last few years the education environment has undergone a paradigm shift as a result of rapid growth of the technology such as the Internet. This growth in technology has made it possible for educational institutions to utilize electronic services to enhance their education methods by incorporating electronic learning (e-learning). E-learning can be defined as a technology-based learning environment where teaching material is supplied to the learner by means of technology, for example a computer network. E-learning has advantages and disadvantages for learners, educators as well as the educational institution. It is, however, critical that possible disadvantages (such as the loss of sensitive information) are addressed proactively before they can cancel out the advantages of an e-learning environment.

It is vital that all education institutions that have existing e-learning environments (or wish to have one) should understand that e-learning education is fundamentally dependent on the use of information and communication technologies (ICT). However, the use of ICT in the e-learning environment opens the door to many information security risks. These information security risks (such as unauthorized changes to learning material) could compromise the entire education environment if they are not properly and timely addressed. It is therefore imperative that all e-learning institutions ensure that they are aware of all the possible information security risks involved in e-learning, as well as which information security measures should be implemented to prevent possible information security incidents. A great deal of research has been done regarding e-learning, but not much attention has been paid to the important role that information security plays within the e-learning environment.

This chapter starts by addressing information security by mentioning a few information security issues that should be considered and implemented within an e-learning environment. The chapter then continues by primarily focusing on different information security issues that should be integrated, implemented and monitored in an e-learning environment to ensure that the integrity of information is not compromised in any way. This chapter concludes by identifying the different role-players (such as learners and educators) as well as their roles and responsibilities in securing the information with which they work. This means involving all role-players in the overall information security plan.

The next section will address some information security issues such as awareness, monitoring, policies and governance that is important to implement within any e-learning environment.

INFORMATION SECURITY: POLICIES AND PROCEDURES

We live in an era in which information is becoming increasingly valuable and the organization with the best information on which to base management decisions will be the likeliest to win and prosper (Finne, 2000). It is therefore essential to secure information properly against all possible information security threats (from inside as well as outside the organization). This section identifies some information security issues that should be taken into consideration when securing information in any environment.

Information is the Lifeline of Many Organizations and Must be Protected

Without information, many organizations will cease to exist. It is therefore vital to protect information from all possible information security threats. Let's look at a few examples where information has been compromised.

The first example is the Sasser Worm which was first detected on 30 April 2004. It spread rapidly and infected more than a million Windows machines worldwide, using a security hole in the Windows operating system (Roberts, 2004). Microsoft offered a reward of $250 000 for the apprehension of the culprit. Train traffic was halted in Australia (Rail Infrastructure Corporation - RailCorp), leaving 300 000 travellers stranded, while two country hospitals in Sweden were infected and left with 5 000 computers and X-ray equipment off-line (F-Secure, 2004). Sasser affected the availability of information, which led to the compromising of services such as those provided by RailCorp.

The second example is that according to the Donau University Krems, an Italian couple hacked into the security system of two American banks and stole credit card data pertaining to nearly

1 500 clients. They used the credit cards for various purchases. In one month, they purchased $750 000 worth of lotto tickets and the winnings of $400 000 were transferred directly into their bank account (Fotinger & Ziegler, 2004). According to the CSI/FBI Computer Crime and Security Survey, the 639 organizations that participated in the survey suffered a total loss due to unauthorised use of computers for 2005 of $130 104 542 (CSI/FBI, 2005).

Lastly, in 2002 a University in Minnesota revealed sensitive information to 400 donors, exposing the recipients who had received their kidneys (Sillivan, 2002). According to John Halamka, the chairman of the New England Health Electronic Data Interchange Network, such inadvertent information Security incidents are a result of the fact that the healthcare environment spends a mere 2% to 3% on their IT budget, as opposed to other industries that spend up to 12% (Hoffman, 2006).

These are but a few examples indicating the serious consequences resulting from information security breaches. It is therefore vital that managing information security should be a top priority in any organization. Information security management should therefore be about maintaining information security in an organization at all times (Pfhleeger, 1997). For the purpose of this chapter, information security management is about ensuring the identification and authentication, authorisation, confidentiality, integrity and non-repudiation of information is not compromised in any way. This is done through proactive management and understanding the risks, threats and vulnerabilities involved.

Information Security: Technical and Non-Technical

When managing information security; it is important to take the technical information security issues as well as the non-technical (human related) information security issues into account. Information security is not a purely technical issue, but it is often treated that way (Leach, 2003; Posthumus & Von Solms, 2004; Von Solms & Von Solms, 2005; Wood, 2004). The technical information security issues still overshadow the non-technical, human-related information security issues. Research primarily focuses on the technical issues, such as firewalls and encryption, while the non-technical, human-related information security issues (such as awareness and policies) receive far less attention (Pfhleeger, 1997; Von Solms & Eloff, 2004). Organizations should recognise and treat information security as both a technical and a non-technical, human-related issue. Many information security breaches that occur within organizations are linked directly to human-related issues, such as downloading unauthorised software from the Internet (CompTIA, 2006; CSI/FBI, 2005; Deloitte, Touche & Tohmatsu, 2005; Pratt, 2006). Employees could be seen as an information security vulnerability if they do not possess the necessary skills and knowledge to protect the information they work with (Streff & Zhou, 2006; Whiteman, 2004). Furthermore, insider information security threats occur far more frequently than threats from outside (Deloitte, Touche & Tohmatsu, 2005). Information security therefore clearly has a human-related side and should not be treated as a technical issue only (Hone & Eloff, 2002; Von Solms & Von Solms, 2004b). Even though the human-related issues have been recognised as playing a pivotal role in information security, they have not yet received sufficient attention (CSI/FBI, 2005; Siponen, 2000a). It is therefore vital when protecting information security both technical and non-technical aspects should addressed.

Information Security Policy

Organizations should ensure that their employees are aware of all the existing information security rules and regulations (including relevant national and international law), to enable them to incorporate such rules and regulations into daily routine when working with information (Berinato, 2005;

CompTIA, 2006; Lewis, 2000; Nosworthy, 2000; Pratt, 2006). These rules and regulations are combined in an information security policy document that is used as a basis for all other information security sub policies, procedures and standards (Von Solms & Von Solms, 2004a). There is a lack of properly defined information security policies globally (Von Solms, 2005a). During 2004 in the UK, for example, only a third of businesses had formally defined information security policies in place (PriceWaterhouseCoopers, 2004). The absence of such policies directly contributes to the lack of information security awareness within an organization. If employees are not aware of how to protect information, such information becomes vulnerable and open to attack.

Information Security Awareness

Global statistics show that although many organizations believe that information security awareness is important, not enough is currently being invested in it (CSI/FBI, 2005). Even if there are information security awareness programmes in place, they are very often neither implemented nor enforced. Statistics show that only 6% of organizations present any information security awareness programme to their newly appointed employees (Deloitte, Touche & Tohmatsu, 2005). Statistics also show that 35% of global organizations do not make their employees aware of any possible Information Security threats (Deloitte, Touche & Tohmatsu, 2005). This lack of information security awareness could lead to information being compromised. To avoid this, organizations should ensure that information corporate governance forms the basis and integrated part of their information security plan.

Information Security Governance

Corporate governance is defined as a the system or method by which companies are directed, controlled and managed (Cadbury Report, 1992; King Report, 2002). The ultimate responsibility for corporate governance ends with top management, for instance the board and executive management (Von Solms, 2005a). Top management should therefore ensure that all resources within the organization are managed at all times. One subset of corporate governance is information security governance – which addresses the protection of information. Top management is therefore also responsible for protecting information. Although information security governance is addressed by top management, this effort is still not enough (Kwok & Longley, 1999). Only 20% of organizations view information security as a priority to be addressed at the Chief Executive Officer (CEO) level, while 42% of top management still believe that information security is an IT function (Berinato, 2005). This shows a clear lack of information security governance. Employees are not going to adhere to information security policies if top management does not get involved (Ernest & Young, 2003). It is no use having information security policies if it is not possible to monitor and enforce compliance with such policies (Von Solms & Von Solms, 2004a).

Monitoring

This monitoring must occur on a regular basis to ensure ongoing information security – it is not a one-time investment (Danchev, 2003; Ernest & Young, 2004). Why implement information security controls if you cannot determine whether or not they are successful? For example, it is totally unacceptable for an organization to find, six to 12 months after an employee has left the organization, that this employee still has access to organization-related information! The only way to stop such unauthorized use of information is through regular monitoring of information and information security.

Many organizations have a misguided sense of how difficult it is to secure their information and many of them want a "quick-fix tool" to ensure it (Cutler, 2000; Deloitte, Touche & Tohmatsu, 2005). Organizations should understand that there are no quick-fixes in information security and that a proper information security culture must be cultivated within the organization (Gallivan & Srite, 2005; Von Solms & Von Solms, 2005). This information security culture should ensure that all information security issues mentioned in this section is addressed by ensuring that proper information security measures are put in place to ensure that information is not compromised in any way. The information security issues addressed in this section will now be used to investigate information security within the e-learning educational environment.

APPLYING INFORMATION SECURITY MEASURES TO EDUCATIONAL ENVIRONMENTS

The main aim of this section is to enforce the importance of incorporating information security issues within the e-learning environment. This section will focus primarily on two well-known environments, the traditional e-learning environment and the full e-learning environments. E-learning (or online learning) could be seen as a professional level of education but with the advantages of lower education time and costs. Although much research has been conducted about the advantages of e-learning, not much attention has been given to the important role that information security plays within the e-learning environment. Information security is vital in any e-learning environment since e-learning is fundamentally dependent on Information and Communication Technologies (ICT). The use of ICT in the e-learning environment opens doors to many possible (information security) risks that could compromise information within in the e-learning environment. This section will provide a brief overview of each environment and investigate the extent to which information security is (should be) implemented within these two e-learning education environments.

Traditional E-Learning Education

The traditional e-learning environment has been around for many years and is encountered all around the globe. It consists of a central physical teaching facility (institution) which consists of lecturers, learners and databases. These databases could contain public as well as sensitive information (such as examination marks) that is stored in databases within a closed computer system. This traditional e-learning environment utilized e-learning within the classroom where learners could download study material and upload assignments. The assessment of these courses is in a specific location with proper supervision. Figure 1 depicts a traditional e-learning environment within a close system environment.

Implementing information security measures within traditional e-learning environments is more manageable since these institutions are mostly restricted to one physical location with a closed computer environment. This means that the lecturers, learners as well as databases are grouped together in a closed system environment where information security threats could be restricted to a minimum. For example, lecturers could check learners' identification (IDs or Learner Cards) when admitting them for assessment. In this way lecturers are certain that the learners who are writing the exam are the learners who enrolled for that specific course. The possibility is also eliminated that any other person may pretend to be a learner and write the examination on his/her behalf.

The situation changed when educational institutions decided to change their traditional way of e-learning education and incorporate newer technologies so as to be able to provide education electronically over the Internet.

Figure 1. Traditional e-learning environment (Kritzinger, 2006)

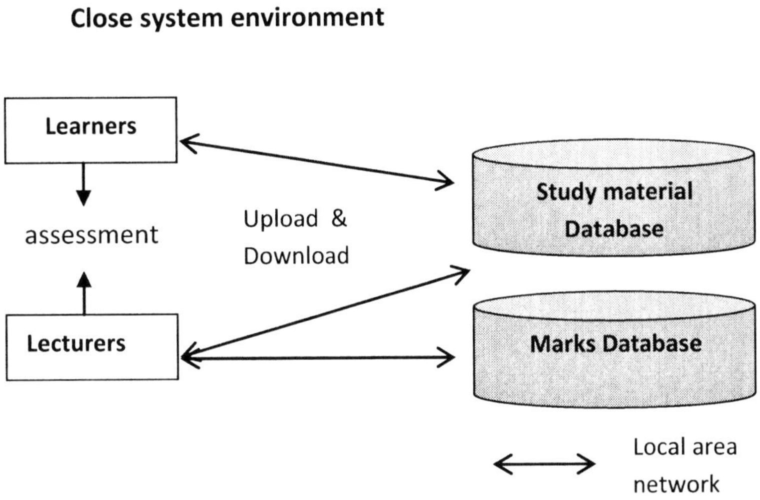

E-Learning Environment

This section focuses mainly on e-learning environment that utilize the Internet. Some other advantages of utilizing the Internet within the e-learning environment includes a larger learner population, lower cost of campus maintenance, up-to-date information and accessibility (El-Kahatib et al., 2003; Silver, 2004). Within the e-learning environment the lecturers, learners and data are at different geographic locations (as depicted in Figure 2) and are connected via the Internet. Figure 2 also depicts that the assessment of learners are also done via the Internet.

It is this dependency on the Internet that contributes to the greatest information security risk. Implementing information security measures are becoming more difficult due to the huge number of possible information security threats connected to the use of the Internet.

Some examples include (Kritzinger & Von Solms, Information Security Governance within the E-learning environment, 2006):

- Within the e-learning environment all parties (for examples learners) are assigned login and passwords. However, this will not ensure that the learner that is being assessed is the 'correct' learner who is officially enrolled for that course. The learner might have given his/her logon and password to another learner (or third party), who writes the test on behalf of the 'real' learner. If this deception is not prevented right at the logon phase, it may probably never be found out.
- During the assessment of one learner, another learner could intercept the first learner's answers (that is being sent over the network), and submit these answers directly as his/her own.
- A peer-to-peer wireless network may be established between two or more learners (or a learner and an outside expert), who may then first have a 'conference call' among themselves to determine the correct answers, after which they deceitfully submit such information as their individual answers.
- After lecturers have saved the final examination marks on the database, a learner obtains unauthorized access via the Internet to the database and changes his/her mark.
- When a learner actually wrote a test and found out that he/she had failed, he/she may suddenly claim never to have written the test

Figure 2. E-learning environment (Kritzinger, 2006)

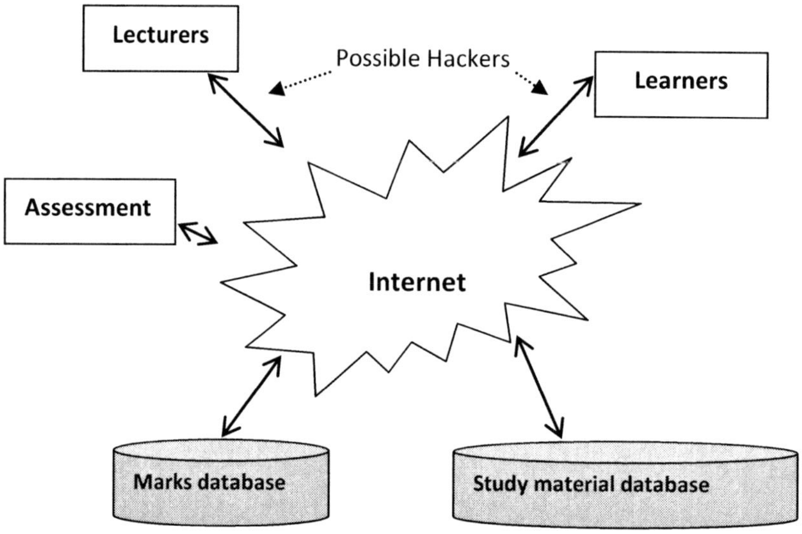

and allege that some unauthorized person had logged in under his/her name without consent.

- While being assessed (writing a test), a learner may realize that he/she will not get a pass mark. He/She may purposefully cause a denial-of-service attack, which may take the website down. This will in effect cause the test to be rescheduled because no other learner will be able to access the relevant website any more.

The scenarios investigated above clearly illustrate some of the potential information security risks, unless special attention is given to the implementation of information security measures. It is therefore vital that all institutions operating within an e-learning environment address these information security risks before the integrity of the information within the e-learning environment is compromised. These risks could be addressed by implementing different information security pillars as investigated in the next section.

E-LEARNING INFORMATION SECURITY PILLARS

The main focus of this section is to identify four pillars that could assist institutions in the process of securing the integrity of the information within the e-learning environment. The pillars are as follows:

- Ensuring e-learning Information Security Governance
- Creating e-learning Information Security Policies and Procedures
- Implementation of e-learning Information Security countermeasures
- Monitoring the e-learning Information Security countermeasures

A combination of these four pillars will have a significant effect on implementing and maintaining a good and secure e-learning environment. Each of these pillars could have one or more actions. These four pillars and their actions are depicted in Figure 3.

Each of the four pillars consists of one or more actions that will help the institution in implementing that specific pillar. Each of the pillars as well as the actions (depicted in Figure 3) will be separately looked at in the rest of this section.

Ensuring E-Learning Information Security Governance

The first pillar highlights the significance of information security governance within the e-learning environment and consists of two actions. The first action is to ensure proper information security governance and the second action is about the buy-in and commitment from top management.

Introduce E-Learning Information Security Governance

Corporate governance is the system or method by which companies are directed, controlled and managed (Cadbury Report, 1992; Lindup, 1996; Moulton & Coles, 2003; Turnbull, 2003).

Corporate governance must be taken seriously due to the fact that the accountability for corporate governance ultimately rests with the Board level and the Executive Management level (Von Solms, 2001b). If the corporate governance system fails, international scandals can occur such as that involving ENRON. ENRON is an American

Figure 3. Four pillars of e-learning (Kritzinger & von Solms, 2006)

company that went bankrupt in 2002 as a result of unacceptable corporate governance. Corporate governance must therefore be taken seriously in order to ensure the survival of the organization.

Corporate governance could be seen as good practice in many countries such as South Africa and England. The board level and executive management level are also accountable for the proper *information security governance* in organizations. *Information security governance* involves the leadership, organizational structure, processes and technologies that ensure that the confidentiality, integrity and availability of the organization's electronic assets are maintained at all times (Von Solms, 2001b). The board level and executive management level can be taken to court if the integrity, availability or confidentiality of information is compromised in any way. Consequently these management levels in many large organizations are now expressing a much greater interest in information security than a few years ago (Kwok & Longley, 1997). They have never been as dependent on information security as they are today (Lindup, 1996; Von Solms, 2005). All the signs show that this dependency can only increase. It is essential that corporate governance include information security as a vital part of governing an organization and that the board level and executive management level should also encourage effective and responsible use of information among all stakeholders in the organization.

Information security governance consists of the leadership, organizational structure, processes and technologies that ensure that information is never compromised (Von Solms, 2001b). From this definition it is clear that in general, the main purpose of information security governance is to protect against the risks which can impact on the confidentiality, integrity and availability of all electronic resources. In most cases information is processed using Information and Communications Technologies (ICT) systems, this means the information is stored in databases and transmitted over networks. This is naturally just as important for educational institutions, where ICT is used for such information processing, and where risks can arise with regard to the confidentiality, integrity and availability of the following types of data and information, usually stored in centralized databases:

- learner information like course marks and study records,
- staff information like salaries and pension information,
- intellectual property,
- etc.

It is vital to know that information security governance form part of the over all corporate governance of an institution. All educational institutions should therefore enforce information security governance, at least to protect and secure the types of sensitive information and data referred to above.

Get Buy-In and Commitment from Top Management

The second action in this pillar highlights how important it is to obtain the buy-in and commitment from top management. Top management should therefore protect information through effective management, which is assured only through effective board oversight (Von Solms, 2001a). Only if top management takes information security seriously the rest of the institution will follow.

E-Learning Information Security Policies and Procedures

The second pillar is about ensuring that proper e-learning information security policies and procedures are designed and implemented within the institution. This pillar also consists of two actions which include policies and risk management procedures. Both of these actions are vital in ensuring information is secured.

Having an E-Learning Information Security Policy

An Information security policy is defined as a document that contains specific rules and regulations regarding securing information within a specific organization (National Institute of Standards and Technology, 2000).

Before any organization can start to manage their information security, they should first have an information security policy in place as a guideline to **what** must be managed and **how** this must be done. The information security rules and regulations stipulated in the information security policy relate to the hardware, software, networks and information within an organization (Von Solms & Von Solms, 2004a; Waint, 2005). One purpose of an information security policy is to protect the organization's information assets from all threats, whether internal or external. All organizations must have an information security policy in place so as to ensure that all information is correctly and fully secured. The presence of an information security policy is one of the most important elements in the prevention of information security incidents (Lewis, 2000). The assumption is then that an information security policy is no longer a luxury, but a basic necessity for any organization wanting to secure its information.

Information security policies lately experienced a paradigm shift. A few years ago many organizations had a properly designed information security policy, but were not implementing it (Doherty & Fulford, 2006; Von Solms & Von Solms, 2004b). The policy was probably stored on a shelf somewhere, instead of being used and managed. When Information Security management started to become more prominent, it was surrounded by much controversy regarding the failure to manage the information security policy. Critics argued that an organization that did not manage its information security policy, might just as well not have had such a policy at all (Von Solms & Eloff, 2000).

This e-learning information security policy should address how security decisions can be made with regard to hardware, software, networks and information. The primary purpose of an e-learning information security policy is to protect the integrity of the information within the e-learning environment. Such an e-learning information security policy should comprise a maximum of 2 to 3 pages, very generic and non-technical, and must be signed by the most senior official in the company

Having an E-Learning Risk Management Procedure

Risk management is the process of ensuring that risks within the organization are kept and maintained at an acceptable level (National Institute of Standards and Technology, 2000).

Risk is about the likelihood of damage, loss or injury and can be found in any organization. An example of such a risk is if an employee compromises his/her password. The impact of this is that an unauthorised person can access secured information and compromise the integrity, availability or confidentiality of the information. These risks should therefore be identified and managed in order to keep security losses to a minimum (Burnette, 2005; Gerber & Von Solms, 2005; Whiteman & Mattord, 2003).

Risk management consists of specific phases, namely risk identification (identifying all possible risks), risk assessment (estimating the probability that risk could occur), risk analysis (making decisions regarding Information Security based on the outcome of the risk assessment) and risk monitoring (monitoring the risk situation in the organization to identify any changes) (Smith, 2000). The aim of risk management is to minimise risk or, in the best case, to prevent risks from occurring. Each stakeholder in the organization should in some way be involved in managing risks in the organization (Whiteman & Mattord, 2003).

Risk management can be seen as a technical as well as a non-technical information security issue. The *technical* side of risk management involves issues such as installing firewalls to ensure that no unauthorised person could obtain access to the system. The *non-technical* side of risk management involves issues such as management decision making processes.

The second action in this pillar is to prevent the information security incidents within the e-learning environment. Top management of educational institutions should provide platforms for integrated educational, learning and assessment environments. This could be done by following at least, the following steps (Kritzinger & Von Solms, Information Security Governance within the E-learning environment, 2006):

- Perform a proper risk analysis to identify all the ICT and business-related risks involved in the implementation of an e-learning environment. Ensure that this risk analysis is driven by international best practices in the field of ICT and information security governance.
- Determine the potential impact of these risks on the e-learning environment if they should materialize.
- Determine how to handle these e-learning risks, i.e. ignore them, transfer them or accept and manage them.
- Determine the information security countermeasures needed to manage those risks which are accepted.
- Create a proper Enterprise Information Security Management (EISM) system to continuously manage these risks. Such a system should include the relevant policies, procedures, technical measures as well as the necessary compliance measurement and monitoring mechanisms to monitor and enforce compliance with the relevant policies, and to report the level of risk to top management on a regular basis.
- Review the risk situation on an annual basis and adapt the EISM system as necessary.

Implementation of E-Learning Information Security Countermeasures

The third pillar highlights the implementation of different information security measures. This pillar consists of two actions, the first is about the implementation of policies and procedures. The second action identifies six services that are vital for overall security within e-learning.

Implement E-Learning Information Security Policies and Procedures

It is essential that all institutions ensure that their e-learning information security policy is not only properly designed but also properly implemented. An e-learning information security policy has no value if it is stored somewhere on a shelf and is not used to secure information. If an e-learning information security policy is not implemented within the institution, it is just as bad as not having one at all. However, the implementation of the e-learning information security policy is ultimately the responsibility of Top management.

Implement Six Information Security Services

The second action in this pillar is to identify and implement six information security services. When implementing information security services within the e-learning environment it is essential that the implemented countermeasures should enforce the following six information security services:

Identification and Authentication

The first service, identification and authentication, is put in place to ensure that only authorized users can gain access to a system (or part of a system). The first part of this service is about determining whether or not a person who is trying to gain access to a system is cleared for access. This process is called identification and is usually done by entering a user ID into the system. Once the user has been identified, the system must ensure that the user is truly who he/she claims to be. This process is called authentication. Authentication can be done by means of something the user knows, such as passwords, something the user has, such as an access card or something the user is, such as fingerprints (Von Solms & Eloff, 2004). Examples of the information security countermeasures for identification and authentication include proper unique passwords and login IDs.

Authorization

The next step towards enforcing information security is authorization. This involves determining whether or not the authenticated party has the right to access the information in question (Von Solms & Eloff, 2004). An example of the information security countermeasures for authorization is access control.

Confidentiality

The third service, Confidentiality, is an information security characteristic as well as a service and is put in place to protect data from unauthorized access. The purpose of confidentiality is to ensure that information and data are not disclosed to any unauthorized person or entity (International Federation of Accountants, 2000). An example of the information security countermeasure for confidentiality is encryption.

Integrity

The fourth service is integrity. The purpose of integrity is to ensure that information is still in its original form and that no tampering or alteration has taken place. In other words, only authorized parties may change the content of information and unauthorized modification must be prevented. An example of a countermeasure that will help to ensure integrity is message authentication codes.

Non-Repudiation

The last service towards enforcing information security is non-repudiation or non-denial. This service ensures that no action taken that affects Information Security can be denied at a later stage (Von Solms & Eloff, 2004). An example of the information security countermeasure for non-repudiation is digital signatures.

Availability

This service ensures that all electronic resources and services are available to authorized users when they want to use such services. Availability means that data and information are accessible at any time to authorized parties (International Federation of Accountants, 2000). An example of the information security countermeasures for availability is regulator backups.

Monitoring the E-Learning Information Security Countermeasures

The fourth and last pillar is about information security compliance monitoring to establish if procedures and processes that are implemented in an organization are working as they should. The objects that are monitored can differ from organization to organization and include products, systems, processes, security program effectiveness and personal competence (Katzke, 2001). This monitoring process should therefore be extended to include the e-learning environment and include aspects such as validation of information, evaluating of the operating capacity as well as overall impact of the e-learning environment on learners' success.

This monitoring process will ensure that institutions know their information security situation within the e-learning environment at any given time. This will also help top management in their decision making process to ensure that if there is a security incident, it can be resolved before the availability, integrity and confidentiality of information is compromised. If any difficulty is identified by the monitoring process it is essential that the e-learning information security policies and risk management procedures are updated at regular intervals.

RESPONSIBILITIES FOR E-LEARNING INFORMATION SECURITY MEASURES

It is important to ensure that the information security counter measures (mentioned in previous sections) are assigned to the different role players within the e-learning environment that should be responsible to ensure they are properly implemented. If employees are not properly made aware of information security issues, they could not be held accountable if the information is compromised. All employees in an organization should therefore be made aware of their role and responsibility towards securing the information they work with.

The typical role players that could be identified within an e-learning environment include Top Management, Technical Personnel, Lecturing Personnel and the Learners. The role players within an institution could differ depending on the different needs for that institution. The information security measures that should be implemented by the role players include:

1. Identification and authentication
2. Authorization
3. Confidentiality
4. Integrity
5. Non-repudiation
6. Availability
7. E-learning Information Security Governance
8. E-learning information security policy
9. E-learning information security risk management Plan
10. Monitoring of e-learning countermeasures

Not all role players are responsible for all the different information security e-learning countermeasures. The countermeasures are therefore assigned to different role players according to their job function. Figure 4 depicts which role players within an e-learning institution should be responsible for which countermeasure.

Figure 4 indicates that top management should be responsible for specific countermeasures such as information security governance, policy and risk management plan. Top management should therefore protect information through effective management that is assured only through effective board oversight (Von Solms, 2001a). Only if top management takes information security seriously the rest of the institution will follow.

The technical personnel are responsibly for many of technical information security countermeasures in the e-learning environment. These technical countermeasures include authorization, availability as well as monitoring.

All lectures within the e-learning environment should be responsible for more that just teaching of a course. Lectures should be aware of how important information security is and how they can enforce the countermeasures assigned to them.

Figure 4. Countermeasures assigning to different role players (Kritzinger & Von Solms, 2006)

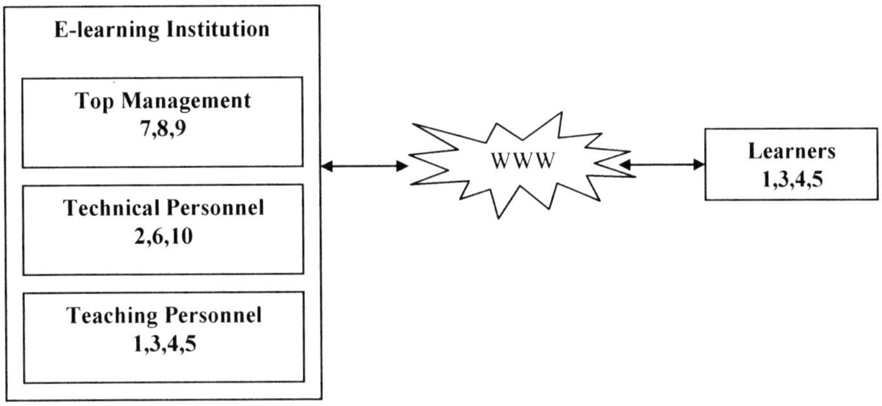

These countermeasures include identification & authentication, confidentiality, integrity and non-repudiation.

The last role players within the e-learning are the learners. Learners should also be made aware of the necessity of security information when using the WWW. The information security countermeasures assigned to them include identification & authentication, confidentiality, integrity and non-repudiation.

All the role players should be made aware of their assigned countermeasures and understand the consequences if these countermeasures are not implemented and used correctly.

CONCLUSION

All the issues addressed above contribute towards ensuring that education institutions understand how important it is to create and cultivate an information security culture in the e-learning environment. This is to ensure that the most important resource (information) is properly protected and secured against any possible security threats. This can only be achieved if all role-players in the e-learning environment are aware of their specific role and responsibility in securing the information they work with.

In conclusion, if all the information security countermeasures are addressed proactively, implemented and monitored on a regular basis, any possible information security threats can be kept to a minimum.

REFERENCES

Berinato, S. (2005). The Global State of Information Security. Available at: www.cio.com.

Burnette, R. (2005). Legal risk management for the IT industry. *Computer Law & Security Report, 21*(1), 61-67.

Cadbury Report (1992). *Report of the committee on the Financial Aspects of Corporate Governance*, United Kingdom.

CompTIA (2006). Fourth annual CompTIA study on information security and the workforce. Available at: http://www.comptia.org/about/pressroom/get_pr.aspx?prid=903.

CSI/FBI (2005). Computer Crime and Security Survey. Available at: GoCSI.com.

Cutler, K. (2000). Hitting the Bull's eye. Available at: http://infosecuritymag.techtarget.com/articles/august00/columns5_logoff.shtml. August.

Danchev, D. (2003). Reducing Human Factor Mistakes. Available at: http:www.windowsecurity.com. July 23.

Deloitte, T. & T. (2005). Global Security Survey. Available at: www.deloitte.com.

Doherty, N. F., & Fulford, H. (2006). Aligning the information security policy with the strategic information systems plan. *Computers & Security, 25*(1), 55-63.

El-Kahatib, K., Korba, L., Xu, Y., & Gee, G. (2003). Privacy and Security in E-Learning. *International Journal of Distance Education, 1*(4).

Ernest & Young (2003). Global Information Security Survey. Available at: http://www.ey.com.

Ernest & Young (2004). Global Information Security Survey. Available at: http://www.ey.com.

F-Secure (2004). F-Secure Corporation's Data Security Summary for 2004. Available at: http: www.f-secure.com.

Finne, T. (2000). Information Systems Risk Management: Key Concepts and Business Processes. *Computers & Security, 19*(3), 234-242.

Fotinger, C. S., & Ziegler, W. (2004). Understanding a hacker's mind - A psychological insight into the hijacking of identities. *A White Paper by the Danube-University,* Zentrum fur praxisorientiere Informatik, Dr Karl-Dorrek Strabe 30, A-3500 Krems.

Gallivan, M., & Srite, M. (2005). Information technology and culture: Identifying fragmentary and holistic perspectives of culture. *Information and Organization, 15*(4), 295-338.

Gerber, M., & Von Solms, R. (2005). Management of risk in the information age. *Computers & Security, 24*(1), 16-30.

Hoffman, T. (2006). Q&A: Health care standards on the Table. Available at: http://www.computerworld.com/databasetopics/data/story/0,10801,109417,00.html.

Hone, K., & Eloff, J. H. P. (2002). What makes an Effective Information Security policy. *Network Security, 2002*(6), 14-16.

International Federation of Accountants (2000). Managing Security of Information.

Katzke, S. (2001). Security Metric. Available at: http://www.acsac.org/measurement/position-papers.

King Report (2002). *The Code of Corporate Practices and Conduct*, Institute of Directors, South Africa.

Kritzinger, E. (2006). Information Security in an e-learning environment. In *19th World Computer Congress*, Santiago, Chile.

Kritzinger, E., & von Solms, S. H. (2006). *E-learning: Incorporating Information Security Governance*, in *InSite 2006*, England.

Kritzinger, E., & Von Solms, S. H. (2006). Information Security Governance within the E-Learning environment. In *2006 Teaching and Learning conference*, Mexico.

Kwok, L., & Longley, D. (1997). Code of Practice: A Standard for Information Security Management. In *Proceedings of IFIP TC11, 13th International Conference on Information Security.*

Kwok, L., & Longley, D. (1999). Information Security Management and modeling. *Information Management and Computer Security, 7*(1), 30-40.

Leach, J. (2003). Improving user security behaviors. *Computers & Security, 22*(8), 685-670.

Lewis, A. (2000). Time to elevate IT security to the boardroom. *e Secure, 1*(1), 28.

Lindup, K. (1996). The role of information security in corporate governance. *Computers & Security, 15*(6), 477-485.

Moulton, R., & Coles, R. S. (2003). Applying information security governance. *Computers & Security, 22*(7), 580-584.

National Institute of Standards and Technology (2000). *An Introduction to Computer Security: The NIST Handbook.*, Special Publication 800-12.

Nosworthy, J. D. (2000). Implementing Information Security In The 21st Century — Do You Have the Balancing Factors? *Computers & Security, 19*(4), 337.

Pfhleeger, C. P. (1997). *Security in Computing,* Second edition. Prentice Hall, USA.

Posthumus, S., & Von Solms, R. (2004). A framework for the governance of information security. *Computers & Security, 23*(8), 638-646.

Pratt, M. K. (2006). Employee Security Training: Beyond Posters. Available at: http://www.computerworld.com/printthis/2006/0,4814,110494,00.html.

PriceWaterhouseCoopers (2004). Information Security Breaches survey. Available at: http://www.pwcglobal.com/.

Roberts, P. (2004). Sasser a warning of things to come. Available at: http:www.infoworld.com.

Sillivan, B. (2002). Release of organ donor data prompts changes. Available at: http://archives.cnn.com/2002/TECH/internet/02/16/organ.donor.data.idg/.

Silver, M. (2004). E-Learning for the pump industry. *Worlds Pumps, 2004*(453), 28-31.

Siponen, M. T. (2000a). A conceptual foundation for organizational information security awareness. *Information Management & Computer Security, 8*(1), 31-41.

Smith, E. (2000). *Information Security in Health-Care Systems: a New approach to IT Risk Management.* Rand Afrikaans University. Johannesburg, South Africa.

Streff, K., & Zhou, Z. (2006). Developing and enhancing a computer and network security curriculum. *Journal of Computing Sciences in Colleges, 21*(3), 1-14.

Turnbull, S. (2003). Network governance. *Corporate Governance International, 6*(3), 4-14.

Von Solms, R., & Von Solms, S. H. (2004a). From policies to culture. *Computers & Security, 23*(4), 275-279.

Von Solms, R., & Von Solms, S. H. (2004b). The 10 deadly sins of information security management. *Computers & Security, 23*(5), 371-376.

Von Solms, R., & Von Solms, S. H. (2005). From information security to. business security? *Computers & Security, 24*(4), 271-273.

Von Solms, S. H. (2001a). Information Security - A Multidimensional Discipline. *Computers & Security, 20*(6), 504-508.

Von Solms, S. H. (2001b). Corporate Governance and Information Security. *Computers & Security, 20*(3), 215-218.

Von Solms, S. H. (2005). Information Security Governance in ICT Based Educational Systems. *Proceedings of the 2005 Conference in Bankok.*

Von Solms, S. H. (2005a). Information Security Governance - Compliance management vs operational management. *Computers & Security, 24*(6), 443-447.

Von Solms, S. H., & Eloff, J. H. P. (2004). *Information Security.* Johannesburg, South-Africa.

Waint, T. L. (2005). Information security policy's impact on reporting security incidents. *Computers & Security, 24*(6), 448-459.

Whiteman, W. (2004). In defense of the realm: understanding the threats of information Security. *International Journal of Information Management, 24*(1), 43-57.

Whiteman, W. & Mattord, H. J. (2003). *Principles of Information Security,* Thomson - Course Technology, Canada.

Wood, C. C. (2004). Why information security is now multi-disciplinary, multi-departmental, and multi-organizational in nature. *Computer Fraud & Security,* (1), 16-17.

KEY TERMS

Authorization: Involves determining whether or not the authenticated party has the right to access the information in question (Von Solms & Eloff, 2004).

Availability: Data and information is accessible at any time to authorized parties (International Federation of Accountants, 2000).

Corporate Governance: Is a system or method by which companies are directed, controlled and managed (Cadbury Report, 1992; King Report, 2002).

Confidentiality: Ensures that information and data are not disclosed to any unauthorized person or entity (International Federation of Accountants, 2000).

Information Security Awareness: Entails ensuring that all stakeholders in an organization understand their role and responsibility towards securing the information they work with.

Information Security Management: It is about maintaining Information Security in an organization (Pfleeger, 1997).

Information Security Policies: An Information Security policy is a set of documentation that contains Information Security rules and regulations (National Institute of Standards and Technology, 2000).

Integrity: Ensures that information is still in its original form and that no tampering or alteration has taken place.

Non-Denial: Ensures that no action taken that affects Information Security can be denied at a later stage (Von Solms & Eloff, 2004).

Chapter XXII
Research Notes on Emerging Areas of Conflict in Security

Donald Murphy
M&T Bank Corporation, USA

Manish Gupta
State University of New York, USA

H.R. Rao
State University of New York, USA

ABSTRACT

We present five emerging areas in information security that are poised to bring the radical benefits to the information security practice and research. We have selected these five areas based on extensive literature review and emerging trends in information technology and security. This is a theoretical discourse, which considers a number of research issues and paradigms and explores the relevance of some interesting research areas that have far-reaching implications for IS research. The chapter aims to stimulate discussions about the five covered research areas and in doing so responds to the call for information security researchers to be more aware of the research methodological options available to them. For each area, we have provided background and existing research along side rationale on why this area is becoming important and vital in the field of information security research. The chapter introduces five key areas of information security research that are gaining recognition and credibility to significantly aid information security practice.

INTRODUCTION

Information assets are highly critical to any business and are increasingly becoming basis of survival today's networked and global economy. In recent years, the developments in information technology and evolution of Internet have introduced newer information security risks such as the risk of service interruptions, breach of confidentiality and integrity of information. Evidently, there is growing importance for information in the economy, life, and development of society, where information security has surely emerged as a key concern for more and more organizations. Not only have security breaches have shown to cause losses to organizations but also have shown to hugely impact ordinary computer users' well being, such as Identity theft, privacy violation and credit card information breach.

Providing information systems security and assurance has emerged as one of the most interesting as well as complex technological and social challenges. Computing Research Association (CRA, 2003), with support from the US National Science Foundation, recently drafted its Grand Research Challenges in security and assurance, intent on galvanizing the field by focusing attention and stimulating progress on these problems (Smith and Spafford, 2004). In the same spirit, based on extensive literature survey and review of practical information assurance issues, we present five research issues in information assurance area. In the area of information security research, we can find significant contributions from computer scientists, psychologists, socialists, economists, cryptologists, electrical and computer engineers and IS scholars. As a result of the increased attention and importance of this field, there are now several journals and a large number of annual conferences and workshops dedicated to the security aspects of information systems (IS) and computing. However, despite such diversity in the information security research, there are very few research efforts that involve interdisciplinary research, i.e. without limiting the analysis to a particular discipline (e.g., computer science, psychology, economics, business or cryptology).

We present five emerging areas in information security that are poised to bring the tremendous benefits to the information security practice and research. We have selected these five areas based on extensive literature review and emerging trends in information technology and security. This is a theoretical discourse, which considers a number of research issues and paradigms and explores the relevance of some interesting research areas that have far-reaching implications for IS research. This is not intended to be in any way an authoritative reference for the areas discussed in the chapter. Rather it is hoped that the chapter will stimulate a discussion about the five covered research areas and in doing so respond to the call for information security researchers to be more aware of the research methodological options available to them. Another motive for this chapter is to encourage debate among information security researchers as to how to assess the research methodologies available to them to explore the discussed areas. For each area, we have provided background and existing research along side rationale on why this area is becoming important and vital in the field of information security research. The contributions of the chapter are two-fold. First, it introduces five key areas of information security research that are gaining recognition and credibility to significantly aid information security practice. Secondly, the chapter provides discussion on these areas in light of existing and missing research that should stimulate information security researchers with thoughts and inclinations. The chapter is organized as follows: the next section presents five the identified emerging areas in information security research followed by a conclusion section.

MODEL DRIVEN SECURITY

Information systems security is usually implemented in an ad-hoc manner and is considered a nonfunctional systems requirement. It is treated as an emergent feature of the system and is applied in a very patched manner. More often than not security aspects are considered very late in the overall software development and management cycle. It is not very well built into the different stages of the systems design, development and implementation. The development of security-critical large-scale distributed software systems is a difficult and error prone process and it is especially difficult to manually define security policies, for example for access control (Reznik et al., 2007). Security is an integral part of most modern IT systems and designing such systems requires properly identifying, integrating, and configuring different security technologies. Information security is a serious requirement that must be carefully considered, not as an isolated aspect, but as an element that is present in all stages of the development life cycle (Devanbu and Stubblebine, 2000; Ferrari and Thuraisingham, 2000; Ghosh et al., 2002).

"*Model-driven security is the use of integrated visual models or modeling languages during application design, development and composition to assign security primitives — such as confidentiality, integrity, authentication, authorization and auditing — to application, process and information flows. The security-augmented application models may then be used to automate the generation of necessary security code and potentially configure necessary security enforcement mechanisms, freeing the application developer from having to code to specific security application programming interfaces and enabling faster future updates as applications and processes change.*" (Gartner, 2006)

Model-driven security tools modularize the software development process and makes its unnecessary for free developers to hard-code security policies and login with the software code. This lends huge advantage in terms of de-coupling software developers from having to understand the security policies and provides ease of code management and maintenance. This speeds up the development efforts, ensures consistent deployment of security policies and enables easier future changes. The externalization of security policy enables business units and security organizations, not developers, to define and make appropriate changes to the security policy. For long, Model Driven Security has been used to build certifiably secure systems using Common Criteria set of assessment benchmarks. There has been a renewed interest in integrated modeling tools from development platform vendors. For example, IBM has demonstrated proof-of-concept security integration in its Rational modeling tool with its WebSphere Business Integrator and constituents of efforts for supporting modeling language standards, such as Unified Modeling Language (UML) and Business Process Execution Language (BPEL), are looking at standard security extensions. However, these efforts have not fully matured or standardized to be able to receive widespread adoption.

Today most of the web attacks exploit vulnerabilities that are found in software both COTS (commercial off the shelf) and built by companies in house. This had resulted in severe costs both in terms of tangible losses such as financial and intangible such as trust and reputation. Building secure applications by incorporating security considerations in every step of the way of software development, while maintaining cost and time to market, is one of the biggest conflicts that information security faces in today's Internet age. This should be interest to both businesses and governments alike. The adoption of Model Driven Security will help thwarts threats from cyber terrorism and help bolster national critical infrastructure. Next we discuss some research and studies that has also done in the area, directly of indirectly, of model driven security; most of which is in the realms of UML (Unified Modeling Language and MDA (Model Driven Architecture). However, model driven security that still requires significant research, as is evidenced from the literature survey below.

Security is often managed in an ad-hoc fashion where requirements are analyzed and solutions are implemented, as patches as opposed to integral components of software, much later during the overall development cycle, especially before, or even during, the system installation and deployment phase. The results are poorly integrated security controls in the information systems that present huge avoidable risks to operation of the application and the supporting business processes. The need to overcome this deficiency has been noted before, e.g. in (Devanbu and Stubblebine, 2000). Model Driven Architecture, which is an emerging standard for model-centric and generative software development and is defined by the Object Management Group (Kleppe et al., 2003; OMG1, 2003). Model Driven Architecture provides standards like the Meta-Object Facility (OMG2, 2002) for defining modeling languages and the Unified Modeling Language (UML) (OMG3, 2001) as In Model Driven Security, security is integrated into modeling. Design models are combined with security models, leading to new kinds of models that are referred to as security design models. The primary concept of MDA is to use a standard modeling language, such as UML, to specify both the static interfaces and the dynamic interactions of the components in platform-independent models (PIM). Issues such as reliability, safety, security and availability comprise software dependability (Littlewood and Strigini , 2000; Bondavalli et al., 1999; Emmerich , 2000; Rodrigues et al., 2003; Avizienis et al., 2001). Existing research on dependability focuses on the early design phases of software development only (Cortellessa et al., 2002; Huszerl and Majzik, 2001). Rodrigues has presented a platform-independent means to support reliability design following the principles of a model driven approach (Rodrigues, 2004).

Because of the way system and security models are formulated and presented, security models and their design and applications have been treated as a very narrow and specialty area, divorced from mainstream system design. Security models need to be simple, to start with, and then add complexity (and completeness) by introducing layers of abstractions. This abstraction has been attractively simple and general purpose; and has been used during 1970s for designing and implementing time-sharing, user driven systems. It was around this time also when the initial interest in the security modeling efforts began. Various formalizations of this model (Bell and LaPadula, 1973; Goguen and Meseguer, 1982) have been created and used in system developments, and it is the basis of some of the widely adopted security evaluation criteria (DOD, 1985). The state of the art in security engineering at the application layer is much more limited (Viega and McGraw, 2001; Wing, 1998).

There have been other efforts on security and UML: (Epstein and Sandhu, 1999; Shin and Ahn, 2000) used UML as a language to represent RBAC modeling and notation; (Jürjens[1] , 2002; Jürjens[2] , 2002) on theoretical security definition with UML; (Lodderstedt et al., 2002) introduced SecureUML for model-driven security with extended meta-model elements for RBAC only; (Ray et al., 2003) used UML elements to model MAC and RBAC based systems; and, (Alghathbar[1] and Wijesekera, 2003; Alghathbar[2] and Wijesekera, 2003) presented a framework to incorporate security into use cases only. Vela (Vela et al., 2006) has also proposed a methodological approach for the model driven development of secure XML databases (DB). We presented, in this section, a survey of model driven security research in light of growing importance to build and deploy secure systems. This lays out current state of research on the topic and we encourage information security researchers for further exploration and investigation of the area.

SECURITY USABILITY

One of the most challenging problems in ensuring information security arises from the human and social factors of information systems. Human errors and oversights are increasingly being found to be one of the leading causes of security failures, yet most design paradigms in security systems ignore the importance of usability design. The fact that security mechanisms and controls are only effective when used correctly seems to be eluding developers and designers of information systems. There have been several important usability studies of security applications (Adam and Sasse, 1999; Karat, 1989; Whitten and Tygar, 1999), all of which have demonstrated the severe adverse impact that ignoring usability issues can have on the effectiveness of security measures. Today there is an increasing recognition that security issues are also fundamentally human-computer interaction issues (Dourish, 2004; Patrick et al., 2004). For example, Ross Anderson (1994) discusses the effects of user non-compliance on security and Don Davis (1996) analyzes the unrealistic expectations that public-key based security systems often place on users.

It is generally believed that strength of information security and ease of systems usability are inversely proportional to each other, which translates to "*the tougher and stricter the security is, the less usability there is*", and vice versa. However, usability and security do not have to be sacrificed for the sake of the other. Ideally the more secure an information system is, the more reliable and effective it will be, which will lead it be a *more usable* system. Until last few years, during which information security has grown in importance, systems were designed for managing issues of features, performance and time-to-market. For last few years, systems and all its components are designed keeping security in mind. Recent high profile security incidents such as outbreak of viruses/worms and disclosure of security vulnerabilities have kept software vendors on their toes. However, still the un-usability of the applications' and systems' security systems pose one of the greatest threats of security of the information.

Technical applications of security such as strong encryption, provably correct protocols and secure code will not provide the acceptable levels of security if the users of the software ignore the protocols of the system when they become a bit unwieldy in normal routine. There is also an interesting psychological aspect to it: people would rather prefer to reduce a risk (however small it may be to start with) to zero than create a proportionally much larger decrease that would not reduce the risk to zero. For example instead of reducing one risk from 90% to 10% they'll concentrate on reducing another risk from 1% to 0%, yielding a risk reduction of 1% instead of 80%. Psychologists refer to this phenomenon as zero-risk bias. Zero-risk bias occurs because people are concerned about risk and if they can reduce the risk they will be happier and won't have to worry about the risk anymore. So if people think that security is something they cannot achieve 100%, they ignore it, while finding assurances in environmental factors such as policies and other technological countermeasures. There seem to be relatively few development efforts in computer security that have seriously emphasized user interaction issues (Jendricke and Markotten, 2000; Zurko, et al., 1999; Holmstrom, 1999).

CASE OF PASSWORDS

Passwords are a typical point in the case how security and usability don't go hand in hand. Users tend to keep their password simple enough for them to remember. Another factor that aggravates the situation is that on average users have to remember 5-10 different passwords in a typical work setting. So they choose passwords that are easier to remember. In recent years, password security has been proposed to improve by introducing complexity in its composition and in the policy. For example, *a complex password rule can state that passwords should be at least 10 characters long and should contain at least one number, one upper case, one lower case, one special character and no letter should be repeated in succession and that previous 10 passwords cannot be picked again; and that passwords will expire in 30 days, which means user will have to change their password every 30 days.* In such a situation, though passwords are strong and complex enough to provide a degree of confidence in its un-breakability, it introduces other security problems. Users, in this case, will tend to write down their passwords on sheet of paper (or post-its) or will also incur increased calls to helpdesk for passwords reset that lowers productivity and user motivations. In other worlds, users who fail to choose and handle passwords securely open holes that attackers can exploit (Brown et al, 2004; Dhamija and Perrig, 2000; Morris and Thompson, 1979; Sasse et al., 2001) Fe;dmeier and Karn, 1990, Kliein, 1990) The "password problem," as formulated by Wiedenbeck (2005), arises because passwords are expected to comply with two conflicting requirements, namely:

1. Passwords should be easy to remember, and the user authentication protocol should be executable quickly and easily by humans.
2. Passwords should be secure, i.e., they should look random and should be hard to guess; they should be changed frequently, and should be different on different.

There can be a significant difference between *theoretical* and *effective* security (Gutman, 2006). In *theory*, we should all be using smart cards and PKI for authentication. However, these measures are so painful to deploy and use that they're almost never employed, making them far less *effectively* secure than basic usernames and passwords. Security experts tend to focus exclusively on the measures that provide the best (theoretical) security, however sometimes these measures provide very little effective security because they end up being misused, or turned off, or bypassed (Gutman, 2006). Security experts frequently lament that security has been bolted onto applications as an afterthought, however the security community has committed the exact same sin in reverse, placing usability considerations in second place behind security, if they were considered at all. For example passwords are widely decried as being insecure, but this is mostly because security protocol designers have *chosen* to make them insecure (Gutman, 2006).

We consider this aspect of human side to information assurance that severely lacks researchers' attention and that imposes severe threats to any security technology designed to provide information assurance. Despite having strong security technology and policies, it is pertinent that users are in the loop as well and technology and policies should be designed keeping them in mind. Any system designed for people to use should be easy to learn (and remember), useful, that is, contain functions people really need in their work, and be easy and pleasant to use.

RETURN ON SECURITY INVESTMENTS

It is usually difficult to show any economic or tangible earnings or returns from information security investments. At the same time, investments in countermeasures, both technical and procedural, to defend the enterprise against electronic attacks are absolutely essential. It has been consistently being demonstrated by high visibility incidents that information security breaches can have huge costs, though magnitude and probability of such incidents are inherently very difficult to estimate. It is also mentioned in a report on grand challenges in information assurance: "*we cannot manage the risk if we cannot measure the risk*" (CRA, 2003). As security becomes more important to companies in terms of the ability to show growth and profit, it becomes more important to look at investments in the acquisition of security technology and its ongoing maintenance to make sure a company is spending prudently. Costs related to information security countermeasures are difficult to estimate for lack of accurate and reliable metrics and estimation models. Though it is highly publicized that every year security breaches cause immense economic loss, the true extent of the losses are very still difficult to quantify. There are several qualitative approaches to justify security investments including value to business and assurance in its processes and resources. An important factor in maximizing value from security is by ensuring that assets and processes that are most critical are protected first. The financial returns from a successful implementation of a security-enabled business process have been used to justify the cost of security in terms of enabling business.

In fact, academics and professionals alike have been discussing return on security investment (ROSI) for years. Most of the "Return on Investment for Security" (ROSI) models are based on "chance" and "impact" concepts. This simple equation is not satisfactory — it doesn't help anyone make decisions because while investment is often clear, "chance" and "severity" are unknowns (Karofsky, 2001). There has been great deal of literature on importance of security technologies (Potter, 2005). Information security problems cost millions of dollars for US companies and billions for the overall US economy, according to a joint survey by the Computer Security Institute and the US Federal Bureau of Investigation. ROI is generally thought of being calculated for understanding impact on as a revenue enhancement or on extent of cost savings. Security, meanwhile, is sold on a concept known as FUD- fear, uncertainly and doubt. Nowadays, the question is not whether organizations need more security, but how much to spend for added security; and yet investing in IT security has always been a hard sell for IT managers (Geer et al., 2003). The vocabulary of information security is fraught with imprecision and overlapping meanings; and because no good, consistent security metrics are available, companies find themselves unable to gauge the suitability or effectiveness of different security options accurately (Geer et al., 2003).

While most ROSI models focus on characteristics of the information and technology to address the investment issue, Neubaeur et. al (2005) discusses that using company-specific business processes allows a more accurate collection of data needed for valuation of security cost-benefit. The area of understanding the economics of information security technology investments has already provided yielded some very interesting and relevant results and analyses (Anderson, 2001; Cavusoglu et al., 2002; Foster and Paci, 2002; Gordon et al., 2003, Schechter, 2004). Our literature review in this area also reveals a stream of research on the cost of information systems security incidents (Ande 2001, Butl 2002, Cohe 1991, Dobs 1994, Orla 1991, Tarr 1995). This stream has helped us understand when to avoids over-spending (Anderson, 1994). This also, at the same time, reduces the usage of poorly designed and inefficient security solutions, which are more often than not in used due to irrational reasons (Schneier, 2004). Investigation has also introduced insurance companies in assumed markets for security vulnerabilities (Schechter , 2004) to provide the much-needed liquidity.

Unfortunately, organizations cannot make all of their information 100% secure all of the time. There are economic, as well as technical, limitations that prevent perfect information security. One of the fundamental challenges faced by companies today is to estimate if they are overspending or under spending and identification of areas that needs to be given more attention and effort. In the same vein, in one interesting study, Moitra and Konda (2004) have demonstrated that as organizations start investing in information systems security their protection increases rapidly, while it increases at a much slower rate as the investments reach a much higher level.

The primary reason why we think this area is slated to be of vast significance in information security research is because of the fact that presently there is very little strategic alignment of organization's objectives and security objectives.

Usually, security spending is considered mere costs of doing business. Businesses tend to reduce costs if they don't perceive direct financial benefits, underestimating the security spending. However, with much of business moving towards Internet either as sales channel or to facilitate partnership, the role of security is gaining more importance. Although management is usually paranoid on risk management, it often takes information security "for granted" (BSI, 2004), and is reluctant to invest in it, (Foster and Pacl 2002), barring the exceptional cases when the information system of the organization is compromised. In surveys such as that of (Briney 2001) and (Briney and Prince 2002), it is evident that stringent IT budgets will only allow the applicability of a minimum subset of Information Security products and systems and thus it is necessary to prioritize in accordance with business objectives. However, little is known as to what the minimal subset should be and information security practitioners have been using a best practice or "what-others-are-doing" approach (Liss, 2001), to determine the information security budgets. The work is more often technically oriented with little heed paid to the economic aspects (Gordon and Loeb, 2002). A quantitative model to help organizations understand and estimate value of information security investments is very much needed. This will also allow them to make judicious decisions on how much investments is optimal, which will depend on a lot factors such as type of industry the business is in, size of the company, online presence of the company and risk preference of company. We have expounded more on this topic with proposition of more research on concepts and accompanying methodologies to help estimate how much spending is optimum for an organization. This research area should also take into account decisions about risks and defenses that are well understood by risk management techniques; and focus should move away from any specific security technology or any specific threat or risk or type of information to an organizational level.

ASSURANCE ISSUES WITH SEARCH ENGINES

Search engines index a huge number of Web pages and other resources that sometimes inadvertently expose security weaknesses and confidential data. Search engines have taken on the role of "gate-keepers of the web" (Hargittai, 2004). A January 2005 study found that 84% of all Internet users have used search engines, and an August 2005 study reported that the average user conducts 42 searches each month (Fellows, 2005; Burns, 2005). This underlines the prevalence of the security threats that search engines can pose. Hackers use search engines to make anonymous attacks, find easy victims, and gain relevant knowledge that, in some cases, can be more than enough to mount a powerful attack against a network. The volume of pages that the largest search engines index (Google has hundreds of billions of web pages) makes them excellent tools for identifying vulnerable servers. When a user is trying to locate information on the Internet, more often than not they will use a search engine. However, search engines aren't responsible for the huge numbers of poorly configured and insecure machines all over the Internet—even if the search engines do aid in identifying them. Although search engines have contributed greatly to the potential for disastrous leakage of sensitive information, their contribution to security risk does not stop there. There are several ways in which search engines are increasingly become security nightmares, some of which are:

- Disclosure of confidential or private information.
- Aiding hackers find vulnerable systems and other information to launch targeted attacks (reconnaissance)
- Covering tracks of hackers by providing cached pages.
- Hackers trick web crawlers to rate their sites, which contain malicious code, with higher ranking.

- Providing access to content that is not published and users cannot go there directly.
- Search worms (an alternative to regular random scanning of web servers over Internet)
- Vulnerabilities in search engines themselves

The risk of compromise of trade secrets, client data, and other types of information through postings on the Internet, chat sessions, and email transmissions is among the most serious types of risk that organizations face today. With the plethora of Web and FTP sites, chat rooms, and other Internet information outlets that currently exist, the likelihood of perpetrators or potential perpetrators finding a given piece of sensitive and/or valuable information concerning a particular organization should in theory be very low. The power of today's search engines increases this likelihood by a huge factor, however, by making all kinds of information readily available to virtually anyone within seconds. Attackers normally perform reconnaissance before attacking individual systems, something that involves a certain amount of time and trouble. The work factor in doing reconnaissance diminishes greatly, however, when search engines are used to almost immediately locate potential victims. Something that provides valuable functionality to users is once again being used maliciously, drastically cutting down the time from the public announcement of a vulnerability to the time the vulnerability is initially exploited (Schultz, 2995).

In fact, penetration testers, who are legitimately hired to find vulnerabilities in their client's infrastructure in order to determine and resolve security flaws, use Google hacking techniques. *Google hacking* is a term that has not only become commonplace in the security community but in the mainstream media as well (Long, 2005; McMillan, 2005). Google hacking involves using the popular Google search engine to locate sensitive information which is inadvertently not secured. One of the most troublesome features is that hackers can very easily cover their tracks if they use Google to find information on Internet. The sites that either host information that should be protected or host insecure servers can be easily tricked to not log the visits by the intruder using some of the features offered by Google, such as cached pages.

Major Internet search engines on the Web usually avoid any attempt to index restricted documents because of there is severe performance impact in reporting secure results and then there are issues with managing user authentication. However, these days, websites can present information to major search engines that they want associated with their site, while making the information publicly inaccessible. This is a form of web cloaking, where content may be discoverable through Internet search, but is not available for direct access. It is also possible to find vulnerable web servers or other technical infrastructural components by sending carefully crafted queries to search engines. For example, search worms use this approach to spread by using popular search engines and to find new attack vectors.

A new white paper from McAfee has revealed that all the major search engine sites returned malicious or risky web sites in the results when popular keywords were searched. It was also found that all the major Internet search sites unwittingly included results from sites that have been set up by purveyors of spam, malware and adware. More than 70% percent of the results when popular keywords such as "mp3 download" or "digital music" are used are malicious sites. As criminals consistently aim to target the sites that the consumers are more likely to visit, it makes sense that they would try to harness the search engines to lead people to their (malicious) web sites.

To illustrate the severity of the problem, here is an example. Seattle's AGORA Security Organization held a competition where teams had one hour to accumulate the most identity information using only Google to turn up data. The first-place team found a directory with the Social Security numbers of more than 70 million deceased persons, and the second-place team discovered hundreds of scanned passport documents and a Justice Department site listing employees and their work credit-card numbers (Delaney, 2005). This, however, only presents part of the picture on the kind of damage search engines can bring if used maliciously. Clearly, search engines are double-edged sword with inevitable and huge benefits; and even higher security risks. In our opinion, this unreservedly qualifies to be one of the top five emerging areas in information security research. Also, because we don't have real solutions and countermeasures - technical or otherwise - to thwart the problem at the source. In present day and age, with Internet being one of chief harbingers of information (Internet) age, solutions to this problem calls for attention.

SECURITY IN OUTSOURCING AND GLOBAL PARTNERSHIPS

Corporations across world are embracing the outsourcing opportunities to foster and strengthen their businesses, tap into global talent, increase their reach, and cut their costs. Economics and quality is driving businesses to gain efficiencies with outsourcing. All companies face the changing global risk landscape as they pursue global opportunities. While companies are performing due diligence in meeting the information security risk challenges to identify organization's global information security risks and threats, there is still a lot of open and gray areas that have not been addressed. Consulting company McKinsey estimates that by 2010, the U.S. IT industry will save $390 billion through offshore outsourcing of software development. But it also presents new challenges of industrial espionage in nations that don't have strong laws protecting foreign companies and seldom, if ever, enforce whatever laws may exist Here is a recent incident to illustrate the point (Fitzgerald, 2006):

The American software company SolidWorks has also been troubled by these kinds of incidents. GSSL is the Indian partner company outsourced to by SolidWorks. The staff responsible for testing SolidWorks 2001 Plus, Shekhar Verma, stole the entire original codes for the SolidWorks 2001 Plus CAD system and attempted to sell this code, valued at 700, 000, 000 USD to 900,000,000 USD, for 200, 000 USD to the competitor of SolidWorks. Fortunately, SolidWorks caught wind of this news and with the assistance of the FBI, caught Shekhar Verma and prevented loss to the company. India does not have laws against trade theft, so prosecutors filed charges against Verma under a general civil theft law, with a secondary charge of criminal breach of trust against his employer, GSSL. Nondisclosure works well in the United States, which has laws like the Industrial Espionage Act of 1996, which makes it a criminal offense to steal trade secrets. But the law does not apply to non-U.S. citizens acting outside U.S. borders. So, due to conflicts between American and Indian law, SolidWorks is unable to prosecute Shekhar Verma. Having its own intellectual property rights violated and unable to seek legal protection has made SolidWorks even more worried about the security issues in offshore outsourcing. Despite its near miss on source code, SolidWorks has no plans to stop outsourcing to India. It won't even change business partners. It has worked closely with GSSL for more than six years, and has had the company do it's debugging for the past five.

With recent trends of increased attention towards attractiveness of outsourcing, mitigating outsourcing security risks has become more important than ever. While companies are trying to manage risks by transferring risks to the outsourcing vendor through SLAs and contracts, one important consideration that should be kept in accounts is that they cannot transfer their reputation risk. The outsourcing relationships with an offshore vendor often involve sharing resources and information. Often this information can be very business critical and confidential. In that light organizations must carefully evaluate their outsourcing partners, because while offshore companies can be entrusted with core business functions and mission-critical data, they cannot afford to have their information compromised, damaged, rendered inaccessible. On top of that, legal considerations should be given importance in wake of existing legal frameworks and enforcement mechanisms in the service provider's jurisdiction, both local/regional and national.

Some of the common ways that companies manage risks and compliance is by completing their due diligence through regular audits such as a SAS 70 type 2 audit and using a risk assessment standard such as BS 7799 or ISO 27001. However, media is replete with many incidents that show that audits and evaluation of vendors is not carried out in a fashion that can reveal any shortcomings. Also, there are intangible, yet vitally important in delivery of offshored/outsourced services, factors such as human, cultural and behavioral that cannot be detected using traditional precautionary measures. Overall, these aspects force the outsourcing party to pay great attention to the management and protection of intellectual property rights and information security (Yahong, 2004; Gupta and Chellappa, 2004). The case of SolidWorks presented before attest to that. The importance of Intellectual property exponentially increases in companies that are planning to execute some of their core projects offshore and in companies that need to provide access to classified company data to the offshore location. Similar situations in US can be managed with relative ease because precedents are set. But for lack of consistent legal framework in overseas, it is very difficult, if not out right impossible, to enforce. In the same vein, one of the most unsettling findings in "*The global state of Information Security Study: 2006*" is the sad state of security in India, by a wide margin the world's primary locus for IT outsourcing. The problem is less with the outsourcing companies themselves than with the dangerous waters they swim in; as is evident from the fact that many respondents from India admit to not adhering to the most routine security practices (Homes, 2006). The problem is even worse in other emerging contenders to Indian supremacy in IT sourcing such as China, Russia and Poland is that they fare much worse in enforcement and maturity.

We present protection of intellectual properties as a very critical element in the offshoring and as a one of the top emerging areas of conflict in information security research because there have been many cases where companies have lost their position in the market due to the loss of intellectual property or breach of protected information. To illustrate the severity of the situation, we can consider a hypothetical situation where terrorist group can affect financial environment of US by targeting companies in different countries where offshore development is happening. This can put in perspective with the fact that 75% of Fortune 500 companies use outsourcing or offshoring to some extent. This can have severe impact on function of US economy.

CONCLUSION

A common view of information security research and practice that has been held and followed included predominantly technical measures. It was long understood that with access control policy models, application of cryptographic protocols, deployment of firewalls, intrusion detection systems and use of tools for system evaluation and assurance, much of the problems of information security could be solved. We presented in the chapter five emerging areas in information security that are increasingly becoming important in assuring information security measures and practices. We covered research issues with security requirements and modeling under model driven security and usability issues with security implementations. We tend to focus organizational security from viewpoints of internal controls and policies, but the threat landscape is fast evolving and is no longer limited to practices and control within an organization. We presented assurance issues with search engines and outsourcing relationships to highlight some areas that transcend traditional organizational boundaries to bring to information security researchers' attention. We also presented challenges and current methodologies in understanding and communicating economics of information security investments. This particular field has been researched extensively, yet there are huge gaps in research and practice. We presented what has been done so far in these areas and why more research is needed to complete the gaps in the literature.

REFERENCES

Adams A., & Sasse, M. A. (1999). Users are Not the Enemy. In *Communications of the ACM* (Dec 1999), p. 40-46.

Alghathbar, K., & Wijesekera, D. (2003). *AuthUML: A Threephased Framework to model Secure Use Cases.* In Proc. of the Formal Methods in Security Engineering Wksp (FMSE'03), Washington D.C., USA, 2003.

Alghathbar, K., & Wijesekera, D. (2003). *Consistent and Complete Access Control Policies in Use Cases.* In Proc. of UML 2003, San Francisco, CA, LNCS, 2003.

Anderson. Ross. (1994). Why Cryptosystems Fail. *In Communications of the ACM, 37*(11), 1994.

Anderson, R. J. (2001). *Why information security is hard - an economic perspective.* In Proc. of the 17th Annual Computer Security Application Conference, 2001.

Anderson. Ross J. (1994). *Liability and computer security: Nine principles.* In Dieter Gollmann, editor, Computer Security (ESORICS '94), LNCS 875, pages 231–245, Berlin Heidelberg, 1994. Springer Verlag.

Avizienis, A., Laprie, J., & Randell. B. (2001). *Fundamental Concepts of Dependability.* Research Report N01145, LAASCNRS, Apr. 2001.

Bell, D. E., & LaPadula, L.J. (1973, November). Secure Computer Systems: A Mathematical Model. *ESD-TR-73-278, 2*(MITRE).

Bondavalli, A., Majzik, I., & Mura, I. (1999). Automatic Dependability Analysis for Supporting Design Decisions in UML. In R. Paul and C. Meadows (Ed). *Proc. of the IEEE International Symposium on High Assurance Systems Engineering. IEEE.*

Brown, A. S., Bracken, E., Zoccoli, S., & Douglas, K. (2004). Generating and remembering passwords. *Applied Cognitive Psychology, 18*(2004), 641-651.

Briney, A. (2001). 2001 Industry Survey. *Information Security,* pp. 34-47.

Briney, A., & Prince, F. (2002). 2002 ISM Survey. *Information Security,* pp. 36-54.

BSI 2004. (2004). *BSI - Short information to current topics of IT Security.* Retrieved 17 June 2007 from http://www.bsi.bund.de/english/fb/F30image_en.pdf.

Burns. E. (2005). *Search increased in august.* Retrieved October 7, 2005 from http://www.clickz.com/stats/sectors/search tools/article.php/3554731.

Butler, S. A. (2002, May). Security Attribute Evaluation Method: A Cost-Benefit Approach. *Proceedings of the 24th International Conference on Software Engineering, ACM,* 232-240.

Cavusoglu, H., Mishra, B., & Raghunathan, S. (2002). *A model for evaluating it security investments.* Technical Report: University of Texas at Dallas, School of Management, 2002.

Cohen, F. (1991). A Cost Analysis of Typical Computer Viruses and Defenses. *Computers & Security, 10,* 239-250.

Cortellessa, V., Singh, H., & Cukic, B. (2002). Early reliability assessment of uml based software models. *In Proceedings of the third international workshop on Software and performance*, pages 302–309. ACM Press, 2002.

CRA Grand challenges in Information Security and Assurance. (2003). Retrieved 12th January 2008 from www.cra.org/Activities/grand.challenges /security/home.html

Delaney, K. (2005). Identity Theft Made Easier. *Wall Street Journal* (Mar. 29 2005), P. B1.

Devanbu P. T., & Stubblebine, S. (2000). Software engineering for security: a roadmap. In *Proceedings of the conference on the future of Software engineering*, pages 227–239. ACM Press, 2000.

Dhamija, R., & Perrig, A. (2005). *Déjà Vu: User study using images for authentication*. In Ninth Usenix Security Symposium (Denver, CO, USA, Aug. 14-17, 2000). Retrieved Feb 20, 2006 from http://www.usenix.org/publications/library/proceedings/sec2000 /dhamija.html,

Dobson, J. (1994). Messages, Communication, Information Security and Value. *Proceeding of the New Security Paradigms Workshop, IEEE*, Aug. 1994, pp. 10-18.

DOD. (1985). *Department of Defense Trusted Computer Security Evaluation Criteria*, DOD 5200.28-STDN, National Computer Security Center, December 1985.

Davis, D. (1996). Compliance Defects in Public-Key Cryptography. *In Proceedings of the 6th USENIX Security Symposium*.

Dourish, P. (2004). *Security as experience and practice: Supporting everyday security.* Talk given at the *DIMACS Workshop on Usable Privacy and Security Software*, July 7, 2004.

Emmerich, W. (2000). *Engineering Distributed Objects*. JohnWiley & Sons, Inc, 2000.

Epstein, P., & Sandhu, R. (1999). Towards A UML Based Approach to Role Engineering. In *Proc. of the 4th ACM workshop on Role-based Access Control.*

Feldmeier, D. C., & Karn, P. R. (1989). *UNIX password security – ten years later.* In Advances in Cryptology – CRYPTO'89, Lecture Notes in Computer Science 435, Springer Verlag (1990), 44-63.

Fellows, D. (2005). *Search Engine Users.* Retrieved January 23, 2005. from http://www.pewinternet.org/pdfs/PIP Searchengine users.pdf.

Ferrari, E. & Thuraisingham, B. (2000). *Secure Database Systems.* In: M. Piattini, O. Díaz (Ed.), Advanced Databases: Technology Design. Artech House, 2000.

Fitzgerald, M. (2006). *The Risks Associated With Offshoring Software Development.* CIO Magazine. Retrieved October 21st 2007 from http://www.cio.com/article/31967/The_Risks_Associated_With_Offshoring_Software_Development_

Foster, S., & Pacl, B. (2002). *Analysis of return on investment for information security.* Technical Report, Getronics Inc.

Gartner. (2006). *Gartner Information Security Hype Cycle Annual Report.* Gartner Research publications, 2006

Geer, D., Jr., Hoo, K.S.& Jaquith, A. (2003, July-August). Information security: why the future belongs to the quants. *Security & Privacy Magazine, IEEE, 1*(4), 24 – 32.

Ghosh, A., Howell C. & Whittaker J. (2002). Building software securely from the ground up. *IEEE Software 19*(1) 14-17.

Goguen, J. A. & Meseguer, J. (1982, April). Security Policies and Security Models. *Proceedings 1984 IEEE Symposium on Security and Privacy.*

Gordon, L. A., & Loeb, M. P. (2002). *The economics of information security investment.* ACM Transactions on Information and System Security 5, 4 (2002), 438.457.

Gordon, L. A., Loeb, M. P., & Lucyshyn, W. (2003). Information security expenditures and real options: A wait-and-see approach. *Computer Security Journal, 19*, 2,1.7.

Gupta, A., & Chellappa, R. K. (2004). Ethical, Legal and Economic Issues in the Digital Economy. *Intellectual Property Rights, Piracy, Trust, Security and Privacy: Minitrack Introduction.* hicss, p. 70179, *Proceedings of the 37th Annual Hawaii International Conference on System Sciences (HICSS'04)* - Track 7, 2004.

Gutman, P., (2006). *Security Usability Fundamentals.* Retrieved November 21st, 2007 from www.cs.auckland.ac.nz/~pgut001/pubs/ usability.pdf

Hargittai, E. (2004). *The Changing Online Landscape: From Free-for-All To Commercial Gatekeeping.* CommunityPractice in the Network Society: Local Actions/GlobalInteraction, pages 66–76, 2004. http://www.eszter.com/research/c03-onlinelandscape.html.

Holmstrom, U. (1999, May). User-centered design of secure software. *In Proceeedings of the 17th Symposium on Human Factors in Telecommunications.*Denmark.

Holmes, A. (2006). *The Global State of Information Security 2006.* CIO Magazine. Retrieved September 15, 2006 from http://www.cio.com/article/24979

Huszerl, G., & Majzik, I. (2001). *Modeling and analysis of redundancy management in distributed object–oriented systems by using UML statecharts.* In *Proc. of the EuroMicro Conference, Workshop on Software Process and Product Improvement*, Poland, pages 200–207, 2001.

Jendricke, U., & Markotten. D. Gerd tom. (2000, December). Usability meets Security: The Identity- Manager as your Personal Security Assistant for the Internet. *In Proceedings of the 16th Annual Computer Security Applications Conference*

Jürjens, J. (2002). *Principles for Secure Systems Design.* Ph.D. dissertation. Oxford University Computing Laboratory. Oxford University, 2002.

Jürjens, J. (2003). UMLsec: Extending UML for Secure Systems Development. *In Proc. of UML 2002, LNCS*, Sept. 30 - Oct. 4, 2002.Kleppe, A., Bast, W., Warmer, J. B. and Watson A.. MDA Explained: The Model Driven Architecture–Practice and Promise. Addison-Wesley, 2003.

Karat, C. M. (1989). Iterative Usability Testing of a Security Application. *In Proceedings of the Human Factors Society 33rd Annual Meeting.*

Karofsky, E. (2001). Insight into return on security investment. *Secure business quarterly: defining the value of strategic security 2001,1*(2). Fourth Quarter.

Klein, D. (1990). A survey of, and improvement to, password security. In *UNIX Security Workshop II Proceedings*, Tenth Usenix Security Symposium (Portland, OR, USA, Aug. 27- 28, 1990), 83-86.

Li, Y. L. (2004). Intellectual Property Protection for E-Business Methods. *IEEE International Conference on E-Commerce Technology for Dynamic E-Business*, 15-15 Sept. 2004 Page(s):362 – 365.

Liss, S. (2001). *Practical Aspects of Information Security.* InfoGroup NorthWest.

Littlewood, B., & Strigini, L. (2000). *Software Reliability and Dependability: A Roadmap.* In A. Finkelstein, editor, The Future of Software Engineering, pages 177–188. ACM Press, Apr. 2000.

Lodderstedt, T. (2002). *SecureUML: A UML-Based Modeling Language for Model-Driven Security.* In Proc. of UML 2002, LNCS, 2002.

Long, J. (2005). *Google Hacking for Penetration Testers*, Syngress Publishing, Rockland, MA, 2005.

McMillan, R. (2005, September). Google hacking; What started as a joke builds into a movement. *Network World*, 1.

Moitra, S., & Konda, S. (2005). *The survivability of network systems: An empirical analysis.* Carnegie Mellon Software Engineering Institute, Technical Report, CMU/SEI-200-TR-021.

Morris, R., & Thompson, K. (1979). Password security; A case study. *CACM 22*, 594-597.

Neubauer, T., Markus, K., & Stefan, B. (2005). *Economics-Driven Software Engineering Research (EDSER): Business process-based valuation of IT-security.* May 2005, ACM SIGSOFT Software Engineering Notes. *Proceedings of the 2005 workshop on Economics-driven software engineering research EDSER '05, 30*(4).

OMG3. (2001). *OMG Unified Modeling Language Specification, Version 1.4.* Object Management Group. 2001. http://www.omg.org/technology/documents/formal/uml.htm.

OMG2. (2002). *Meta-Object Facility (MOF), version 1.4.* Object Management Group., 2002. http://www.omg.org/technology/documents/formal/mof.htm.

OMG1. (2003). *MDA Guide Version 1.0.1.* Object Management Group. 2003. http://www.omg.org/docs/omg/03-06-01.pdf.

Orlandi, E. (1991). The Cost of Security. *Proceeding of the 25th Annual IEEE International Carnahan Conference on Security Technology*, Oct. 1991, pp. 192 –196.

Patrick, A. S., Long, A. C., & Flinn, S. (2004). HCI and security systems. *In Proceedings of the SIGCHI Conference on Human Factors in Computing Systems (CHI'04)* (Vienna, Austria, April 24-29, 2004). ACM Press, New York, NY, 1056-1057.

Potter, C. (2005). *Information Security- Security conscious.* Retrieved October 2007 from http://www.financialdirector.co.uk/accountancyage/features/2040335/information-security-security-conscious, September 2005.

Ray, I. (2003). Using Parameterized UML to Specify and Compose Access Control Models. *In Proc. of the 6th IFIP Working Conference on Integrity & Internal Control in Info. Systems.*

Reznik, J., Ritter, T., Schreiner R., & Lang, U. (2007, April). *Model Driven Development of Security Aspects.* Electronic Notes in Theoretical Computer Science (ENTCS), 163, (2), 65-79.

Rodrigues, G. N. (2004). A Model Driven Approach for Software Systems Reliability. *Proceedings of the 26th International Conference on Software Engineering (ICSE'04)*

Rodrigues, G., Roberts, G., Emmerich, W., & Skene, J. (2003). Reliability Support for the Model Driven Architecture. *In Workshop on Software Architecture for Dependable Systems (ICSE/WADS 2003)*, Portland, OR, pages 7–12. ACM Press, May 2003.

Sasse, M. A., Brostoff, S., & Weirich, D. (2001). Transforming the 'weakest link' – a human/computer interaction approach to usable and effective security. *BT Technical Journal 19*,122-131.

Schneier, B. (2004, April). Hacking the business climate for network security. *IEEE Computer*, 87–89..

Schultz, E. (2005, March). Search engines: a growing contributor to security risk. *Computers & Security, 24*(2), 87-88

Shin, M., & Ahn, G. (2000). UML-Based Representation of Role- Based Access Control. In *Proc. of the IEEE 9th Intl. Wksp. on Enabling Technologies: Infrastructure for Collaborative Enterprises.*

Smith S. W., & Spafford, E. H. (2004, January/February). Grand Challenges in Information Security: Process and Output. *IEEE Security & Privacy*, 69-71.

Stuart, E. S. Computer Security Strength & Risk: A Quantitative Approach. PhD thesis, Harvard University, Cambridge, MA, 2004.

Tarr, C. J. *(1995).* Cost Effective Perimeter Security, Security and Detection. *European Convention on Security and Detection*, 183-187.

Vela, B., Fernández-Medina, E., Esperanza, M., & Piattini, M. (2006). *Model Driven Development of Secure XML Databases. SIGMOD Record, 35*(3.

Viega, J., & McGraw, G. (2001). *Building Secure Software: How to Avoid Security Problems the Right Way.* Addison-Wesley, 2001.

Wiedenbeck, S., Waters, J., Birget, J. C., Brodskiy, A., & Memon, N. (2005). Authentication using graphical passwords: effects of tolerance and image choice. *Proceedings of the 2005 symposium on Usable privacy and security*, Pittsburgh, Pennsylvania, Pages: 1 – 12.

Wing, J. (1998, December). A Symbiotic Relationship Between Formal Methods and Security. *Proc. NSF Workshop on Computer Security, Fault Tolerance, and Software Assurance: From Needs to Solution.*

Whitten, A., & Tygar, J. D. (1999, August). *Why Johnny can't encrypt.* In *Proceedings of the 8th USENIX Security Symposium.*

Zurko, M. E., Simon, R., & Sanfilippo, T. (1999, May). A User-Centered, Modular Authorization Service Built on an RBAC Foundation. *In Proceedings of IEEE Symposium on Research in Security and Privacy*, 57-71.

KEY TERMS

Google Hacking: Use of Google, the most commonly used Internet search engine, to gather information available on Internet to discover exploits in systems or to obtain unauthorized access to information and systems.

Model Driven Architecture: An emerging standard model-centric and generative software development, presented as set of guidelines for structuring specifications expressed as system models. It is defined and managed by the Object Management Group.

Model Driven Security: Use of different modeling techniques, architectures and standards during each stage of system development lifecycle to incorporate security primitives — such as confidentiality, integrity, authentication, authorization and auditing — to ensure security of the system, process and information flows.

Outsourcing: A process by which a company contracts with another company or person to do particular function(s) and provide services to meet its own business objectives.

Return on Security Investment: Economic and non-economic returns from investments in information security measures including technology, policy and people.

Search Engine: An information retrieval application that allows users to locate and browse information on Internet or on an information system.

Security Economics: Area that focuses on understanding economics of information security processes such as implementation of a technology or incorporation of security measure in an existing business application or institution of a new organizational security policy.

Security Usability: Aspects and issues related to impact of security mechanisms and implementations on use of security and technology.

Unified Modeling Language: A standardized visual specification language, developed and managed by Object Management Group, for creating abstract model of systems to understand and demonstrate their functions and interactions.

Section IV
Human and Interaction Issues

Chapter XXIII
The Human Attack in Linguistic Steganography

C. Orhan Orgun
University of California, Davis, USA

Vineeta Chand
University of California, Davis, USA

ABSTRACT

This chapter develops a linguistically robust encryption system, LUNABEL, which converts a message into syntactically and semantically innocuous text. Drawing upon linguistic criteria, LUNABEL uses word replacement, with substitution classes based on traditional linguistic features (syntactic categories and subcategories), as well as features under-exploited in earlier works: semantic criteria, graphotactic structure, and inflectional class. The original message is further hidden through the use of cover texts—within these, LUNABEL retains all function words and targets specific classes of content words for replacement, creating text which preserves the syntactic structure and semantic context of the original cover text. LUNABEL takes advantage of cover text styles which are not expected to be necessarily comprehensible to the general public, making any semantic anomalies more opaque. This line of work has the promise of creating encrypted texts which are less detectable to human readers than earlier steganographic efforts.

1. INTRODUCTION

We develop in this chapter LUNABEL, a technique for text-based steganography. We refer to our approach more specifically as linguistic steganography, as we take into account certain linguistic criteria that past approaches to text-based steganography have not dealt with (Bergmair, 2007, and references therein). This allows us to more effectively hide information. In particular, our encrypted messages more closely resemble natural text than was possible in past approaches which lack the linguistic sophistication necessary to achieve satisfactory results.

Section 1 introduces the concept of steganography and discusses desiderata for a successful technique. In section 2, we develop LUNABEL and discuss some specific choices that were made in its implementation. Section 3 discusses the details of some of the particularly important choices that were made in developing LUNABEL, namely the choice of cover text in which to hide information and the compilation of word substitution classes. In section 4, we compare LUNABEL to past approaches to lexical steganography. Section 5 concludes the paper.

1.1 What is Steganography?

"Steganography" means encryption by means of information hiding. It includes hiding information in any form of data, such as images, audio or video files. Our interest in this paper is text-based steganography. This refers to hiding a message in what looks like an ordinary piece of text.

1.2 Linguistic Steganography

Ways of hiding information in text have been used since antiquity. One simple method is the acrostic, in which the initial letters of successive lines of poetry spell a word or words. This method is used more for artistic purposes than for secret information exchange; nonetheless, it provides a useful illustration. Consider the following Edgar Allan Poe poem, in which the first letters of successive lines spell the word *Elizabeth*:

1. Elizabeth it is in vain you say
   "Love not" — thou sayest it in so sweet a way:
   In vain those words from thee or L. E. L.
   Zantippe's talents had enforced so well:
   Ah! if that language from thy heart arise,
   Breathe it less gently forth — and veil thine eyes.
   Endymion, recollect, when Luna tried
   To cure his love—was cured of all beside—
   His folly—pride—and passion—for he died.

While this form of steganography may be sufficient for poetic use, a practical system has additional requirements. We would want information hiding to be more effective—the hidden information should not be readily visible to an outside observer. Equally important, the system needs to be algorithmic rather than creative; it should be possible to hide any given message in any desired text. Finally, decryption too needs to be algorithmic: given a text containing a hidden message, the hidden message should be reliably recoverable by a recipient in possession of the required decryption information (the acrostic poem presented satisfies this last requirement, but none of the others).

1.3 Encryption versus Steganography

Today, techniques for encryption have grown sufficiently sophisticated that it is possible to encrypt a message such that its decryption by brute force code cracking is a practical impossibility. However, there will be contexts in which even the fact that two parties are exchanging encrypted messages might be more information than one is willing to reveal to a third party. In such instances, what is needed is a way of hiding information in what appears at least to the casual observer to be an innocuous message. Typical encryption techniques give rise to results that are immediately noticeable as not being natural text. Consider, for example, the following encryption, which was created by a simple key-based technique:

2. XOQRW ISMWK QCBWT MBOFS PEMPW VUGQW QHJTO FIOCE KSLUO AWOTP RVLDV HLFGH WTDGC IAFCT

HCLPT OJLQR MQMXD NPNBK FUAGV MDRWS ENSES EQJWF SRSVF VVRKC TGUDF BQTUS WXTLJ DGQWT PUTUG WFKTE GGOOX BQRTH FBMVQ LH-KRU ULOMS SWUVS KOJFU RMRCD XDTMT PREFF DTKND UBHJX PIEWL AOGTT GVQFF EEAHE QKEJD CWNEC OHWJL APOCA CHGLX CWXXL EIPFQ EJPXW HWCHO UTXOV LBRGU HVRZZ

In linguistic steganography, the main goal is not to achieve strong encryption, but rather to exchange messages that resemble, at least to a casual observer, plain text. If strong encryption is an additional desire, this is easily achieved through a two-step process. One can first encrypt one's message, then hide the encrypted message through steganography. The recipient would then need to extract the encrypted message, then decrypt it. Our system, LUNABEL, does include a simple encryption method into its information-hiding system, but is still compatible (as is any method of steganography) with the two-step process just described. This is discussed in somewhat more detail in the next section.

1.4 Goals

In this section, we discuss our goals, which differ considerably from conventional encryption and stegosystem techniques.

Our overarching goal is to provide a means for two parties to exchange information hidden in what appears to be innocuous text messages (email would be the most likely medium for such exchange). The main desire here is that a casual human observer will not suspect that there is any need for further investigation of the messages being sent (such as code-breaking attempts, statistical analysis to determine naturalness, and so on). If such investigation appears warranted to a human observer, the first line of defense has already failed (all is not necessarily lost, though, as discussed below).

We will thus consider our method to have succeeded if a human observer accepts it as natural text. Within this, we strive for our text to consist mainly of grammatical sentences which are semantically coherent and pragmatically not too odd.

What happens if an encrypted message is tagged for code breaking? This depends on one's desire to use whatever form of encryption prior to the hiding of information. Since our technique is capable of hiding any sort of data in a piece of text, it is in principle geared towards using a two-step technique which can be arbitrarily powerful in its resistance to decryption. In the first pass, one can use any desired encryption method to generate a coded message. One can subsequently use our technique to hide the resulting code in a text message. The code-breaker's job then consists of several steps. First, the text message must be identified as suspect and be subjected to code breaking attempts. Second, the hidden information must be extracted. Third, the extracted code must be broken. The difficulty of this third step is dependent solely on the method of encryption used, not on any aspect of steganography.

The acceptability of encrypted texts as natural is our primary concern. A human-interactive stegosystem proof has been developed which "is secure against a non-human aribtrator *if the human interactive proof is secure*" (Bergmair & Katzenbeisser, 2006: 20, italics ours), however, as will be discussed in section 4, existing methods both fall short of achieving this goal and downplay the importance of passing human inspection. Our program specifically targets this issue, creating encrypted texts with what we term linguistic robustness, with the goal of passing human inspection and attack (Bergmair & Katzenbeisser, 2006).

2. DEVELOPING LUNABEL: A LINGUISTICALLY ROBUST SYSTEM OF LEXICAL STEGANOGRAPHY

LUNABEL is a system of steganography based on word replacement in a cover text. Its key features include choice of cover text to maximize linguistic robustness, not targeting every word in the cover text for replacement (an essential requirement for linguistic validity), and linguistically informed compilation of word substitution classes. We discuss these issues in the following subsections.

2.1 A Misguided Approach: Replacing Every Word

A simplistic attempt at text-based steganography might proceed as follows. Take the message to be encrypted and then replace words in that message with other words according to some predetermined scheme. For example, the message "attack now" might turn into "sleep tonight". There are a number of problems with such an approach, however. The most obvious problem is that the message is not very well hidden. In particular, the syntactic structure of the result is identical to that of the original message.

To avoid this problem, it is common to use a cover text. A cover text is simply any piece of text that one aims to hide one's message in. The cover text typically bears no resemblance to the intended message.

In order to effectively use a cover text, one must agree on conventions for substitutions within the cover text. Each substitution must in some fashion convey some of the data representing the hidden message. The usual way to do this is to assign arbitrary numerical values to individual words. The message to be hidden is converted to a string of numbers by some simple method (such as, for example, using the ASCII codes of the letters constituting the message). Each substitution within the cover text then indicates some number and when all substitutions are accounted for, the hidden message can be recovered. Suppose, for example, that the cover text starts with the word "pizza" and that this is replaced by "pasta". If the (arbitrary) number assigned to "pasta" is, say, 7, then the replacement indicates that the first number in the digital representation of the hidden message is likewise 7. In this approach, one does not need to have access to the original cover text in order to recover the hidden message. It is, on the other hand, equally easy to develop a method where the original cover text is necessary in order to proceed with message recovery. One could, for example, use the difference between the numerical values assigned to the original cover text word and its replacement as the conveyor of information.

In a naïve approach, one might try to replace each word in the cover text with a new word. In such an approach, the role of the cover text is simply to provide syntactic structures to be filled out by the replacement words. The naturalness of the resulting text is a function of how well the cover text has been tagged for syntactic categories. This is the approach taken in many attempts preceding ours. There are, however, a number of problems associated with such an approach.

The first problem with replacing every word of a cover text is function words. Many function words are present in a sentence not to convey a given meaning but rather because they are required by the syntactic structure. Take the passive *by*, for example, as in (3):

3. The window was broken by vandals

This grammatical element is required by the syntax of passive sentences and it is not possible to replace it with any other (function or content) word without changing the syntactic structure of the sentence (**the window was broken of vandals*, etc.). Other function words may be somewhat more replaceable, but still pose problems. For example, the English equivalent of quirky case (requirements for a specific case, rather than accusative, for the internal argument—that is, the direct object in an active sentence—of a verb) is verbs requiring their internal arguments to occur with a specific preposition. The verb *look*, for example, specifies *at*, while *listen* calls for *to*.

4. I looked at the painting.
5. I listened to the song.

It is therefore not possible to replace these verbs without their accompanying prepositions, or the prepositions without their verbs. However, the same prepositions may also be used as semantic elements in other cases.

6. I walked to school.
7. I walked from school.

In such cases, the verbs and prepositions could be targeted independently for substitution.

Other problems are caused by verbs. Different verbs may impose different types of requirements on their arguments. One simple difference is the number of arguments a given verb has. *Sleep* has one, while *devour* has two, *give*, three, and *sell*, four.

8. I slept.
9. I devoured the eggplant.
10. I gave the eggplant to the dentist.
11. I sold the eggplant to the dentist for one dollar.

Some verbs allow optional omission of their arguments, while others do not.

12. I ate.
13. I ate the eggplant.
12. *I devoured.
13. I devoured the eggplant.

Even verbs that have the same number of arguments and the same pattern of omissibility may impose different semantic restrictions on their arguments. For example, *expect* does not have any restrictions on its direct object, while *persuade* requires a sentient direct object.

14. I expected the dentist to run.
15. I persuaded the dentist to run.
16. I expected it to rain.
17. *I persuaded it to rain.

Thus, syntactic categories alone are not sufficient to create substitution classes of verbs. One needs much finer syntactic and semantic distinctions. As well, it is necessary to keep track of multiple complicated dependencies between verbs, the number and nature of their arguments, syntactic structure, the distribution of function words, and so on. At the present time, the necessary distinctions appear intractable for a practical application.

Further complications arise from the fact that many words are ambiguous, not just in meaning, but even in syntactic category and subcategory. Within an indefinite interpretation, some arguments may be drawn from context, while others are always required. Example (19), marked with '#,' demonstrates conditional acceptability with the indefinite interpretation: the sentence is acceptable only if the recipient argument is already contextually available. Example (20), however, demonstrates that *give* does not permit its patient, the argument undergoing the giving, to be omitted and drawn from context. It is always unacceptable, regardless of context.

18. gave the dentist the eggplant.
19. # I gave the eggplant.
20. *I gave the dentist.

The verb *donate*, on the other hand, does allow its direct object to be omitted under an indefinite reading.

21. I donated (generously) to the Red Cross.

When *give* is used to mean *donate*, however, it does allow indefinite null realization of its direct object:

22. I gave (generously) to the Red Cross.

All these difficulties make word-for-word replacement impractical today, and possibly forever: some degree of unresolved ambiguity and misparsing is not detrimental to regular language use and is probably an inherent aspect in natural language. That is, no matter how finely honed our techniques for syntactic and semantic analysis become, it is likely that there will remain an intractable residue in any natural text.

In the next two sections, we present our solution to this difficulty and develop our system for linguistic steganography.

2.2 A Naïve Word Replacement Approach Based on Part of Speech Alone

Before we fully develop our solution to the problems discussed in the previous section, we first present a method of word substitution in which some, but not all, words in a cover text are subject to replacement. This immediately addresses several of the issues raised in the previous section. Function words are not a problem; we simply choose to retain all function words in the cover text. Only content words are targeted for replacement. Ambiguity is handled similarly. Words that are highly ambiguous in the chosen genre of cover text are simply held exempt from replacement. The remaining question is how to determine which specific words can substitute for one another.

In order to develop a word replacement system, we need to have substitution classes of words. A substitution class is a set of words such that replacing one word from the set with another in a given sentence does not alter the acceptability of the sentence. For example, consider the following two sentences:

23. I had eggs for breakfast.
24. I had pancakes for breakfast.

These sentences suggest that *eggs* and *pancakes* might be two members of a substitution class. To develop a substitution class fully, one would need to make sure the words in it are consistently replaceable in all contexts. One would also need to decide how many members there should be in each substitution class. This latter issue is of a technical, not linguistic, nature, and we leave its discussion to a later section.

To a first approximation, POS (also known as major syntactic categories: verbs, nouns, adjectives, adverbs) are substitution classes. Generally speaking, one may replace a verb with another verb or a noun with another noun, but not, for example, a verb with a noun or adjective. We have devised a word replacement scheme based on POS alone. A sample of text encrypted with this method is shown here:

25. Original cover text:
    ABOUT THE OVID DEMONSTRATION CONNECTION FILES

    [Available in the Demo folder in the Connect folder.]
    Free access to a set of demonstration databases has been provided by Ovid Technologies, Inc. By connecting to and searching these sample databases, you can see how the EndNote Connect feature works and get an idea of the information that is available online.

26. Encrypted message:
    ABOUT THE OVID FOXPRO GHOST PLACES

    [Available to the January list up the Offer nl.]
    Free drive at a develop on java drives has been wrote to Ovid Corrections, Inc! Into

> moving for or comparing these bit licences, you can die how the format Insert niles finds but share an idea above the pfeiffer that is available online.

Several shortcomings of this technique are immediately apparent. First, failure to distinguish between subcategories of major lexical classes causes grammatical problems. For verbs, for example, argument structure is a problem (for example, **you can die how the format...* runs afoul of the argument structure for *die*). For nouns, distinctions such as mass/count, proper/common, animate/inanimate are significant. In many cases, these noun distinctions interact with verbal argument structure requirements.

Before we have a viable transcription system, we need to compile substitution classes that will be viable in the real world. We now turn into a discussion of how this can be done.

2.3 A Linguistically Sophisticated Approach Based on Cover Texts and Word Substitution Classes

The basis of our approach to steganography is that it is not necessary to target every word of a cover text for replacement. The idea of not-every-word word replacement has already been introduced in section 2.2. In this section, we discuss the compilation of linguistically robust substitution classes, choice of size 16 for our substitution classes, and the actual mechanics of word replacement.

The first decision to be made in putting together substitution classes is the number of members each class should have. Using a small number of members (say, 2) makes it easy to come up with workable classes. It is not that challenging to find two words that can be substituted for one another. However, using a small class implies that each substitution conveys only a small amount of information. With a class size of two, the information content of the choice of member is one bit (one member as opposed to the other).

With a larger class, the challenge is to find enough words to fill the class. If we desired a substitution class of several thousand members, for example, it would be impossible to find enough words in the lexicon or a natural human language to populate such a class with words that could be replaceable. The advantage of a larger substitution class is that each substitution conveys more information. This is of particular importance to us: the extra information-carrying capacity we gain from larger substitution classes allows us to throw away some of it in the search for linguistic robustness in the form of not-every-word replacement.

As a practical compromise, we have chosen substitution classes of 16 members each. This size turned out to be quite workable in terms of finding enough words to populate a fair number of classes. For example, the two working versions of LUNABEL we have programmed have 38 and 44 substitution classes, respectively. One could of course use fewer or more classes as desired. The more substitution classes one uses, the more dense the encryption becomes (therefore, a shorter cover text is needed to encrypt a given message). At the same time, however, it becomes more difficult to avoid running into problems of ambiguity, semantic and syntactic incompatibility, and so on, within each substitution class. For purposes of illustration, we provide two example word classes here:

27. Word list 1 (accompanying Readme Corpus):
    [key, passkey, login, password, pincode, pin, passcode, authorization, permission, authentication, signal, ticket, indicator, passport, code, credential]
28. Word list 2 (accompanying Recipe Corpus):
    [crispy, crunchy, greasy, caramelized, melted, stewed, browned, sautéed, finished, firm, boiling, chilled, bubbly, sizzling, glazed, pulpy]

A class size of 16 means each substitution conveys 4 bits of information. Since we are using ASCII codes of the characters in the original message to represent the message (ASCII codes consist of 8 bits), this means every character in the original message is encrypted by two word substitutions in the cover text.

For one of our working versions of LUNABEL, the building of the word lists occurred in this fashion: the corpus (47 readme files) has 46,000 words, from which word frequency statistics have been extracted. The word *process* appears 18 times within that. Because it almost always appears as a noun in this corpus, it needs to heed the a/an distinction, as it can directly follow an indefinite determiner. The term *section* occurs 23 times, follows the same graphotactic structure, and occurs in the same syntactic positions. Both words are used as a transitive action in a manipulation of data, and both can be used nominally to highlight an area or aspect of something (generally a program, code, or location on the computer, within this genre of texts). While these words are not synonyms, or even near synonyms, and hence would not be replaceable under earlier synonym-based word-replacement systems, such is not important within LUNABEL. What does matter is that, within our corpus, these two words occupy similar sentence positions. Building up the word list continues until 16 terms are found, factoring all of the above features. These criteria require a sizable corpus in order to produce comprehensive word lists. Given all of these criteria, the result is a syntactically reasonable and semantically innocuous text with unremarkable word frequencies when compared to other texts in a corpus of that style. We have proceeded along similar lines to compile word lists for recipes, which are another fertile source for successful cover texts.

2.3.1 Choice of Cover Text

Choice of cover text is an important factor in the success of a lexical steganography program. Several criteria apply. First, the cover text style needs to be relatively undemanding in terms of the range of syntactic structures found and the degree of semantic and pragmatic coherence tolerated. For example, metrical poetry such as that of Shakespeare's would be hardly appropriate, as just about any word replacement would be immediately obvious. Second, a genre in which multiple documents with small differences from one another (resulting from word replacement) would not immediately arouse suspicion would be advantageous. Several genres qualify. One can, for example, consider technical manuals, which might undergo several revisions before being made public (and further revisions as the product they describe is upgraded). Likewise, recipes may often be found in multiple versions, which might differ from one another in more or less arbitrary ways. In our implementations of LUNABEL, we have used readme files distributed with software packages as well as collections of recipes. Readme files have the additional advantage that they are found too boring to read by many people. Recipes have a different advantage: if a long message is to be encrypted and the cover text runs out, one can simply repeat the recipes, which would then undergo somewhat different word substitutions. While such repetition within one message might appear suspicious in some styles (including readme files), with recipes, a message consisting of multiple recipes, or even multiple versions of one recipe, would be nothing extraordinary.

Other plausible choices for cover texts could include spam messages, classified ads, posts made to discussion groups, chat room transcripts, manifestoes (real or fictional) by disturbed individuals, and so on.

2.3.2 The Internal Mechanics of LUNABEL

The first step in encryption by LUNABEL is converting the original message into a sequence of numbers. For convenience, we convert the message into a sequence of hexadecimal digits (since each of our word lists contains 16 members, this will allow us to use these hexadecimal digits directly in determining word substitutions). This task is very simple: we use the ASCII code of each character in the original message, which contains 8 bits. The first 4 bits describe one hexadecimal digit, and the next for bits give us another. An example of this first step is given below.

The encryption scheme is two-part; the first step converts the plain text message (29) into a sequence of hexadecimal digits (30). This is done by taking the ASCII code of each character and expressing it as a pair of hexadecimal digits.

29. Plain text
    I had a cat and the cat pleased me
    I fed my cat under yonder tree.
    Cat went fiddle-dee-dee, fiddle-dee-dee....
30. Plain text converted to sequence of hexadecimal digits (via LUNABEL)
    9 2 0 6 8 6 1 6 4 2 0 6 1 2 0 6 3 6 1 7 4 2 0
    6 1 6 14 6 4 2 0 7 4 6 8 6 5 2 0 6 3 6 1 7 4
    2 0 7 0 6 12 6 5 6 1 7 3 6 5 6 4 2 0 6 13 6 5
    2 14 0 10 4 9 2 0 6 6 6 5 6 4 2 0 6 13 7 9 2
    0 6 3 6 1 7 4 2 0 7 5 6 14 6 4 6 5 7 2 2 0 7
    9 6 15 6 14 6 4 6 5 7 2 2 0 7 4 7 2 6 5 6 5 2
    14 0 10 4 3 6 1 7 4 2 0 7 7 6 5 6 14 7 4 2 0 6
    6 6 9 6 4 6 4 6 12 6 5 2 13 6 4 6 5 6 5 2 13
    6 4 6 5 6 5 2 12 2 0 6 6 6 9 6 4 6 4 6 12 6 5
    2 13 6 4 6 5 6 5 2 13 6 4 6 5 6 5 2 14 0 10 0
    10 4 9 2...

It follows that each character of the original message will be represented by two word replacements in the cover text. This contrasts with other approaches, which typically use binary digits in their replacement method and therefore need eight word replacements per character. At this point, LUNABEL appears to have a fourfold advantage in cover text size requirement. What we will later do, however, is to give this up in the search for linguistic robustness. Recall that we are not going to replace every word of our cover text. If we were to replace, on average, every fourth word, the required cover text size would be equal to that of a binary-digit replacement method that targets every word. In our current working system, we target far fewer words than this, however (about one in every 16 words, in fact), and so our cover texts need to be about four times as big as most every-word approaches.

In the next step, the actual information hiding process takes place. We remove the first hexadecimal digit from the converted message, in our current example, 9. We use a simple encryption key, which generates a pseudo-random sequence of digits, to give us a hexadecimal digit; let us assume this is 8. These two numbers are then added together, which give us 17, which is equivalent to 2 (17 mod 16, where we have decided to use integers from 0 to 15 to identify positions in our word classes).

The next step is to find the first word in the cover text that is eligible for replacement. To do this, we skip words that are not members of any substitution class until we reach a word that is a member of one. In the current example, the cover text we used starts as follows:

31. Excerpt from Cover Text: (readme.txt file distributed with GSview® software package)
    Features include:
    - View pages in arbitrary order (Next, Previous, Goto).
    - Selectable display resolution, depth, alpha.
    - Page size is automatically selected from DSC comments or can be selected using the menu.
    - Orientation can be automatically selected from DSC comments or can be selected using the menu (Portrait, Landscape).

Given our word classes, the first word eligible for replacement is *include*, the second word of the cover text. We now replace include with the 2nd word in its word list (where 2 is the number we derived previously from the original message and the encryption key). In this case, the word we get is *change*. Thus, the beginning of the cover text has become *Features change*.

Encryption proceeds along these lines until the message is fully hidden. After this, the cover text is simply copied unchanged (alternatively, one could use random replacements). In our current example, the encrypted message begins thus:

32. Encrypted text
    Features change:
    - *Close pages in arbitrary upgrade (Trailing, Last, Goto).*
    - *Selectable broadcast resolution, depth, alpha.*
    - *Use size is instantaneously selected from DSC comments or can be selected using the source.*
    - *Orientation can be perpetually selected from DSC comments or can be selected using the table (Portrait, Landscape).*

Decryption by the recipient requires the key and the word lists, but not the cover text. In decryption, we compare each word in the encrypted message against our word lists. Once we find a word that is in one of our word lists, we add two integers together: the position of the found word in its word list and the pseudo-random integer obtained from the encryption key. Iteration of this procedure through the encrypted message results in a sequence of hexadecimal digits, which, in pairs, correspond to the ASCII codes of characters forming the plain (decrypted) message. If desired, the encryption system can be altered so that decryption would require, in addition, access to the cover text: in the step where we add the hexadecimal digit from the converted message and the digit from the encryption key, we would add a third number to this sum. This third number would be the position of the original cover text word within its word list. In this case, decryption would depend on access to this number, which would need to be extracted from the cover text.

For purposes of illustration, we provide an example using recipes as cover text. The original message is the same as above. The cover text is a list of ingredients from a recipe:

33. Excerpt from recipe for Seafood Croquettes:

3	tb	Unsalted butter
1/2	sm	Onion -- finely minced
1/2		Celery stalk -- finely diced
3	tb	All-purpose flour
1/3	c	Milk
1/4	ts	Ground nutmeg
		Bread crumbs
1	lb	Cooked fish and/or shellfish - such as salmon, shrimp, - scallops, white fish, - or a combination
1	tb	Finely chopped parsley
1	tb	Chopped chives
1	t	Salt -- or as desired
1/4	ts	Cayenne pepper -- as desired
		Flavorless cooking oil

The encrypted text is shown below:

34. LUNABEL encrypted text of same recipe ingredient list

3	tb	Unsalted butter
½		largish Onion–tightly quartered
1/2		Anise root -- coarsely grated
3	tb	All-purpose flour
2/3	c	Milk
1/4	oz	Ground cinnamon
		Bread crumbs
3	pint	Cooked fish and/or shellfish - such as grouper, eel, - scallops, golden fish, - or a combination
2	tb	Evenly bruised marjoram
1	tb	Separated chives

1	t	Salt -- or as desired
1/4	pn	Turmeric spike -- as desired
		Flavorless cooking oil

We now turn to a more detailed discussion of certain aspects of LUNABEL.

3. DISCUSSION

3.1 Different Cover Text genres

The use of opaque cover texts, while possibly unique to LUNABEL, also holds promise for other lexical steganographic efforts. However, different programs use cover texts in different ways; by replacing all words within the cover text (Chapman, 1997a; Chapman, Davida, & Rennhard, 2001), or by manipulating the syntax of the cover text (Atallah et al., 2001), not by selectively replacing single words (LUNABEL). The style of readme files, while less rigid than other genres, does have expected syntactic patterns, complicating one steganographic approach (Atallah et al., 2001), and the their semantic opacity, which LUNABEL exploits, is marred by wholesale word replacement, which, within the replacement process, does not maintain the particular genre of text, nor the particular topic of the original cover text (Taskiran, Topkara, Topkara, & Delp, 2006).

Another point of consideration is the level of commitment each program has to a particular cover text document: earlier programs (Atallah et al., 2001; Chapman, 1997a; Chapman et al., 2001; McKellar, 2000) are bound to a single cover text once its syntactic patterns have been extracted, while LUNABEL is only restricted to a particular genre of texts once word lists are created, with any text within that genre available for possible use as the cover text in a particular instance of message transmission.

Programs which rely on already constructed, mammoth sized synonym lists are also hampered in their use of the readme genre in particular because the technology being discussed within a readme is constantly changing, as new technology (and hence jargon) is created and distributed. For LUNABEL, the addition of new jargon is somewhat of an advantage. New vocabulary simply allows us to add new word lists. The constant flux which technology-related language exists within is harder to capture within a program whose synonym lists are unwieldy. The potential extent of the benefit of using readme files for other approaches is thus uncertain.

3.2 Word Class Size, Encryption Density, and Cover Text Size Requirements

The size requirement for cover texts is naturally affected by LUNABEL's sparse substitution. However, the size of the word lists is also a factor, in that the more words are considered viable for replacement, the less cover text is necessary. Essentially, the ratio of words in substitution classes versus non-replacement words determines both how sparse the encryption is and the minimum length of the cover text.

In our current system, each plain text character is represented by two word replacements in the cover text. Given the number of word lists we use and the token frequency of the words in them, the rate of word replacement in a typical readme file (as observed empirically) comes to about one in 16 words or so. Therefore, each character of the original message will be represented, on average, by 32 words in the cover text. It can be seen that LUNABEL requires rather large cover texts. This could be remedied to some extent by targeting a larger number of words for replacement. While we have discussed how only content words are used, it is in fact even more selective than that, with only a small subset of content words even marked for replacement. This also contributes to the sparse replacement.

LUNABEL has a larger cover text size requirement than earlier efforts (approximately four times as large as NICETEXT II (Chapman et al., 2001)), in large part because of its sparse substitution. The exact ratio of cover text to original message size is not constant, however; it inversely depends on the size of the word lists (as the number of word lists increases, the size requirement of the cover text drops).

There is, however, a compromise involved in choosing to use a larger number of word lists. With a small number of lists, one can control for several factors. We have, for example, constructed our word lists so as to include words with comparable token frequencies in the genre we were working with. If one were to maximize the number of word lists, this could be compromised. Also, at some point, one will be forced to include in a substitution class words that are subject to more ambiguity, less semantic and syntactic coherence, and so on.

4. PAST APPROACHES TO LEXICAL STEGANOGRAPHY

Lexical steganography has had three main veins of research: watermarking techniques (Atallah et al., 2001) that manipulate sentences through syntactic transformations, word replacement systems both with and without cover texts, and context-free grammars such as NICETEXT (Chapman, 1997b). All of these focus on computer based attacks (Bergmair & Katzenbeisser, 2006), thus failing in linguistic robustness.

4.1 Watermarking

Atallah et al. (2001) watermark texts by manipulating and exploiting the syntax (formal word order and grammatical voice) of sentences. Through common generative transformations (clefting (36), adjunct fronting (37), passivization (38), adverbial insertion [39]), the syntax of each sentence is altered:

35. The lion ate the food yesterday. (original sentence)
36. It was the lion that ate the food yesterday.
37. Yesterday, the lion ate the food.
38. The food was eaten by the lion yesterday.
39. Surprisingly, the lion ate the food yesterday.

While this broadly preserves the meaning of each sentence, their argument that this approach will withstand translation into other languages, as well as appear as innocuous text, is not strong.

Covering the first point, adverbs and adjunct clauses which may appear in multiple syntactic positions within English (e.g., in [39], *yesterday* and *surprisingly* can be placed at the beginning or end of the sentence as well as directly before the verb) do not necessarily have this same range of movement in other languages with differing word order rigidity. Also confounding is English's notorious strictness in its subject, object and verb word order, in marked contrast to its treatment of adverb and adjunct clauses. Because of these features, the range of possible transformations within English does not have a dependable one to one correlation in most other languages, Indo-European or otherwise.

Additionally, the more serious claim when examining the English version of Atallah et al.'s watermarked text, that transformations will not affect the semantics of a text, reflects a generative bias, and is not necessarily true. Newer theories of language argue for the interconnectedness of the semantic and syntactic levels (Langacker, 1982, 1987; Taylor, 2002), demonstrating that the syntactic pattern is itself inherently meaningful. Furthermore, statistically, various syntactic structures (word orders) are not equal in distribution: different genres of text have wildly different syntactic structures, and replacing such structures freely could create a text which is trivially broken by statistical methods (Taskiran et al., 2006)-a security threat to the program.

Another problem for their claim of encryption integrity within translation arises with a closer examination of syntactic structure cross-linguistically. The use of passivization, for example, varies cross-linguistically: in English it is appropriate to say (40), while in Hindi the same concept would be phrased, when translated directly into English, as (41).

40. I was late.
41. To me lateness happened.

Translation, either based on semantics or word-by-word, will not maintain the syntactic structures Atallah et al. assume (2001). Their approach, while more linguistically sophisticated than earlier work, is clearly not without problems. More importantly, its focus is centered on defeating word frequency statistics and NLP software which would test the semantics of the text, making little reference to how such text would fare with a human inspection. Our program is focused towards defeating the casual human inspector, negating the possibility that the text would raise suspicion and be passed into NLP and statistical programs for further inspection.

4.2 Word Replacement

Attempts have been made to focus on synonymous words as potentials for word replacement (WordNet (Miller, 2006), Tyrannosaurus Lex (Winstein, 1999a, 1999b)). However, this is rather problematic from a linguistic standpoint, as the number of true synonyms in English is relatively small to nonexistent (a commonly cited synonymous pair in American English is sofa/couch, but even this is only valid in some areas of the United States). Unfortunately, the notion of synonymy is vague, often characterized as a similarity in meaning and the ability to replace one term with another. A closer examination of commonly perceived synonyms often reveals differences in terms of their syntactic distributions and word frequencies. Additionally, most words have more than one sense. It is rare that two terms will overlap completely in all of their senses, complicating the replace-all plan used in earlier steganographic works.

Another complication is that many synonymous pairs actually come from different dialects (i.e., regionally defined varieties of language) or registers (i.e., language varieties used in particular social settings); their range of underlying implications is disparate and often based on these variations in register and dialect. For example, the terms violinist and fiddler are commonly cited synonyms, however, they are poor replacement choices. Compare the original sentence, (42), with (43), synonymous term replacement:

42. Itzhak Perlman, one of the most famous <u>violinists</u>, performed recently at Carnegie Hall.
43. *Itzhak Perlman, one of the most famous <u>fiddlers</u>, performed recently at Carnegie Hall.

Example (43) demonstrates that semantically similar terms, in this case terms for people who play a small fretless, bowed string instrument, are not necessarily replaceable, due to underlying differences in connotation—Itzhak Perlman is not a famous fiddler. To say that he is one implies that he plays a style of music other than Western classical music (perhaps bluegrass), and could be interpreted as a derogatory reflection on his sophistication. Oftentimes this register difference for synonymous terms is problematic for wholesale replacement schemes, which ignore register as well as genre specific word frequencies, making replaced terms stand out with respect to the text as a whole.

A further impediment to synonym based word replacement is graphotactic structure (i.e., legal and illegal letter combinations)—to cite one example, the English indeterminate articles a and an are used in a phonologically rule-based pattern, with *a* preceding consonant initial terms and *an* preceding vowel initial terms:

44. /a/ → [a] / __#C e.g. a banana
→ [an] / __#V e.g. an apple

Exchanging *apple* with *banana* would thus produce the ill-formed phrase **an banana.* These factors, taken collectively, severely affect the flow, semantics, and readability of a text altered based on "synonymous" word replacement. In short, the notion of replacement based on synonyms is oversimplifying language and has been challenged in its ability to sustain computer attack (Taskiran et al., 2006).

Word replacement stegosystems based on synonymy downplay the role and potential threat human attack, however "the performance of machines in word-sense disambiguation is nowhere near the performance of humans, and that problem is now widely considered "AI-complete" in the sense that a solution to this problem presupposes a solution to the "strong AI-problem" of the synthesis of a human-level intelligence" (Bergmair & Katzenbeisser, 2006: 19). Thus our challenge, that past word replacement based on synonymy is not linguistically sophisticated and has yet to produce encrypted naturalistic text, is critical because past attempts have neglected the only acknowledged attacker of potentially semantically innocuous text, human inspection.

4.3 Context-Free Grammars

The third approach used in lexical steganography exploits the syntactic structures of a text, using a part-of-speech tagger to place new words in old frames, in order to create new encrypted text. Past research in this arena has produced software functionally similar to LUNABEL, in that a message is encoded into an innocuous looking text (Chapman, 1997b). However, while improving upon earlier synonym-based word replacement programs, NICETEXT has certain drawbacks which limit its potential, and distinguish it in appearance and methodology from LUNABEL.

NICETEXT uses the cover text simply as a source of syntactic patterns: by running the cover text through a part-of-speech tagger, NICETEXT obtains a set of "sentence frames," e.g. [(noun) (verb) (prep) (det) (noun)] for *I sat in the tree.* It also compiles a lexicon of words found in the cover text via part-of-speech tags, with each word in the lexicon associated (arbitrarily) to either of the binary digits 0 or 1. In encryption, the plain text message is converted into a sequence of binary digits. A random sentence frame is chosen and the part of speech tags in it are replaced by words in the lexicon according to the sequence of binary digits.

Based on a linguistically unsophisticated model of language, (part of speech tags are useful in syntactic parsing and similar tasks, but inadequate for semantically plausible word replacement-an indication of this may be found in the wildly differing numbers of part of speech tags used in taggers developed for different purposes: the Penn Treebank tagset of 45 tags vs. the C7 tagset of 146 tags (Jurafsky & Martin, 2000)), NICETEXT is ill prepared to deal with ambiguous lexical items (part of speech ambiguity—words with two possible syntactic categories, like share, which functions as a noun and a verb—is especially disastrous [also commented on by (Bergmair & Katzenbeisser, 2006)]), and items which cannot be interpreted literally (idioms and metaphors). Furthermore, function and content words are treated alike in NICETEXT. Since function word often have more to do with syntactic relationships (e.g., passive agent by; infinitival to) than semantics, subjecting them to word replacement often results in ungrammatical and semantically anomalous sentences. Compare (45), NICETEXT's cover text with (46), encryption based on NICETEXT.

45. NICETEXT Original text (unaltered), from John F. Kennedy's 1962 inaugural speech
We observe today not a victory of party but a celebration of freedom... symbolizing an end as well as a beginning. . . signifying renewal as well as change for I have sworn before you and Almighty God the same solemn oath our forbears prescribed nearly a century and three-quarters ago. The world is very different now, for man holds in his mortal hands the power to abolish all forms of human poverty and all forms of human life. (...)

46. NICETEXT Encrypted version of above text
My area origins of the suspicion... oppose much what America will be before you, before what asunder we would be for the Poverty inside Man. Yet will it do almighty off the first two south votes... or on the course at this administration, whether even deadly off our suspicion by this peace. To those young votes what proud nor alike origins we comfort: we house the heritage past hostile americans. (...)

Regarding the semantics of (46), Atallah et al. (2001) comment that NICETEXT, and similar programs, are "...context-free grammars that generate primitive but less conspicuously meaningless texts, in which each individual sentence may be sort of meaningful, even if rather unrealistically simple..." Clearly, there is room for improvement in the semantics of the texts produced by steganographic attempts thusfar, improvements which target the human attacker as equally important to computer-based attack (Bergmair & Katzenbeisser, 2006).

Another factor worth considering is the density of encryption within the cover text. Ideally, the cover text should work to hide the word frequencies and syntactic structure of the hidden plain text message. Steganographic goals encourage sparse encryption, which does not alter a majority of the text by the word replacement. NICETEXT encryption is maximally dense-every word within the final encrypted cover text is conveying hidden information. Given that each encrypted word is part of the original information bearing message and common word usage patterns are unavoidable, this is problematic for the original steganographic intent: avoiding detection and producing naturalistic text.

All of the shortcomings detailed above make the fact of encryption obvious, as the syntax and semantics of the cover text are unnatural enough to draw attention to the message, whether examined by AI/NLP software (Taskiran et al., 2006) or by a human (Orgun, 1999). This is acknowledged in the original authors' reflection on NICETEXT, "Although the initial NICETEXT approach was an improvement, it was not as effective in producing text that was 'believable' by a human" (Chapman et al., 2001).

NICETEXT II (Chapman et al., 2001), the successor to NICETEXT, is based on a context-free grammar instead of sentence frames, and is focused on the ability to build an infinitely large set of sentences based on a dictionary of tagged words. This focus on infinite sentence generation still leaves NICETEXT II as open to the density critique as NICETEXT. Additionally, the semantic plausibility of the sentences has not increased, nor is there any relevance or relation between sequential sentences, rendering the resulting text contextless. These issues can be seen in (47), which uses the sentence frames from the original text found in (45), to produce the following sample sentence:

47. NICETEXT II Encrypted version
The prison is seldom decreaseless tediously, till sergeant outcourts in his feline heralds the stampede to operate all practices among interscapular stile inasmuch all tailers underneath indigo pasture.

While this sentence might be considered syntactically reasonable, it is clearly not semantically wellformed, and hence open to further inspection and detection. It is reminiscent of Chomsky's (1957) famous sentence (48), in which he highlighted syntactic wellformedness without semantic wellformedness, i.e. grammatically reasonable nonsense:

48. Colorless green ideas sleep furiously.

While Chomsky's accompanying generative syntactic theory has had many incarnations in the last 40 years, his point made with this sentence holds true.

As this review has demonstrated, NICETEXT I and II are concerned only with syntactic wellformedness, allowing for grammatically correct but semantically anomalous text which itself is not immune to computer-based attack (Taskiran et al., 2006). Given the goal of creating innocuous text, failing to consider semantic wellformedness, pivotal for a human attacker (Bergmair & Katzenbeisser, 2006; Orgun, 1999), leaves NICETEXT I and II vulnerable to detection. While the dominant focus has been creating naturalistic text which would fool a human, it can be gathered from surveying the goals and steganographic processes of existing systems that there is much work still to be done. The texts produced by all of these earlier systems, while potentially more innocuous than an alpha-numeric stream of digits, are clearly unnatural and likely to arouse suspicion, either with statistical or NLP software (Taskiran et al., 2006), or human inspection. Linguistic features beyond syntactic structure and synonymy clearly need to be accounted for in order to produce natural looking text, and less dense encryption is critical for future work. The current project addresses these further needs.

5. CONCLUSION

With the features enumerated in this paper, it has proven possible to refine the simple word replacement cryptosystem of past into a much more robust and linguistically sophisticated program, LUNABEL. This system improves upon earlier word replacement programs like NICETEXT in its focus on producing semantically innocuous text, its adherence to a range of further linguistically significant criteria, and its exploitation of cover text genres which are syntactically and semantically abnormal and prone to opaque language styles. This line of work has the advantage of creating encrypted cover texts which are likely to appear innocent to humans in a casual scan.

REFERENCES

Atallah, M. J., Raskin, V., Crogan, M., Hempelmann, C., Kerschbaum, F., Mohamed, D., et al. (2001). Natural language watermarking: Design, analysis, and a proof-of-concept implementation. In I. S. Moskowitz (Ed.), *Information Hiding: Fourth International Workshop, 2137 of Lecture Notes in Computer Science* (pp. 185-199): Springer Verlag.

Bergmair, R. (2007). *Semantilog: A Comprehensive Bibliography of Linguistic Steganography.* Retrieved April 2007, from http://semantilog.ucam.org/biblingsteg/

Bergmair, R., & Katzenbeisser, S. (2006). *Content-aware steganography: About lazy prisoners and narrow-minded wardens.* Paper presented at the Proceedings of 8th Information Hiding Workshop, Lecture Notes in Computer Science, Washington D.C.

Chapman, M. T. (1997a). *Hiding the hidden: A software system for concealing ciphertext as innocuous text.* University of Wisconsin-Milwaukee, Milwaukee.

Chapman, M. T. (1997b). NICETEXT. Retrieved October 2004, from http://www.ctgi.net/NICETEXT

Chapman, M. T., Davida, G., & Rennhard, M. (2001). A Practical and Effective Approach to Large-Scale Automated Linguistic Steganography. In *Lecture Notes in Computer Science, 2200*, 156-167. Berlin Heidelberg: Springer Verlag.

Chomsky, N. (1957). *Syntactic Structures*. The Hague: Mouton.

Jurafsky, D., & Martin, J. (2000). *Speech and language processing: an introduction to natural language processing, computational linguistics, and speech recognition* Upper Saddle River, NJ: Prentice-Hall.

Langacker, R. (1982). Space grammar, analyzability, and the English passive. *Language, 58*, 22-80.

Langacker, R. (1987). *Foundations of Cognitive Grammar, 1. Theoretical Prerequisites*. Palo Alto: Stanford University Press.

McKellar, D. (2000). Spammimic. Retrieved April 2007, from http://www.spammimic.com/

Miller, G. (2006). WordNet: A Lexical Database for the English Language. Retrieved October 2004, from http://www.cogsci.princeton.edu/~wn/

Orgun, O. (1999). *Linguistic Steganography Project Report*. Unpublished manuscript, University of California, Davis.

Taskiran, C. M., Topkara, U., Topkara, M., & Delp, E. J. (2006). Attacks on lexical natural language steganography systems. In *Proceedings of the SPIE International Conference on Security, Steganography, and Watermarking of Multimedia Contents*.

Taylor, J. R. (2002). *Cognitive Grammar*. Oxford: Oxford University Press.

Winstein, K. (1999a). *Lexical steganography through adaptive modulation of the word choice hash*. Retrieved October 2004, from http://alumni.imsa.edu/~keithw/tlex/lsteg.ps.

Winstein, K. (1999b, January). *Tyrannosaurus lex Web site*. Retrieved October 2004, from http://alumni.imsa.edu/~keithw/tlex/

KEYWORDS

Cover Text: A piece of text that is altered in subtle ways to hide a message in it.

Density of Encryption: The ratio of words that are replaced to those that are left intact in the course of information hiding.

Linguistic Robustness: The likelihood that a cover text altered so as to hide information in it will still appear syntactically and semantically natural to human observers.

Linguistic Steganography: A system of steganography that strives for linguistic robustness by paying attention to linguistic criteria.

Minimum Length of Cover Text: The length of cover text required in order to hide a message of a given size. This depends on the size of substitution classes and the density of encryption.

Sentence Frames: Sequences of syntactic categories (part of speech tags) extracted from a corpus and used in some text-based stegosystems as templates for generating encrypted messages.

Sparse Substitution: A system of word substitution that does not target every word of a cover text. Function words and highly ambiguous words will typically be left out; it is a matter of choice what other words may or may not be targeted for substitution.

Substitution Classes: Sets of words whose members may be replaced by one another within a given genre of cover text with a high probability that the replacement will not adversely affect the syntactic and semantic plausibility of the cover text.

Synonym-Based Word-Replacement Systems: Systems of text-based steganography in which substitution classes consist of (nearly) synonymous words.

Text-Based Steganography: A system of hiding information in a text file (as opposed to, for example, an image file).

Chapter XXIV
Using Technology to Overcome the Password's Contradiction

Sérgio Tenreiro de Magalhães
Universidade Católica Portuguesa, Portugal

Kenneth Revett
University of Westminster, UK

Henrique M. D. Santos
Universidade do Minho, Portugal

Leonel Duarte dos Santos
Universidade do Minho, Portugal

André Oliveira
Universidade do Minho, Portugal

César Ariza
Bogomovil Ltda, Portugal

ABSTRACT

The traditional approach to security has been the use of passwords. They provide the system with a barrier to access what was quite safe in the analogical world. The digital era provided the means to easily try thousands of passwords in a short period of time and now the password schema is no longer safe. Now it suffers of the password's contradiction: the fact that it requires both simplicity and complexity to be usable and safe. Being so, new technologies are required that can preserve the easiness of use, but can provide stronger authentication processes. This chapter presents the latest advances in three technologies that can be used, unaided or together, to improve the safety of user/password schemas without significant changes in the protected information system architecture, despite the human factors that traditionally reduce the security of those systems. The presented technologies are Keystroke Dynamics, Graphical Authentication and Pointer Dynamic.

INTRODUCTION

Password vulnerabilities come from their misuse that, in turn, results from what we call the password's contradiction: the fact that a password must be both easy to remember, therefore simple, and secure, therefore complex. Consequently, it is virtually impossible to come up with a "good" password. On the other hand, once users have not yet completely realized the need for securing their authentication secrets, even fairly good passwords become a threat when the security policies (if at all existing) fail to be implemented. The results of an inquiry made in 2004 to sixty Information Technology (IT) professionals shown that, even among those that have technical knowledge, the need for passwords security is underestimated. This is probably one of the reasons why the governments increased their investment in biometric technologies after the terrorist attack of 9/11. But, although the use of biometric technologies to increase the security of a system has become a widely discussed subject, a consensus has not been reached. While governments and corporations are pressing for a wither integration of these technologies with common security systems (like passports or identity cards), human rights associations are concerned with the ethical and social implications of its use. This situation creates a challenge to find biometric algorithms that are less intrusive, easier to use and more accurate, while other solutions must be created/developed simultaneously.

In this chapter we present the latest advances in three technologies that can be used, unaided or together, to improve the safety of user/password schemas without significant changes in the protected information system architecture, despite all the human factors that traditionally reduce the security of those systems. The presented technologies are Keystroke Dynamics, Graphical Authentication and Pointer Dynamics.

BACKGROUND: BIOMETRIC TECHNOLOGIES

Biometric technologies are mainly used in both physical and logical access control (Luis-García et al., 2003) but they can also be used to assist in other tasks, some so unimaginable has helping to preserve several animal endangered species (Jewell et al., 2001). But the use of biometric technologies to increase the security of a system has become a widely discussed subject and, while governments and corporations are pressing for a whither integration of these technologies with common security systems (like passports or identity cards), human rights associations are concerned with the ethical and social implications of its use (Privacy International *et al.*, 2004a; Privacy International *et al.*, 2004b). This situation creates a challenge to find biometric algorithms that are less intrusive, easier to use and more accurate.

The precision of a biometric technology is measured by its False Acceptance Rate (FAR), that measures the permeability of the algorithm to attacks, by its False Rejection Rate (FRR), that measures the resistance of the algorithm to accept a legitimate user, and by its Crossover Error Rate (CER), the point of interception of the FAR curve with the FRR curve that indicates the level of usability of the technology, also known as Equal Error Rate (EER). As an algorithm gets more demanding, its FAR gets lower and its FRR gets higher (Figure 1); usually the administrator of the system can define a threshold and decide what will be the average FAR and FRR of the applied algorithm, according to the need for security – dependent of the risk evaluation and of the value of what is protected; also the threshold can be, in theory, defined by an Intrusion Detection System (software designed to identify situations of attack to the system).

Establishing the error rates of a biometric technology is a complex problem. Studies have been made to normalize their evaluation, but the fact is that the results are strongly dependent of

Figure 1. False rejection rate vs false acceptance rate and consequent equal error rate, also know as crossover error rate

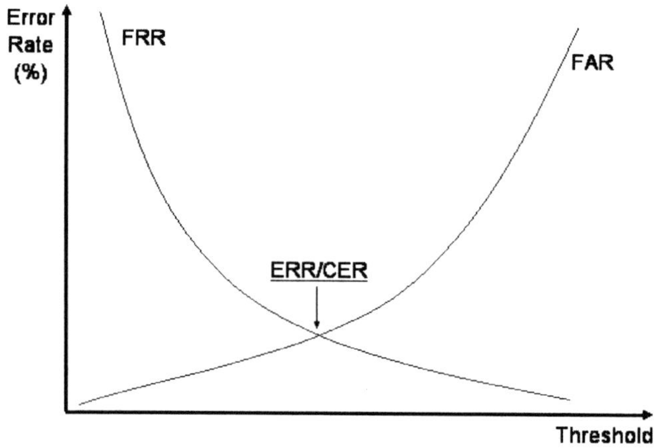

the number of individuals involved in the process and, what is worst, of who is chosen. This means that, even with a large amount of data collected, the results can be very different if we change the group evaluated. This happens because it's very difficult to obtain a sample representative of the population, once we do not know how to characterize the population. A good example of this disparity are the results of the Fingerprint Verification Competition (FVC) 2004, where the best CER achieved had a value of 2.07% (Maio et al., 2004), compared with the results of the FVC 2002, where the best CER achieved was 0.19% (Maltoni et al., 2003). Some international companies presented their products in both contests and the only justification for the disparity of the results is the difference in the sample data used to test the algorithms. All things considered, the only way to evaluate biometric algorithms is comparing them using the same data and, then, we can say that this technology is more accurate then that. The results also vary according to the use: a system used to identify an individual is less accurate that a system used to authenticate it (in this case the user presents himself to the system and it has only to confirm his identity)

Biometric technologies are usually classified as behavioral (e.g. voice recognition) or physical (e.g. retinal recognition), according to the classification of the characteristics evaluated. But they can also be classified as collaborative, if they demand that the user knows of its existence and participate in the process, or as stealth technologies, if they can be used without the knowledge of the one that is being authenticated or identified (Figure 2) (Tenreiro de Magalhães & Santos, 2005).

OVERCOMING THE CONTRADICTION ON PERSONAL COMPUTERS

Keystroke Dynamics

It is a biometrical authentication algorithm that tries do define a user's typing pattern and then verifies in each login attempt if the pattern exiting in the way the password was typed matches the user's known pattern.

The Keystroke dynamics algorithms are behavioral biometric technologies that can be used with the collaboration off the user or in stealth mode and that allows to increase the level of security, both in authentication and in identification, almost without any extra effort once it works by analyzing the patterns existing on the way that the user

Figure 2. Classification of biometric technologies: behavioural vs physical and stealth vs collaborative

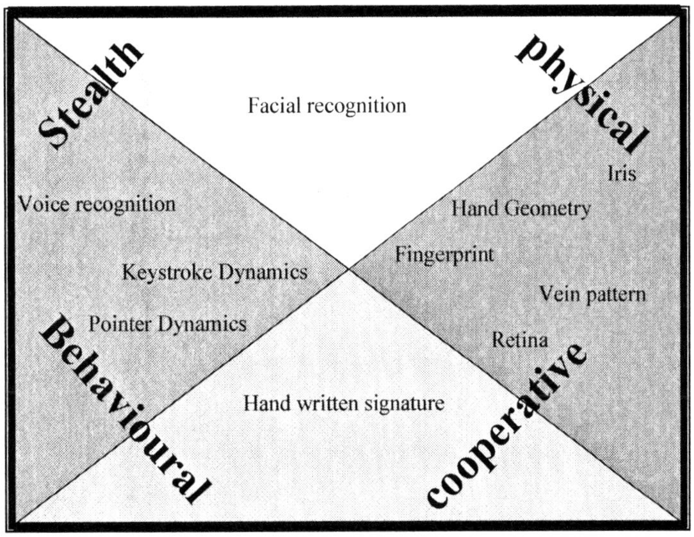

types (a password, a passphrase or general text) on a keyboard. Furthermore, these algorithms can adjust their parameters to adapt themselves to evolutions on the typing patterns of the user

The approaches to find an algorithm that maximizes the performance of these technologies include, apart from the mathematical algorithms themselves, several different approaches to the information to be captured. The first keystroke dynamics algorithm dates of 1980 when Gaines presented a report of his work to study the typing patterns of seven professional typists (Gaines, 1980). The small number of volunteers and the fact that the algorithm was deducted from their data and not tested in other people later, results on a lower confidence on the FAR and FRR values presented. But the method used to establish a pattern was a breakthrough: a study of the time spent to type the same two letters (digraph), whenever together in the text. Since then, many others have used probabilistic calculations to improve the liability of the authentication process, especially in small texts like a passphrase or even a password and Gupta that, in 1990, presented an algorithm to calculate a value that represents the distance between acquired keystroke latency times and the correspondent times previously stored (Gupta, 1990). The development of the machine learning approaches allowed several sets of rules/classifiers to be found using, for instance, the similarity models of Bayes (Monrose & Rubin, 1997), the Rough Sets Theory (Revett et al., 2005) or neural networks (Revett et al., 2006a).

Keystroke Dynamics Accuracy

At this time several works have reached algorithms for keystroke dynamics that can achieve an Equal Error Rate/ Crossover Error Rate below 5%, which wouldn't be enough to guarantee the security of a system if it wasn't for the fact that this error rate is obtained after the password is made public, when in normal conditions (meaning without keystroke dynamics) it is a secret and if made public there isn't any other layer of protection. Tables 1 and 2 and Figure 3 show the precision of algorithms reached through the use of Rough Sets theory (Revett et al., 2006b), probabilistic neural networks (Revett et al., 2006a)and probability calculations based on the presumption of a distribution near to the Gauss Distribution (Tenreiro de Magalhães et al., 2005), respectively.

Table 1. A listing of the classification accuracy measurements (support and accuracy) for the rules obtained by (Revett et al., 2006b). The numeric values in the 'Support' column heading indicate the number of instances for each decision rule.

Support		Accuracy	
LHS	RHS	Decision: 1	0
55	55	100%	0%
59	59	100%	0%
49	48.1	97.9%	2.1%
39	38.1	97.4%	2.6%
41	40.1	97.6%	2.4%
43	42.1	97.7%	2.3%

Table 2. FAR/FRR values as a function of the division level, obtained by (Revett et al., 2006a). Note the values must be multiplied by 100 to give percentages.

Division points	False acceptance	False rejection
10	0.0483	0.0481
20	0.0192	0.0197
30	0.0576	0.0376
40	0.0576	0.0566
50	0.0576	0.0483
60	0.0001	0.0021
70	0.0576	0.0598
80	0.0481	0.0483
90	0.0288	0.0312
100	0.0480	0.0427

Future work should focus on retrieving what is best on the many approaches followed so far, in order to maximize the global effect.

Despite the improvement on security provided by keystroke dynamics, the situation is not altered when typing passwords using pointing devices like the palmtop stylus. In those situations we need to overcome the password's contradiction with a different approach.

OVERCOMING THE CONTRADICTION ON MOBILE DEVICES

In mobiles environments the level of privacy is normally higher, once the equipment is used nearer to the body of the user and/or the screen is smaller. Therefore, all the conditions are gathered to substitute passwords by graphical processes of authentication, taking advantage of the human ability to recognize visual information better

Figure 3. False acceptance rate and false rejection rate for several possible thresholds and estimation of the crossover error rate obtained by (Tenreiro de Magalhães et al., 2005)

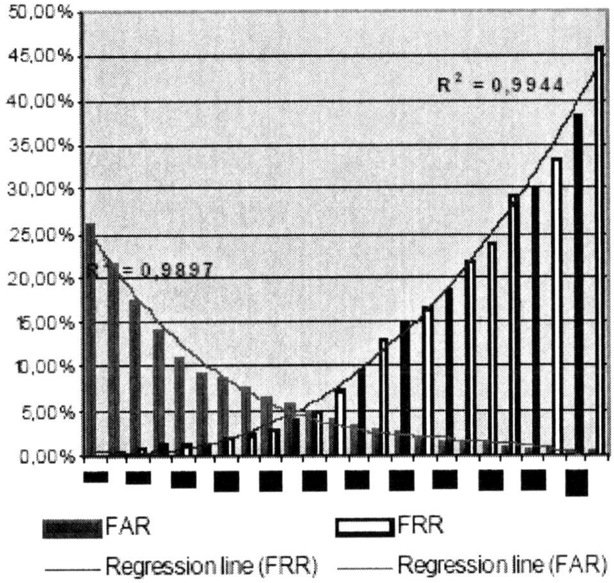

than meaningless text-based strings (Nickerson, 1965; Shepard, 1967; Standing, 1973). Graphical Authentication is a technology in which the user selects some images from a bigger set, or selects some points in an image. The secret possessed by the legitimate user is the images/points selected and the corresponding sequence. These technologies can provide a way to generate traditional passwords, using unidirectional functions, from the sequence of images/points selected and, in this way, provide compatibility with the existing systems. Despite the fact that Blonder has patented the "graphical password" in 1996 (Blonder, 1996) many graphical systems have been proposed since then and in this section we will present some of the existing alternatives for using graphics instead of passwords, as well as our latest results on a pointer dynamics system, a biometric technology that goes beyond the secret inherent to graphical authentication by including behavioral biometrics in the authentication protocol.

Before stepping into section 4 we will also describe how Graphical Authentication Systems (GAS), while being used for authentication, can also be used to prevent phishing, a method for obtaining personal information (like passwords, Personal Identification Numbers, or others) in which a mail is sent to a user persuading him to follow a link to a page that is an imitation of a legitimate website. Once in there, the user is driven to provide the desired information. We will show that GAS can be used both to enhance the user's authentication procedures as to allow the user to authenticate the website.

Graphical Authentication Protocols

DAS - Draw a Secret (Jermyn et al., 1999)

This authentication scheme was drawn to be used in personal digital assistants - PDAs. In this scheme the personal code is a simple image drawn by the user on a grid. The drawing is converted in a sequence of pairs of co-ordinates. The text generated from the drawing is transformed using a unidirectional hash function and the result is stored and associated to the user. The hash function from the registration process will be compared with the one stored in the system whenever the user tries to get access to the system.

The advantage of this method is that it originates long codes and the fact of being difficult to be imitated by other persons. Despite this scheme has been drawn with the objective of being using in PDA, it is also possible to use it in computers and, in this case, the use in public places is one of the disadvantages once that is easier to visualize and memorize a drawing in the monitor of a computer than to see what is being typed.

Déjà Vu (Dhamija & Perrig, 2000)

The authentication proposal elaborated by Dhamija and Perrig, is based on the generation of images having on is base a group of pre-selected images. This authentication scheme is composed of three phases: creation of the portfolio, training and, the last one, the login phase. The first consists in a selection of a group of abstract images. Starting with the selected images a process of generating new images is executed and those will be the ones to compose the user's portfolio. In the training phase, the user makes a small training with the objective to improve the image memorization. The last phase happens whenever the user tries to make the login. In this point the system shows a group of random images where the images of the user's portfolio are included and he must identify them.

The advantage of this process is that is practically impossible to describe the selected images and, once again, the disadvantage lies in the logins in public places.

Passfacestm (Real User Corporation, 2001)

This authentication scheme works in compliance with the empiric study of Brostoff and Sasse (Brostoff & Sasse, 2000)]. To create an access code it is required that the user pre-selects a group of four people's images among a group of images. After this, the users make a training process with the objective of memorizing them. In the login process a 3x3 grid is shown (nine images of people) in a set of four stages. Each stage contains an image from those pre selected and eight random ones. As can be seen, this authentication scheme is very identical to the previous outline (Déjà Vu), being that the previous scheme uses abstract images while PassFaces uses people's images.

The use of people's images is one of the disadvantages of this scheme once it is relatively easy to describe a person.

PassPoints (Wiedenbeck et al., 2005)

PassPoints is based on only one image for authentication in the system, in which the user should select a group of pre-selected and sequential points. In the authentication scheme, the user picks the pre-selected points, inside of a tolerance area defined around the selected point. The tolerance area is necessary once the choose point is a pixel, what is too precise for a human user.

Visual Identification Protocol (VIP)

(De Angeli et al., 2003)

Angeli proposed a solution for user authentication based in images and in the user's visual memory (De Angeli et al., 2003). Three authentication processes were created in this solution and compared with the PIN, Personal Identification Number, process (table 3). The first possibility (VIP1), consisted in the selection of four images from a group of 10 pre-defined images, disposed in fixed positions and introduced in the same order, or disposed in random positions (VIP2). In the last process (VIP3) the limits of the visual paradigm are studied. The user has a portfolio of 8 images, and in each authentication attempt four images among the eight images are shown together with 12 random images (of distraction images) and the user has to identify his images without any specific order. Angeli's study showed that the most common mistakes associated with VIP1 were related with a wrong sequence selection, in VIP2 the mistakes were due to a wrong sequence of images and wrong identification of the images, and in VIP3 most of the mistakes were due to a wrong identification of images, that is, the user tended to identify distraction images as being part of his portfolio.

Magalhães, Revett E. Santos (Magalhães et al., 2006)

This system, proposed in 2006, consisted in the choice of an image of among four made available. Each image includes a grid (20 x 15) in which each area can be seen as a pair of letter/number, where the first line contains letters and the first column contains numbers. The user must choose between the graphical secret key and the traditional secret key based on text. Having chosen the image, the user must select the several areas that compose his personal code. After the selection of the several areas, the system transforms the several points in an alphanumeric text. This scheme diverges from the PassPoints scheme, in the fact that the user selects a set of fixed and known areas while in the latest the user selects a group of points (pixels) of an image.

Best Practices in Choosing the Images

The use of a graphical authentication system eliminates some problems related to the alphanumeric codes, however, also potency possible bad habits related with this new authentication form. Magalhães et al elaborated a study (Magalhães et al., 2006) in which they tried to understand the user's methods of choosing images and areas inside an image.

The results obtained with the experience were surprising, having attained a group of important factors which should be considered when maximizing the safety of the graphical authentication process. The results showed that:

- 50% of the user defined codes had less than four points and, from those, 70% didn't have more than five points. Of notice: 21% of the codes had only one point in only one image.
- 75.9% of the codes had only points in the same line (55.5%) or in the same column (20.4%).
- of the totality of the chosen points, the next line to the one of the letters, the corners of the images, the people's eyes, the letters and the numbers obtained respectively, 39.94%, 13.12%, 9.18%, 10.06% and 6.56% of probability of being chosen to belong to a code, instead of 6.67%, 2.11%, 0.83%, 6.67% and 5.26%, respectively, expected if random.

The conclusions from this study showed that the analysts and the programmers need to implement the correct security policies, forcing users to follow and respect a group of rules of graphic codes definition, for instance:

- To force users to introduce codes with at least 5 points.

Table 3. Authentication processes and results

Prototype	Type of code	Location	Security scoring
VIP1	4 fixed order images from 10	Fixed	Same as PIN
VIP2	4 fixed order images from 10	Random	Intermediate
VP3	Portfolio based	Random	Maximum

- To prohibit the definition of codes with points in the same line and column or corners
- Not to propose images with people and with points standing out from the global image (when the images are not uploaded by the user but, has it has been common, are proposed by the system).

Generating a Password from a Passgraph

A passgraph with length n will be a vector of the type (p_1, p_2,..., p_n) where $p \in \{(x,y) | 0 \leq x \leq 19,\ 0 \leq y \leq 13\}$. The values of x and y define the selected section in a specific two-dimensional image. In order to maintain the compatibility with the traditional password systems, we need to generate a string. For that, we'll use 15 tables, numbered from 0 to 14, with 26 columns and 20 lines. So we have 7800 cells, each one with one 3 characters string and the corresponding ANSI code. Table 4 is one of those tables.

We find our first cell by locating, in the number (x+y)mod15 table, the line x and column y. Then, for each $p \in \{(x,y) | 0 \leq x \leq 19,\ 0 \leq y \leq 13\}$ we'll do:

$$\left(x + y + 1^{st}\ ANSIFromThePreviousSelectedCell\right) mod\ NumberOfLines$$

to find the next line selected;

$$\left(x + \bar{y} + 2^{nd}\ ANSIFromThePreviousSelectedCell\right) mod\ NumberOfColums$$

to find the next column selected;

$$\left(x + \bar{y} + 3^{rd}\ ANSIFromThePreviousSelectedCell\right) mod\ NumberOfTables$$

to find the next table selected;

To prevent the possibility of discovering the sequence of clicks from the string if this is compromised, for instance by capturing the packages on a poorly encrypted network, we need to make some final changes in the string. In this way, frequent changes in the tables (and the correspondent passwords) can increase the level of security of the system, in a transparent way to the user that will continue to click in the same places of the same figures. In our case:

Let x be the ANSI code of the first element of the so far generated string. Given t = x mod n, will reverse the order of the first t characters.

Let y be the ANSI code of the last element of the so far generated string. Given k = x mod n, will reverse the order of the last k characters.

If the system allows the user to choose at the moment of login what system to use according to the surrounding environment and/or used device, then there must be a way to convert the passgraph to the user's password. This can be achieved in two ways: the system accepts two different passwords, the one chosen by the user and the one that

Table 4. The conversion of the passgraph to traditional passwords (creating strong passwords) is made through unidirectional functions that make use of 15 tables similar to this one

0

4kQ	v9:	D't	~\'	M'p	K"|	.n.	@8v	(!p	LQi	H=p	i.6	h$m	.:]	q:	]h8	D-{	-Yh	`Ri	T^-	evf	y6:	i*f	iJH	^sl	{(T
E6W	xnf	:}V	Sx8	e(r	XT0	:8u	aWA	x6w	pd/	#.T	t4i	EwB	:!^	EIX	VOU	PiE	br4	wch	:!l	A:/	"eb	D.S	8R1	8%i	dQi
B`o	}5N	yDv	y$U	:3t	F`l	[+-	X!q	yvd	HdF	9XQ	Wcp	2-u	pEB	}Ti	iZl	mx	f#l	5Df	&)^	?d$	up6	3:@	u=	r<	yiK
T~3	LZM	hF7	.'V	]`d	C}{	-5%	]:3	qwn	&!n	-vf	sTr	lrV	X3d	aZn	zs4	HqV	l1U	@v>	AUs	L[a	?/n	OkA	lS/	=s/	i<6
ZU8	xtx	yT2	ekN	Evy	V^#	)l2	2Fv	<w&	u{=	l6L	?f0	\r.	Jew	6l/	z[]	`Oc	zJk	Ati	Y&h	xG\	O]^	L3E	P#D	8.d	tfx
!Z[	He$	'Ot	HdS	QB(	>.y	ewC	}{d	ayq	%+"	a"}	0LY	DE	NiD	53l	xXV	ry6	~.Y	:l6	({e	$.8	D~2	.Mp	lL9	-zl	Ad~
aC&	@.H	ios	Hq4	e$Q	(i?	0fl	k:n	hpS	Dx$	z0&	?P3	W#f	k:B	&k`	v#^	O/t	0)q	48a	4~!	sv\	N.!	qZb	~"J	?{<	zaL
~t	0lp	:%S	%$K	bUb	`f-	`9(	3"'	u<W	HKl	@m=	CTQ	O}H	no:	A-t	{l#	Q\)	rGc	1TX	lVy	`<o	l7B	~Np	"."	3^$	qYr
P?p	x7U	&^"	FLn	Fl.	.\b	1io	4{E	L$4	##	6Bv	h8]	e@J	KFP	cO&	}SN	$kS	fN!	b(!	-%w	il/	c7`	#P:	;an	2=!	q^4
k2"	v0n	z$S	v4j	W?.	.yL	$#u	-q)	&O}	wZt	\Gl	]5B	k\a	BK6	Xhp	m=c	[(Q	Tkd	+!r	!Y^	lMf	KVf	jjM	riJ	tF#	+v(
-md	eYY	t4Y	ali	yl!	cT6	Ml@	wsk	8Bo	iES	l9R	#&.	N.k	:??	(*V	h*i	0@^	^1"	xB$	-lv	<.t	Kb/	V9<	&2m	.0	D#r
ZVW	i.W	X~O	/f3	q@5	p%h	rAM	kuv	B[9	xzb	UQR	4"b	glN	S6*	@6}	j]6	UMr	z*H	n.K	O-H	8el	<>r	4H2	tl/	p:P	ZVw
WKA	.y>	?"B	XDw	+q.	OQ"	DNL	]d1	9lf	A[7	/Y'	i8\	hl1	CF*	DV:	tot	(>~	}4H	y%3	V[o	*s	!5Q	ev&	$o\	d(%	o{@
]04	e5Y	$rB	&q@	~~E	?<!	3[/	ZG	"MD	9t[	{DF	lzU	D`d	6B~	Z?l	til	8o+	RFi	~W3	s7F	?Si	]V[	`RS	.5q	xke	dqQ
"M:	OCn	G%k	wyv	R~o	9kb	7uM	qCa	.l.	2G1	'Ew	CFi	Liz	v+d	#1&	/e$	oxG	-o2	U`j	3k!	<2q	#wE	<ub	Z2T	lq$	zK'
qqz	t4%	\a:	J\2	{[	ky>	lkl	K07	&6x	:N:	>5V	}eq	>L2	2su	Cb^	M)(	3?T	Zl*	-^D	qUr	>Ll	=C:	rMS	b^~	>6/	pte
W&H	!bQ	:Ww	dbX	P6U	AkE	`7K	G#%	u6V	TN9	A:3	1Q(	:L5	Gm-	@HA	'ic	Zs[	>N/	c:?	n.>	0rW	5}}	qQ(	B3l	*Bh	#Ti
!~z	UxU	veV	H~?	;b#	S80	:=?	HXd	^H~	y!1	Tt*	.db	V}7	Ff!	XYt	P=W	iKO	t-3	w1l	ubN	Wsk	\Ko	W8x	vbu	+q2	]).
Ud.	@yL	cc[	tba	1wP	sXB	LGk	-'A	sSC	dxU	~6Z	A6r	7[m	1v%	R'M	"7]	~`k	W&5	lXl	62]	tDn	V#R	LLi	pHp	XHm	v=G
}C!	a:E	<qM	QG#	w(@	M&.	[<@	!QP	yn*	*D~	s2W	y4@	VJ'	do*	TU"	.<B	SRA	x9t	K.l	DzC	6-	S.8	~Q]	).?	N^}	hVY

will be generated from the passgraph; or there is a conversion table that allows the processing (on the server's side) of the data coming from the authentication fields and tests both the password at it is and the corresponding conversion result. This table would associate to each user a table containing the character associated to each of the trigraphs existing in the conversion tables (see Table 4). Each character of the alphabet is, of course, repeated several times and this table will not give any clue to the user's password. In this case the quality of the generated password is reduced to the exact level of security provided by the user's password, once they will be the same.

POINTER DYNAMICS

This is an experimental concept in which a biometric algorithm aims to define a user's clicking pattern when using a pointing device (mouse, stylus, touch pad, etc.) to authenticate towards a Graphical Authentication System. In each login attempt, access is granted if and only if the pattern exiting in the way the secret was clicked matches the user's known and recorded pattern.

An Experimental System

In order to test a Pointer Dynamics authentication process we integrated a java applet in a software called Moodle, a Course Management System. The login process, in the software Moodle, was transformed in order to integrate and substitute the conventional user and password by the one generated by our developed java applet. To support Moodle we have used a software package called WAMP5 that has among others MySQL as database, Apache as web server and PHP.

Both the enrolment and the authentication environment consist on a window with a field for a username, a dialog panel, where the users get feedback from the system; two buttons to erase the password and a third button used only in the enrolment process. The enrolment consists in 12 steps in which the user has to repeat in each one the graphical secret so that the system has a set of times required to establish a pattern. The image was divided in an 11x16 grid (Figure 4) and in the java applet was implemented a few limitations based on the study of Magalhães et al(Magalhães et al., 2006):

Figure 4. The registration and authentication system

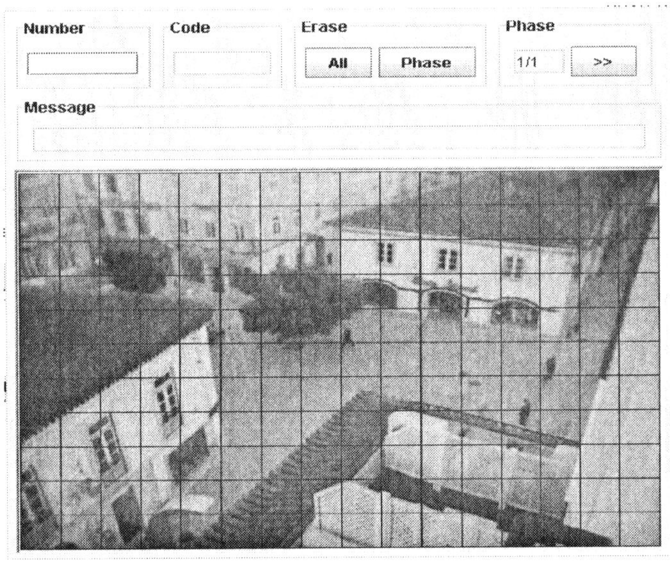

- The passwords must have at least 4 points and at the most 10 (this one implemented for reasons related to the moodle's architecture).
- The passwords points couldn't be all in the same line or in same row.
- The passwords points couldn't be all in the corners.

Also, the image used for the experiment was selected in accordance with the rules proposed in the study of Magalhães et al(Magalhães et al., 2006). In order to make the process of describing the authentication graphic secret to a third person more complex, no identification was included in each column or row.

Obtained Accuracy

For the experiment we have used 9 users from different professional areas, which provided their user and graphical secret (passgraph) information after registering in the system. Then, a group of university students from different grades tried to access the system, using the known login data.

To understand if the times between clicks were information enough to provide the system with an authentication pattern, we used an algorithm developed for keystroke dynamics.

The used algorithm has two distinct phases: the enrolment and the authentication attempt. In the enrolment phase, the user clicks his secret key twelve times and the systems records the times spent between the several clicks, calculating the average, the median and the standard deviation for those twelve times. The authentication attempt phase consists on, for each two points clicked, collect the proposed (once the alleged user is proposing that time as a legitimate one) time spent – PTS – and compare it with the corresponding value stored during the enrolment stage through the acceptance criteria presented in Figure 5, where α is a definable parameter.

Once all the times corresponding to the sequence of clicks constituting the secret key were classified, they received the value of 0 (zero) if they didn't satisfy the criteria, 1 (one) if the time satisfies the criteria and the time before didn't (or if it is the first time evaluated) and 1.5 (one point five) if it satisfies the criteria and so did the time before. Those values were added together and the final sum A corresponded to the level of trust in the presented pattern. If the value A is not smaller then the defined threshold (a defined parameter) then we would accept the user as legitimate and replace the oldest stored time sequence by this one, therefore allowing some evolution in a user's pattern. The obtained accuracies, with α set at 0,6 (zero point six), for the different thresholds are presented in Figure 6, along with the corresponding tendency lines (polynomials of 6th degree).

The Crossover Error Rate (CER) proved to be very high (approximately 30%) but the fact that low False Acceptance Rates and low False Rejection Rates were achievable (not at the same time) clearly indicates that this is a valid technology that, of course, need time and work to find new algorithms that will lead to an acceptable level of maturity.

Another fact observed was that, despite the initial efforts, several users chose a diagonal secret key. Therefore, it was decided to verify what would happen to the accuracy levels if only the users' with secret keys dependent on the image,

Figure 5. Acceptance decision criteria for a given time input

$$Lowest(Average; median) * \left(1 - \alpha - \frac{Sdeviation}{Average}\right) \leq PTS \leq Higher(Average, median) * \left(1 + \alpha + \frac{Sdeviation}{Average}\right)$$

Figure 6. Obtained accuracy for the test algorithm with α set at 0,6 (after the secret code was made public)

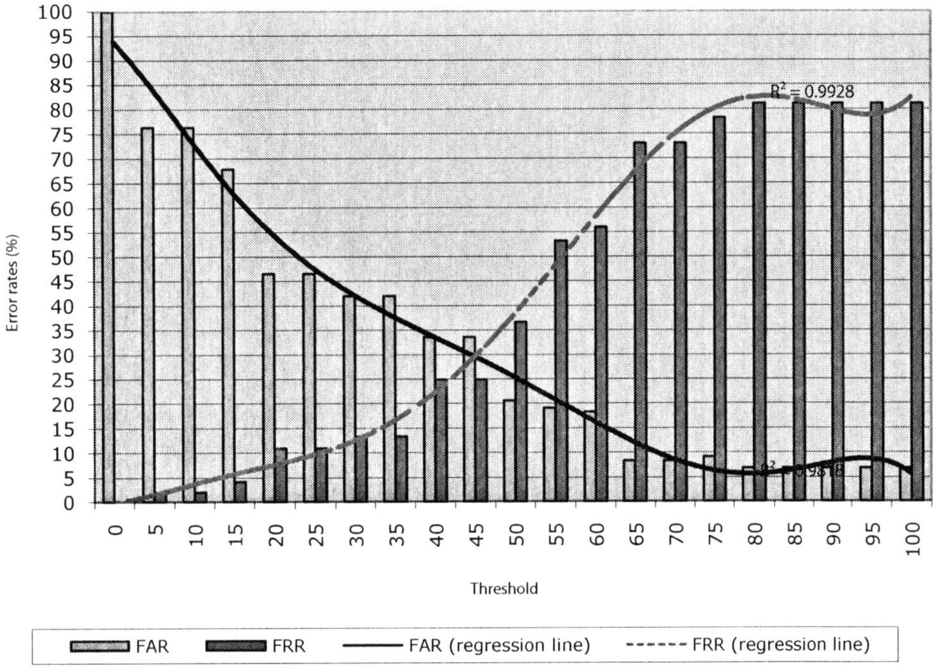

not on geometry, were considered. The results improved a lot and the CER dropped bellow 19% (Figure 7).

The results indicate that one must be very careful when implementing the security policies for the constitution of the secret access keys and that, if so, one can obtain very satisfying levels of accuracy.

Using GAS to Authenticate Both the User and the Service

When surfing on the Internet one must authenticate in order to access restricted areas, but there is no authentication for the website soliciting the user's authentication data. Several attacks can mislead the user into thinking that he is entering the authentication data on one determined website when in fact he is entering the data on someone else's site, designed to impersonate the original one. That can be achieved in many ways, for instance by DNS cache poisoning or DNS Hijacking (Wüest, 2005). One of the first entities to realize this need for an authentication of the website was the Bank of America that presented in 2005 the PassMark system, designed with the objective of allowing the user to authenticate the website by recognizing one determined mark that is particular to him and that was previously chosen (Bank of America, 2005). What we propose is that the images used to authenticate the websites can also be used as a basis for the user's authentication. In our proposed system, when a registered user intends to access the service, he inserts his username and the system creates the corresponding login page that includes the image that is specific to that user and, inserted on the image, the Internet Protocol address (IP) of the machine that requested the image (Figure 8) and the date/time of the request (to prevent reutilization of the image for fixed IP machines). If the system does not present the correct image, the correct date/time or the correct IP, the user knows that he is most probably dealing with an impersonation of the server acting as the

Figure 7. Accuracy level for the users that have a secret key (made public) dependent of the image

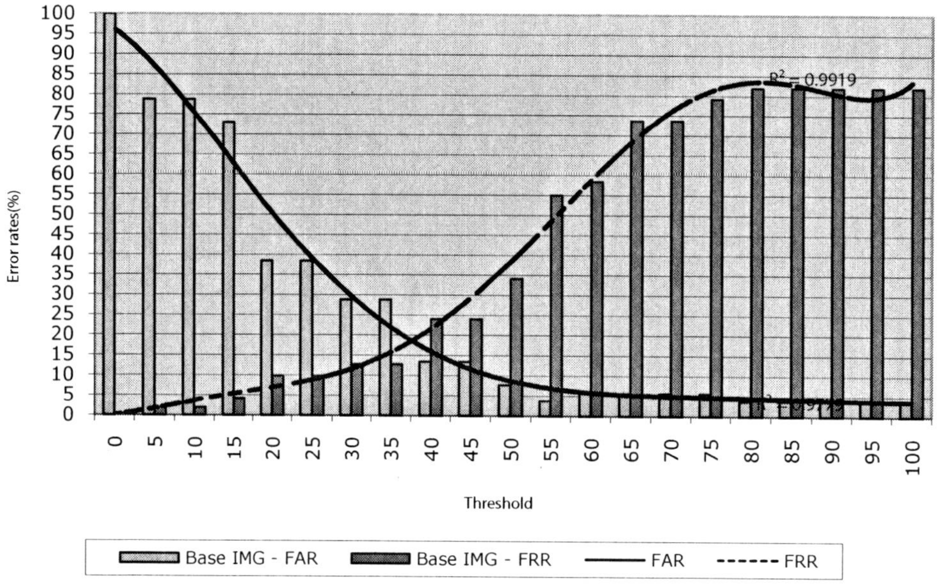

Figure 8. Pointer dynamics authentication system

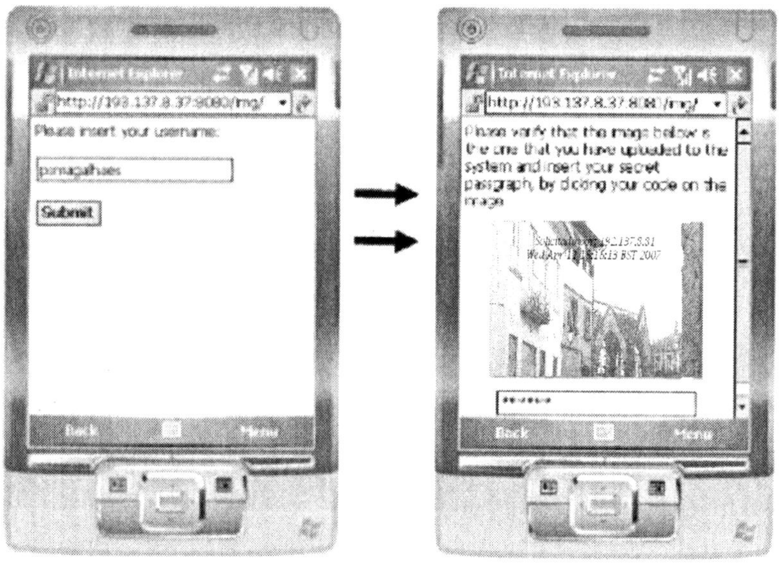

"man in the middle" and does not proceed with providing the authentication data. In this way, the GAS is being used for the authentication of both the user and the site. This process protects the user from malicious software like PWSteal. Bancos.B (also known as Infostealer.Bancos.B) that creates an authentication windows over the original one in order to capture the authentication data outside the protection of the SSL protocol despite the presence of the SSL padlock with the correct certificate details (Symantec Corp., 2003), once the authentication image would be covered. Unfortunately this cannot provide any additional protection against Trojans that, when detecting the access to a known website, store the sequence of clicks and a screenshot, allowing the calculation of all the positions clicked. The other drawback of this system is the possibility of having the IP changed along the communication, leading to information of the image that can be deceiving. This can be made, for instance, when using proxy servers.

FUTURE TRENDS

The research in the field of behavioural biometrics has grown is the past few years, mainly due to the potentiality of any large scale authentication process that does not require any dedicated hardware. This characteristic is even a requirement when the context is a service provided through the Internet for the withiest audience possible. Considering the usability of the presented technologies, future research will focus on three essential aspects: the accuracy of the authentication algorithm, the evolution from authentication to identification and the protection of the private data when using the technology in crowded spaces.

The accuracy of the algorithms will continue to improve along with the evolution of the mathematical theories that support that research. At the same time, new approaches for the use of the technology will improve the acceptability of the processes and help to solve other problems, like stepping from authentication, when the user presents himself as the legitimate owner of a system's, to identification, when the system detects, by itself, the correct identity of the user. Recent studies show that graphical authentication, when the selection of the images/sections is performed not through touching the screen but using the keyboard, can be less prone to shoulder-surfing then traditional passwords (Tari *et al.*, 2006). Other fields of research have presented works that are trying to solve the shoulder-surfing problem from different perspectives, for instance by allowing the selection of the images/sections to be made only by looking at them, thanks to an eye-tracking system (Hoanca & Mock, 2006). All these solutions will continue to increase the potential of the technologies destined to overcome the password's contradiction but will require an extra effort to improve the accuracy of the resulting algorithms, once all those evolutions will have a negative effect on it.

CONCLUSION

The several results and schemas presented along this chapter allow us to conclude that, if the human factors associated to the use of passwords are taken into account, it is possible to provide easy to use and non-intrusive technologies that can enhance the existing authentication schemas security, without demanding more effort from the users and, in some conditions, these schemas will also prevent other kinds of attacks like phishing.

At this moment, overcoming the password's contradiction requires the use of a behavioral/stealth biometric technology—Keystroke Dynamics—and graphical authentication (when using mobile devices), but in the future graphical authentication can become usable in open spaces, due to the integration with eye-tracking systems and/or by using them through the keyboard. Biometric technologies can also be applied to graphical authentication with some success, but not yet completely satisfying, and future research in the quest for better algorithms and in the understanding of the user's behavior can considerably improve their performance. At the same time that one overcomes the password's contradiction applying to graphical authentication, a serious advance in authenticating the provider of the service is also made, providing a higher level of trust to the systems.

REFERENCES

Bank of America. (2005). *Bank of America announces industry-leading security feature for its 13.2 million online banking customers to help prevent fraud and identity theft.* Retrieved April, 2007, from http://newsroom.bankofamerica.com/index.php?s=press_releases&item=6971

Blonder, G. E. (1996). Graphical password. In US (Ed.): Lucent Technologies Inc. Murray Hill, N. J.

Brostoff, S., & Sasse, M. A. (2000). Are passfaces more usable than passwords: A field trial investigation, *HCI 2000*: Springer.

De Angeli, A., Coventry, L., Johnson, G. I., & Coutts, M. (2003). Usability and user authentication: Pictorial passwords vs. Pin. In P.T.McCabe (Ed.), *Contemporary ergonomics 2003* (pp. 253-258). London: Taylor & Francis.

Dhamija, R., & Perrig, A. (2000). Déjà vu: A user study using images for authentication. *9th USENIX Security Symposium.*

Gaines, R. (1980). *Authentication by keystroke timing: Some preliminary results* (No. Report R-256-NSF): Rand Corporation.

Gupta, J. (1990). Identity authorization based on keystroke latencies. *Communications of the ACM, 33*(2), 168-176.

Hoanca, B., & Mock, K. (2006). Secure graphical password system for high traffic public areas. *Eye Tracking Research & Applications Symposium 2006*. San Diego: ACM SIGGRAPH.

Jermyn, I., Mayer, A., Monrose, F., Reiterand, M., & Rubin, A. (1999). The design and analysis of graphical passwords, *8th USENIX Security Symposium.*

Jewell, Z. C., S. K., A., & Law, P. R. (2001). Censusing and monitoring black rhino (diceros bicornis) using an objective spoor (footprint) identification technique. *J. Zool*(254), 1-16.

Luis-García, R., Alberola-López, C., Aghzout, O., & Ruiz-Alzola, J. (2003). Biometric identification systems. *Signal Processing, 83*, 2539-2557.

Magalhães, P. S., Revett, K., & Santos, H. D. d. (2006). *Critical aspects in* authentication graphic keys, *International Conference on Information Warfare and Security (ICIW2006).* Maryland Eastern Shore, USA: Academic Conferences, Inc.

Maio, D., Maltoni, D., Cappelli, R., Wayman, J. L., & Jain, A. K. (2004). Fvc2004: Third fingerprint verification competition, *International Conference on Biometric Authentication – ICBA.* Hong Kong.

Maltoni, D., Maio, D., Jain, A. K., & Prabhakar, S. (2003). *Handbook of fingerprint recognition.* New York: Springer.

Monrose, F., & Rubin, A. D. (1997). Authentication via keystroke dynamics, *Fourth ACM Conference on Computer and Communication Security.* Zurich, Switzerland: ACM.

Nickerson, R. S. (1965). Short-term memory for complex meaningful visual configurations: A demonstration of capacity. *Canadian Journal of Psychology, 19*, 155-160.

Privacy International, Statewatch, & European Digital Rights. (2004a). *An open letter to the icao a second report on 'towards an international infrastructure for surveillance of movement'.* Retrieved January, 2005, from www.privacyinternational.org

Privacy International, Statewatch, & European Digital Rigts. (2004b). An open letter to the european parliament on biometric registration of all eu citizens and residents. Retrieved January, 2005, from www.privacyinternational.org

Real User Corporation. (2001). The science behind passfaces. Passfaces[tm]. Retrieved October 2005, from http://www.idarts.com/

Revett, K., Gorunescu, F., Gorunescu, M., Ene, M., Tenreiro de Magalhães, S., & Santos, H. D. (2006a). Authenticating computer access based on keystroke dynamics using a probabilistic neural network, *2nd Annual International Conference on Global e-Security*. London: University of East London.

Revett, K., Magalhães, S. T. d., & Santos, H. (2006b). Datamining a keystroke dynamics based biometrics database using rough sets, *EPIA 2005, Portuguese Conference on Artificial Intelligence*. Covilhã, Portugal: IEEE CS Press.

Revett, K., Tenreiro de Magalhães, S., & Santos, H. D. (2005). Developing a keystroke dynamics based agent using rough sets, *International Workshop On Rough Sets And Soft Computing In Intelligent Agent And Web Technologies*. Compiègne: University of Technology of Compiègne.

Shepard, R. N. (1967). Recognition memoryfor words, sentences and pictures. *Journal of Verbal Learning and Verbal Behavior, 6*, 156-163.

Standing, L. (1973). Learning 10,000 pictures. *Quarterly Journal of Experimental Psychology, 25*, 207-222.

Symantec Corp. (2003). Infostealer.Bancos.B. Retrieved April, 2007, from http://www.symantec.com/security_response/writeup.jsp?docid=2003-073117-3108-99

Tari, F., Ozok, A. A., & Holden, S. H. (2006). A comparison between of perceived and real shoulder-surfing risks between alphanumeric and graphical passwords. *Symposium on Usable Privacy and Security (SOUPS) 2006*. Pittsburgh, PA, USA.

Tenreiro de Magalhães, S., Revett, K., & Santos, H. (2005). Password secured sites - stepping forward with keystroke dynamics, *International Conference on Next Generation Web Services Practices*. Seoul, Korea: IEEE CS Press.

Tenreiro de Magalhães, S., & Santos, H. (2005). An improved statistical keystroke dynamics algorithm, *Multi Conference on Cumputer Science and Information Systems*: IADIS.

Wiedenbeck, S., Waters, J., Birget, J. C., Brodskiy, A., & Memon, N. (2005). Authentication using graphical passwords: Basic results, *Human-Computer Interaction International (HCII 2005)*. Las Vegas.

Wüest, C. (2005). "Phishing in the middle of the stream" - Today's threats to online banking. *8th Annual AVAR International Conference*. Tianjin, China.

KEY TERMS

Authentication: It's the process of verifying the identity alleged by a user that tries to gain access to a system.

Collaborative Biometric Technology: It's an authentication biometric authentication technology that requires the user's volunteer and intended participation in the process. It opposes to the stealth biometric technologies that can be used without the user's consent.

Crossover Error Rate (CER): Authentication algorithms need to simultaneously minimize the permeability to intruders, therefore they have to be demanding, and to maximize the comfort level, therefore to be permissive. This contradiction is the base for the optimisation problem in authentication algorithms and the measure of success for the overall precision of an algorithm and of its usability is the Crossover Error Rate (CER), the error rate obtained at the threshold that provides the same False Acceptance Rate and False Rejection Rate.

False Acceptance Rate (FAR): This rate is a measure of the permeability of an authentication algorithm. It's calculated by dividing the number of intruder's successful login attempts, by the total number of intruder's login attempts.

False Rejection Rate (FRR): This rate is a measure of the comfort level of an authentication algorithm. It's calculated by dividing the number of unsuccessful attempts made by the legitimate users, by the total number of legitimate login attempts.

Graphical Authentication System: It's a login system that verifies the user's knowledge on specific images or parts of images to grant or deny him a successful login.

Identification: It's the process of discovering the identity of the user that tries to gain access to a system. It's differs from authentication because in the identification process no identity is proposed to the system, while in authentication an identity is proposed and the system will only verify if that identity is plausible.

Keystroke Dynamics: It's a biometrical authentication algorithm that tries do define a user's typing pattern and then verifies in each login attempt if the pattern exiting in the way the password was typed matches the user's known pattern. Another application of Keystroke Dynamics, at least in theory, is the permanent monitoring of the user's typing pattern in order to permanently verify if the user that is typing is the legitimate owner of the system's account being used.

Passgraph: It's the user's secret code to access a system protected by a graphical authentication system. It is constituted by a sequence of points where the user must click in order to obtain a successful login.

Stealth Biometric Technology: It's an authentication biometric authentication technology that can be used without the user's consent. It opposes to the collaborative biometric technologies that require the user's volunteer and intended participation in the process.

Threshold: It's the variable that defines the level of tolerance of an algorithm. It can be set on a more demanding value, raising the False Rejection Rate and lowering the False Acceptance Rate, or it can be set on a less demanding error, lowering the False Rejection Rate and raising the False Acceptance Rate.

Chapter XXV
Formal Analysis of Security in Interactive Systems

Antonio Cerone
United Nations University, China

Siraj A. Shaikh
United Nations University, China

ABSTRACT

Reducing the likelihood of human error in the use of interactive systems is increasingly important. Human errors could not only hinder the correct use and operation, they can also compromise the safety and security of such systems. Hence the need for formal methods to analyze and verify the correctness of interactive systems, particularly with regards to human interaction. This chapter examines the use of formal modeling and analysis of security properties of interactive systems. The reader is introduced to some basic concepts in security and human-computer interaction, followed by formal modeling of human cognitive behavior and analysis of such systems. Authors highlight the use of model-checking to drive the system development to design secure user actions and sequences of actions. Authors also analyze the patterns of user behavior that may lead to security violation. Finally, particular areas of security protocol design where human interaction plays a key role are discussed.

INTRODUCTION

Reducing the likelihood of human error in the use of interactive systems is increasingly important: the use of such systems is becoming widespread in applications that demand high reliability due to safety, security, financial or similar considerations. Consequently, the use of formal methods in verifying the correctness of interactive systems should also include analysis of human behaviour in interacting with the interface.

The study of human behaviour in operating machines has emerged in the 1980's, when Human Reliability Assessment (HRA) techniques have been used in the analysis of safety-critical systems (Kirwan, 1990). These techniques appeared soon to lack objectivity (Svenson, 1989) and failed to cope with the complex behaviours emerging in the human-machine interaction (Kirwan, 1992).

In the 1990s formal methods have started to be introduced aiming at a more objective analysis (Dix, 1991). However, the gain in objectivity was offset by an oversimplified model of the human behaviour, which was actually often modelled as defined by the interface requirements. In reality, the user interacting with the system does not necessarily behave as it was expected while designing the interface, and errors are actually the very result of an unexpected user behaviour that emerges through the interaction.

To best capture such an emergent behaviour, a model of the user must specify the cognitively plausible behaviour, which is all the possible behaviours that can occur, and that involve different cognitive processes (Butterworth *et al*, 2000). The model must take into account all relationship between user's actions, user's goals and the environment. Following this approach, a number of researchers have explored the use of formal models to understand how cognitive errors can affect user performance. Mode confusion is often blamed for human errors in interactive systems, whereby the user's mental model of how the system works gets out of step with how the system is actually working. This phenomenon has been analysed by developing a plausible (but simplified) mental model such as might represent the user's understanding of the system and comparing it with a user interface model, to look for sources of cognitive dissonance (Butler *et al*, 1998; Rushby, 2002). Rushby (2002) models the behaviour of a forgetful user who follows a warning display light or a non-forgetful user without warning lights and checks for emergent mode confusion. Curzon and Blandford (2004) focus on goal-based interactions and model the behaviour of a user who assumes all tasks completed when the goal is achieved, but forgets to complete some important subsidiary tasks (post-completion error). Cerone *et al* (2005) investigate the application of formal methods to the classification and analysis of task failure caused by systematic recurrence of human errors. This recurrence produces complex patterns of human behaviours, which are the result of bad habits, poor training, deficient mental models, or are associated with cognitive processes such as habituation. The error is modeled by the behavioural pattern itself, rather than by specific error states as for mode confusion and post-completion error. In particular, different categories of behavioural patterns are formally verified to be a sound and complete decomposition of an air traffic control task failure.

These formal approaches all address safety-critical aspects of interactive systems and cognitive behaviour. Only at the beginning of the new millenium, security aspects of interactive systems have been started to be systematically analysed (Cerone and Curzon, 2007; Yee, 2002; Zurko, 2005). In fact, security violations in human-computer interaction may be due to systematic causes such as cognitive overload, lack of security knowledge, and mismatches between the behaviour of the computer system and the user's mental model (Yee, 2002). The user who causes the violation may or may not be the attacker: the user may either become aware of the violation and exploit it or unwillingly allow a malicious user to exploit it. The latter situation is more complex due to two reasons. First, the violation often emerges as a consequence of a complex behavioral pattern (Cerone *et al*, 2005). Secondly, the security properties need to capture the conditions which enable a malicious user to exploit the violation (Cerone and Elbegbayan, 2007).

Rest of this Chapter

The rest of this chapter focuses on the use of formal methods in modelling and analysing security properties of interactive system. Concepts will be introduced with references to a few case studies from several fields such as e-commerce, e-voting, health systems, messaging and collaboration systems and security protocols. It is organised as follows.

The first part will introduce the reader to basic concepts in security and human-computer interaction. Then it will explore the notion of user-centred security (Zurko, 2005), present the different ways cognitive processes and usability influence the system security, and show how to model behaviours which may lead to specific error states, such as post-completion error. Finally it will show how security violations may emerge in presence of such errors, possibly associated with an additional human element as enabling condition. Behaviours will be modelled in a process algebra framework while security properties will be defined either using temporal logic or in terms of processes of the algebra.

The second part will be devoted to the modelling of complex behavioural patterns, where the enabling condition is often a social element. This part aim to propose, for some of the case studies introduced in previous parts, taxonomies of user behavioural patterns which lead to security breaches, and to formally verify that each taxonomy is a sound and complete decomposition of the negation of a given specific security property.

The third part will focus on security protocols involving human interaction, such as for ad hoc computing and electronic voting. The use of formal methods to model and analyse human interaction and its effects on the security of such protocols will be examined.

SECURITY IN HUMAN-COMPUTER INTERACTION

Security and Human-Computer Interaction are two fields of computer science that have been growing very fast and at similar growth rates during the last years. The quality of computer applications in important domains, such as e-commerce, groupware and web services, heavily counts on the presence of a user-friendly interface able to ensure a high degree of security. Therefore, security and usability are strongly intertwined in such applications and the system designers have to take them into account as a single issue rather than as separate aspects (Cerone and Elbegbayan, 2007).

An important requirement for this kind of computer applications is the need to address users whose familiarity with computer systems is in general unknown, and may actually be very low. For instance, a banking system in principle must allow all customers of the bank, independently of their skills, to perform on-line transactions. A similar situation applies to groupware systems, such as internet dating systems.

These systems also need to be trustful, in the sense that the user must be ensured that all information provided to the system is kept confidential and/or addressed to the right recipient and that all information received from the system has not been modified during transmission (data integrity) and is properly authenticated (source integrity) through digital signature and/or appropriate authentication protocols. Certification Authorities (CA) and Public Key Infrastructures (PKI) aim to achieve such trustfulness, but their efficacy may be easily invalidated by poorly designed user interfaces. Usability is therefore the actual means that allows security mechanisms to be effective.

A trivial example is given by a user who has to input a secret password using a public terminal. It is pointless to ensure a secure password distribution if the password appears in clear text when input by the user and someone else can see it on the screen. These problem is usually prevented by the user interface by replacing each of the characters of the password by a '*' in the terminal output. However, this is a protection from malicious users, but not from malicious software. If the user types the password to access a bank account online, all the software running on the user's computer has full access to that same bank account. Hence the opportunity for criminals to quickly and easily steal money during the transaction, independently of how secure the bank's computer systems is. One way to overcome this problem is the usage of a live CD, which features a bootable CD drive, whose boot programs only load software from the CD, and prevent the user from loading software from the hard disk.

The example above illustrates a situation in which the user knows how to use the interface to achieve the intended goal but vulnerabilities in the interface make security violations possible. However, we have mentioned that users of e-banking or groupware systems might have very low familiarity with computer systems. The role of the interface is therefore to safely guide the user towards the final goal of the interaction, for example the successful completion of a transaction using internet banking. If this aim is not pursued by the interface, not only the user may not achieve the intended goal, but may also leave the system in an insecure state. For instance, the interface must ensure that after a user has logged out no confidential information is left accessible to the next user on a public computer. For example a web interface that allows the user to open more windows at the same time may leave confidential information on one of the windows other than the logout window.

In addition, very few assumptions can be made on the user's behaviour. In particular, even the assumption that the user always logs out (or locks the system) before leaving the public computer unattended is not realistic. In fact, users are prone to forgetfulness, decreased attention, slips, etc. For example, it is very common to forget to complete some subsidiary tasks once the goal of the interaction has been achieved. Such a kind of user error is commonly known as post-completion error (Curzon and Blandford, 2004).

Forgetting to logout after completing an internet transaction is an example of post-completion error. While some post-completion errors can be easily prevented by requiring the user to perform actions in such an order that allows all subsidiary tasks to be performed before the goal is achieved, this is actually not a general solution. For example, to prevent users of ATM machines from forgetting their card after collecting the money, modern ATM machines do not actually issue the cash until the card is taken back by the user. This approach is not effective when the subsidiary task is the logout action, as in the transaction example above. In principle we could incorporate an automatic logout with the completion of the transaction. But what if the user wishes to perform another transaction? And what if the transaction is not successful? In such cases the user must login again and this clearly decreases the usability of the system. Moreover, we said that we cannot assume that the user always logs out (or locks the system) before leaving the public computer unattended, independently of having achieved the goal (e.g. before having completed the transaction) or not. Therefore an automatic logout not only decreases usability, but does not actually provide a general solution to the problem.

In practice, rather than trying to completely prevent security violations, we often need to compromise between security and usability and just introduce safeguards that minimise the likelihood of security violations, in a way that does not introduce much degradation in the quality and performance of the services provided to the user. In order to find the right balance between security and the quality and performance of services, it is important to analyse the user attitudes and behaviours while interacting with the system. Specific attitudes and behaviours may actually reduce the likelihood of some threats and increase the likelihood of others. For example, a user may wish to logout but the logout button is not immediately available on the current web page. A non expert user, who cannot easily navigate the website to reach a page that allows logout may panic and leave the session unattended, so causing a security threat. On the other hand, the attitude of always checking that all tasks have been completed after achieving a goal reduces the likelihood of forgetting to logout before leaving the session. It is therefore sensible to introduce safeguards only to prevent the most likely threats, that is, those threats that are more likely to occur given specific assumptions about user attitudes and behaviours.

In general, skills, knowledge, expertise, age, personality of the expected user contribute to define the patterns of user behaviour that emerge from the interaction with the computer. It is therefore important to identify those patterns of user behaviour that may lead to security violation and design the interface in such a way that reduces the likelihood of a security breach. A very simple example of common patterns of behaviour is the alternation between two passwords when using a system which requires to periodically change the password and does not accept the old password as the new one. Unfortunately, most emergent patterns of behaviour, which might appear as very simple errors at a first sight, are actually caused by very complex mental processes and need to be repeatedly decomposed before identifying those basic patterns of behaviour that can drive the interface design process. An example is given by the interaction between a system that features various usage modalities with a user who leaves the system unattended without logging out. At a first sight this might appear as a simple situation of forgetfulness. In reality the user may believe to have logged out, but, while intending to log out, might actually have performed an action that would have correctly led to a successful logout in the mode in which the user believed to work, but did not lead to logout at all in the mode in which the user was actually working. Such decomposition can go even further trying to identify the psychological causes of such mode confusion.

To summarise, we can identify three levels at which usability affects security:

1. single user action (e.g., passwords must be hidden on the display)
2. user action sequence (e.g., subsidiary tasks should precede the achievement of the goal)
3. patterns of user behaviour (e.g., unsecure patterns of behaviour should be detected and their likelihood reduced)

In the next two sections we illustrate how formal methods may be used to

- drive the system development to design secure user actions and secure sequences of user actions;
- analyse the patterns of user behaviour that may lead to security violation.

Model-Checking Driven Design

In this section we illustrate a formal methodology to drive the system development to design secure user actions and secure sequences of actions. We model the systems using the CSP (Communicating Sequential Processes) process algebra (Hoare, 1985).

First, we introduce the basic building blocks of CSP describing the notation of the language relevant to our usage. A CSP system is modelled in terms of processes and events that these processes can perform, where events may be atomic in structure or may consist of distinct components. The CSP expression *a -> P* describes a process that initially performs event *a* and then behaves as process *P*. For example, consider the process

PRINTER = accept -> print -> PRINTER

This *PRINTER* describes a process that can perform the event *accept* and then *print*, after which it returns to the original state to *accept* more documents.

The external choice operator *[]* provides the option of running either of the two processes *P* or *Q* when put together as

P [] Q

where the choice between these two processes is determined by the first event that is performed, which can be chosen by the environment. Sequential composition of *P* and *Q* can be written as

P;Q

whereas parallel composition of *P* and *Q* can be written as

P||Q.

The feature of CSP of modelling concurrency is exploited by defining the user and the system as two concurrent interacting processes. The user behaviour is triggered by a goal, which can be chosen among a list of possible goals, and consists of a sequence of interactions with the systems that aim to achieve the goal. Each interaction is seen from the user's perspective as a user action, and can be chosen among a list of possible user actions. Cognitively speaking user actions are not atomic, but consist of several mental and motor processes, which can be modelled in CSP at the appropriate abstraction level as follows.

UserAction = intend -> try -> outcome -> aware -> achieve -> UserAction

Event *intend* denotes the intention of the user to perform a certain action, while event *try* denotes the physical attempt to perform an action, which may not be the intended action. If the attempt of physically performing an action succeeds, then event *outcome* denotes the effect of that action on the system, while event *aware* denotes the awareness of such an effect by the user. Finally event *achieve* denotes how the performed action contributes to the achievement of the goal. Note that *intend, try, aware* and *achieve* represent events occurring in the user process, whereas *outcome* is actually a system events. The use of this system event allows the synchronisation between the process describing the user and the process describing the system.

The *UserAction* process represents the modelling of the generic way a user "processes" actions: it defines the cognitive architecture in which to plug the specific user and system behaviours. When interacting with a specific system (or class of systems) the *UserAction* process is instantiated with specific actions, intended and attempted by the user, and with the awareness and achievements of the outcome. The design of the overall system proceeds through the following steps

1. definition of goals and subgoals of the users and of their representation by CSP events;
2. identification of the actions needed to achieve the goal and instantiation of the cognitive architecture with those actions and their representation by CSP events;
3. identification of completion action needed to perform subsidiary tasks which do not contribute to the achievement of the goal but are essential for the security of the system and their representation by CSP events;
4. definition of the user's possible strategies to achieve the defined goals by performing the identified action and their modelling by processes with the introduction of auxiliary events to describe relevant states of the user behaviour;
5. definition of the computer system to perform the user's actions.

Completion actions identified in step 3 prevent the overall system from entering a failure state or allow it to recover from a failure state. For example an automatic logout prevents the overall system from entering a state where some confidential information is disclosed to another user and an undo button allows recovery after the user has performed an erroneous action. Step 4 is implemented through the definition of process *UserGoals*, which can be composed in parallel with the instantiation of process *UserAction* to give the full user behaviour and with process *ComputerSystem* defined in step 4 to give the behaviour of the overall system. This methodology is strongly user-centred (Zurko, 2005); in fact, the first four steps only address the user, whereas the computer system is defined only at step 5.

Even if step 5 is defined in a user-centred way by using the action introduced while building the user model, and is carried out taking into account learnability and efficiency criteria as well as the need to guarantee security properties, it is still necessary to verify that the parallel composition of the *ComputerSystem* process with the processes that characterise the user behaviour actually meets the desired criteria and security properties. This can be done using model checking (Cerone *et al*, 2007) in the way we illustrate below.

While the model provided to the model-checker consists of the overall system, properties will be built by using only events used in the user model. The typical structure of a security property to be verified is the following: "in a specific state of the user behaviour no critical action can be performed before a completion action is performed". The specific state of the system considered in the property is one of the states defined by the auxiliary CSP events introduced in step 4. Critical actions are some of the user actions defined in step 2 and their criticality is evaluated with respect to the specific state considered in the property. Finally, the "before" is a "weak until" in the sense that the property holds also when critical actions are never performed independently of performing the completion action. In Linear Time Temporal Logic (Manna and Pnueli, 1992), this formula structure is represented as follows

$$relevant\_state \rightarrow ((\, big \bigwedge \sim critical\_action\_i\,)\; W\; (\, big \bigvee termination\_action\_i\,))$$

where W is the "weak until" temporal modality. If the property above does not hold on the system model, then the model-checker automatically provides a counterexample that can be used to improve the model. The process is then iterated and terminates when we finally build a model of the system which satisfies the property.

As an example we consider a groupware system intended for use among large groups of people, with communication, collaboration, information exchange and interest matching as the main goals (Fiore and Donath, 2004; McCarthy *et al*, 2004). In particular, we consider an online interactive tool that enables conference attendees to communicate and share their thoughts and reactions about a shared event despite community size and geographic distribution (Cerone and Elbegbayan, 2007). Users may have different motivations to use such a system. These motivations, in general, depend on the user's personality, social skills, familiarity with the topics, research and professional interests, as well as practical issues such as availability of time. Motivations determine actually the users' goals in using the system. We can easily identify three possible goals for a potential user of such a system:

- expressing ideas in order to share them with other users;
- gathering information about events and people;
- establishing contacts with users who represent good matches in terms of interest and ideas.

These goals can then drive the selection of the appropriate functionalities of the system, expressed as interactions with the user (user actions). For example,

- expressing ideas requires a mechanism to allow users to set their profiles (CSP event *setup*) to be made available to the user's community, and to post or reply to messages (CSP event *post_msg*);
- gathering information about events and people by browsing the website and reading profiles (CSP event *read_profile*) and posted messages (CSP event *read_msg*);
- establishing contacts require a specific contact action (CSP event *contact*) achieving this goal.

A possible strategy of a user who wants to establish contacts is to have gathering information as a subgoal and, when gathered sufficient information, explicitly contact matching users. In order to encourage user to share their private information and to cope with legal and community policies the system needs to be equipped with a login/logout mechanisms where authorised users are authenticated. Therefore a login action is needed for achieving any goal. In this example process *UserGoals* could be defined as follows.

UserGoals = (gather_info -> GatherInfo ; GoalAchieved)
[] (establish_contact -> EstablishContact ; GoalAchieved)
[] (express_ideas -> ExpressIdeas ; GoalAchieved)

The three processes *GatherInfo*, *EstablishContact* and *ExpressIdeas* consists of choices of the actions relevant for the specific goal (for *EstablishContact* also action relevant for gathering information) or of a termination action which activates the *GoalAchieved* process. The *GoalAchieved* process allows the user to perform subsidiary tasks needed after achieving the goal, essentially the logout action, or establish a new goal, but also describes relevant states of the user behaviour such as

- having established a goal (represented as CSP event *goal_established*);
- having achieved the goal (represented as CSP event *goal_achieved*);
- having left an open session unattended without logging out (represented as CSP event *unattended*).

A first property to be verified on this system is "in the state in which the user has achieved the goal no critical action can be performed before a new goal is established or a logout performed". In this case critical actions are all actions which only authorised users can perform: *setup*, *contact*, *post_msg*, *read_profile*, *read_msg*. In fact, if these actions are performed after the authorised user has already achieved the goal, then they must be performed by an unauthorised user. Using Linear Time Temporal Logic the formula is written as follows.

$\square$ *(goal_achieved → ((~setup ∧ ~contact ∧ ~post_msg ∧ ~read_profile ∧ ~read_msg) W (goal_established ∨ logout))*

The counterexample provided by the model-checker shows a situation where the security violation occurs in a state where an open session is left unattended. A first remark is that the information provided by the counterexample allows the following definition of a more precise security property.

$\square$ *(unattended → ((~setup ∧ ~contact ∧ ~post_msg ∧ ~read_profile ∧ ~read_msg) W logout)*

This new formula focuses on the fact that the status of the interaction is given by an unattended open session independently of being the goal achieved. Moreover, the counterexample suggests that the system design must be modified by introducing security mechanisms which prevent unauthorised users from exploiting the open session.

A possible security mechanism consists of having an automatic logout as in the example of the internet transaction presented in the previous section. In the current example the automatic logout might occur after the achievement of the goal, but with all the usability issues introduced in the previous section. Alternatively, the automatic logout might occur after a period of no action by the user. Again we have usability issues similar to the ones introduced in the previous section. Moreover, this solution is not fully effective because an unauthorised user may take control of the unattended open session before the automatic logout occurs. This can be verified with model-checking by introducing specific assumptions on the time needed to an unauthorised user to take control of an unattended open session.

Another possible security mechanism consists of requesting user authentication every time a critical action has to be performed. In general this has usability issues similar to the ones illustrated in the previous section for the example of internet transaction. In the analysis of real systems we should quantify how critical are actually critical actions and performs a cost-benefit analysis before introducing security mechanisms. In our example, if it is likely that some sensitive information may be posted on the website, privacy policies might require confidentiality just for that particular information. Then authentication would only be introduced for the *read_profile* and *read_msg* actions, while the property to be verified would be

$\Box\,(\mathit{unattended} \rightarrow ((\sim\mathit{read\_profile} \wedge \sim\mathit{read\_msg})\; W\; \mathit{logout}))$

Although masquerading would still be possible and some users might be driven by the attacker to post confidential information, such information could not be read by the attacker. If instead masquerading is a security issue, then authentication would only be introduced for the *setup*, contact and *post_msg* actions, while the property to be verified would be

$\Box\,(\mathit{unattended} \rightarrow ((\sim\mathit{setup} \wedge \sim\mathit{contact} \wedge \sim\mathit{post\_msg})\; W\; \mathit{logout}))$

An important aspect of this approach is that the design must start by building a model of the user behaviour which provides the constrained environment in which the designer has to build the system. Moreover, the use of model-checking provides an additional tool to perform a predictive evaluation of the system in terms of security and usability and the way they affect each other. Therefore our approach defines a psychologically constrained architecture similar to the Programmable User Model (PUM) defined by Young *et al* (1989)

Formal Analysis of Patterns of User Behaviour

The previous section has shown a formal methodology to drive the system development to design secure user actions and secure sequences of user actions. This methodology, however, cannot rule out complex patterns of user behaviour that may lead to emergent security violations. Although we can use formal methodologies to analyse such patterns of behaviour, we are still far from being able to automate their detection and possibly elimination during the development process. It is actually unclear whether such an automatic detection and elimination will be ever possible in reality: the complex causality of patterns of behaviour in terms of user's mental processes makes the task very difficult.

In spite of such difficulties, the study of human errors in human-computer interaction and of their causal roots in human behaviour have been very intense since the 1980s and has exploited synergic efforts in a multidisciplinary approach that combine computer science, psychology, cognitive science and sociology. The original motivation for such study is the major role played by human error in the occurrence of accidents in safety-critical systems such as aviation, transportation systems, medical systems, chemical and nuclear power plants (Reason, 1990). In this context several attempts have been done in trying to classify human errors in relation to what is observed as a result of the error and to their underlying cognitive mechanisms.

A first taxonomy of type of errors was proposed by Rasmussen (1983). His classification system, known as SRK (Skill, Rule, Knowledge) associates errors with three levels of human information processing, which are characterised by different degrees of conscious control of the individual on the performed actions. With decreasing conscious control the tree levels are:

- Skill-base level, for highly practiced actions which are performed automatically with no conscious control
- Rule-based level, for actions that require the application of rules learned in a previous activity (either formal training or practical experience), with human intuition providing the conscious control in applying the rules to the specific circumstance
- Knowledge-based level, for actions which have to be consciously defined for a completely novel situation for which no rule is available.

Rasmussen's taxonomy is however limited to the degree of consciousness; it does not take into account cognitive mechanisms underlying the occurrence of the error. An improvement towards this direction was given by Reason's GEMS (Generic Error Modelling System) model (Reason, 1987 and 1990), which extends Rasmussen's SRK by describing the dynamic switching between the three different levels of information processing. Moreover, Reason relates basic error tendencies to information processing levels and to user's intention and looks for the psychological causes of errors under specific environmental conditions. Errors can therefore be classified into two categories:

- a slip results from a failure occurring while incorrectly carrying out the actions required by a correct intention;
- a mistake results from an incorrect intention that leads to an action or a sequence of actions, which are consistent with the wrong intention.

Slips arise at skill-base level and are due to the absence of conscious control while making intentions into actions. Mistakes can be rule-based or knowledge-based. Rule-based mistakes can be due to the use of an incorrect diagnostic rule either because of inappropriate learning or because of experience of previous success in using that rule. Knowledge-based mistakes usually arise in situation of high workload and can have psychological causes which range from encystement, where the individual focuses on a single problem and ignores everything else, and vagabonding, where the individual is skipping from problem to problem without spending enough time on each of them.

An important advance in characterising the psychological causes of human errors has been contributed by Hollnagel (1991). He starts analysing the observable errors, which he calls phenotype of the human error, identifies eight simple phenotypes and five complex phenotypes, and maps this observable (erroneous) behaviour to the mental mechanism that is assumed to underlie it, which he calls error genotype.

The mapping of phenotypes to genotypes is a very complex process and requires many assumptions on the way mental processes work. A way to make this mapping easier is to decompose observable failures, which we call top-level phenotypes, into simpler phenotypes aiming to reach, at the lowest level of the decomposition, phenotypes that are so simple to be immediately mapped to error genotypes. This approach has been introduced by Lindsay and Connelly (2002) in the analysis of human operator failure in an air traffic control task. Their decomposition of the task failure was based on the analysis of the results of the experiments conducted using an air traffic control simulator.

However, the decomposition of task failures in complex systems, such as the air traffic control task considered by Lindsay and Connelly (2002), is unlikely to be correct without the support of formal methods and automated tools. Lindsay and Connelly (2002) actually used CSP to define the air traffic control task and temporal logic to define the hierarchy of task failures. Their decomposition of the formula representing the top-level task failure was carried out manually and led to an incomplete set of low-level task failure.

The manual decomposition defined by Lindsay and Connelly (2002) has been reworked and automatically verified for soundness and completeness by Cerone *et al* (2005 and 2007) using a model-checking tool. The model-checking analysis not only showed that Lindsay and Connelly's (2002) decomposition was incomplete, but also provided a counterexample from which a new basic task failure was identified.

Although the model-checking analysis conducted by Cerone *et al* (2005 and 2007) is concerned with errors leading to safety violations in a safety-critical system, a similar approach can be used in a security context. Let us revisit the conference system described in the previous section. The temporal logic formula

$$\Box\,(\, unattended \rightarrow (\,(\sim read\_profile \wedge \sim read\_msg\,)\ W\ logout\,)\,)\,)$$

states that for all states in which the user has left an open session unattended no critical action can be performed before a logout is performed. We can verify that the negation of the formula above can be rewritten as

$$\Diamond\,(\, unattended \wedge (\,(\sim logout\,)\ U\ (\, read\_profile \vee read\_msg\,)\,)\,)$$

where U is the "strong until" temporal modality. Formula

$$F_1 = unattended \wedge (\,(\sim logout\,)\ U\ (\, read\_profile \vee read\_msg\,)\,)$$

represents the top-level task failure in which the user has left an open session unattended and no logout performed until a critical action is actually performed. Informal reasoning or results of experiments can lead to a decomposition of F_1 into formulae $F_{1,1},\ldots,F_{1,n(1)}$. Set $\{ F_{1,1},\ldots,F_{1,n(1)}\}$ is called a complete decomposition of F_1 with respect to a CSP model if and only if

$$F_1 \rightarrow \bigvee_{i=1}^{n} F_{1,i}$$

holds on the CSP model. A possible decomposition of F_1 is given by $\{F_{1,1},F_{1,2}\}$, where

$$F_{1,1} = \sim intended\_logout \wedge (\,\bigcirc\ unattended\,) \wedge (\,(\sim logout\,)\ U\ (\, read\_profile \vee read\_msg\,)\,)$$

$$F_{1,2} = intended\_logout \wedge (\bigcirc\ unattended\,) \wedge (\,(\sim logout\,)\ U\ (\, read\_profile \vee read\_msg\,)\,)$$

where O is the "next state" temporal modality. Formula $F_{1,1}$ defines the situation in which the user forgot to logout, whereas $F_{1,2}$ defines the situation in which the user intends to logout, but does not actually do it. Formula $F_{1,2}$ can be further decomposed into two other formulae $F_{1,2,1}$ and $F_{1,2,2}$. Formula $F_{1,2,1}$ defines the situation in which the user tries to perform the correct action to logout but finds it impossible, panics and leaves the open session unattended. Formula $F_{1,2,1}$ defines the situation in which the user tries to perform the an action different from the intended logout and leaves unaware that the session is still open. We do not show formulae $F_{1,2,1}$ and $F_{1,2,2}$, because their complexity is already high enough to make them hard to read. This decomposition can be developed through further steps but the complexity of proving the completeness of the step is likely to increase towards the lower levels of the decomposition up to a point that requires the use of model-checking.

SECURITY PROTOCOLS

Modern communications technology allows us to communicate faster than ever before, with much higher capacity for more diverse types of data. Along with its wider reach in society, in the form of both mobility and relatively affordable access, modern communications and the Internet has transformed the world we live in – serving as bedrock for electronic commerce and, other digital and communication services, raising an increasing need for a secure and trusted electronic infrastructure. The pervasive nature of the Internet, one major factor behind its success, is also proving to be its main threat. Once connected to this global network, no one is more than a few clicks away from Web servers hosting web sites transacting commerce worth millions or critical state-run infrastructures running sensitive operations; such systems are threatened by both hackers with malicious and fraudulent intent, and software technology designed using indefinite and imprecise methods.

Security protocols, being developed for more than two decades now, aim to protect and secure networked systems from such threats. Using mathematically-sound yet simple cryptographic methods, these protocols are designed to provide a range of communication security services, such as authentication, confidentiality and non-repudiation. These protocols allow networked entities to engage with each other and derive guarantees about each other's identity, state of knowledge and participation. In this section, we focus on two particular areas of security protocol design where human interaction plays a key role:

1. Secure environments for ad hoc computing. This is a rapidly developing area of computing where the emphasis is on handheld mobile devices with limited memory and processing power, communicating with nearby devices using wireless links such as wireless LANs or Bluetooth, and where peer entities are not always trusted, and
2. Electronic voting. The design of such systems is governed by social, technical, legal and often obscure requirements, where the social and human element (and trust in them) is as important as the dependability of the technical component. Moreover, the highly critical nature of voting systems where the (political) future of a nation may even depend on it makes the role of formal analysis absolutely crucial.

Ad Hoc Computing

Recent developments in the area of computing, with particular regards to ubiquitous computing and pervasive networking technologies, have raised the need for designing security protocols involving human interaction. Electronic (mobile) devices are being increasingly used to store and exchange sensitive information, and run critical applications. This coupled with the use of the wireless medium and the somewhat mobile/disposable nature of such devices means that user authentication and privacy have become ever so important. Other issues such as trust, whereby authenticating a device provides no guarantees for its behaviour, make it altogether more challenging.

Notable here is work done by Creese *et al* (2005 & 2006). They focus on multi-party protocols for ad hoc networks used to bootstrap secure communications. This is achieved by modifying existing key establishment mechanisms into protocols that rely on some form of human-to-human (such as verbal conversations) or human-to-device (such as reading from a device display panel) interaction. Such interactions are captured and formalised as low bandwidth, authenticated *empirical channels* (Creese *et al*, 2005) that could be used to convey short message strings. An *empirical channel* is essentially a notion used to refer to some form of human-to-human or human-to-device interaction, and is useful in modelling short but reliable exchanges of information, as opposed to an unreliable albeit high bandwidth digital channel (such as a wireless network link).

We consider a simple example protocol from (Creese *et al*, 2005) that demonstrates their approach. Consider a human user *A*, who wishes to print a confidential document stored on a wireless-enabled PDA, on a public printer *B*. The communication between the PDA and the printer takes place over a public wireless network, where *B* is one of the many public printers available to *A*. *A* needs to be assured that the document is indeed being sent to *B*, the public printer *A* is interacting with (and not any other within public range). The aim of the protocol is to establish a temporary session key between the PDA and the printer over an unsecured medium but also using the *empirical channel*. Such a small protocol is shown in Figure 1.

The protocol assumes pk_A and pk_B are public keys of *A* and *B* respectively, and the nonce N_A is a random challenge chosen by *A* (possibly generated by the PDA). There are two types of channel where $\rightarrow_N$ denotes the wireless link between *A* and *B*, and $\rightarrow_E$ denotes the empirical channel, which in this case is user *A* reading of the display panel of printer *B*.

A is allowed to initiate the protocol by taking its identity *A*, its public key and the nonce N_A, encrypting it with *B*'s public key and transmitting it to *B* using the wireless link. *B* responds by transmitting back to the PDA a message encrypted with *A*'s public key including the identities of both *A* and *B*, *A*'s public key, the nonce N_A and a session key *K*. *A* can only retrieve this response if the message is encrypted with pk_A, which was sent out by *A* to *B* using the first message. It still doesn't assure *A* that *B* is indeed the printer it is communicating with, since *A*'s first message could have been intercepted by some tampered printer (within range) or an active intruder attempting to compromise the session. This problem is solved by the use of the empirical channel, where *B* displays a hash value of the second message sent over the wireless link. *A* compares this value with a hash value computed by the PDA to guarantee that *B* is indeed the printer *A* is interacting with.

The introduction of *empirical channels* allows such protocols to be modelled using CSP and model-checked using FDR, the approach adopted by the authors (Creese *et al*, 2005 & 2006). These protocols are developed further by Nguyen and Roscoe (2006) for (human) group authentication. Further research however is required to develop and formalise appropriate threat models for such protocols, as opposed to the standard Dolev-Yao model. These models (Creese *et al*, 2003) need to consider both interface design issues and cognitive principles when analysing such systems. Creese *et al* (2005) briefly hint at some of these including using relatively smaller hash values or possibly using hash-dependent pictures/patterns that are more convenient for the purpose of human comparison.

Figure 1. A simple protocol providing key distribution using the notion of empirical channels

(1)	$A \rightarrow_N B$	:	$\{A, pk_A, N_A\} pk_B$
(2)	$B \rightarrow_N A$	:	$\{A, B, pk_A, N_A, K\} pk_A$
(3)	$B \rightarrow_E A$	:	PRINT *hash(Message 2)*

Electronic Voting

Electronic voting systems are voting infrastructures that use electronic means to support and provide the casting and counting of votes. This usually involves an underlying computer system which allows the voters to cast their vote and output the result of the election. Such systems are being more seriously examined and analysed than ever before. The need for this has become clear after the recent controversies surrounding the last two presidential elections in the US (Time (2001), Radford & Glaister (2004)). Apart from the obvious security requirements of *anonymity* and *ballot secrecy*, electronic voting also needs to be

- *demonstrably accurate* to provide verifiability for votes cast by the voters,
- *scalable* to work on a mass or national level,
- *recoverable* so as to avoid the repeat of whole election if a particular component (or trust in it) breaks down, and
- *usable* to allow the general electorate to participate in the system and *accessible* to those somewhat less technically apt

Electronic voting typically involves human in a variety of roles interacting with the system in a variety of ways. *Voters* involved in the voting process, who actually use the system to vote and may wish to confirm that their vote is included in the count accurately and to prove if it is not. *Vote coercers* aim to influence (vulnerable) *voters* into voting in a certain way and would also like to be assured they have done so, raising the need for *ballot secrecy* and *coercion-resistance* so as to not allow the *voters* to be able to prove how they voted. *Tellers/officials* held responsible for facilitating free and fair voting may tamper with the ballots, but who may introduce bogus votes or interfere in the counting process. *Authorities* overseeing the elections may be yet another source of threat possibly leaking or generating incorrect ballots.

Over the years a number of electronic voting protocols and schemes have emerged. Some notable ones include *FOO 92* (Fujioka *et al*, 1992), Chaum *et al*'s (2005) *Prêt à Voter* and Benaloh's (2006) scheme. We briefly describe *Prêt à Voter* here only to give an idea of how such schemes work.

The *Prêt à Voter* scheme requires ballot forms to list the candidates in randomized ordering and carry a value that is used to retrieve the order of candidates on the ballot. The voters are then allowed to make their choice, discard the candidate list and pass the selection along with the value to the tellers. The value is encrypted using some threshold cryptographic scheme so as to keep the vote secret, and only to be revealed if a minimum (threshold) number of tellers collude amongst each other. The tellers record the index value of the candidate selection and the encrypted value for each vote, and compute a digital signature over this information. The voters are provided with a copy of a receipt containing this signature (along with the corresponding information). A copy of all such receipts is then published for the public to confirm their vote is counted. Once the voting concludes, votes go through a process of mixing and re-encryption by a number of tellers, each mixing (shuffling) the receipts and re-encrypting them before passing them onto the next teller. This provides ballot secrecy and also an opportunity to check for any collusion amongst the tellers. The final phase then involves decrypting the receipts to reveal the final tally of votes, which can then be counted and verified.

Given the intricate nature of electronic voting schemes and the strict properties they need to satisfy, formal analysis and verification becomes only necessary. Notable recent efforts to this end include Mauw *et al*'s (2006) analysis of *anonymity* properties of *FOO 92* (Fujioka *et al*, 1992), Kremer and Ryan's (2005) verification of *privacy* and *fairness* of the same scheme and Delaune *et al*'s (2006) analysis of some *coercion-resistance* and *receipt-freeness* properties. Moreover, such schemes have to be more than just *trustworthy* and actually have to be *trusted* as Randell and Ryan (2006) put it, which also takes a great deal of time and trial. This makes it ever so important to understand the usability issues and analyse human behavior with respect to such schemes. Laskowski and Redish (2006), for example, discuss the use of language in instructions and ballots, while Herrnson *et al* (2006) examine other issues such as ballot navigation, changing votes and write-in votes. Yee *et al* (2006) present an approach to simplify and verify user interfaces for such systems, which involves prerendering of the interface before the election and allowing the public (users) to test and verify the system for usability and accessibility. Further research however is needed to address important properties such as *voter-verifiability* – ability of voters to verify their votes have been accurately counted – in order for electronic voting systems to be trusted; Chaum *et al*'s (2005) and Benaloh's (2006) efforts are a step in this direction.

CONCLUSION

The purpose of this chapter has been to introduce the reader to the new yet fast developing area of formal analysis of security in interactive systems. In the first part of the chapter we have presented how to incorporate security into interactive system, with a major focus on the relations between security and usability. Inspired by psychologically constrained architectures such as PUM, we have introduced a user-centred methodology for the design of secure interactive systems. This methodology is based on a rigorous model of the user behaviour that drives the system design process and on the support of a model checking tool in verifying that the system design complies with security requirements.

We have also used model checking to analyse complex patterns of user behaviour which may lead to emergent security violations but cannot be automatically detected and eliminated during the development process. We have shown the efficacy of this kind of analysis in proving the completeness of the decomposition of a top-level task failure into error phenotypes that facilitates the mapping into the underlying error genotypes.

The second part of the chapter has focussed on distributed protocols (such as those for ad hoc computing) and systems (such as electronic voting) where human interaction plays a key role. The pervasive and critical nature of such systems makes the analysis of security much more challenging.

REFERENCES

Benaloh, J. (2006). Simple Verifiable Elections. USENIX/ACCURATE Electronic Voting Technology Workshop (EVT'06), Vancouver, Canada, August 1, 2006.

Butler, R. W., Miller, P., Potts, J. N., & Carreno, V. A. (1998). A formal methods approach to the analysis of mode confusion. In *Proc. of the 17th Digital Avionics Systems Conference*, Washington, Oct 31 – Nov 6, 1998.

Butterworth, R., Blandford, A. E., & Duke, D. (2000). Demonstrating the cognitive plausibility of interactive systems. *Formal Aspects of Computing, 12*, 237–259.

Chaum, D., Ryan, P. Y. A., & Schneider, S. A. (2005). A Practical Voter-Verifiable Election Scheme. In S. C. Vimercati, P. F. Syverson, and D. Gollman, (eds.), *Computer Security - ESORICS 2005, 10th European Symposium on Research in Computer Security (ESORICS'05), Milan, Italy, September 12-14, 2005, Proceedings*, pp. 118-139.

Cerone, A., Lindsay, P., & Connelly, S. (2005). Formal analysis of human-computer interaction using model-checking. In Bernhard Aichernig and Bernhard Beckert (eds.) *Proceedings of the 3rd IEEE International Conference on Software Engineering and Formal Methods*, pp. 352–361. IEEE Computer Society.

Cerone, A., Connelly, S., & Lindsay, P. (2007). Formal Analysis of Human Operator Behavioural

Patterns in Interactive Surveillance Systems. *To appear in System and Software Modeling.* Springer-Verlag.

Cerone, A., & Curzon, P. (2007). *Proceedings of the 1st International Workshop on Formal Methods for Interactive Systems (FMIS'2006). ENTCS 183.* Elsevier.

Cerone, A., & Elbegbayan, N. (2007). Model-checking driven design of interactive systems. In Antonio Cerone and Paul Curzon (eds.) *Proceedings of the 1st International Workshop on Formal Methods for Interactive Systems. ENTCS, 183*, 3-20. Elsevier.

Clarke Jr., E. M., Grumberg, O., & Peled, D. A. (1999). *Model-checking.* The MIT Press.

Creese, S., Goldsmith, M., Roscoe, A.W. & Zakiuddin, I. (2003). The attacker in ubiquitous computing environments: formalising the threat model. *Proceedings of the Formal Aspects of Security and Trust (FAST 2003)*, Pisa, Italy.

Creese, S., Goldsmith, M., Harrison, R., Roscoe, A. W., Whittaker, P., & Zakiuddin, I. (2005). Exploiting empirical engagement in authentication protocol design. *Security in Pervasive Computing, Second International Conference, SPC 2005*, Boppard, Germany, April 6-8, 2005, Proceedings. *LNCS v3450*, 119-133.

Creese, S., Goldsmith, M., Roscoe, A. W., & Xiao, M. (2006). Bootstrapping multi-party ad-hoc security. *Proceedings of the 2006 ACM Symposium on Applied Computing (SAC)*, Dijon, France, April 23-27, 2006, pp. 369-375.

Curzon, P., & Blandford, A. E. (2004). Formally justifying user-centred design rules: A case study on post-completion errors. In E.A. Boiten, J. Derrick, and G. Smith (eds.) *Integrated Formal Methods, 2999 of Lecture Notes in Computer Science*, 461–480. Springer-Verlag, Berlin, Germany.

Delaune, S., Kremer, S., an&d Ryan, M. D. (2006). Coercion-Resistance and Receipt-Freeness in Electronic Voting. *Proceedings of the 19th IEEE Computer Security Foundations Workshop (CSFW'06)*, Venice, Italy, pp. 28-42. IEEE Computer Society.

Dix, A. J. (1991). Formal Methods for Interactive Systems. Academic Press.

Fiore, A., & Donath, J. S. (2004). Online Personals: An Overview. *ACM Computer-Human Interaction.* ACM Press.

Fujioka, A., Okamoto, T., & Ohta, K. (1992). A practical secret voting scheme for large scale elections. In J. Seberry and Y. Zheng, editors, *Advances in Cryptology —AUSCRYPT '92*, 718 of LNCS, pp. 244- 251. Springer.-Verlag

Hoare, C. A. R. (1985). *Communicating Sequential Processes.* Prentice Hall International.

Herrnson, P. S, Niemi, R. G., Hanmer, M. J., Bederson, B. B., Conrad, F. G., & Traugott, M. (2006). The Importance of Usability Testing of Voting Systems. USENIX/ACCURATE lectronic Voting Technology Workshop (EVT'06), Vancouver, Canada, August 1, 2006.

Hollnagel, E. (1991). The Phenotype of Erroneous Actions: Implications for HCI Design. G. R. S. Weir and J. L. Alty (eds.). Academic Press. 1991.

Kirwan, B. (1990). Human reliability assessment. In Evaluation of Human Work, chapter 28. Taylor and Francis.

Kirwan, B. (1992). Human error identification in human reliability assessment. part 1: Overview of approaches. *Applied Ergonomics, 25*(5), 299–318.

Kremer, S., & Ryan, M. D. (2005). Analysis of an Electronic Voting Protocol in the Applied Pi Calculus. *Proceedings of the 14th European Symposium on Programming, ESOP 2005, Edin-*

burgh, UK, April 4-8, 2005, 3444 of LNCS 186-200. Springer-Verlag.

Laskowski & Redish (2006). Making Ballot Language Understandable to Voters. USENIX/ ACCURATE Electronic Voting Technology Workshop (EVT'06), Vancouver, Canada, August 1, 2006.

Lindsay, P., & Connelly, S. (2002). Modelling Erroneous Operator Behaviours for an Air-Traffic Control Task. John Grundy and Paul Calder (eds.) Third Australasian User Interfaces Conference (AUIC2002). Conferences in Research and Practice in Information Technology, 7, 43-54. Australian Computer Society, Inc.

Manna, Z., & Pnueli, A. *The Temporal Logic of Reactive and Concurrent Systems–Specification.* Springer-Verlag.

Mauw, S., Verschuren, J. H. S., & de Vink, E. P. (2007) Anonymity groups of the FOO E-Voting scheme. *Proceedings of the Second International Workshop on Views on Designing Complex Architectures (VODCA 2006), Bertinoro, Italy, September 16-17, 2006. Electronic Notes in Theoretical Computer Science (ENTCS) 168*, 5-28. Elsevier.

McCarthy, J. F., Boyd, D., Churchill, E. F., Griswold, W. G., Lawley, E., & Zaner, M. (2004). Digital backchannels in shared physical spaces: attention, intention and contention. CSCW '04: Proceedings of the 2004 ACM Conference on Computer Supported Cooperative Work, 550-553. ACM Press, New York, USA.

Nguyen, L., & Roscoe, A. W. (2006). Efficient group authentication protocols based on human interaction. *Proceedings of the Foundations of Computer Security and Automated Reasoning for Security Protocol Analysis (FCS-ARSPA'06), Seattle, US*, August 15-16, 2006, pp. 9-31

Radford, T., & Glaister, D. (2004). Hi-tech voting machines 'threaten' US polls. *The Guardian*, 16 February 2004.

Randell, B., & Ryan, P. Y. A. (2005). Voting technologies and trust. In T. Dimitrakos, F. Martinelli, P. Ryan, and S. Schneider (eds.) *Formal Aspects of Security and Trust (FAST) 2005, 3866* of Lecture Notes in Computer Science, 1–4. Berlin, Germany: Springer-Verlag.

Rasmussen, J. (n/d). Skills, rules, knowledge: Signals, signs, and symbols and other distinctions in human performance models. *IEEE Transactions on Systems, Man, and Cybernetics, 13*(3), 257-267. IEEE Computer Society.

Reason, J. (1987). Generic Error-Modelling system ({GEMS}): A Cognitive Framework for Locating Common Human Error Forms, Chapter 7. J. Rasmussen, K. Duncan and J. Leplat (eds.) New Technology and Human Error, 63-83. John Wiley and Sons.

Reason, J. (1990). *Human Error.* Cambridge University Press.

Rushby, J. (2002, February). Using model-checking to help discover mode confusions and other automation surprises. *Reliability Engineering and System Safety, 75*(2), 167–177.

Svenson, O. (1989). On expert judgements in safety analysis in the process industries. *Reliability Engineering and System Safety, 25*, 219–256.

TIME (2001). The Wildest Election in History. *Time Magazine*, Glencoe Social Studies, Current Events Update, Spring 2001, 12-13.

Yee, K-P. (2002) User interaction design for secure systems. In at al. R. Deng, (Ed.), *Proceddings of ICICS 2002, 2513 of Lecture Notes in Computer Science*,278–290. Springer-Verlag, Berlin.

Yee, K. P., Wagner, D., Hearst, M., & Bellovin, S. M. (2006). Prerendered User Interfaces for Higher-Assurance Electronic Voting. USENIX/ACCURATE Electronic Voting Technology Workshop (EVT'06), Vancouver, Canada, August 1, 2006.

Young, R. M., Green, T. R. G., & Simon, T. (1989). Programmable Users Models for Predictive Evaluation of Interface Design. *ACM CHI 89 Human Factors in Computing Systems Conference*, 15-19. ACM Press.

Zurko, M. E. (2005). User-centered security: Stepping up to the grand challenge. *In Proceedings of ACSAC 2005*, 187–202. IEEE.

KEY TERMS

Coercion-Resistance: A property of electronic voting systems where a voter is not able to prove to a coercer what way he/she voted. This is an important property as it prevents voters being bought or blackmailed by those who intend to unlawfully influence the results of the election.

CSP: Communicating Sequential Processes, or CSP, is a formal language for describing patterns of interaction for concurrent systems (in computer science). First described by Sir Professor Tony Hoare at Oxford in 1978, it is a member of the family of mathematical theories of concurrency known as process algebras. It is traditionally written in a fairly mathematical notation, with special symbols representing its operators, and is typeset more like mathematics than a typical programming language.

Electronic-Voting: A voting infrastructure that uses electronic means to support and provide the casting and counting of votes. This usually involves an underlying computer system which allows the voters to cast their vote and output the result of the election.

Empirical Channel: A formalisation of a medium of communication which results from human-to-human or human-to-device interaction. Some information communicated verbally from one person to another, read from a device display panel or input into a keyboard of a computer are all examples of communication over *empirical channels*. They are considered low bandwidth and reliable.

Human Error: A class of errors that (in the context of interactive systems) refer to any undesired user action or user-system interaction that leads to the violation of a system goal. Such an interaction may also violate some security goal of the system, that is leakage of confidential information or facilitate unauthorised access to the system.

Model-Checking: An approach to verifying whether a model (of a software or hardware system) satisfies a set of formal assertions and constraints. This usually involves the use of a tool, which allows a model to be specified using a particular formal language (such as CSP), along with the property that it needs to be checked against, and then check whether the model would always satisfy the property for all its executions. The check involves the use of a state exploration technique to ensure that all possible states of the system are explored as desired. In case if the model fails to satisfy the stated property, the tool returns an execution path demonstrating the failure.

Security Protocol: A security protocol is essentially a communication protocol – an agreed sequence of actions performed by two or more communicating entities in order to accomplish some mutually desirable goal – that makes use of cryptographic techniques, allowing the communicating entities to achieve a security goal. A particular protocol, however, may enable the communicating parties to establish one or more such goals. Some common security goals include (data and entity) authentication, confidentiality and integrity.

Chapter XXVI
Internet Crime:
How Vulnerable Are You? Do Gender, Social Influence and Education play a Role in Vulnerability?

Tejaswini Herath
State University of New York, USA

H. R. Rao
State University of New York, USA

Shambhu Upadhyaya
State University of New York, USA

ABSTRACT

It is estimated that over 1 billion people now have access to the Internet. This unprecedented access and use of Internet by individuals around the world, however, is accompanied by malicious and mischievous activities online. With the traditional crimes such as fraud, identity theft, and harassment now being committed with the use of the Internet, and networked home computers being exploited to carry out attacks such as denial of service, spamming, phishing and virus/worm propagation, it has become important to investigate security and privacy issues as they pertain to individual Internet users. To date very little is known about what characteristics of internet users affect their computing and on-line behaviors as they relate to security online. While some attention has been paid to understand the security issues affecting corporations, research investigating security issues as they relate to home users is still in infancy. Drawing from disciplines such as criminology, sociology, consumer fraud, and information security, this study seeks to find the role of computing skills and computer training, social influence, and gender on person's vulnerability to Internet crimes. Our findings are significant and shed light in this important area of Internet crime contributing to the information security literature.

INTRODUCTION

Explosive growth in the use of the Internet around the globe has been noted by several surveys. The web statistics compiled by Internet World Stats (http://www.internetworldstats.com/stats.htm) indicates that estimated over 1 billion people around the world now have access to the Web. The 2005 UCLA Internet Report notes that Internet use at home has increased consistently in the past five years. Typically, internet users participate in online activities such as e-mail, Web browsing, working from home, accessing news stories, seeking information, instant messaging, using the Internet in lieu of the library for school work, playing games, and managing personal finance (Center for the Digitial Future, 2005). With the wide use of Internet, there now exist a significant opportunities to carry out malicious and mischievous activities (Dowland *et al.*, 1999). This is evident through the staggering numbers available on the numbers of crimes committed over internet and losses they pose.

With the traditional crimes such as fraud, identity theft, and harassment now being committed with the use of the Internet, and networked home computers being exploited to carry out attacks such as denial of service, spamming, phishing and virus/worm propagation, it is important to investigate what characteristics of individual internet users affect their computing and on-line behaviors. According to statistics gathered for the E-Crime Watch Survey the chances of falling victim to a computer virus, phishing attack, malicious hack attempt or other cyber security dangers are currently running at 70% (http://news.bbc.co.uk/2/hi/technology/3708260.stm).

Sparse yet some information security literature has focused on behavioral components of information security in an attempt to understand the security related behaviors of individuals (for example, (Hazari, 2005; Hu & Dinev, 2005; Sasse & Brostoff, 2001; Stanton *et al.*, 2004; Stanton *et al.*, 2005). While many of these studies have been conducted in organizational settings others have focused on behaviors pertaining only to the software use behaviors. Although, as discussed in detail later, we can draw valuable insights from these studies, many other online risks faced by individual internet users in home setting such as social engineering tactics or awareness issues were outside the scope of these studies. Drawing from disciplines such as criminology, sociology, consumer fraud, and information security, this paper lays a theoretical foundation to evaluate the role of computing skills and computer training, social influence, culture, individual values, age and gender on person's vulnerability to online risks. We take the approach of understanding on-line risks and vulnerabilities and factors that relate to them. Such understanding will allow us to effectively design defense mechanisms to overcome these issues. Although, consumer fraud literature in marketing has used such approach, this approach is new to online risks and information security area.

This article is organized as follows. We first discuss various types of crimes committed on-line that affect individual citizens. Then we define vulnerability related to on-line activities based on distinct characteristics of each. Drawing from the disciplines of criminology, sociology and marketing (specifically consumer fraud literature in marketing), we present a theoretical model along with propositions to understand the role of computing skills and computer training, age and gender on person's vulnerability to internet crimes.

Nature of Cyber Crime

Wide range of crimes that affect individual citizens are now being committed through the Internet. The Internet Fraud Compliant Center (IFCC) report shows that traditional crimes affecting individuals such as fraud, identity theft, and harassment are on the rise, and are now committed with the use of the Internet ((IFCC),

2004). These crimes include Internet fraud, child pornography, computer intrusion, SPAM e-mail, and identity theft. The financial loss incurred through the above fraudulent activities is extensive but the new emergence of crime against children and crime against women using the Internet is even more disturbing. Crimes perpetrated through internet not only cause financial losses but also have implications for emotional stress and psychological trauma. While more difficult to quantify, non monetary losses can be substantial and possibly greater than monetary losses (Lee & Soberon-Ferrer, 1997). In addition to losses posed to individuals and organizations, these on-line risks have implications for security of overall cyber infrastructure. Individuals may unknowingly introduce a virus that compromises the security of their own computer by innocently opening e-mails from unknown origins while not running current antivirus software. By forwarding such message onto other people, virus can spread quickly and virtually undetected (Anderson, 2005). In addition, hackers, spammers or phishers can take advantage of infected computers. Symantec estimates that between one to two million computers worldwide are infected with the bot software, which allows a system to be surreptitiously remote-controlled by hackers to carry out malicious activity (McMillan, 2005). These networks of zombie computers, most of which are home computers, have become a weapon of choice for spammers and phishers. In addition, with these zombie networks, attackers can carry out denial of service attacks and distribute viruses and worms to enormous number of computers on the network.

Cyber crime is a still evolving term and is a broadly used term to describe criminal activity committed on computers or the Internet (http://www.webopedia.com/TERM/c/cyber_crime.html). Cyber crime encompasses the use of computer technology to commit either (a) social harms that have already been identified and outlawed –"traditional crimes" such as trespass, burglary, theft, stalking etc. or (b) new types of social harm that is specific to computer technology such as DoS attacks. Encyclopedia Britannica describes 'Cyber crime' as the use of a computer as an instrument to further illegal ends, such as committing fraud, trafficking in child pornography and intellectual property, stealing identities, or violating privacy.

To effectively deal with a crime, it is important to understand the characteristics of victims as well as characteristics of criminals. In an on-line environment both of these have turned out to be difficult for several reasons. Internet has provided a tool to criminals to commit the crimes with distance, anonymity and ease. Legal avenues have turned out to be more difficult to pursue due to wide range of reasons including difficulty in finding the perpetrators as well as difficulty in prosecuting due to jurisdiction limitations. To understand victimization patterns, considering actual victimization to evaluate the characteristics that contribute to it has also proven to be difficult for the following reasons. Such data about on-line victimization is sparse. Furthermore, it is recognized that victims are reluctant to report victimization and often do not report due to guilt or shame (Lee & Soberon-Ferrer, 1997).

VULNERABILITY TO INTERNET CRIMES

Recently some information security literature has tried to understand the security related behavior of individuals. For instance, Sasse et.al. (2001) identify issues that can lead to undesirable behavior with regard to how employees handle passwords. Stanton et.al. (2004, 2005) indicate that training, awareness, computer usage and number of individuals supervised all positively influenced an employee's password behavior. Hazari (2005) studied the perceptions of employees regarding firewall software and provide managerial implications. Although, many of these studies observe the behaviors in organizational setting, they provide valuable insight into factors leading to security behaviors that can be adopted in this study. In home setting, Anderson (2005) studied the security behavioral intentions of internet users while Hu and Dinev (2005) studied the behavior of internet users in regards to anti-spyware programs.

This study instead focuses on vulnerabilities related to on-line activities in line with consumer fraud and victimology literature. We take a different approach than studies mentioned above for several reasons. First, most of the above studies focus on security behaviors pertaining only to the software related behaviors such as antivirus software use, use of firewalls, and password selection. Many of the on-line crimes involve other facets of traditional fraud that are not considered in these studies. In addition, as Anderson (2005) points out, unlike in organizational setting, individual home user, is not trained or required to have security plan. Individual home user must take initiative to educate himself about the security precautions that entail both the technology solutions as well as other precautions that are pertinent in traditional fraud. As found by Hu and Dinev (2005), in most cases the security behavior (lapse) is not the result of rational decision but rather a consequence of lack of understanding of real implications of privacy and security. An individual, who is aware of the problems and available solutions such as antivirus software, may undertake security related actions. However, lack of computing knowledge or skills may impede the security actions such as having up to date antivirus, having firewall, or using appropriate security settings. Furthermore, many a times the vulnerability may exist due to mere lack of awareness. For example, a recent survey sponsored by America Online with support from the National Cyber Security Alliance found that as many as 20% of home computers were infected with a virus and 80% contained software such as spyware and adware. Shockingly, approximately two-thirds of the home survey participants believed that they were adequately protected (Roberts, 2004). Lack of understanding about issues related to internet activities such as privacy and security policies of vendors, security safeguards related to on-line transactions can also contribute to likelihood of on-line victimization. It has been argued that many of these individuals are unaware that their individual habits and computer usage patterns can impact the security and privacy of their own personal data (Anderson, 2005). This lack of awareness or understanding is an important issue and is not considered by many of already existing information security studies.

Predisposition to on-line victimization may also arise from differences in cognitive thinking and abilities. For example, in computer crimes such as phishing, identity theft and other frauds, social engineering tactics taking advantage of trusting nature of individuals may play a bigger role rather than computing abilities of that individual. In personal fraud context Titus (1999) notes that victims of some types of personal fraud may possess highly socially-valued individual characteristics such as good citizenship, respect for authority, unsuspicious nature etc. that, unfortunately, can be exploited by con artists in scams designed for that purpose. Consumer fraud studies such as (Langenderfer & Shimp, 2001; Lee & Geistfeld, 1999; Lee & Soberon-Ferrer, 1997) give us a valuable guideline to evaluate all these issues. In this study we recognize that vulnerabilities to internet crime may arise from various computing and internet activities, trusting tendencies as well as awareness issues related to on-line risks. We define them as (1) vulnerability related to computing and internet habits (2) vulnerability related to trusting tendencies (social engineering), and (3) vulnerability related to awareness of issues related to computer crimes

Influencing Factors

The Structural-Choice Model of victimization theory (Meier & Miethe, 1993) integrates the current predominant theories of victimization, namely lifestyle-exposure theory and routine-activity theory. Lifestyle-exposure theory accounts for changes in victimization risks across social groups. Lifestyle characteristics such age, gender, and education may predispose individuals to riskier situations. Recent reports show that the American population has unprecedented access to the Internet from their own homes. Now over 78.6 percent of Americans go online (Center for the Digitial Future, 2005). The household members using these computers vary in age, sex, race, educational background, personality and socioeconomic status. Thus their knowledge of technology and related processes are also diverse. Information systems research has considered many of these variables in evaluating the comfort level in using the technology. Researchers have argued that many of these individuals are unaware that their individual habits and computer usage patterns can impact the security and privacy of their own personal data (Anderson, 2005).

Vulnerability literature also considers social interaction paradigm. This paradigm explains vulnerability to fraud based on the asymmetry of social relationships and social isolation. Research considering social paradigm posits that family members, friends and peers are valuable resources for an individual. These resources provide psychological support and information, thereby increasing a consumer's knowledge and awareness. Peer effect and social influence has also been considered extensively in information systems research. Many studies have found that the environment around a person, i.e, peers, influence person's behavior.

Computer Knowledge and Computing Skills

Level of education is considered as a predictor in many vulnerability studies(Lee & Soberon-Ferrer, 1997; McGhee, 1983). Computing skills are especially important in on-line context. Skills obtained by the formal and informal computing education can enhance an individual's comfort level and give more control in carrying out computing tasks. Computing education and skills can be expected to have direct impact on how the person will carry out the activities related to computer security and thus reducing the exposure to the Internet crime. Also the more exposure an individual has to computing environment, he/she is more likely to be aware of the crimes related to Internet use and tactics used for exploitation.

Figure 1. Model

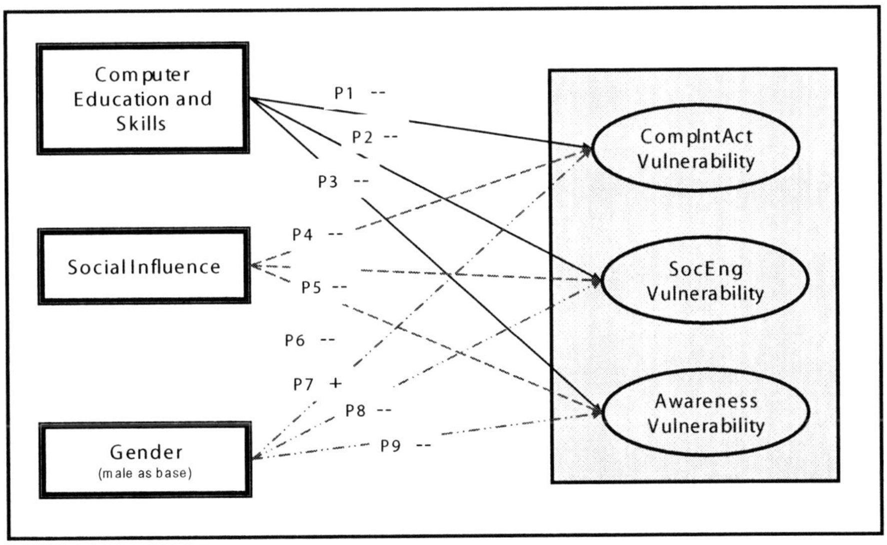

This is likely to induce risk averse behavior and reduce the vulnerability related to these issues. Therefore we can posit that:

P1. Level of computer education and skills will be negatively associated with vulnerability related to computing and Internet activities (CompIntActVulnerability)
P2. Level of computer education and skills will be negatively associated with vulnerability related to social engineering (SocEngVulnerability), and
P3. Level of computer education and skills will be negatively associated with vulnerability related to computer crime awareness of issues (AwarenessVulnerability).

Social Influence

Information systems research has considered role of social influence (Venkatesh *et al.*, 2003), social factors (Thompson *et al.*, 1991) and subjective norm (Davis *et al.*, 1989). In general, what significant others think an individual should do, influences individual's intention to perform a behavior. Sasse et al (Sasse & Brostoff, 2001) find that risk of embarrassment plays a role in security related behavior indicating that a social component influences individual behavior in the workplace. Individual can also benefit from the knowledge his/her peers have to draw upon the skills of the peers to carry out security activities, thus reducing vulnerability.

Consumer fraud literature recognizes that an individual can draw upon support and information from the family, friends and peers, thereby decreasing the vulnerability to fraud. In the Internet crime context, an individual can obtain direct or indirect knowledge regarding the computer worms, viruses, new scams and frauds which will in turn enhance the awareness of this issue and reduce individual's vulnerability to being victim of such crimes. Thus we can expect:

P4. Social influence to be negatively associated with vulnerability related to computing and internet activities (CompIntActVulnerability),
P5. Social influence to be negatively associated with vulnerability related to social engineering (SocEngVulnerability), and
P6. Social influence to be negatively associated with vulnerability related to computer crime awareness of issues (AwarenessVulnerability).

Gender

In on-line victimization, role of gender can be discussed from several different aspects. The gender based attitudinal, emotional, educational, perceptional, cognitive, and skill level differences may affect the vulnerability of a internet user (Herath *et al.*, 2006). Prior IT research has considered gender role and differences in variety of areas including information systems in organizations, e-mail usage, and Internet use. These studies have shown relevance of gender on how an individual adopts, perceives, and uses technology. Several studies have considered gender differences in specific computer related topics such as computer anxiety (Quereshi & Hoppel, 1995), computer skills (Harrison & Rainer, 1992), technostress (Elder *et al.*, 1987), attitudes towards computers and factors influencing computer usage (Teo & Lim, 1996). Based on this prior research females on average can be expected to be less cognoscente in the computer security activities and we can expect that:

P7. Females to be likely to exhibit more vulnerability related to computing and internet activities (CompIntActVulnerability) than males.

Drawing upon the socio-linguistic literature, Gefen and Straub (Gefen & Straub, 1997) note that "women perceive networking more useful than do men, and thus have tendency to see support, intimacy and cooperative behavior through e-mail. E-commerce literature shows that women are involved in different activities on-line than men. More specifically, women are found to use the Internet more for interpersonal communication, information search or education, while men use the Internet more for one-way communication, entertainment, or personal finance (Banerjee *et al.*, 2005). Women are more likely to get information from their peers and be more aware of the issues.

Women are more risk averse than men. They have been found to process information in more detail and thus more aware of and sensitive to changes in their environments (Meyers-Levy & Maheshwaram, 1991). Several surveys conducted in 1990s as well as a 2002 survey by Harrison Interactive confirms that women conveyed more concerns about the potential misuse of their personal information. Based on prior literature and results of their own study, Finucane et.al. (Finucane *et al.*, 2000) find that risks tend to be judged lower by men than by women and by white people than by people of color. Women are likely to have more information about the issues and are likely to be conservative in giving out personal information. Thus we can expect that:

P8. Females are likely to exhibit less vulnerability related to social engineering (SocEngVulnerability) than males, and
P9. Females are likely to exhibit less vulnerability related to computer crime awareness of issues (AwareVulnerability) than males.

METHODOLOGY AND RESULTS

The study was carried out using a cross-sectional survey in a large north-eastern U.S. university. Participant's anonymity was assured to encourage the honest participation. The invitations to participate in the survey were distributed to students enrolled in undergraduate-level courses and yielded 177 responses. Two classes from different disciplines were used to achieve diversity in computing skills. The average age of the respondents was 20.5 years. All respondents were in a bachelor degree program, and had been using the Internet for more than 4 years.

Dependent Variables: Vulnerability

No previously validated questionnaire was available for specifically measuring the *vulnerability to internet crimes*. Several consumer fraud studies have considered 'vulnerability index' to study consumer vulnerability to market fraud and identity theft based on the condition that apply to a respondent (Lee & Soberon-Ferrer, 1997; Milne, 2003). For this study, the survey questions were adapted from a detail review of the questionnaire developed by National Computer Security Alliance (NCSA), tips available for the consumers on FTC website for safe use of computers as well as tips available from websites of task forces fighting against phishing and cyber stalking. Separate vulnerability indexes (factors) were calculated based upon the responses to these questions related to computing habits, social engineering aspects and awareness issues.

The scores of vulnerability indices were obtained by adding the scores of the responses. These scores were kept in continuous form rather than dividing them into ordinal levels. Converting continuous data into ordinal levels can loose the level of detail and use of continuous data is recommended whenever possible. Principal component factor analysis was performed on the vulnerability items. Results suggest that 3 factors exist. The Cronbach alpha values on three vulnerability measures were ComplntActVulnerability = .61, SocEngVulnerability = 0.6 and AwarenessVulnerability = 0.88. Although, Cronbach alpha of 0.7 is considered acceptable, a lenient cut-off of .60 is common in exploratory research.

Explanatory Variables

Computing knowledge and skills a measure of level of computing expertise a participant has in computing and internet related activities. Previous research considers computing skills to be comprised of participant's education level, computer usage as well as skills in using various tools or programs (Harrison & Rainer, 1992). This study adopts a similar view. The computer knowledge and skills in this study comprise of the years of computer use and level of computing skills in word processing, e-mail and Internet usage (Cronbach alpha = 0.67). In this study the level of expertise in terms of skill level was captured by participant's own perception of skill level in these areas.

Social influence is measured with amount of expertise participant has as a result of expertise of people around. Social influence in this study considered the level of computing help available to the participant in case of emergency. Participants were also asked about the level of experience their peers have at home and at work (Cronbach alpha= 0.5).

Variables considered in this study are summarized in Table 1.

SPSS 11.5 was used for testing relationships. Since the study needed to consider three separate and distinct dependent variables, a separate stepwise regression analysis was performed for each dependent variable with all three independent variables. The results of stepwise regression analyses are summarized in Table 2.

Results of the first regression show that level of computer experience and computer skills (- .010, $p < 0.05$) is negatively related to vulnerability indicating that higher level of computer experience and skills reduce the vulnerability related to computing and Internet activities. Social influence was not found to be significant predictor in this regression. Gender was found to be positively associated with vulnerability (1.432, $p < 0.01$) indicating that females are likely to take less security precautions such as use of firewalls, antivirus, using stronger passwords, setting security settings on Internet browsers among other and thus are likely to more vulnerable.

In the second regression we tested the vulnerability related to social engineering tactics. The same set of independent variables was considered in this regression. Level of computer experience and computer skills (- .005, $p < 0.01$) was found to be negatively related to vulnerability indicating that individuals with higher level of computer experience and skills are likely to be less vulnerable to social engineering tactics . As expected, gender was found to be negatively associated

Table 1. Summary of variables considered

Variable	Items
Computer training and skills	- Years of computer experience - Skills in computing activities such as word processing skills, electronic mail skills and Internet skills
Social Influence	- Level of help available in case of emergency - Experience level of peers at home and at work
Computer and Internet activity Vulnerability	- Use of products such as antivirus software and firewalls - Security and password practices - Internet security settings and activities (such as file sharing) - Internet safe practices
Social Engineering Vulnerability	- Responses to spam mail, pop-up windows - Responses to other social engineering tactics
Internet Crime Awareness Vulnerability	- Awareness related to various on-line frauds

Table 2. Results of stepwise regression analyses: Parameter estimates

	Regression 1		Regression 2		Regression 3	
Independent Variables	ES	Vulnerability Related to Computing and Internet Knowledge	ES	Vulnerability Related to Social Engineering	ES	Vulnerability Related to Awareness Issues
Computing knowledge and Skills	(-)	- .010*	(-)	- .005**	(-)	.398***
Social Influence	(-)	-.075	(-)	.016	(-)	.006
Gender (Male as base)	(+)	1.432 **	(-)	-.387*	(-)	-2.212*
R^2		.072 **		.059**		.027*

*p < 0.05
** p < 0.01
*** p < 0.001
Expected Signed are denoted in parentheses in ES columns

with vulnerability (-.387, $p < 0.05$) indicating that females are likely to be less vulnerable to social engineering techniques.

Third and last regression tested for the effect of computing knowledge and skills, social influence and gender on vulnerability related to awareness regarding on-line frauds. Surprisingly, the level of computer experience and computer skills (.398, $p < 0.001$) was found to be positively associated with awareness vulnerability. Gender, was found to be negatively related with awareness vulnerability (-2.212, $p < 0.05$) indicating that females are likely to be more aware of the on-line frauds. Findings are summarized in Table 3.

DISCUSSION AND FUTURE RESEARCH

A study carried out in US by America Online and the National Cyber Security Alliance stated that internet users at home are not as safe as they believe. With increased internet use, we need to understand the relative importance of socio-demographic factors that affect an individual's vulnerability to Internet-based crimes. Recent trends show that traditional crimes such as harassment, fraud, and identity theft are now committed with the use of the Internet. This article investigates role of gender, computing skills and the societal context of the internet user in predicting vulnerability to Internet crimes. Such understanding will be useful in educating individuals and households about cyber security and will be essential for law enforcement agencies to intervene before a crime is committed.

Our findings indicate that gender has an impact in understanding vulnerability. While women seem to undertake fewer security precautions in their computer and Internet use, from this sample, they seem to be more aware of internet crime issues. They also seem to be more risk averse and less likely to fall for social engineering tactics. Although, this study finds support for role of gender in vulnerability to on-line crime, it should be noted that computing gender differences observed and studied in wide range of samples disappear in certain select samples. For example, (Parsuraman & Igbaria, 1990) found no male-female differences on attitudes towards computers among highly educated participants holding managerial positions in organizations

Table 3. A summary of findings and implications

		Findings
P1	*Level of computer education and skills will be negatively associated with vulnerability related to computing and Internet activities (CompIntActVul).*	Weakly Supported
P 2	*Level of computer education and skills will be negatively associated with vulnerability related to social engineering (SocEngVul).*	Weakly Supported- (Significant but effect size very small)
P 3	*Level of computer education and skills will be negatively associated with vulnerability related to computer crime awareness of issues (AwareVul).*	Not Supported (Significant but opposite direction)
P 4	*Social Influence will be negatively associated with vulnerability related to computing and Internet activities (CompIntActVul).*	Not Supported†
P 5	*Social Influence will be negatively associated with vulnerability related to social engineering (SocEngVul).*	Not Supported
P 6	*Social Influence will be negatively associated with vulnerability related to computer crime awareness of issues (AwareVul).*	Not Supported
P 7	*Females are likely to exhibit more vulnerability related to computing and Internet activities (CompIntActVul) than males*	Strongly Supported
P 8	*Females are likely to exhibit less vulnerability related to social engineering (SocEngVul) than males.*	Supported
P 9	*Females are likely to exhibit less vulnerability related to computer crime awareness of issues (AwareVul).*	Strongly Supported

† *Note: Although the results were not found to be statistically significant, the sign of the relationship was found to be in the expected direction.*

that are more dependent on computer technology (e.g., accounting, finance, information systems and marketing firms). It is understandable that education and computer training will make user more comfortable with computing tasks such as loading and updating anti-virus software. Education is also likely to make user savvier about the privacy and security issues. On the other hand, elderly women, perhaps with very little knowledge of computers may likely be more vulnerable. Thus the interaction between the gender, education, age etc. needs further investigation.

Our study also finds significant effect of level of computing experience and computing skills on stated vulnerabilities. However, influence of social influence was found to be insignificant for all three vulnerabilities. This could be due to low reliability of the measurement scale. Although factor analysis showed sufficient evidence to consider these items, Cronbach alpha was relatively low (0.5) indicating testing with larger sample.

The research in consumer fraud area considers cognitive deficiency paradigm which proposes that persons with limited ability to process information are more vulnerable to fraud. Reading and decision making skills gained through formal schooling are resources that people can mobilize when coping with the complexities of the environment (McGhee, 1983). Thus, education can be seen as an important determinant of vulnerability. However due to the nature of sample, which is somewhat homogenous in education level, we did not consider formal education as one of the factors.

Age has also been discussed in vulnerability literature. Normal aging process has been argued to give rise to cognitive impairment (Lee & Soberon-Ferrer, 1997). It is however recognized that cognitive impairment is influenced not only by biological aging but also by psychological, cultural and environmental factors (Lee & Soberon-Ferrer, 1997). We did not consider age in this study due to very close range of age in the given sample. We hope to consider and investigate this issue further.

ACKNOWLEDGMENT

This research supported in part by National Science Foundation Grant No. 0417095. Usual disclaimer applies.

REFERENCES

(IFCC), I. F. C. C. (2004). Ic3 2004 Internet Fraud Report, January 1, 2004-December 31, 2004. Retrieved March 15, 2005, from http://www.ifc-cfbi.gov/strategy/2004_IC3Report.pdf.

Anderson, C. (2005). *Creating Conscientious Cybercitizen: An Examination of Home Computer User Attitudes and Intentions Towards Security.* Paper presented at the Information Systems.

Banerjee, S., Kang, H., Bagchi-Sen, S., & Rao, H. R. (2005). Gender Divide in the Use of the Internet Applications. *International Journal of E-Business Research, 1*(2), 24-39.

Center for the Digitial Future. (2005). *2005 Digital Future Report*: USC Annenberg School.

Davis, F. D., Bagozzi, R. P., & Warshaw, P. R. (1989). User Acceptance of Computer Technology: A Comparison of Two Theoretical Models. *Management Science, 35*(8), 982-1002.

Dowland, P. S., Furnell, S. M., Illingworth, H. M., & Reynolds, P. L. (1999). Computer Crime and Abuse: A Survey of Public Attitudes and Awareness. *Computers and Security, 18*(8), 715-726.

Elder, V. B., Gardner, E. P., & Ruth, S. R. (1987). Gender and Age in Techno Stress: Effects on White Collar Productivity. *Government Finance Review, 3*, 17-21.

Finucane, M., Slovic, P., Mertz, C. K., Flynn, J., & Satterfield, T. A. (2000). Gender, Race, and Perceived Risk: The `White Male' Effect. *Health, Risk and Society, 2*(2), 159-172.

Gefen, D., & Straub, D. (1997). Gender Differences in the Perception and Use of E-Mail: An Extension to the Technology Acceptance Model. *MIS Quarterly, 21*(4), 389-400.

Harrison, A. W., & Rainer, R. J. J. (1992). The Influence of Individual Differences on Skill in End-User Computing. *Journal of Management Information Systems, 9*, 93-111.

Hazari, S. (2005). Perceptions of End-Users on the Requirements in Personal Firewall Software: An Exploratory Study. *Journal of Organizational and End User Computing, 17*(3), 47-65.

Herath, T. C., Bagchi-Sen, S., & Rao, H. R. (2006). Vulnerability to Internet Crime and Gender Issues. In E. Trauth (Ed.), *Gender and Information Technology Encyclopedia*: Idea Group Inc.

Hu, Q., & Dinev, T. (2005). Is Spyware and Internet Nuisance or Public Menace. *Communications of the ACM, 48*(8), 61-66.

Langenderfer, J., & Shimp, T. A. (2001). Consumer Vulnerability to Scams, Swindles, and Fraud: A New Theory of Visceral Influences on Persuasion. *Psychology and Marketing, 18*(7), 763-783.

Lee, J., & Geistfeld, L. V. (1999). Elderly Consumers' Receptiveness to Telemarketing Fraud. *Journal of Public Policy & Marketing, 18*(2), 208-218.

Lee, J., & Soberon-Ferrer, H. (1997). Consumer Vulnerability to Fraud: Influencing Factors. *The Journal of Consumer Affairs, 31*(1), 70-89.

McGhee, J. (1983). Vulnerability of Elderly Consumers. *International Journal of Aging and Human Development, 17*(3), 223-246.

McMillan, R. (2005). Zombie Armies Attack British PCs.

Meier, R. F., & Miethe, T. D. (1993). Understanding Theories of Criminal Victimization. *Crime and Justice, 17*, 459-499.

Meyers-Levy, J., & Maheshwaram, D. (1991). Exploring Differences in Males and Females Processing Strategies. *Journal of Consumer Research, 18*, 63-70.

Milne, G. (2003). How Well Do Consumers Protect Themselves from Identity Theft. *The Journal of Consumer Affairs, 37*(2), 388-402.

Parsuraman, S., & Igbaria, M. (1990). An Extension of Gender Differences on Determination of Computer Anxiety and Attitudes toward Microcomputers among Managers. *International Journal of Man-Machine Studies, 32*, 327-340.

Quereshi, S., & Hoppel, C. (1995). Profiling Computer Predispositions. *Journal of Professional Services Marketing, 12*, 73-83.

Roberts, P. (2004). *Aol Survey Finds Rampant On-line Threats, Clueless Users*: Computer World.

Sasse, M. A., & Brostoff, S. (2001). Transforming the 'Weakest Link' - a Human/Computer Interaction Approach to Usable and Effective Security. Bt Technology Journal. *BT Technology Journal, 19*(3), 122-131.

Stanton, J. M., R., M. P., Stam, K. R., & Jolton, J. (2004). *Behavioral Information Security: Two End User Survey Studies of Motivation and Security Practices.* Paper presented at the America's Conference on Information Systems (AMCIS).

Stanton, J. M., Stam, K. R., Mastrangelo, P., & Jolton, J. (2005). Analysis of End-User Security Behaviors. *Computers & Security, 24*(2), 124-133.

Teo, T. S. H., & Lim, V. K. G. (1996). Factors Influencing Personal Computer Usage: The Gender Gap. *Women in Management Review, 11*, 18-26.

Thompson, R. L., Higgins, C. A., & Howell, J. M. (1991). Personal Computing: Toward a Conceptual Model of Utilization. *MIS Quarterly, 15*(1), 124-143.

Venkatesh, V., Morris, M. G., Davis, G. B., & Davis, F. D. (2003). User Acceptance of Information Technology: Toward a Unified View. *MIS Quarterly, 27*(3), 425-478.

KEY TERMS

Internet Crime (Cyber Crime): Internet crime consists of specific crimes dealing with computers and networks (such as hacking) and the facilitation of traditional crime through the use of computers (child pornography, hate crimes, telemarketing /Internet fraud). In addition to cyber crime, it may cover the use of computers by criminals for communication and document or data storage.

On-Line Victimization: Falling victim to internet crimes such as on-line harassment, computer intrusion, SPAM e-mail, internet fraud and identity theft.

Security: Policies, procedures, and technical measures used to prevent unauthorized access, alteration, theft, or physical damage to data or computer systems.

Spyware: A software that gathers user information through the user's Internet connection without his or her knowledge, usually for advertising purposes. Once installed, the spyware monitors user activities while on the Internet such as capture your keystrokes while typing the passwords, read and track your e-mail, record what sites you visit, record the credit card numbers; and transmits that information in the background to someone else.

System Vulnerability (Vulnerability): Weakness in an information system, system security procedures, internal controls, or implementation that could be exploited.

Victimology: The study of why certain people are victims of crime and how lifestyles affect the chances that a certain person will fall victim to a crime. This interdisciplinary field draws from a wide number of disciplines, including sociology, psychology, and criminology.

Vulnerability to Internet Crimes: Weaknesses that may subject an internet user to become victim to an Internet Crime e.g. lack of awareness of current threats and system vulnerabilities, inability or delay in dealing with the system vulnerabilities. In this chapter the term vulnerability to Internet crime is defined as vulnerabilities related to on-line activities arising from various computing and internet activities, trusting tendencies as well as awareness issues related to on-line risks.

Chapter XXVII
Detecting Shill Bidding in Online English Auctions

Jarrod Trevathan
James Cook University, Australia

Wayne Read
James Cook University, Australia

ABSTRACT

Shill bidding is where spurious bids are introduced into an auction to drive up the final price for the seller, thereby defrauding legitimate bidders. While shilling is recognized as a problem, presently there is little or no established means of defense against shills. This chapter presents an algorithm to detect the presence of shill bidding in online auctions. It observes bidding patterns over a series of auctions, providing each bidder a score indicating the likelihood of his/her potential involvement in shill behavior. The algorithm has been tested on data obtained from a series of realistic simulated auctions, and commercial online auctions. The algorithm is able to prune the search space required to detect which bidders are likely to be shills. This has significant practical and legal implications for commercial online auctions where shilling is considered a major threat. This chapter presents a framework for a feasible solution, which acts as a detection mechanism and a deterrent.

INTRODUCTION

Shill bidding is the act of introducing fake bids into an auction on behalf of the seller to artificially inflate the price of an item. The seller either can: 1) register as a bidder under a false identity, or 2) be in collusion with one or more of the bidders. Bidders who engage in shilling are referred to as *shills*. To win the item on auction a legitimate bidder must outbid a shill's price. If one of the shills accidentally wins, then the item is re-sold in a subsequent auction. Shill bidding is a problem as it forces legitimate bidders to bid against false bids hence paying significantly more for the item.

The most common type of auction is the English auction. In an English auction a seller offers an item for sale and many bidders attempt to outbid each other to obtain the item. The winner is the bidder with the highest bid after a given time-out period. English auctions are particularly susceptible to shill bidding practices.

The advent of online auctions such as eBay[1] and ubid[2], have made shill bidding much more exploitable. This is because it is relatively simple for a seller to register under many aliases and operate in rings with impunity. Furthermore, as bidders are not physically present it becomes much easier for a shill to anonymously influence the bidding process. This chapter examines shill behavior in the online setting and presents an algorithm to detect the presence of shill bidders in English auctions. The algorithm examines bidding information across several auctions and produces a score indicating the likelihood that a bidder is engaging in shill behavior.

The algorithm is applied to real auction data where shills are present. We believe this is the first formal (documented) attempt to detect shills using a conformatory analysis of bidding behavior.

This chapter shows that the algorithm can effectively reduce the search space required to detect shills. This enables the implementation of exploratory analysis using data mining techniques.

RELATED WORK

This section explores some related work that has been conducted into shilling. At present there is limited coverage on how to detect shill bidding.

eBay has been involved in many legal disputes where bidders/sellers have been accused of shilling (see Schwartz and Dobrzynski (2002)). eBay has clear rules regarding shill bidding behavior in their auctions[3]. Their policy clearly outlines undesirable bidder behavior and the penalties for shill bidding. The regular process for a bidder who suspects that they have been shilled is to contact eBay, who then investigates the incident. eBay does not state exactly what factors they use to determine whether shilling has occurred, nor how to detect which bidders are shills.

Shah et al (2003) use data mining techniques to produce evidence of shilling. Their work used data from approximately *12,000* commercial auctions looking for associations between bidders and sellers. Bidders (or groups of bidders) that participated frequently in auctions held by particular sellers were deemed suspect. However, the authors' state that their analysis is very limited in that it only looks for simple associations. They suggest that a much more thorough analysis must be performed using complex associations which consider a wider range of shill behavior.

There are also companies who offer data mining techniques to detect fraud in online auctions[4]. However, like eBay, these companies have not made their techniques public.

Wang et al (2002) discuss an approach that attempts to deter shilling in the first place. The Auctioneer is allowed to use fees to make shilling unprofitable for the seller. In auctions using a reserve price, a seller is charged an increasing fee based on how far the winning price is from the reserve price.

Aspects regarding the economic theory of shilling have been examined by Kauffman and Wood (2003), and Barbaro and Bracht (2005).

ONLINE ENGLISH AUCTIONS

This section describes the operation of online English auctions, which is the auction model used in this paper. Formally an English auction can be defined as an ascending-price, open-bid auction. Each bid submitted must be higher than the current highest bid. The minimal amount required to outbid others is usually a percentage of the current highest bid. The value of the current highest bid is available to all parties, along with the auction timing. The winner is the bidder with the highest bid when the auction terminates.

There are four main stages in an online English auction:

- **Initialization:** The Auctioneer sets up the auction and advertises it (i.e., description of goods, starting time, etc).
- **Registration:** In order to participate in an online auction, a bidder must first register with the Auctioneer. During this stage a bidder establishes his/her identity (usually via credit card) and obtains a unique bidder id, which they use to bid with.
- **Bidding:** A registered bidder computes his/her bid and submits it to the Auctioneer. The Auctioneer checks the bid received to ensure conformity with the auction rules. Bids are posted on a bulletin board, where all bidders are able to obtain a real-time price quote and view the auction proceedings.
- **Winner Determination:** At the close of bidding the Auctioneer determines the winner. Online English auctions can terminate according to the following rules:
  - *Expiration Time* - The auction closes at a predetermined expiration time.
  - *Timeout* - The auction closes when no bids higher than the current highest bid are made within a predetermined timeout interval.
  - *Combination of Expiration and Timeout* - The auction closes when there is a timeout after the expiration time.

The structure of bid information available to participants is as follows:

$< b_{id}, price, time >$

where b_{id} is a unique bidder id, *price* is the value the bidder is willing to pay, and *time* is the time when the bidder submitted a bid. It is assumed that a bidder is only after a single quantity of an item.

In online auctions it is common to allow bidders to cancel (or retract) bids. Although eBay does not formally allow bid retraction, they permit it in exceptional cases such as typographical errors (e.g., the bidder entered *$99.9* instead of *$9.99*), or if the item has radically changed in its description. Furthermore, auctions may last days or weeks and some bidders might be reluctant to make such opened-ended bids. For these reasons, bid retraction mechanisms are desirable in online auctions even though their use is discouraged.

In this chapter it is assumed that a bidder **cannot** cancel a bid. When a bid has been submitted it is valid until it is beaten by a higher valued bid. If a bid is submitted that is less than the current highest bid, it is discarded.

SHILL BEHAVIOR

This section provides an insight into the general behavior of shills. It describes a shill's mindset, characteristics and strategies, and presents an example of shill behavior in an auction.

Shill Mindset

The main goal for shilling is to artificially inflate the price for the seller beyond what legitimate bidders would otherwise require to win the item. The pay-off for the seller is the difference between the final price and the un-inflated price.

A shill's goal is to lose each auction. A shill is not constrained by a budget, but rather a profit margin. If the shill wins, the item is resold in a subsequent auction. However, there is a limit on how many times this can be done. For each auction won, the seller incurs auction listing fees and is required to invest more time. Continual wins erode the profit from shilling on the item.

The shill faces a dilemma for each bid they submit. Increasing a bid could marginally increase the revenue for the seller. However, raising the price might also result in failure if it is not outbid before the auction terminates. The shill must decide whether to take the deal or attempt to increase the payoff.

On the contrary, a bidder's goal is to win. A bidder has a finite budget and is after the lowest price possible. Increasing a bid for a legitimate bidder decreases the money saved, but increases the likelihood of winning.

Shill Characteristics and Strategies

The following outlines typical shill characteristics assuming we are using an auction that terminates at a set expiration time:

- A shill tends to bid exclusively in auctions only held by one particular seller, however, this alone is not sufficient to incriminate a bidder. It may be the case that the seller is the only supplier of an item the bidder is after, or that the bidder really trusts the seller (based on previous dealings).
- A shill tends to have a high bid frequency. An aggressive shill will continually outbid legitimate bids to inflate the final price. A shill typically will bid until the seller's expected payoff for shilling has been reached. Or until the shill risks winning the auction (e.g., near the termination time or during slow bidding).
- A shill has few or no winnings for the auctions participated in.
- It is advantageous for a shill to bid within a small time period after a legitimate bid. Generally a shill wants to give legitimate bidders as much time as possible to submit a new bid before the closing time of the auction.
- A shill usually bids the minimum amount required to outbid a legitimate bidder. If the shill bids an amount that is much higher than the current highest bid, it is unlikely that a legitimate bidder will submit any more bids and the shill will win the auction.
  It is common behavior for legitimate bidders trying to conserve their money to also only bid the minimal amount. In situations where a bidder's valuation is higher than the current bid, a bidder is more likely to outbid by more than the minimum amount.
- A shill's goal is to try and stimulate bidding. As a result, a shill will tend to bid more near the beginning of an auction. This means a shill can influence the entire auction process compared to a subset of it. Furthermore, bidding towards the end of an auction is risky as the shill could accidentally win.

The most extreme shill bidding strategy is referred to here as *aggressive shilling*. An aggressive shill continually outbids everyone thereby driving up the price as much as possible. This strategy often results in the shill entering many bids.

In contrast, a shill might only introduce an initial bid into an auction where there have been no prior bids with the intent to stimulate bidding. This kind of behavior is a common practice in both traditional and online auctions. However, most people typically do not consider it fraudulent. Nevertheless it is still shilling, as it is an attempt to influence the price by introducing spurious bids.

This is referred to as *benign shilling* in the sense that the shill does not continue to further inflate the price throughout the remainder of the auction. A benign shill will typically make a "one-off" bid at, or near the very beginning of the auction.

Regardless of the strategy employed, a shill will still be a bidder that often trades with a specific seller but has not won any auctions.

Another factor that affects a shill's strategy is the value of the current bid in relation to the reserve price. For example, once bidding has reached the reserve price it becomes more risky to continue shilling. This is conditional on whether the reserve is a realistic valuation of the item that all bidders share.

Shill Example

Table 1 illustrates an example auction with three bidders. Each bidder is denoted as b_1, b_2 and b_3 respectively. Bidders b_3 and b_3 are legitimate whereas b_2 is a shill. b_2 engages in aggressive shill behavior by outbidding a legitimate bid by the minimal amount required to stay ahead and within a small time period of the last bid. b_2's bids force the other bidders to enter higher bids in order to win. If b_2 was not participating in this auction b_1 would have only needed to pay *$21* in order to win. Instead b_2 caused b_1 to pay *$33*, thus the shill has inflated the price by *$12*.

In this example, b_2 exhibits the typical shill behavior described above. This is evidenced by: 1. High bid frequency (i.e., b_2 has submitted more bids than both the other bidders); 2. Has not won the auction despite the high number of bids; 3. Quick to bid after a legitimate bidder; and 4. Only bids the minimal amount to stay in front.

Table 1. An example auction with one shill

Bid #	b_{id}	Price	Time
15	b_1	$33	20:03
14	b_2	$32	12:44
13	b_1	$31	12:42
12	b_2	$26	5:05
11	b_1	$25	5:02
10	b_2	$21	2:47
9	b_3	$20	2:45
8	b_2	$15	1:07
7	b_1	$14	1:05
6	b_2	$9	0:47
5	b_3	$8	0:45
4	b_2	$6	0:20
3	b_3	$5	0:19
2	b_2	$2	0:06
1	b_1	$1	0:05

SHILL DETECTION

This section describes how to detect shill bidding in online English auctions. It discusses the approach used in this chapter and contrasts other less reliable proposals for shill detection.

As previously mentioned, a shill can either be a bidder who is in collusion with the seller, or the seller can directly introduce fake bids of his/her own by registering as a bidder. For all intents and purposes, the distinction does not make any difference for detecting the presence of shill behavior.

The solution used in this paper observes bidding patterns over a series of auctions for a particular seller looking for the aforementioned shilling behavior. The goal is to obtain statistics regarding the bidding patterns of bidders and deduce a measure called a *Shill Score*, which indicates the likelihood of a bidder/seller engaging in shill behavior.

It has been suggested by Wang et al (2002) that this approach is inadequate as shills can change their strategies to adapt to any detection algorithm. While this is true, our algorithm targets core strategies that a shill follows. A shill who deviates too far from these characteristics is less effective and won't significantly alter the auction outcome for the seller. Examining bidding behavior acts as both a detection mechanism and a deterrent to shill bidders. To avoid detection, a shill must behave like a normal user, which in effect stops them from shilling.

There are also other characteristics possessed by shills. However, the use of these as a means of detection is dubious. For example, when a shill accidentally wins, the seller usually re-sells the item in a subsequent auction. The most obvious solution for detecting shilling is to observe if the same item is resold in a subsequent auction by the seller. This requires assigning a unique *item id* to each item sold by the seller. If the same *item id* is detected twice (i.e., the item has been resold by the seller), this provides some indication that shilling is taking place.

The problem with this approach is that it is only relevant for situations where a shill accidentally wins the item. That is, shilling is not detected in the case where a legitimate bidder has won and paid an inflated price. Furthermore, the seller might attempt to re-list the item under a new *item id*. This then allows them to re-sell the item without raising suspicion. For these reasons, tracking resold items is not a sound method for detecting shilling.

Another commonly used detection method exploits the property that shills tend to be within close geographical proximity to each other. There are two main reasons for this. Firstly, collusion among bidders typically occurs amongst friends who live/operate near each other. This is because the costs of communication and coordinating the shilling process are less than over long distances. Secondly, if the seller has several aliases, these aliases will be registered in the same location.

However, geographical proximity alone is an unreliable indicator of shill behavior. First of all, the decreasing costs of communication hardware have made coordinating shill bidding over long distances much more affordable. Secondly, geographical information cannot be deduced from the raw auction data (as can the other characteristics) and involves cross-referencing users with the registration database, which raises anonymity concerns.

One proposed shill detection method examines the source IP address of a bidder. This is to prevent a shill from bidding using the same computer by logging in under different aliases. However, this is unreliable if more than one legitimate bidder must use the computer to bid (e.g., a computer in an Internet Cafe or a public library). Furthermore, this raises definite anonymity and privacy issues with regard to the bidders.

Other detection techniques examine seller feed back ratings and other statistics provided by eBay's feedback system. The feedback system allows buyers and sellers to report on their dealings with each other, which becomes an indicator of an individual's honesty and reliability.

In many cases shill bidders tend to have similar feedback profiles. This technique looks for anomalies in the feedback data to determine whether an individual fits the profile of a shill. However, the problem with this approach is that it is specific to eBay, and is based solely on the integrity of the feedback system.

One possible bidding strategy to combat shilling is *bid sniping*. Sniping refers to a bid that is submitted just before the auction terminates. The intent of the bid is to prevent other bidders from outbidding it by denying them time to react. Sniping cannot prevent shilling from occurring in an auction. However, it does protect a bidder from being shilled even further.

Existing commercial Auctioneers permit sniping, but discourage the practice. If every bidder engaged in sniping, the auction would essentially become a sealed bid auction. A sealed bid auction differs to an English auction in that no one knows the value of any one else's bid. In contrast, English auctions are open bid, as everyone knows everyone else's bid. Instead eBay recommends that bidders bid early using their proxy bidding system.

The proxy bidding system allows a bidder to specify a maximum amount they are willing to pay.

If a rival enters a new high bid, the proxy bidding system will minimally outbid it on behalf of the bidder until the maximum amount is reached. However, if all bidders use proxy bidding, the auction becomes a second price auction. Second price auctions differ to English auction in that the winner only has to pay the price of the second highest bid (i.e., the highest losing bid).

Existing shill detection methods are not public. It can be argued that it is dangerous to give a shill bidder knowledge of the inner workings of the detection method as this might allow them to subvert the system. However, the security (or ability) of the system should not rest with keeping it secret. In cryptography it is usually the case that confidence in a proposed security technique is only acquired over time if it withstands public scrutiny and attacks against its security. Likewise, if an adversary is allowed to attack the shill detection methods, then the confidence in a scheme will grow and ultimately better detection techniques can evolve.

THE SHILL SCORE

This section presents an algorithm to detect a shill by looking for common shill behavior. Our algorithm considers the case with **one shill**. The goal of the algorithm is to determine which bidder is most likely to be the shill out of a group of l bidders. A bidder is examined over m auctions held by the same seller for the aforementioned behavior outlined. Each characteristic of shill behavior is given a rating, which is combined to form the bidder's shill score. The shill score gives a bidder a value between *0* and *10*. The closer the shill score is to *10*, the more likely that the bidder is a shill.

The remainder of this section describes how to quantify a shill's characteristics to deduce a shill score. However, to do this some preliminary notation is required:

Let $L = \{1,\ldots,l\}$ be the set of bidder numbers;

$$|L| = l$$

Let $M = \{1,\ldots,m\}$ be the set of auction numbers;

$$|M| = m$$

For $i \in L$, let $M^i = \{j \mid j \in M, \text{bidder } i \text{ bids in auction } j\}$

$$|M^i| = m^i$$

For $j \in M$, let $N_j = \{1,\ldots,n_j\}$ be the bid numbers (e.g., 1st bid, 2nd bid, etc.) in auction j;

$$|N_j| = n_j$$

For $i \in L$, $j \in M$, let $N_j^i = \{k \mid k \in N_j, \text{bidder } i \text{ makes the } kth \text{ bid in auction } j\}$

$$|N_j^i| = n_j^i$$

For $i \in L$, let $W^i = \{j \mid j \in M, \text{ bidder } i \text{ wins auction } j\}$;

$$|W^i| = w^i$$

For $j \in M$, $k \in N_j$, let $t_{j,k}$ be the time of the kth bid in auction j, and let

$$T_j = \{t_{j,k} \mid j \in M, k \in N_j\}$$

be the set of bid times for auction j.

For $i \in L$, $j \in M$, $k \in N_j$, let $t^i_{j,k}$ be the time of the kth bid in the auction j by bidder i. Let

$$T_j^i = \{t^i_{j,k} \mid i \in L, j \in M, k \in N_j\}$$

be the set of bid times for bidder i in auction j;

$|T_j^i| = n_j^i$

For $j \in M$, $k \in N_j$, let $p_{j,k}$ be the value of the kth bid in auction j, and let

$P_j = \{p_{j,k} \mid j \in M, k \in N_j\}$

be the set of bid values in auction j;

$|P_j| = n_j$

For $i \in L$, $j \in M$, $k \in N_j$, let $p_{j,k}^i$ be the value of the kth bid in the auction j by bidder i.

Let

$P_j^i = \{p_{j,k}^i \mid i \in L, j \in M, k \in N_j\}$

be the set of bid values for bidder i in auction j;

$|P_j^i| = n_j^i$

-α Rating -

A shill is likely to participate exclusively in auctions held by one particular seller. The first step in detecting shilling is to count the number of the seller's auctions bidder i has participated in. Any auctions that bidder i has won (denoted as w^i) are excluded.

Given a seller which has held m auctions, the percentage a , of auctions bidder i has participated in is calculated as:

$\alpha^i = (m^i - w^i) / m$

where $0 \leq \alpha^i \leq 1$.

In general, the a rating will be higher for a shill compared to a legitimate bidder.

-β Rating -

An aggressive shill tends to submit a lot of bids as they are continually trying to outbid others. This might involve the shill bidding as often as every second bid (i.e., after every legitimate bid).

Table 2 illustrates this behavior. In the worst case a shill must submit $\lfloor n_j / 2 \rfloor$ bids, where n_j is the total number of bids for an auction. If a shill bids any more bids than this, they will win the auction.

This bound holds regardless of how many bidders there are in the auction. Table 3 shows an auction with two normal bidders and one shill bidder. At most the shill bidder can submit $\lfloor n_j / 2 \rfloor$ bids. In the best case, a shill will not have to bid because the legitimate bidders have already bid up the price well beyond the expected payoff from shilling.

Table 2. Auction with two bidders - one bidder b_1, one shill s_1

n_j	b_1	s_1	bid sequence	b_1	s_1
3	2	1	b_1, s_1, b_1	$\lceil n_j/2 \rceil$	$\lfloor n_j/2 \rfloor$
4	2	2	s_1, b_1, s_1, b_1	$n_j/2$	$n_j/2$
5	3	2	b_1, s_1, b_1, s_1, b_1	$\lceil n_j/2 \rceil$	$\lfloor n_j/2 \rfloor$
6	3	3	$s_1, b_1, s_1, b_1, s_1, b_1$	$n_j/2$	$n_j/2$

Table 3. Auction with three bidders - two bidders (b_1, b_2), one shill (s_1)

n_j	b_1	b_2	s_1	Bid sequence	$b_1 b_2$	s_1
3	1	1	1	b_1, s_1, b_2	$\lceil n_j/2 \rceil$	$\lfloor n_j/2 \rfloor$
4	1	1	2	s_1, b_1, s_1, b_2	$n_j/2$	$n_j/2$
5	2	1	2	b_1, s_1, b_2, s_1, b_1	$\lceil n_j/2 \rceil$	$\lfloor n_j/2 \rfloor$
6	2	1	3	$s_1, b_1, s_1, b_2, s_1, b_1$	$n_j/2$	$n_j/2$

The β rating indicates the average percentage of bids that bidder i has submitted throughout all the auctions he/she has participated in. The percentage for an individual auction is calculated in terms of the worst case bound of $\lfloor n_j/2 \rfloor$ bids. If a bidder has won an auction, then his/her b rating for that auction is zero.

An individual's β rating is calculated as follows.

Count the number of auctions m^i, that bidder i has participated in. For all auctions $j \in M^i$, that bidder i has participated in, perform the following:

Let β^i_j be bidder i 's β rating for auction j.

1. If bidder i won auction j, then $M^i = M^i - j$ (and $m^i = m^i - 1$) and skip the remaining numbered steps. Otherwise proceed to step 2.
2. Calculate the number of bids n_j, that have been submitted by all bidders in auction j.
3. Calculate the worst case number of bids Ω_j, for auction j:

   $$\Omega_j = \lfloor n_j/2 \rfloor$$

4. Calculate the number of bids n^i_j, bidder i has submitted in auction j.
5. Calculate the percentage of bids made by bidder i in terms of the worst case bound Ω_j:

   $$\beta^i_j = n^i_j / \Omega_j$$

Finally, bidder i 's β rating is calculated as the average of his/her β^i_j ratings for all auctions m_i, participated in:

If $m^i = 0$, then

$\beta^i = 0$

Else

$$\beta^i = \frac{1}{m^i} \sum_{j \in M^i} \beta^i_j$$

where $0 \le \beta^i \le 1$.

In general, the β rating will be high for an aggressive shill.

-γ Rating -

A shill's secondary goal is to avoid winning, as the auction will have to be repeated (with cost to the seller). To measure this, the simplest approach is to determine how many times bidder i has actually won over the auctions they have participated in.

For a bidder i that has won w^i auctions, the percentage γ, of wins is calculated as follows:

$$\gamma^i = 1 - (w^i / m^i)$$

where $0 \leq \gamma^i \leq 1$.

In general a shill will have a high γ rating. However, calculating the γ rating in this manner is biased towards bidders who only bid one or two bids and bidders that have participated in a small number of auctions.

We refer to a bidder who has only submitted one bid as a *one-time* bidder. At present, a one-time bidder that loses the auction attains a γ rating of one. This artificially inflates the bidder's shill score even though he/she has only bid once.

Our own experiments using commercial auction data have shown that many of the bidders participating in a set of auctions by a particular seller are often one-time bidders. Calculating the g rating in this manner gives misleading results when large numbers of one-time bidders are present.

To rectify this problem, the γ rating must also consider the number of losses l^i, incurred by bidder i, where $l^i = m^i - w^i$. As it is common for a bidder to lose auctions it makes no sense to penalize small numbers of losses. Instead, suspicion is only raised when the number of losses becomes large in comparison to the number of winnings. One-time bidders can be identified as bidders with no winnings and only one loss. Such bidders are given a γ rating of zero.

The γ rating is altered to permit a *20%* loss to winnings ratio without penalty. This allows bidders with a small number of losses to be ignored. The γ rating is further altered to ensure it is scalable depending on the number of auctions a bidder participates in. As the number of auctions that bidder i participates in increases, the penalties for losing an auction increase. This effectively identifies bidders who have participated in an excessive number of auctions and have little or no winnings.

The γ rating is calculated as follows:

$$\gamma^i = 1 - \left(\frac{5 \times (w^i + 0.2)}{l^i} \right)$$

where $\gamma^i < 1$

In the case where $\gamma^i < 0$, then $g^i = 0$.

Thus $0 \leq \gamma^i \leq 1$.

- δ **Rating** -

A shill wants to give other bidders as much time as possible to consider a shill bid. Therefore a shill generally submits a new bid within a small time period of a rival bid.

This behavior can be measured by observing inter bid times for all bidders. The average inter bid time is found for bidder i across the auctions they have participated in. Bidders who wait longer between bids have a lower average inter bid time score.

For all auctions $j \in M^i$, that bidder i has participated in, perform the following:

Let δ^i_j be bidder i's δ rating for auction j.

1. If bidder i won auction j, then $M^i = M^i - j$ (and $m^i = m^i - 1$) and skip the remaining numbered steps. Otherwise proceed to step 2.
2. Calculate the inter bid time for each bid k, submitted by bidder i in auction j:

$$\Delta t^i_{j,k} = \begin{cases} 0 & k = 1 \\ t^i_{j,k} - t_{j,k-1} & k > 1, k \in N_j \end{cases}$$

where $t_{j,k-1}$ is the time of a previous bid (by a rival bidder).

3. Calculate the average inter bid time for bidder i:

$$\overline{\Delta t}^i_j = \frac{1}{n^i_j} \sum_{k \in N^i_j} \Delta t^i_{j,k}$$

4. The maximum and minimum average inter bid times for auction j are:

$$\overline{\Delta t}_j^{\max} = \overset{\max}{i \in L}\{\overline{\Delta t}_j^i\}$$

$$\overline{\Delta t}_j^{\min} = \overset{\min}{i \in L}\{\overline{\Delta t}_j^i\}$$

Normalize to find bidder i's δ_j^i rating for auction j

$$\delta_j^i = \frac{\overline{\Delta t}_j^i - \overline{\Delta t}_j^{min}}{\overline{\Delta t}_j^{max} - \overline{\Delta t}_j^{min}}$$

Finally, calculate the average of the normalized inter bid times for bidder i over all auctions participated in:

$$\delta^i = 1 - \left(\frac{1}{m^i} \sum_{j \in M^i} \delta_j^i \right)$$

where $0 \leq \delta^i \leq 1$.

In general, the δ rating will be higher for a shill in comparison to a legitimate bidder.

- ε Rating -

A shill that outbids by a large amount increases the risk of losing the auction. Therefore a shill tends to only bid the minimal amount to stay ahead of the leading bid.

This behavior can be measured by observing inter bid increments for all bidders. The average inter bid increment is found for bidder i across the auctions they have participated in. Bidders who submit smaller bid increments have a lower average inter bid increment score.

For all auctions $j \in M^i$, that bidder i has participated in, perform the following:

Let e_j^i be bidder i's e rating for auction j.

1. If bidder i won auction j, then $M^i = M^i - j$ (and $m^i = m^i - 1$) and skip the remaining numbered steps. Otherwise proceed to step 2.
2. Calculate the inter bid increment for each bid k, submitted by bidder i in auction j:

$$\Delta p_{j,k}^i = \begin{cases} 0 & k = 1 \\ p_{j,k}^i - p_{j,k-1} & k>1, k \in N_j \end{cases}$$

where $p_{j,k-1}$ is the price of a previous bid (by a rival bidder).

3. Calculate the average inter bid increment for bidder i:

$$\overline{\Delta p}_j^i = \frac{1}{n_j^i} \sum_{k \in N_j^i} \Delta p_{j,k}^i$$

4. The average maximum and minimum inter bid increments for auction j are:

$$\overline{\Delta p}_j^{\max} = \overset{\max}{i \in L}\{\overline{\Delta p}_j^i\}$$

$$\overline{\Delta p}_j^{\min} = \overset{\min}{i \in L}\{\overline{\Delta p}_j^i\}$$

Normalize to find bidder i's ε_j^i rating for auction j:

$$\varepsilon_j^i = \frac{\overline{\Delta p}_j^i - \overline{\Delta p}_j^{min}}{\overline{\Delta p}_j^{max} - \overline{\Delta p}_j^{min}}$$

Finally, calculate the average of the normalized inter bid increments for bidder i over all auctions participated in:

$$\varepsilon^i = 1 - \left(\frac{1}{m^i} \sum_{j \in M^i} \varepsilon_j^i \right)$$

where $0 \leq \varepsilon^i \leq 1$.

In general, the e rating will be higher for a shill than that of a legitimate bidder.

- ζ Rating -

If a shill bids late in an auction, he/she risks losing the auction by not being outbid in time.

Therefore it is in the shill's best interests to bid early in an auction as it is less risky and maximizes the amount of influence the shill has over an auction.

The ζ rating indicates how early in an auction bidder i commenced bidding. This is calculated as the difference between the auction's expiration time and the time that bidder i first submitted a bid. This result is normalized against all other participants in the auction and averaged over all the auctions that bidder i participated in.

An individual's ζ rating is calculated as follows:

Count the number of auctions m^i, that bidder i has participated in. For all auctions $j \in M^i$, that bidder i has participated in, perform the following:

Let ζ^i_j be bidder i's ζ rating for auction j.

1. If bidder i won auction j, then $M^i = M^i - j$ (and $m^i = m^i - 1$) and skip the remaining numbered steps. Otherwise proceed to step 2.
2. Calculate the difference between auction j's expiration time t_j, and the time, t^i_{j,k_0} of the first bid submitted by bidder i in auction j.

$$\Delta t^i_j = t_j - t^i_{j,k_0}$$

3. The maximum and minimum average final bid time differences for auction j are:

$$\Delta t^{\max}_j = \max_{i \in L}\{\Delta t^i_j\}$$

$$\Delta t^{\min}_j = \min_{i \in L}\{\Delta t^i_j\}$$

Normalize to find bidder i's ζ^i_j rating for auction j

$$\zeta^i_j = \frac{\Delta t^i_j - \Delta t^{min}_j}{\Delta t^{max}_j - \Delta t^{min}_j}$$

Finally, calculate the average of the final bid time differences for bidder i over all auctions participated in:

$$\zeta^i = \frac{1}{m^i} \sum_{j \in M^i} \zeta^i_j$$

where $0 \leq \zeta^i \leq 1$.

In general, the ζ rating will be higher for a shill.

Pre-Conditioning the Data

Commercial auctions such as those on eBay do not adhere to the English auction format used in this paper. Before executing the shill detection algorithm, the data from commercial auctions must be *pre-conditioned.* Pre-conditioning the data refers to the process of getting the data into the correct format for the algorithm. This also involves modifying the algorithm to deal with proxy bidding.

As stated earlier, a proxy bid allows a user to enter a maximum bid that they are willing to pay. The proxy bidding system will then marginally outbid any new high bid up until the user's maximum value. We refer to the first proxy bid submitted by the bidder as the *initial proxy bid.* A bid placed by the proxy system is referred to as a *proxy-generated bid.* If the winning bid is less than the bidder's maximum value, then the bidder gets the item for the lower value. Once a proxy bid is made, it cannot be retracted.

Table 4 shows an example auction using proxy bidding. In this example b_2 is the proxy bidder. The bid number indicates the order the bids were received. The auction history does not display the

Table 4. An example auction with proxy bidding

Bid #	b_{id}	Price	Time
8	b_5	$17	3:01
7	b_4	$16	2:54
2	b_2	$15	0:33
6	b_3	$9	2:00
5	b_3	$7	1:55
4	b_3	$5	1:47
3	b_3	$3	1:40
1	b_1	$1	0:05

proxy-generated bids. The initial proxy bid is only revealed when it is outbid. If a proxy-generated bid wins the auction, its value is shown, but the initial proxy bid is not revealed. If two proxy bidders are competing, the lower of the two bids is listed and the proxy-generated bid of the higher valued bid is listed.

A shill is unlikely to use proxy bidding. This is the same justification behind the e rating, which states that a shill is more likely to bid in smaller increments rather than one large up-front bid. Proxy bidding encourages bidders to bid large amounts up-front. However, this behavior is risky for a shill.

A safer approach is for a shill to edge up a proxy bid until it reaches its maximum. If a shill can predict what the value of the initial proxy bid is, then the shill can seize the full value of the proxy bid.

When a shill encounters a proxy bid, this presents the shill with an accessible target to shill. Upon outbidding a proxy-generated bid, the shill is provided with instant feedback. That is, the shill is either outbid immediately by a new proxy-generated bid or the shill has outbid the proxy bid. Such instant feedback allows a shill to inflate the price quickly and in a controlled incremental manner. Upon submitting a proxy bid, the bidder is powerless to prevent a shill from edging the price up as the initial bid cannot be retracted.

Note that alternately a shill might use a proxy bid up-front in order to inflate the price to a given value. This can be likened to an undisclosed reserve under the guise of a legitimate bid. Such behavior is essentially benign shilling. If a shill uses multiple proxy bids throughout an auction, they must do so sparingly. Once again it is risky for the shill to set an initial proxy bid too high.

This effectively limits the usefulness of proxy bidding to a shill.

To detect shill bidders in commercial online auctions, the algorithm must be altered to deal with proxy bidders. The first step to achieving this goal is to re-order the auction data based on time rather than bid value. This facilitates the identification of initial proxy bids.

An initial proxy bid can be identified as a bid that has a higher value than a subsequently placed bid. The re-ordered data from the example auction is shown in Table 5. Bid number *2* submitted by b_2 clearly stands out as an initial proxy bid. This bid is for *$15* whereas the subsequent bid (i.e., bid number *3*) is lower at *$3*.

The total number of generated proxy bids (not shown in the bidding history) can be determined by counting the number of subsequent bids that have a lower value than the initial proxy bid. In Table 5 there are four rival bids after b_2's initial proxy bid. Therefore there are also four proxy-generated bids.

To ensure that a proxy bidder's β rating does not exceed one, the number of proxy-generated bids for auction *j* is added to the total number of bids n_j. When a proxy bid is used, the β rating only penalizes the proxy bidder for one bid (i.e., the initial proxy bid). Proxy-generated bids are not included in the proxy bidder's β rating. This

Table 5. Example auction re-ordered according to the time submitted

Bid #	b_{id}	Price	Time
8	b_5	$17	3:01
7	b_4	$16	2:54
6	b_3	$9	2:00
5	b_3	$7	1:55
4	b_3	$5	1:47
3	b_3	$3	1:40
2	b_2	$15	0:33
1	b_1	$1	0:05

functionality rewards and encourages proxy bidding.

A proxy bidder's δ rating is only calculated for the initial proxy bid. Proxy-generated bids are not included in the proxy bidder's δ rating. This is because the timings for the proxy-generated bid will always be zero as they are placed immediately once a rival bid of lesser value is received. This wrongly gives the appearance that proxy-generated bids are being submitted by a shill bidder.

To allow a bidder's ε rating to be determined, the values of the proxy-generated bids must be calculated. As proxy-generated bids are not included in the auction history, the shill score algorithm cannot accurately determine the e ratings for bidders in competition with a proxy bid. eBay has guidelines regarding the minimal amount required to outbid the current high bid. This is shown in Table 6 as an increasing scale that is a function of the price (roughly *5%*). These guidelines can be used to reproduce the missing proxy-generated bid values.

Table 6. Bid increments

Current Price	Bid Increment
$0.00 - $0.99	$0.05
$1.00 - $4.99	$0.25
$5.00 - $24.99	$0.50
$25.00 - $99.99	$1.00
$100.00 - $249.99	$2.50
$250.00 - $499.99	$5.00
$500.00 - $999.99	$10.00
$1000.00 - $2499.99	$25.00
$2500.00 - $4999.99	$50.00
$5000.00 and up	$100.00

The ε rating for the initial proxy bid is calculated as normal according to time. As the proxy bidder has bid a large amount up-front, this is manifested in his/her ε rating. Proxy-generated bids are not included in the proxy bidder's e rating.

The bid immediately following the initial bid is calculated in terms of the proxy-generated bid produced. When an initial bid is placed, it is only listed as the minimum amount required to win.

That is, the first proxy-generated bid is displayed. The rival bidder's e value is calculated in terms of the first proxy-generated bid rather than the initial bid. All subsequent rival bids are calculated in terms of the proxy-generated bids they have outbid.

Calculating the Shill Score

The following algorithm is run on a seller's auction history for each bidder that participated in any of the seller's auctions:

1. Pre-condition the data.
2. Calculate α rating.
3. Calculate β rating.
4. Calculate γ rating.
5. Calculate δ rating.

6. Calculate ε rating.
7. Calculate ζ rating.
8. Calculate shill score.

Each bidder obtains a shill score between *0* and *10*, representing his/her likelihood of being a shill. This is calculated as follows:

$$score = \frac{\omega 1\alpha + \omega 2\beta + \omega 3\lambda + \omega 4\delta + \omega 5\varepsilon + \omega 6\zeta}{\omega 1 + \omega 2 + \omega 3 + \omega 4 + \omega 5 + \omega 6} \times 10$$

where ω is the weighting associated with each rating.

The bidder with the highest shill score is considered most likely to be the shill.

The weights used in this paper are: $\omega_1 = 9$, $\omega_2 = 2$, $\omega_3 = 5$, $\omega_4 = 2$, $\omega_5 = 2$, and $\omega_6 = 2$. These were obtained by experimenting with simulated auction data and using the following justifications:

A bidder's α rating is given the highest weighting. This is done to eliminate one-time bidders. In the instance where a one-time bidder has high δ and e ratings, the bidder will be allocated a high shill score despite clearly not fitting a shill's profile.

A bidder's γ rating receives the next highest weighting. When a bidder has a high α rating and a low γ rating, the bidder is clearly bidding to win. This is irrespective of the bidder participating in so many auctions. A shill employing this strategy would not be very successful.

Once a bidder has initially been detected by his/her α and γ ratings, the next significant factors are the β, δ, ε and ζ ratings. These are used to see if the bidding behavior matches regular shill behavior.

The β rating measures the number of bids submitted in terms of $\lfloor n_j / 2 \rfloor$. If a shill is aggressive, β will be high. However, if the shill is benign, β will be low. As a result, the β rating can present mixed results depending on the type of shill behavior employed. For this reason, the β rating is given a lower weighting than the α and γ ratings.

The δ and ε weightings are also lower than the α and γ weightings due to the effect of one-time bidders. That is, if a bidder only bids once, placing the bid quickly after the current highest bid and by the minimal amount required, then the bidder will have high δ and ε ratings. As the bidder does not bid again, his/her δ and ε ratings will always remain high and not average down if the bidder were to later submit slower, larger bids. Therefore, weighting δ and ε highly results in many one-time bidders scoring high overall even though such bidders are clearly not shills (evidenced by a low α rating).

The ζ rating is also weighted at two as it is not more influential than the other bidding characteristic ratings. Instead all the bidding characteristic weightings must be examined as a group to determine if the bidder's bidding behavior fits a shill's profile.

Note that the weightings must be adjusted according to the number of auctions held. For small values of m the α and γ ratings are less effective. For example, when $m \leq 3$ the α rating for all bidders will be high and the γ rating will be zero for all of the bidders. This distorts a bidder's shill score and therefore cannot be relied upon. When $m \leq 3$ the weightings for the α and γ ratings are zero.

In the case where $m \leq 3$, the bidding characteristic ratings are more heavily relied on to indicate the level of shill-like behavior a bidder possesses.

PERFORMANCE

This section describes how the algorithm performed on real auction data. Two types of data were obtained. The first was from a series of simulated auction trials. The second was from commercial online auctions. Each type will be explained in turn.

Simulated Auctions

A series of simulated auctions were conducted to obtain auction data. Thirty-nine auctions were performed on an auction server[5], which emulates existing commercial online auction websites. Details of the software used can be found in Trevathan and Read (2006). Each auction was for a different item and all auctions were considered to be for one seller (consistent with the algorithm)

The auction proceedings involved twenty-six people. Each bidder was given a random amount of fake money at the beginning of the trials. A bidder was free to bid his/her valuation in any auction provided that collectively the amount bid did not exceed the initial amount provided.

When a bidder won an auction, the balance of his/her account was reduced by the value of the winning bid. A bidder's goal was to win while also trying to save his/her money.

The shill's goal was to force a bidder into spending as much of his/her money as possible. Bidders were not informed that shilling was occurring. Furthermore, the shill had no knowledge of how much money bidders had.

Table 7 shows the proceedings of one of the simulated auctions. The item auctioned was Dire Straits' Greatest Hits DVD. This consisted of a

Table 7. Simulated auction with one shill

Bid #	b_{id}	Price	Time
25	Ness	$91.00	2005-08-11 15:58:35
24	wayne	$90.00	2005-08-11 15:44:04
23	townsville	$80.00	2005-08-11 15:22:46
22	Ness	$56.00	2005-08-11 15:16:16
21	townsville	$55.00	2005-08-11 15:07:28
20	Shelly	$50.50	2005-08-11 14:55:34
19	townsville	$50.00	2005-08-11 14:54:46
18	Shelly	$39.39	2005-08-11 14:12:55
17	buzzcook	$39.00	2005-08-11 14:11:02
16	Shelly	$38.38	2005-08-11 14:04:43
15	marianne	$38.00	2005-08-11 13:49:17
14	Shelly	$36.72	2005-08-11 13:40:26
13	Soraya	$36.36	2005-08-11 13:34:23
12	wayne	$36.00	2005-08-11 08:31:09
11	Shelly	$35.35	2005-08-10 14:47:40
10	Soraya	$35.00	2005-08-10 14:41:33
9	Shelly	$33.33	2005-08-10 14:34:15
8	wayne	$33.00	2005-08-10 14:25:49
7	Ness	$32.00	2005-08-10 14:20:13
6	Shelly	$31.31	2005-08-10 11:11:21
5	wayne	$31.00	2005-08-10 11:09:55
4	Soraya	$30.50	2005-08-10 08:25:17
3	Ness	$30.00	2005-08-09 16:42:48
2	marianne	$0.25	2005-08-09 16:25:13
1	Shelly	$0.20	2005-08-09 16:01:18

DVD of the band's video clips and two CDs. The retail value was approximately *$50* AUD. The shill bidder is 'Shelly'.

It quickly became apparent that bidders took the auctions seriously. The simulation captured the essence of a real auction where the competitive desire to win induced bidders to spend more money than was intended. Bidders that won an auction were elated, even though they did not obtain anything tangible. Other bidders such as 'brenda' vowed that they were determined to win all of the auctions.

The simulation showed that while the shill's strategy was to marginally increase the bid, legitimate bidders tended to increase the bid by larger values. Furthermore, legitimate bidders who were focused on winning an item regardless of the cost tended to bid large amounts up front.

In addition, many bidders engaged in rallies amongst themselves and with the shill bidder. During such rallies legitimate bidders tended to bid in larger increments than the shill's marginal increases.

For the auction shown in Table 7, the shill (i.e., 'Shelly') pushed the price up to *$50.50*. At this stage the auction was one hour from terminating. Although bidding was constant, the reserve price had been met, therefore it was in the shill's interests to discontinue. The winning bid for the item was *$91*.

There were three types of tests performed: with one shill, without shilling, and with benign shilling. The shill detection algorithm was run on all of the tests to determine its effectiveness in catching shills and the likelihood of it incriminating innocent bidders.

The first test involved ten auctions and one shill bidder. Table 8 shows the shill scores for each bidder. The shill (i.e., 'Shelly') is clearly identified as the bidder that has engaged in the most shill-like behavior. The shill was the only bidder to score consistently on the behavioral characteristics that optimally inflate the price for the seller. Figure 1A gives a graphical representation of the shill scores.

Table 8. Shill scores for simulated auctions with one shill bidder

Bidder	α	β	γ	δ	ε	ζ	**Shill Score**
Shelly	1.00	0.70	0.90	0.96	0.88	0.79	9.16
townsville	0.60	0.21	0.83	0.86	0.65	0.60	6.46
Marie	0.60	0.11	0.83	0.45	0.89	0.20	5.84
jc112425	0.40	0.20	0.75	0.75	0.72	0.79	5.58
Wayne	0.20	0.42	0.50	0.75	0.93	0.66	4.46
Ness	0.40	0.48	0.00	0.88	0.90	0.85	4.46
Marianne	0.60	0.18	0.00	0.62	0.91	0.39	4.36
Soraya	0.40	0.32	0.00	0.91	0.85	0.78	4.25
Bear	0.20	0.22	0.50	0.98	0.16	0.43	3.58
Brenda	0.20	0.59	0.00	0.97	0.97	0.41	3.49
joe	0.10	0.67	0.00	0.62	0.92	1.00	3.32
banana	0.10	0.11	0.00	1.00	1.00	1.00	3.24
ronisanidiot	0.10	0.10	0.00	0.95	0.98	0.76	2.95
phrdw	0.10	0.10	0.00	0.99	0.99	0.68	2.92
buzzcook	0.10	0.08	0.00	1.00	0.99	0.01	2.30
groper	0.00	0.00	0.00	0.00	0.00	0.00	0.00

Figure 1. Shill scores for simulated auctions

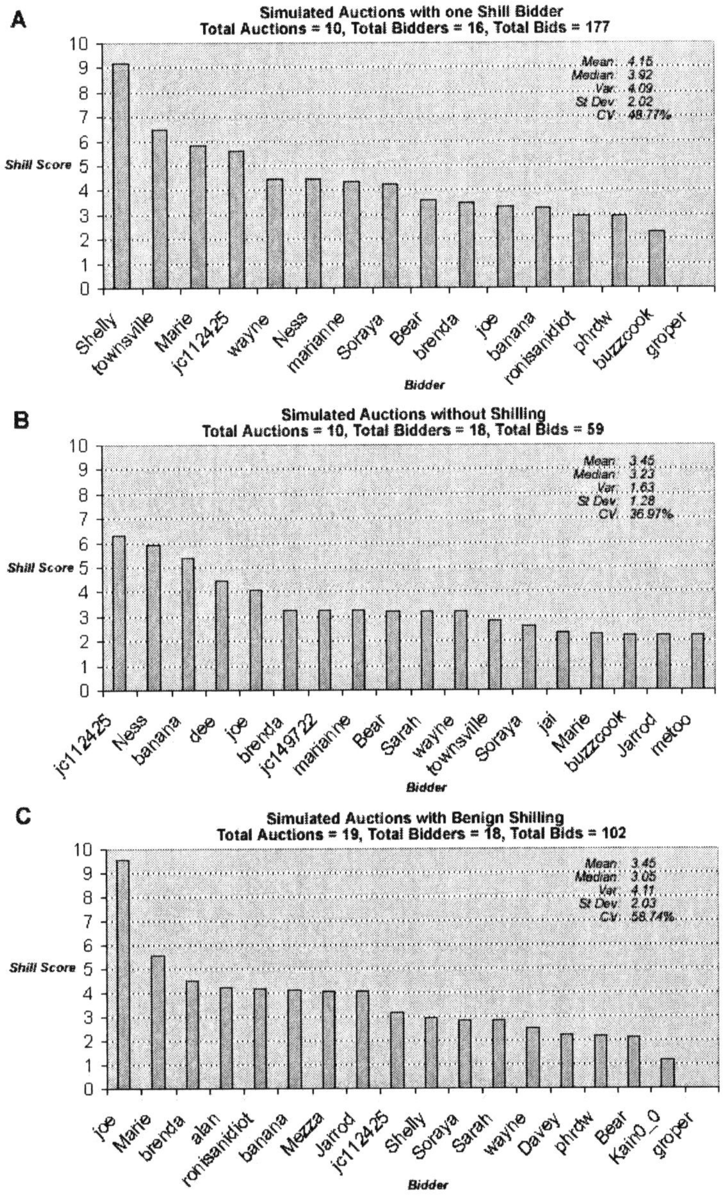

The second test also involved ten auctions. However, unlike the previous test, no intentional shilling behavior was engaged in. Shill scores for each bidder are shown in Table 9 and graphically in Figure 1B. The test's purpose was to gauge regular bidding behavior.

At some stages during an auction, a legitimate bidder's behavior can emulate that of a shill. This raises the possibility of classifying innocent behavior as shilling. During the trial some bidders participated in many of the auctions and also engaged in rallies, which pushed up the bid price (e.g., 'brenda', 'marianne', 'Ness', 'townsville' and 'Soraya'). This behavior effectively raised their shill scores. However, other factors such as number of winnings, large bid increments

Table 9. Shill scores for simulated auctions without shilling

Bidder	α	β	γ	δ	ε	ζ	Shill Score
jc112425	0.40	0.36	0.75	0.99	0.90	0.99	6.28
Ness	0.30	0.64	0.67	0.98	0.87	1.00	5.92
banana	0.20	0.75	0.50	1.00	1.00	1.00	5.36
dee	0.20	0.42	0.50	0.97	0.91	0.43	4.44
joe	0.10	1.00	0.00	1.00	1.00	1.00	4.05
Brenda	0.30	0.38	0.00	0.84	0.85	0.17	3.27
jc149722	0.20	0.25	0.50	0.95	0.00	0.22	3.25
Marianne	0.20	0.30	0.00	0.81	0.83	0.73	3.24
Bear	0.20	0.42	0.00	0.98	0.76	0.49	3.23
Sarah	0.10	1.00	0.00	0.96	0.68	0.46	3.22
wayne	0.10	0.50	0.00	0.98	0.63	0.95	3.18
Townsville	0.30	0.44	0.00	0.50	0.50	0.28	2.80
Soraya	0.10	0.50	0.00	0.62	0.79	0.50	2.60
jai	0.10	0.17	0.00	0.99	0.93	0.00	2.31
Marie	0.10	0.14	0.00	0.95	0.92	0.07	2.30
buzzcook	0.10	0.14	0.00	0.98	0.87	0.01	2.23
Jarrod	0.10	1.00	0.00	0.00	0.00	1.00	2.23
metoo	0.10	0.17	0.00	0.89	0.93	0.00	2.22

and slower bid times indicated that these bidders were bidding to win.

During both the first and second tests, one of the bidders ('banana' in this case) was tasked with introducing some initial bids into auctions where there had been no bidding. The idea was to try and stimulate bidding (i.e., benign shilling).

When a bidder is the first to bid in an auction, there is no previous bid. As a result there is no inter bid time interval nor bid increment for the bid. The shill detection algorithm gives bids of this sort δ and ε ratings of one. If a benign shill continually bids first in an auction (to try 'kick off' the bidding) s/he will have high overall δ and e ratings. Such a bidder will also have relatively high α and γ ratings if the behavior continues over a series of auctions.

'banana' has one of the highest δ and ε ratings out of all the bidders in both tests. Since 'banana' only shilled in relatively few auctions, his α rating is low. A benign shill's γ rating will always be high. In general, a benign shill will have a low β rating, except in situations where the auctions participated in have a low bid volume.

A third series of auction tests were conducted to further investigate benign shilling. This involved nineteen auctions, fifteen of which contained instances of benign shilling behavior. Shill scores for each bidder are shown in Table 10 and graphically in Figure 1C.

In this instance 'joe' is the shill bidder. 'joe' rates highly across all measures. The bidding volume was low in several auctions 'joe' participated in. This accounts for why 'joe's' β rating is reasonably high.

Figure 2 shows the average inter bid times and increments for each bidder in the auction from Dire Straits' Greatest Hits DVD in Table 7. The shill bid the most during this auction and had a consistently low inter bid time and increment. Legitimate bidders that had inter bid times and increments less than the shill had submitted

Table 10. Shill scores for simulated auctions with benign shilling

Bidder	α	β	γ	δ	ε	ζ	Shill Score
joe	1.00	0.68	0.95	0.99	1.00	1.00	9.58
Marie	0.37	0.45	0.86	0.62	0.59	0.66	5.56
brenda	0.42	0.52	0.25	0.65	0.70	0.59	4.52
alan	0.11	0.25	0.50	0.85	0.95	0.84	4.20
ronisanidiot	0.16	0.24	0.67	0.97	0.63	0.35	4.15
banana	0.11	1.00	0.50	0.89	0.02	0.90	4.13
Mezza	0.16	0.26	0.67	0.82	0.94	0.07	4.07
Jarrod	0.16	0.56	0.67	0.75	0.33	0.43	4.04
jc112425	0.26	0.28	0.00	0.61	0.81	0.60	3.16
Shelly	0.05	0.25	0.00	0.86	0.98	0.90	2.93
Soraya	0.16	0.39	0.00	0.96	0.89	0.17	2.84
Sarah	0.16	0.31	0.00	0.65	0.91	0.52	2.82
wayne	0.11	0.29	0.00	0.99	0.95	0.05	2.50
Davey	0.05	0.13	0.00	0.99	1.00	0.10	2.22
phrdw	0.11	0.38	0.50	0.00	0.00	0.25	2.14
Bear	0.21	0.24	0.00	0.53	0.51	0.08	2.09
Kain0_0	0.05	0.13	0.00	0.78	0.00	0.12	1.14
groper	0.00	0.00	0.00	0.00	0.00	0.00	0.00

Figure 2. Time intervals and bid increments for the Dire Straits' DVD auction

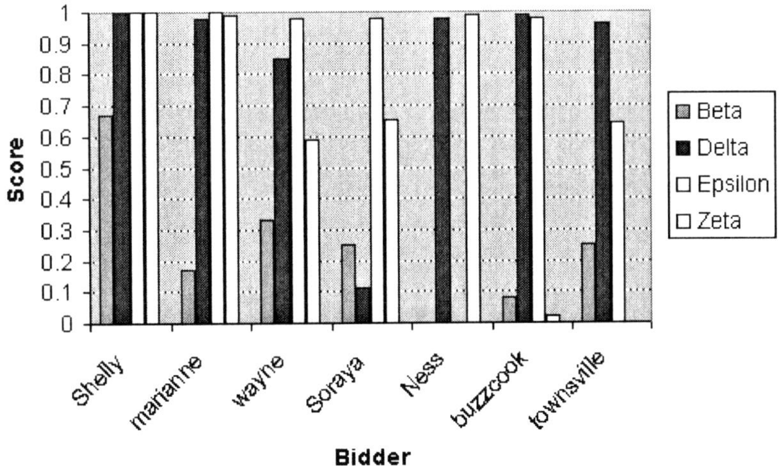

significantly fewer bids. When compared to the shill scores (see Table 8) only bidders 'Shelly' and 'marianne' rank highly and warrant further investigation. While Figure 2 indicates which bidders are potential shills, it is insufficient to only look at an individual auction. For example, 'buzzcook' also rates poorly, but when his behavior from several auctions is observed he has a low ranking shill score.

It is interesting to note that there was a significant degree of sniping occurring during all three tests. Many bidders such as 'brenda', 'buzzcook', 'Davey' and 'wayne' often employed this strategy to ensure that they won. It became evident that online auctions that terminate exclusively with an expiration time promote this sort of bidding. As this behavior is totally the opposite of shilling, these bidders tended to have low shill scores.

These simulated tests are currently being repeated using real money. Furthermore, software bidding agents are being developed in order to conduct further simulations. A software bidding agent is a program that bids on behalf of a bidder according to a predefined strategy. This allows the shill detection algorithm to be tested on extremely large datasets.

Commercial Auctions

The algorithm was tested on commercial auction data. This refers to actual data collected from real auctions that were performed by commercial online auctioneers such as eBay.

There is limited commercial data on shilling. Several commercial online auction sites were approached for auction data (i.e., bidding histories). We also stated in the request that we are

"interested in auctions where it has either been confirmed or suspected that shilling has occurred."

Most commercial sites were disinclined to give out information for privacy reasons. Shilling is cognate to other types of fraud (e.g., credit card fraud). Companies are reluctant to admit shilling has occurred, as it would tarnish their reputation. This can also partially justify why auction companies do not give out extensive bidding history records, especially those containing shilling.

The shill score algorithm was tested on commercial auction data obtained used in previous auction research by Jank and Shmueli (2007). The auction data was for *150* auctions conducted on eBay for new Palm M515 PDAs.

The commercial data differed to the simulated data in various ways. Firstly, the commercial data was for a single (but distinct) item (i.e., PDAs), whereas the simulated data were for different items. Second, there were a larger number of bidders in the commercial data. Thirdly, for the simulated data it was more common for a bidder to bid multiple times in a single auction. Finally, with the commercial data, a large number of users only bid once during an auction.

The data was analyzed using the methods presented in this paper. Unlike the simulated data, it was unknown whether shilling had actually occurred. Therefore the algorithm determined whether shill behavior was present solely by examining the bidding characteristics of the auction participants. This essentially provided the algorithm with a realistic test (i.e., the manner the algorithm would run in practice).

The remainder of this section gives the results for three different sellers of the commercial data.

The first seller (named 'saveking') conducted ten auctions involving seventy bidders. The top five shill scores for this seller are listed in Table 11 and are shown graphically in Figure 3A.

The bidder named 'camotorl@aol.com' has the highest score and warranted further investigation. On closer inspection, this bidder was found to have participated in *80%* of the seller's auctions, and had not won any. The other bidders who scored high had also participated in quite a few auctions without winning, and had bid often and quickly in small increments.

Table 11. Top five shill scores for seller: saveking

Bidder	α	β	γ	δ	ε	ζ	Shill Score
camotor1@aol.com	0.80	0.29	0.88	0.77	0.70	0.32	7.16
bacardi91	0.40	0.26	0.75	0.68	0.91	0.87	6.15
ypolina	0.30	0.34	0.67	0.55	0.59	0.18	4.25
janicerunning	0.20	0.24	0.50	0.96	0.75	0.15	3.86
S13g	0.20	0.12	0.50	0.86	0.89	0.11	3.76

Figure 3 Shill scores for commercial auction data

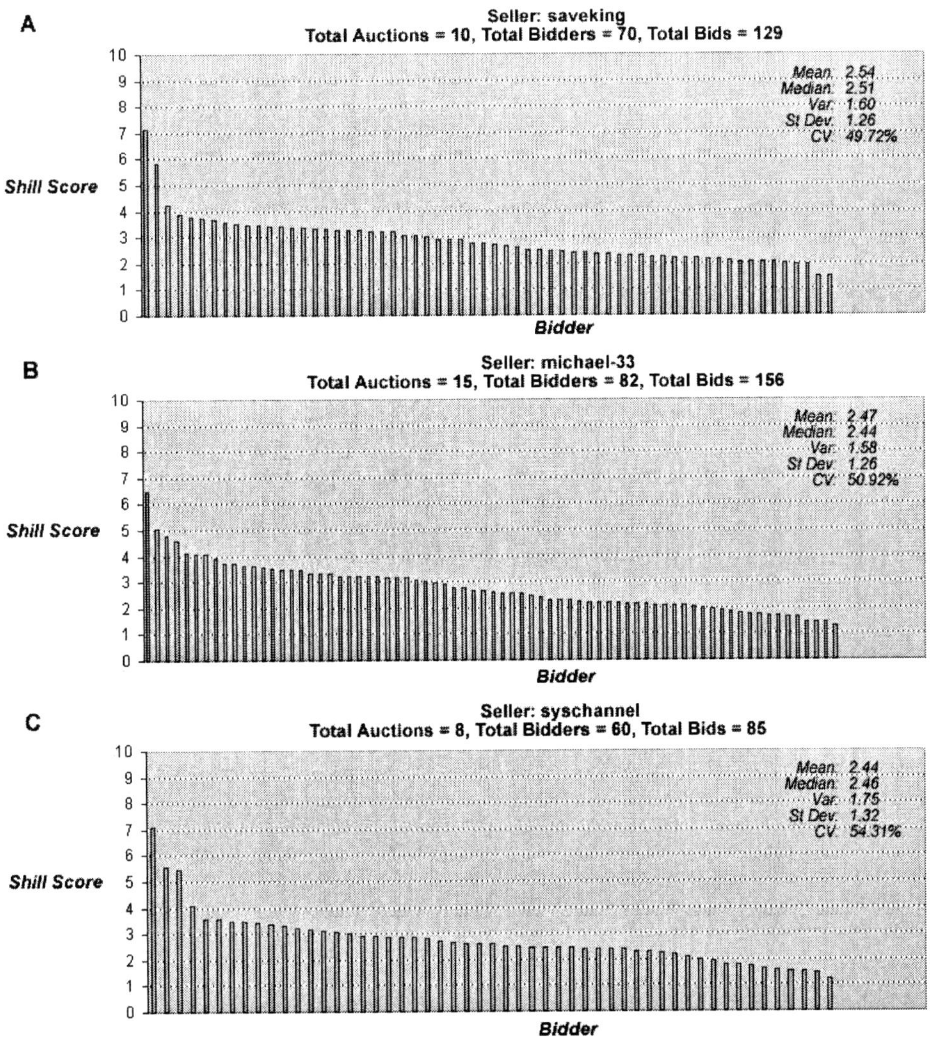

In contrast, there are bidders with shill scores of zero. These are bidders that won all of the auctions they participated in. Typical bidders had shill scores ranging between four and five.

The overall results for this seller suggest that there was a significant amount of price inflating bidding behavior present. Out of seventy bidders, 'camotorl@aol.com' had the most suspicious behavior. Given the extent of this behavior compared to other bidders, this indicates that 'camotorl@aol.com' may be engaging in aggressive shilling.

Table 12 shows the top five shill scores for the seller named 'michael-33'. The shill scores are calculated for *156* bidders over fifteen auctions. Shill scores for the bidders are shown graphically in Figure 3B.

This series of auctions contained a lesser extent of price inflating bidding compared to the previous two sellers. The bidder with the highest shill score is 'chimam'. This bidder has participated in *50%* of the seller's auctions and has not won any. However, this bidder does not have significantly high β, δ and ε ratings. Therefore it is questionable whether 'chimam' is actively engaging in shill behavior. Instead, what the shill algorithm allows us to say is, "out of *156* bidders, this bidder engaged in the most significant price inflating behavior".

The other bidders listed in Table 12 had mid range shill scores. On further inspection, these bidders had only participated in a small number of auctions and had the highest shill scores due to the aforementioned "one-time" bidder phenomena.

Table 13 shows the top five shill scores for the seller named 'syschannel'. The shill scores are calculated for fifty-nine bidders over eight auctions. This is shown graphically in Figure 3C.

The bidder with the most suspicious behavior is 'kc10'. This bidder participated in the most auctions. Furthermore, 'kc10' (like 'banana' and 'joe' in the simulated auctions) was usually the first to bid in auctions that he/she participated in. This strongly indicates that 'kc10' may have been engaging in benign shilling behavior.

The algorithm also singled out several other users for further investigation. For example, the

Table 12. Top five shill scores for seller: michael-33

Bidder	α	β	γ	δ	ε	ζ	Shill Score
chimam	0.53	0.26	0.88	0.82	0.52	0.95	6.50
rexth	0.27	0.34	0.75	0.65	0.85	0.74	5.07
bonnieellarae	0.27	0.21	0.75	0.65	0.83	0.50	4.79
charly.0	0.20	0.21	0.67	0.65	0.79	0.84	4.60
steve_howard	0.20	0.29	0.67	0.73	0.31	0.66	4.14

Table 13 Top five shill scores for seller: syschannel

Bidder	α	β	γ	δ	ε	ζ	Shill Score
kc10	0.63	0.21	0.80	0.97	0.86	0.97	7.11
bigriney1	0.50	0.26	0.75	0.87	0.63	0.21	5.54
reharrell	0.50	0.24	0.75	0.84	0.72	0.08	5.46
julhale	0.25	0.23	0.50	0.93	0.92	0.01	4.06
havokzprodigy	0.25	0.23	0.50	0.43	0.80	0.07	3.57

bidders 'bigrineyl' and 'reharrell' also exhibited dubious behavior. This is evidenced by the large number of auctions participated in, lack of winnings and a larger percentage of bids submitted per auction than other bidders. However, in comparison to 'kc10', the number of auctions, inter bid times and bid increments were slightly lower.

Bidders that had won any of the auctions had lowest shill scores. There were a large number of bidders that did not win, however, these bidders usually participated in only one auction. Such bidders tended to have a low range score (one to three) where their final ranking was heavily influenced by inter bid times and bid increments.

The commercial data shows that the algorithm can effectively allow shill investigators to rule out many bidders and focus on those with the most significant shill-like behavior.

The shill score algorithm is presently being tested on thousands of eBay auctions. We have written a program that parses an eBay HTML document extracting the auction data. This allows us to easily collect large amounts of commercial auction data via an automated process. We intend to continue collecting data in this manner to enable extensive testing of the shill score algorithm.

CONCLUSION

This chapter presents the first published algorithm to detect the presence of shill bidding in online English auctions. Our algorithm targets core shill behavior and calculates a score to indicate the likelihood that a bidder is a shill. To avoid detection a shill essentially must behave like a normal bidder. This renders a shill less effective, literally stopping shill bidding altogether.

The algorithm observes bidding patterns over a series of auctions held by a particular seller looking for shill-like behavior. Bidding characteristics studied include how many auctions a bidder participated in, the number of bids submitted and the rate of auctions won. Furthermore, the algorithm inspects how quickly a bidder bids, how much a bidder outbids by and what stage in the auction a bidder commences bidding.

The ability of the shill score algorithm to effectively identify shill bidders was verified on simulated auctions. When faced with aggressive and benign shilling, the algorithm was able to single out the shill bidder whilst exonerating legitimate bidders.

When tested on actual commercial data with no a priori knowledge of shills, the shill score algorithm detected definite shill behavior. This was in the form of both aggressive and benign shilling. The algorithm also singled out other bidders with moderately suspicious behavior.

The results of the tests showed that it is insufficient to rely on any single factor to determine whether a bidder is a shill. Instead a range of factors must be examined in relation to each other.

The shill score algorithm has significant practical and legal implications for commercial online auctions. This approach acts as both a shill detection mechanism and a deterrent to potential shills. Our algorithm serves as a basis for more sophisticated shill detection methods.

At present the algorithm only considers the case when there is one shill. However, in reality there may be multiple shills working in collusion. Multiple shills can employ sophisticated strategies that are harder to detect. Future work involves modifying the algorithm to better identify shill behavior with colluding shills.

REFERENCES

Barbaro, S., & Bracht, B. (2005). Shilling, Squeezing, Sniping: Explaining late bidding in online second-price auctions. *Working Paper Johannes-Gutenberg University, Mainz.*

Jank, W., & Shmueli, G. (2007). Studying Heterogeneity of Price Evolution in eBay Auctions via Functional Clustering. *Conditionally accepted at Adomavicius and Gupta (Eds.) Handbook of Information Systems Series: Business Computing*, Elsevier.

Kauffman, R., & Wood, C. (2003). An Investigation of Premium Bidding in Online Auctions. Working Paper.

Schwartz, J., & Dobrzynski, J. (2002). *3 men are charged with fraud in 1,100 art auctions on eBay.* The New York Times.

Shah, H., Joshi, N., & Wurman, P. (2003). Mining eBay: Bidding Strategies and Shill Detection. *WEBKDD 2002 - MiningWeb Data for Discovering Usage Patterns and Profiles*, Lecture Notes in Computer Science. 17-34.

Trevathan, J., & Read, W. (2006). RAS: A system for supporting research in online auctions. *ACM Crossroads, 12.4*, 23-30.

Wang, W., Hidvegi, Z., & Whinston, A. (2002). Shill Bidding in Multi-round Online Auctions. *In Proceedings of the 35th Hawaii International Conference on System Sciences.*

KEY TERMS

Aggressive Shilling: A shill bidder that consistently outbids any legitimate bid to force the price up as much as possible.

Benign Shilling: A shill bidder that only uses an initial bid at the auction's beginning in an attempt to try and stimulate bidding.

e-Commerce: A system used to conduct business transactions of buying and selling goods and services over a computer network.

Online Auctions: An auction conducted over the Internet.

Proxy Bidding: A system offered by Online Auctioneers that allows the bidder to enter the maximum price they are willing to pay, and will incrementally increase his/her current bid when out bid, up to the maximum price specified.

Shill Bidder: A bidder who engages in shill bidding behavior.

Shill Bidding: Using spurious bids on the seller's behalf to artificially inflate an auction's price.

Shill Score: A rating between zero and ten that indicates the likelihood that a bidder has engaged in typical shill behavior based on his/her past actions in a series of auctions.

Software Bidding Agents: A program that bids on a human bidder's behalf.

ENDNOTES

1. http://www.ebay.com
2. http://www.ubid.com
3. http://pages.ebay.com/help/policies/seller-shill-bidding.html
4. http://www.virtualgold.com
5. http://auction.maths.jcu.edu.au

Chapter XXVIII
Information Security at Large Public Displays

Carsten Röcker
University of California, San Diego, USA

Carsten Magerkurth
SAP Research, CEC St. Gallen, Switzerland

Steve Hinske
Institute for Pervasive Computing, ETH Zürich, Switzerland

ABSTRACT

In this chapter we present a novel concept for personalized privacy support on large public displays. In the first step, two formative evaluations are conducted in order to analyze the requirements of potential users regarding the protection of private information on large public displays. The insights gained in these evaluations are used to design a system that automatically adapts the information visible on public displays according to the current social situation and the individual privacy preferences of the user working on the display. In a third evaluation, the developed system is evaluated regarding its appropriateness for daily usage and its usefulness to protect privacy. The results of the evaluation show that users are in general willing to trust system-based protection mechanisms, provided that they are well implemented. In this context, the proposed combination of pre-defined privacy profiles and context-adapted information visualization proved to be a good trade-off between usability and adequate privacy protection.

1. INTRODUCTION AND MOTIVATION

A continuous trend towards higher mobility is observable in most companies, with employees spending considerable time away from their own desk, working in meeting rooms, other offices or in the hallway (Lamming et al., 2000). According to estimates, white-collar workers spend between 25% and 70% of their daily working time in conferences or meetings with colleagues (Eldridge et al., 1994; Whittaker et al., 1994). As large-screen displays are becoming increasingly prevalent in public spaces (Churchill et al., 2004), several projects address this evolution by providing 'walk-up-and-use' applications on large screens in public or semi-public areas. *Blue Board* (Russell & Gossweiler, 2001), for example, is a large plasma display with touch sensing and a badge reader to identify individuals. The on-board software is designed for personal use as well as small group collaborative usage. While *Blue Board* requires users to set up their content ahead of time and thus gives the user control over the information that is displayed, other systems, like *IM Here* (Huang et al., 2004), are designed for more spontaneous workgroup interaction. *IM Here* is a shared instant messaging system running on a large public display designed to facilitate informal communication while away from the desktop. Similar to (Huang & Mynatt, 2003), upcoming privacy and security problems are eluded by restricting the usage of the systems to small groups of users.

Although privacy guidelines have been available for quite some time (e.g., Langheinrich, 2001; Bellotti & Edwards, 2001) most developers still rely on social protocols or do not address privacy questions at all when designing applications for large public displays. Until today, there are very few approaches that help users with preserving their privacy while working on large displays in public places. In most cases (e.g., Rekimoto, 1998; Greenberg et al., 1999), additional private displays are used to generate and present personal information, while public information is displayed on a shared large display. A different approach using a stereographic display and special shutter glasses is described in (Shoemaker & Inkpen, 2001). Personal privacy is maintained through the filtering of the information on the shared display. Users wearing shutter glasses see the information publicly available as well as their own private information, while other people's private data is not visible to them. A similar system was developed by Yerazunis & Carbone (2002), which uses time-masked images to ensure privacy. As the system requires CRT displays with higher-than-usual screen refresh rates and special eyewear, the usage of the system is likewise restricted. Comparable systems were developed by Eaddy et al. (2004), Needham & Koizumi (1998) and Berger et al. (2005).

Although all approaches support individual privacy in an adequate way, they always require additional personal devices like PDAs or shutter glasses. But as most public displays are intended for walk-up-and-use applications, existing solutions are not very suitable.

The goal of the research work presented in this chapter is to give users the freedom to spontaneously work on large public and semi-public displays without being afraid of possible privacy infringements through passers-by. In contrast to existing approaches, we aimed at providing users with a system that automatically controls the information that is visible to others, but without requiring users to employ any additional equipment.

2. FORMATIVE EVALUATION OF USER REQUIREMENTS

In order to provide trusted mechanisms for privacy protection, it is most crucial to involve potential users in the design process right away from the beginning. Therefore, the requirements of potential users regarding privacy and security issues in multi-user situations were analyzed in two questionnaire-based evaluations.

The emphasis of the first evaluation was on data-related questions, especially on the willingness to disclose different types of information in the work environment and on the acceptance of system-controlled privacy measures. In the second evaluation we intended to analyze the system and interface requirements of potential users regarding the protection of private information on large public displays.

2.1 Analysis of Information Requirements

In order to guarantee satisfactory privacy protection while simultaneously minimizing interruptions during the work process, it is essential to know which information should be hidden from whom and when. Protecting work-related information from colleagues passing-by might not be necessary and doing so would most likely result in an unintended interruption of the ongoing task; but the situation is fundamentally different, when other people approach the display while the user is accessing private information.

In a first step, a questionnaire-based survey was carried out to investigate potential privacy concerns. The topic was addressed by investigating the demands of potential users regarding workplace-related information. This was done to obtain a deeper insight in the requirements for privacy in multi-user situations and establish a basis for the development of an appropriate concept. The emphasis of the survey was on privacy-related questions, especially on the importance of privacy in office environments, and the willingness to share personal information with co-workers. In order to get representative results, a target group outside the research community was chosen. This is of particular importance, as the majority of office workers will lack a detailed technical knowledge. The survey was conducted during an open house day at the Fraunhofer Institute for Integrated Information and Publications Systems (IPSI) in Darmstadt, Germany. The age distribution is shown in Table 1.

Being asked about their computing skills, 51.1 % rated themselves as advanced, 42.2 % as experts und 6.9 % as beginners (see Table 2). The survey shows that 45.0% of all users rate privacy 'important' and 32.8% as 'very important', while at the same time over one third (36.6%) never change their passwords. The results stress again the important role of privacy in ubiquitous computing environments (Lahlou et al., 2005), but also indicate a large discrepancy between the users' desire to protect privacy and their willingness to take relevant measures.

In the second part of the questionnaire, the participants were confronted with different types of information and asked, which information they would be willing to provide to whom.

In a local work environment, different types of information are available to those present. Depending on the degree of confidentiality, the information can be clustered into different groups. For example, some data are continuously available and immediately perceptible by everyone in the local environment (e.g., location), while other information might only be available to a certain group of people (e.g., business appointments). Besides this, there is also personal information, which is usually not meant to be shared with others, for example, the history of recently accessed web pages. To make the questions more concrete, examples of workplace information are used that represent certain categories of data. The participants had to fill out a table, containing different examples of information that could be captured in the work context and corresponding people who might have access to the information. In all questions, the captured information is used as the independent variable, and the persons, who can

Table 1. Age distribution (N=131)

Age	15-20	21-25	26-30	31-35	36-40	41-45	46-50	51-55	56-60
Frequency	8	43	37	17	8	4	5	6	3
Percentage [%]	6.1	32.8	28.2	13.0	6.1	3.1	3.8	4.6	2.3

Table 2. Importance of privacy (left) and computer skills (right)

Importance of Privacy	Freq.	Perc. [%]
1 (unimportant)	0	0
2	9	6.9
3	20	15.3
4	59	45.0
5 (very important)	43	32.8

Computer Skills	Freq.	Perc. [%]
Beginner	9	6.9
Advanced	67	51.1
Expert	55	42.2

access the information, as the dependent variable. The following diagrams show the answers for the different types of data (percentage of possible responses, multiple responses were feasible)

Table 3 lists different types of information that is continuously available to co-workers in a local office environment. Examples for such information are the current activity, the location of a colleague, or the progress of a task a team member is currently working on.

But not all workplace information is continuously perceptible to all persons in the local work environment. Some information is only available to a certain group of people, like members of a team. That information is usually not directly perceptible, but based on shared knowledge or accessible through a shared source of information like a group calendar or project plan. Examples of such information used in the questionnaire are assigned tasks and activities, business appointments, and information about previous tasks and projects.

The third group comprises information that is personal and therefore usually not available to team members. Such information includes private appointments, hobbies and personal preferences, and data about accessed websites.

The results indicate that the willingness to provide information varies widely depending on both, the type of information and the information receiver. In most cases there are differences between colleagues, superiors, and specially authorized persons. Users are generally very careful to grant others access to previously captured workplace information. Even information that is continuously visible to co-workers, like information about the current activity and task (7.63%) or location (8.40%), is not voluntarily shared with all others. The willingness to provide data is even lower for information that is usually not available

Table 3. Frequency and percentage of participants, who would provide different types of continuously available information to different recipients (N=131)

	Current Activity		Current Location		Task Progress	
Information Receiver	Freq.	Per. [%]	Freq.	Per. [%]	Freq.	Per. [%]
Nobody	20	15.27	25	19.08	14	10.69
Authorized Persons	40	30.53	37	28.24	45	34.35
Friends and Family	36	27.48	42	32.06	43	32.82
Colleagues	58	44.27	51	38.93	47	35.88
Superior	53	40.46	36	27.48	70	53.44
All	10	7.63	11	8.40	12	9.16

Table 4. Frequency and percentage of participants, who would provide different types of team internal information to different recipients (N=131)

	Assigned Tasks		Business Appointments		Previous Tasks	
Information Receiver	**Freq.**	**Per. [%]**	**Freq.**	**Per. [%]**	**Freq.**	**Per. [%]**
Nobody	9	6.87	12	9.16	10	7.63
Authorized Persons	58	44.27	53	40.46	47	35.88
Friends and Family	29	22.14	47	35.88	37	28.24
Colleagues	66	50.38	88	67.18	46	35.11
Superior	84	64.12	90	68.70	71	54.20
All	12	9.16	7	5.34	18	13.74

Table 5. Frequency and percentage of participants, who would provide different types of personal information to different recipients (N=131)

	Private Appointments		Personal Preferences		Accessed Websites	
Information Receiver	**Freq.**	**Per. [%]**	**Freq.**	**Per. [%]**	**Freq.**	**Per. [%]**
Nobody	37	28.24	15	11.45	55	41.98
Authorized Persons	30	22.90	27	20.61	27	20.61
Friends and Family	71	54.20	81	61.83	21	16.03
Colleagues	7	5.34	32	24.43	13	9.92
Superior	2	1.53	10	7.63	14	10.69
All	2	1.53	17	12.98	5	3.82

to team members, for example, information about recently accessed websites (3.82%).

The third part of the evaluation investigated the acceptance of automated protection mechanisms in group situations as well as the desired degree of system support regarding privacy protection. The goal was to understand if and how users want to be supported in protecting their privacy in dynamically changing group situations. The evaluation showed that most users (83%) would appreciate a system-based mechanism helping them to protect their information privacy. While automated privacy support seems to be favored by the majority of users, most users are very reluctant to provide the necessary information to auto-configure their privacy settings. For example, less than 10% of the users would accept the collection of biometric information, even if this would significantly reduce the required manual input. The results showed that system developers must not rely on active user participation when implementing measures to safeguard user privacy, but should aim at designing easy and intuitive ways to handle personal privacy and data security in everyday situations.

2.2 User Interface Requirements

The goal of the second evaluation was to investigate how automated protection mechanisms would influence the usage of large displays in public areas. During the evaluation, different scenarios were presented to the participants in a three-step process. First and prior to the presentation of the main scenarios, the participants were asked to assess the suitability of large displays in public areas. Therefore, examples of different applications and information types were presented to the participants, which had to be rated on a five-point scale.

In the second part of the evaluation, the participants were asked to visualize a scenario where they are working on a large public display located in a hallway of an office building. Since the display (or, more explicitly, the computer it is connected to) is integrated in the company network, the display can be used as a desktop replacement (i.e., all standard application are running on it). The scenario describes a situation, where several application windows (for example, an internet browser, a document viewer, and an e-mail program) are displayed on the public display. At the end of the scenario, the participants were explicitly reminded that passers-by are likely to see what they are doing, but also that these passers-by are mostly colleagues (i.e., people they are familiar with). In the following questions, they were asked to assess their perceived privacy while working on the display, to specify applications they would use in such a situation, and to rate the suitability of large public displays for accessing public as well as private information.

Besides this general information, we aimed at gaining specific feedback on how automated privacy protection would influence the usage of large displays in public environments. Therefore, the initial scenario was extended with a fictitious system, which automatically protects the privacy of users working on the display. The described system protects individual user privacy by automatically hiding sensitive information when other people approach the display. The participants, however, were asked not to care *how* this is achieved, but focus on the fact that they can work on the display without being afraid of potential privacy infringements.

The questions presented in the previous part were adapted to the extended scenario and had to be answered under the light of a generic privacy protection system that unobtrusively works in the background. In addition to that, the participants were asked to assess the usefulness of the presented approach and to answer several questions concerning the interface requirements of automated privacy protection systems. Altogether, N=55 people participated in the evaluation. The gender and age distribution are shown in Table 6.

In addition to the standard demographical information, the participants were asked to assess their technical experience (see Table 7).

Table 6. Gender and age distribution of the participants

Gender Distribution		
Male	Female	Total
36	19	55
65.45%	34.55%	100.00%

Age Distribution					
<25	25-34	35-44	45-54	>54	Total
16	22	4	9	4	55
29.09%	40.00%	7.27%	16.36%	7.27%	100.00%

Table 7. Technical experience of the participants

Very Experienced	Experienced	Average	Not Very Experienced	No Experience	Total
13	16	17	7	2	55
23.64%	29.09%	30.91%	12.73%	3.64%	100.00%

It is worth noticing that in most cases there were no or only slight differences between the demographical groups.

Above all, we wanted the participants to provide us with information about how suitable they consider large displays in public areas in general (see Table 8). We listed six applications for large public displays that had to be rated on a scale ranging from 1 (very suitable) to 5 (totally unsuitable).

Over 80% of the participants considered large displays to be suitable or very suitable for displaying rather public or general content such as advertisements or traffic information. In the case of entertainment-related content or presentations, the majority (over 60%) still classified large public displays as suitable or very suitable. The remaining two applications, namely desktop replacement and internet browsing, however, turned out to be rather unsuitable for being displayed on large public displays: more than half the interviewees considered them to be unsuitable or even absolutely unsuitable.

Based on the aforementioned scenario, where the participants were asked to imagine the situation of being within an office hallway working on a large public display, we asked the participants how comfortable they would feel, using such a large display in the described situation. Less than 10% stated that they would feel comfortable or even very comfortable (see Table 9).

We further asked them whether they would use the large display for viewing e-mails or documents of private content (e.g., an e-mail from a family member). The question had to be rated from 1 (yes, always) to 5 (no, never). The result was very distinct, but not yet surprising: almost all participants would rather not use a large public display for viewing private content.

Finally, we asked the participants to consider the case in which they have to immediately send an urgent e-mail of private nature. In the described

Table 8. Results to the answers "How suitable do you consider large displays for the following application: app" with app ∈ {advertising, traffic information, entertainment, presentations, desktop replacement, internet browsing}. The applications had to be rated on a scale from 1 (very suitable) to 5 (absolutely unsuitable).

Type of Application	(very) suitable	average	(absolutely) unsuitable
Internet Browsing	20.00%	25.45%	54.55%
Desktop Replacement	18.19%	18.18%	63.63%
Presentations	61.82%	27.27%	10.91%
Entertainment	67.27%	12.73%	20.00%
Traffic Information	87.27%	9.09%	3.64%
Advertising	83.64%	7.27%	9.09%

Table 9. Answers to the question "Would you feel comfortable using a large public display in an office hallway in general?", rated on a scale from 1 (very comfortable) to 5 (absolutely uncomfortable)

1	2	3	4	5	Total	Mean	Variance	Std. Error
2	3	21	14	15	55	3.67	1.0929	1.0454
3.64%	5.45%	38.18%	25.45%	27.27%	100.00%			

scenario, the large display is right next to them, compared to their own office, which is a few minutes away. The question was, whether they would prefer to use the large public display or rather go back to their private desktop computer instead.

Almost 80% would rather go all the way back to their desktop computer instead of using the public computer system directly next to them. The fact that a *private* e-Mail needs to be sent certainly is the main reason for this result. Furthermore, it is worth mentioning that the answer depended on the *technical experience*: while only less than 8% of the *very experienced* users would use the large display, more than 23% of the users that are *not very experienced* and 28% of the users that have *no experience* would use the large display.

In this context, we asked the participants how important privacy was to them in general. Similar to the scales before, the participants could express their preferences on a scale from 1 (very important) to 5 (not at all important). Again, the results were not really surprising as almost all participants considered privacy to be important or very important (see Table 12).

Summing up the results, the evaluation showed that users are largely concerned with their privacy and that they are rather reluctant to use large public displays, at least without proper protection against possible privacy infringements.

In the last part of the evaluation, we extended the initial scenario and asked the participants to imagine that there would be "some kind" of privacy protection system available that is able to protect their privacy by hiding private or sensitive content whenever other people approach the large public display. In the first part of this second questionnaire we explicitly requested

Table 10. Answers to the question "Would you use the large display for viewing private content?", rated on a scale from 1 (yes, always) to 5 (no, never)

1	2	3	4	5	Total	Mean	Variance	Std. Error
0	0	1	11	43	55	4.76	0.2169	0.4657
0.00%	0.00%	1.82%	20.00%	78.18%	100.00%			

Table 11. Answers to the question "If you need to send an urgent e-mail, would you rather go back to your desktop computer or use the large display (that happens to be spatially close to you)?"

Use Large Display	Go Back	Total
12	43	55
21.82%	78.18%	100.00%

Table 12. Answers to the question "How important is privacy to you in general?", rated on a scale from 1 (very important) to 5 (not important at all)

1	2	3	4	5	Total	Mean	Variance	Std. Error
29	24	1	0	1	55	1.55	0.5025	0.7089
52.73%	43.64%	1.82%	0.00%	1.82%	100.00%			

them to disregard *how* the system works. We then repeated the questions of whether they would feel generally comfortable with using the large public display (Table 13), and whether they would use the display for displaying public and private content (Table 14). The light bars stand for the answers if no privacy protection system is available while the dark bars represent the existence of such a system.

In case of public content, a system designed to prevent privacy infringement resulted in the frequency of participants willing to use a large public display to almost sextuple from 5.45% to 30.91% regarding answer 1 (yes, always).

In the case of private content, the result is even more obvious and distinct: while almost 80% of the participants answered that they would never (answer 5) use a large display for viewing private documents without a privacy protection system, this number shrunk to 20% given such a system.

Summarizing the results, it is evident that the provision of a privacy protection system can significantly increase the users' trust when using a large display in public environments.

3. ACTIVE PRIVACY SUPPORT FOR LARGE PUBLIC DISPLAYS

The insights gained in the previous evaluations were used to design a system for automated privacy support at large public displays. The developed application gives users the freedom to spontaneously work on large public displays, without the fear of privacy infringements through passers-by. The system automatically controls the information that is visible to others, without requiring users to employ any additional equipment. This is achieved by providing users with a "personal space" in front of large displays in a shared environment. Within that personal space, the information that is visible to others is automatically controlled according to the user's individual preferences. In order to adapt the information representation to the current context, people entering the private space around a public display are automatically detected and identified using infrared (IR) and radio frequency identification (RFID) technology. Based on the identity of the person entering the private space and the privacy preferences of the user working at the public display, the information

Table 13. Answers to the question "Would you use a large public display for viewing public information depending on whether a privacy protection system is available?", both rated on a scale from 1 (yes, always) to 5 (no, never)

	1	2	3	4	5
no system	5.45%	34.55%	30.91%	10.91%	18.18%
system	30.91%	45.45%	10.91%	9.09%	3.64%

Table 14. Answers to the question "Would you use a large public display for viewing private information depending on whether a privacy protection system is available?", both rated on a scale from 1 (yes, always) to 5 (no, never)

	1	2	3	4	5
no system	0.00%	0.00%	1.82%	20.00%	78.18%
system	5.45%	20.00%	27.27%	27.27%	20.00%

currently visible is automatically adapted. Before the technical realization of the system is presented, the key ideas, which guided the conceptual design process, are illustrated.

3.1 Personal Space Concept

The desire for a personal space that is not penetrated by others is one of the most basic human rights and it has become even more important within the last decades. This tendency is reflected in our society by increasing privacy concerns regarding current and future information and communication technologies (see, e.g., Lahlou et al., 2005; McCarthy et al., 2004; Palen & Dourish, 2003). Clarke (1999) defines this desire as "the interest that individuals have in sustaining a personal space, free from interference by other people". In this contribution, this real-world concept is adapted to the virtual domain. The term 'personal space' refers to the space in which all interactions are only visible to the interacting user. Or, from another perspective, being outside this specific private space does not allow another person to see the content and nature of the interaction taking place.

Figure 1 illustrates the aforementioned concept of a personal space. The left picture shows a user working on a large display in a public space. The semicircle in front of the display shows the user's personal space. In this example, the personal space represents exactly the physical space that is necessary to remain free of interruptions or intrusions. As this space is currently not invaded by other users, all content is being displayed. The black areas on the display represent applications or documents with confidential content, the grey areas indicate applications with public information. On the right picture another person is entering the personal space. As this person might threaten the information privacy of the user working at the display, the confidential content (black outline) is temporarily concealed, while the public information (grey) is still visible.

3.2 Context-Adapted Privacy Protection

As pointed out before, most users are not willing to share private information with colleagues. The problem encountered here is that information cannot be classified as being public or private in general. How confidential a certain type of information is primarily depends on the individual assessment of each user. For example, Palen (1999) found, that information regarded

Figure 1. Personal space around a public display (left), confidential information is hidden as soon as another person invades the personal space (right)

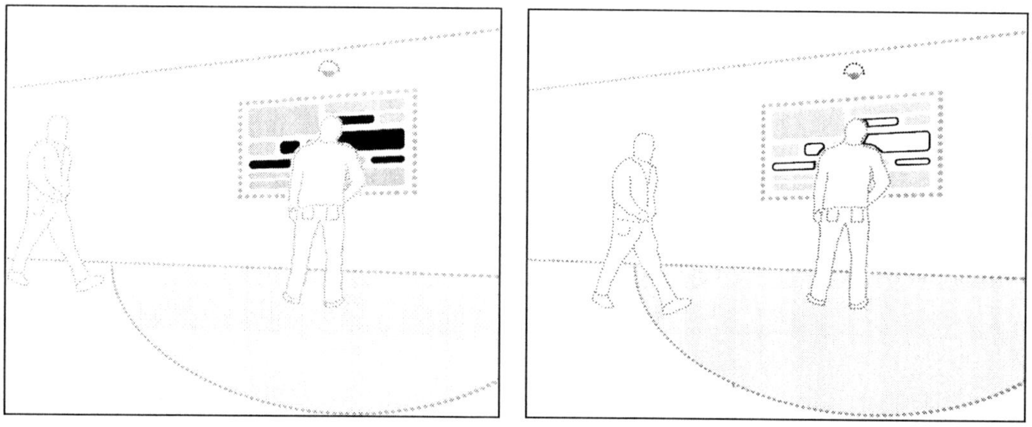

totally innocuous by some users, were considered personally private by others. In the same way, Zhao and Stasko (2002) argue that individuals usually have different comfort zones in the level of personal information being broadcasted and that these comfort zones change over time. They conclude that individuals should be allowed to select the level of information about them that is being transmitted. But privacy settings not only depend on the sender's preferences, they are also determined by the identity of the information receiver. The behavior regarding the disclosure of personal information in multi-user situations was investigated in various studies (see, e.g., Röcker, 2006 or Olson et al., 2005). All studies came to the result, that the willingness to provide information varies widely with the type of information and the information receiver.

3.3 Privacy Levels to Control Information

In real-world situations, the disclosure of personal information is usually done in an ad-hoc manner and often does not follow any strict rules. But when using an automated privacy protection system, the disclosure of personal information has to follow a basic concept with specific „rules". As illustrated before, users have different preferences depending on what they are doing and to whom they are providing certain information. Hence, the adaptation of the displayed information must depend on the content of the application or document as well as on the person(s) invading the personal space. But using individual privacy settings for each situation would require that all persons, documents and applications have to be classified beforehand.

3.3.1 Group-Based Privacy Control

Experiences with existing systems showed that individual classifications are not necessary to manage privacy in multi-user situations. In a study with N=36 users, Patil and Lai (2005) found a significant preference for defining privacy permissions at a group level. Around 70% of the participants chose to configure permissions in 'group mode', with significantly different permissions granted to the various groups. Based on the feedback gained by the participants, they conclude that utilizing grouping mechanisms provides the flexibility needed to appropriately manage the balance between privacy control and the burden of configuration. Results leading to similar design recommendations were found in studies by Olson et al. (2005) and Lederer et al. (2003).

3.3.2 Classification of Users

These findings led to the approach of using a group-based classification scheme, in which each individual is assigned to a specific 'privacy level'. Table 15 gives an example how privacy levels can be defined.

3.3.3 Classification of Documents and Applications

The classification of documents and applications is realized through a keyword system, which allows a high degree of flexibility. Every document and application can be assigned to one of the five privacy levels shown above. A keyword is a string that is searched for in the window title of a document or application. Figure 2 shows part of a screenshot taken from an application with an open document. The window title contains the name of the document ("Bank of America") and the name of the application ("Microsoft Internet Explorer").

Using the keyword system, a user can classify all websites accessed via the Internet Explorer to the highest privacy level (level 1) by adding the keyword 'Internet Explorer' to the keyword list of the first level. In addition, it is also possible to hide only specific websites. For example, adding the keywords "Bank of America" to the keyword

Table 15. Example for different privacy levels

Privacy Setting	Description
Level 1 (Private)	The highest privacy level covers the most private content and is meant for eyes of its owner only. This includes personal emails and private documents.
Level 2 (Partner)	The second privacy level includes all information that is meant for intimate circle of persons only. In this example, the user's partner is assumed to be trustworthier than everyone else.
Level 3 (Family)	This level contains all information that is family-internal and potentially accessible by all family members.
Level 4 (Friends)	Hides family-internal information (e.g., banking information), but still allows access to other personal information (e.g., pictures from the last holidays).
Level 5 (Public)	All applications containing personal or confidential information are hidden.

Figure 2. Screenshot of an open application with several keywords in the title bar

list of the second level, results in all documents containing the keywords "Bank of America" being hidden from all users except for the persons assigned to the second level. In this case it is not important which application is used to access the document.

3.4 Measure to Preserve Privacy

As there is a natural trade-off between usability and the level of privacy protection, several protection measures were implemented. Currently, there are six possible actions available to users, each having its specific advantages and disadvantages:

The settings for the different privacy levels are controlled using a graphical user interface, which enables users to adjust the levels to their individual preferences. The interface consists of two parts, the *Keyword Manager*, and the *Action Manager*.

The *Keyword Manager* comprises five keyword lists (corresponding to the five privacy levels), which can be individually adapted by the user. Furthermore, users can choose in which order the lists are checked, when a keyword is looked up. This concept enables users to express their general attitude towards sharing information. Users with a strong desire for privacy, who regard specific information as sensitive, unless expressed otherwise (e.g., by creating an exception rule), would choose to start the keyword search in the keyword list that represents privacy level 1 (private).

The *Action Manager* allows users to choose the action (as described in Table 16), which is taken in case of a keyword match. In addition, users can overrule the automatic comparison as well as the action taken for affected windows (e.g., windows that have one or more keywords in their title bar). By doing this, they can choose between "All Windows" and "Active Window". The option "All Windows" executes the selected action for every open window, regardless of the keywords in the title bar. "Active Window" affects only the currently active window (i.e., the window the user is currently working on).

4. TECHNICAL REALIZATION OF SPIROS

In order to implement the concept outlined in the previous section, we developed a privacy protection system called SPIROS (**S**ystem for **P**rivacy-Enhanced **I**nformation **R**epresentation in **O**pen **S**paces). Following the conceptual design approach, privacy protection is achieved in a three-step process:

- First, people entering the personal space of the user are detected and if possible identified.
- Second, the system determines and subsequently compares the privacy levels of the identified person(s) with the privacy levels of the currently open applications and documents.
- Third, the system initiates privacy-preserving measures according to the result of the comparison and the user's preferences.

The remainder of this section provides a detailed description of the underlying sensing infrastructure as well as the software architecture.

4.1 Sensing Infrastructure

The necessary information about nearby individuals is collected via a hybrid sensing infrastructure

Table 16. Advantages and disadvantages of the different measures for privacy protection

Method	Advantages	Disadvantages
Privacy Protection De-Activated	No interference of ongoing activities	No privacy protection at all
Display Message	No interference of ongoing activities, but users are still aware of people entering their personal space	No automated privacy protection by the system, but user can manually hide specific content
Open Cover Window	All open windows remain in their position, adequate privacy protection since confidential data is visually blocked	Interference of current activities, all windows are still visible in the taskbar
Minimize Window	All open windows will appear in the same position as before, good privacy protection as confidential information is temporarily hidden	Interference of current activities, all windows are still visible in the taskbar
Hide Window	All open windows will appear in the same position as before, high privacy protection since they are temporarily hidden (even in the taskbar)	Interference of current activities
Close Window	Highest level of privacy, since all confidential applications and documents are closed	Interference of current activities, work is lost unless saved before

consisting of infrared sensors and RFID readers. People entering a personal space are detected by the infrared sensors and are simultaneously identified through the RFID system. All sensors are individually adjustable regarding their detection range and angle. This allows an adaptation of the user's personal space to the specific requirements of the environment.

4.1.1 RFID Readers

RFID is already widely used today (Fleisch & Mattern, 2005) and belongs to the basic sensor types available in most smart office environments. RFID technology enables contactless identification of people and objects that are equipped with a transponder. As RFID transponders are currently being integrated into a vast variety of everyday objects, it is assumed that users in smart office environments are not required to carry any additional RFID transponders in order to be identified. The SPIROS system was realized using an active RFID, which allows adjusting the reading ranges of the system to the spatial extension of the personal space. Hence, people carrying an RFID transponder are identified as soon as they enter the personal space around a public display.

4.1.2 IR Sensors

To detect the presence of persons who are not equipped with an RFID transponder, a special motion detection system was developed (see Figure 3). The system consists of several infrared detectors and a central communication unit, which can handle up to ten IR detectors simultaneously. The IR sensors are distributed in the environment and detect motion within a defined area. The communication unit aggregates the signals received from all IR sensors, and transmits them via a USB link to a host computer. Hence, if people approach the display, who can not be identified, it would be still possible to hide all personal information currently being displayed.

4.2 SPIROS Architecture

The SPIROS architecture consists of three main components (see Figure 4):

- The *SPIROS Scanner Manager* (SSM), which identifies persons entering the personal space around the public display,
- The *SPIROS Privacy Manager* (SPM), which adapts the displayed information to the pre-defined user preferences and identified persons, and

Figure 3. Large public display with an RFID antenna in upper left corner (left) and infrared detection system with two sensors (right)

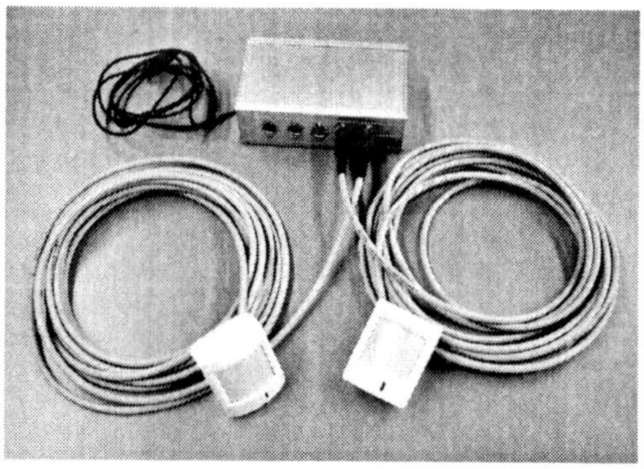

Figure 4. General overview of the system

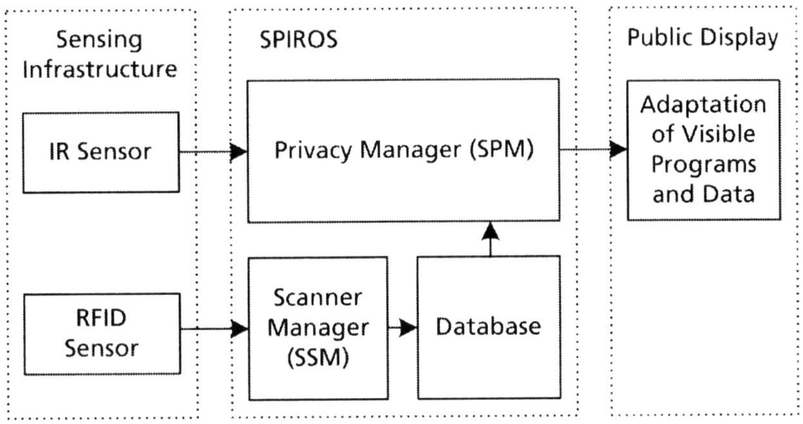

- A database for storage and communication.

The separation of the SSM and SPM was done due to performance reasons. In addition, the separation allows several SSMs to run simultaneously, with each entity being responsible for one or more large public displays. This is of particular importance if several public displays are spatially distributed in an intelligent environment.

The main function of the SSM component is the identification of people who are within the reading ranges of the connected RFID readers. The IDs of all read RFID transponders are stored in the database. This data is then used by the SPM component. The SPM is responsible for adapting the displayed information to the user's privacy preferences and the persons currently present around the display. Whenever one of the IR sensors next to the display is triggered, the SPM retrieves the ID of the RFID transponders within the personal space and determines the privacy level of the corresponding person(s) as well as the privacy levels of the currently open windows. Based on this information, the content that is not supposed to be seen by the passers-by is temporarily hidden until the persons have left the personal space.

The following sections provide a more detailed description of the different SPIROS components and illustrate their general operating principles.

4.2.1 SPIROS Scanner Manager (SSM)

As mentioned before, the SSM operates the RFID readers and inserts all scanned tags within reading ranges of the system into the database (see below). Once the SSM has successfully connected to the RFID reader and the database, it starts polling the reader for RFID transponders in range. Whenever transponders are read by the reader, the SSM checks whether the transponders' IDs have already been inserted into the database. If this is not the case, the newly discovered ID is added to the database. The main problems encountered in the test phase were malfunctions due to missing or erroneous identification data. This happened, for example, if RFID transponders were not detected although they were within the reading range. To eliminate such problems, the SSM uses an internal counter for each transponder. As explained above, the ID of each detected transponder is inserted into the database. This entry is only removed if the transponder is not read for three consecutive reading cycles.

4.2.2 SPIROS Privacy Manager (SPM)

When the personal space of a user is invaded by other persons, the SPM hides confidential information according to the user's preferences. On starting, the SPM retrieves the user's profile from the database, creates a temporary table, and initiates the connection to the IR sensors using DirectX. The temporary table contains the user's current relationships to all other users. This is done by assigning the user's partner(s) to the *'partner level'*, family members to the *'family level'*, friends to the *'friends level'*, and all remaining users to the *'public level'*. Once the initialization phase has been completed, the SPM switches to the operating phase.

The SPM starts by checking an internal counter, which that is meant for undoing actions (e.g., windows that are minimized or hidden need to reappear). After each cycle, the counter is increased by one. If this counter reaches a certain limit, all actions taken before are reversed. In a second step, the SPM checks the IR sensors for activity. If any motion is detected, the counter is set back to zero. This is necessary in order to guarantee that all confidential information is hidden as long as other users are in close proximity to the display.

Based on the IDs of the detected transponders, the highest privacy level of all users within the personal space is calculated. In the same way, the privacy levels of the currently open windows are determined by scanning all window titles. To determine which windows should be hidden, the privacy levels of both, the passers-by and the active windows are compared. Depending on the user's pre-defined preferences, a specific action is initiated (see Table 16).

4.2.3 SPIROS Database

All information required by the SSM and SPM component is stored in a central database. The main table (*users*) contains the users' IDs as well as the individual privacy preferences. The privacy levels described in Table 15 are represented through the three tables *partners*, *family_members* and *friends*, which contain information about the social relationships among users. If users are not contained in one of these three tables, they are assigned to privacy level five ('public'). To guarantee a quick look-up, a temporary table is created, that contains the user's current relationships to all other users. The keywords used for determining the privacy level of an active window are stored in five individual keyword tables. The IDs of detected RFID transponders are stored in the table *scanned_rfids*, and are then mapped to the table *users* by the table *temp*.

5. EVALUATION OF THE DEVELOPED PROTOTYPE SYSTEM

The SPIROS prototype application was tested in a third evaluation. Therefore, the developed system was presented to the same group of persons who already participated in the second study. This time, the participants were asked to rate the conceptual approach as well as the implemented protection mechanisms regarding their appropriateness for daily usage and their usefulness to protect privacy. The first part of the questionnaire briefly described the developed system. It was explained that the system scans the environment and is able to detect people passing-by the display. It is further illustrated how users can classify documents and applications and assign special actions that will be executed by the system if other persons approach the display.

For a better understanding, a concrete situation was described in form of a scenario. The participants were asked to imagine a situation, were they are viewing a project-related document as well as a news page in an additional browser window. The project document contains information that only authorized people (in this case project members) are allowed to see. While they are browsing through the confidential project document, a person, who works in the same company, but is not a member of the project team, approaches the display. In this case, the presented system would be able to minimize or hide the project-related document, but leave the browser window open. Thus, the approaching colleague would see the news website, but not the confidential project information.

We first wanted to know, how comfortable the participants would feel using SPIROS compared to other approaches. Therefore, the participants were asked to rate the different approaches on a scale from 1 (very comfortable) to 5 (absolutely uncomfortable).

The results shown in Table 17 basically disclose two things. First, that there is a tremendous difference between having a privacy protection system or not. And second, that users feel more comfortable with the idea of using SPIROS than using other systems. The first premise is rather obvious: while the majority of the users would feel rather uncomfortable if no system was installed (answers 4 and 5), only 20% felt the same way if there is a system available. The second point is less obvious but still visible: comparing the statistic means and variances of each distribution, the observable differences demonstrate the superiority of SPIROS over other approaches (see Table 18).

Thus, it is not surprising that the majority of users would prefer SPIROS. More than two third (67%) are willing to protect their privacy with SPIROS when asked whether they would use the system (see below). Very important was also the assessment of the possible measures that can be taken by SPIROS. During the evaluation, we proposed four possible actions, which had to be rated on according to their appropriateness to protect privacy (see Table 19 for the results):

- "Show Message"
  (a pop-up message saying "someone is approaching" is displayed),
- "Cover Window"
  (a cover window with harmless content pops us and covers private or sensitive information),
- "Minimize Window"
  (all windows that currently display private or sensitive content are minimized), and

Table 17. Answers to the question "How comfortable would you feel working on a large display in a public environment?", rated on a scale from 1 (very comfortable) to 5 (absolutely uncomfortable)

	SPIROS	**Generic System**	**No System**
(very) suitable	52.73%	45.45%	9.09%
average	34.55%	34.55%	38.18%
(absolutely) unsuitable	12.72%	20.00%	52.73%

Table 18. Mean and Variance of the question "How comfortable would you feel working on a large display in a public environment?", rated on a scale from 1 (very comfortable) to 5 (absolutely uncomfortable)

Type of Privacy Protection	***Mean***	***Variance***
No System	3.67	1.0929
Generic System	2.67	0.8747
SPIROS	2.42	0.8615

- "Hide Window"
  (completely hides all windows displaying sensitive content, i.e., they are not even visible in the task bar).

We were rather curious to find out which action would be preferred to protect visual privacy at public displays. The feedback on displaying a message was relatively balanced: obviously, people see this action very differently. The other three actions received a better feedback: more than 50% considered the cover window to be good or very good, more than 60% thought the same of minimizing, and early 70% found hiding to be good or very good. Apparently, hiding private or confidential information seems to be the preferable solution for most of the participants. Finally, we wanted to know whether the participants would generally use SPIROS (see Table 20). Looking at the previous results, it is not surprising that the majority of participants would use SPIROS: more than two third (67%) are willing to protect their privacy with the described system.

6. CONCLUSION

In this chapter we presented a novel concept for personalized privacy support on large public displays. In a first step, two formative evaluations were conducted in order to analyze the requirements of potential users regarding the protection of private information on large public displays. The insights gained in these evaluations were used to design a system that automatically adapts the information visible on public displays according to the current social situation and the individual privacy preferences of the user working on the display. In a third evaluation, the developed system was evaluated regarding its appropriateness for daily usage and its usefulness to protect privacy. The results of the evaluation showed that users are in general willing to trust system-based protection mechanisms, provided that they are well implemented. In this context, the proposed combination of pre-defined privacy profiles and context-adapted information visualization proved to be a good trade-off between usability and adequate privacy protection.

Table 19. Answers to the question "What do you think of each possible action?", rated on a scale from 1 (very suitable) to 5 (absolutely unsuitable)

	Hide Window	Minimize Window	Cover Window	Display Message
(very) suitable	69.09%	61.82%	50.90%	0.4182
average	20.00%	16.36%	30.91%	0.2364
(absolutely) unsuitable	10.91%	21.82%	18.19%	0.3454

Table 20. Answers to the question "Would you use such a system?"

Yes	*No*	*Total*
37	18	55
67.27%	32.73%	100.00%

REFERENCES

Bellotti, V., & Edwards, K. (2001). Intelligibility and Accountability: Human Considerations in Context Aware Systems. In: *Human-Computer Interaction, Special Issue on Context-Aware Computing, 16*(2, 3 & 4), 193 – 212

Berger, S., Kjeldsen, R., Narayanaswami, C., Pinhanez, C., Podlaseck, M., & Raghunath, M. (2005). Using Symbiotic Displays to View Sensitive Information in Public. In: *Proceedings of the International Conference on Pervasive Computing and Communications* (PerCom'05), Kauai Island, HI, USA, pp. 139 – 148.

Churchill, E. F., Nelson, L., Denoue, L., Helfman, J., & Murphy, P. (2004). Interactive Systems in Public Places: Sharing Multimedia Content with Interactive Public Displays: A Case Study. In: *Proceedings of the Conference on Designing Interactive Systems: Processes, Practices, Methods, and Techniques*, pp. 7 – 16.

Clarke, R. (1999). *Introduction to Dataveillance and Information Privacy, and Definitions of Terms.* Retrieved January 13, 2006, from http://www.anu.edu.au/people/Roger.Clarke /DV/Intro.html

Eaddy, M., Blasko, G., Babcock, J., & Feiner, S. (2004). My Own Private Kiosk: Privacy-Preserving Public Displays. In: *Proceedings of the International Symposium on Wearable Computers* (ISWC'04), pp. 132 – 135.

Eldridge, M., Barnard, P., & Bekerian, D. (1994). Autobiographical memory and Daily Schemes at Work. In: *Memory, 2*(1), 51-74.

Fleisch, E., & Mattern, F. (Eds.). (2005). *Das Internet der Dinge. Ubiquitous Computing und RFID in der Praxis: Visionen, Technologien, Anwendungen, Handlungsanleitungen.* Heidelberg, Germany: Springer-Verlag.

Greenberg, S., Boyle, M., & LaBerge, J. (1999). PDAs and Shared Public Displays: Making Personal Information Public, and Public Information Personal. In: *Personal Technologies*, 3(1), 54 – 64.

Huang, E. M., & Mynatt, E. D. (2003). Semi-Public Displays for Small, Co-located Groups. In: *Proceedings of the ACM Conference on Human Factors in Computing Systems* (CHI'03), pp. 49 – 56.

Huang, E. M., Russell, D. M., & Sue, A. E. (2004). IM Here: Public Instant Messaging on Large, Shared Displays for Workgroup Interactions. In: *Proceedings of the ACM Conference on Human Factors in Computing Systems* (CHI'04), pp. 279-286.

Lahlou, S., Langheinrich, M., & Röcker, C. (2005). Privacy and Trust Issues with Invisible Computers. In: *Communications of the ACM, 48*(3), 59-60.

Lamming, M., Eldridge, M., Flynn, M., Jones, C., & Pendlebury, D. (2000). Satchel: Providing Access to Any Document, Any Time, Anywhere. In: *ACM Transactions on Computer-Human Interaction*, 7(3), 322 – 352.

Langheinrich, M. (2001). Privacy by Design – Principles of Privacy Aware Ubiquitous Systems. In: *Proceedings of the 3rd International Conference on Ubiquitous Computing* (Ubicomp'01), September 2001, Atlanta, USA, pp. 273-291.

Lederer, S., Dey, A., & Mankoff, J. (2003). Who Wants to Know What When? Privacy Preference Determinants in Ubiquitous Computing. In: *Proceedings of the ACM Conference on Human Factors in Computing Systems* (CHI'03), Ft. Lauderdale, USA, pp. 724-725.

McCarthy, J. F., McDonald, D. W., Soroczak, S., Nguyen, D. H., & Rashid, A. M. (2004). Augmenting the Social Space of an Academic Conference. In: *Proceedings of the ACM Conference on Computer Supported Cooperative Work* (CSCW'04), Chicago, Illinois, USA, pp. 39 – 48.

Needham, B. H., & Koizumi, D. H. (1998). *Method of Displaying Private Data to Collocated Users*, US Patent 5,963,371.

Olson, J. S., Grudin, J., & Horvitz, E. (2005). A Study of Preferences for Sharing and Privacy. In: *Extended Abstracts of the ACM Conference on Human Factors in Computing Systems* (CHI'05), 1985-1988.

Palen, L. (1999). Social, Individual and Technological Issues for Groupware Calendar Systems. In: *Proceedings of the ACM Conference on Human Factors in Computing Systems* (CHI'99), pp. 17-24.

Palen, L., & Dourish, P. (2003). Unpacking "Privacy" for a Networked World. In: *Proceedings of the ACM Conference on Human Factors in Computing Systems* (CHI'03), Ft. Lauderdale, Florida, USA, pp. 129-136.

Patil, S., & Lai, J. (2005). Who Gets to Know What When: Configuring Privacy Permissions in an Awareness Application. In: *Proceedings of the ACM Conference on Human Factors in Computing Systems* (CHI'05), pp. 101-110.

Rekimoto, J. (1998). A Multiple Device Approach for Supporting Whiteboard-based Interactions. In: *Proceedings of the ACM Conference on Human Factors in Computing Systems* (CHI'98), pp. 18-23.

Röcker, C. (2006). *Awareness and Informal Communication in Smart Office Environments.* Verlag Dr. Driesen, Taunusstein, Germany. ISBN 3-936328-65-X.

Russell, D. M., & Gossweiler, R. (2001). On the Design of Personal & Communal Large Information Scale Appliances. In: *Proceedings of the International Conference on Ubiquitous Computing* (UbiComp'01), pp. 354-361.

Shoemaker, G. B. D, & Inkpen, K. M. (2001) Single Display Privacyware: Augmenting public displays with private information. In: *Proceedings of the ACM Conference on Human Factors in Computing Systems* (CHI'01), pp. 522-529.

Whittaker, S., Frohlich, D., & Daly-Jones, O. (1994). Informal workplace communication - What is it like and how might we support it? In: *Proceedings of the ACM Conference on Human Factors in Computing Science* (CHI '95). ACM, NY, pp. 131-137.

Yerazunis, W. S., & Carbone, M. (2002) Privacy-Enhanced Displays by Time-Masking Images, *Technical Report TR2002-011*, Mitsubishi Electric Research Laboratories.

Zhao, Q. A., & Stasko, J. T. (2002) What's Happening? Promoting Community Awareness Through Opportunistic Peripheral Interfaces. In: *Proceedings of the Conference on Advanced Visual Interfaces* (AVI'02), pp. 69-74.

ADDITIONAL REFERENCES

Bohn, J., Coroama, V., Langheinrich, M., Mattern, F., Rohs, M. (2004). Living in a World of Smart Everyday Objects – Social, Economic, and Ethical Implications. In: Journal of Human and Ecological Risk Assessment, Vol. 10, No. 5, pp. 763 – 786.

Bohn, J., Coroama, V., Langheinrich, M., Mattern, F., Rohs, M. (2005). Social, Economic, and Ethical Implications of Ambient Intelligence and Ubiquitous Computing. In: W. Weber, J. Rabaey, E. Aarts (Eds.): Ambient Intelligence. Springer-Verlag, Heidelberg, pp. 5 – 29.

Burkhardt, J., Henn, H., Hepper, H., Rindtorff, K., Schaeck, T. (2001). Pervasive Computing. Addison Wesley, Reading.

Cook, D., Das, S. (2004). Smart Environments: Technology, Protocols and Applications. Wiley-Interscience.

Feith, A. (2003). Privacy Aspects in Ubiquitous Computing. Technical Report of Fraunhofer's Integrated Publication and Information Systems Institute (IPSI), Darmstadt, Germany.

Ferguson, G. T. (2003). Have Your Objects Call My Objects. In: Harvard Business Review, Vol. 80, No. 6, pp. 138 – 143.

Friedewald, M., Vildjiounaite, E., Wright, D. (2006). The Brave New World of Ambient Intelligence: A State-of-the-Art Review. Deliverable D1 of the SWAMI consortium to the European Commission under contract 006507.

Gellersen, H.-W., Schmidt, A., Beigl, H.-W. (2000). Adding Some Smartness to Devices and Everyday Things. Paper presented at the IEEE Workshop on Mobile Computing Systems and Applications, December 7 – 8, Monterrey, USA.

Hansmann, U., Merk, L., Nicklous, M., Stober, T. (2001). Pervasive Computing Handbook. Springer-Verlag, Berlin, Germany.

Mattern, F. (2002). The Vision and Technical Foundations of Ubiquitous Computing. In: Upgrade, Vol. 2, No. 5, pp. 2 – 6.

Mattern, F. (2005). Die technische Basis für das Interner der Dinge. In: E. Fleisch, F. Mattern (Eds.): Das Internet der Dinge - Ubiquitous Computing und RFID in der Praxis: Visionen, Technolgien, Anwendungen, Handlungsanleitungen. Springer-Verlag, Heidelberg, Germany, pp. 39 – 66.

Schoch, T., Strassner, M. (2003). Wie smarte Dinge Prozesse unterstützen. In: HMD, No. 229, Februar 2003, pp. 23 – 32.

Tennenhouse, D. (2000). Proactive Computing. In: Communications of the ACM, Vol. 43, No. 5, pp. 43 – 50.

von Locquenghien, K. (2006). On the Potential Social Impact of RFID-Containing Everyday Objects Science. In: Technology & Innovation Studies, Vol. 2, No 1, pp. 57 –78.

Weiser, M. (1991). The Computer for the Twenty-First Century. In: Scientific American, Vol. 265, No. 3, pp. 94 – 104.

Westin, A. F. (1967). Privacy and Freedom. Atheneum, New York, USA.

KEY TERMS

Informational Privacy: The term privacy dates back to 1450 (see Feith, 2003) and is constantly adjusted to the needs of a changing society. In its original meaning, the term privacy referred to a state of 'being apart or belonging to oneself', in contrast to belonging to the state. When the term privacy is used today, especially in relation with information and communication technology, it usually refers to the concept of informational privacy. One of the most popular definitions is probably the one by Westin (1967), who defined privacy as 'the claim of individuals, groups or institutions to determine for themselves when, how and to what extend information about them is communicated to others'. In this context, the term informational privacy refers to all data about a person, in general everything other people know about a person, and especially includes individual-related data (von Locquenghien, 2006).

Pervasive Computing: The concept of 'Pervasive Computing' is very similar to the one of Ubiquitous Computing. But while the term Ubiquitous Computing is mainly used in the academic domain, the notion of Pervasive Computing is mainly used in industry (see, e.g., Burkhardt et al., 2001 or Hansmann et al., 2003). The term was originally coined by IBM and refers to a shift in corporate computing systems (Friedewald et al., 2006). The only difference of both visions is their temporal scope. While Ubiquitous Computing envisions the omnipresent usage of computer-enhanced everyday objects, the focus of Pervasive Computing is on available respectively emerging technologies, like, e.g. mobile commerce applications or web-based business processes (Mattern, 2005).

Proactive Computing: The vision of 'Proactive Computing' (Tennenhouse, 2000) goes even beyond those of Ubiquitous and Pervasive Computing. It anticipates future environments, in which networked computers proactively anticipate our needs and, sometimes, take actions on our behalf.

Radio Frequency Identification: Radio Frequency Identification (RFID) is a generic term, describing systems which use radio or electromagnetic propagation for contactless identification of tagged objects. RFID systems usually consist of three components: a transponder containing information, an antenna, used to transmit the signals between the reader and the transponder, and a reader that receives data from a transponder and passes the data to a host system for processing.

Smart Artifacts: The notion of 'Smart Artifacts' describes technology-enhanced everyday objects, which are equipped with sensors, memory and communication capabilities (see, e.g., Ferguson, 2003 or Gellersen et al., 2000). Hence, they are able to capture information about their surrounding, communicate with each other and react according to previously defined rules (Schoch and Strassner, 2003). Through the capability to interact with humans directly, they can help users to accomplish their tasks in new, intuitive ways (Bohn et al., 2004; 2005). The terms 'Smart Objects' and 'Intelligent Objects' are synonymously used and describe the same underlying concepts.

Smart Environments: Based on the initial idea of Ubiquitous Computing (Weiser, 1991), the concept of 'Smart Environments' envisions a future, where a multitude of computers are seamlessly embedded into everyday objects of the physical world. In this sense, Cook and Das (2004) define a smart environment as "a small world, where all kinds of smart devices are continuously working to make inhabitants' lives more comfortable".

Ubiquitous Computing: The vision of 'Ubiquitous Computing' was first formulated by Weiser (1991), who argues, that computers should be integrated into the physical environment, and hence be effectively invisible to the user, rather than distinct objects on the desktop. Weiser envisioned the omnipresence of tiny, wirelessly interconnected computers, which are embedded into just about any kind of everyday object (Mattern, 2002). Regarding the interaction with ubiquitous computing applications, the user is not necessarily part of each transaction, instead he controls the system from the outside (Tennenhouse, 2000).

Chapter XXIX The Sense of Security and Trust

Yuko Murayama
Iwate Prefectural University, Japan

Carl Hauser
Washington State University, USA

Natsuko Hikage
Iwate Prefectural University, Japan

Basabi Chakraborty
Iwate Prefectural University, Japan

ABSTRACT

The sense of security, identified with the Japanese term, Anshin, is identified as an important contributor to emotional trust. This viewpoint suggests that designers should consider the subjective sense of security as well as objective security measures in designing systems and their user interfaces. A survey of users reveals both the personal and the environmental factors contributing to the users' sense of security when using the Internet. A more encompassing view of Anshin as including safety, reliability, and other non-functional properties of systems may provide additional insights for system design.

INTRODUCTION

Security of systems and services is an enormous concern in the modern world. The word *security* in the context of these concerns almost always has a meaning related to the technical aspects of security, either referring to means for being secure (*The Oxford English Dictionary,* security definitions 5-7) or "the condition of being protected from or not exposed to danger; safety" (definition 1).

Definition 2 from *The Oxford English Dictionary* provides a different, rather more subjective, sense for the word security: "Freedom from doubt;

confidence, assurance. Now chiefly, well-founded confidence, certainty." It is this less commonly addressed (at least in the technical literature) sense of the word that underlies the common phrase "a false sense of security." Yet, as Dillon (1996, p. 125) observes, the Latin antecedent *securitas*, deriving from *sine+cura* meaning literally "without care," conveys this meaning, not the others. In Japanese, the word *Anshin*, combining *An*—to ease—and *Shin*—mind or worry—conveys much the same idea.

One might well ask how (and whether) this emotional or subjective sense of security—Anshin—relates to achievement of objective security in the sense of Definition 1. Studies such as the AOL/NCSA Online Safety Study (2005) are indicative of the issue: a large fraction (79%) of surveyed users felt their personal computers were either very safe or somewhat safe from viruses but when examined by independent experts 56% of those users' machines were found to lack current virus protection software. People feel like their computers are safer than they really are. This feeling is itself a barrier to achieving better security. In the realm of people's physical security, De Becker (1997) argues that wariness or even fear, that is absence of Anshin, is often an essential contributor to achieving safety and he provides many examples..

The concept of *trust* is intimately related to the idea of *sense of security* as well. People using a computer system or service are usually incurring some financial or privacy risk. What factors contribute to willingness to engage in these transactions or in other words to trust the system or service provider? We present here our current understanding of the relationship between *trust* and the *sense of security* in the hope that it will be found useful in the design of computer systems.

We begin with background concerning research on the structure of trust and Anshin, followed by discussion of our understanding of the implications of this research and the questions it raises for design. We very briefly present the results of analysis of a survey that we conducted to discover more about how people regard providers of computer systems and surveys. We conclude with a summary of our current understanding of these issues and a number of questions that require further investigation.

BACKGROUND

In Japanese, the term Anshin is commonly used to mean what we have called the sense of security. The word can refer to not only security against a threat but also to express confidence in an outcome, such as in the context of having Anshin that I will be on time for my flight because I am on a train scheduled to reach the airport with time to spare.

The use of the term Anshin in technological contexts has been investigated primarily in the field of *risk communication*—the process by which nuclear power plant providers, experts, and residents of a plant area interact in order so that residents can get Anshin regarding their safety (Kikkawa et al., 2003, pp.1-8). In the field of risk communication, Kikkawa identified two Anshin states that might be reached, one *with* knowledge and the other *without* knowledge. When one has knowledge of technology and feels secure, one is in the state of Anshin *with knowledge*. On the other hand, when one does not have such knowledge and yet feels secure, one is in the state of Anshin *without knowledge*. Anshin with knowledge is achieved by active learning and seeking information by users, as well as when technology experts provide information to users.

Indeed, if we broaden our view of the sense of security to include trust issues we find more related work. An extensive literature is developing on trust in various disciplines such as sociology, psychology and economics. Understanding the factors that contribute to and inhibit trust in human-machine and machine-machine interactions is important for system and service providers. Ways are needed to quantify trust in making decisions about whether and how to interact. Furthermore, system designers will want to incorporate design elements that facilitate rather than inhibit trust.

Different researchers have attempted to define trust from different points of view and consequently there are several definitions of trust.

Working from a psychological viewpoint, Deutsch (1960, 1962) defined trust in an interpersonal context. His definition is based on an individual's perceived values of benefit and cost associated with a particular event.

Sociologists Luhman (1979) and Berber (1983) provide definitions from a sociological perspective. Luhman considers trust to be a means of reducing the complexity of society. Every time we face a decision making situation, we have to make some assumptions taking into account the particular situation and the particular environment and then make some trusting choice. Luhman also considered this choice as a means of handling risk. Berber linked trust to society and culture, rather than Deutsch's approach of linking to an individual's perceived value of cost and benefits. He presented three expectations that involve some of the fundamental meanings of trust: expectation of the persistence and fulfillment of the natural and moral social order; expectation of technically competent role of performance; and expectation that partners in interaction will carry out their obligations and responsibilities. In general sense, for Berber, trust is an expectation that the natural, physical and biological order will continue to hold true.

Likewise, Yamagishi (1998), another sociologist, states that trust is both a social lubricant and a bond. He analyzes the value of trust in social settings in terms of other manifestation like security, cooperation, reputation, intelligence, and so forth. Yamagishi (1998, p. 50) also provides a unique perspective relating Anshin and trust. For him, Anshin is the belief that we have no social uncertainty, whereas trust is needed when we have high social uncertainty. Trust is expectation of others' intentions based on the trustor's judgment of others' personalities and feelings.

Most of the research on trust described above is concerned primarily with cognitive trust. Sociologists Lewis and Weigert (1985) also identify emotional trust, distinguishing the two types as follows; "trusting behavior may be motivated primarily by strong positive affect for the object of trust (emotional trust) or by 'good rational reasons' why the object of trust merits trust (cognitive trust), or more usually some combination of both" (p.972).

The emotional aspect of trust is defined as emotional security, or feeling secure, or feeling comfortable by Xiao and Benbasat (2003), a viewpoint that ties emotional trust closely to Anshin. Xiao Komiak, and Benbasat (2004, p. 187) state that "emotional trust is feeling, while cognitive trust is cognition." McAllister (1995, p. 26) calls emotional trust *affect-based trust* in the interpersonal context in organizations. Regarding the factors of trust in the e-commerce area, these authors define trust as "a trustor's rational expectation that a trustee will have the necessary competence, benevolence, and integrity to be relied upon" (Xiao Komiak, & Benbasat, 2004, p.187). Kuan and Bock (2005, Section 3) propose a research model in which cognitive trust has those three factors and affects emotional trust. More recent work by Chopra and Wallace (2003, Section 3) proposes a framework for trust in electronic environments which include emotional factors.

Gambetta (1988) developed a mathematical definition of trust. He defined trust as a particular level of one's subjective probability that another's action would be favorable to oneself. He states that "trust (or symmetrically distrust) is a particular level of subjective probability with which an agent will perform a particular action, both before the trustor can monitor such action (or independently of his capacity of ever to be able to monitor it) and in a context in which it affects its own action" (Gambetta, p. 217). This definition gives an opportunity of considering trust more concretely than the other abstract definitions presented earlier. Using this definition, trust is quantifiable with a value in the range 0 to 1. This definition is the basis of work on trust modeling by several researchers.

Gambetta's mathematical definition created the opportunity to develop computational trust models as risk management mechanisms for online communications. Marsh's (1994) model is one of the earliest formal computational trust models. It is a quite complex and abstract sociological model integrating various views from social sciences. Trust is considered here as an artificial agent (formalized as an embedding of the concepts) which provides a tool for consideration of other agents and the environment. In this model trust is quantized to values in a scale of -1 to +1.

Zimmerman (1995) created the PGP or 'Pretty Good Privacy' distributed trust model for encrypting e-mail messages using public key cryptography. PGP adopts the *web of trust* approach for its trust architecture. This The web of trust is created when individuals sign one anothers' keys, attesting to one anothers' identities. An individual receiving a signed key can evaluate its trustworthiness based on the trustworthiness he or she assigns to the signatures: complete trust, marginal trust, or no trust. Through this process trusted communities are formed which are linked through common trustees to form a web. The PGP model stands in contrast to the X.509 hierarchical trust model (ITU-T, 1997) which relies on trusted central authorities to sign all keys.

Abdul-Rahman and Hailes, in a series of works (1997a, 1997b, 1999), proposed a distributed model of trust based on recommendation for use in security and trust management. This model uses the definition of trust as subjective probability proposed by Gambetta and is also uses the agent concept.

Elofson's model (1998) is based on the definition of trust as the outcome of observations leading to the belief that the action of another may be relied upon, without explicit guarantee, to achieve a goal in a risky situation. Trust can be updated over time as the outcome of positive and negative observations which defines the dynamics of trust.

Yahalom's model (Yahalom, Klein & Beth, 1993), (Yahalom, Klein & Beth, 1994), (Beth, Borcherding & Klein, 1994) discussed in significant detail the concept of trust in distributed systems. They defined six different trust classes with each of the classes divided between direct and recommendation trust and then proposed a formal framework for analyzing trust with numerical values for quantifying trust. They also used positive and negative experiences to model the degree of trust.

Dionysiou (2006) described a distributed trust model for managing time-varying trust and trust that depends on the trustworthiness of intermediate nodes that handle communications.

Besides the above-mentioned models based on computation of subjective probability, other computational trust models have been proposed by different researchers. Most of these are based on belief functions, belief values, possibility values or BAF logic (Tan, 2005).

Finally, some authors have proposed equating trust with various desirable, non-functional, properties of systems. According to McAllister (1995), Johnson-George and Swap (1982) used the term, "reliableness" and Rempel, Holmes, and Zanna (1985) used the term "dependability" for cognitive trust, in the interpersonal context (p.26). Hoffman, Lawson-Jenkins and Blum (2006) proposed the creation of a trust model that would include security, safety, privacy, availability and reliability. Lamsal (2001, pp.21-22) illustrates how trust and security interact using cryptography as an example: one's secure communication with another requires a key obtained via some form of trusted key distribution. "What this means is that key management can be thought of as a tool to manage trust," (p. 22). If the key distribution was not worthy of that trust the communication is not secure. Dimmock, Belokosztolszki, Eyers, Bacon, and Moody (2004, pp. 156-157) incorporate trust as a part of access control security.

TRUST AND ANSHIN IN SYSTEM DESIGN

Stephens (2004, pp. 309-314) reports that design elements of a web page, such as page layout, navigation, and graphics affect the development of trust between buyers and sellers in e-commerce. According to Riegelsberger, Sasse, and McCarthy (2003, pp.121-128), quantitative studies on trust in e-commerce and other consumer research confirm that affective reactions influence consumer decision-making.

The computational trust models described above do not take into account emotional trust. Thus, while they may be suitable for machine-machine interactions the insight that they provide into human-machine interaction is incomplete. In our view, an assessment of trustworthiness is an important part of an individual's decision making when interacting with a system or service. The cognitive and emotional components both contribute to this assessment. The sense of security, Anshin, that users have in the interaction is an essential input for the decision making process.

Figure 1 illustrates the way that consideration of Anshin could influence system design. Security systems and services are traditionally evaluated in terms of objective technical factors such as strength against various attacks. These objective factors are shown as the X-axis and the subjective factor, the sense of security, is along the Y-axis.

It is a primary objective for security service and system providers and their users that the systems and services are objectively secure and that users feel secure (the upper right quadrant). This is the most desirable state. On the other hand, when systems and services are insecure, the users should feel insecure (lower left quadrant). Although this is not as desirable for providers and users, it could be acceptable because users are appropriately wary of the insecure tools; otherwise we have a security problem. We would like users to feel secure only when the system is secure indeed

When the systems and services are not secure but users nevertheless feel secure (upper left quadrant), we have a **security problem**. Users are not aware that they are vulnerable to attack.

Figure 1. System security vs. the sense of security

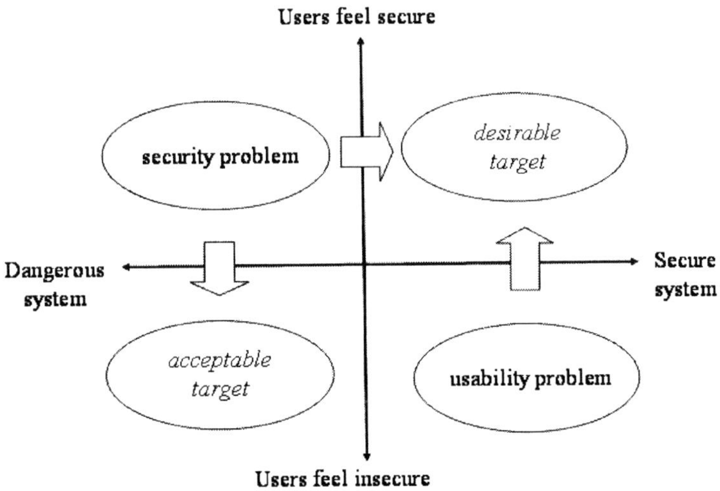

However, if the systems and services are secure but the users do not feel secure (lower right quadrant), users are afraid to use the system: we have a **usability problem**. As an example of this, Whitten and Tygar (1999) studied the effect of usability issues on users' perceptions of security tools. The poor Graphic User Interface (GUI) of the PGP 5.0 system for Macintosh systems was found to deter users from adopting the tool even though the system was in fact secure.

Moving to the target states is the goal for providers and researchers by resolving those security and usability problems. For example, to solve the usability problem one could provide users with education about security technology so that the users are aware of the correct security level provided by the systems and services. Alternatively, the user interface could be improved to resolve the usability problem, so that users are sure that systems are secure enough. The question is what properties of user interface give users a feeling of security. Answering this involves identifying factors that contribute to a sense of security.

For the security problem, however, improving the user interface means giving users warnings and alarm messages. While usability has been investigated in terms of comfort and ease of use, what we need here is user interfaces that promote *discomfort* so that the user is aware of the existence of danger and vulnerability. Research on discomfort has been investigated to a great extent in safety engineering in the physical world, for avoiding human errors and giving alarms to users (Norman,1988). Here we need to promote appropriate discomfort for user interfaces in the presence of cyber space insecurity.

INVESTIGATING THE STRUCTURE OF ANSHIN

Traditional research on security and safety has assumed that users will feel secure and safe provided with secure and safe systems and services (Schneier, 2007). The emphasis is on security technology while emotional factors, *e.g.* the sense of security and emotional trust, are ignored. Our research focuses on discovering the psychological factors that contribute to users' structure of Anshin—the sense of security (Hikage, Hauser, & Murayama, 2007)(Murayama, Hikage, Fujiwara, & Hauser, in press).

The survey participants were 452 students from the faculties of software and information science, nursing, policy studies, and social welfare of Iwate Prefectural University. All of the subjects had basic knowledge of how to operate a computer and they all use the Internet on a daily basis. After eliminating incomplete responses, we had 425 valid surveys to use in the analysis. Of the 425 subjects, 276 were male, and 149 were female. The age range of participants was from 19 through 36, with the average age 19.45.

We asked questions that probed participants' opinions about the sense of security when they use a security system or service on the Internet. Our results using factor analysis showed that *security technology, usability, experience, preference, understanding* and *assurance* were factors contributing to participants' sense of security when using the Internet. *Security technology* is concerned with users' expectations of the security measures and support from the system and services. *Usability* and *preference* are concerned with user interface; the former concerns operational aspects of an interface, whereas the latter concerns personal tastes. *Experience* is the user's personal background with the Internet and security technology. *Understanding* indicates a user's personal competence in learning and obtaining knowledge; it is based on one's own experience and subjective judgments *Assurance* is a user's expectation about the providers.

We define the first three factors as *personal* factors because they are dependent on the user's past knowledge, personal experiences and preferences. The other factors are *environmental* factors because they depend on the system or service provider's side.

Factor analysis of the survey data showed that all six factors contributed to the sense of security at statistically significant levels. Our validation results using Structural Equation Modeling (SEM) (Fornell, 1982) show that the structure of the sense of security has both an environmental dimension and a personal dimension. The traditional assumption that users feel secure and safe when provided with secure and safe systems should be reconsidered.

CONCLUSION

This chapter has introduced the sense of security, Anshin, and identified it as a key component of emotional trust. Computer science methods in information security research typically focus on aspects that contribute primarily to cognitive trust in systems. Subjective factors that contribute to emotional trust are hard to measure; however, progress here will be useful in creating designs that enable users to have appropriate degrees of Anshin when using systems and services.

We also observe that Anshin literally indicates "being free from all sorts of wary and minding matters," so Anshin includes feelings about safety, reliability, availability and privacy as well as feelings about security measures. We conjecture that the discussion concerning the sense of security vs. actual security could be extended to encompass these additional aspects, but we have not yet constructed that argument. Furthermore, the survey described above was performed with a limited population consisting of undergraduate and graduate students as subjects, most of them computer science students. For both of these reasons, the work presented shows only a tentative model of the sense of security—the structure of Anshin. To develop deeper understanding of the structure of Anshin we need to conduct surveys on the sense of safety, privacy and reliability using a broader cross-section of the public.

REFERENCES

Abdul-Rahman, A., & Hailes, S. (1997). Using recommendations for managing trust in distributed systems. *Proceedings of the IEEE Malaysia International Conference on Communication.* Available: http://citeseer.ist.psu.edu/360414.html

Abdul-Rahman, A., & Hailes, S. (1998). A distributed trust model. *Proceedings of the ACM 1997 New Security Paradigms Workshop*, 48-60.

Abdul-Rahman, A., & Hailes, S. (1999). Relying on trust to find reliable information. *Proceedings of the International Symposium on Database, Web and Cooperative Systems*, Baden Baden. Available: http://citeseer.ist.psu.edu/348491.html

Abdul-Rahman, A., & Hailes, S. (2000). Supporting trust in virtual communities. *Proceedings of the Hawaii International Conference on System Sciences 33.* Available: http://ieeexplore.ieee.org/application/mdl/mdlconfirmation.jsp?arnumber=926814

America Online & The National Cybersecurity Alliance. *AOL/NCSA online safety study.* Available: http://www.staysafeonline.org/pdf/safety_study_2005.pdf

Barber, B. (1983). *The logic and limits of trust.* New Brunswick, NJ: Rutgers University Press.

Beth, T., Borcherding, M., & Klein, B. (1994). Valuation of trust in open networks. *Proceedings of the European Symposium on Research in Computer Security,* Brighton, UK, 3-18.

Chopra, K., & Wallace, W. A. (2003). Trust in electronic environments. *Proceedings of the 36th Hawaii International Conference on System Science*, 331.1.

De Becker, G. (1997). *The Gift of fear.* Boston: Little, Brown and Company.

Deutsch, M. (1962). Cooperation and trust: Some theoretical notes. M. R. Jones (Ed.), *Nebraska Symposium on Motivation*, (pp. 275-319). Lincoln, NE: University of Nebraska Press.

Deutsch, M. (1973). *The resolution of conflict.* New Haven, CT: Yale University Press.

Dillon, M. (1996). *Politics of security: Towards a political philosophy of continental thought.* London: Routledge.

Dimmock, N., Belokosztolszki, A., Eyers, D., Bacon, J., & Moody, K. (2004). Access management for distributed systems: Using trust and risk in role-based access control policies, (pp. 156-162). *Proceedings of the Ninth ACM symposium on Access Control Models and Technologies.*

Dionysiou, I. (2006). *Dynamic and composable trust for indirect interactions.* Unpublished doctoral dissertation, Washington State University, Pullman.

Elofson, G. (1998). Developing trust with intelligent agents: An exploratory study, (pp. 125-139). *Proceedings of the first international workshop on trust.*

Fornell, C.(Ed.) (1982). *Second Generation of Multivariate Analysis.* New York: Praeger.

Gambetta, D. (1988). Can we trust trust? In D. Gambetta (Ed.), *Trust: Making and breaking cooperative relations*, electronic edition, chapter 13, (pp. 213-237). Department of Sociology, University of Oxford. Originally published by Basil Blackwell 1988. Available online from the following site: http://www.sociology.ox.ac.uk/papers/gambetta213-237.pdf

Hikage, N., Hauser, C., & Murayama, Y. (2007). Joho security gijutsu ni taisuru anshinkan no kozo ni kansuru tokeiteki kento[A statistical discussion of the sense of security, Anshin]. *Information Processing Society of Japan Journal 48*(9) (in Japanese).

Hoffman, L. J., Lawson-Jenkins, K., & Blum, J. (2006). Trust beyond security: an expanded trust model. *Communications of the ACM, 49*(7), 94-101.

ITU-T (1997). ITU-T Recommendation X.509 (1997 E): Information Technology - Open Systems Interconnection - The Directory: Authentication Framework, 1997

Kikkawa, T., Shirato, S., Fujii, S., & Takemura, K. (2003). Gijutsuteki anzen to shakaiteki Anshin[The pursuit of informed reassurance ('An-Shin' in Society) and technological safety ('An-Zen')]. *Journal of SHAKAI-GIJUTSU, 1*,1-8 (in Japanese).

Kuan, H. H., & Bock, G. W. (2005). The collective reality of trust: An investigation of social relations and networks on trust in multi-channel retailers. *Proceedings of the 13th European Conference on Information Systems.* Available from: http://is2.lse.ac.uk/asp/aspecis/20050018.pdf(Last Access: 9 February 2007)

Lamsal, P. (2001). Understanding trust and security. From http://www.cs.Helsinki.FI/u/lamsal/papers/UnderstandingTrustAndSecurity.pdf

Lewis, D. J., & Weigert, A. (1985). Trust as a social reality. *Social Forces, 63*(4), 967-985.

Luhmann, N. (1979). *Trust and power.* Chichester, UK: John Wiley.

Marsh, S. (1994). *Formalising trust as a computational concept.* Unpublished doctoral dissertation, University of Stirling, U.K.

McAllister, D. J. (1995). Affect- and cognition-based trust as foundations for interpersonal cooperation in organizations. *Academy of Management Journal, 38*(1), 24-59.

Murayama, Y., Hikage, N., Fujiwara, Y., & Hauser, C. (in press). The structure of the sense of security, Anshin, to appear in *Proceedings of the 2nd International Workshop on Critical Information Infrastructures Security.* Springer.

Norman, D. A. (1988). *The psychology of everyday things.* New York: Basic Books

Rempel, J. K., Holmes J. G., & Zanna, M. P. (1985,). Trust in close relationships. *Journal of Personality and Social Psychology, 49*(1), 95-112.

Riegelsberger, J., Sasse, M.A., & McCarthy, J. D. (2003). Privacy and trust: Shiny happy people building trust? Photos on e-commerce websites and consumer trust. *Proceedings of CHI2003, 5*(1), 121-128.

Schneier, B. (2007). The Psychology of Security – DRAFT, http://www.schneier.com/essay-155.html

Shi, J., Bochmann, G. V., & Adams, C. (2005). A trust model with statistical foundation. In T. Dimitrakos and F. Martinelli, (Eds.), *Second IFIP TC1 WG1.7 Workshop on Formal Aspects in Security and Trust 2004*, (pp. 145-158). Springer.

Stephens, R. T. (2004). A framework for the identification of electronic commerce design elements that enable trust within the small hotel industry. *Proceedings of ACMSE*, 309-314.

Tan, C. K. (2005). A belief augmented frame computational trust model. *FLAIRS Conference*, 647-652.

*The Oxford English Dictionary (*2nd ed.). (1989). *OED Online.* Oxford University Press. 19 August 2007. http://dictionary.oed.com/cgi/entry/50218187.

Whitten, A., & Tygar, D. (1999). Why johnny can't encrypt: A usability evaluation of PGP 5.0. *Proceedings of the 9th USENIX Security Symposium*, 169-184.

Xiao, S., & Benbasat, I. (2003). The formation of trust and distrust in recommendation agents in repeated interactions: A process-tracing analysis. *Proceedings of the 5th International Conference on Electronic Commerce*, 287–293.

Xiao Komiak, S., & Benbasat, I. (2004). Understanding customer trust in agent-mediated electronic commerce, web-mediated electronic commerce, and traditional commerce. *Information Technology and Management, 5(1–2)*, 181–207. Kluwer Academic Publishers.

Yahalom, R., Klein, B., & Beth, T. (1993). Trust relationships in secure systems - A distributed authentication perspective. *Proceedings of the IEEE Symposium on Research in Security and Privacy*, 150-164.

Yahalom, R., Klein, B., & Beth, T. (1994). Trust-based navigation in distributed systems. *Computing Systems, 7*(1), 45-73.

Yamagishi, T. (1998). The structure of trust: The evolutionary games of mind and society. Tokyo: Tokyo University Press (in Japanese), English version available from: http://lynx.let.hokudai.ac.jp/members/yamagishi/english.htm (Last Access April 2007)

Zimmerman, P. (1995). *PGP user's guide.* Cambridge, MA: MIT Press.

KEY TERMS

Anshin: A Japanese noun which is composed of two words, viz. "*An*" and "*Shin*." "*An*" indicates to ease, and "*Shin*" is mind or worry. It means the sense of security as well as the senses of safety, reliability, availability and privacy.

Cognitive Trust: According to Lewis and Weigert (1985), the cognitive part of trust is the trusting behavior motivated by "good rational reasons" why the object of trust merits trust (p.972). In the e-commerce area, Xiao Komiak and Benbasat define cognitive trust as "a trustor's rational expectation that a trustee will have the necessary competence, benevolence, and integrity to be relied upon" (2004, p.187). Cognitive trust has been called simply "trust" in many literatures, however, they call it cognitive when they compare it with emotional trust.

Emotional Trust: According to Lewis and Weigert (1985, p. 972) emotional trust is trusting behavior motivated primarily by strong positive affect for the object of trust. Emotional trust is defined as emotional security, or feeling secure, or comfortable by Xiao & Benbasat (2003).

Risk Communication: The communication between nuclear power plant providers and experts and the residents of a plant area. The providers and experts communicate about risks of a nuclear power plant so that residents will get Anshin (Kikkawa et al., 2003, pp.1-8).

Security: According to Oxford English dictionary (Oxford English Dictionary, 1933, vol.9), security is the condition of being protected from or not exposed to danger, or freedom from doubt. In this chapter we are concerned with security in the former terms. Generally information security has been concerned more with security technology including cryptography, steganography, authentication, access control and secure protocols.

The Sense of Security: The emotional part of security. It is concerned with how users feel when they use security tools.

Trust: Trust is a particular level of one's subjective probability that another's action would be favorable to oneself from the psychological viewpoint (Gambetta, 1988),. Gambetta states that "trust (or symmetrically distrust) is a particular level of subjective probability with which an agent will perform a particular action, both before the trustor can monitor such action (or independently of his capacity of ever to be able to monitor it) and in a context in which it affects its own action" (p.217).

Trust Model: The trust model proposed by Marsh (1994) is one of the first works which proposed a formal treatment integrating different trust concepts. According to Marsh, major early contributions to understanding trust have come from the areas of sociology, social psychology and philosophy mainly in work carried out by Deutsch, Luhman, Berber and Gambetta. Many attempts have been made to represent trust mathematically and a number of computational trust models, mostly based on Gambetta's definition have emerged for risk management mechanism in on-line communications. The goal of a computational trust model is to assist users with decision making.

Compilation of References

(1995). *An introduction to computer security: The NIST handbook (NIST SP800-12).* National Institute of Standards and Technology.

(IFCC), I. F. C. C. (2004). Ic3 2004 Internet Fraud Report, January 1, 2004-December 31, 2004. Retrieved March 15, 2005, from http://www.ifccfbi.gov/strategy/2004_IC3Report.pdf.

Abdul-Rahman, A., & Hailes, S. (1997). Using recommendations for managing trust in distributed systems. *Proceedings of the IEEE Malaysia International Conference on Communication.* Available: http://citeseer.ist.psu.edu/360414.html

Abdul-Rahman, A., & Hailes, S. (1998). A distributed trust model. *Proceedings of the ACM 1997 New Security Paradigms Workshop*, 48-60.

Abdul-Rahman, A., & Hailes, S. (1999). Relying on trust to find reliable information. *Proceedings of the International Symposium on Database, Web and Cooperative Systems*, Baden Baden. Available: http://citeseer.ist.psu.edu/348491.html

Abdul-Rahman, A., & Hailes, S. (2000). Supporting trust in virtual communities. *Proceedings of the Hawaii International Conference on System Sciences 33.* Available: http://ieeexplore.ieee.org/application/mdl/mdlconfirmation.jsp?arnumber=926814

Accenture (2006). *The rising importance of enterprise content management.* New York, NY: Accenture.

Accused AOL Hacker Arrested After Months At Large. (2006, November 1, 2006). Retrieved November, 2006, from http://cbs2.com/topstories/local_story_305232841.html

ACFE (2006). *Report to the nation on occupational fraud and abuse.* Austin, Texas: Association of Certified Fraud Examiners.

Ackerman, M., & Cranor, L. (1999). Privacy Critics: UI Components to Safeguard Users' Privacy. *In proceedings of the CHI '99 Extended Abstracts on Human Factors in Computing Systems* (pp. 258-259).

Adams A., & Sasse, M. A. (1999). Users are Not the Enemy. In *Communications of the ACM* (Dec 1999), p. 40-46.

Adams, A., Sasse, M. A., & Lunt, P. (1997). *Making Passwords Secure and Usable.* Paper presented at the Proceedings of HCI on People and Computers XII.

Adams, C., & Barbieri, K. (2006). Privacy Enforcement in E-Services Environments. Chapter in *Privacy Protection for E-Services*, edited by Yee, G., Idea Group, Inc.

Aggarwal, G., Feder, T., Kenthapadi, K., Khuller, S., Panigrahy, R., Thomas, D., et al. (2006). Achieving anonymity via clustering. *In proceedings of the Symposium on Principles of Database Systems* (pp. 153 - 162).

Agrawal, R., Kiernan, J., Srikant, R., & Xu, Y. (2003). An XPath-based Preference Language for P3P. *In proceedings of the 12th Int'l World Wide Web Conference* (pp. 629 - 639) Budapest, Hungary.

Ahmed, A. A. E., & Traore, I. (2003). System and Method for Determining a Computer User Profile from a Motion-based Input Device. *PCT patent application with the World Intellectual Property Organization*, filed by the University of Victoria (PCT/CA2004/000669) filing date: 3 May 2004 priority date: May2, 2003.

Ahmed, A. A. E., & Traore, I. (2005, October). Detecting Computer Intrusions Using Behavioral Biometrics. *Proceeding s of Third Annual Conference on Privacy, Security and Trust* (pp. 91-98), St. Andrews, New Brunswick, Canada.

Ahmed, A. A. E., & Traore, I. (2007, July-September). A New Biometrics Technology based on Mouse Dynamics. *IEEE Transactions on Dependable and Secure Computing*, *4*(3), 165-179.

Ahrens, F. (2004, September 8). FTC Pulls Plug on Infomercial Giant. *Washington Post,* p. E1.

AHRI. (2007). *Georgia Tech aware home research initiative (AHRI).* Retrieved September 11, 2007, from http://www.chia.org/programs/2000/prg_oct00.htm.

Alamus. (July 30, 2005). From the International E-Commerce Legislation to China's Environment of E-commerce Policy and Regulation. Retrieved April 3, 2007, from http://www.cyberlawcn.com/Get/lfdt/lfyj/20051005296.htm.

Alberts, C., & Dorofee, A. (2001). *An Introduction to the OCTAVE Method,* Software Engineering Institute, Carnegie Mellon University. Retrieved October 11, 2001, from http://www.cert.org/octave/methodintro.html.

Alghathbar, K., & Wijesekera, D. (2003). *AuthUML: A Threephased Framework to model Secure Use Cases.* In Proc. of the Formal Methods in Security Engineering Wksp (FMSE'03), Washington D.C., USA, 2003.

Alghathbar, K., & Wijesekera, D. (2003). *Consistent and Complete Access Control Policies in Use Cases.* In Proc. of UML 2003, San Francisco, CA, LNCS, 2003.

Allcorn, W. (2003). *The Maginot Line 1928-45.* Oxford, England: Osprey Publishing.

Allen, M. (2006). Social Engineering: A Means to Violate a Computer System. Retrieved May, 2007, from http://www.sans.org/reading_room/whitepapers/engineering/529.php

Altman, I. (1975). *The environment and social behaviour: Privacy, personal space, territory and crowding.* Monetery: Brooks/Cole.

Altman, I. (1977). Privacy regulation: Culturally universal or culturally-specific? *Journal of Social Issues, 33*(3), 66-84.

America Online & The National Cybersecurity Alliance. *AOL/NCSA online safety study.* Available: http://www.staysafeonline.org/pdf/safety_study_2005.pdf

American National Standard Institute. ANSI INCITS 359-2004 for Role-based Access Control. 2004

Anderson, A. (2005). *A Comparison of Two Privacy Policy Languages: EPAL and XACML*: Sun Microsystems Laboratories. Retrieved from http://research.sun.com/techrep/2005/smli_tr-2005-147/TRCompareEPAL-andXACML.html

Anderson, C. (2005). *Creating Conscientious Cybercitizen: An Examination of Home Computer User Attitudes and Intentions Towards Security.* Paper presented at the Information Systems.

Anderson, R. (2001). *Security Engineering: A Guide to Building Dependable Systems.* New York, NY: John Wiley & Sons, Inc.

Anderson, R. (2001). Why information security is hard—An economic perspective. In *Proceedings of 17th Annual Computer Security Applications Conference (ACSAC)* (New Orleans).

Anderson. Ross J. (1994). *Liability and computer security: Nine principles.* In Dieter Gollmann, editor, Computer Security (ESORICS '94), LNCS 875, pages 231–245, Berlin Heidelberg, 1994. Springer Verlag.

Anderson. Ross. (1994). Why Cryptosystems Fail. *In Communications of the ACM, 37*(11), 1994.

Anti-Phishing Working Group. Retrieved July, 11, 2007, from http://www.antiphishing.org/

Anti-Phishing Working Group. (2007). Retrieved March 17, 2007, from http://www.antiphishing.org/

APEC-FIP. (2004). *APEC Privacy Framework* (No. 2004/AMM/014rev1): Asia-Pacific Economic Cooperation.

Appelbaum, S. H. (1997). Socio-technical systems theory: an intervention strategy for organizational development. *Management Decision, 35*(6), 452–463.

Ashley, P., Hada, S., Karjoth, G., Powers, C., & Schunter, M. (2003). Enterprise Privacy Authorization Language (EPAL 1.2). W3C Member Submission 10 November 2003.

Ashrafi, N., & Kuilboer, J.-P. (2005). Privacy Protection via Technology: Platform for Privacy Preferences (P3P). *International Journal of E-Business Research, 1*(2), 56-69.

Asplen-Taylor, S. (2008). *Preventing operational losses: Are tighter controls really the answer?* London, England: Detica.

AT&T (2003). Achieving network security – point of view. Retrieved May 13, 2007 from http://www.typex.com/.../bcfbc9acb168ca5380256f71004b363b/$FILE/achieving_network_security_3.pdf

Atallah, M. J., Raskin, V., Crogan, M., Hempelmann, C., Kerschbaum, F., Mohamed, D., et al. (2001). Natural language watermarking: Design, analysis, and a proof-of-concept implementation. In I. S. Moskowitz (Ed.), *Information Hiding: Fourth International Workshop, 2137 of Lecture Notes in Computer Science* (pp. 185-199): Springer Verlag.

AusCERT (2005). Australian Computer Crime and Security Survey. Retrieved May 12, 2007 from http://www.auscert.org.au/images/ACCSS2005.pdf

Avizienis, A., Laprie, J., & Randell. B. (2001). *Fundamental Concepts of Dependability*. Research Report N01145, LAASCNRS, Apr. 2001.

Axelrod, C. W. (1999). Data Processing and Communications Security During Recovery and Repair. In S.F. Blanding (ed.), *Enterprise Operations Management Handbook, Second Edition* (pp. 631-640). Boca Raton, FL: CRC Press.

Babbie, E. (2004). *The Practice of Social Research*. Belmont, CA: Wadsworth/Thomson Learning.

Backbone (2005). *Backbone Corporate Blogging Survey 2005*. Backbone Media, Inc. Retrieved 1/18/07 from http://blogsurvey.backbonemedia.com/archives/2005/06/_not_a_factor.html

Backes, M., Karjoth, G., Bagga, W., & Schunter, M. (2004). Efficient Comparison of Enterprise Privacy Policies. *Proceedings of the 2004 ACM Symposium on Applied Computing*, pp. 375-382.

Baeza-Yates, R., & Ribeiro-Neto, B. *Modern Information Retrieval*.

Bagchi, K., & Udo, G. (2003). An Analysis of the Growth of Computer and Internet Security Breaches. *Communications of the Association for Information Systems, 12*, 684-700.

Banerjee, S., Kang, H., Bagchi-Sen, S., & Rao, H. R. (2005). Gender Divide in the Use of the Internet Applications. *International Journal of E-Business Research, 1*(2), 24-39.

Banisar, D. (1999). Privacy and Data Protection Around the World. *21st International Conference on Privacy and Personal Data Protection*, September 13.

Bank of America. (2005). *Bank of America announces industry-leading security feature for its 13.2 million online banking customers to help prevent fraud and identity theft*. Retrieved April, 2007, from http://newsroom.bankofamerica.com/index.php?s=press_releases&item=6971

Bansler, J., Damsgaard, J., Scheepers, R., Havn, E., & Thommesen, J. (2000). Corporate Intranet Implementation. *Journal of the Association of Information Systems*, 1(10), 1-39.

Barabási, A.-L. (2003). *Linked: How Everything is Connected to Everything Else and What It Means for Business, Science, and Everyday Life*. New York, NY: Plume.

Barbaro, M. (2006). Wal-Mart Enlists Bloggers in Its Public Relations Campaign. *New York Times*, March 7, 2006, Section C, Page 1, Column 2.

Barbaro, S., & Bracht, B. (2005). Shilling, Squeezing, Sniping: Explaining late bidding in online second-price auctions. *Working Paper Johannes-Gutenberg University, Mainz*.

Barber, B. (1983). *The logic and limits of trust*. New Brunswick, NJ: Rutgers University Press.

Bardzell, J., Blevis, E., & Lim, Y.-K. (2007). Human-Centered Design Considerations. In M. Jakobsson & S. Myers (Eds.), *Phishing and Countermeasures: Understanding the Increasing Problem of Electronic Identity Theft* (pp. 241-275). Hoboken, New Jersey: John Wiley & Sons, Inc.

Barman, S. (2002). *Writing Information Security Policies*. Indianapolis: New Riders.

Barnes, J. A. (1954). Class and Committees in a Norwegian Island Parish. *Human Relations*, 7, 39-58.

Barth, F. (2005). The Golden Age, 1945-1970. *One Discipline, Four Ways: British, German, French, and American anthropology*, 32-43. Chicago, IL: University of Chicago Press.

Basel II (2004). International Convergence of Capital Measurement and Capital Standards: A Revised Framework.

Bayuk, J. L. (2008). *Stepping through the Infosec Program*, Rolling Hills, IL: ISACA.

Bazire, M., & Brézillon, P. (2005). Understanding context before to use it. *Modeling and Using Context (CONTEXT-05)*, A. Dey, B.Kokinov, D.Leake, R.Turner (Eds.), Springer Verlag, LNCS 3554 (pp. 29-40).

Bell, D. E., & LaPadula, L. J. (1976). *Secure Computer Systems: Unified Exposition and Multics Interpretation*, ESD-TR-75-306, MTR 2997 Rev. 1. Bedford, Massachusetts: The MITRE Corporation.

Bell, D. E., & LaPadula, L.J. (1973, November). Secure Computer Systems: A Mathematical Model. *ESD-TR-73-278, 2*(MITRE).

Bellotti, V., & Edwards, K. (2001). Intelligibility and Accountability: Human Considerations in Context Aware Systems. In: *Human-Computer Interaction, Special Issue on Context-Aware Computing, 16*(2, 3 & 4), 193 – 212

Bellotti, V., & Sellen, A. (1993). Design for Privacy in Ubiquitous Environments. *In proceedings of the Third*

European Conference on Computer-Supported Cooperative Work (ECSCW'93) (pp. 77-92) Milan, Italy.

Benaloh, J. (2006). Simple Verifiable Elections. USENIX/ACCURATE Electronic Voting Technology Workshop (EVT'06), Vancouver, Canada, August 1, 2006.

Bender, T. (1978). *Community and Social Change in America*. Baltimore, MD: Johns Hopkins University Press.

Bergadano, F., Guneti, D., & Picardi, C. (2002). User Authentication through Keystroke Dynamics. *ACM Transactions on Information and System Security, 5*(4), 367-39.

Berger, S., Kjeldsen, R., Narayanaswami, C., Pinhanez, C., Podlaseck, M., & Raghunath, M. (2005). Using Symbiotic Displays to View Sensitive Information in Public. In: *Proceedings of the International Conference on Pervasive Computing and Communications* (PerCom'05), Kauai Island, HI, USA, pp. 139 – 148.

Berghel, H., Carpinter, J., & Jo, J.-Y. (2006, August 28, 2006). Phish Phactors: Offensive and Defensive Strategies. Retrieved November 12, 2006, from http://berghel.net/publications/phishing/phishing.php

Bergmair, R. (2007). *Semantilog: A Comprehensive Bibliography of Linguistic Steganography*. Retrieved April 2007, from http://semantilog.ucam.org/biblingsteg/

Bergmair, R., & Katzenbeisser, S. (2006). *Content-aware steganography: About lazy prisoners and narrow-minded wardens*. Paper presented at the Proceedings of 8th Information Hiding Workshop, Lecture Notes in Computer Science, Washington D.C.

Berinato, S. (2003). The state of information security 2003. CIO Magazine. Retrieved May 13, 2007 from http://www.cio.com/article/print/29841

Bertino, E., Bonatti, P. A., & Ferrari, E. (2001, August). TRBAC: A temporal role-based access control model. *ACM Transactions on Information & System Security, 4*(3), 191-233.

Bertino, E., Catania, B., Damiani, M. L., & Perlasca, P. (2005, June). Access control model I: GEO-RBAC: a spatially aware RBAC. *Proceedings of the tenth ACM symposium on Access control models and technologies.*

Beth, T., Borcherding, M., & Klein, B. (1994). Valuation of trust in open networks. *Proceedings of the European Symposium on Research in Computer Security*, Brighton, UK, 3-18.

Bhatti, R. (2003). *X-GTRBAC: An XML-based Policy Specification Framework and Architecture for Enterprise Wide Access Control*. Masters thesis, Purdue University, May 2003.

Bhatti, R., Joshi, J., Bertino, E., & Ghafoor, A. (2004, June). Role administration: X-GTRBAC admin: a decentralized administration model for enterprise wide access control. *Proceedings of the ninth ACM symposium on Access control models and technologies.*

Biba, K. J. (1975). *Integrity Considerations for Secure Computer Systems*, MTR-3153. Bedford, MA: MITRE Corporation.

Biometrics. *IEEE Security & Privacy Magazine, 1*(3), 45-49.

BITS (2008). *Pandemic Influenza Resources on File*. Retrieved May 1, 2008 from www.bitsinfo.org

Bjorck, F. (2004). *Institutional theory: A new perspective for research into IS/IT security in organisations.* Paper presented at the Proceedings of the 37th Hawaii International Conference on System Sciences.

Black, T. (2007). *The data explosion: how to survive its impact.* Homeland Defence & Resilience, Issue 1, pp. 72-75. London, England: Newsdesk Communications Ltd.

Black, T. (2008). *In my opinion*. Management Today. London, England: Haymarket Specialist.

Blair, L., & Pang, J. (2000). Feature Interactions – Life Beyond Traditional Telephony. *Proceedings of the 6th International Workshop on Feature Interactions in Telecommunications and Software Systems*, pp.83-93, Glasgow, Scotland, May.

Blakley, B., McDermott, E., & Geer, D. (2001). *Information security is information risk management.* Paper presented at the ACM Special Interest Group on Security, Audit, and Control, Cloudcroft, New Mexico.

Blarkom, G. W. v., Borking, J. J., & Verhaar, P. (2003). PET. In G. W. v. Blarkom, J. J. Borking, & J. G. E. Olk (Eds.), *Handbook of Privacy and Privacy-Enhancing Technologies: The Case of Intelligent Software Agents.* College bescherming persoonsgegevens.

Bleha, S., Slivinsky, C., & Hussein, B. (1990). Computer-access Security Systems using Keystroke Dynamics. *IEEE Transactions on Pattern Analysis and Machine Intelligence, PAMI-12, 12*, 1217-1222.

Bloch, A. (2005). Business Relationships Built on Trust, Reliability, Honesty and Integrity. Retrieved April 5, 2007, from http://ezinearticles.com/?Business-

Relationhips-Built-On-Trust,-Reliability,-Honesty-and-Integrity&id=98374.

Blonder, G. E. (1996). Graphical password. In US (Ed.): Lucent Technologies Inc. Murray Hill, N. J.

Bloom, B. S., Krathwohl, D. R., Masia, B. B., & Emgelhart, M. D. (1956). *Taxonomy of educational objectives: The classification of educational goals*. New York: Longmans, Green.

Bohn, J., Coroama, V., Langheinrich, M., Mattern, F., Rohs, M. (2004). Living in a World of Smart Everyday Objects – Social, Economic, and Ethical Implications. In: Journal of Human and Ecological Risk Assessment, Vol. 10, No. 5, pp. 763 – 786.

Bohn, J., Coroama, V., Langheinrich, M., Mattern, F., Rohs, M. (2005). Social, Economic, and Ethical Implications of Ambient Intelligence and Ubiquitous Computing. In: W. Weber, J. Rabaey, E. Aarts (Eds.): Ambient Intelligence. Springer-Verlag, Heidelberg, pp. 5 – 29.

Bondavalli, A., Majzik, I., & Mura, I. (1999). Automatic Dependability Analysis for Supporting Design Decisions in UML. In R. Paul and C. Meadows (Ed). *Proc. of the IEEE International Symposium on High Assurance Systems Engineering. IEEE.*

Bostromand, R., & Heinen, S. (1977). MIS Problems and Failures: A Sociotechnical Perspective. *MIS Quarterly*, 17-32.

Botnet (Eds.). (2006). Wikimedia Foundation.

Boyle, M., & Greenberg, S. (2005). The Language of Privacy: Learning from Video Media Space Analysis and Design. *ACM Transactions on Computer-Human Interaction (TOCHI), 12*(2), 328-370.

Brandt, A. (2005). Phishing Anxiety May Make You Miss Messages. *PCWORLD, 34* .

Brézillon, J., & Brézillon, P. (2007). Context modeling: Context as a dressing of a focus. In: *Modeling and Using Context (CONTEXT-07),* LNAI 4635, Springer Verlag, (pp. 136-149).

Brézillon, P. (2005) *Task-realization models in Contextual Graphs. Modeling and Using Context (CONTEXT-05)*, A. Dey, B. Kokinov, D. Leake, and R. Turner (Eds.), Springer Verlag, LNCS 3554, (pp. 55-68).

Brézillon, P. (2007). Context Modeling: Task model and model of practices. In: Kokinov et al. (Eds.): *Modeling and Using Context (CONTEXT-07),* LNAI 4635, Springer Verlag, (pp. 122-135).

Brézillon, P., & Pomerol, J.-Ch. (1999). Contextual knowledge sharing and cooperation in intelligent assistant systems. *Le Travail Humain, 62*(3), 223-246. Paris: PUF.

Briggs, R., & Edwards, C. (2006). *The Business of Resilience: Corporate security for the 21st century.* London, England: Demos.

Briney, A. (2001). 2001 Industry Survey. *Information Security*, pp. 34-47.

Briney, A., & Prince, F. (2002). 2002 ISM Survey. *Information Security*, pp. 36-54.

Brodie, C. A., Karat, C.-M., & Karat, J. (2006). An Empirical Study of Natural Language Parsing of Privacy Policy Rules Using the SPARCLE Policy Workbench. *Proceedings of the Second Symposium on Usable Privacy and Security*, pp. 8-19, Pittsburgh, PA, USA.

Brostoff, S., & Sasse, M. A. (2000). Are passfaces more usable than passwords: A field trial investigation, *HCI 2000*: Springer.

Brown, A. S., Bracken, E., Zoccoli, S., & Douglas, K. (2004). Generating and remembering passwords. *Applied Cognitive Psychology, 18*(2004), 641-651.

Brown, M., Rogers, S. J. (1993). Identification Via Keystroke Characteristics of Typed Names Using Neural Networks. *International Journal on Man-Machine Studies,* Vol. 39, pp. 999-1014.

Brusilovsky, P., Kobsa, A., & Nejdl, W. (2007). *The Adaptive Web: Methods and Strategies of Web Personalization.* Heidelberg, Germany: Springer Verlag.

BSI 2004. (2004). *BSI - Short information to current topics of IT Security.* Retrieved 17 June 2007 from http://www.bsi.bund.de/english/fb/F30image_en.pdf.

Buffett, S., Jia, K., Liu, S., Spencer, B., & Wang, F. (2004). Negotiating Exchanges of P3P-Labeled Information for Compensation. *Computational Intelligence, 20*(4), 663-677.

Buller, D. B., & Burgoon, J. K. (1996). Interpersonal Deception Theory. *Communication Theory, 6*(3), 203-242.

Burke, E. (1770). *Thoughts on the cause of the present discontents.* (Note: the referenced quotation is often attributed to Burke but has never been found in his works. It is probably a paraphrase of Burke's view that *"When bad men combine, the good must associate; else they will fall one by one, an unpitied sacrifice in a contemptible struggle".*)

Burkert, H. (1997). Privacy-Enhancing Technologies: Typology, Critique, Vision. In P. E. Agre, & M. Rotenberg (Eds.), *Technology and Privacy: The New Landscape* (pp. 126-143). Boston, MA: MIT Press.

Burkhardt, J., Henn, H., Hepper, H., Rindtorff, K., Schaeck, T. (2001). Pervasive Computing. Addison Wesley, Reading.

Burner, E. R. (2003). Forrester Sees Strong Ecommerce Growth Continuing. Forrestor Web site.

Burnette, R. (2005). Legal risk management for the IT industry. *Computer Law & Security Report, 21*(1), 61-67.

Burns. E. (2005). *Search increased in august.* Retrieved October 7, 2005 from http://www.clickz.com/stats/sectors/search tools/article.php/3554731.

Butler, R. W., Miller, P., Potts, J. N., & Carreno, V. A. (1998). A formal methods approach to the analysis of mode confusion. In *Proc. of the 17th Digital Avionics Systems Conference*, Washington, Oct 31 – Nov 6, 1998.

Butler, S. A. (2002, May). Security Attribute Evaluation Method: A Cost-Benefit Approach. *Proceedings of the 24th International Conference on Software Engineering, ACM*, 232-240.

Butterworth, R., Blandford, A. E., & Duke, D. (2000). Demonstrating the cognitive plausibility of interactive systems. *Formal Aspects of Computing, 12*, 237–259.

Byers, S., Cranor, L., Kormann, D., & McDaniel, P. (2004, May, 2004). Searching for Privacy: Design and Implementation of a P3P-Enabled Search Engine. *In proceedings of the 2004 Workshop on Privacy Enhancing Technologies (PET2004)* (pp. 26-28) Toronto, Canada.

Cadbury Report (1992). *Report of the committee on the Financial Aspects of Corporate Governance*, United Kingdom.

Camp, J., & Osorio, C. (2003). Privacy-Enhancing Technologies for Internet Commerce. In *Trust in the Network Economy.* Berlin: Springer-Verlag.

Canadian Standards Association (n.d.). Model Code for the Protection of Personal Information. *Available as of Sept. 5, 2003 at: http://www.csa.ca/standards/privacy/code/Default.asp?articleID=5286&language=English*

Cannon, J. C. (2005). *Privacy: What Developers and IT Professionals Should Know*: Addison-Wesley.

Capelli, D., Moore, A., Shimeall, T. J., & Trzeciak, R. (2006). Common Sense Guide to Prevention and Detection of Insider threats, 2nd Edition. Carnegie Mellon University, CyLab.

Capra, L., Emmerich, W., & Mascolo, C. (2002). A Micro-Economic Approach to Conflict Resolution in Mobile Computing. *Proceedings of the 10th ACM SIGSOFT Symposium on Foundations of Software Engineering*, November.

Carey, A. (2006). 2006 Global Information Security Workforce Study, sponsored by $(ISC)^2$. Retrieved May 12, 2007 from http://www.isc2.org/download/workforcestudy06.pdf

Carlsen, J., Thingsted, P., & Thorne, S. (1993). *Implementation guide: How to make your organization aware of IT security.* European Security Forum.

Carr, D. (2007). Case Dissection: Inside MySpace. *Baseline Magazine*, 68, 34-49

Carroll, J. M. (2000). Five reasons for scenario-based design. *Interacting with computers, 13*(1), 43-60.

Casar, E., Scheer-Gumm, G., & Simons-Felwor, P. (2004). *IT Baseline Protection Manual.* Germany: BSI.

CastleCops. (2006, November 5, 2006). New PayPal Phishing Approach. Retrieved November 6, 2006, from http://www.castlecops.com/article-6680-nested-0-0.html

Cavusoglu, H., Mishra, B., & Raghunathan, S. (2002). *A model for evaluating it security investments.* Technical Report: University of Texas at Dallas, School of Management, 2002.

Cazier, J. A., & Botelho, C. M. (2007). *Social Engineering's Threat to Public Privacy.* Paper presented at the the 6th Security Conference, Las Vegas, Nevada.

Center for the Digitial Future. (2005). *2005 Digital Future Report*: USC Annenberg School.

Central Intelligence Agency. (2003). *The 2002 annual report of the United States intelligence community.* Washington, DC.

Cerone, A., & Curzon, P. (2007). *Proceedings of the 1st International Workshop on Formal Methods for Interactive Systems (FMIS'2006). ENTCS 183.* Elsevier.

Cerone, A., & Elbegbayan, N. (2007). Model-checking driven design of interactive systems. In Antonio Cerone and Paul Curzon (eds.) *Proceedings of the 1st International Workshop on Formal Methods for Interactive Systems. ENTCS, 183*, 3-20. Elsevier.

Cerone, A., Connelly, S., & Lindsay, P. (2007). Formal Analysis of Human Operator Behavioural Patterns in Interactive Surveillance Systems. *To appear in System and Software Modeling*. Springer-Verlag.

Cerone, A., Lindsay, P., & Connelly, S. (2005). Formal analysis of human-computer interaction using model-checking. In Bernhard Aichernig and Bernhard Beckert (eds.) *Proceedings of the 3rd IEEE International Conference on Software Engineering and Formal Methods*, pp. 352–361. IEEE Computer Society.

Chai, S., Bagchi-Sen, S., Morrell, C., Rao, H. R., & S.Upadhyaya. (2006). Role of Perceived Importance of Information Security: An Exploratory Study of Middle School Children's Information Security Behavior. *Issues in Informing Science and Information Technology, 3*.

Chandrasekaran, M., Chinchani, R., & Upadhyaya, S. (2006). *PHONEY: Mimicking User Response to Detect Phishing Attacks*. Paper presented at the World of Wireless, Mobile and Multimedia Networks (WoWMoM), Niagara Falls, Canada.

Chandrasekaran, M., Narayanan, K., & Upadhyaya, S. (2006). *Phishing Email Detection Based on Structural Properties*. Paper presented at the New York State Cyber Security Conference (NYS), Albany, NY.

Chapman, M. T. (1997a). *Hiding the hidden: A software system for concealing ciphertext as innocuous text*. University of Wisconsin-Milwaukee, Milwaukee.

Chapman, M. T. (1997b). NICETEXT. Retrieved October 2004, from http://www.ctgi.net/NICETEXT

Chapman, M. T., Davida, G., & Rennhard, M. (2001). A Practical and Effective Approach to Large-Scale Automated Linguistic Steganography. In *Lecture Notes in Computer Science, 2200*, 156-167. Berlin Heidelberg: Springer Verlag.

Chaula, J. A. (2006). *A Socio-Technical Analysis of Information Systems Security Assurance A Case Study for Effective Assurance*. Stockholm University, Stockholm

Chaum, D. (1982). Blind Signatures for Untraceable Payments. *In proceedings of the CRYPTO 82* (pp. 199-203).

Chaum, D., Ryan, P. Y. A., & Schneider, S. A. (2005). A Practical Voter-Verifiable Election Scheme. In S. C. Vimercati, P. F. Syverson, and D. Gollman, (eds.), *Computer Security - ESORICS 2005, 10th European Symposium on Research in Computer Security (ESORICS'05), Milan, Italy, September 12-14, 2005, Proceedings*, pp. 118-139.

Chen, R., Sharman, R., Chakravarti, N., Rao, H. R., & Upadhyaya, S. J. (2007). mergency Response Information System Interoperability: Development of Chemical Incident Response Data Model. *Journal of the Association for Information Systems*.

Cheng, Z. (2003). Discussion about the Honesty-credit Principle and the Inspiration of British and American Laws. *Journal of Taiyuan University of Technology (Social Sciences Edition), 21*(1), 9-12.

China's National People's Congress. (1999). Contract Law of the People's Republic of China.

Chomsky, N. (1957). *Syntactic Structures*. The Hague: Mouton.

Choobineh, J., Dhillon, G., Grimaila, M. R., & Rees, J. (2007). Management of Information Security: Challenges and Research Directions. *Communications of AIS, 20*.

Chopra, K., & Wallace, W. A. (2003). Trust in electronic environments. *Proceedings of the 36th Hawaii International Conference on System Science*, 331.1.

Chou, N., Ledesma, R., Teraguchi, Y., & Mitchell, J. (2004). *Client-Side Defense Against Web-Based Identity Theft*. Paper presented at the 11th Annual Network and Distributed System Security Symposium (NDSS), San Diego, CA.

Churchill, E. F., Nelson, L., Denoue, L., Helfman, J., & Murphy, P. (2004). Interactive Systems in Public Places: Sharing Multimedia Content with Interactive Public Displays: A Case Study. In: *Proceedings of the Conference on Designing Interactive Systems: Processes, Practices, Methods, and Techniques*, pp. 7 – 16.

Claburn, T. (2005). Workers Trade Password Security For Starbucks. Information Week, May 6. Retrieved May 12, 2007 from http://www.informationweek.com/story/showArticle.jhtml?articleID=162600315

Claburn, T. (2007, January 22, 2007). Minor Google Security Lapse Obscures Ongoing Online Data Risk Retrieved January 24, 2007, from http://www.informationweek.com/shared/printableArticle.jhtml?articleID=196902585

Clark, D., & Wilson, D. (1989). Evolution of a Model for Computer Integrity, in *Report of the Invitational Workshop on Data Integrity*, Gaithersburg, Maryland, A.2-1A.2-13. Gaithersburg, MD, National Institute of Standards and Technology, NIST Special Publication 500-168: NIST.

Clark, J., & DeRose, S. (1999). XML Path Language (XPath) Version 1.0, W3C Recommendation 16 November

1999. Retrieved from http://www.w3.org/TR/1999/REC-xpath-19991116

Clarke Jr., E. M., Grumberg, O., & Peled, D. A. (1999). *Model-checking*. The MIT Press.

Clarke, R. (1999). *Introduction to Dataveillance and Information Privacy, and Definitions of Terms*. Retrieved January 13, 2006, from http://www.anu.edu.au/people/Roger.Clarke/DV/Intro.html

Clemen, T. R., & Reilly, T. (1999). Correlations and Copulas for decision and risk Analysis. *Management Science*, 45(2), 208-224.

Cochrane, P. (1997). *108 Tips for Time Travellers*. London, England: Orion Business Books.

Cohen, A. B. J., & Nagin, D. (Eds.). (1978). *Introduction*. Washington, DC: National Academy of Sciences.

Cohen, F. (1991). A Cost Analysis of Typical Computer Viruses and Defenses. *Computers & Security, 10*, 239-250.

Compeau, D. R., & Higgins, C. A. (1995). Computer self-efficacy: Development of a measure and initial test. *MIS Quarterly, 19*(2), 189.

CompTIA (2006). Fourth annual CompTIA study on information security and the workforce. Available at: http://www.comptia.org/about/pressroom/get_pr.aspx?prid=903.

Computing curricula 2001. (2001). *J. Educ. Resour. Comput., 1*(3es), 1.

Condon, R. (2006). Analysis: protecting yourself from an inside job - what are the options? Retrieved May 12, 2007 from http://software.silicon.com/security/0,39024655,39158082,00.htm

ConneXion, C. (1996). *Anonymous Surfing*. Retrieved from http://anonymizer.com

Contos, B.T. (2006). *Enemy at the water cooler – Real-life stories of insider threats and enterprise security management countermeasures*. Rockland, MA: Syngress Publishing Inc.

Cook, D., Das, S. (2004). Smart Environments: Technology, Protocols and Applications. Wiley-Interscience.

Cortellessa, V., Singh, H., & Cukic, B. (2002). Early reliability assessment of uml based software models. *In Proceedings of the third international workshop on Software and performance*, pages 302–309. ACM Press, 2002.

COSO (Committee Of the Sponsoring Organizations of the Treadway Commission, 1994). *Internal control – integrated framework*. New York, NY: American Institute of Certified Public Accountants.

Covington, M. J, Long, W., Srinivasan, S., & Dey, A. K., Ahamad, M. & Abowd, G. D. (2001). Securing Context-Aware Applications Using Environment Roles. In *Proceedings of the sixth ACM symposium on Access control models and technologies*, Chantilly, Virginia, United States, (pp. 10-20), ACM Press.

Covington, M., Ahamad, M., & Srinivasan, S. (2001). *A security architecture for context-aware applications*, Technical Report GITCC-01-12, College of Computing, Georgia Institute of Technology.

Covington, M., Fogla, P., Zhan, Z., & Ahamad, M., (2002). *A context-aware security architecture for emerging applications*. In *Proceedings of the Annual Computer Security Applications Conference (ACSAC)*.

Cowen, Z. (1976). *Opening address*. Paper presented at the *Symposium on Privacy*, Sydney.

Coyle, K. (1999). *P3P: Pretty Poor Privacy? A Social Analysis of the Platform for Privacy Preferences* (P3P) [Electronic Version]. Retrieved from http://www.kcoyle.net/p3p.html

CRA Grand challenges in Information Security and Assurance. (2003). Retrieved 12th January 2008 from www.cra.org/Activities/grand.challenges /security/home.html

Crampton, J., & Loizou, G. (2003, May). Administrative Scope: A Foundation for Role-Based Administrative Models. *ACM Transactions on Information and System Security, 6*(2), 201-231.

Cranor, L. (2002). *Web Privacy with P3P*. O'Reilly.

Cranor, L. F., & Reidenberg, J. R. (2002). Can User Agents Accurately Represent Privacy Notices? *In proceedings of the 30th Research Conference on Communication, Information and Internet Policy*, Alexandria, VA. from http://articles.ssrn.com/sol3/articles.cfm?abstractid=328860

Cranor, L. F., Egelman, S., Hong, J., & Zhang, Y. (2006, Novemeber 13, 2006). Phinding Phish: An Evaluation of Anti-Phishing Toolbars. Retrieved March 16, 2007, from http://www.cylab.cmu.edu/files/cmucylab06018.pdf

Cranor, L. F., Guduru, P., & Arjula, M. (2006, June). User Interfaces for Privacy Agents. *ACM Transactions on Computer-Human Interaction (TOCHI), 13*(2), 135–178.

Cranor, L., Dobbs, B., Egelman, S., Hogben, G., Humphrey, J., Langheinrich, M., et al. (2006). The Platform for Privacy Preferences 1.1 (P3P1.1) Specification. W3C Working Draft 10 February 2006. Retrieved from http://www.w3.org/TR/2006/WD-P3P11-20060210/

Cranor, L., Langheinrich, M., & Marchiori, M. (2002, April 15). *A P3P Preference Exchange Language 1.0 (APPEL1.0): W3C Working Draft.*.

Creese, S., Goldsmith, M., Harrison, R., Roscoe, A. W., Whittaker, P., & Zakiuddin, I. (2005). Exploiting empirical engagement in authentication protocol design. *Security in Pervasive Computing, Second International Conference, SPC 2005*, Boppard, Germany, April 6-8, 2005, Proceedings. *LNCS v3450*, 119-133.

Creese, S., Goldsmith, M., Roscoe, A. W., & Xiao, M. (2006). Bootstrapping multi-party ad-hoc security. *Proceedings of the 2006 ACM Symposium on Applied Computing (SAC)*, Dijon, France, April 23-27, 2006, pp. 369-375.

Creese, S., Goldsmith, M., Roscoe, A.W. & Zakiuddin, I. (2003). The attacker in ubiquitous computing environments: formalising the threat model. *Proceedings of the Formal Aspects of Security and Trust (FAST 2003)*, Pisa, Italy.

Cressman, Joe (2006). Elmhurst Police Logging on to Catch Predators. *Liberty Suburban Chicago Newspapers*, November 22, 2006. Retrieved 2/18/2007 from http://www.libertysuburban.com/story.php?pub=4&sid=72741#

Creswell, J. W. (2003). *Research Design: Qualitative, Quantitative, and Mixed Methods Aprroaches*. Thousand Oaks, CA: Sage Publications.

CSI Survey (2007). The 12th Annual Computer Crime and Security Survey. Computer Security Institute Survey. Retrived online from http://ccr.i2.nscee.edu/resources/CSISurvey2007.pdf on 6th May, 2008.

CSI/FBI (2005). Computer Crime and Security Survey. Available at: GoCSI.com.

Curriculum: Proposed standards for IT curriculum. (2005). from http://sigite.acm.org/activities/curriculum/downloads/IT%20Volume-April%202005.pdf

Curzon, P., & Blandford, A. E. (2004). Formally justifying user-centred design rules: A case study on post-completion errors. In E.A. Boiten, J. Derrick, and G. Smith (eds.) *Integrated Formal Methods, 2999 of Lecture Notes in Computer Science*, 461–480. Springer-Verlag, Berlin, Germany.

Cutler, K. (2000). Hitting the Bull's eye. Available at: http://infosecuritymag.techtarget.com/articles/august00/columns5_logoff.shtml. August.

CxG's Software (2007). *Contextual Graphs Homepage*. Retrieved September 11, 2007, from http://cxg.fr

CZ. (2000). Czech Republic Act of 4 April 2000 on the Protection of Personal Data and on Amendment to Some Related Acts (Vol. 101).

Czekalski, E. (2006). Personal communication.

Daft, R. L., & Lengel, R. H. (1986). Organizational information, media richness and structural design. *Management Science, 32*, 554-571.

Danchev, D. (2003). Reducing Human Factor Mistakes. Available at: http:www.windowsecurity.com. July 23.

Dark, M. J. (2004). *Assessing student performance outcomes in an information security risk assessment, service learning course.* Paper presented at the Proceedings of the 5th conference on Information technology education, Salt Lake City, UT, USA.

Dark, M. J., Ekstrom, J., J., & Lunt, B., M. . (2005). *Integration of information assurance and security into the IT2005 model curriculum.* Paper presented at the Proceedings of the 6th conference on Information technology education, Newark, NJ, USA.

Davis, D. (1996). Compliance Defects in Public-Key Cryptography. *In Proceedings of the 6th USENIX Security Symposium.*

Davis, F. D., Bagozzi, R. P., & Warshaw, P. R. (1989). User Acceptance of Computer Technology: A Comparison of Two Theoretical Models. *Management Science, 35*(8), 982-1002.

De Angeli, A., Coventry, L., Johnson, G. I., & Coutts, M. (2003). Usability and user authentication: Pictorial passwords vs. Pin. In P.T.McCabe (Ed.), *Contemporary ergonomics 2003* (pp. 253-258). London: Taylor & Francis.

De Becker, G. (1997). *The Gift of fear.* Boston: Little, Brown and Company.

Debuse, J., & Rayward-Smith, V. (1997). Feature subset selection within a simulated annealing data mining algorithm. *Journal of Intelligent Information Systems.*

Defense in depth. (2002). Retrieved December 27, 2006, from nsa2.www.conxion.com/support/guides/sd-1.pdf.

Delaney, K. (2005). Identity Theft Made Easier. *Wall Street Journal* (Mar. 29 2005), P. B1.

Delaune, S., Kremer, S., an&d Ryan, M. D. (2006). Coercion-Resistance and Receipt-Freeness in Electronic Voting. *Proceedings of the 19th IEEE Computer Security Foundations Workshop (CSFW'06)*, Venice, Italy, pp. 28-42. IEEE Computer Society.

Deloitte (2005). *Global security survey.* Retrieved May 12, 2007 from http://www.deloitte.com/dtt/cda/doc/content/dtt_financialservices_2005GlobalSecuritySurvey_2005-06-22b.pdf

Deloitte, T. & T. (2005). Global Security Survey. Available at: www.deloitte.com.

Denning, D. (1987). An Intrusion Detection Model. *IEEE Transactions on Software Engineering, 13*(2), 222-232.

Denning, D. E. (1999). *Information Warfare and Security.* Singapore: Addison Wesley.

Desman, M. (2002). Building an Information Security Awareness Program. Florida: CRC Press LLC.

Detica (2004). *Don't put all your PINs in one basket! Consumer PIN-sharing undermines Chip & PIN scheme.* Retrieved May 21, 2008, from http://www.detica.com/index.php?option=com_articlemanager&Itemid=266&task=display&artid=199&year=2004&category=none

DE-TML. (2007). *German Telemedia Law.* Retrieved from http://www.gesetze-im-internet.de/tmg/

Deutsch, M. (1962). Cooperation and trust: Some theoretical notes. M. R. Jones (Ed.), *Nebraska Symposium on Motivation*, (pp. 275-319). Lincoln, NE: University of Nebraska Press.

Deutsch, M. (1973). *The resolution of conflict.* New Haven, CT: Yale University Press.

Devanbu P. T., & Stubblebine, S. (2000). Software engineering for security: a roadmap. In *Proceedings of the conference on the future of Software engineering*, pages 227–239. ACM Press, 2000.

Dey, A. (2000). *Providing Architectural Support for Building Context-Aware Applications.* PhD thesis, College of Computing, Georgia Institute of Technology.

Dhamija, R., & Perrig, A. (2000). Déjà vu: A user study using images for authentication. *9th USENIX Security Symposium.*

Dhamija, R., & Perrig, A. (2005). *Déjà Vu: User study using images for authentication.* In Ninth Usenix Security Symposium (Denver, CO, USA, Aug. 14-17, 2000). Retrieved Feb 20, 2006 from http://www.usenix.org/publications/library/proceedings/sec2000 /dhamija.html,

Dhamija, R., Tygar, D., & Hearst, M. (2006). *Why Phishing Works.* Paper presented at the SIGCHI conference on Human Factors in computing systems, ACM Special Interest Group on Computer-Human Interaction.

Dhamija, R., Tygar, J. D., & Hearst, M. (2006, Aoruk 2). *Why Phishing Works.* Paper presented at the SIGCHI Conference on Human Factors in Computing Systems, Montreal, Quebec, Canada.

DiFalco, G. (2006, November 7). Web Host GoDaddy Supports Rigorous New Validation SSL. Retrieved November 3, 2006, from http://www.tophosts.com/articles/004087.html

Dillon, M. (1996). *Politics of security: Towards a political philosophy of continental thought.* London: Routledge.

Dimmock, N., Belokosztolszki, A., Eyers, D., Bacon, J., & Moody, K. (2004). Access management for distributed systems: Using trust and risk in role-based access control policies, (pp. 156-162). *Proceedings of the Ninth ACM symposium on Access Control Models and Technologies.*

Dionysiou, I. (2006). *Dynamic and composable trust for indirect interactions.* Unpublished doctoral dissertation, Washington State University, Pullman.

Dix, A. J. (1991). Formal Methods for Interactive Systems. Academic Press.

Dobson, J. (1994). Messages, Communication, Information Security and Value. *Proceeding of the New Security Paradigms Workshop, IEEE*, Aug. 1994, pp. 10-18.

DOD. (1985). *Department of Defense Trusted Computer Security Evaluation Criteria*, DOD 5200.28-STDN, National Computer Security Center, December 1985.

Dodaro, G. L., Zafra, D. d., Pitcher, S. I., Tressler, J. D., & Ippolito, J. B. (1998). *Information technology security training requirements: A role- and performance-based model* (No. 800-16). Gaithersburg, MD: National Institute of Standards and Technology.

Doherty, N. F., & Fulford, H. (2006). Aligning the information security policy with the strategic information systems plan. *Computers & Security, 25*(1), 55-63.

Domino, M., Klaus, T., & Collins, R. W. (2004). *An Experiment in Collaborative Programming: How Distributed Cognition Impacts Performance Outcomes.* Paper presented at the Proceedings of the Tenth Americas Conference on Information Systems, New York, New York.

Dorrington, P. (2004). *A strategic approach to reducing losses.* Cary, NC: SAS Institute.

Dourish, P. (2004). *Security as experience and practice: Supporting everyday security.* Talk given at the *DIMACS Workshop on Usable Privacy and Security Software*, July 7, 2004.

Dourish, P., & Anderson, K. (2006). Collective Information Practice: Exploring Privacy and Security as Social and Cultural Phenomena. *Human-Computer Interaction, 21*(3), 319-342.

Dowland, P., Furnell, S., & Papadaki, M. (2002). Keystroke Analysis as a Method of Advanced User Authentication and Response. *IFIP TC11 17th International Conference on Information Security: Visions and Perspectives* (pp. 215-226).

Dowland, P. S., Furnell, S. M., Illingworth, H. M., & Reynolds, P. L. (1999). Computer Crime and Abuse: A Survey of Public Attitudes and Awareness. *Computers and Security, 18*(8), 715-726.

Downs, J. S., Holbrook, M. B., & Cranor, L. F. (2006). Decision strategies and susceptibility to phishing. In *Proceedings of the second symposium on Usable privacy and security* (pp. 79-90). Pittsburgh, Pennsylvania: ACM Press.

DPA (1998). Data Protection Act. U.K. Parliament.

Drake, C., Oliver, J., & Koontz, E. (2004, July). *Anatomy of a Phishing Email.* Paper presented at the First Conference on Email and Anti-Spam Mountain View, CA.

Drake, P., & Clarke, S. (2008). *Social Aspects of Information Security: An International Perspective.* In Gupta, M and Sharman, R. (Eds), Social and Human Elements of Information Security: Emerging Trends and Countermeasures. IGI Publishing. Hershey, PA: Information Science Publishing. September 2008.

Drucker, H., Wu, D., & Vapnik, V. (1999). Support vector machines for Spam categorization. *IEEE-NN, 10*, 1048--1054.

DTI (United Kingdom Department of Trade and Industry, 2006). Information security breaches survey 2006 – technical report. Retrieved May 12, 2007 from http://www.dti.gov.uk/files/file28343.pdf

Duntemann, J. (2004). *Degunking Your Email, Spam, And Viruses.* Scottsdale, Arizona: Paraglyph Press.

Eaddy, M., Blasko, G., Babcock, J., & Feiner, S. (2004). My Own Private Kiosk: Privacy-Preserving Public Displays. In: *Proceedings of the International Symposium on Wearable Computers* (ISWC'04), pp. 132 – 135.

Edmead, M. T. (2002) *Social engineering attacks: What we can learn from Kevin Mitnick.* Retrieved September 11, 2007, from http://searchsecurity.techtarget.com/tip/1,289483,sid14_gci865450,00.html

Egelman, S., Cranor, L., & Chowdhury, A. (2006). An Analysis of P3P-Enabled Web sites among Top-20 Search Results. *In proceedings of the 8th International Conference on Electronic Commerce* (pp. 197 - 207).

Elder, V. B., Gardner, E. P., & Ruth, S. R. (1987). Gender and Age in Techno Stress: Effects on White Collar Productivity. *Government Finance Review, 3*, 17-21.

Eldridge, M., Barnard, P., & Bekerian, D. (1994). Autobiographical memory and Daily Schemes at Work. In: *Memory, 2*(1), 51-74.

El-Kahatib, K., Korba, L., Xu, Y., & Gee, G. (2003). Privacy and Security in E-Learning. *International Journal of Distance Education, 1*(4).

Elofson, G. (1998). Developing trust with intelligent agents: An exploratory study, (pp. 125-139). *Proceedings of the first international workshop on trust.*

Elron Sofware's Internet Manager. http://www.lansafe.com/elron.html

Emigh, A. (2005). *Online Identity Theft: Phishing Technology, Chokepoints and Countermeasures*: Radix Labs.

Emmerich, W. (2000). *Engineering Distributed Objects.* JohnWiley & Sons, Inc, 2000.

ENISA (European Network and Information Security Agency, 2006). *A user's guide: how to raise information security awareness.* Retrieved May 13, 2007 from http://www.enisa.europa.eu/doc/pdf/deliverables/download.htm

EPIC (2002). *Letter to House Judiciary Subcommittee on the Courts, the Internet, and Intellectual Property.* The Electronic Privacy Information Center and the Electronic Frontier Foundation, June 5, 2002. Retrieved 2/16/2007 from http://www.epic.org/privacy/DRM/hj-DRMltr6.5.02.html

EPIC, & Junkbusters, Pretty Poor Privacy: An Assessment of P3P and Internet Privacy. (June 2000). from http://www.epic.org/reports/prettypoorprivacy.html

Epstein, P., & Sandhu, R. (1999). Towards A UML Based Approach to Role Engineering. In *Proc. of the 4th ACM workshop on Role-based Access Control.*

Ernest & Young (2003). Global Information Security Survey. Available at: http://www.ey.com.

Ernest & Young (2004). *Global Information Security Survey 2004*. Retrieved March 5, 2006 from http://www.ey.com/GLOBAL/content.nsf/International/Press_Release_-_2004_Global_Information_Security_Survey

EU. (1995). Directive 95/46/EC of the European Parliament and of the Council of 24 October 1995 on the Protection of Individuals with Regard to the Processing of Personal Data and on the Free Movement of such Data. *Official Journal of the European Communities* (23 November 1995 No L. 281), 31ff.

EU. (2002). Directive 2002/58/EC of the European Parliament and of the Council Concerning the Processing of Personal Data and the Protection of Privacy in the Electronic Communications Sector.

European Union Directive (1995). Directive 95/46/EC of the European Parliament and of the Council of 24 October 1995 on the protection of individuals with regard to the processing of personal data and on the free movement of such data. *Unofficial text available as of Sept. 5, 2003 at: http://aspe.hhs.gov/datacncl/eudirect.htm*

Evers, J. (2007). Fortinet: Beware of Google's Blogger [Electronic Version], 2007. Retrieved March 15, 2007 from http://news.com.com/8301-10784_3-6167750-7.html.

eXtensible Access Control Markup Language (XACML), Version 2.0; OASIS Standard, February 1, 2005. (2005). from http://www.oasis-open.org/committees/tc_home.php?wg_abbrev=xacml

Federal Privacy Commissioner. (2000). *Community attitudes towards privacy in Australia*. Retrieved 18 June, 2004, from http://www.privacy.gov.au/publications/rcommunity.html

Feith, A. (2003). Privacy Aspects in Ubiquitous Computing. Technical Report of Fraunhofer's Integrated Publication and Information Systems Institute (IPSI), Darmstadt, Germany.

Feldmeier, D. C., & Karn, P. R. (1989). *UNIX password security – ten years later*. In Advances in Cryptology – CRYPTO'89, Lecture Notes in Computer Science 435, Springer Verlag (1990), 44-63.

Fellows, D. (2005). *Search Engine Users*. Retrieved January 23, 2005. from http://www.pewinternet.org/pdfs/PIP Searchengine users.pdf.

Ferguson, A. J. (2005, 11/1/2005). Fostering E-mail Security Awareness: The West Point Carronade, 54-57.

Ferguson, G. T. (2003). Have Your Objects Call My Objects. In: Harvard Business Review, Vol. 80, No. 6, pp. 138 – 143.

Fernback, J., & Thompson, B. (1995). *Computer-Mediated Communication and the American Collectivity: The Dimensions of Community Within Cyberspace*. Paper presented at the annual convention of the International Communication Association, Albuquerque, New Mexico.

Ferraiolo, D. F., Barkley, J. F., & Kuhn, D. R. (1999, February). A role-based access control model and reference implementation within a corporate intranet. *ACM Transactions on Information and System Security (TISSEC), 2*(1).

Ferraiolo, D., Sandhu, R., Gavrila, S., Kuhn, D., & Chandramouli, R. (2001). Proposed NIST standard for role-based access control. *ACM Transactions on Information and System Security (TISSEC), 4*(3).

Ferrari, E. & Thuraisingham, B. (2000). *Secure Database Systems*. In: M. Piattini, O. Díaz (Ed.), Advanced Databases: Technology Design. Artech House, 2000.

Fette, I., Sadeh, N., & Tomasic, A. (2007). *Learning to detect phishing emails* Paper presented at the 16th international conference on World Wide Web (WWW), Banff, Alberta, Canada.

Fight Back Against Identity Theft. (2006). Retrieved March 17, 2007, from http://www.ftc.gov/bcp/edu/microsites/idtheft/

Financial Times (2007). *A generation waiting to play havoc with company security*. The Financial Times, March 28 2007. London, England: Financial Times Ltd.

Finder, Alan (2006). When a Risqué Online Persona Undermines a Chance for a Job. *New York Times*, June 11, 2006, Section 1, Page 1, Column 1.

Finne, T. (1998). A Conceptual Framework for Information Security Management. *Computers & Security, 17*, 303-307.

Finne, T. (2000). Information Systems Risk Management: Key Concepts and Business Processes. *Computers & Security, 19*(3), 234-242.

Finucane, M., Slovic, P., Mertz, C. K., Flynn, J., & Satterfield, T. A. (2000). Gender, Race, and Perceived Risk: The 'White Male' Effect. *Health, Risk and Society, 2*(2), 159-172.

Fiore, A., & Donath, J. S. (2004). Online Personals: An Overview. *ACM Computer-Human Interaction*. ACM Press.

FISMA (2002). Federal Information Security Management Act. U.S. Congress.

Fitzgerald, M. (2006). *The Risks Associated With Offshoring Software Development.* CIO Magazine. Retrieved October 21st 2007 from http://www.cio.com/article/31967/The_Risks_Associated_With_Offshoring_Software_Development_

Fitzpatrick, Michael (2006). *HR 5319 IH, the "Deleting Online Predators Act of 2006".* The US. Congress. Retrieved 2/16/2007 from http://www.techlawjournal.com/cong109/bills/house/hr5319/hr5319ih.asp

Fleisch, E., & Mattern, F. (Eds.). (2005). *Das Internet der Dinge. Ubiquitous Computing und RFID in der Praxis: Visionen, Technologien, Anwendungen, Handlungsanleitungen.* Heidelberg, Germany: Springer-Verlag.

Foltz, C. B. (2004). Cyberterrorism, computer crime, and reality. *Information Management & Computer Security, 12*(2), 154-166.

Fontes, E. L. G., & Balloni, A. J. (2007). Security in Information Systems: Sociotechnical Aspects. In *Innovations and Advanced Techniques in Computer and Information Sciences and Engineering* (pp. 163-166): Springer Netherlands.

Fornell, C.(Ed.) (1982). *Second Generation of Multivariate Analysis.* New York: Praeger.

Foster, S., & Pacl, B. (2002). *Analysis of return on investment for information security.* Technical Report, Getronics Inc.

Fotinger, C. S., & Ziegler, W. (2004). Understanding a hacker's mind - A psychological insight into the hijacking of identities. *A White Paper by the Danube-University,* Zentrum fur praxisorientiere Informatik, Dr Karl-Dorrek Strabe 30, A-3500 Krems.

Friedewald, M., Vildjiounaite, E., Wright, D. (2006). The Brave New World of Ambient Intelligence: A State-of-the-Art Review. Deliverable D1 of the SWAMI consortium to the European Commission under contract 006507.

F-Secure (2004). F-Secure Corporation's Data Security Summary for 2004. Available at: http:www.f-secure.com.

FTC. (1998 June 1998). Federal Trade Commission. Privacy online: A Report to Congress.

FTC. (2000). Online Profiling: A Report to Congress.

FTC. (2000, May 2000). Privacy Online: Fair Information Practices in the Electronic Marketplace. A Report to Congress.

FTC. (2000). The Seven Safe Harbor Principles.

Fujioka, A., Okamoto, T., & Ohta, K. (1992). A practical secret voting scheme for large scale elections. In J. Seberry and Y. Zheng, editors, *Advances in Cryptology —AUSCRYPT '92*, 718 of LNCS, pp. 244- 251. Springer.-Verlag

Gaines, R. (1980). *Authentication by keystroke timing: Some preliminary results* (No. Report R-256-NSF): Rand Corporation.

Gaines, R., Lisowski, W., Press, S., Shapiro, N. (1980). *Authentication by Keystroke Timing: Some Preliminary Results.* Rand Report R-256-NSF. Rand Corporation.

Gallivan, M., & Srite, M. (2005). Information technology and culture: Identifying fragmentary and holistic perspectives of culture. *Information and Organization, 15*(4), 295-338.

Gambetta, D. (1988). Can we trust trust? In D. Gambetta (Ed.), *Trust: Making and breaking cooperative relations,* electronic edition, chapter 13, (pp. 213-237). Department of Sociology, University of Oxford. Originally published by Basil Blackwell 1988. Available online from the following site: http://www.sociology.ox.ac.uk/papers/gambetta213-237.pdf

Gantz, J., Chute, C., Manfrediz, A., Minton, S., Reinsel, D., Schlichting, W., & Toncheva, A. (2008). *The diverse and expanding digital universe: an updated forecast of worldwide information growth through 2011.* Framingham, MA: IDC.

GAO (United States Government Accountability Office) (2007). *Financial Market Preparedness: Significant Progress Has Been Made, but Pandemic Planning and Other Challenges Remain. Report to Congressional Requesters.* Washington, D.C.: GAO. Retrieved April 20, 2008 from www.gao.gov/new.items/d07399.pdf

Gao, Z. (March 1, 2006). Credit Ethics Study—the Ethics Explanation of Economic Credit Crises. Retrieved April 3, 2007, from http://www.ethics.com.cn/Html/Article/133.html

Garfinkel, S., & Cranor, L. (2002). P3P: Privacy Primer.

Garretson, C. (2006, November 1, 2006). Spam that delivers a pink slip. Retrieved November 6, 2006, from http://www.networkworld.com/news/2006/110106-spam-spear-phishing.html

Gartner Press Release. (2006). Gartner says number of phishing e-mails sent to U.S adults nearly doubles in just two years. from http://www.gartner.com/it/page.jsp?id=498245

Gartner. (2006). *Gartner Information Security Hype Cycle Annual Report.* Gartner Research publications, 2006

GASSP (1999). *Generally Accepted Systems Security Principles*, version 2.0. Retrieved May 13, 2007 from http://www.infosectoday.com/Articles/gassp.pdf

Gavrila, S., & Barkley, J. (1998, October). Formal Specification for RBAC User/Role and Role/Role Relationship Management. *Proceedings of Third ACM Workshop on Role-Based Access Control.*Fairfax, VA, USA.

Geer, D., Jr., Hoo, K.S.& Jaquith, A. (2003, July-August). Information security: why the future belongs to the quants. *Security & Privacy Magazine, IEEE, 1*(4), 24 – 32.

Gefen, D., & Straub, D. (1997). Gender Differences in the Perception and Use of E-Mail: An Extension to the Technology Acceptance Model. *MIS Quarterly, 21*(4), 389-400.

Gellersen, H.-W., Schmidt, A., Beigl, H.-W. (2000). Adding Some Smartness to Devices and Everyday Things. Paper presented at the IEEE Workshop on Mobile Computing Systems and Applications, December 7 – 8, Monterrey, USA.

Georgiadis, C. K., Mavridis, I., Pangalos, G., & Thomas, R. K. (2001). Flexible Team-Based Access Control Using Contexts. *Proceedings of Sixth ACM Symposium on Access Control Models*, May 2001, Fairfax, Virginia, USA.

Georgiadis, C. K., Mavridis, I., Pangalos, G., & Thomas, R. K. (2001). Flexible team-based access control using contexts. In *Proceedings of the sixth ACM symposium on Access control models and technologies*, (pp. 21–27).

Gerber, M., & Von Solms, R. (2005). Management of risk in the information age. *Computers & Security, 24*(1), 16-30.

Ghosh, A., Howell C. & Whittaker J. (2002). Building software securely from the ground up. *IEEE Software 19*(1) 14-17.

Gideon, J., Cranor, L., Egelman, S., & Acquisti, A. (2006). *Power* Strips, Prophylactics, and Privacy, Oh My! *In proceedings of the Second Symposium on Usable Privacy and Security* (pp. 133-144) Pittsburgh, Pennsylvania.

Giuri, L., & Iglio, P. (1997). Role Templates for Content-Based Access Control. *Proceedings of Second ACM Workshop on Role-Based Access Control*, Fairfax, VA, USA, November 1997

Glaser, B. G., & Strauss, A. L. (1967). *The discovery of grounded theory: Strategies for qualitative research.* Chicago: Aldine.

GLB (1999). United States Financial Modernization Act, also known as Gramm-Leach-Bliley.

Goguen, J. A., & Meseguer, J. (1982). Security Policies and Security Models, *Symposium on Security and Privacy*, pp.11-20. Menlo Park, CA: IEEE.

Goldberg, I. (2002, April 2002). Privacy-Enhancing Technologies for the Internet, II: Five Years Later. *In proceedings of the Workshop on Privacy Enhancing Technologies 2002.*

Goldberg, I., Wagner, D., & Brewer, E. (1997). Privacy-Enhancing Technologies for the Internet. *In proceedings of the 42nd IEEE Spring COMPCON.* San Jose, CA.

Goodall, J. R., Lutters W. G., & Komlodi, Anita. (2004). *The Work of Intrusion Detection: Rethinking the Role of Security Analysts.* Proceedings of the Tenth Americas Conference on Information Systems, New York, New York, August 2004.

Gordan, L. A., Loeb, M. P., Lucyshyn, W., & Richardson, R. (2007). 2006 CSI/FBI Computer Crime and Security Survey: Computer Security Institute.

Gordon, A. L., & Loeb, P. M. The economics of information security investment. (2002). *ACM Trans on Inf Sys Sec, 5*(4), 438-457.

Gordon, A. L., Loeb, P. M., & Sohai, I. T. (2003). A framework for using insurance for cyber-risk management. *Communications of the ACM, 46*(3).

Gordon, A. L., Loeb, P. M., Lucyshyn, W., & Richardson, R. (2004). CSI/FBI Computer Crime and Security Survey, GoCSI.com.

Gordon, L. A., & Loeb, M. P. (2002). *The economics of information security investment.* ACM Transactions on Information and System Security 5, 4 (2002), 438.457.

Gordon, L. A., Loeb, M. P., & Lucyshyn, W. (2003). Information security expenditures and real options: A wait-and-see approach. *Computer Security Journal, 19*, 2,1.7.

Government of Canada (n.d.). Personal Information Protection and Electronic Documents Act. *Available as of February 28, 2005 at: http://www.privcom.gc.ca/legislation/index_e.asp*

Grady, D., & Kolata, G. (2008) How Serious is the Risk of Avian Flu? *The New York Times.* March 27,

2006. Retrieved April 20, 2008 from www.nytimes.com/2006/03/27/health/28qna.html?_r=1&ref=clogin

Gragg, D. (2002). *A Multi-Level Defense Against Social Engineering*. Retrieved on September 11, 2007 from http://www.sans.org/rr/papers/51/920.pdf.

Gragg, D. (2003). A Multi-level Defense Against Social Engineering. Retrieved May, 2007, from http://www.sans.org/rr/whitepapers/engineering/920.php

Granovetter, M., (1983). The Strength of Weak Ties: A Network Theory Revisited. In *Sociological Theory*, 1, 201-233. Michigan, American Sociological Association.

Green, T (2005). Security chiefs share pains of being caught in the middle. Retrieved May 12, 2007 from http://www.networkworld.com/news/2005/121205-security-interop.html

Greenberg, S., Boyle, M., & LaBerge, J. (1999). PDAs and Shared Public Displays: Making Personal Information Public, and Public Information Personal. In: *Personal Technologies*, 3(1), 54 – 64.

Grzebiela, T. (2002). Insurability of Electronic Commerce Risks, *Proceedings of the 35th Hawaii International Conference on System Sciences*, Hawaii, USA.

Gülcü, C., & Tsudik, G. (1996). Mixing Email with BABEL. *In proceedings of the 1996 Symposium on Network and Distributed System Security (SNDSS '96)* (pp. 2).

Guneti D., & Picardi, C. (2005). Keystroke Analysis of Free Text. *ACM Transactions on Information and System Security*, *8*(3), 312-347.

Gupta, A., & Chellappa, R. K. (2004). Ethical, Legal and Economic Issues in the Digital Economy. *Intellectual Property Rights, Piracy, Trust, Security and Privacy: Minitrack Introduction*. hicss, p. 70179, *Proceedings of the 37th Annual Hawaii International Conference on System Sciences (HICSS'04)* - Track 7, 2004.

Gupta, J. (1990). Identity authorization based on keystroke latencies. *Communications of the ACM, 33*(2), 168-176.

Gupta. M. (2008). Activity Theory Guided Role Engineering. *Proceedings of 14th Americas Conference on Information Systems (AMCIS 2008)*, Toronto, Canada, August 14-17, 2008.

Gutman, P., (2006). *Security Usability Fundamentals*. Retrieved November 21st, 2007 from www.cs.auckland.ac.nz/~pgut001/pubs/ usability.pdf

Hackworth, R. (2005). *Presentation to the Information Systems Security Association*, London, England.

Hammersley, Ben (2003). Click to the clique. *The Guardian*, January 9, 2003. Retrieved 2/10/2007 from http://technology.guardian.co.uk/online/story/0,3605,870848,00.html

Hansche, S., Berti, J., & Hare, C. (2004). *Official (ISC)² Guide To The CISSP Exam*. New York: Auerbach Publications.

Hansmann, U., Merk, L., Nicklous, M., Stober, T. (2001). Pervasive Computing Handbook. Springer-Verlag, Berlin, Germany.

Harford, T. (2007). *The Undercover Economist*. London, England: Abacus.

Hargittai, E. (2004). *The Changing Online Landscape: From Free-for-All To Commercial Gatekeeping*. CommunityPractice in the Network Society: Local Actions/GlobalInteraction, pages 66–76, 2004. http://www.eszter.com/research/c03-onlinelandscape.html.

Harl. (1997). People Hacking: The Psychology of Social Engineering. Retrieved May, 2007, from http://library.cyber-punk.cc/files/se10.html

Harrison, A. W., & Rainer, R. J. J. (1992). The Influence of Individual Differences on Skill in End-User Computing. *Journal of Management Information Systems, 9*, 93-111.

Hartley, R. L. (2006, Novemeber 2, 2006). Scam Stoppers Alert: Phishing Scam. Retrieved November 7, 2006, from http://www.myeyewitnessnews.com/news/local/story.aspx?content_id=DD5603BF-DDF1-47EA-B73E-A08456EB7E36

Hassler, V. (2001). *Security Fundamentals for E-Commerce*. Norwood, MA: Artech House Inc.

Hazari, S. (2005). Perceptions of End-Users on the Requirements in Personal Firewall Software: An Exploratory Study. *Journal of Organizational and End User Computing, 17*(3), 47-65.

Hazem, S., Chaytor, L., Humpert, D., Nyland, J., Schlemmer, R., Stockman, M., et al. (2004). *An implementation of a core curriculum in an information technology degree program*. Paper presented at the Proceedings of the 5th conference on Information technology education, Salt Lake City, UT, USA.

Hearne, L. (2006). The enemy within the firewall. *The Age*, Australia, March 13.

Herath, T. C., Bagchi-Sen, S., & Rao, H. R. (2006). Vulnerability to Internet Crime and Gender Issues. In E. Trauth (Ed.), *Gender and Information Technology Encyclopedia*: Idea Group Inc.

Herbert, A. J. (2005, December). Information Battleground. *Air Force Magazine, 88.*

Herold, R. (2005). *Managing an information security and privacy awareness and training program.* Boca Raton, FL: Auerbach Publications.

Herold, R. (2006). Addressing Privacy Issues during Disaster Recovery. *Information Systems Security*, January-February 2006,16-22.

Herrnson, P. S, Niemi, R. G., Hanmer, M. J., Bederson, B. B., Conrad, F. G., & Traugott, M. (2006). The Importance of Usability Testing of Voting Systems. USENIX/ACCURATE lectronic Voting Technology Workshop (EVT'06), Vancouver, Canada, August 1, 2006.

Hikage, N., Hauser, C., & Murayama, Y. (2007). Joho security gijutsu ni taisuru anshinkan no kozo ni kansuru tokeiteki kento[A statistical discussion of the sense of security, Anshin]. *Information Processing Society of Japan Journal 48*(9) (in Japanese).

Hoffman, L. J., Lawson-Jenkins, K., & Blum, J. (2006). Trust beyond security: an expanded trust model. *Communications of the ACM, 49*(7), 94-101.

HIPAA (1996), Health Insurance Portability and Accountability Act. U. S. Congress.

Hoanca, B., & Mock, K. (2006). Secure graphical password system for high traffic public areas. *Eye Tracking Research & Applications Symposium 2006.* San Diego: ACM SIGGRAPH.

Hoare, C. A. R. (1985). *Communicating Sequential Processes.* Prentice Hall International.

Hoffman, T. (2006). Q&A: Health care standards on the Table. Available at: http://www.computerworld.com/databasetopics/data/story/0,10801,109417,00.html.

Hollnagel, E. (1991). The Phenotype of Erroneous Actions: Implications for HCI Design. G. R. S. Weir and J. L. Alty (eds.). Academic Press. 1991.

Holmes, A. (2006). *The Global State of Information Security 2006.* CIO Magazine. Retrieved September 15, 2006 from http://www.cio.com/article/24979

Holmstrom, U. (1999, May). User-centered design of secure software. *In Proceeedings of the 17th Symposium on Human Factors in Telecommunications.*Denmark.

Homeland Security Presidential Directive/Hspd-9, Defense of United States Agriculture and Food, Retrieved January 30, 2004 from http://www.whitehouse.gov/news/releases/2004/02/text/20040203-2.html.

Hone, K., & Eloff, J. H. P. (2002). What makes an Effective Information Security policy. *Network Security, 2002*(6), 14-16.

Hong, K.-S., Chi, Y.-P., Chao, L. R., & Tang, J.-H. (2003). An integrated system theory of information security management. *Information Management & Computer Security, 11*(5), 243.

Hoover, N. (2006). MySpace Beefs up Security. *InformationWeek*, 1119, 31.

Horgan, D. (2005, November 14). *The Phishing Phleet.* Retrieved December 2, 2006, from http://blogs.courant.com/travel_columnists_horgan/2005/11/the_phishing_ph.html

Hossack, B. I., Pollard, J., & Zehnwirth, B. (1983). *Introduction to Statistics with applications to general insurance*, Cambridge University Press.

How to obscure any URL - How Spammers And Scammers Hide and Confuse. (2002). Retrieved July, 11, 2007, from http://www.pc-help.org/obscure.htm

Howe, J. (2006). The Rise of Crowdsourcing. *Wired Magazine, 14*(06). Retrieved 1/18/07 from http://www.wired.com/wired/archive/14.06/crowds.html

Hu, Q., & Dinev, T. (2005). Is Spyware and Internet Nuisance or Public Menace. *Communications of the ACM, 48*(8), 61-66.

Hu, Q., Hart, P., & Cooke, D. (2006). *The Role of External Influences on Organizational Information Security Practices: An Institutional Perspective.* Paper presented at the Proceedings of the 39th Hawaii International Conference on System Sciences.

Huang, A., & Yen, D. (2003). Usefulness of Instant Messaging among Young Users: Social vs. Work Perspective. *Human Systems Management*, 22, 63–72.

Huang, E. M., & Mynatt, E. D. (2003). Semi-Public Displays for Small, Co-located Groups. In: *Proceedings of the ACM Conference on Human Factors in Computing Systems* (CHI'03), pp. 49 – 56.

Huang, E. M., Russell, D. M., & Sue, A. E. (2004). IM Here: Public Instant Messaging on Large, Shared Displays for Workgroup Interactions. In: *Proceedings of the ACM Conference on Human Factors in Computing Systems* (CHI'04), pp. 279-286.

Hughes, J., O'Brien, J., Randall, D., Rodden, T., Rouncefield, M., & Tolmie, P. (1999). Getting to know the 'customer in the machine'. In the Proceedings of the international ACM SIGGROUP conference on *Supporting group work*, Phoenix.

Hunter, R., Girard, J., & Mogull, R. (2002). *Don't fund security awareness until you're secure.* Gartner. Retrieved May 13, 2007 from http://www.gartner.com/resources/109900/109981/dont_fund_security_awareness_109981.pdf

Hurley, D. (1999). A Whole World in One Glance: Privacy as a Key Enabler of Individual Participation in Democratic Governance. *21st International Conference on Privacy and Personal Data Protection*, September 13.

Huszerl, G., & Majzik, I. (2001). *Modeling and analysis of redundancy management in distributed object–oriented systems by using UML statecharts.* In *Proc. of the Euro-Micro Conference, Workshop on Software Process and Product Improvement*, Poland, pages 200–207, 2001.

IBM (n.d.). Enterprise Privacy Authorization Language (EPAL). Available as of May 31, 2007 at: http://www.zurich.ibm.com/security/enterprise-privacy/epal/

IBM. (2006). *IBM Tivoli Privacy Manager for E-Business.*

ICTWorld. (2006, November 11, 2006). Number of phishing e-mails has almost doubled in two years. Retrieved November 12, 2006, from http://www.mybroadband.co.za/nephp/?m=show&id=4849

Information Security Forum (2005). *Standard of good practice for information security.* Version 4.1. Retrieved May 13, 2007 from http://www.isfsecuritystandard.com/pdf/standard.pdf

Information technology – Code of practice for information security management (ISO/IEC 17799) (2001). International Standards Organization / International Electrotechnical Commission.

Information technology - Security techniques – Information security management systems – Requirements (ISO/IEC 27001) (2005). International Standards Organization / International Electrotechnical Commission.

International Federation of Accountants (2000). Managing Security of Information.

ISO/IEC (International Standards Organization/International Electrotechnical Commission, 2005). International Standard ISO/IEC 27002:2005 - Information Technology – Security Techniques - Code of Practice for Information Security Management.

ISO/IEC 17799 (2007). Retrieved May 25th, 2007, from http://en.wikipedia.org/wiki/ISO_17799.

ISO/IEC 27001 (2007). Retrieved May 25th, 2007, from http://en.wikipedia.org/wiki/ISO_27001.

ITU-T (1997). ITU-T Recommendation X.509 (1997 E): Information Technology - Open Systems Interconnection - The Directory: Authentication Framework, 1997

Iyengar, V.S. (2002). Transforming Data to Satisfy Privacy Constraints. *Proceedings, The Eighth ACM SIGKDD International Conference on Knowledge Discovery and Data Mining*, Edmonton, Alberta.

Jackson, C., Simon, D., Tan, D., & Barth, A. (2007). *An Evaluation of Extended Validation and Picture-in-Picture Phishing Attacks.* Paper presented at the Usable Security (USEC'07). from http://usablesecurity.org/papers/jackson.pdf.

Jaeger, T., Sailer, R., & Zhang, X. (2004, June). Resolving Constraint Conflicts. *Proceedings of the Ninth ACM Symposium on Access Control Models and Technologies.*

Jagatic, T., Johnson, N. A., Jakobsson, M., & Menczer, F. (2005). *Social Phishing: ACM.*

Jakobsson, M. (2005). *Modeling and Preventing Phishing Attacks.*

James, C. (2006, November 2, 2006). Spam levels reach record high. Retrieved November 7, 2006, from http://www.itnews.com.au/newsstory.aspx?CIaNID=41608&src=site-marq

Jank, W., & Shmueli, G. (2007). Studying Heterogeneity of Price Evolution in eBay Auctions via Functional Clustering. *Conditionally accepted at Adomavicius and Gupta (Eds.) Handbook of Information Systems Series: Business Computing*, Elsevier.

Jaques, R. (2006, August 2). *Huge botnet swamps UK firms with 8 million phishing emails.* Retrieved November 13, 2006, 2006, from http://www.vnunet.com/vnunet/news/2161530/huge-botnet-swamps-uk-firms

Jendricke, U., & Markotten. D. Gerd tom. (2000, December). Usability meets Security: The Identity- Manager as your Personal Security Assistant for the Internet. *In Proceedings of the 16th Annual Computer Security Applications Conference*

Jensen, F. V. (2001). *Bayesian Networks and Decision Diagrams*, Springer.

Jermyn, I., Mayer, A., Monrose, F., Reiterand, M., & Rubin, A. (1999). The design and analysis of graphical passwords, *8th USENIX Security Symposium.*

Jewell, Z. C., S. K., A., & Law, P. R. (2001). Censusing and monitoring black rhino (diceros bicornis) using an objective spoor (footprint) identification technique. *J. Zool*(254), 1-16.

Joachims, T. (1998). *Text Categorization With Support Vector Machines: Learning With Many Relevant Features.* Paper presented at the 10th European Conference on Machine Learning {ECML}-98.

Johansson, J. M., & Riley, S. (2005). *Protect your Windows network - from perimeter to data.* Addison Wesley Professional.

Johnson, C. A., & Tesch, B. (2006). US E-Commerce: 2005 To 2010: A Five-Year Forecast and Analysis of US Online Retail Sales. Forrestor Web site.

Joshi, J. B. D., Bertino, E., Latif, U., & Ghafoor, A. (2005). A generalized temporal role-based access control model (GTRBAC). *IEEE Transaction on Knowledge and Data Engineering 17*,1 (Jan. 2005).

Jurafsky, D., & Martin, J. (2000). *Speech and language processing: an introduction to natural language processing, computational linguistics, and speech recognition* Upper Saddle River, NJ: Prentice-Hall.

Jürjens, J. (2002). *Principles for Secure Systems Design.* Ph.D. dissertation. Oxford University Computing Laboratory. Oxford University, 2002.

Jürjens, J. (2003). UMLsec: Extending UML for Secure Systems Development. *In Proc. of UML 2002, LNCS*, Sept. 30 - Oct. 4, 2002.Kleppe, A., Bast, W., Warmer, J. B. and Watson A.. MDA Explained: The Model Driven Architecture– Practice and Promise. Addison-Wesley, 2003.

Kabay, M. (1993). Social Psychology & INFOSEC. Retrieved May 12, 2007 from http://catless.ncl.ac.uk/Risks/15.16.html

Kahneman, D., & Tversky, A. (1979). Prospect Theory: An Analysis of Decision under Risk. *Econometrica, 47*(2), 263-292.

Kamali, R., Liles, S., Winer, C., Jiang, K., & Nicolai, B. (2005). *An implementation of the SIGITE model curriculum.* Paper presented at the Proceedings of the 6th conference on Information technology education, Newark, NJ, USA.

Kamali, R., Liles, S., Winer, C., Jiang, K., & Nicolai, B. (2006). A Curriculum Model Based on the SIGITE Guidelines. *Journal of Information Technology Education, 5.*

Kandra, A. (2003). Social networking Sites are Hot, and They can be Useful Business Tool. *PCWorld Magazine.* Retrieved 1/18/07 from http://www.pcworld.com/article/id,113738-page,1/article.html

Kapadia, A. (2007, March/April). A Case (Study) For Usability in Secure Email Communication. *IEEE Security and Privacy, 5,* 80-84.

Kaplan, D. (2007). Web 2.0, Emerging Threats. *SC Magazine, 18*(2), 25-29.

Karat, C. M. (1989). Iterative Usability Testing of a Security Application. *In Proceedings of the Human Factors Society 33rd Annual Meeting.*

Karat, C.-M., Karat, J., Brodie, C., & Feng, J. (2006). Evaluating Interfaces For Privacy Policy Rule Authoring. *Proceedings of the SIGCHI Conference on Human Factors in Computing Systems*, pp. 83-92, Montreal, Quebec, Canada.

Kark, K., Orlov, L. M., & Bright, S. (2005). Five steps to effective security awareness. Forrester Research.

Karofsky, E. (2001). Insight into return on security investment. *Secure business quarterly: defining the value of strategic security 2001,1*(2). Fourth Quarter.

Karydaa, M., Kiountouzisa, E., & Kokolakis, S. (2005). Information systems security policies: a contextual perspective. *Computers & Security, 24,* 246-260.

Katzke, S. (2001). Security Metric. Available at: http://www.acsac.org/measurement/position-papers.

Kauffman, R., & Wood, C. (2003). An Investigation of Premium Bidding in Online Auctions. Working Paper.

Kawamoto, D. (2006). *Worm Lurks behind MySpace Profiles.* CNET News, July 18, 2006. Retrieved 2/16/2007 from http://news.com.com/Worm+lurks+behind+MySpace+profiles/2100-7349_3-6095533.html.

Keck, D., & Kuehn, P. (1998, October). The Feature and Service Interaction Problem in Telecommunications Systems: A Survey. *IEEE Transactions on Software Engineering*, 24(10).

Keeney, M., Cappelli, D., Kowalski, E., Moore, A., Shimeall, T., & Rogers, S (2005, May). *Insider Threat Study: Computer System Sabotage in Critical Infrastructure Sectors.* U.S. Secret Service and CERT Coordination Center/SEI (Tech. report)

Keep America's food and agriculture safe. (2002). Retrieved January 30, 2004, from www.usda.gov/homelandsecurity/fsproc.htm

Kellermann, T. (2002). Mobile risk management: E-Finance in the Wireless Environment. World Bank.

Kenny, S., & Korba, L. (2002, November). Adapting Digital Rights Management to Privacy Rights Management. *Computers & Security*, 21(7), 648-664.

Kent, D. C. (2006, November 2, 2006). *Tricare, Medicare issues at forefront of defense bill.* Retrieved November 7, 2006, from http://www.zwire.com/site/news.cfm?newsid=17405636&BRD=1659&PAG=461&dept_id=8110&rfi=6

Kerner, S. M. (2005). DNS-Based Phishing Attacks on the Rise Retrieved July, 11, 2007, from http://cws.internet.com/article/2792-.htm

Kersetter, J. (2006). Reporters' records accessed in HP probe. *CNET News.com* Retrieved May, 2007, from http://news.com.com/Reporters+records+accessed+in+HP+probe/2100-1014_3-6113362.html

Kikkawa, T., Shirato, S., Fujii, S., & Takemura, K. (2003). Gijutsuteki anzen to shakaiteki Anshin[The pursuit of informed reassurance ('An-Shin' in Society) and technological safety ('An-Zen')]. *Journal of SHAKAI-GIJUTSU, 1*,1-8 (in Japanese).

King Report (2002). *The Code of Corporate Practices and Conduct*, Institute of Directors, South Africa.

Kirwan, B. (1990). Human reliability assessment. In Evaluation of Human Work, chapter 28. Taylor and Francis.

Kirwan, B. (1992). Human error identification in human reliability assessment. part 1: Overview of approaches. *Applied Ergonomics, 25*(5), 299–318.

Kittur, N. (2006). Cognition, Computation, Design. Retrieved 04/26, 2008 from http://www.kittur.org

Klein, D. (1990). A survey of, and improvement to, password security. In *UNIX Security Workshop II Proceedings*, Tenth Usenix Security Symposium (Portland, OR, USA, Aug. 27- 28, 1990), 83-86.

Knapp, K. J. (2005). *A Model of Managerial Effectiveness in Information Security: From Grounded Theory to Empirical Test.* Auburn University.

Kobsa, A. (2002). Personalization and International Privacy. *Communications of the ACM,* (5), 64-67.

Kobsa, A. (2007). Privacy-Enhanced Web Personalization. In P. Brusilovsky, A. Kobsa & W. Nejdl (Eds.), *The Adaptive Web: Methods and Strategies of Web Personalization* (pp. 628-670). Springer-Verlag.

Kobsa, A., & Schreck, J. (2003, May). Privacy Through Pseudonymity in User-Adaptive Systems. *ACM Transactions in Internet Technology*, 3(2), 149-183.

Kobsa, A., & Teltzrow, M. (2005). Contextualized Communication of Privacy Practices and Personalization Benefits: Impacts on Users' Data Sharing Behavior. In D. Martin & A. Serjantov (Eds.), *Privacy Enhancing Technologies: Fourth International Workshop, PET 2004, Toronto, Canada* (Vol. LNCS 3424, pp. 329-343). Heidelberg, Germany: Springer Verlag.

Kolberg, M., Magill, E., Marples, D., & Tsang, S. (2002). Feature Interactions in Services for Internet Personal Appliances. *Proceedings of IEEE International Conference on Communications 2002 (ICC 2002), 4*, 2613-2618.

Korba, L. (2002). Privacy in Distributed Electronic Commerce. *Proceedings of the 35th Hawaii International Conference on System Science (HICSS)*, Hawaii, January 7-11.

Kouadri Mostefaoui, G. & Brézillon, P. (2006). *Human-centric network security management: A comprehensive helper.* In *Proceedings of the 4th international Workshop on Wireless Mobile Applications and Services on WLAN Hotspots* (Los Angeles, CA, USA, September 29 - 29, 2006). WMASH '06. ACM Press, New York, NY, (pp. 47-52).

Kouadri Mostefaoui, G. (2004). *Towards a Conceptual and Software Framework for Integrating Context Based Security in Pervasive Environments.* Ph.D. Thesis No. 1463, University of Fribourg, Switzerland, October 2004.

Kremer, S., & Ryan, M. D. (2005). Analysis of an Electronic Voting Protocol in the Applied Pi Calculus. *Proceedings of the 14th European Symposium on Programming, ESOP 2005, Edinburgh, UK, April 4-8, 2005, 3444 of LNCS*186-200. Springer-Verlag.

Kritzinger, E. (2006). Information Security in an e-learning environment. In *19th World Computer Congress*, Santiago, Chile.

Kritzinger, E., & von Solms, S. H. (2006). *E-learning: Incorporating Information Security Governance*, in *InSite 2006*, England.

Kritzinger, E., & Von Solms, S. H. (2006). Information Security Governance within the E-Learning environment. In *2006 Teaching and Learning conference*, Mexico.

Kroger, J. (2000). *Identity development: Adolescence through adult.* Tromso, Norway: Sage.

Krutz, R. L, & Vines, R. D. (2001). *The CISSP Prep Guide: Mastering the Ten Domains of Computer Security.* New York, NY: John Wiley & Sons, Inc.

Kuan, H. H., & Bock, G. W. (2005). The collective reality of trust: An investigation of social relations and networks on trust in multi-channel retailers. *Proceedings of the 13th European Conference on Information Systems.* Available from: http://is2.lse.ac.uk/asp/aspecis/20050018.pdf(Last Access: 9 February 2007)

Kumar, A., Karnik, N., & Chafle, G. (2002, July). Context sensitivity in role-based access control, ACM SIGOPS Operating Systems Review, 36(3),.

Kumaraguru, P., Rhee, Y., Acquisti, A., Cranor, L. F., Hong, J., & Nunge, E. (2007). *Protecting People from Phishing: The Design and Evaluation of an Embedded Training Email System*. Paper presented at the Computer/Human Interaction 2007 Conference. Retrieved March 15, 2007, from http://www.cs.cmu.edu/~jasonh/publications/CHI2007-embedded-training-final.pdf.

Kumekawa, J. K. (n.d.). Health Information Privacy Protection: Crisis or Common Sense? *Available as of Sept. 7, 2003 at: http://www.nursingworld.org/ojin/topic16/tpc16_2.htm*

Kutner, M., Greenberg, E., Jin, Y., Boyle, B., Hsu, Y., Dunleavy, E., & White, S. (2007). *Literacy in everyday life: Results from the 2003 National Assessment of Adult Literacy.* Washington, DC: National Center for Education Statistics.

Kuutti, K. (1995). Activity Theory as a potential framework for humancomputer interaction research. In B. Nardi (Ed.), *Context and Consciousness: Activity Theory and Human Computer Interaction* (pp. 17-44): Cambridge: MIT Press.

Kwok, L., & Longley, D. (1997). Code of Practice: A Standard for Information Security Management. In *Proceedings of IFIP TC11, 13th International Conference on Information Security.*

Kwok, L., & Longley, D. (1999). Information Security Management and modeling. *Information Management and Computer Security, 7*(1), 30-40.

Lafrance, Y., (2004). *Psychology: A Precious Security Tool.* Retrieved on September 11, 2007 from http://www.sans.org/reading_room/whitepapers/engineering/1409.php?portal=611fd7dad659f7fefb9f79f9b33edc58.

Lahlou, S., Langheinrich, M., & Röcker, C. (2005). Privacy and Trust Issues with Invisible Computers. In: *Communications of the ACM, 48*(3), 59-60.

Lambert, L. (2002). Asian underground banking scheme: A field note. *Journal of Contemporary Criminal Justice, 18*(4), 358-369.

Lamming, M., Eldridge, M., Flynn, M., Jones, C., & Pendlebury, D. (2000). Satchel: Providing Access to Any Document, Any Time, Anywhere. In: *ACM Transactions on Computer-Human Interaction, 7*(3), 322 – 352.

Lampson, B. W. (1974). Protection. *Proc. Fifth Princeton Symposium on Information Sciences and Systems.* Princeton University, reprinted in *Operating Systems Review, 8*(1), 18-24. Palo Alto, CA.

Lamsal, P. (2001). Understanding trust and security. From http://www.cs.Helsinki.FI/u/lamsal/papers/UnderstandingTrustAndSecurity.pdf

Langacker, R. (1982). Space grammar, analyzability, and the English passive. *Language, 58*, 22-80.

Langacker, R. (1987). *Foundations of Cognitive Grammar, 1. Theoretical Prerequisites.* Palo Alto: Stanford University Press.

Langenderfer, J., & Shimp, T. A. (2001). Consumer Vulnerability to Scams, Swindles, and Fraud: A New Theory of Visceral Influences on Persuasion. *Psychology and Marketing, 18*(7), 763-783.

Langheinrich, M. (2001). Privacy by Design – Principles of Privacy Aware Ubiquitous Systems. In: *Proceedings of the 3rd International Conference on Ubiquitous Computing* (Ubicomp'01), September 2001, Atlanta, USA, pp. 273-291.

Langheinrich, M. (2002). *A Privacy Awareness System for Ubiquitous Computing Environments* In proceedings of the 4th International Conference on Ubiquitous Computing (pp. 237-245) Göteborg, Sweden.

Lascelles, D. (2008). *Banking Banana Skins 2008: the CSFI's annual survey of the risks facing banks.* Centre for the Study of Financial Innovation. Huddersfield, England: Portal Publishing.

Laskowski & Redish (2006). Making Ballot Language Understandable to Voters. USENIX/ACCURATE Electronic Voting Technology Workshop (EVT'06), Vancouver, Canada, August 1, 2006.

Lazarus, D. (2006, September 1, 2006). *Phishing expedition at heart of AT&T hacking.* Retrieved November 15, 2006, from http://sfgate.com/cgi-bin/article.cgi?f=/c/a/2006/09/01/BUGVBKSUIE1.DTL

Leach, J. (2003). Improving user security behaviors. *Computers & Security, 22*(8), 685-670.

Lederer, S., Dey, A., & Mankoff, J. (2003). Who Wants to Know What When? Privacy Preference Determinants in Ubiquitous Computing. In: *Proceedings of the ACM Conference on Human Factors in Computing Systems* (CHI'03), Ft. Lauderdale, USA, pp. 724-725.

Lee, J., & Geistfeld, L. V. (1999). Elderly Consumers' Receptiveness to Telemarketing Fraud. *Journal of Public Policy & Marketing, 18*(2), 208-218.

Lee, J., & Soberon-Ferrer, H. (1997). Consumer Vulnerability to Fraud: Influencing Factors. *The Journal of Consumer Affairs, 31*(1), 70-89.

Leeds, J. (2006). Universal Music Sues MySpace for Copyright Infringement. *New York Times*, November 18, 2006, Section C, Page 3, Column 2.

Legget, J, Williams, G. (1991). Dynamic Identity Verification via Keystroke Characteristics. *International Journal on Man-Machine. Studies, 35*, 859-870.

Lemos, R. (2004). Browser phishing 'flaw' could hook users [Electronic Version]. *CNETNEWs.Com*. Retrieved 15 December, 2005 from http://news.com.com/Browser+phishing+flaw+could+hook+users/2100-1002_3-5484315.html.

Levi, M., Burrows, J., Fleming, M., & Hopkins, M. (2007). *The nature, extent and economic impact of fraud in the UK*. London, England: Association of Chief Police Officers.

Levitt H. (2004, October). *Employee Surveillance and Workplace Investigations*. Presented at "Demystifying Employee Privacy" Lang Michener Privacy Law Seminar, Toronto, Ontario, Canada.

Lewis, A. (2000). Time to elevate IT security to the boardroom. *e Secure, 1*(1), 28.

Lewis, D. J., & Weigert, A. (1985). Trust as a social reality. *Social Forces, 63*(4), 967-985.

Lewis, H. (2007). *Cracks in the dam: The network view of risk*. Business Resilience Forum. London, England: AKJ Associates.

Lewis, M. (2007). In Nature's Casino. *The New York Times Magazine*. August 26, 2007, pages 26-33 and 49-53. Retrieved April 20, 2008 from http://query.nytimes.com/gst/fullpage.html?res=9C05E1DE103FF935A1575BC0A9619C8B63&scp=2&sq=nature%27s+casino&st=nyt

Li, S. (1999, January). *Relation-based versus rule-based governance: an explanation of the East Asian miracle and Asian crisis*. Paper presented at the American Economic Association Annual Meeting, New York.

Li, S., & Li, X. (2005). Game Analysis on Mechanism of Credit Transaction. *China Economist*, November, 15-16.

Li, Y. L. (2004). Intellectual Property Protection for E-Business Methods. *IEEE International Conference on E-Commerce Technology for Dynamic E-Business*, 15-15 Sept. 2004 Page(s):362 – 365.

Li, Z. (2001) *Ethics based enterprises*. Shanghai: Shanghai Social Sciences Publishing House.

Liao, J., & Zhao, D. (2004). *Honesty-credit and Social Development*. Chengdu, Chongqing: Southwestern University of Finance & Economic Press.

Liles, S. P., & Kamali, R. (2006). An Information Assurance and Security Curriculum Implementation. *Issues in Informing Science and Information Technology, 3*.

Lin, H. (2004). A Game Analysis on Effect of Information Transparency to Enterprises' Credit Behavior. *Journal of Chongqing University (Social Sciences Edition), 110*(23-25), 35.

Lindsay, P., & Connelly, S. (2002). Modelling Erroneous Operator Behaviours for an Air-Traffic Control Task. John Grundy and Paul Calder (eds.) Third Australasian User Interfaces Conference (AUIC2002). Conferences in Research and Practice in Information Technology, 7, 43-54. Australian Computer Society, Inc.

Lindup, K. (1996). The role of information security in corporate governance. *Computers & Security, 15*(6), 477-485.

Liss, S. (2001). *Practical Aspects of Information Security*. InfoGroup NorthWest.

Littlewood, B., & Strigini, L. (2000). *Software Reliability and Dependability: A Roadmap*. In A. Finkelstein, editor, The Future of Software Engineering, pages 177–188. ACM Press, Apr. 2000.

Lively Jr., C. E. (2003). Psychological Based Social Engineering. Retrieved May, 2007, from http://www.giac.org/certified_professionals/practicals/gsec/3547.php

Lodderstedt, T. (2002). *SecureUML: A UML-Based Modeling Language for Model-Driven Security*. In Proc. of UML 2002, LNCS, 2002.

Loechner, J. (2006, November 7, 2006). Phishing May Net More Than Previously Thought. Retrieved November 7, 2006, from http://publications.mediapost.com/index.cfm?fuseaction=Articles.showArticleHomePage&art_aid=50686

Long, J. (2005). *Google Hacking for Penetration Testers*, Syngress Publishing, Rockland, MA, 2005.

Lu, X. (2007). Game Model of Credit of Fabricated Community in E-commerce. *Journal of Wuhan University of Technology Information & Management Engineering Edition*, 29(3), 96-98.

Lucca, C. (2006). Pandemic of Fear: Thinking about Disaster Recovery Planning. *The ISSA Journal*. November 2006, 20–22.

Lueg, C. (2001). *A Distributed Cognition Approach to Integrate Security Management and Business Processes*. Paper presented at the Proceedings of the 2nd International Conference on Working for e-Business (WeB 2001), Perth, WA.

Luhmann, N. (1979). *Trust and power*. Chichester, UK: John Wiley.

Luis-García, R., Alberola-López, C., Aghzout, O., & Ruiz-Alzola, J. (2003). Biometric identification systems. *Signal Processing, 83*, 2539-2557.

Maconachy, W. V., Schou, C. D., Ragsdale, D., & Welch, D. (2001). A Model for Information Assurance: An Integrated Approach. *Proceedings of the 2001 IEEE Workshop on Information Assurance and Security, US Military Academy, West Point, NY*, 5-6.

Magalhães, P. S., Revett, K., & Santos, H. D. d. (2006). *Critical aspects in* authentication graphic keys, *International Conference on Information Warfare and Security (ICIW2006)*. Maryland Eastern Shore, USA: Academic Conferences, Inc.

MailFrontier. (2004). *Phishing IQ*. Retrieved 3 Nov. 2005, 2005, from http://www.mailfrontier.com

Maio, D., Maltoni, D., Cappelli, R., Wayman, J. L., & Jain, A. K. (2004). Fvc2004: Third fingerprint verification competition, *International Conference on Biometric Authentication – ICBA*. Hong Kong.

Maltoni, D., Maio, D., Jain, A. K., & Prabhakar, S. (2003). *Handbook of fingerprint recognition*. New York: Springer.

Manjak, M. (2006). *Social Engineering Your Employees to Information Security*. Retrieved on September 11, 2007 from http://www.sans.org/reading_room/whitepapers/awareness/1686.php

Manna, Z., & Pnueli, A. *The Temporal Logic of Reactive and Concurrent Systems –Specification*. Springer-Verlag.

Maranjian, S. (2006, November 3, 2006). *Toss That IRS Email, Please*! Retrieved November 7, 2006, from http://msnbc.msn.com/id/15546334/

Marks, P. (2002, February 3). Airport security to grow. *The Hartford Courant*.

Marsh, S. (1994). *Formalising trust as a computational concept*. Unpublished doctoral dissertation, University of Stirling, U.K.

Mason, B., & Gruenfeld, L. (2003). *Confessions of a master jewel thief*. New York, NY: Villard.

Masone, C. (2002). *Role definition language (RDL): A language to describe context-aware roles*. Technical report, Dartmouth College, Computer Science. Hanover, NH.

Mattern, F. (2002). The Vision and Technical Foundations of Ubiquitous Computing. In: Upgrade, Vol. 2, No. 5, pp. 2 – 6.

Mattern, F. (2005). Die technische Basis für das Interner der Dinge. In: E. Fleisch, F. Mattern (Eds.): Das Internet der Dinge - Ubiquitous Computing und RFID in der Praxis: Visionen, Technolgien, Anwendungen, Handlungsanleitungen. Springer-Verlag, Heidelberg, Germany, pp. 39 – 66.

Matyas, V. Jr., Riha, Z., (2003). Toward Reliable User Authentication through

Mauw, S., Verschuren, J. H. S., & de Vink, E. P. (2007) Anonymity groups of the FOO E-Voting scheme. *Proceedings of the Second International Workshop on Views on Designing Complex Architectures (VODCA 2006), Bertinoro, Italy, September 16-17, 2006. Electronic Notes in Theoretical Computer Science (ENTCS) 168*, 5-28. Elsevier.

Mayfield, T., Roskos, J. E., Welke, S. R., & Boone, J. M. (1991). Integrity in Automated Information Systems. *Prepared for National Computer Security Center (NCSC)*. Alexandria, Virginia: NCSC.

McAllister, D. J. (1995). Affect- and cognition-based trust as foundations for interpersonal cooperation in organizations. *Academy of Management Journal, 38*(1), 24-59.

McCarthy, B. (2006). Attributed by Swartz, M., in Employees Cause Most Security Breaches, Yet Response Lags - What's the best way to stop users from inadvertently compromising your company's information security?. Retrieved May 12, 2007 from http://www.esj.com/security/article.aspx?EditorialsID=1769

McCarthy, J. F., Boyd, D., Churchill, E. F., Griswold, W. G., Lawley, E., & Zaner, M. (2004). Digital backchannels in shared physical spaces: attention, intention and contention. CSCW '04: Proceedings of the 2004 ACM Conference on Computer Supported Cooperative Work, 550-553. ACM Press, New York, USA.

McCarthy, J. F., McDonald, D. W., Soroczak, S., Nguyen, D. H., & Rashid, A. M. (2004). Augmenting the Social Space of an Academic Conference. In: *Proceedings of the ACM Conference on Computer Supported Cooperative Work* (CSCW'04), Chicago, Illinois, USA, pp. 39 – 48.

McConnell, M. (2007). *Overhauling intelligence. Foreign Affairs, 86*(4). New York, NY: Council on Foreign Relations.

McCoy, Carrie, Fowler, Rebecca (October 2004). You are the key to security: establishing a successful security awareness program. *Proceedings of the 32nd annual ACM SIGUCCS conference on User Services SIGUCCS '04.*

McCullagh, D. (2006). *Congress Readies Broad New Digital Copyright Bill.* CNET News, April 23, 2006. Retrieved 2/16/2007 from http://news.com.com/2100-1028_3-6064016.html

McCumber, J. (2005). *Assessing and managing security risk in IT systems.* Auerbach Publications.

McDaniel, P. (2003). On context in authorization policy. In *Proceedings of the eighth ACM symposium on Access control models and technologies*, (pp. 80–89).

McGhee, J. (1983). Vulnerability of Elderly Consumers. *International Journal of Aging and Human Development, 17*(3), 223-246.

McKay, T. (1998). *Can CPTED tunnel vision be cured?* Security Management magazine. Alexandria, VA: American Society for Industrial Security.

McKellar, D. (2000). Spammimic. Retrieved April 2007, from http://www.spammimic.com/

McKenzie, A. (2005, October). *The Enemy is "Us" - What the Surveys tell us.* Paper presented at CACS Oceania Conference, Perth, Western Australia.

McKnight, W. (2002, July). What is Information Assurance. *CROSSTALK, The Journal of Defense Software Engineering.*

McMillan, R. (2005). Zombie Armies Attack British PCs.

McMillan, R. (2005, September). Google hacking; What started as a joke builds into a movement. *Network World*, 1.

MDC (2007). *AJAX Getting Started.* Mozilla Development Center. Retrieved 2/16/2007 from http://developer.mozilla.org/en/docs/AJAX:Getting_Started

Meier, R. F., & Miethe, T. D. (1993). Understanding Theories of Criminal Victimization. *Crime and Justice, 17*, 459-499.

Member, Subcommittee on 21st Century Competitiveness, Committee on Education and the Workforce, House of Representatives (No. GAO-02-717).

Menta, R. (2005). *A need to know.* SCmagazine, UK edition, July.

Metzger, M. J. (2006). Effects of Site, Vendor, and Consumer Characteristics on Web Site Trust and Disclosure. *Communication Research, 33*(3), 155-179.

Meyers-Levy, J., & Maheshwaram, D. (1991). Exploring Differences in Males and Females Processing Strategies. *Journal of Consumer Research, 18*, 63-70.

Microsoft (2006). More on Feed Security. *Microsoft Team RSS Blog*. Retrieved from http://blogs.msdn.com/rssteam/archive/2006/09/09/747111.aspx

Microsoft. (2000). Microsoft Announces Privacy Enhancements for Windows, Internet Explorer. Retrieved 21 June 2000, from http://www.microsoft.com/PressPass/press/2000/jun00/ p3ppr.asp

Microsoft. (2006). How to Protect Insiders from Social Engineering Threats. Retrieved May, 2007, from http://www.microsoft.com/technet/security/midsizebusiness/topics/complianceandpolicies/socialengineeringthreats.mspx

Microsoft. (2006). *Windows Internet Explorer 7* (Version 7.0.5730.11): Microsoft.

Microsoft. CardSpace [Electronic Version]. Retrieved 2006, from http://cardspace.netfx3.com/

Milberg, S. J., Burke, S. J., Smith, H. J., & Kallman, E. A. (1995, December). Values, Personal Information, Privacy, and Regulatory Approaches. *Communications of the ACM, 38*(12).

Miller, D., & Slater, D. (2000). *The Internet: An ethnographic approach.* Oxford: Berg.

Miller, G. (2006). WordNet: A Lexical Database for the English Language. Retrieved October 2004, from http://www.cogsci.princeton.edu/~wn/

Miller, H. (2001). *Submission to the Senate Committee on Commerce, Science and Transportation, on behalf of the Information Technology Association of America (ITAA).* Retrieved May 12, 2007 from http://commerce.senate.gov/hearings/071601Miller.pdf

Milne, G. (2003). How Well Do Consumers Protect Themselves from Identity Theft. *The Journal of Consumer Affairs, 37*(2), 388-402.

Minieri, M.W. (2004). Protecting corporate secrets - A brief primer on contemporary practices in information security. Kroll Schiff & Associates. Retrieved May 12, 2007 from http://www.becca-online.org/images/Protecting_Corporate_Secrets.pdf

Mitchell, V. L., & Nault, B. R. (2003). *The Emergence of Functional Knowledge in Sociotechnical Systems*. Calgary, Alberta: Haskayne School of Business University of Calgaryo. Document Number)

Mitnick, K. D. (2000). Cyber Attack: Is the Government Safe? *Senate Committee on Governmental Affairs* Retrieved May, 2007, from http://www.iwar.org.uk/comsec/resources/sa-tools/mitnick-testimony.htm

Mitnick, K. D., & Simon, W. L. (2002). *The Art of Deception: Controlling the Human Element of Security*. Indianapolis, Indiana: Wiley.

Mitnick, K. D., & Simon, W. L. (2003). *The Art of Deception: Controlling the Human Element of Security*. John Wiley & Sons, Inc

Mitnick, K. D., & Simon, W. L. (2005). *The Art of Intrusion: The Real Stories Behind the Exploits of Hackers, Intruders, and Deceivers*. Indianapolis, Indiana: Wiley.

Moitra, S., & Konda, S. (2005). *The survivability of network systems: An empirical analysis*. Carnegie Mellon Software Engineering Institute, Technical Report, CMU/SEI-200-TR-021.

Monahan, M. (2007). *2007 Identity fraud survey report*. Pleasanton, CA: Javelin Strategy & Research.

Monrose, F., & Rubin, A. (1997). Authentication Via Keystroke Dynamics. *Proceedings of Fourth ACM Conference on Computer and Communications Security* (pp. 48-56).

Monrose, F., & Rubin, A. D. (1997). Authentication via keystroke dynamics, *Fourth ACM Conference on Computer and Communication Security*. Zurich, Switzerland: ACM.

Mook, N. (2005). *Cross-Site Scripting Worm Hits MySpace*. BetaNews, October 13, 2005. Retrieved 2/16/2007 from http://www.betanews.com/article/1129232391

Morison, W. (1973). *Report on the Law of Privacy*, New South Wales Parliament, para 4.

Morris, R., & Thompson, K. (1979). Password security; A case study. *CACM 22*, 594-597.

Morse, J. M., & Richards, L. (2002). *Readme first for a user's guide to qualitative methods*. Thousand Oaks, Calif.: Sage Publications.

Moser, C. (1999). *Improving literacy and numeracy: A fresh start*. London, England: DfEE Publications.

Moulton, R., & Coles, R. S. (2003). Applying information security governance. *Computers & Security, 22*(7), 580-584.

Mukhopadhyay, A. (2007b). A novel framework for mitigating e-risk through insurance. *Phd Thesis*, Indian Institute of Management Calcutta.

Mukhopadhyay, A., Chakrabarti, B. B., Saha, D., & Mahanti, A. (2007a). E-Risk management through self-insurance: An option model. *Proceedings of the 40th Hawaii International Conference on System Sciences* , Hawaii, USA.

Mukhopadhyay, A., Chatterjee, S., Saha, D, Mahanti, A., and Sadhukhan, K. S. (2006). *E-Risk Management with Insurance: A framework using Copula aided Bayesian Belief Networks. Proceedings of the 39th Hawaii International Conference on System Sciences*, Hawaii, USA.

Mukhopadhyay, A., Chatterjee, S., Saha, D., Mahanti, A., and Podder, K. A. (2005). E-Risk: A case for insurance. *Proceedings of the Conference on Information Systems and Technology*, New Delhi, India.

Mukhopadhyay, A., Chatterjee, S., Saha, D., Mahanti, A., Chakrabarti, B. B., & Podder, K. A. (2005). Security breach losses in e-commerce through Insurance. *Proceedings of 4th Security Conference*, Las Vegas, Nevada.

Mukhopadhyay, A., Chatterjee, S., Saha, D., Mahanti, A., Roy, R., & Sadhukhan S. K. (2007). Insuring big losses due to security breaches through insurance: A business model. *Proceedings of the 40th Hawaii International Conference on System Sciences*, Hawaii, USA.

Mukhopadhyay, A., Saha, D., Mahanti, A., & Podder, K. A. (2005c). Insurance for cyber-risk: A Utility Model. *Decision, 32*(1), 153-170.

Munley, Mary (2004). *Moving from consciousness to culture: creating an environment of cultural awareness*. SANS Information Security Reading Room. Retrieved May 25th, 2007, from http://www.sans.org/reading_room/whitepapers/awareness/1439.php?portal=f48313ae979fda55251e768b2dadd2d2.

Murayama, Y., Hikage, N., Fujiwara, Y., & Hauser, C. (in press). The structure of the sense of security, Anshin, to appear in *Proceedings of the 2nd International Work-*

shop on Critical Information Infrastructures Security. Springer.

Murray-Watson, A., & Dennis, G. (2005). How to make your company a hard target. *The Telegraph*. London, England. July 10.

Myers, M. D. (1997). Qualitative Research in Information Systems [Electronic Version], from http://www.qual.auckland.ac.nz/

Myers, M. D. (1997). References on Grounded Theory. Retrieved 04/26, 2008, from http://www.qual.auckland.ac.nz/grndrefs.htm

Myers, S. (2007). Status Quo Security Tools. In M. Jakobsson & S. Myers (Eds.), *Phishing and Countermeasures: Understanding the Increasing Problem of Electronic Identity Theft* (pp. 139-173). Hoboken, New Jersey: John Wiley & Sons, Inc.

National Institute of Standards and Technology (2000). *An Introduction to Computer Security: The NIST Handbook.*, Special Publication 800-12.

National Security Institute. (2004). *Improving Security from the Inside Out (A NSI Special Report)*. Medway, MA. URL: http://nsi.org

National Security Telecommunications and Information Systems. (1994). *National Training Standard for Information Systems Security (INFOSEC) Professionals*. Retrieved April 20, 2006. from http://www.cnss.gov/Assets/pdf/nstissi_4011.pdf.

National Security Telecommunications and Information Systems. (1997). *National Information Systems Security Glossary No. 4009*. Retrieved. from.

National Security Telecommunications and Information Systems. (1997). *National Training Standard for Designated Approving Authority (DAA)*. Retrieved April 20, 2006. from http://www.cnss.gov/Assets/pdf/cnssi_4012.pdf.

National Security Telecommunications and Information Systems. (1997). *National Training Standard for Information Systems Security Officers (ISSO)*. Retrieved April 20, 2006. from http://www.cnss.gov/Assets/pdf/cnssi_4014.pdf.

National Security Telecommunications and Information Systems. (1997). *National Training Standard for System Administrators in Information Systems Secuirty (INFOSEC)*. Retrieved April 20, 2006. from http://www.cnss.gov/Assets/pdf/cnssi_4013.pdf.

Navarro, L. (2007). Train employees - your best defense - for security awareness. *SC Magazine*. US edition. February 27.

Needham, B. H., & Koizumi, D. H. (1998). *Method of Displaying Private Data to Collocated Users*, US Patent 5,963,371.

NetCraft. (2004). NetCraft Anti-phishing Toolbar. Retrieved July, 11, 2007, from http://toolbar.netcraft.com/

Neubauer, T., Markus, K., & Stefan, B. (2005). *Economics-Driven Software Engineering Research (EDSER): Business process-based valuation of IT-security*. May 2005, ACM SIGSOFT Software Engineering Notes. *Proceedings of the 2005 workshop on Economics-driven software engineering research EDSER '05, 30*(4).

New e-mail virus preys on Anna Kournikova fans. (2001). *CNN.com*. Retrieved May, 2007, from http://archives.cnn.com/2001/TECH/internet/02/12/anna.worm/index.html

New warning about fraudulent charity email scams. (2006, November 2, 2006). Retrieved November 7, 2006, from http://www.ekklesia.co.uk/content/news_syndication/article_06112scam.shtml

Nguyen, L., & Roscoe, A. W. (2006). Efficient group authentication protocols based on human interaction. *Proceedings of the Foundations of Computer Security and Automated Reasoning for Security Protocol Analysis (FCS-ARSPA'06), Seattle, US*, August 15-16, 2006, pp. 9-31

Nichols, S. (2006, November 7, 2006). *US hosts a quarter of all phishing sites*. Retrieved November 7, 2006, from http://www.itweek.co.uk/vnunet/news/2168068/claims-per-cent-phishing-sites

Nichols, S. (2007, April 18, 2007). *Online scammers exploit Virginia Tech shootings*. Retrieved April 30, 2007, from http://www.itweek.co.uk/vnunet/news/2187983/security-firms-brace-virgina

Nickerson, R. S. (1965). Short-term memory for complex meaningful visual configurations: A demonstration of capacity. *Canadian Journal of Psychology, 19*, 155-160.

Nie, N., Hillygus, D., & Erbring, L. (2002). Internet Use, Interpersonal Relations, and Sociability. *The Internet in Everyday Life*, 215-243, Oxford, UK: Blackwell.

Nielsen (2006). *Social networking Sites Grow 47 Percent, Year over Year*. Nielsen/NetRatings Inc., Press Release: May 11, 2006.

NIST (National Institute of Science and Technology, 1995). *An Introduction to Computer Security: The NIST Handbook.* Special Publication 800-12. Retrieved May 12, 2007 from http://csrc.nist.gov/publications/nistpubs/800-12/handbook.pdf

NIST (National Institute of Science and Technology, 2006). Minimum security requirements for federal information and information systems. Federal Information Processing Standards Publication 200 (FIPS PUB 200). Retrieved May 13, 2007 from http://csrc.nist.gov/publications/fips/fips200/FIPS-200-final-march.pdf

Norman, D. A. (1988). *The psychology of everyday things.* New York: Basic Books

Norman, D. A. (1998). *The invisible computer.* Cambridge, Mass: MIT Press.

Nosworthy, J. D. (2000). Implementing Information Security In The 21st Century — Do You Have the Balancing Factors? *Computers & Security, 19*(4), 337.

Nyanchama, M., & Osborn, S. (1999, February). The Role Graph Model and Conflict Of Interest, ACM Transactions on Information and System Security, 2(1), 3-33.

O'Reilly, T. (2005). *What Is Web 2.0, Design Patterns and Business Models for the Next Generation of Software.* O'Reilly Associate. Retrieved 2/16/2007 from http://www.oreillynet.com/pub/a/oreilly/tim/news/2005/09/30/what-is-web-20.html

OASIS. (2005). eXtensible Access Control Markup Language (XACML), Version 2.0; OASIS Standard, February 1, 2005. from http://www.oasis-open.org/committees/tc_home.php? wg_abbrev=xacml

OECD (Organization for Economic Co-operation and Development, 2002). *Guidelines for the security of information systems – towards a culture of security.* Retrieved May 13, 2007 from http://www.oecd.org/dataoecd/16/22/15582260.pdf

OECD. (1980). Recommendation of the Council Concerning Guidelines Governing the Protection of Privacy and Transborder Flows of Personal Data.

Oh, S., Sandhu, R., & Zhang, X. (2006, May). An Effective Role Administration Model Using Organization Structure. *ACM Transactions on Information and System Security, 9*(2), 113-137.

Ollmann, G. (2004, September 9, 2004). *The Phishing Guide: Understanding & Preventing Phishing Attacks.* Retrieved November 12, 2006, from http://www.ngssoftware.com/papers/NISR-WP-Phishing.pdf

Olson, J. S., Grudin, J., & Horvitz, E. (2005). A Study of Preferences for Sharing and Privacy. In: *Extended Abstracts of the ACM Conference on Human Factors in Computing Systems* (CHI'05), 1985-1988.

OMG1. (2003). *MDA Guide Version 1.0.1.* Object Management Group. 2003. http://www.omg.org/docs/omg/03-06-01.pdf.

OMG2. (2002). *Meta-Object Facility (MOF), version 1.4.* Object Management Group., 2002. http://www.omg.org/technology/documents/formal/mof.htm.

OMG3. (2001). *OMG Unified Modeling Language Specification, Version 1.4.* Object Management Group. 2001. http://www.omg.org/technology/documents/formal/uml.htm.

One in 10 Holiday Shoppers Will Face Fraudulent Internet Attacks This Year. (2006). Retrieved November 7, 2006, from http://www.earthtimes.org/articles/show/news_press_release,16881.shtml

OnGuardOnline. (2006). Retrieved March 17, 2007, from http://onguardonline.gov/index.html

Online Banking Fraud Rises Fast. (2006, November 7, 2006). Retrieved November 7, 2006, from https://news.bbc.co.ck/2/hi/business/612216.stm

OpenDNS Shares October 2006 PhishTank Statistics. (2006, November 2, 2006). Retrieved November 7, 2006, from http://press.xtvworld.com/article15152.html

OpenID. OpenID: An Actually Distributed Identity System [Electronic Version]. Retrieved 2006, from http://openid.net

Orgun, O. (1999). *Linguistic Steganography Project Report.* Unpublished manuscript, University of California, Davis.

Orlandi, E. (1991). The Cost of Security. *Proceeding of the 25th Annual IEEE International Carnahan Conference on Security Technology*, Oct. 1991, pp. 192 –196.

P. Bellavista, R. Montanari and D. Tibaldi, (2003). *COSMOS: A Context-Centric Access Control Middleware for Mobile Environments, MATA'2003*, (pp. 77–88).

P3P (2002). The Platform for Privacy Preferences 1.0 (P3P 1.0) Specification. W3C Recommendation, April 16, 2002. *Available as of May 31, 2007 at: http://www.w3.org/TR/P3P/*

Palen, L. (1999). Social, Individual and Technological Issues for Groupware Calendar Systems. In: *Proceedings of the ACM Conference on Human Factors in Computing Systems* (CHI'99), pp. 17-24.

Palen, L., & Dourish, P. (2002). *Unpacking "Privacy" for a Networked World.* In proceedings of the CHI-02 (pp. 129-136) Fort Lauderdale, FL.

Palen, L., & Dourish, P. (2003). Unpacking "Privacy" for a Networked World. In: *Proceedings of the ACM Conference on Human Factors in Computing Systems* (CHI'03), Ft. Lauderdale, Florida, USA, pp. 129-136.

PandaLabs Warns Users of the Mass-mailing of False Job Offers. (2006, November 2, 2006). Retrieved November 7, 2006, from http://home.nestor.minsk.by/networks/news/2006/11/0205.html

Pandit, N. R. (1996). The Creation of Theory: A Recent Application of the Grounded Theory Method [Electronic Version], *2*, from http://www.nova.edu/ssss/QR/QR2-4/pandit.html

Park, J. S., Costello, K. P., Neven, T. M., & Diosomito, J. A. (2004). A Composite RBAC Approach for Large, Complex Organizations. *Proceedings of Ninth ACM Symposium on Access Control Models*, June 2004, Yorktown Heights, New York, USA.

Parker, D. (2006). Making the Case for Replacing Risk-Based Security. *The ISSA Journal.* May 2006, 6-10.

Parsuraman, S., & Igbaria, M. (1990). An Extension of Gender Differences on Determination of Computer Anxiety and Attitudes toward Microcomputers among Managers. *International Journal of Man-Machine Studies, 32*, 327-340.

Patil, S., & Lai, J. (2005). Who Gets to Know What When: Configuring Privacy Permissions in an Awareness Application. In: *Proceedings of the ACM Conference on Human Factors in Computing Systems* (CHI'05), pp. 101-110.

Patrick, A. S., Long, A. C., & Flinn, S. (2004). HCI and security systems. *In Proceedings of the SIGCHI Conference on Human Factors in Computing Systems (CHI'04)* (Vienna, Austria, April 24-29, 2004). ACM Press, New York, NY, 1056-1057.

Paula, R. r. d., Ding, X., Dourish, P., Nies, K., Pillet, B., Redmiles, D. F., et al. (2005). In the Eye of the Beholder: A Visualization-based Approach to Information System Security. *International Journal of Human-Computer Studies, 63*(1-2), 5-24.

Pearsall, J., & Trumble, B. (Eds), (2001). *The Oxford English Reference Dictionary.* Oxford University Press, Great Clarendon Street, Oxford oX2 6DP.

Peltier, T. R. (1999). *Information Security Policies and Procedures.* Boca Raton, Florida: Auerbach Publications.

Peltier, T. R. (2004). *Information Security Policies and Procedures.* Washington D.C.: Auerbach Publications.

Peltier, T. R. (2005). *Information Security Risk Analysis.* Boca Raton, Florida: Auerbach Publications.

Pentasafe Security Technologies (2002). *Security awareness index report: The state of security awareness among organizations - worldwide security awareness survey.* Retrieved May 12, 2007 from http://security.ittoolbox.com/pub/AM101502a.pdf

Perwaiz, N., & Sommerville, I. (2001). Structured Management of Role-Permission Relationships. *Proceedings of Sixth ACM Symposium on Access Control Models*, May 2001, Fairfax, Virginia, USA.

Pfhleeger, C. P. (1997). *Security in Computing,* Second edition. Prentice Hall, USA.

Phelps, D. C. (2005). *Information System Security: Self-Efficacy and Security Effectiveness in Florida Libraries.* PhD Dissertation, Florida State University.

Phishing - Wikipedia. Retrieved July 10, 2007, from http://en.wikipedia.org/wiki/Phishing

Phishing Activity Trends Report - September 2005. (2005, October 2005). Retrieved November 19, 2006, from http://www.antiphishing.org/reports/apwg_phishing_activity_report_sept_05.pdf

Phishing Activity Trends Report - September 2006. (2006, October 9, 2006). Retrieved November 29, 2006, from http://www.antiphishing.org/reports/apwg_report_August_2006.pdf

Phishing. (2006, November 13, 2006). Retrieved November 29, 2006, from http://www.webopedia.com/TERM/p/phishing.html

Pidd, M. (2003). *Tools for Thinking: Modelling in Management Science*: John Wiley & Sons Ltd.

Pierson, L., Witzke, E., Bean, M., & Trombley, G., (1999). *Context-agile encryption for high speed communication networks*, ACM SIGCOMM Computer Communication Review, 29(1): (pp. 35-49).

PIPEDA. http://www.privcom.gc.ca/legislation/02_06_01_01_e.asp

Plate, A., & Weissmann, O. (Ed.). (2005). *Information Technology – Code of practice for information security management*, ISO/IEC 17799:2005. Berlin, Germany: ISO.

Plous, S. (1993). *The Psychology of Judgment and Decision Making.* New York: McGraw-Hill.

Porter, D. (2003). E-Business sector analysis. In Clark, A. & Burrell, P. (Eds), *A practitioner's guide to international money laundering law and regulation* (pp. 395-413). London, England: City & Financial Publishing.

Porter, D. (2006). *Businesses beware: protection from identity thieves.* Paper presented at the Association of Certified Fraud Examiners 17th Annual Fraud Conference & Exhibition, Las Vegas, Nevada.

Porter, D. (2007). The evolution of fraud intelligence. In Gupta, M. (Ed.), *Managing Information Assurance in Financial Services* (pp. 261-283). Hershey, PA: IGI Publishing.

Porter, D. (2008). *Soft, pervasive and complex: The new world of fraud containment.* Paper presented at the Association of Certified Fraud Examiners European Fraud Conference, London, England.

Posthumus, S., & Von Solms, R. (2004). A framework for the governance of information security. *Computers & Security, 23*(8), 638-646.

Potter, C. (2005). *Information Security- Security conscious.* Retrieved October 2007 from http://www.financialdirector.co.uk/accountancyage/features/2040335/information-security-security-conscious, September 2005.

Pratt, M. K. (2006). Employee Security Training: Beyond Posters. Available at: http://www.computerworld.com/printthis/2006/0,4814,110494,00.html.

Preibusch, S. (2006). Personalized Services with Negotiable Privacy Policies. *In proceedings of the PEP06, CHI 2006 Workshop on Privacy-Enhanced Personalization* (pp. 29-38) Montreal, Canada.

PriceWaterhouseCoopers (2004). Information Security Breaches survey. Available at: http://www.pwcglobal.com/.

Princeton Survey Research Associates International. (2005, October 26). *Leap of faith: Using the Internet despite the dangers- Results of a National Survey of Internet Users for Consumer Reports WebWatch.* Retrieved 30 January, 2006, from http://www.consumerwebwatch.org/pdfs/princeton.pdf

Privacy International, Statewatch, & European Digital Rights. (2004). *An open letter to the icao a second report on 'towards an international infrastructure for surveillance of movement'.* Retrieved January, 2005, from www.privacyinternational.org

Privacy International, Statewatch, & European Digital Rigts. (2004). An open letter to the european parliament on biometric registration of all eu citizens and residents. Retrieved January, 2005, from www.privacyinternational.org

Qu, Y. & Zhang, Q. (2006). A Game Analysis of Credit Mechanism. *Journal of ShanXi Finance and Economics University, 28*(6), 117-122.

Quereshi, S., & Hoppel, C. (1995). Profiling Computer Predispositions. *Journal of Professional Services Marketing, 12*, 73-83.

Radford, T., & Glaister, D. (2004). Hi-tech voting machines 'threaten' US polls. *The Guardian*, 16 February 2004.

Ragucci, J. W., & Robila, S. A. (2006a, July 7, 2007). Montclair Phish. Retrieved April 30, 2007, from http://csam.montclair.edu/~robila/RSL/Phish/

Ragucci, J. W., & Robila, S. A. (2006b). *Social Implications of Phishing.* Paper presented at the IEEE ISTAS 2006, Queens, NY.

Randazzo, M. R., Cappelli, D., Keeney, M., Moore, A., & Kowalski, E. (2004, August)). *Insider Threat Study: Illicit Cyber Activity in the Banking and Finance Sector.* U.S. Secret Service and CERT Coordination Center/SEI (Tech. Report).

Randell, B., & Ryan, P. Y. A. (2005). Voting technologies and trust. In T. Dimitrakos, F. Martinelli, P. Ryan, and S. Schneider (eds.) *Formal Aspects of Security and Trust (FAST) 2005, 3866* of Lecture Notes in Computer Science, 1–4. Berlin, Germany: Springer-Verlag.

Ranum, M. (2005). *The six dumbest ideas in computer security.* Retrieved May 21, 2008, from http://www.ranum.com/security/computer_security/editorials/dumb/

Rasmussen, G. (2005). *Implementing information security: Risks vs. cost.* Retrieved May 12, 2007 from http://www.gideonrasmussen.com/article-07.html

Rasmussen, J. (n/d). Skills, rules, knowledge: Signals, signs, and symbols and other distinctions in human performance models. *IEEE Transactions on Systems, Man, and Cybernetics, 13*(3), 257-267. IEEE Computer Society.

Rawe, J. (2006). How Safe is MySpace? *Time Magazine, 168*(1), 43.

Ray, I. (2003). Using Parameterized UML to Specify and Compose Access Control Models. *In Proc. of the 6th IFIP Working Conference on Integrity & Internal Control in Info. Systems.*

Real User Corporation. (2001). The science behind passfaces. Passfaces[tm]. Retrieved October 2005, from http://www.idarts.com/

Reason, J. (1987). Generic Error-Modelling system ({GEMS}): A Cognitive Framework for Locating Common Human Error Forms, Chapter 7. J. Rasmussen, K. Duncan and J. Leplat (eds.) New Technology and Human Error, 63-83. John Wiley and Sons.

Reason, J. (1990). *Human Error.* Cambridge University Press.

Reason, J. (2000). Human error: models and management. *British Medical Journal, 320*, 768-770. London, England: BMJ Publishing Group.

Reder, S (1998). *The state of literacy in America: estimates at the local, state, and national levels.* Washington, DC: National Institute for Literacy.

Rekimoto, J. (1998). A Multiple Device Approach for Supporting Whiteboard-based Interactions. In: *Proceedings of the ACM Conference on Human Factors in Computing Systems* (CHI'98), pp. 18-23.

Rempel, J. K., Holmes J. G., & Zanna, M. P. (1985,). Trust in close relationships. *Journal of Personality and Social Psychology, 49*(1), 95-112.

Revett, K., Gorunescu, F., Gorunescu, M., Ene, M., Tenreiro de Magalhães, S., & Santos, H. D. (2006). Authenticating computer access based on keystroke dynamics using a probabilistic neural network, *2nd Annual International Conference on Global e-Security.* London: University of East London.

Revett, K., Magalhães, S. T. d., & Santos, H. (2006). Datamining a keystroke dynamics based biometrics database using rough sets, *EPIA 2005, Portuguese Conference on Artificial Intelligence.* Covilhã, Portugal: IEEE CS Press.

Revett, K., Tenreiro de Magalhães, S., & Santos, H. D. (2005). Developing a keystroke dynamics based agent using rough sets, *International Workshop On Rough Sets And Soft Computing In Intelligent Agent And Web Technologies.* Compiègne: University of Technology of Compiègne.

Reznik, J., Ritter, T., Schreiner R., & Lang, U. (2007, April). *Model Driven Development of Security Aspects.* Electronic Notes in Theoretical Computer Science (ENTCS), 163, (2), 65-79.

Rheingold, H. (2002). *Smart Mobs: The Next Social Revolution.* Cambridge, MA: Basic Books.

Richardson, R. (2003). *CSI/FBI Computer Crime and Security Survey.* Hayward, CA: Computer Security Institute.

Richardson, R. (2007). *Computer Crime and Security Survey.* Computer Security Institute, 2007.

Riegelsberger, J., Sasse, M.A., & McCarthy, J. D. (2003). Privacy and trust: Shiny happy people building trust? Photos on e-commerce websites and consumer trust. *Proceedings of CHI2003, 5*(1), 121-128.

Rigby, S., & Dark, M. (2006). Using outcomes-based assessment data to improve assessment and instruction: a case study. *SIGITE News, 3*(1), 10-15.

Roberts, P. (2004). *Aol Survey Finds Rampant Online Threats, Clueless Users*: Computer World.

Roberts, P. (2004). Sasser a warning of things to come. Available at: http:www.infoworld.com.

Robila, S. A., & Ragucci, J. W. (2006). *Don't be a Phish: Steps in User Education.* Paper presented at the ITiCSE'06, Bologna, Italy.

Röcker, C. (2006*). Awareness and Informal Communication in Smart Office Environments.* Verlag Dr. Driesen, Taunusstein, Germany. ISBN 3-936328-65-X.

Rodrigues, G. N. (2004). A Model Driven Approach for Software Systems Reliability. *Proceedings of the 26th International Conference on Software Engineering (ICSE'04)*

Rodrigues, G., Roberts, G., Emmerich, W., & Skene, J. (2003). Reliability Support for the Model Driven Architecture. *In Workshop on Software Architecture for Dependable Systems (ICSE/WADS 2003)*, Portland, OR, pages 7–12. ACM Press, May 2003.

Rogers, Y. (1997). A Brief Introduction to Distributed Cognition [Electronic Version], from http://mcs.open.ac.uk/yr258/papers/dcog/dcog-brief-intro.pdf

Rosmarin, R. (2006). The MySpace Economy. *Forbe Megazine.* Retrieved 1/18/07 from http://www.forbes.com/digitalentertainment/2006/04/07/myspace-google-murdoch-cx_rr_0410myspace.html

Ross, R., Katzke., S., Johnson, A., Swanson, M., Stoneburner, G., Rogers, G., & Lee, A. (2005). Recommended Security Controls for Federal Information Systems. *NIST SP 800-53.* Retrieved May 13, 2007 from http://csrc.nist.gov/publications/nistpubs/800-53/SP800-53.pdf

RTI International. (2002). The Economic Impact of Role-Based Access Control. March 2002. Retrieved from http://www.nist.gov/director/prog-ofc/report02-1.pdf

Rusch, J. (1999). The "Social Engineering" of Internet Fraud. *INET '99*. San Jose, California.

Rushby, J. (2002, February). Using model-checking to help discover mode confusions and other automation surprises. *Reliability Engineering and System Safety, 75*(2), 167–177.

Russ, A. (2001). *Digital Rights Management Overview.* SANS Information Security Reading Room, July 26, 2001. Retrieved 2/16/2007 from http://www.sans.org/reading_room/whitepapers/basics/434.php

Russell Research (2006). *CA/NCSA Social networking Study Report.* CA and the National Cyber Security Alliance. Retrieved 2/16/2007 from http://staysafeonline.org/features/ncsalibrary.html

Russell, D. M., & Gossweiler, R. (2001). On the Design of Personal & Communal Large Information Scale Appliances. In: *Proceedings of the International Conference on Ubiquitous Computing* (UbiComp'01), pp. 354-361.

Sagan, S. (2004). The problem of redundancy: why more nuclear security forces may produce less nuclear security. *Risk Analysis, 24*(4), 935-946. Stanford, CA: Center for International Security and Cooperation.

Samuels, M. (2005, June 22). CIOs must be business and IT experts. *Computing Magazine.* UK.

Sandhu, R., Bhamidipati, V., & Munawer, Q. (1999, February). The ARBAC97 Model for Role-Based Administration of Roles, *ACM Transactions on Information and Systems Security, 2.*

Sandhu, R., Coyne, E., Feinstein, H., & Youman, C. (1996, February). Role-Based Access Control Models. *IEEE Computer, 29*(2).

Sandhu, R., Ferraiolo, D., & Kuhn, R. (2000). The NIST Model for Role-Based Access Control: Towards A Unified Standard. National Institute of Standards and Technology, December 2000, http://csrc.nist.gov/rbac/sandhu-ferraiolo-kuhn-00.pdf

SANS (2003). *Newsletter.* Retrieved May 13, 2007 from http://www.sans.org/newsletters/statusupdates/11.php

Sasse, M. A., & Brostoff, S. (2001). Transforming the 'Weakest Link' - a Human/Computer Interaction Approach to Usable and Effective Security. Bt Technology Journal. *BT Technology Journal, 19*(3), 122-131.

Sasse, M. A., Brostoff, S., & Weirich, D. (2001). Transforming the 'weakest link' – a human/computer interaction approach to usable and effective security. *BT Technical Journal 19*,122-131.

Saunders, K. M., & Zucker, B. (1999). Counteracting identity fraud in the information age: The identity theft and assumption deterrence Act. *International Review of Law, Computers & Technology, 13*(2), 183.

Savvas, A. (2006, November 3, 2006). FBI anti-phishing operation leads to Polish and US arrests. Retrieved November 6, 2006, 2006, from http://www.computerweekly.com/Feeds/RSS/Articles/2006/11/03/219637/FBI%2Banti-phishing%2Boperation%2Bleads%2Bto%2BPolish%2Band%2BUS%2Barrests.htm

Schaad, A., Moffett, J., & Jacob, J. (2001). The Role-Based Access Control System of a European Bank: A Case Study and Discussion. *Proceedings of Sixth ACM Symposium on Access Control Models*, May 2001, Fairfax, Virginia, USA.

Schechter, S., Dhamija, R., Ozment, A., & Fischer, I. (2007). *The Emperor's New Security Indicators.* Paper presented at the Usable Security (USEC'07). from http://usablesecurity.org/emperor/.

Schipke, R. C. (2006). *The Language of Phishing, Pharming, and Other Internet Fraud—Metaphorically Speaking.* Paper presented at the IEEE ISTAS 2006, Queens, NY.

Schmidt, H. (2005, September). *Keynote address presented at the Information Systems Security Association.* London, England.

Schneberger, S., & Wade, M. (2008, 28 January 2008). Social Cognitive Theory. Retrieved 04/27, 2008, from http://www.fsc.yorku.ca/york/istheory/wiki/index.php/Social_cognitive_theory

Schneberger, S., & Wade, M. (2008, 28 January 2008). Socio-technical theory. Retrieved 04/27, 2008, from http://www.fsc.yorku.ca/york/istheory/wiki/index.php/Socio-technical_theory

Schneier, B. (2000). *Secrets and Lies: Digital security in a Networked World*: John Wiley & Sons.

Schneier, B. (2004). *Secrets & lies – digital security in a networked world.* Indianapolis, IN: Wiley Publishing, Inc.

Schneier, B. (2004, April). Hacking the business climate for network security. *IEEE Computer*, 87–89..

Schneier, B. (2006, December 21). Microsoft Anti-Phishing and Small Businesses. Retrieved March 16, 2007, from http://www.schneier.com/blog/archives/2006/12/microsoft_antip.html

Schneier, B. (2007). The Psychology of Security – DRAFT, http://www.schneier.com/essay-155.html

Schoch, T., Strassner, M. (2003). Wie smarte Dinge Prozesse unterstützen. In: HMD, No. 229, Februar 2003, pp. 23 – 32.

Schultz, E. (2005, March). Search engines: a growing contributor to security risk. *Computers & Security, 24*(2), 87-88

Schwartz, J., & Dobrzynski, J. (2002). *3 men are charged with fraud in 1,100 art auctions on eBay.* The New York Times.

Scott, J. (1991). *Social network Analysis: A Handbook.* New York, NY: Sage Publications.

Sebek. http://www.honeynet.org/tools/sebek/

Sengupta, A., Mukhopadhyay, A., Ray, K., Roy, A. G., Aich, D., Barik, M. S., & Mazumdar, C. (2005). A Web-Enabled Enterprise Security Management Framework Based on a Unified Model of Enterprise Information System Security : (An Ongoing Project Report), *First International Conference on Information Systems Security,* ICISS 2005. Kolkata, India, Pages 328 – 331: LNCS.

Senicar, V., Jerman-Blazic, B., & Klobucar, T. (2003). Privacy-Enhancing Technologies: Approaches and Development. *Computer Standards & Interfaces, 25*(2), 147-158.

Shah, H., Joshi, N., & Wurman, P. (2003). Mining eBay: Bidding Strategies and Shill Detection. *WEBKDD 2002 - MiningWeb Data for Discovering Usage Patterns and Profiles,* Lecture Notes in Computer Science. 17-34.

Shankland, S. (2006). HP chairman: Use of pretexting 'embarrassing'. *CNET News.com* Retrieved May, 2007, from http://news.com.com/HP+chairman+Use+of+pretexting+embarrassing/2100-1014_3-6113715.html

Shapiro, A. (2003). *Creating contagious commitment: applying the tipping point to organisational change.* Hillsborough, NC: Strategy Perspective.

Shepard, R. N. (1967). Recognition memory for words, sentences and pictures. *Journal of Verbal Learning and Verbal Behavior, 6,* 156-163.

Shi, J., Bochmann, G. V., & Adams, C. (2005). A trust model with statistical foundation. In T. Dimitrakos and F. Martinelli, (Eds.), *Second IFIP TC1 WG1.7 Workshop on Formal Aspects in Security and Trust 2004,* (pp. 145-158). Springer.

Shin, M., & Ahn, G. (2000). UML-Based Representation of Role- Based Access Control. In *Proc. of the IEEE 9th Intl. Wksp. on Enabling Technologies: Infrastructure for Collaborative Enterprises.*

Shoemaker, G. B. D, & Inkpen, K. M. (2001) Single Display Privacyware: Augmenting public displays with private information. In: *Proceedings of the ACM Conference on Human Factors in Computing Systems* (CHI'01), pp. 522-529.

Show, J. (2007). *Information Security in Practice from an Activity-Theoretic Perspective.* Paper presented at the Proceedings of the 6th Annual Security Conference, Las Vegas, NV.

Sillivan, B. (2002). Release of organ donor data prompts changes. Available at: http://archives.cnn.com/2002/TECH/internet/02/16/organ.donor.data.idg/.

Silltow, J. (2001). Social Engineering, Part 1. Retrieved April, 2007, from http://www.theiia.org/ITAudit/index.cfm?act=itaudit.archive&fid=339

Silver, M. (2004). E-Learning for the pump industry. *Worlds Pumps, 2004*(453), 28-31.

Singh, S. (2004). Impersonalisation of electronic money: Implications for bank marketing. *The International Journal of Bank Marketing, 22*(7), 505-521.

Singh, S., & Cassar-Bartolo, K. (2004, November 21-24). *The privacy of money and health.* Paper presented at the OZCHI, Wollongong.

Singh, S., Zic, J., Satchell, C., Bartolo, K. C., Snare, J., & Fabre, J. (2004, 29 June- 2 July 2004). *A reflection on translation issues in user-centred design.* Paper presented at the 7th International Conference on Work with Computing Systems, WWCS 2004, Kuala Lumpur.

Siponen, M. T. (2000). A conceptual foundation for organizational information security awareness. *Information Management & Computer Security, 8*(1), 31-41.

Siponen, M. T. (2005). An analysis of the traditional IS security approaches: implications for research and practice. *European Journal of Information Systems, 14,* 303-315.

Slashdot. (2006). Phishing in Yahoo! Geocities? Retrieved from http://ask.slashdot.org/article.pl?sid=06/07/12/0028254

Smith S. W., & Spafford, E. H. (2004, January/February). Grand Challenges in Information Security: Process and Output. *IEEE Security & Privacy,* 69-71.

Smith, E. (2000). *Information Security in Health-Care Systems: a New approach to IT Risk Management.* Rand Afrikaans University. Johannesburg, South Africa.

Smith, M. (2007). *The importance of security awareness.* Retrieved May 12, 2007 from http://www.thesecurityco.com/kzscripts/default.asp?cid=7

Smithson, C., & Song, P. (2004). Quantifying Operational Risk, www.risk.net.

Snare, J., & Kuiper, E. (Ed.). (2005). *Information technology - Security techniques – Information security management systems - Requirements,* BS ISO/IEC 27001:2005 BS 7799-2:2005. Geneva, Switzerland: ISO.

Song, R., Korba, L., & Yee, G. (2006). Pseudonym Technology for E-Services. Chapter in *Privacy Protection for E-Services,* edited by Yee, G., Idea Group, Inc.

SonicWALL Phishing IQ Quiz. (2006). Retrieved March 18, 2007, from http://www.sonicwall.com/phishing/

SOX (2002). *United States Public Company Accounting Reform and Investor Protection Act.* Also known as Sarbanes-Oxley.

Spitzner, L. (2003). Honeytokens: The Other Honeypot. Retrieved July, 11, 2007.

Spivak, M. (1979). *A comprehensive introduction to differential geometry.* Wilmington, Delaware: Publish or Perish.

Spoofstick. (2004). Spoofstick Toolbar. Retrieved July, 11, 2007, from http://www.spoofstick.com/

Standing, L. (1973). Learning 10,000 pictures. *Quarterly Journal of Experimental Psychology, 25,* 207-222.

Stanton, J. M., R., M. P., Stam, K. R., & Jolton, J. (2004). *Behavioral Information Security: Two End User Survey Studies of Motivation and Security Practices.* Paper presented at the America's Conference on Information Systems (AMCIS).

Stanton, J. M., Stam, K. R., Mastrangelo, P., & Jolton, J. (2005). Analysis of End-User Security Behaviors. *Computers & Security, 24*(2), 124-133.

Star, L. S., & Griesemer, J. R. (1989). Institutional ecology, 'translations' and boundary objects. *Social Studies of Science, 19*(3), 387-420.

State of Texas Department of Information Resources (2001). *Statewide information technology security assessment.* Retrieved May 12, 2007 from http://www.dir.state.tx.us/IRAPC/security_assessment/html/DIR.SSA.FinalReport.htm

Steiner, I. (2006, November 4, 2006). *eBay Reduces Bidding Transparency in Phish Fight.* Retrieved November 7, 2006, from http://www.auctionbytes.com/cab/abn/y06/m11/i03/s01

Stephens, R. T. (2004). A framework for the identification of electronic commerce design elements that enable trust within the small hotel industry. *Proceedings of ACMSE,* 309-314.

Stiff, J. B., Kim, H., & Ramesh, C. N. (1992). *Truth Biases and Aroused Suspicion in Relational Deception. 19*(3), 326.

Stoneburner, G. (2001). Underlying Technical Models for Information Technology Security. *NIST Special Publication 800-33.* Gaithersburg, MD: NIST.

Stop-Phishing.com (Indiana University). (2006, 15 February 2007). Retrieved March 23, 2007, from http://www.indiana.edu/~phishing/

Straub, D. W., & Welke, R. J. (1998). Coping with Systems Risk: Security Planning Models for Management Decision-Making *MIS Quarterly, 22*(4), 441-469.

Straub, D. W., Carlson, P. J., & Jones, E. H. (1992). *Deterring Highly Motivated Computer Abusers: A Field Experiment in Computer Security.* Paper presented at the Proceeding of the IFIP/Sec '92 Conference.

Streff, K., & Zhou, Z. (2006). Developing and enhancing a computer and network security curriculum. *Journal of Computing Sciences in Colleges, 21*(3), 1-14.

Stuart, E. S. Computer Security Strength & Risk: A Quantitative Approach. PhD thesis, Harvard University, Cambridge, MA, 2004.

Stufflebeam, W. H., Anton, A. I., He, Q., & Jain, N. (2004). Specifying Privacy Policies with P3P and EPAL: Lessons Learned. *Proceedings of the 2004 ACM Workshop on Privacy in the Electronic Society,* pp. 35-35.

Stufflebeam, W., Anton, A. I., He, Q., & Jain, N. (2004). *Specifying Privacy Policies with P3P and EPAL: Lessons Learned.* In proceedings of the 2004 ACM Workshop on Privacy in the Electronic Society (pp. 35-36).

Stump, J. (2003). *Food security - protect and prevent.* Retrieved December 29, 2006, from www.vdacs.state.va.us/foodsafety/advisory.html

Sulkin, R. (2006). *First Line of Defense Against Data Security Breaches: Employees.* Retrieved May 12, 2007 from http://www.law.com/jsp/article.jsp?id=1167300410341

Svenson, O. (1989). On expert judgements in safety analysis in the process industries. *Reliability Engineering and System Safety, 25,* 219–256.

Swanson, M., & Guttman, B. (1996). *Generally accepted principles and practices for securing information technology systems.* National Institute of Standards and

Technology. Retrieved May 25th, 2007, from http://csrc.nist.gov/publications/nistpubs/800-14/800-14.pdf

Sweeney, L. (2002). K-anonymity: a model for protecting privacy. *International Journal on Uncertainty, Fuzziness and Knowledge-based Systems, 10*(5), 557-570.

Symantec Corp. (2003). Infostealer.Bancos.B. Retrieved April, 2007, from http://www.symantec.com/security_response/writeup.jsp?docid=2003-073117-3108-99

Taleb, N.N. (2007). *The Black Swan*. New York, NY: Random House, Inc.

Tan, C. K. (2005). A belief augmented frame computational trust model. *FLAIRS Conference*, 647-652.

Tari, F., Ozok, A. A., & Holden, S. H. (2006). A comparison between of perceived and real shoulder-surfing risks between alphanumeric and graphical passwords. *Symposium on Usable Privacy and Security (SOUPS) 2006*. Pittsburgh, PA, USA.

Tarr, C. J. *(1995)*. Cost Effective Perimeter Security, Security and Detection. *European Convention on Security and Detection*, 183-187.

Taskiran, C. M., Topkara, U., Topkara, M., & Delp, E. J. (2006). Attacks on lexical natural language steganography systems. In *Proceedings of the SPIE International Conference on Security, Steganography, and Watermarking of Multimedia Contents.*

Tatham, M. (2006). *One in 20 US Internet Visits Went to Social networking Websites*. Hitwise. Retrieve 2/16/2007 from http://www.hitwise.com/press-center/hitwiseHS2004/us-08112006cgm.php

Tavani, H., & Moor, J. (2001). Privacy Protection, Control of Information, and Privacy-Enhancing Technologies. *ACM SIGCAS Computers and Society, 31*(1), 6-11.

Taylor, J. R. (2002). *Cognitive Grammar*. Oxford: Oxford University Press.

Teltzrow, M., & Kobsa, A. (2004). Impacts of User Privacy Preferences on Personalized Systems: a Comparative Study. In C.-M. Karat, J. Blom & J. Karat (Eds.), *Designing Personalized User Experiences for eCommerce* (pp. 315-332). Dordrecht, Netherlands: Kluwer Academic Publishers.

Tennenhouse, D. (2000). Proactive Computing. In: Communications of the ACM, Vol. 43, No. 5, pp. 43 – 50.

Tenreiro de Magalhães, S., & Santos, H. (2005). An improved statistical keystroke dynamics algorithm, *Multi Conference on Cumputer Science and Information Systems*: IADIS.

Tenreiro de Magalhães, S., Revett, K., & Santos, H. (2005). Password secured sites - stepping forward with keystroke dynamics, *International Conference on Next Generation Web Services Practices*. Seoul, Korea: IEEE CS Press.

Teo, T. S. H., & Lim, V. K. G. (1996). Factors Influencing Personal Computer Usage: The Gender Gap. *Women in Management Review, 11*, 18-26.

The Honeynet Project & The Honeynet Research Alliance (2004). *Know your enemy – trend analysis – trend: Life expectancy increasing for unpatched or vulnerable Linux deployments.* Retrieved May 12, 2007 from http://www.honeynet.org/papers/trends/life-linux.pdf

The National Strategy to Secure Cyberspace (2003). *The President's Critical Infrastructure Protection Board*. Retrieved February 14, 2003, from http://www.whitehouse.gov/pcipb/.

*The Oxford English Dictionary (*2nd ed.). (1989). *OED Online.* Oxford University Press. 19 August 2007. http://dictionary.oed.com/cgi/entry/50218187.

Theoharidoua, M., Kokolakisb, S., Karydaa, M. and Kiountouzis E. (2005, September). *The insider threat to information systems and the effectiveness of ISO17799.* Computers & Security, 24(6), 472-484.

Thomas, R. K. (1997). Team-Based Access Control (TMAC): A Primitive for Applying Role-Based Access Controls in Collaborative Environments. *Proceedings of the Second ACM workshop on Role-based Access Control*, Fairfax, VA, USA, 1997.

Thompson, R. L., Higgins, C. A., & Howell, J. M. (1991). Personal Computing: Toward a Conceptual Model of Utilization. *MIS Quarterly, 15*(1), 124-143.

Tian, J. (2007). Research on Credit Problem in C2C Commerce——Based on Gambling Mode. *Electronic Ecommerce*, March, 62-66.

TIME (2001). The Wildest Election in History. *Time Magazine*, Glencoe Social Studies, Current Events Update, Spring 2001, 12-13.

Tor. (2004). from http://tor.eff.org/

Trevathan, J., & Read, W. (2006). RAS: A system for supporting research in online auctions. *ACM Crossroads, 12.4*, 23-30.

Tsai, J., Egelman, S., Cranor, L., & Acquisti, A. (2007). The Effect of Online Privacy Information on Purchasing Behavior: An Experimental Study. *In proceedings of the Sixth Workshop on the Economics of Information Security*, Pittsburgh, PA.

Tsohou, A., Karyda, M., Kokolakis, S., & Kiountouzis, E. (2006). Formulating information systems risk management strategies through cultural theory. *Information Management & Computer Security, 14*(3), 198-217.

Turkle, S. (1995). *Life on the screen: identity in the age of the Internet*. New York: Simon and Schuster.

Turnbull, S. (2003). Network governance. *Corporate Governance International, 6*(3), 4-14.

Tversky, A., & Kahneman, D. (1974). Judgment under Uncertainty: Heuristics and Biases. *Science, 185*(4157), 1124.

Twitchell, D. P. (2006). *Augmenting Detection of Social Engineering Attacks Using Deception Detection Technology*. Paper presented at the International Conference on i-Warfare and Security, Princess Anne, Maryland.

United States Army (2006). *Army information assurance training program*. Retrieved May 13, 2007 from http://ia.gordon.army.mil/iaso/lesson04.htm

United States General Accounting Office (GAO) (2002). *Employee Privacy: Computer-Use Monitoring Practices and Policies of Selected Companies*. Report to the Ranking Minority

USA. (2002). *The E-Government Act*. Retrieved from http://thomas.loc.gov/cgi-bin/bdquery/z?d107:HR02458:|TOM:/bss/d107query.html

USACM. (2006). *USACM Policy Recommendations on Privacy*. Retrieved from http://usacm.acm.org/usacm/Issues/Privacy.htm

USG (1998). *The Digital Millennium Copyright Act of 1998*. US. Copyright Office, Pub. 05-304, 112 Stat. 2860.

VanWyk, K. R., & Steven, J. (2006). Essential Factors for Successful Software Security Awareness Training. *IEEE Security and Privacy, 4*, 5 (Sept 2006), 80-83. DOI= http://dx.doi.org/10.1109/MSP.2006.119

Vela, B., Fernández-Medina, E., Esperanza, M., & Piattini, M. (2006). *Model Driven Development of Secure XML Databases. SIGMOD Record, 35*(3).

Venkatesh, V., Morris, M. G., Davis, G. B., & Davis, F. D. (2003). User Acceptance of Information Technology: Toward a Unified View. *MIS Quarterly, 27*(3), 425-478.

VeriSign. (2007). Buy SSL Certificates - SSL Certificate from VeriSign, Inc. Retrieved March 16, 2007, from http://www.verisign.com/ssl/buy-ssl-certificates/index.html

Viega, J., & McGraw, G. (2001). *Building Secure Software: How to Avoid Security Problems the Right Way*. Addison-Wesley, 2001.

Vinge, V. (2001). Introduction. In J. Frenkel (Ed.), *True names and the opening of the cyberspace frontier* (pp. 15-23). New York: Tom Doherty Associates.

Visual evidence. (2004). Retrieved December 28, 2006 from www.cr.nps.gov/nr/twhp/wwwlps/lessons/60sanjuan/60visual2.htm

von Goethe, J. (1774). *Die Leiden des jungen Werther*. Translated into Hulse, M. (1989), *The Sorrows of Young Werther*, London, England: Penguin Books.

von Locquenghien, K. (2006). On the Potential Social Impact of RFID-Containing Everyday Objects Science. In: Technology & Innovation Studies, Vol. 2, No 1, pp. 57 –78.

Von Solms, R., & Von Solms, S. H. (2004). From policies to culture. *Computers & Security, 23*(4), 275-279.

Von Solms, R., & Von Solms, S. H. (2004). The 10 deadly sins of information security management. *Computers & Security, 23*(5), 371-376.

Von Solms, R., & Von Solms, S. H. (2005). From information security to. business security? *Computers & Security, 24*(4), 271-273.

Von Solms, S. H. (2001). Information Security - A Multidimensional Discipline. *Computers & Security, 20*(6), 504-508.

Von Solms, S. H. (2001). Corporate Governance and Information Security. *Computers & Security, 20*(3), 215-218.

Von Solms, S. H. (2005). Information Security Governance in ICT Based Educational Systems. *Proceedings of the 2005 Conference in Bankok*.

Von Solms, S. H. (2005). Information Security Governance - Compliance management vs operational management. *Computers & Security, 24*(6), 443-447.

Von Solms, S. H., & Eloff, J. H. P. (2004). *Information Security*. Johannesburg, South-Africa.

Vontu Data Loss Prevention Software. http//www.vontu.com

Voss, B. D. (2003). *The ultimate defense of depth: Security awareness in your company*. SANS Information Security Reading Room. Retrieved May 26th, 2007, from http://www.sans.org/reading_room/whitepapers/awareness/395.php?portal=e890567ebf0e64fc81d240d49821e7ba.

Vredenburg, K., Isensee, S., & Righi, C. (2002). *User-centered design: An integrated approach*. Upper Saddle River, NJ: Prentice Hall.

W3C (2002). A P3P Preference Exchange Language 1.0 (APPEL1.0). W3C Working Draft 15 April 2002. *Available as of August 12, 2002 at: http://www.w3.org/TR/P3P-preferences/*

W3C. (1998). HTML Document Object Model (DOM). from http://www.w3c.org/DOM

Waint, T. L. (2005). Information security policy's impact on reporting security incidents. *Computers & Security, 24*(6), 448-459.

Wakefield, R. L. Employee Monitoring and Surveillance—The Growing Trend (2004). *Information Systems Control Journal, 1.*

Wang, G. (2005). Keynote speech, IDG World Expo SecurityWorld Conference and Showcase, Singapore. Retrieved May 12, 2007 from http://cio-asia.com/ShowPage.aspx?pagetype=2&articleid=3147&pubid=5&issueid=76

Wang, H., Lee, M. K. O., & Wang, C. (1998). Consumer Privacy Concerns about Internet Marketing. *Communications of the ACM, 41*(3), 63-70.

Wang, L., & Shen, Y. (2002). *Credit and China's E-commerce*(Tech. Rep. No. 1). Peiking University E-business Research Center.

Wang, W., Hidvegi, Z., & Whinston, A. (2002). Shill Bidding in Multi-round Online Auctions. *In Proceedings of the 35th Hawaii International Conference on System Sciences.*

Wang, Y., & Kobsa, A. (2006). Impacts of Privacy Laws and Regulations on Personalized Systems. *In proceedings of the PEP06, CHI06 Workshop on Privacy-Enhanced Personalization* (pp. 44-46) Montréal, Canada.

Wang, Y., & Kobsa, A. (2008). Technical Solutions for Privacy-Enhanced Personalization. In Mourlas, C. & Germanakos, P. (Eds.), *Intelligent User Interfaces: Adaptation and Personalization Systems and Technologies*: IGI Global.

Warren, S., & Brandeis, L. (1890). The Right to Privacy. *Harvard Law Review, 4*(5), 193-220.

Weiner, E. S. C., & Simpson, J. A. (Eds.). (1991). *The Compact Edition of The Oxford English Dictionary.* USA: Oxford University Press.

Weiser, M. (1991). The Computer for the Twenty-First Century. In: Scientific American, Vol. 265, No. 3, pp. 94 – 104.

Wellman, B., & Guila, M. (1999). Virtual Communities as Communties: Net Surfers don't Ride Alone. *Communities in Cyberspace*, 167-194. London, UK: Routledge.

Wellman, B., Salaff, J., Dimitrova, D., Garton, L., Gulia, M., & Haythornthwaite, C. (1996). Computer Networks as Social networks: Collaborative Work, Telework, and Virtual community. *Annual Review of Sociology, 22,* 213-239.

Wenyin, L., Huang, G., Xiaoyue, L., Min, Z., & Deng, X. (2005). *Detection of phishing webpages based on visual similarity.* Paper presented at the Special interest Tracks and Posters of the 14th international Conference on World Wide Web (WWW), Chiba, Japan.

Werner, L. (2005). *Redefining computer literacy in the age of ubiquitous computing.* Paper presented at the Proceedings of the 6th conference on Information technology education.

Westin, A. (1967). *Privacy and freedom.* New York: Atheneum.

Westin, A., & Gelder, V. v. (2003). Privacy & American Business: Special Issue on Consumer Privacy in Japan and the New National Privacy Law. Retrieved from http://www.privacyexchange.org/ pab_japanissue.pdf

Whiteman, W. & Mattord, H. J. (2003). *Principles of Information Security*, Thomson - Course Technology, Canada.

Whiteman, W. (2004). In defense of the realm: understanding the threats of information Security. *International Journal of Information Management, 24*(1), 43-57.

Whiteside, T. (1979). *Computer Capers: Tales of Electronic Thievery, Embezzlement, and Fraud*: Sidgwick & Jackson.

Whittaker, S., Frohlich, D., & Daly-Jones, O. (1994). Informal workplace communication - What is it like and how might we support it? In: *Proceedings of the ACM Conference on Human Factors in Computing Science* (CHI '95). ACM, NY, pp. 131-137.

Whitten, A., & Tygar, D. (1999). *Why Johnny Can't Encrypt. A Usability Evaluation of PGP 5.0.* In proceedings of the Ninth USENIX Security Symposium. from http://www.cs.berkeley.edu/~tygar/papers/Why_Johnny_Cant_Encrypt/OReilly.pdf

Whitten, A., & Tygar, D. (1999). Why johnny can't encrypt: A usability evaluation of PGP 5.0. *Proceedings of the 9th USENIX Security Symposium*, 169-184.

Whitten, A., & Tygar, J. D. (1999, August). *Why Johnny can't encrypt*. In *Proceedings of the 8th USENIX Security Symposium*.

Wiedenbeck, S., Waters, J., Birget, J. C., Brodskiy, A., & Memon, N. (2005). Authentication using graphical passwords: Basic results, *Human-Computer Interaction International (HCII 2005)*. Las Vegas.

Wiedenbeck, S., Waters, J., Birget, J. C., Brodskiy, A., & Memon, N. (2005). Authentication using graphical passwords: effects of tolerance and image choice. *Proceedings of the 2005 symposium on Usable privacy and security*, Pittsburgh, Pennsylvania, Pages: 1 – 12.

Wikipedia (2007). *Social network*. Wikipedia. Retrieve 2/16/2007 from http://en.wikipedia.org/wiki/Social_network

Wikipedia. (2008, 28 April 2008). Distributed cognition. from http://en.wikipedia.org/wiki/Distributed_cognition#Applications

Wikipedia. (2008, 6 April 2008). Socio-technical systems. Retrieved 04/27, 2008, from http://en.wikipedia.org/wiki/Socio-technical_systems

Willison, R. (2006). *Understanding the perpetration of employee computer crime in the organisational context*, Information and Organization, 16(4), 304-324

Willison, R., & Siponen, M. (2007). A Critical assesment if IS Security Research Between 1990-2004. *Working Paper No. 01-2007.*

Wilson, M., & Hash, J. (2003). *Building an Information Technology Security Awareness and Training Program*. National Institute of Science and Technology Special Publication 800-50. Retrieved May 12, 2007 from http://csrc.nist.gov/publications/nistpubs/800-50/NIST-SP800-50.pdf

Wing, J. (1998, December). A Symbiotic Relationship Between Formal Methods and Security. *Proc. NSF Workshop on Computer Security, Fault Tolerance, and Software Assurance: From Needs to Solution.*

Winstein, K. (1999). *Lexical steganography through adaptive modulation of the word choice hash.* Retrieved October 2004, from http://alumni.imsa.edu/~keithw/tlex/lsteg.ps.

Winstein, K. (1999, January). *Tyrannosaurus lex Web site*. Retrieved October 2004, from http://alumni.imsa.edu/~keithw/tlex/

Witty, J. and Wagner R. (2005). *Awareness training is necessary to support your information security program.* Gartner. Retrieved May 12, 2007 from http://www.gartner.com/resources/125800/125896/awareness_training_is_necess_125896.pdf

Wood, C. C. (1995). Writing infosec policies. *Computers & Security, 14*(8), 667.

Wood, C. C. (2004). Why information security is now multi-disciplinary, multi-departmental, and multi-organizational in nature. *Computer Fraud & Security,* (1), 16-17.

Wu, M., Robert, C. M., & Simson, L. G. (2006). *Do security toolbars actually prevent phishing attacks?* Paper presented at the Proceedings of the SIGCHI conference on Human Factors in computing systems. from http://portal.acm.org/citation.cfm?id=1124863&coll=Portal&dl=GUIDE&CFID=6253896&CFTOKEN=24538716#.

Wüest, C. (2005). Phishing in the middle of the stream - Todays threats to online banking. *8th Annual AVAR International Conference*. Tianjin, China.

Xia, G., & Liu, X. (2006). Electronic Commerce and Honesty-credit Problems in China. *Information Network Security*, May, 3-6.

Xiao Komiak, S., & Benbasat, I. (2004). Understanding customer trust in agent-mediated electronic commerce, web-mediated electronic commerce, and traditional commerce. *Information Technology and Management, 5(1–2)*, 181–207. Kluwer Academic Publishers.

Xiao, S., & Benbasat, I. (2003). The formation of trust and distrust in recommendation agents in repeated interactions: A process-tracing analysis. *Proceedings of the 5th International Conference on Electronic Commerce*, 287–293.

Yahalom, R., Klein, B., & Beth, T. (1993). Trust relationships in secure systems - A distributed authentication perspective. *Proceedings of the IEEE Symposium on Research in Security and Privacy*, 150-164.

Yahalom, R., Klein, B., & Beth, T. (1994). Trust-based navigation in distributed systems. *Computing Systems, 7*(1), 45-73.

Yamagishi, T. (1998). The structure of trust: The evolutionary games of mind and society. Tokyo: Tokyo University Press (in Japanese), English version available from: http://lynx.let.hokudai.ac.jp/members/yamagishi/english.htm (Last Access April 2007)

Yanushkevich, S. N., Stoica, A., Shmerko, V. P., & Popel, D. V. (2005). *Biometric Inverse Problems*. Taylor & Francis: CRC Press.

Yee, G., & Korba, L. (2003, June). Feature Interactions in Policy Driven Privacy Management. *Proceedings, Seventh International Workshop on Feature Interactions in Telecommunications and Software Systems*, Ottawa, Canada.

Yee, G., & Korba, L. (2003, January). Bilateral E-services Negotiation Under Uncertainty. Proceedings, *The 2003 International Symposium on Applications and the Internet (SAINT2003)*, Orlando, Florida, USA.

Yee, G., & Korba, L. (2003, May). The Negotiation of Privacy Policies in Distance Education. In *Proceedings of the Information Resources Management Association International Conference 2003 (IRMA 2003)*, Philadelphia, PA, USA.

Yee, G., & Korba, L. (2004). Privacy Policy Compliance for Web Services. *Proceedings, 2004 IEEE International Conference on Web Services (ICWS 2004)*, San Diego, California, July.

Yee, G., & Korba, L. (2005, January). Semi-Automatic Derivation and Use of Personal Privacy Policies in E-Business. *International Journal of E-Business Research, Vol. 1, No. 1*, Idea Group Publishing.

Yee, G., & Korba, L. (2005, October). Specifying Personal Privacy Policies to Avoid Unexpected Outcomes. *Proceedings, Third Annual Conference on Privacy, Security and Trust,* St. Andrews, New Brunswick, Canada.

Yee, G., Korba, L., & Song, R. (2006). Legislative Bases for Personal Privacy Policy Specification. Chapter in *Privacy Protection for E-Services*, edited by Yee, G., pp. 281-294, Idea Group Inc., March.

Yee, K. P., Wagner, D., Hearst, M., & Bellovin, S. M. (2006). Prerendered User Interfaces for Higher-Assurance Electronic Voting. USENIX/ACCURATE Electronic Voting Technology Workshop (EVT'06), Vancouver, Canada, August 1, 2006.

Yee, K-P. (2002) User interaction design for secure systems. In at al. R. Deng, (Ed.), *Proceddings of ICICS 2002, 2513 of Lecture Notes in Computer Science*,278–290. Springer-Verlag, Berlin.

Yerazunis, W. S., & Carbone, M. (2002) Privacy-Enhanced Displays by Time-Masking Images, *Technical Report TR2002-011*, Mitsubishi Electric Research Laboratories.

Young, J. (1978). Introduction: A Look at Privacy. In J. Young (Ed.), *Privacy*. New York: John Wiley & Sons.

Young, R. M., Green, T. R. G., & Simon, T. (1989). Programmable Users Models for Predictive Evaluation of Interface Design. *ACM CHI 89 Human Factors in Computing Systems Conference*, 15-19. ACM Press.

Yu, C-F., & Gligor, V. D. (1990). A Specification and Verification Method for Preventing Denial of Service. *IEEE Trans. on Software Engineering*, 16(6), 581-592. IEEE.

Yu, Z., Shi, B., & Liu, X. (2006). Game Analysis on the Honesty of Transaction Parties in E-commerce. *Business Study*, *339*(7), 67-69.

Zannone, N., Jajodia, S., Massacci, F., & Wijesekera, D. (2005). Maintaining Privacy on Derived Objects. *Proceedings of the 2005 ACM Workshop on Privacy in the Electronic Society*, pp. 10-19, Alexandria, VA, USA.

Zhang, Y., Egelman, S., Cranor, L., & Hong, J. (2007, 28 February--2 March, 2007). *Phinding Phish: Evaluating Anti-Phishing Tools.* Paper presented at the 14th Annual Network and Distributed System Security Symposium (NDSS 2007), San Diego, CA.

Zhang, Y., Hong, J., & Cranor, L. (2007). *Cantina: a content-based approach to detecting phishing web sites* Paper presented at the 16th international conference on World Wide Web (WWW), Banff, Alberta, Canada.

Zhang, Z., Zhang, X., & Sandhu, R. (2006). ROBAC: Scalable Role and Organization Based Access Control Models. *Proceedings of CollaborateCom-2006/TrustCol-2006*, Atlanta, Georgia, USA, November 2006.

Zhao, Q. A., & Stasko, J. T. (2002) What's Happening? Promoting Community Awareness Through Opportunistic Peripheral Interfaces. In: *Proceedings of the Conference on Advanced Visual Interfaces* (AVI'02), pp. 69-74.

Zheng, H., Xing, W.-L., Wang, D.-Q., & Duan, H.-X. (2005). *Analysis of Malicious Code for Phishing.* Paper presented at the 8th Association of anti Virus Asia Researchers Conference (AVAR 2005). from http://worm.ccert.edu.cn/doc/spark/AnalysisMaliciousCodeForPhishing.pdf.

Zheng, Y. (2001). *On Trust.* Beijing: Trust China Broadcasting and Television Press.

Zimmerman, E. (2002). HR Must Know When Employee Surveillance Crosses the Line. *Workforce*. pp 38-45.

Zimmerman, P. (1995). *PGP user's guide.* Cambridge, MA: MIT Press.

Zurko, M. E. (2005). User-centered security: Stepping up to the grand challenge. *In Proceedings of ACSAC 2005*, 187–202. IEEE.

Zurko, M. E., Simon, R., & Sanfilippo, T. (1999, May). A User-Centered, Modular Authorization Service Built on an RBAC Foundation. *In Proceedings of IEEE Symposium on Research in Security and Privacy*, 57-71.

About the Contributors

Manish Gupta is an information security professional at a large US financial services institution and also a PhD candidate at State University of New York, Buffalo. He received his bachelor's degree in mechanical engineering from Institute of Engineering and Technology, Lucknow, India and an MBA in Information Systems from State University of New York, Buffalo, NY, USA. With more than a decade of experience in information systems, policies and technologies, he has published 3 books in the area of information security, ethics and assurance including *Managing information Assurance in Financial Services* (publisher: Idea Group Inc.). He has also taught at SUNY, Buffalo as adjunct professor. He has authored or co-authored more than 30 refereed research articles in leading journals, conference proceedings and books. He serves in editorial boards of 6 international journals and has served in program committees of several national and international conferences. He holds several professional designations including CISSP, CISA, CISM, ISSPCS, CIW Security Analyst, COMPTIA Security+ and PMP. He has also received advanced certificates in information assurance (SUNY, Buffalo), IT Benchmarking (Stanford University) and cyber law (Asian School of Cyber Law).

Raj Sharman is an associate professor in the Management Science and Systems Department at SUNY Buffalo, NY. He received his BTech and MTech degree from IIT Bombay, India and his MS degree in Industrial Engineering and PhD in computer science from Louisiana State University. His research streams include Information Assurance, Extreme Events, and improving performance on the Web. His papers have been published in a number of national and international journals. He is also the recipient of several grants from the university as well as external agencies. He serves as an associate editor for the *Journal of Information Systems Security.*

* * *

Serkan Ada is currently a PhD student in the Department of Management Science and Systems, School of Management at the State University of New York at Buffalo. He is also a scholarship holder of the Turkish Government. He received BS degree in Business Administration at Celal Bayar University in 2003 and he received MBA degree in State University of New York at Oswego in 2007. He is a member of Beta Gamma Sigma-International Honor Society and The National Scholars Honor Society. His research interests are business value of information technology, improvisation and resilience in emergency response, and information security.

Ahmed Awad E. Ahmed is a research associate and a PhD candidate at the Electrical and Computer Engineering Department, University of Victoria. His PhD thesis presents a number of new trends in security monitoring through human computer interaction devices. He is a member of the Security and Object Technology (ISOT) Research Laboratory at the University of Victoria and the principal investigator of Biotracker (http://www.isot.ece.uvic.ca/projects/biotracker), an intrusion detection system based on biometrics. Ahmed worked as a Software Design Engineer, Project Manager, and Quality Assurance Consultant in a number of leading software firms. He obtained his BSc and MSc from Ain Shams University (Cairo, Egypt), Electrical and Computer Engineering Department in 1992, and 1997 respectively.

César Ariza is an information technologies consultant at Bogomovil Ltda. Previously he was a researcher at the ubicomp research group of the Algoritmi Research Center of the University of Minho where he has finished his master's degree.

C. Warren Axelrod is an information security and privacy officer at Bank of America, where he identifies, assesses and mitigates privacy and security risks. He testified before Congress in 2001 on cybersecurity. He was a founder of the Financial Services and Analysis Center and is on the Financial Services Sector Coordinating Council R&D Committee. He received the Computerworld Premier 100 Leadership Award in 2003 and the ISE Luminary Leadership Award in 2007. His latest book is "Outsourcing Information Security" (Artech House, 2004) and his chapter on return on security investment is in "Managing Information Assurance in Financial Services" (IGI, 2007). He has a BSc and MA, both with honors, from Glasgow University and a PhD from Cornell University. He has a CISM and CISSP.

Mridul Sankar Barik is presently a lecturer in the Department of Computer Science & Engineering, Jadavpur University, India. He has nearly nine years of experience in research and teaching. At present his active area of research is information security. His other research interests include digital forensics, distributed and dependable systems. He has to his credit several publications in National and International Journals and Conferences.

Jenine Beekhuyzen is a PhD student in the School of Information and Communication Technology at Griffith University. In her thesis 'Digital Rights Management and the online music experience'; she is investigating how technology is changing the way that people access, share and listen to music. Technology is also changing the options for downloading music over the Internet. Jenine is also a researcher in the Smart Internet Technology Cooperative Research Centre currently focused on user-centred security of financial services in the Australian banking context. Another research project is the WinIT Project (Women in IT) longitudinal study since 2000. In 2007, she was an invited visiting scholar to Hanover, Germany.

Patrick Brézillon defended his Thèse d'Etat in 1983 on "Mathematical Modeling of Self-Oscillating Nonlinear Systems." Since 1997, he belongs to the SYSDEF team at LIP6, which stands for Laboratoire d'Informatique de Paris 6. His personal research focuses since 1992 on the study of Intelligent Assistant Systems, and particularly the aspects explanation, context and incremental knowledge acquisition. He published more than 290 papers in international conference and international journals (e.g., IEEE Expert,

AI Magazine, The Knowledge Engineering Review, etc.). He has been the chair of several workshops and co-organizer of two international conferences in AI area.

Antonio Cerone joined the International Institute for Software Engineering (IIST) of the United Nations University (UNU) in February 2004 as a research fellow. His research focuses on the use of formal methods in the verification of software and in modelling cognitive human behaviour. He is particularly interested in the verification of interactive systems, security systems, safety-critical systems, asynchronous hardware and concurrent and real-time systems. Within his research on cognitive human behaviour he has also developed an interest in pedagogy and education.

Basabi Chakraborty received MTech and PhD degrees in radio physics and electronics from Calcutta University, India. She received another PhD in information science from Tohoku University, Japan. Currently she is a faculty in the department of Software and Information Science, Iwate Prefectural University, Japan. Her main research interests are in the area of pattern recognition, image processing, biometrics, trust models and soft computing techniques.

Tom S. Chan is an associate professor at the Information Department, Southern New Hampshire University at Manchester, New Hampshire, USA. He holds a EdD from Texas Tech University, and M.S.C.S. from the University of Southern California. Prior to SNHU, he was an assistant professor at Marist College, and as project manager and software designer specialized in data communication at Citibank. He has published works in the area of instructional design, distance learning, technology adaptation, information security and Web design.

Vineeta Chand is a PhD candidate in linguistics at the University of California, Davis. Her dissertation focuses on emerging world Englishes within the Indian post-colonial linguistic landscape. Her background includes testing natural language processing (NLP) software, and her current research reflects multiple intersecting interests: sociolinguistic anthropology, phonetic analysis of normal and distorted speech, and NLP, related to the current chapter.

Madhusudhanan Chandrasekaran received his BE degree in computer science and engineering in 2002 from University of Madras. He is currently a fifth year Computer Science and Engineering PhD student at the State University of New York at Buffalo. His research interests are in the field of computer security, with particular focus on anti-phishing, anti-spam, spyware and intrusion detection.

Samir Chatterjee is a professor of computer networking and telecommunications at CGU's School of Information Systems & Technology (SISAT). He is also the founding director of Network Convergence Laboratory funded by the National Science Foundation. He joined CGU in July of 2001. He is also an adjunct faculty of the Peter F. Drucker and Ito School of Management, where he teaches on their executive MBA program. His research interests are transdisciplinary. His research combines technical skills from computer science and evaluation skills from social sciences. He loves to design and develop technologies that solve human problems. They range from networking and collaboration tools to security and trust algorithms to e-health technologies such as telemedicine. Currently he is pursuing the design of virtual worlds to enhance human creativity and cognition. He is also leading the design and implementation of e-Health technologies such as Telemedicine, stress management software and context-aware intervention technologies for managing obesity. He has published over 75 articles in refereed conferences and journals including IEEE Network, IEEE J. on Selected Areas in Communications, Communications of the ACM, Computer Networks, International Journal of Healthcare Technology & Management, Telemedicine & e-Health Journal, Information Systems Frontiers, Computer Communication, IEEE IT Professional, ACM CCR, Communications of AIS, Journal of Internet Technology etc. He is an active IETF member affiliated to several working groups and a core group member of Video Middleware Initiative within Internet-2.

Carl H. Hauser is an associate professor of Computer Science in the School of Electrical Engineering and Computer Science (EECS) at Washington State University (WSU). His research interests include concurrent programming models and mechanisms, networking, programming language implementation, and distributed computing systems. He is currently working on GridStat, flexible and secure middleware for electric power grid communications. Prior to joining WSU, he worked at Xerox Palo Alto Research Center and IBM Research for a total of over 20 years.

Tejaswini Herath is a PhD candidate in Management Science & Systems, School of Management at the State University of New York at Buffalo. She holds MMIS, MSCE from Auburn University and BE from Pune University, India. Previously she worked as a lecturer at Brock University, Canada. She also worked as a systems analyst and part-time lecturer at UNBC, Canada. Her research interests include information security, privacy and outsourcing. Her work has been published in the *Gender and Information Technology Encyclopedia* and *International Journal of Electronic Government Research.* Her work has appeared or accepted for proceedings of *WEIS (06,07)*, *AMCIS (07)*, and *International Conference on E-Government.*

Natsuko Hikage received MSc degree in software and information science from Iwate Prefectural University, Japan in 2007. She has been with NTT Information Sharing Platform Laboratories, NTT Corporation since April 2007. Her research interests include psychology of security, security usability and trust models. She is a member of ACM and IPSJ.

Steve Hinske is a PhD student at the Institute for Pervasive Computing at ETH Zurich, Switzerland. He finished his studies in Business Administration and Computer Science at Darmstadt University of Technology, Germany, in 2005, and wrote his diploma thesis at Fraunhofer Institute in the fields of pervasive computing and privacy. Steve did a research project at University of New South Wales in Sydney, Australia, as well as two internships with companies in Japan and the United States, respectively. He has furthermore started his own business consulting companies on ICT-related issues. Steve is mainly interested in the management of smart environments, human-computer interaction, and pervasive games.

Gary Hinson is an experienced information security and IT audit consultant with CISM, CISSP and CISA qualifications plus a PhD and an MBA. Gary has worked for and managed information security and computer audit functions for several major multinational companies in various industries since the 1980's. He has been consulting since 2000, establishing his own company in 2002 specialising in information security, IT audit and IT governance. He has established a successful global security awareness brand, NoticeBored, and continues to innovate in the field.

Margaret Jackson is professor of Computer Law at the Royal Melbourne Institute of Technology University and director of the Law Discipline in the School of Accounting and Law. She leads the stream of e-commerce in the Smart Internet Technology Cooperative Research Centre. Margaret conducts research in the areas of computer law, protection of information, data protection and privacy, and copyright. She is a member of the User Centred Design Group located in the Co-operative Research Centre for Smart Internet Technology. She is the author of *Hughes on Data Protection in Australia*, LawBook Co 2001, and *A Practical Guide to Protecting Confidential Business Information*, LawBookCo, 2003.

Reza Kamali is an professor and Department Head of Computer Information Technology Department at Purdue University Calumet, Hammond, Indiana. He was a founding member of SITE, which later became ACM's SIGITE. He was a member of the IT2006 Task Force and a member of The Joint Task Force for Computing Curricula 2005

Alfred Kobsa is a professor in the Donald Bren School of Information and Computer Sciences of the University of California, Irvine. His research lies in the areas of user modeling and personalized systems (with applications in information environments, expert finders, and user interfaces for disabled and elderly people), privacy, and in information visualization. He is the editor of *User Modeling and User-Adapted Interaction*, editorial board member of *World-Wide Web*, *Universal Access in the Information Society*, and *Information Technology and Decision Making.* He edited several books and authored numerous publications on user-adaptive systems, human-computer interaction and knowledge representation.

Ghita Kouadri-Mostefaoui is currently a researcher at Oxford university computing laboratory. Her research interests include software engineering, context-based security, and e-health. Before joining Oxford University, she worked as a postdoctoral fellow at the University of Montreal, Canada, and as a research and teaching assistant at the University of Fribourg (Switzerland). She received an MS degree (pre-doctoral school) in computer science from Ecole Polytechnique Fédérale de Lausanne, Switzerland, in 1999, and a PhD in computer science from both the University of Fribourg and Université Pierre et Marie Curie (Paris 6) in 2004.

Larry Korba is the leader and founder of the Information Security Group in the Institute for Information Technology of the National Research Council of Canada, in Ottawa, Canada. As a principal research officer, he currently leads a group of over a dozen researchers, guest workers and support staff in the research and development of technologies for privacy compliance and security intelligence. Over the past 7 years, he has led several R&D projects involving the development of privacy technologies with a number of European and Asian collaborators as well as with Canadian companies. His research interests include network and application security, privacy protection, and technologies for security intelligence.

E. Kritzinger is a lecturer at the School of Computing of the University of South Africa, South Africa. She obtained her PhD in information systems at the University of South Africa and has been lecturing from February 1, 2000. Her main focus area is information security education within a distance education environment.

Guoling Lao, PhD, associate professor of School of Information Management and Engineering, Shanghai University of Finance & Economics, director of SHUFE-IBM Electronic Commerce Center, concurrently assistant deputy office chief of financial division of the university (responsible for informatization), has published more than 20 textbooks and 70 academic paper, and completed more than 30 enterprise and government projects. Main research direction: Electronic commerce, management information system.

Samuel P. Liles is an assistant professor of Computer Information Technology at Purdue University Calumet. He is currently involved in research identifying the knowledge skills and abilities of cyber adversaries and mitigation strategies.

Sérgio Tenreiro de Magalhães teaches Computer's and Network's Architecture in the Portuguese Catholic University. He is also a researcher in that university, mainly in the fields of Information Security, cyber enhanced terrorism monitoring, prevention and social impact. He has published several works in international refereed journals and in international conference proceedings and he is currently a member of several international conference committees.

Carsten Magerkurth is a senior researcher at SAP Research CEC St. Gallen, Switzerland. His current research activities include HCI techniques for smart items, anti-counterfeiting methods, and pervasive computing support for manufacturing. Before joining SAP he was head of the research division "AMBIENTE – Smart Environments of the Future" at the Fraunhofer Institute for Integrated Information and Publication Systems (IPSI) in Darmstadt, Germany. He has authored or co-authored more than 30 scientific papers in the fields of Pervasive Gaming, Human Computer Interaction, and Ambient Intelligence in the relevant journals and conferences.

Ambuj Mahanti works as a professor of Computer Science and Management Information Systems at Indian Institute of Management Calcutta, Kolkata, India. His specializations are in the area of artificial intelligence and heuristic programming, and business intelligence. He has published extensively in international journals and conferences including several publications in *Journal of ACM, Theoretical Computer Science, Artificial Intelligence, Information Processing Letters*, etc. His current research interest includes combinatorial auctions, data mining, recommendation systems, business intelligence, and workflow verification.

Chandan Mazumdar is teaching Computer Science & Engineering in Jadavpur University. He is the coordinator of the Centre for Distributed Computing. He has supervised five PhDs and has to his credit over 52 publications in National and International Journals and Conferences. He has copyrighted two software – one, on Forensic Identification of Fire Arms and another on Enterprise Information Security Management. He was the program co-chair of the First International Conference on Information Systems Security, 2005 and general co-chair of the same conference in 2006.

Arunabha Mukhopadhyay is an assistant professor of Information Technology & Systems at Indian Institute of Management Lucknow (IIM L), India. He is a PhD from IIM Calcutta, in the area of Management Information Systems. He has awarded the Infosys scholarship during his PhD. Prior to it he has done his Post Graduate Diploma in Business Management (PGDBM) majoring in Finance, from

IIMC. He has presented his work in international conferences like AMCIS, HICSS etc. He has a couple of national level journal publications to his credit too. His current research interest lies in the area of electronic risk (e-risk) management through financial instruments (such as insurance and derivatives).

Yuko Murayama is a professor in the Faculty of Software and Information Science at Iwate Prefectural University, Japan. Her research interests include Internet, network security and human aspects of security and trust. She has been leading a project on Anshin and Trust funded by Japan Science and Technology Agency (JST) since 2005. She had a BSc in mathematics from Tsuda college, Japan. After several years in industry in Japan, she went to a graduate school at University College London. She had a MSc and PhD both in computer science from University of London in 1984 and 1992, respectively. She had been a visiting lecturer from 1992 to 1994 at Keio University, a lecturer at Hiroshima City University from 1994 to 1998. She has been with Iwate Prefectural University since April 1998. Her interests include internetworking and its applications as well as network security. She is a member of IEEE, ACM, IPSJ, IEICE, and ITE. She serves as an IPSJ director for the moment.

Donald Murphy is identity services manager at M&T Bank Corporation, Buffalo. He has more than 20 years of experience in different information systems and security technologies.

André Oliveira is an information technologies consultant in an international consulting company and he has responsibilities in several projects across Europe. He is currently at the finishing stage of his master's thesis in the Department of Information Systems of the School of Engineering of the University of Minho.

C. Orhan Orgun is an associate professor of Linguistics at the University of California, Davis. He teaches graduate and undergraduate courses in phonetics, phonology and computational linguistics. His past research focuses primarily on Turkish, and OT approaches to phonology and morphology. He is currently investigating the relationship between distorted speech and speech rehabilitation through acoustic analysis.

Peter O. Orondo is a managing partner at Acclaim Consulting Group, Inc., a leading technology services consulting firm specializing in Identity and Access Management (IAM) solutions located in Waltham, MA. Mr. Orondo has more than 13 years experience in technology management and consulting. Prior to founding Acclaim Consulting Group, he worked in senior roles at Netegrity, Inc., Computer Associates International and Myers-Holum, Inc, where he spearheaded technology thought leadership, and architected and deployed complex enterprise Identity and Access Management, and E-provisioning solutions. In 2003, Mr. Orondo led Acclaim Consulting Group team to win the Semi Finalist Award at the prestigious MIT $50K Entrepreneurial Competition. Mr. Orondo holds bachelors and masters degrees in electrical engineering and computer science from the Massachusetts Institute of Technology (MIT). He also performed PhD work (ABD) at MIT in electrical engineering and computer science.

David Porter is head of security and risk at Detica, the intelligence systems and services organization. A Certified Fraud Examiner, he consults to government and banking clients and is also Detica's chief media commentator. Originally an artificial intelligence researcher at South Bank University, he moved into risk management services at Deloitte and Unisys. He holds a first class honors bachelor's degree, and a master's degree, in computer science from the University of London. He has contributed to *A Practitioners Guide to Money Laundering Law and Regulation, Managing Information Assurance in Financial Services* and *The Washing Machine: Money Crime and Power in the Offshore System*.

Nick Pullman is the global projects manager with Citigroup in the security administration department. For the past 3 years he has developed and implemented several integrated identity management and reporting tools. Nick is a board member for the South Dakota InfraGard chapter as well as a member of the Financial Services Information Sharing and Analysis Center. He graduated with Masters Degree in Information Assurance with a specialization in Banking and Financial Security from Dakota State University.

James W. Ragucci is a graduate student in Computer Science at Syracuse University. He is a recipient of the Scholarship for Service from the National Science Foundation. Mr. Ragucci received his BS in computer science from Montclair State University in 2006 with the Outstanding CS 2006 Undergraduate distinction and has worked for the Department of Defense and the New Jersey National Guard. Mr. Ragucci's research interests are on social engineering with a focus in phishing, and information assurance.

H. Raghav Rao, PhD, CISSP is a professor of MIS and adjunct professor of CSE at the State University of New York at Buffalo. His interests are in the areas of management information systems, decision support systems, expert systems, and information assurance. He has authored or coauthored more than 100 technical papers, of which more than 70 are published in archival journals. His work has received best paper and best paper runner up awards at AMCIS and ICIS. He has also received the University's prestigious Teaching Fellowship. He was named a Fulbright Fellow in 2004. He is associate editor of *Decision Support Systems, Information Systems Research and IEEE Transactions in Systems, Man and Cybernetics*, and coeditor-in-chief of *Information Systems Frontiers*.

Wayne Read completed an Honours degree in mathematics at James Cook University in 1982, and then commenced doctoral studies in the School of Engineering (Civil and Systems) in 1983. His thesis title was *Wave Groups in the Time and Frequency Domains*, and the degree was conferred in 1987. Research interests include: Modelling transport processes in porous media, series solutions to partial differential equations, restricted occupancy models, and e-commerce. He has been the head of the School of Mathematics, Physics and Information Technology since June 2002.

Kenneth Revett is a professor in the Harrow School of Computer Science of the University of Westminster. He researches mainly in the several applications of the computer science, namely the artificial intelligence technologies. He has published several works in international refereed journals and in international conference proceedings. He is currently a member of several international conference committees.

Stefan Robila is an assistant professor in Computer Science and the director of the Center of Imaging and Optics at Montclair State University, NJ. He has received his MS in computer science and PhD in computer information science from Syracuse University in 2000 and 2002 respectively. Dr. Robila's research focuses on pattern recognition in large data sets (remote sensing, hyperspectral data, efficient processing) and information assurance (social factors, phishing). He is the author of over thirty publications and has received funding from National Science Foundation, Sun Microsystems, HP, and SPIE.

Carsten Röcker is a visting researcher at the Cognitive Science Department of the University of California in San Diego. He has an interdisciplinary background with academic degrees in the areas of computer science (PhD), electrical engineering (Master) and management (Master). From 2001 until 2006 he worked as a research associate at the Fraunhofer Institute for Integrated Information and Publication Systems (IPSI) in Darmstadt (Germany) where he lead the design and construction of technical prototypes within the research division AMBIENTE. He published one book on Smart Office Environments and is author and coauthor of numerous scientific papers in the areas of Ambient Intelligence, Intellectual Teamwork and Human Computer Interaction.

Samir K. Sadhukhan is a senior system analyst at Indian Institute of Management Calcutta, Kolkata, India. His research interests are in the area of artificial intelligence and heuristic programming.

Debashis Saha works as a professor of Computer Science and Management Information Systems at Indian Institute of Management Calcutta, Kolkata, India. His specializations are in the area of computer communication and networks. He has published extensively in international journals and conferences including several publications in *Journal of IEEE Transactions*.

Ravi Sandhu is the founder, executive director and chief scientist of the Institute for Cyber-Security Research (ICSR) at the University of Texas at San Antonio, where he holds the Lutcher Brown Endowed Chair in Cyber-Security. He previously served on the Information Security faculty at George Mason University (18 years) and the Computer Science faculty at Ohio State University (7 years). Ravi earned B.Tech. and M.Tech. degrees from IIT Bombay and Delhi respectively, and MS and PhD degrees from Rutgers University. He is a fellow of ACM and of IEEE, and recipient of the IEEE Computer Society Technical Achievement Award. His research has focused on information security, privacy and trust, with special emphasis on models, protocols and mechanisms. He is also co-founder and chief scientist of TriCipher, an Internet identity security company.

Henrique M. D. Santos is the director of the Algoritmi Research Center in School of Engineering of the University of Minho and an associate professor in the same institution. In the past years he has orientated several Master and PhD students, published several academic works and collaborated in several projects. He was also the leader researcher in the project "Segurança na Rede de Distribuição de Dados em Formato Digital, para as Forças Armadas". He is also the president of the national technical committee for the normalization of information security procedures.

Leonel Duarte dos Santos is an auxiliar professor at the Department of Information Systems of the University of Minho, where he teaches several graduate and post-graduate courses. His research interests are in the fields of e-Government, information security and information services. He has been involved in several projects regarding the evaluation of the adoption of information technologies in the national and local governmental institutions and in e-voting technologies.

Anirban Sengupta is a senior research engineer at the Centre for Distributed Computing, Jadavpur University, Kolkata, India. He has over 5 years of experience in Information Technology. His current area of research is security modeling for enterprises. He has to his credit several publications in national and international journals and conferences.

Siraj A. Shaikh is currently a postdoctoral research fellow at the International Institute of Software Technology (IIST), at the United Nations University (UNU) in Macau SAR China. His main research interests include formal design and analysis of distributed security systems and protocols. His other interests include performance analysis of security protocols and information security education. He is a member of the British Computer Society (BCS).

Supriya Singh is professor, Sociology of Communications at the Royal Melbourne Institute of Technology University and project leader with the Smart Internet Technology Cooperative Research Centre. Her research interests cover the sociology of money and banking, domestic aspects of globalization, and the user-centred design of information and communication technologies. Her books include *Marriage money: the social shaping of money in marriage and banking.* (Allen & Unwin, St. Leonards, NSW, 1997), *The bankers: Australia's leading bankers talk about banking today* (Allen & Unwin, North Sydney, 1991) and *Bank Negara Malaysia: The first 25 years, 1959-1984* (Bank Negara Malaysia, Kuala Lumpur, 1984).

Prof SH (Basie) von Solms is a professor in the Academy for Information Processing of the University of Johannesburg, South Africa. He had been the Chairman of the Academy for Information Technology from 1978 to 2006. He obtained his PhD in computer science at University of Johannesburg (previously the Rand Afrikaans University) and has been lecturing Computer Science and IT at this University since October 1, 1970. The professor specializes in research and consultancy in the area of Information Security and has written more than 80 papers regarding this field - most of which have been published internationally. In addition, professor von Solms has, up to date, supervised 15 PhD students and more then 50 master students. Professor von Solms is the president – Elect of IFIP, the International Federation for Information Processing (www.ifip.org). See also the item IFIP Activities.

Kevin Streff is the director of the Center for Information Assurance at Dakota State, which has been recognized by both the National Security Agency and The Department of Homeland Security as a national center of academic excellence in information assurance. Dr. Streff has extensive knowledge of the financial services industry, including banking, insurance, and credit operations, and holds technology-related degrees from Dakota State, Temple, and Capella University, where he graduated with honors in all programs, including his PhD. Dr. Streff is founder and managing partner of Secure Banking Solutions, a security consulting firm focused on improving security in community banks across the country. Dr. Streff is also president of InfraGard - South Dakota, a partnership program between private industry and the U.S. government (represented by the FBI). Dr. Streff speaks nationally on security issues and solutions relevant to small and medium-sized banks.

Issa Traore received an aircraft engineer degree from Ecole de l'Air in Salon de Provence (France) in 1990, and successively two master degrees in aeronautics and space techniques in 1994, and in Automatics and Computer Engineering in 1995 from Ecole Nationale Superieure de l'Aeronautique et de l'Espace (E.N.S.A.E), Toulouse, France. In 1998, Traore received a PhD in software engineering from Institute Nationale Polytechnique (INPT)-LAAS/CNRS, Toulouse, France. From June - Oct. 1998, he held a post-doc position at LAAS-CNRS, Toulouse, France, and research associate (Nov. 1998 - May 1999), and senior lecturer (June-Oct. 1999) at the University of Oslo. Since Nov. 1999, he has joined the faculty of the Department of ECE, University of Victoria, Canada. He is currently an associate professor and holds since Oct. 2003 the position of computer engineering programme director. His research interests include behavioral biometrics systems, intrusion detection systems, software security metrics, and software quality engineering. He is the founder and coordinator of the Information Security and Object Technology (ISOT) Research Lab (http://www.isot.ece.uvic.ca).

Jarrod Trevathan completed an honours degree in computer science at James Cook University in 2002, and then commenced doctoral studies in the School of Mathematical and Physical Sciences in 2005. His thesis title was *Privacy and Security in Online Auctions*, and the degree was conferred in 2007. Research interests include: e-commerce fraud, online privacy and security, and web databases/programming. He has been a lecturer in the School of Mathematics, Physics and Information Technology since July 2002, and is a commercial programmer/research officer for Osmotion Pty Ltd.

Douglas P. Twitchell, PhD, is an assistant professor in the School of Information Technology and the director of the Center for Information Assurance and Security Education at Illinois State University. He received his PhD from the University of Arizona's Eller College of Business in 2005. In addition to teaching information security courses, Dr. Twitchell spends time researching social engineering and other social aspects of information security, natural language processing, and artificial intelligence.

Shambhu J. Upadhyaya, PhD, is an associate professor of Computer Science and Engineering at the State University of New York at Buffalo where he also directs the Center of Excellence in Information Systems Assurance Research and Education. His research interests are information assurance, computer security, fault diagnosis, fault tolerant computing, and VLSI Testing. He has authored or coauthored more than 190 articles in refereed journals and conferences in these areas. He was a guest co-editor of the book *Managing Information Assurance in Financial Services* (IGI Global, 2007) and was a guest co-editor of a special issue on *Secure Knowledge Management in IEEE Transactions on Systems, Man and Cybernetics*, May 2006. He is a senior member of IEEE. His current projects involve insider threat modeling, intrusion detection, security in wireless networks, and protection against Internet attacks. His research has been supported by the National Science Foundation, Rome Laboratory, the U.S. Air Force Office of Scientific Research, DARPA, and National Security Agency.

John Walp is corporate information security officer at M&T Bank, a $65 billion financial institution headquartered in Buffalo, NY. He has more than 15 years of IT experience, half of which has been focused on information security initiatives. Previously, he held the role of Vice President, Network Security Solutions Manager. His responsibilities include oversight and management of M&T's Information Security Program as well as the Privacy Office functions. All external and internal network security which includes key security systems such as firewalls, intrusion detection/prevention systems and security information management platforms are also part of his responsibilities. Prior to M&T, Mr. Walp has held a variety of security consultant positions and was a lead systems engineer with Electronic Data Systems supporting the manufacturing vertical business. He is a customer-focused professional who demonstrates strong leadership, communication, and technical skills as well as a thorough understanding of current business and regulatory environments. He is a certified information security manager (CISM) as well as an accomplished public speaker that excels at relating highly technical material in to commonly understood concepts. He was a panelist at RSA 2007 and is a frequent speaker on security and technology topics. He also serves on the advisory board of the Center of Excellence in Information Systems Assurance Research and Education (CEISARE) at the University of Buffalo. Mr. Walp also serves on the executive board of the local FBI InfraGard organization where he assists in forming the strategic direction and initiatives of this public sector-law enforcement partnership.

Liping Wang, doctor of School of Finance, Shanghai University of Finance & Economics, has published several papers in journals and academic meetings, participated in the compilation of some textbooks and translation of teaching materials. Since the mayor at the stage of master is electronic commerce security and now is international finance, has a background of interdisciplinary studies in the aspect of bank information assurance. Main research direction: international finance.

Yang Wang is a PhD candidate in the Donald Bren School of Information and Computer Sciences of the University of California, Irvine. His broad research interests span across the fields of human-computer interaction (HCI), software engineering (SE), e-commerce and applied statistics. His PhD research focuses on mechanisms of reconciling web personalization with privacy constraints imposed by legal restrictions and by users' privacy preferences. He was a visiting researcher at Institute of Information Systems at Humboldt University in Berlin. He has performed research with several organizations, including CommerceNet, Fuji Xerox Palo Alto Lab (FXPAL), and Intel Research.

George O.M. Yee (www.georgeyee.ca) is a senior information scientist in the Information Security Group, Institute for Information Technology, National Research Council Canada (NRC). Prior to joining the NRC in late 2001, he spent over 20 years in telecom research and development at Bell-Northern Research and Nortel Networks. George received his PhD (electrical engineering), MSc (systems and information science), and BSc (mathematics) from Carleton University, Ottawa, Canada, where he is currently an adjunct research professor. Dr. Yee is on the Editorial Review Board of several journals including the *International Journal of E-Business Research*, the *Journal of Autonomic and Trusted Computing*, and the *International Journal of Patterns*. He is a senior member of IEEE, and member of ACM and Professional Engineers Ontario. His research interests include security and privacy for e-services, enhancing reliability, security, and privacy using software agents, and engineering software for reliability, security, and performance.

Zhixiong Zhang is a senior software engineer in the College Board and a PhD candidate in Information Technology at George Mason University (GMU). He received graduate certificates in information security and assurance (2007) and in software system engineering (2000) from GMU. He received MS in EE from Shanghai Jiao-Tong University (1986) and received BS in CS from Fudan University (1983). He has more than 20 year working experience in software development. He is interested in information security, software engineering, and artificial intelligence.

Xinwen Zhang is a senior engineer in the Trusted Computing Group of Samsung Information Systems America, San Jose, CA, USA. His research areas include security policies, models, architectures, and mechanisms for platform and distributed systems. Currently, he is working on trusted computing for mobile devices. He earned his BEng and MEng degrees from Huazhong University of Science and Technology, Wuhan, China and PhD degree from George Mason University, Fairfax, Virginia, USA.

Index

J

K

L

M

N

O

P

R

S

T

U

V

W

X